A Manual for
Holy Relationship

Nouk Sanchez

THE END OF DEATH - Volume Two
The deeper teachings of *A Course in Miracles*

Praise for A Manual for Holy Relationship
by kironJ Gardner

A Manual for Holy Relationship is not just another *A Course in Miracles* based book, and it's certainly not a skim-through read. I see it as a transformational call to students who have a deep and committed desire to experience and live from the *Course's* teachings. This eloquent and engrossing Volume Two of *The End of Death* trilogy sets out a clear and welcoming map of the journey from special relating to holy relationship. Nouk writes in the prologue: *'When we individually learn to genuinely forgive, we will heal. But when two people consciously join with one another, and their priority is to forgive together, a quantum healing of the entire dream of fear is affected...the collapse of time (suffering) is immeasurable.'*

Almost 100 pages are devoted to a comprehensive and truly radical teaching on the area of sex. I'm not aware of any other *ACIM* material that comes even close to providing such insights and support for healing our ego use of the body for illusions of union.

There is an unmistakable power that comes through this Manual, arising from Nouk's own profound embrace of holy relationship and her lifelong connection with and dedication to Jesus. Volume Two is a radiant star, shining practical and clarifying light on the central teaching of the *Course*, that we are One and that our nature is pure Love. I highly recommend this Love offering from Nouk to anyone feeling called to the divine purpose of holy relationship, be it with a friend/miracle buddy or family member or partner.

Towards the end of the Manual, Nouk writes: *'There is an almost entirely unknown level of mastery which Jesus beckons us to embrace in the Course.'* I'd like to suggest that Nouk's work will be a beautiful and mighty companion to any student who is drawn to new levels of mastery in Love. Volume One was groundbreaking, and I can only imagine that Volume Three will be a miraculous culmination of *The End of Death* trilogy.

I end this review with perfect encouragement from the *Course* to offer all our relationships to holy purpose: *'Your newborn purpose is nursed by angels, cherished by the Holy Spirit and protected by God Himself...it is deathless, and within it lies the end of death.'* Amen!

kironJ Gardner is an *A Course in Miracles* teacher and healer, passionate about an experiential approach to *ACIM*. kironJ works with groups in the UK and internationally, and offers online webinars, study groups, support sessions and 1-1 spiritual support. kironJ is a former Events Manager for the *Miracle Network*.

Please note: Neither the publisher nor the author is able to render professional advice or services to the individual reader. The teachings in this book are not intended to diagnose, treat, cure or prevent any condition, whether spiritual, medical, psychological, emotional, physical or health-related. They are intended to be complimentary to and supportive of you and of any treatment you might choose from your licensed health care professional.

Most quotes within this book are excerpted from *A Course in Miracles,* FIP edition, unless otherwise noted. The author has made every attempt possible to provide accurate information, such as quote location notations for the many *A Course in Miracles* quotes used in this book. In the event errors are discovered after publication, we sincerely apologize.

ISBN 978-0-578-70688-7

Printed in the United States of America, Australia and in the UK

Cover painting created by: Mwanga
Edited by: Nancy Light

ABSOLUTE CERTAINTY　　　　　The DEATH of DEATH

"Your newborn purpose is nursed by angels, cherished by the Holy
Spirit and protected by God Himself. It needs not your protection;
it is [yours.] For it is deathless, and within it lies the end of death."
T-19.IV.C.9:4-6

This book contains diagrams and exercises that are available in
printable format from the Holy Relationship website. In addition,
a guided (audio) meditation, *The End of Fear* can be found in the
Supplemental Materials link at: www.HolyRelationship.com

ACKNOWLEDGMENTS

This manual was truly a collaborative venture! While much of the content came via direct transmissions, my dear friend, colleague and sister, Coreen Walson, reviewed the entire book and made a multitude of helpful suggestions that were instrumental in making this material easier to read and understand.

My editor and dear friend, Nancy Light, played a major role in guiding the practical formation of this manual. She polished this book through her editing and provided finishing touches with various graphics and diagrams.

I wish to thank Simon Wang for his dedication to helping me record and produce the audio-book version of this manual. And a big thank you to Mwanga who created the stunning image of devotion for the front cover.

I want to extend my deepest gratitude to our entire online (TTC) Total Transformation Course family. They have supported me greatly over the last four years and have helped to teach and heal me. Also, I'd like to thank all those individuals who have encouraged and supported me over the years through our nonprofit, Take Me to Truth, Inc. I Love you all!

All throughout the writing of this book I felt my soul buddy Tomas Vieira's Spirit presence. He resides with me eternally and our communication remains entirely unbroken.

My own healing would not have been as certain and joyous had it not been for my precious daughter, Rikki Vieira. Our Holy Relationship continues to reveal many miracles due to her abundant willingness to embody this pathway. We see in her son Yarrow, even at two years old, the unmistakable imprint of Tomas' level of devotion with us all.

My full time Holy Relationship partner, Daniel Boissevain, heard Jesus' call clearly. For me, Daniel has consistently shown up as the Christ in helping me to navigate through and heal the last vestiges of ego self doubt. I am kissing his precious feet.

One more Loving angel to thank, my little doggie Neesie. She stuck by me no matter what. Neesie played the part of my blessed guardian for the many years before Daniel came along.

And deep in my heart lays my undying gratitude for our beloved Brother, Jesus. He blazed the path Home for us all. This is the great Awakening. And we are coming Home!

CONTENTS

FOREWORD

By Coreen Walson

1. There has been a growing anticipation along with a consensus among spiritual seekers that the time for the final tipping in consciousness from fear to Love is closer than ever before. In 1976, Jesus gave us the metaphysics and absolute Truth within *A Course in Miracles.* Since then, teachers of God are being called continually to extend these teachings to earnest seekers for Truth.

2. There is a teacher among us who has willingly undertaken the enormous calling of setting forth Jesus' deeper teachings as they pertain to the literal overcoming of the belief in death. She has discerned within the *Course* the indispensable and supreme message that when Divine Love and Absolute Truth combine as one, the result is the consistent experience of the Power of God in which the belief in material bodies, and therefore death, are overcome.

3. She reveals, step by step, just how and why the Holy Relationship is the means by which to access this Divine Love, for it is safely nestled and protected within every authentic, Holy Relationship. This relationship, when practiced honestly, is the means by which Truth and Love will flood our consciousness and bring this precarious dream of separation down like the house of cards it is.

4. Entirely humble and meek in this undertaking, this teacher of God has been patiently and with uncompromising devotion, communing with Jesus around the clock for many years to bring this final message of deliverance, via Holy Relationship, to the world. While Jesus speaks of how crucial the Holy Relationship is throughout the last third of the *Course's* text, no one has been willing it seems, to undertake these teachings on a very literal and practical level; that is, until now.

5. Nouk Sanchez, along with her husband Daniel Boissevain and myself, have, with the guidance of Jesus, implemented these teachings with the most profound results. Our living examples demonstrate that the Holy Relationship is not only the fast track to awakening but is literally the Holy Grail to total transcendence *from* the dream of separation.

6. With radical transparency and vulnerability, Nouk shares her journey with us from special relating to Holy Relating, by including her fears and doubts along with her revelations and victories. She opens the way for us to experience our Holy Self through this miraculous relationship, which results in our memory and awareness of our beloved relationship with the Father. She further illustrates that contained within the Holy Relationship are both the direct experience of transcending identification as a material body and the miraculous effects that flow from this understanding.

7. Since time began, ego has boasted that the dream of death is the inevitable end for the Son of God. It has protected its *home*, the body, with viciousness and all the arsenal that it thinks it possesses. Even in the face of Jesus' demonstration and victory over this seeming obstacle, it argues that while Jesus did it, we are not as worthy and would be foolish to try. Even those master teachers who have followed in Jesus' footsteps with much success have still succumbed to this belief, i.e. that death is the inevitable outcome of life.

8. Despite insults, threats, ridicule, and mockery, Nouk still stands calling for the final destruction of this boastful imposter, death. She has selflessly given us the "how" in such articulate teachings that it can only be *our own unwillingness* that could deter this final victory.

9. When one considers the impact of these teachings, I have often asked myself how I could ever begin to thank her. When Nouk asked me to write a Foreword, I was struck by the depth and meaning behind her request. My appreciation and gratitude to and for Nouk can only be expressed through my full commitment in support of these teachings.

10. So, my precious Sis, I take your hand unswervingly, unreservedly, and with deepest devotion and reverence. I say "yes," and I place our Holy Relationship as the North Star in my life, allowing the Truth and Love that flows from it to be my Guide. No matter what, and no matter who seems to come between us, I will never forsake or abandon you. I vow to finish His work standing shoulder to shoulder with you. It is the greatest honor and blessing of my Life and my only purpose.

Your Devoted Sister,
Coreen R. Walson

To those who are called to read these pages and feel the import and Truth of these teachings, we thank you, and call you to join with us through our nonprofit *Take Me to Truth, Inc.* to undo the final obstacles to the complete awakening from the dream. We look forward to the celebration as we enter into the final Victory Lap with joyous laughter, and arm in arm with our Brother, Jesus Christ.

Beyond the body
that you interposed
between you and your brother,
and shining in the golden light
that reaches it from the bright,
endless circle that extends forever,
is your holy relationship,
beloved of God Himself.
How still it rests, in time
and yet beyond,
immortal yet on earth.
How great the power
that lies in it.
Time waits
upon its will,
and earth will be
as it would have it be.
Here is no separate will,
nor the desire that
anything be separate.
Its will has no exceptions,
and what it wills is true.
Every illusion brought to its
forgiveness is gently overlooked
and disappears.
For at its center Christ has been reborn,
to light His home with vision that overlooks the world.
Would you not have this holy home be yours as well?
No misery is here, but only joy.

T-22.II.12

PROLOGUE

A Manual for Holy Relationship

By Nouk Sanchez

1. This manual presents a sacred blueprint for interpersonal relationship healing which eventually leads us to Self-Realization of the unified Identity we all share. This healing is the undoing of our deeply coveted belief in separation. Bringing to light the deeper teachings in *A Course in Miracles*, this manual is given as a living legacy. Its gifts are destined to touch countless individuals as they learn to receive the Kingdom of Heaven through union.

2. This is not just a book. It is a series of transmissions which came from my long, close, and continued relationship with Jesus. The teachings contained in this manual are holographic. They reveal many facets of meaning which will unpack itself to the degree that our mind begins to drop its defenses to Love.

3. The contents of this book were delivered in a multi-layered, circular fashion. Because this teaching represents no less than the complete undoing of all that we have erroneously valued, it will be met with fierce resistance by the false identity, the ego. The sheer magnitude of our profound confusion between Love and fear cannot be underestimated. But sadly, it often is. Due to the intense resistance to these teachings, Jesus has again used repetition and recurring themes as a valuable means by which to bypass this resistance and provide the way for these truths to become ingrained in our consciousness. Like *A Course in Miracles*, the reaffirming of essential *reality-reversal* principles is made only to attempt to bypass the ego and its defenses.

4. That being said, the material in this book was not written in a linear fashion. It was largely "given" to me organically through transmissions in individual essay format. Each essay was not pre-planned, or written in consecutive order, although we've tried to place the contents in such a way as to build upon one another. I have kept these transmissions as pure and unadulterated as possible.

5. The world we see, along with the thought system that made it, was not made in Love. Its source is fear. However, much of this fear is unconscious and furthermore, is often cleverly disguised as love itself. Because of this extraordinary confusion between Love and fear we are also largely unable to distinguish between joy and pain. Consequently, the unconscious split mind is attracted to pain and labels it as love.

6. If a relationship that once appeared to be loving turns to hate, then it was not really Love but fear which underpinned it. The teachings in this manual can help in revealing the miracle behind all grievances and in uncovering the actual Love (not special love) which is beneath the fear that appears to hold "special" relationships together.

7. This manual genuinely encourages and prepares us to open to the real meaning and *experience* of changeless, perfect *Love* which cannot be threatened by anyone or anything. This Love completely transcends the ego's highly deceptive and unreliable concept of human love. Perfect Love is the very center of our true Identity, yet it cannot be recognized in our Self and others until we unlearn what Love is *not*. Before we can hope to begin opening to the experience of perfect Love, we need to *unlearn* the rules of special relating which present a heavy block to conscious Love and union.

8. The human experience of the ego's illusory version of love arises from a very deeply hidden and profound confusion. It is not Love because its foundation is rooted in unconscious fear. And this is why it appears that love *can* change, hurt, turn to hate, or that love can even be lost.

   a. *"The course does not aim at teaching the meaning of love, for that is beyond what can be taught. It does aim, however, at removing the blocks to the awareness of love's presence, which is your natural inheritance." T-in.1:6-7*

   b. *"Your task is not to seek for love, but merely to seek and find all of the barriers within yourself that you have built against it. It is not necessary to seek for what is true, but it IS necessary to seek for what is false." T-16.IV.6:12*

9. For some readers, the first few chapters may raise more questions than they seem to answer. Please know that your valid questions more than likely will be answered in later chapters, particularly as we delve into the "practical" aspects of Holy relating. It may be helpful at this point to actually keep a journal where you can list your questions as they arise in your awareness. Remember that Holy Spirit is attuned to your meaningful questions and will always answer them when you are genuinely *willing* to receive His answer. His answers cannot be received while you are in fear because fear is *resistance* to Love.

10. Since these teachings will challenge the ego's identity *as* the body, along with its core beliefs and values, it will attempt to block comprehension. Anger is one way it does this. Keeping a journal helps, especially when we commit to noting reactions of resistance, as these represent the ego's strong hold on "idols" which it refuses to surrender. This is not personal. The ego thought system is relentlessly opposed to being exposed.

11. Journaling about our triggers (spikes of fear or anger, as resistance) without self-judgment, allows the false self concept to diffuse its initial outrage. This clears the airways to create a safe space for the "open-mindedness" necessary for us to make the epic shift from fear to Love.

A. My Relationship with Jesus

1. Anyone who is genuinely willing to recognize and forgive their fears in the form of their limits, judgments, grievances, beliefs and values, and who wholeheartedly desires to transcend *self*-interests, can cultivate a conscious relationship with Jesus. He has offered us all abundant help and no one is excluded. From my experience, I've learned that as we progress in our own transfer from fear to Love, the ego's dark veil of fear, through which we've erroneously perceived our self, others, the body, the past and the world, becomes exceedingly thin; so thin in fact, that the brilliant light of truth eventually shines right through it.

a. *Jesus shares with us: "I take the journey with you. For I share your doubts and fears a little while, that you may come to me who recognize the road by which all fears and doubts are overcome. We walk together. I must understand uncertainty and pain, although I know they have no meaning. Yet a savior must remain with those he teaches, seeing what they see, but still retaining in his mind the way that led him out, and now will lead you out with him. God's Son is crucified until you walk along the road with me." – A Course in Miracles, W-rV. in.6*

2.   My relationship with Jesus goes back a long way in the illusion of time. At a certain point in my own journey it was clearly revealed to me by Jesus that I was to *complete* my role and purpose with Him. But there was a challenge. Apart from the one unmistakable message I received just before I turned five, I did not recall any details of just what my purpose and role were. And yet somehow I had agreed to them. There was a resolute acknowledgment of the immense *value* of this agreement, however the specific means by which it was to develop had escaped me.

3.   There was absolutely no road map. It had something to do with forgiveness and Love, not "human" love, but perfect and changeless Love. This was a Love that could not be threatened, although clearly I had no concept of how to go about this shift from fear to Love. In addition, there was no conscious knowledge of the fact that this "purpose" I had signed up for would involve a massive undoing of all I thought I knew, including the identity I had presumed was me. I was abundantly *willing* to embark upon this journey and that's about all I knew in my younger years.

4.   In this lifetime, around the age of two, Jesus was already attempting to remind me of my role and purpose as best He could. Sometimes as I sat alone in my room, He would visit and sit with me, always dressed in a familiar blue robe. Although I don't recall specific messages of that time, my experience during these meetings was of perfect fulfillment and ever-present peace. Jesus was certainly no stranger to me and through these earlier meetings I realized that He was entirely accessible to anyone who sincerely desired open communication, and was not afraid of Him.

5.   Apparently, there were instances, as I was later told, where my

non-religious grandparents would come rushing into the room asking me "who" I was talking with. I would tell them that my Friend had come to visit again.

6. And then at four and a half, He tried again. I recall a vivid scene, a highly emotional moment that thoroughly transcended my awareness of current time, place and identity. In this one recognition of light, I acknowledged that I did indeed have a divine purpose and it was by no means random. It was this epiphany that gave me my first timeless glimpse into not just *my* purpose, but "our" united purpose as the beloved Children of God.

7. This one experience in particular, was responsible for breaking through the ego's dense amnesia, the forgotten memory of my singular Identity and purpose which sadly follows almost all physical births within this dream.

8. I was sitting on the floor in front of my grandparent's newly acquired black and white TV. While my family was busily distracted preparing a holiday banquet for extended family, I sat watching an epic Easter scene of Jesus' crucifixion.

9. While watching this scene, my heart became so totally engulfed; I remember being overcome with an excruciating sadness that vastly exceeded memory of my own short life. The striking moment of being transported beyond this present incarnation came in one Holy Instant, as I heard Jesus utter the words, *"Father, forgive them for they know not what they do."* The quantum G-force of Jesus' invocation pierced my memory so greatly that I experienced a significant merging or blurring of lifetimes. For me, it felt as if the gap of time, between me being a child in this lifetime and the time of Jesus' incarnation two thousand plus years ago, had disappeared entirely.

10. That moment of sudden insight impacted me so greatly that I felt this truth reverberate throughout all the dimensions of time. This was a Holy Instant outside of time, one that shook me to my core. The message itself was "known" so deeply, so presently. It was incredibly familiar! For me it was a single light shining amongst the cloudy meaninglessness of my early childhood. This was indeed a moment beyond and yet encompassing all of time, and one which

became instrumental later as my understanding of its implications increased greatly over time.

11. I have had a few remarkable healing encounters with Jesus, too many to include here. But by the time my adolescent years were experienced, I had consciously opened my heart to learn of the changeless Love that I had earlier glimpses of with Jesus. And somehow, I knew that the vehicle through which this changeless Love would be known fully was a *Holy Relationship* with someone who was equally willing to undo special or fearful love.

12. I do believe that this was the essential encouragement required for me to release my investment in special love and to pursue Holy Relationship which came in the form of a miraculous relationship journey with Tomas Vieira, beginning in 1984, six years before I found *A Course in Miracles*. It was this relationship that provided the initial boot camp classroom for us both to embark upon an epic transition from special to Holy Love.

13. For us both, this shared experience was responsible for reminding us of our higher purpose. There was indeed a divine and perfect Love that completely transcended the highly volatile "love" of this world. That Love, the one that Jesus revealed to me, was the one that would literally heal the world.

14. If you have read *The End of Death, Volume One* then you may recall the story about my Holy Relationship partner, Tomas' passing in 2010. Shortly after Tomas left the body I descended into a hellish state. This was the darkest of all dark nights of the soul for me. Extreme confusion beset me, where death itself seemed my only way out. It was during this event that Jesus intervened at my heartfelt plea for clarity.

15. Shortly after, I began to receive some startling transmissions from Jesus which I wrote down. They were about the unreality of death. A few months passed and I was told by Jesus that these transmissions were to be instrumental in disseminating His deeper teachings within *A Course in Miracles*. He shared that these teachings would form a book trilogy.

16. At the time I had no idea how there would be a trilogy when I didn't even know what the title of this first book would be. Apparently,

there was one overarching title for all three books yet to come, despite the fact that I was absolutely clueless about what that title would be.

17. In October 2011, ten months after my soul buddy Tomas had passed, I received a strange email from a domain company called Name.com. It was addressed to Tomas. And here is what it said:

18. *"Dear Tomas Vieira, It looks like the following products in your email account are expiring in October of 2011. Please take a moment to renew them now to avoid service interruptions. Your domain name – EndOfDeath.com – is due for renewal."*

19. Just weeks before his passing, and completely unknown to me, Tomas had bought the End of Death domain name and not told a soul. He obviously knew things that I did not, before he left his form. I remember the instant that I saw this notification. I was overcome with grace, with tears and a certainty of God's Love for us. Here it was…the trilogy's title, *The End of Death!* And it was Tomas who had already purchased the domain for the book's website as well.

20. Some have asked me about how I receive these transmissions with Jesus. So, I'll attempt to give a brief overview here. It seems that when I join with Jesus in my mind, He recognizes my willingness to enter a state where I must trust Him implicitly to give me His ideas. Then usually it's up to me to articulate those ideas. Sometimes I will receive very direct words or sentences which I write down. Most of this occurs in my mind and sometimes I hear Jesus speaking.

21. A greater portion of these transmissions are given to me in such a way that they bypass my intellectual mind, which was very frustrating at first. For me, it seemed that it would be beneficial to actually know in advance the subject that I may write about. But this is rare. Joining with Jesus has taught me that I have no idea what will be written about. I begin to write and the material teaches *me* first. I've often said that writing these transmissions has become the breadcrumb trail that I throw forward in order to lead my mind out of the darkness.

a. *"Communication is not limited to the small range of channels the world recognizes. If it were, there would be little point in trying to teach salvation. It would be impossible to do so. The limits the world places on communication are the chief barriers to direct experience of the Holy Spirit, Whose Presence is always there and Whose Voice is available but for the hearing. These limits are placed out of fear, for without them the walls that surround all the separate places of the world would fall at the holy sound of His Voice. Who transcends these limits in any way is merely becoming more natural. He is doing nothing special, and there is no magic in his accomplishments."* ... *"God gives no special favors, and no one has any powers that are not available to everyone." M-25.2:2-8,3:7*

b. *Jesus calls to us: "For this alone I need; that you will hear the words I speak, and give them to the world. You are my voice, my eyes, my feet, my hands through which I save the world. The Self from which I call to you is but your own. To Him we go together. Take your brother's hand, for this is not a way we walk alone. In him I walk with you, and you with me. Our Father wills His Son be one with Him." W-rV.in.9:2-8*

22. Why should we engage in a Holy Relationship? What is a Holy Relationship for?

23. When we individually learn to genuinely forgive, we will heal. But when *two people* consciously join with one another, and their priority is to *forgive together,* a quantum healing of the entire dream of fear is affected. When two or more unite in the goal of forgiveness the collapse of time (suffering) is immeasurable. Awakening from the ego's dream of separation cannot be attained alone in isolation. Salvation is a collaborative venture, as Jesus explains in the following passage:

a. *"Your gratitude to your brother is the only gift I want. I will bring it to God for you, knowing that to know your brother [is] to know God. If you are grateful to your brother, you are grateful to God for what He created. Through your gratitude you come to know your brother, and one moment of real recognition makes everyone your brother because each of them is of your Father." ... "As you come closer to a brother you approach me, and as you withdraw from him I become distant to you. Salvation is a collaborative venture. It cannot be undertaken successfully by those who disengage themselves from the Sonship, because they are disengaging themselves from me." T-4.VI.7:2-5,8:1-3*

24. A Holy Relationship need *not* be romantic. It is not exclusive but *inclusive*. Holy Relationship is the sacred union in which we develop unshakable gratitude for each other. It is within this mutual union of blamelessness that we finally come to behold the exquisite sanctity and invulnerability of our forgotten innocence. In this union the ego's dreadful unconscious attraction to its cycle of sin, guilt and fear is abolished. Guilt and unworthiness give way to breathtaking innocence... so much so, that we yearn to behold this innocence and we will learn to protect it from the ego's quick damnation.

25. So, treasured friends, it is with utmost faith and trust that those who are ready for these teachings will receive them into their hearts and recognize the power that Holy Relationship has to heal the world. This Holy Grail of all time is the divine Love of God here in the dream. When coupled with the undivided truth as given by Jesus in the *Course*, there is no power on earth, including death, that can withstand the Holy Relationship's influence. I offer this manual with the greatest Love and devotion. Many students and teachers have a strong *intellectual* understanding of the *Course's* teachings. Reading and implementing this manual into your life demonstrates a sincere desire to *experience* its teachings. I earnestly thank you, not only for *hearing* the Call to awaken but for *responding* to the Call with your genuine desire to *answer* it.

"Think what a holy relationship can teach! Here is belief in differences undone. Here is the faith in differences shifted to sameness. And here is sight of differences transformed to vision. Reason now can lead you and your brother to the logical conclusion of your union. It must extend, as you extended when you and he joined. It must reach out beyond itself, as you reached out beyond the body, to let you and your brother be joined. And now the sameness that you saw extends and finally removes all sense of differences, so that the sameness that lies beneath them all becomes apparent. Here is the golden circle where you recognize the Son of God. For what is born into a holy relationship can never end." T-22.in.4

CHAPTER ONE

C–I.   PATH TO HOLY SELF

Introduction

1. This chapter lays a crucial foundation for the rest of the manual. It is vital and instrumental in helping to recognize and heal the split mind, which in turn opens us to the peace required to access guidance from Holy Spirit. The intent is to prepare us for the purification which necessarily drives our desire to shift our mind from fear to Love. With this shift in our beliefs and values we increase our trust in our true Identity as the Holy Self. This becomes a springboard for us, making it more likely for us to join meaningfully in Holy Relationship.

2. From decision making, to forgiving triggers, to healing anger and releasing all sense of guilt and unworthiness, this chapter takes on the major obstacles that attempt to block our return to Love as our one, shared Holy Self. We cannot hope to extend the Love, acceptance and healing that we have not yet *accepted* for ourselves.

3. This chapter offers a fast track to lifting the ego's filter of fear and separation. It will hopefully encourage readers to develop the willingness and readiness required to truly join in Holy Relationship. Our desire and willingness for Holy Relationship is accepted by Holy Spirit, however, a fundamental purification of our beliefs and values is necessary first.

I. THE UNEQUIVOCAL SECRET THAT SOLVES EVERY SINGLE PROBLEM

1.   When we are truly eager and willing to see and heal the single cause of all suffering in our self, relationships, the body, the world and the past, we will be ready to *receive* the single remedy and witness the overwhelmingly miraculous consequences. But we cannot receive this healing while we still choose to value our belief in fear. And while we continue to attempt to problem-solve what does not exist, we will unwittingly use our fears to mask and reject healing of the single secret *cause* that spawns all fear.

2.   All fear including fear of conflict, loss, scarcity, aging or pain is fear of the future. Fear is never just *now*. We cannot be wholly present now *and* feel fear or concern. The belief in fear can only occur when we are absent from the present moment in which there exists only Love as our most Holy Self. This Self rests entirely uninterrupted within our present and incorruptible innocence. When we believe a fear or problem, all that is missing is our *awareness* of Love which returns to us as a result of *accepting* the miracle, the Atonement as the correction of fear.

3.   We are either fully present, now, resting or acting from our deeply felt alignment in and as God's changeless Love, peace and innocence – *or* – we're consumed in a bubble of imagined threat. The now moment *and* fear are mutually exclusive. They cannot coexist. Either one or the other is our *choice* in any one moment. Therefore, all fear is really a projection outward into an imaginary future.

4.   This is a bold statement; however all our fears are believed in order to obscure the *one* fear that underpins them all. Our greatest fear, and the final one we will release, is the fear of *"present joining."* This is the gap of fear (guilt) we choose to keep, to separate from our brothers, our Holy Self and God.

5.   Fear of loss, disease, aging or pain, together with all relationship conflicts, are all merely a massive smokescreen made to conceal our single most coveted fear, the fear of joining, of complete forgiveness, of closing the gap with God totally. If we would heal this right here and *now* – we would completely eradicate *all* fear and guilt along with every illusory problem which fear was made to feed.

6. In closing the gap with our Holy Self, others (living or passed on) and God, we cannot experience fear at all, in relation to anyone or anything. It is impossible to fear once this gap of unforgiveness is erased. Even our slightest fears are meant to keep us from knowing our true Holy Self. When we close that gap within our own heart it eradicates the need for fear along with its results – problems.

7. If we fear at all, the cause is never in the past, the future, in another, the body or the world, no matter what the *form* of the seeming problem we face. It dwells solely in the gap we have abandoned to darkness, as unforgiveness. And that dark space is always the same. It represents our fear of joining. It's the ancient fear of forgiving our self completely for having perceived that we are separate from our eternal Source, as Love itself. And we will continue to attract fear and reject our healing while we still prefer to condemn anyone, past or present, including our self.

8. Judgment, grievances, self-doubt, anger, resentment, sacrifice, conflict, pain, sickness, lack, etc., are just a few of the most common expressions of fear. Every fear, no matter how well disguised, arises from just one unseen and well defended wish – *to be separate*. Separate from our brothers, from our Holy Self and from God.

9. In a nutshell this translates to the wish to believe in sin and therefore, to experience guilt and fear. This is also the desire to be special, with its mistaken attraction to special relationships. It's a choice to be completely exiled from the resounding peace, Love and infinite security which rest within our incorruptible innocence, shared with all our brothers.

A. Fear is not Natural

1. This unforgiven wish to be a separate body self with a private mind, is the source of *all* fears and suffering. Contrary to common belief, fear is not involuntary. It is not a natural *reflex*, although it seems so. Fear is something we taught our self throughout the illusory dimensions of time. As the imagined opposite of all-encompassing and unopposed Love (God), fear does *not* exist. Yet we have manufactured our bodies and an entire dream world based on fear. However, only our *belief* in fear sustains it in our awareness, and thus in our experience.

2. Jesus explains that the correction of fear is *our* responsibility. Don't ask for release from fear and the problems we've attracted from it (pain, illness, relationship conflict, financial lack, etc.). Holy Spirit does not acknowledge either fear or its effects which do not exist. If He did acknowledge the disastrous effects of fear, then He would also have to believe their cause – fear – was real too. If fear and its effects were real, then God as Love would not exist. Only one is true. Only Love is real.

   a. *"Nothing and everything cannot coexist. To believe in one is to deny the other. Fear is really nothing and love is everything. Whenever light enters darkness, the darkness is abolished."* T-2.VII.5:1-4

   b. *"The correction of fear [is] your responsibility. When you ask for release from fear, you are implying that it is not. You should ask, instead, for help in the conditions that have brought the fear about. These conditions always entail a willingness to be separate. At that level you [can] help it. You are much too tolerant of mind wandering, and are passively condoning your mind's miscreations."* T-2.VI.4:1-6

   c. *"It is obvious, then, that when you are afraid, you have placed yourself in a position where you need Atonement."*... *"As long as you recognize only the need for the remedy, you will remain fearful. However, as soon as you accept the remedy, you have abolished the fear. This is how true healing occurs."* T-2.VI.8:3,7-9

B. Healing the Fear of Union

1. To find where the deepest core of quantum healing rests, look right here in the Holy Instant in which we *choose* to *overlook* the mistaken consequences of fear. These are now seen as problems we have manifested as constant smokescreens, clever diversions to lure us away from healing the single source of them all.
2. Now, we can choose to recognize that the presence of worry or fear and the appearance of problems are immediate signs that we

are masking what *really* needs healing – *our wish to be separate.* This insane wish is the sole condition that requires correction, as healing. And we heal this separation by accepting the Atonement. The forgiveness process can be found in *The Seven Essential Principles of Quantum Forgiveness (Atonement)* on page 591.

3.   Healing will follow once this distorted wish is seen and offered over to Spirit in exchange for the miracle as God's certain Will. His Will *is done already*. His Will is always for perfect healing of both cause and effect, of both mind and body. It does not require time, although we may.

4.   Our doubt seems to prolong the "appearance" that healing is not immediate. Yet God's Will is already accomplished despite what the body's eyes may witness. The only thing that seems to take time is our unequivocal conviction that God's Will as healing is done; and that we, as God's most beloved Child, are *worthy* of it.

5.   The false self is terrified to forgive completely, to fuse entirely with another. It sees the eradication of the separate space between us as self-annihilation. This fear – to close the gap – is so great that it actually eclipses all our fears of future loss or pain and even death. Jesus tells us that present joining is really our greatest dread. This is the fear of Love, the fear of God as the rejection of our Self, our brothers and God. And this fear of *joining* in full forgiveness is the reason why healing seems to take time.

6.   Yet, salvation is *immediate.* And we will witness the immediacy of salvation as we practice looking past the *appearance* of problems in whatever form they take, and hold steadfast to healing the underlying cause of them all – our hidden wish to be separate.

   a. *"Salvation [is] immediate."*... *"Salvation [would] wipe out the space you see between you still, and let you instantly become as one. And it is here you fear the loss would lie. Do not project this fear to time, for time is not the enemy that you perceive. Time is as neutral as the body is, except in terms of what you see it for. If you would keep a little space between you and your brother still, you then would want a little time in which forgiveness is withheld a little while."* ...*"Future loss is not your fear. But present joining is your dread." T-26.VIII.3:1,4-8,4:3-4*

C. One Problem – One Solution

1. When we are triggered by anyone or anything including the body, the trigger is always a mask to conceal the fundamental problem – *our hidden wish to be separate*. Jesus says that all this complexity is a desperate attempt not to recognize and thus heal the only problem.

   a. *"All this complexity is but a desperate attempt not to recognize the problem, and therefore not to let it be resolved. If you could recognize that your only problem is separation, no matter what form it takes, you could accept the answer because you would see its relevance. Perceiving the underlying constancy in all the problems that seem to confront you, you would understand that you have the means to solve them all. And you would use the means, because you recognize the problem."* W-79.6.

2. There are no problems in God's Love, which is Who we are. Therefore, there literally can be no problems for us when we choose to forgive the ego's many and varied decoys of fear to seduce and distract us from the one defense that caused them all – *our wish to be separate*.

3. This is all that need be seen and forgiven in one genuine, heartfelt Holy Instant in which we accept that God has *already* healed it for us. The cause of *whatever* problem, is already solved. Trust then, that the seeming *effects* in whatever form they may appear must also be healed, because effects (body/world) and cause (mind) are never separate.

4. All seeming problems are always the same in *content* although they express in a multitude of different *forms*. This is why there is no hierarchy of illusions, no hierarchy of problems, sickness or pain. And thankfully, this is why the miracle heals them all equally. Remember the *Course's* number one miracle principle, *"There is no order of difficulty in miracles."*

5. The unequivocal secret that solves every single problem is our genuine desire to close the gap with our Holy Self, others and God. And watch for the free-flowing abundance of miracles as fear then falls away.

a. *"[The sole responsibility of the miracle worker is to accept the Atonement for himself.] This means you recognize that mind is the only creative level, and that its errors are healed by the Atonement. Once you accept this, your mind can only heal. By denying your mind any destructive potential and reinstating its purely constructive powers, you place yourself in a position to undo the level confusion of others." T-2.V.5:1-4*

6. Just a reminder that our fears and seeming problems arise from what the ego sends our physical senses to retrieve, in order to prove the illusory separation is real. This is very important. All relationship conflicts, disease, pain, lack and loss fall into this category. We must learn *not* to trust our physical senses, but to look past them and ask to see *with Christ Vision* the miracle, which always lies beneath the appearance. The five physical senses represent convincing decoys made to obscure both the single cause of all our problems and its sole remedy – the Atonement, or the "closing of the gap."

a. *"The fear of healing arises in the end from an unwillingness to accept unequivocally that healing is necessary. What the physical eye sees is not corrective, nor can error be corrected by any device that can be seen physically. As long as you believe in what your physical sight tells you, your attempts at correction will be misdirected. The real vision is obscured, because you cannot endure to see your own defiled altar. But since the altar has been defiled, your state becomes doubly dangerous unless it [is] perceived." T-2.V.8:1-5*

D. Exercise: All My Problems Have Been Solved

1. Here is a helpful self-inquiry process designed to unearth just where you prefer to hide your secret wish to be unfairly treated. This is your unseen fear of "present joining," or the wish to be separate. When you're able to identify it, you can then choose to exchange it for healing, for the miracle. It's a good idea to find some quiet time in which you won't be disturbed. Perhaps journal your answers and allow your Holy Self to deliver some powerful insights as well.

2. Above all, honor your process. If emotions rise, give them space to surface and be felt thoroughly. Try to embrace yourself without judgment or censoring. Don't try to suppress these emotions, as they are gateways to freedom. Anger and grief must be felt before you can genuinely transcend them. If you find it difficult to forgive a particular person or experience, take the time to allow the small self to express its emotions and beliefs. Set your intent to forgive, but ask Holy Spirit to help you to observe these old beliefs, and ask Him to help you repurpose them.

3. Begin with a particular problem or challenge you may be facing. It may even be an issue from the past, such as childhood abuse, etc. And then unearth the "real issue" underlying it. There is a good chance that you will discover the connection between the real issue and the particular problem as you've been seeing it. Also, notice how the ego defines the superficial problem and then attempts to problem-solve it, making sure you never discover its one underlying cause.

1) **What appearance has the problem taken?** Is it relationship conflict, illness, pain, depression, self-doubt, financial lack, aging, weight gain/loss, concern for the future, concern for the wellbeing of another, etc.?

2) **Are you willing to recognize that this problem is nothing but a smokescreen made to conceal your only problem?** You believe you are separate from your Holy Self, God and your brothers. Your only problem is the lack of heartfelt desire to close the gap; to forgive totally.

3) **What is the underlying issue that constitutes the gap (problem**)? What do you believe you need (value) more than closing the gap via forgiveness (accepting the Atonement)? This is your hidden desire to be separate, the denied cause of the problem. Until this has been identified and sincerely offered up in exchange for the miracle, the problem cannot be solved. Take yourself through these possible clues with radical self-honesty:

4. The need to be right, the need to believe you were victimized (abused, abandoned or betrayed), the need to believe you were a perpetrator (guilty), the need to hold grievances, the need to believe your anger is justified, the need to believe you are a victim of the body, pain, disease, weight gain/ loss or aging, the need to condemn the body and its appetites, the need to idolize the body and its appetites, the need to believe you are suffering from financial lack, the need to believe you're alone, unseen or lonely, the need to believe you must defend yourself, the need to believe you are unworthy, the need to believe you must plan and control apart from Holy Spirit's guidance, the need to believe that your concern or worry for another's wellbeing is helpful, the need to believe that sacrifice and struggle are valuable or necessary, the need to believe that special relationship rules, roles and laws are necessary (parent, child, spouse, friend, etc.), the need to believe you must earn your worthiness, the need to believe you must judge others, etc.

1) **Is there anyone present or from your past whom you have not forgiven completely (including yourself)? Why do you desire to keep these beliefs, grievances and fears over forgiveness and freedom from fear?** What is it that these beliefs give you? What is it that they protect you from?

2) **Are you willing to recognize that all your beliefs, fears, grievances, problems and concerns are there for *one* reason only and that is to act as a smokescreen, a shield of fear; to obscure your resistance to healing the single cause, resistance to genuinely close the gap? Do you genuinely want to see your brother/sister as sinless, as guiltless?** Healing (forgiveness) is achieved by first admitting that you were *mistaken,* that by choosing to believe your fears, grievances and problems, you valued the gap and being separate. And now you wish to close it by accepting the Atonement.

3) **Desire the miracle above all else!** Desire above all else to close the gap which this fear, grievance or problem was made to conceal. Your healing depends on recognizing this one problem and then accepting God's Will that it has been solved.

One problem, one solution! Healing is done because your only problem has been solved.

5. If you believed with unwavering conviction that you are indeed God's innocent Child, then you could not suffer. There could never be any problems. Suffering and problems only appear when you abandon your Self to the wish to be separate from another, from Self and from God. They are merely symptoms of the choice to be separate.

6. To heal any problem all the Holy Spirit needs from you are:

    1) Your recognition that the only problem, regardless of its form, is your mistaken choice to believe you're separate from all-encompassing Love and healing.

    2) Your heartfelt consent to have Him "close the gap" in your heart and mind.

    3) Your sincere acceptance that He has already healed the problem in the instant you gave Him consent to heal it.

E. Healing Prayer to Undo the Cause of All Problems

1. "This problem (fear, guilt, anger, conflict, betrayal, confusion, self-doubt, pain, illness, scarcity, unworthiness, etc.) is purely a smokescreen to hide its singular cause – my mistaken wish to be separate from Love and healing as my incorruptible Holy Self. In this most Holy Instant, I now cancel this painful wish to separate myself from Love. I choose now to "will *with* God" to close the gap responsible for causing this problem. I take in the breath of Love's perfect healing as I open my heart to accept, receive and trust the certainty of His healing. Amen."

2. ONE MESSAGE – ONE PURPOSE

1. Having spent many years with *A Course in Miracles* I can say that I recognize the *Course* itself is already complete. There is nothing left to add. However, there are still vastly unrecognized and therefore unembodied teachings within its earthly pages. After all, Jesus does say that we will come to do as He did – *and more*. And that has not yet occurred in the dream of time. The "and more" aspect of this statement is yet to be witnessed in this particular phase of the dream; although time is collapsing comprehensively as abundant miracles are now piercing its flimsy defense.

2. There appear to be a few differing interpretations of the one complete, singular and total teaching of the *Course*. The reason for different interpretations of the *Course* is because each interpretation arises from that particular individual's level of trust, their demonstration of trust. The more our trust is transferred from fear to Love the more undiluted and literal Jesus' message becomes. There is just one message, one truth and one purpose.

3. We all read, absorb and begin applying the principles of the *Course* through the mechanism of our own ego filter at first. We initially embark on these teachings through fear more than through Love. Only gradually do we begin to loosen the fear and open to surrendering our tightly defended beliefs, our values, our stories, our identity, our bodies, our past and all our relationships to the Holy Spirit.

4. Jesus explains that we have carefully taught our self to trust the ego to tell us what reality is. We trust its fear paradigm and what it seems to see through the body's five senses as well as our past. The ego unconsciously and consistently wishes to be unfairly treated so it can perpetuate separation. What it sees and hears will always confirm exactly what it's looking for; a sense of separation from Love, from God. This doesn't seem to be conscious at first, at least not until we desire to become aware of it and to heal it.

5. The ego holds onto pain and drags it forward into the imagined future. Out of fear, it obscures the present moment, which is the only place healing can occur. What we believe was done to us was not done *to* us. It looks as if it happened in the past but it appeared

in our mind as a memory of fear to separate us from our present safety (innocence) in God's Love.

6. The holographic nature of miracles extends to every facet of life, even to people and situations that seem impossible to reach from the ego's limited scope of awareness. The miracle *quite literally* heals the past. It undoes the false memory by removing it from the split mind because that is the only place the past exists – in memory. It does not exist in truth.

7. I have come to know the *Course* as immensely holographic. It reveals itself in my awareness to the exact extent that I have shifted my trust from fear to Love. One truth, recognized, just continues to unpack itself in a multidimensional way as my resistance falls away and open mindedness replaces it. It is not that the words of the *Course* have changed in the years I've been reading it, but that my *experience* of what it is pointing to has changed. When I *believe* that I was mistreated in the past, and there is an emotional charge remaining, then I unwittingly project my painful memories of mistreatment onto the future. I have stashed the illusory cause in the past. This is separating cause from effect and blocks my awareness of the miracle. Remember that all cause and effect remain together in the mind. They can never be separate.

8. If I blame someone for something or I hold a grievance, I have isolated the *real cause* in my own mind from the effect, which is the situation or the person along with the behavior. Both the offending person (or situation) and my mind are one. That person is not external to me, nor are they doing things independent of what *my own mind directs* them to do. The degree to which I am triggered tells me the extent to which the cause arises from my own unconscious wish to be unfairly treated.

9. To receive the gift of *liberation* we begin to recognize that we cannot be attacked unless there is a conscious or unconscious decision to be unfairly treated. We can only accept healing and demonstrate it to the degree our own fear has been replaced by Love in our awareness. And this comes from valuing the gifts forgiveness gives above valuing attack and taking things personally. Every area of our life must be given over to Spirit for divine repurposing and reinterpretation.

10. If I still attempt to keep some areas of my life compartmentalized from Spirit (relationships, past, body, financial affairs, career, family, etc.) that shows I must still trust the ego *more* than I trust in Spirit. I will then read the *Course* through a filter of fear and will only be willing to see, accept and practice that which does not threaten my present beliefs and values. I will be valuing and boosting my false identity.

A. Transfer from Fear to Love

1. My own development of trust has been a gradual letting go of my limited, fear-based beliefs and values. As I willingly release fear, Love's clarity further reveals the depth of Jesus' teaching. This for me has been an experiential process rather than an intellectual one. I don't however regret the years spent gaining an understanding of the metaphysics of the *Course* on an intellectual level. That understanding now serves as a foundation from which I can feel secure as I *experience* the *Course*. I trust now that when I drop fear and guilt and invite Holy Spirit's Help, I not only receive His Help and listen to His Guidance, I am also courageous enough to act on it.

2. The miracle is perfectly applicable in every facet of life. For instance, like most, I despised being triggered. Yet now when it occurs I am quick to accept a miracle, to recognize that it's a divine opportunity to forgive yet another layer of the false self's previously unseen self-hatred and unworthiness. Why then would I defend myself from it? Why would I react to a trigger if it is a literal gateway to my infinite liberation? This movement toward liberation inspires me to not exclude any part of my relationships or my life from God's all-inclusive and comprehensive transformation.

3. This process has involved the demolition of many of my unseen misidentifications; my miscreations both in belief and form. These were used as idols to block me from resting in the infinite safety and security of God's Love as my Holy Self. My fear-filter is falling away. I really appreciate now exactly what all these fears were initially made to hide from my real vision. As trust is extended to all aspects of my life, the miracles which had been hidden behind my guilt and fear spring forth far and wide.

4. As we practice turning over to Holy Spirit all the areas of our life which we previously held back we develop and strengthen our trust in *only* Spirit. This divine transition in trust moves us *significantly* from fear to Love. This mighty shift is facilitated from within and inevitably affects every single aspect of our miraculous life.

B. Only One Truth, Not Many

1. As our trust is transferred from the ego self to our Holy Self, we learn that there is only *one* truth. And that means we recognize there to be just one purpose for all our perceived challenges and triggers. This fact is consolidated in our experience as we literally recognize that we all share one mind. As our own mind is healed we will see healing in others as well. We never heal alone because there is only one mind to heal.

2. Given its nature, it is logical for the ego self to interpret the *Course* as highly metaphoric and to assume that parts of the *Course* are not to be taken literally. Even some highly respected and sincere teachers of the *Course* have approached the teachings in this manner. As an example, emphasis has been greatly diminished on physical miracles such as healing the sick and raising the dead. The idea of physical death is still accepted by the ego self as the natural, inevitable and legitimate outcome of all life. For many years I was among those who interpreted the *Course* in this way.

3. Our own "fear-filter," especially when we first embark on our *Course* journey, can deny us access to Jesus' deeper teachings. Our belief in death as the natural outcome of all life is indeed the denial of God as Love and Life. Death is the central dream from which all illusions stem. In a nutshell, if we believe that death is natural then we are unknowingly still terrified of God (Love), of Life Itself. And we will continue to try to escape from Love (God and Life) through our attraction to sickness, special relationships, conflict and death. We will also believe unconsciously that death actually comes from God. In addition, there is a widespread misconception that we go home to God *through* the ego's dream of death. We have to ask then, "Who would turn their body, their relationships and their life completely over to a god if he wills our death? Who can trust a god

like this?"

4. Think about this: If death is real there is no God. If God is real there is no death. Death is the fear of awakening to our Holy Self. We don't go home through death as many mistakenly believe.

5. As Jesus tells us:

   a. *"The world is not left by death but by truth…" T-3.VII.6:11*

   b. *"All forms of sickness, even unto death, are physical expressions of the fear of awakening. They are attempts to reinforce sleeping out of fear of waking. This is a pathetic way of trying not to see by rendering the faculties for seeing ineffectual." T-8.IX.3:2-4*

6. Another logical conclusion that the ego self reaches is that death offers the peace that we have been seeking but which life has denied us. Death is seen as the end of conflict. When someone passes away and it's posted on social media, we see *Course* students and teachers who seem to not yet see or accept Jesus' uncompromising message about the unreality of death. Either that, or they may lack the confidence to express their views honestly.

7. It can feel safer to talk freely among like-minded, fellow *ACIM* students and teachers about important subjects like this. But if we could be more unafraid to express truth, even in an open forum like social media, truth *will* be recognized at the Christ level. The more often that *undiluted* truth is expressed, the more natural it feels and the easier it is to drop the façade of the ego self.

C. Good Intentions Are Not Enough

1. Often, we witness messages of sympathy being offered with good intentions. But the common blessing, "may they rest in peace," is an example of confusion over the central message in the *Course*. I made this common mistake repeatedly in my earlier years. Jesus gently corrects us:

   a. *"Rest in peace" is a blessing for the living, not the dead, because rest comes from waking, not from sleeping. Sleep is withdrawing; waking is joining" T-8.IX.3:5-6*

2. The holographic message of the *Course* is gradually unpacked, seen, accepted and finally embodied in increments according to our own release from guilt and fear. I predict that as we release our own fear-filter, we will all see that there is only *one* complete and ultimately simple truth of Jesus' message in the *Course*. There will be just one interpretation then because there will be only one consistent *experience*. And it is this experience and demonstration that speaks louder than a thousand words. Only Love is real. *"Nothing real can threatened. Nothing unreal exists. Herein lies the peace of God."* T-in.2-4

3. In my experience, the need to learn to clearly delineate between the real and the unreal is paramount. We cannot possibly discern Love until we have learned to identify and release everything that is not Love. The false self has never known Love without fear, guilt or loss (which is not Love). It cannot know Love because its existence depends on fear. The experience of Love, like light shining away darkness, obliterates the false self.

4. Unknowingly we are terrified of God (Love) hence our obsession with the personal self and the erroneous belief that it can be attacked. We see this unfortunate dynamic played out in every special relationship that was ever made.

5. God is Love without any form of conflict or fear. This is "What" we are beneath our superficial and illusory self. We cannot trust God (Holy Self) implicitly until we first uncover our secret beliefs (fears) about God and His intent. And when we do, we will be shocked. *The "Fear of God" exercise is a good place to begin:* https://nouksanchez.com/wp-content/uploads/2020/06/2-Are-you-fearful-of-God.pdf

6. The unconscious terror of Love (God) has such a grip on our split mind that we choose suffering and physical death over awakening to the changeless Love we are with all our brothers and sisters. This unrecognized resistance to Love and the attraction to conflict, suffering and death is what prolongs the illusions of time and separation.

7. The greatest single contributor to this ongoing attraction to separation is the lure of "special relationships." Everyone in the

world has special relationships. Because the ego uses these relationships as its predominant means to abandon our Self, they become the primary dumping ground for unseen and unforgiven self-hatred and unworthiness. Yet these relationships offer us the *greatest opportunities* for quantum healing since the beginning of the separation. The key to releasing ourselves from our unconscious fear of Love (God) is found in our brothers, and specifically in the transfer of special relationship to Holy Relationship.

8. While we insist on believing that we were, are, or could be unfairly treated, then we must equally desire to maintain *the guilt* that prolongs our unconscious fear of God. Our unforgiven grievances against our brothers ensure the guilt – as blame – the ego needs to protect itself from the memory of union, the light of God's Love and healing. This fear of God equates to the ego's hidden attraction to pain, sickness, relationship conflict, scarcity and death as its defenses to the Love we are. Whereas when we genuinely forgive our self for having unwittingly chosen to use others to attack our self, our fear of Love and union is healed.

9. From the false self the only love we know is "special," a changing love, which means it is heavily imbued with guilt, fear, sacrifice, change, conflict and loss. We cannot really imagine real, changeless Love until we've at least had an experience of contrast learning by repurposing our special relationships to Holy Relationships. As we do this, we can begin to drop our unconscious fear of genuine union (Love), and of the one continuous Christ Mind we share with our brothers.

10. Contrast learning is an important process where we begin to learn what Love is *not*. With Holy Spirit we learn how to discern the valuable from the valueless, and how to distinguish Love from fear. The ego is always in strong resistance to this because its false identity depends on the insane belief that Love *is* fear, and that fear (sin and guilt) is Love.

11. The ego rejects sincere forgiveness because *forgiveness eradicates* sin, guilt and fear, which the ego regards as the *tragic loss of "its" twisted form of love,* and the very sustenance it requires to maintain separation. In quantum forgiveness, we recognize that no one hurt

us. It was the ego's projection of guilt that "used" another to hurt us. As we forgive our self for having believed in the separation as real, the guilt and fear as "effects," are erased. Without belief in sin, guilt and fear, our projections cease and the gap in which our fear of our brothers and God was maintained, collapses.

12. As we open to undoing special relating (guilt), we find that we are given more opportunities to experience a Holy Relationship with one or more companions. It is in our experience of this blinding contrast between special relating and Holy relating, that we drop our deeply hidden fear of Love.

13. It is in a Holy Instant of selflessness with a brother that we initiate our return to innocence. It is in those "joint" Holy Instants where we truly join with a brother, that incorruptible innocence and changeless union are returned to our awareness. In this blinding light of perfect Love, bodies are eclipsed, and the ancient memory of Home, God, and union are experienced. This is when we come to understand that through the miracle of Holy Relationship, we overcome the belief in bodies *as well as death*, the ego's final obstacle to peace, and we advance toward union and to God.

a. *"The form of the course varies greatly. So do the particular teaching aids involved. But the content of the course never changes. Its central theme is always, "God's Son is guiltless, and in his innocence is his salvation." M-1.3:2-5*

3. AWAKENING – SEPARATING TRUTH FROM ILLUSION

1. Did you know that the ego's most heavily guarded block to awakening entirely *from* the separation dream of space-time, is our unwillingness to accept that only the truth is true and that quite literally, *nothing else* is true? This simple truth can be very easy for us to overlook. We think of it as something that is quite obvious and as something we *already* understand. We are apt to

ignore the importance of *really* exploring it. We move our thoughts towards more "complicated" ideas, without really delving into what a powerful truth it is. Until we learn to recognize and actively separate truth *from* illusion in our daily thoughts and relationship interactions, we will unfortunately continue to attract conflict, disease, pain, lack and loss.

2.   All suffering that we seem to encounter occurs because we still believe (and therefore accord value to) both the truth *and* the ego's hallucinations. We mistakenly believe these two mutually exclusive systems of belief are *equally true*. In our split mind there is a pervasive confusion in the distorted belief that we are both human *and* divine; both the body *and* Spirit.

3.   We have made the ego's illusory projections of guilt – as conflict, sickness, pain, aging, lack, loss and death – equally as real as their *true counter fact* as peace, Love, health, harmony, perfection, wholeness and eternal life . We have also made the ego's *substitutes* for Love real, things considered to be pleasurable or desired such as bodies with their sensual appetites and special relationships. No wonder we're still cycling in the dream! Nearly all spiritual teachings including popular, non-dual teachings have made this common mistake. They passively condone the disastrous blend of truth with untruth which always protects the belief in physical bodies and ultimately leads to death.

a.   *"Salvation is the recognition that the truth is true, and nothing else is true. This you have heard before, but may not yet accept both parts of it. Without the first, the second has no meaning. But without the second, is the first no longer true. Truth cannot have an opposite. This can not be too often said and thought about. For if what is not true is true as well as what is true, then part of truth is false. And truth has lost its meaning. Nothing but the truth is true, and what is false is false."* ... *"This is the simplest of distinctions, yet the most obscure."* W-152.3,4:1

4.   The relative world / universe is seen according to our desire. Projection always precedes what we appear to see and experience. It is imperative to recognize that to experience something pleasurable or

painful, we must have first *desired it*. This desire remains unconscious until we've begun to heal the split mind through forgiveness.

5. Everything we seem to experience is seen either through the ego's filter of guilt (body's senses and its distorted memory), or we literally *see through it* with Christ Vision, to the healed, Real World shining behind it. The first is viewed and thus manifested through its own belief in fear and death, while the second is valued and thus welcomed by its unequivocal *dismissal* of all forms of sin as unreal, and the joyful acceptance of God's perfection in its place. Because the Mind looks clear past all illusions of fear, it is at peace and therefore, is able to embrace all-inclusive Love. All-inclusive Love cannot be known consistently – as the Will of God – until its illusory opposite has been recognized and erased through forgiveness.

6. To truly know and demonstrate the Love and Laws of God as miracles, we must eventually learn to discern the true *from* the false. This, by necessity, involves learning to discern between ego's so-called laws *and* God's Laws, the human *from* the divine, the body *from* Spirit, and the ego's insane wishes *from* God's Will. We do this not with the ego but by learning *with Holy Spirit* to make the positive separation between them.

7. We cannot "love" what is untrue and then expect to demonstrate consistent and miraculous healing of both cause (guilt) and its effects (suffering) in our mind. If we *accept* and attempt to *love* the untrue, we believe it to be real. Instead of asking Holy Spirit to reveal the miracle behind the *appearance*, we actually compound our *confusion* between what is true and what is illusion.

8. The miracle, as healing, does not affect anything real, it merely *undoes the interference* or block to our *awareness* of truth. But this healing cannot happen while we still prefer to glorify an illusion by: 1) seeing it as something desired or real, 2) believing it is something fearful from which we need defense, or 3) submitting or surrendering *to* the illusion. The illusion is entirely neutral. It has no power of itself. It is an illusory effect of our own untrue and unforgiven belief that we deserve punishment because we are guilty. We give the illusion power to affect us by our investment in its reality, which blocks the miracle.

9. The miracle cannot be genuinely welcomed until, with Holy Spirit, we've reached our own inner neutrality about the issue – free of resistance or submission *to it*. To reach this degree of neutrality, we must be willing to make the positive separation between truth and illusions in our mind. This is accepting the Atonement, and results in acceptance of the miracle in place of the illusion.

10. What we deem as natural through the ego, such as conflict, pain, disease, aging, scarcity, loss, death and violent acts of nature, etc., are not "natural" at all. These are *miscreations* projected by our fearful split mind. While we passively condone these illusions as either good or bad, and while we build our life around them, we are destined to perpetuate the separation dream. True healing arises from our comprehensive forgiveness which by necessity requires the uniform *dismissal of unreality*. We cannot forgive nor heal something that we choose to maintain *is* real, did in fact happen, or can harm us in any way.

a. *"The ego's plan is to have you see error clearly first, and then overlook it. Yet how can you overlook what you have made real? By seeing it clearly, you have made it real and [cannot] overlook it." ... "Forgiveness through the Holy Spirit lies simply in looking beyond error from the beginning, and thus keeping it unreal for you. Do not let any belief in its realness enter your mind, or you will also believe that you must undo what you have made in order to be forgiven. What has no effect does not exist, and to the Holy Spirit the effects of error are nonexistent. By steadily and consistently cancelling out all its effects, everywhere and in all respects, He teaches that the ego does not exist and proves it." T-9. IV.4:4-6,5:3-6*

11. In the process of awakening, some spiritual modalities teach that healing involves learning to welcome, allow, accept, trust and love "what is," whether it is mental, emotional or physical. These modalities don't explain however that "what is" is actually an "untruth." In this approach, the relative body and world are mostly viewed and taught as being *causative* rather than as "effects" emanating from unforgiveness in our mind.

12. On a more positive note, this approach of non-resistance can prove helpful by reducing the ego's temptation to go into denial or do a spiritual bypass. The ego wants to intellectually argue that if the body, sickness or apparent adversity is not real anyway, it consequently need not be addressed. This denial is a common ego ploy to ensure that the student never goes beyond a *concept* into the *direct knowing* and *experience* of what the teaching represents: We share God's outright dominion over all phenomena the ego projected. The ego wants to convince us that we are *not* God's beloved Child, but instead, we are a mere body destined for suffering and death. We may tend to learn the metaphysical principles of the *Course* intellectually, but at the application or experience level our trust is often weak in applying them practically in all our relationships and with the body.

13. Bypassing occurs when we deny the fact that we *do* believe that untruth is real and that we *are* clearly fearful of harm. Instead of denying our belief that we're a body which can suffer and die, we need to exercise radical self-honesty so we can unearth these denials without guilt or self-judgment. These denials are the very cause of all suffering, and we cannot employ the ego's means to heal. We must learn to give them to Holy Spirit for forgiveness. Our trust transfers exponentially from fear to Love as we *unlearn* the ego's beliefs, and in particular, as we relinquish our *special* relating, while practicing *authentic* relating. The means by which we engage in this is via forgiveness and the *Seven Key Principles of Authentic Relating* which you can find in Chapter VI, page 572, simply referred to throughout this manual as the *Seven Keys*.

A. The Split Mind – Perception and Knowledge

1. The entire realm of consciousness is exclusive of God's realm of Knowledge. Consciousness (or perception) *and* Knowledge have no meeting place. The Holy Spirit in our Mind is the only mediator between them.

2. We made a vast dream of perception (consciousness), of time and space, birth and death, etc. It's called the separation. Even the highest states of spiritual awakening, including the Real World, remain still *within* the realm of perception/consciousness. Progressive levels of awareness and awakening are not known in the realm of God's Knowledge where our Soul abides.

3. No real creation occurs here in the realm of perception. The highest attainment in the dream of perception is *true perception*. True perception allows the last step to take place, one which is taken by God Himself – the transfer from perception to God's Knowledge.

4. The relative world is fiction, a massive dream all occurring in our mind (not brain). Included in this dream of perception/consciousness are bodies, the past, the dream of death, reincarnation, mother nature and its cycles, the astral realm, inter-dimensional beings and states, space-time, extraterrestrials and UFO's, etc. None of these phenomena exist outside our mind.

5. Consequently, we do not awaken from the ego thought system through the dream of physical death. Death, as an illusory construct and defense against true union, is the ego's central dream, without which there would be no space-time or separation. In renouncing our belief in death, we are recognizing that only the truth is true. The realm of perception would cease to exist in our mind because death *and* God are absolutely irreconcilable. Only one exists. In other words, our unquestioned belief in death as a natural and inevitable part of life (God), maintains the dream of separation. *"Death is the central dream from which all illusions stem."* M-27.1:1

   a. *"This is the darkest veil, upheld by the belief in death and protected by its attraction. The dedication to death and to its sovereignty is but the solemn vow, the promise made in secret to the ego never to lift this veil, not to approach it, nor even to suspect that it is there. This is the secret bargain made with the ego to keep what lies beyond the veil forever blotted out and unremembered. Here is your promise never to allow union to call you out of separation; the great amnesia in which the memory of God seems quite forgotten; the cleavage of your Self from you;--[the fear of >God,] the final step in your dissociation."* T-19.IV.D.3.

6. Death is the ego's obsessive and non-negotiable escape route from Love, life, healing and union; all to ensure we never awaken altogether from the body identity and overcome its dream. However, we will eventually awaken from the separation dream through comprehensive forgiveness of our *choice* to perceive a dream apart from God's Love. This is why, in His short incarnation, Jesus overcame the dream of death through His resurrection. He came to teach us that we too, can and will overcome the body and death. This is where the thinking of the world (as miscreation) is literally reversed.

   a. *"The ego wants [you] dead, but not itself. The outcome of its strange religion must therefore be the conviction that it can pursue you beyond the grave." T-15.I.3:3-4*

7. *"Nothing the world believes is true. It is a place whose purpose is to be a home where those who claim they do not know themselves can come to question what it is they are. And they will come again until the time Atonement is accepted, and they learn it is impossible to doubt yourself, and not to be aware of what you are." W-139.7.* The relative, neutral body and world exist exclusively within our mind as do the experiences of death, NDE's and the after-life. These are dreams we choose that exist within our vast dream of perception or consciousness. The unquestioned and mistaken belief that death ends life is at the seat of the perpetuation of time itself.

B. Split Mind Horizontal Timeline Diagram

1. In the Horizontal Split Mind Timeline diagram on the opposite page, we see a simple horizontal timeline depicting the ego's repetitious dream cycle of birth, amnesia and death.

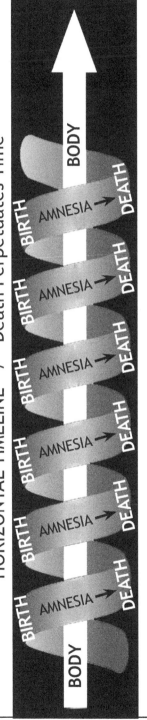

SPLIT MIND

HORIZONTAL TIMELINE / Death Perpetuates Time

BODY

BIRTH · AMNESIA → DEATH
BIRTH · AMNESIA → DEATH
BIRTH · AMNESIA → DEATH
BIRTH · AMNESIA → DEATH
BIRTH · AMNESIA → DEATH
BIRTH · AMNESIA → DEATH

BODY

AMNESIA = Ego's attempts to replace God & our Holy Self in our awareness

The BODY = Ego's central idol as substitute for God

DEATH = The central dream of the entire perceptual realm (consciousness)

C. The Realm of Knowledge vs. The Realm of Illusions Plus
   a Diagram *(Please see the diagram on the opposite page)*

1. While *Creation* is our natural function in Heaven *outside* our dream of space-time, *healing* is our function while our mind's awareness journeys through its dream of perception. No co-creating with God occurs in our dream of duality. Healing is attained exclusively by forgiveness of our own projections of untruth, as the removal of blocks to our awareness of Love's presence. All healing is forgiveness. It is the undoing of our investment in sin, guilt and fear and is thus the undoing of belief in bodies and death.

2. Our Soul dwells in the Absolute, eternally with God in the realm of Knowledge, even though we've chosen that our split mind dreams of duality, of perception/consciousness. Consciousness does not "know" with certainty, because it is still essentially judgmental, containing the questioning aspect which God's unequivocal and indivisible Knowledge does not. The realm of Knowledge knows of no consciousness/perception because it is unified as one with God and our brothers. It is only here, in the realm of Knowledge, where co-creation with God occurs. The Soul continues its extension in Creation with God: *"Creation continues unabated because that is the Will of God. This Will is always unified and therefore has no meaning in this world. It has no opposite and no degrees."* C-1.4:3-5

3. The mind divided between truth and untruth cannot Love. The closest we can come to the experience of changeless Love in the dream is to sincerely forgive all grievances and adversity, forgiving their singular source – as our own *choice* to perceive separation. This healing process is accelerated through the Holy Relationship. From our consistent forgiveness, the divided mind is returned to innocence and wholeness, which *is* Love. *"This is the shift that true perception brings: What was projected out is seen within, and there forgiveness lets it disappear."* C-4.6:1. Only the unified Will of God knows perfect Love, and this perfect Love casts out all fear.

4. The highest healing we can attain whilst still remaining in the realm of perception is true perception, which leads to Christ Vision and the Real World dream. In truth, there is no attainment of One-Mindedness – as the unified Will of God – within the dream of perception and

GOD
REALM OF KNOWLEDGE

- Sons (Souls) of God
- Certainty only
- No perception
- No consciousness
- Christ Mind Whose Will is one with God
- State of undivided Communion
- Heaven/Eternity
- Oneness/Singularity
- Co-Creation with God
- Changeless, perfect Love
- God's Mind / Christ Mind is invincible because it is undivided

and God Himself Takes the Final Step

Portal of
ASCENSION →

True Perception via
Forgiveness/Atonement
Real World Dream
Holy Relationship

The Highest State possible
before God takes the
Last Step

REALM OF ILLUSIONS

The Dream of:

- Perception/consciousness
- Duality/partial awareness
- Choice to perceive apart from God
- The death realm, NDE's and the after life
- All dimensions of time
- The astral realm
- The physical universe and its "laws" (ego laws)
- The dream of "life" apart from God
- The body & all physical form
- The "laws" of nature (ego laws)
- Extraterrestrials/UFO's

In this realm of illusions there is no order of difficulty in miracles because there is no hierarchy of illusions. All illusions are equally UNREAL.

consciousness. The accomplishment of true perception heralds the joyful decision to end our free will "choice" to dream of an identity, will and world apart from God. The option of choice still resides in the realm of consciousness, which involves the possibility of doubt. To perceive then, in absolute terms, is to *not Know*.

5. Whereas in God's realm of Knowledge, free of consciousness, there is *no doubt*, only the *certainty* of knowing. There is no choice to perceive an alternative to what we are as God's all-encompassing Love. Maybe we can see now just why the entire separation is purely a *dream only*. The Son of God *we are* remains completely untouched by this *dream* of the choice to experience a fictional reality apart from God.

6. When we consent to heal our split mind, returning to our whole Mind as the unified Will of God, nothing remains to choose *between*. There is no alternative to God, or to Love as our unified Holy Self. This is One-Mindedness as the *end* of illusions. This is the end of perception or consciousness, and our return to Creation and Knowledge.

7. In the absence of our willing choice to miscreate by perceiving something *apart* from the Love of God we are, our Mind is returned to wholeness. Here, it knows only God and *nothing other* than God. We actively Will *with* God because we know we *are* the Will of God. The Will of God knows no division, and therefore no suffering. There is no point to dream of consciousness or perception any longer, as its purpose lies exclusively in our choice to perceive a dream of something *other than* the Will of God, as our shared and Holy Self. Who then would choose to fabricate and value an alternate identity and world?

a. *"[Wrong-mindedness] listens to the ego and makes illusions; perceiving sin and justifying anger, and seeing guilt, disease and death as real. Both this world and the real world are illusions because right-mindedness merely overlooks, or forgives, what never happened. Therefore it is not the [One-mindedness] of the Christ Mind, Whose Will is One with God's."*

"In this world the only remaining freedom is the freedom of choice; always between two choices or two voices. Will is not involved in perception at any level, and has nothing to

do with choice. [Consciousness] is the receptive mechanism, receiving messages from above or below; from the Holy Spirit or the ego. Consciousness has levels and awareness can shift quite dramatically, but it cannot transcend the perceptual realm. At its highest it becomes aware of the real world, and can be trained to do so increasingly. Yet the very fact that it has levels and can be trained demonstrates that it cannot reach knowledge." C-1.6,7

8. Consciousness is still within the realm of perception and duality. Neither consciousness nor perception is in the realm of Knowledge, where true Creating is. We won't be aware of true co-creating with God until we ascend out of the dream of perception/consciousness and into Knowledge. This is something that most, if not all, spiritual teachings do not realize.

   a. *"Consciousness is thus the level of perception, but NOT of knowledge. Again, to PERCEIVE is NOT to know."* ... *"Consciousness was the first split that man introduced into himself. He became a PERCEIVER rather than a creator in the true sense." Urtext, Chapter 3, Conflict and the Ego*

9. I feel that the following excerpt from chapter 4 in the Urtext is an especially clear and valuable teaching on the fundamental contrast between the ego and the Soul, and between the states of perception and Knowledge.

   a. *"The Soul in its knowledge is unaware of the ego. It does NOT attack the ego. It merely cannot conceive of it at all. While the ego is equally unaware of the Soul, it DOES perceive itself as rejected by something which is greater than itself. This is why self-esteem in ego terms MUST be a delusion." Urtext, Chapter 4*

   b. *"Perception did not exist until the Separation had introduced degrees, aspects and intervals. The Soul has no levels, and ALL conflict arises from the concept of levels."* ... *"Only the levels of the Trinity are capable of Unity. The levels which man created by the Separation are disastrous. They cannot BUT conflict." Urtext, Chapter 4*

c. *"The mind is very active because it has will-power. When it willed the Separation it willed to perceive. Until it chose to do this, it willed only to know. Afterwards, it had to will ambiguously, and the only way out of ambiguity IS clear perception. Urtext, Chapter 4, The Loss of Certainty*

d. *The ability to perceive made the body possible, because you must perceive SOMETHING, and WITH something. This is why perception involves an exchange, or a translation, which knowledge does NOT need. The interpretive function of perception, (actually, a distorted form of creation), then permitted man to interpret the body as HIMSELF, which, although depressing, was a way out of the conflict he induced." Urtext, Chapter 4*

D. The Mind is the Mechanism of Decision

1. Knowledge is the realm of certainty with God and thus it is entirely free of the differing levels within perception/consciousness. It is free from the impossible choice to perceive *apart* from God. It is comprised of and Knows only the thoughts of God, and is therefore *in* and *as* God, as One. The world of form is the dream of duality, a dream of being split between the true and the untrue. Thus, perception is our choice to dream "apart" from God's Certainty. Our Souls dwell eternally within the realm of undivided Knowledge and know of no separation and no choice, no thoughts, no form, and no reality or experience *apart* from God.

2. In order for the Soul to dream of the realm of perception or consciousness, it required a "mind" with which to do so. Mind is the mechanism for decision, and is required for the illusion of choice in the realm of consciousness. The Soul is *free* of choice. Perception *involves choice*, while no choice is necessary in God's Knowledge since there is just one unified Will with God. In God's realm of Knowledge there is no "decision making" faculty required, as there is in the split-minded dream of perception. Our Soul is entirely impervious to all delusional dreams the mind is dreaming.

3. In the realm of perception, we are presented with constant choices to remember that the truth (God) is true, and that *nothing else* is true. In each moment we are making micro decisions about what we desire, many of which are unconscious. Everything we choose to believe, either painful or joyful, constitutes the value it has for us, and is exactly what we desire.

4. Given the free will to choose to dream of an opposite of Love, we imagine that we can think *without* Holy Spirit, without His Truth and Love. In other words, we may say that we agree that God's Truth is true…but we prefer to forget that *nothing but* the Will of God is true, that everything else we perceive through the body's senses is actually untrue. With free will to choose to dream *apart* from God, we hallucinate that fear is *just as real* and as powerful as God. Yet only the truth is true, and nothing else (fear, sickness, conflict, death) is true! We cannot truly know that the truth is true… until we make an undivided commitment to accept and demonstrate that *nothing else* (as fear) is true. Holy Spirit needs our willingness and our permission before He can help us with this process.

5. The ego's illusory laws of chaos, such as nature, conflict, time, sickness, health, biological laws, nutrition, medicine, scarcity, loss and death, are *not* the Laws of God. And while we still choose to believe and value them, we elect to be imprisoned *by* them. We will depend on these chaotic laws and forms of magic until our trust in *only* God's Laws is well advanced and established.

6. God's Will as Love is the only Cause. And we are His Loving Effects. As His Effects, there is absolutely no cause in the body or the world that can harm us, once we wholeheartedly accept this via our forgiveness of everyone and everything.

7. The relative body/world is entirely neutral. These phenomena exist purely *as ideas* in our split mind. The body/world is not causative as it seems. If we are the Effects of God and share His exclusive dominion over all illusions, then nothing in our relative dream world, including the ego's central dream of physical death, can possibly threaten us. Think about that. But better still, "feel"

the truth in this: What would change or heal if we absolutely knew that we cannot be threatened by anyone or anything? In our deep acceptance of this "knowing," is the Will of God.

8.   In the Holy Instant of our wholehearted welcome of this knowing… we return our will to fuse as One with the Will of God. And joyous celebration in Heaven abounds as we receive this knowing.

9.   Even in the realm of Heaven (Knowledge) we each have an individual Soul and that Soul expresses itself uniquely. We are not just one unidentifiable blob of light in truth. Jesus says that there are many Sons of God all with their own Godly expressions. They all share God's Certainty and all-Knowingness.

10. As for mystics and saints who had awakened *in* the realm of perception, many of them are still "recycling" in the dream of birth/death/amnesia because they had not overcome the body and death through their misperception of them *as causative*. Therefore, they had not reversed "effect and cause," to realize and demonstrate their complete sinlessness, and therefore their immunity to all phenomena they made in the dream, including the body and death. But there are some who awoke *from* the dream of separation entirely, and it's comforting to know their image and help is available for us to call on.

a.   *"There are those who have reached God directly, retaining no trace of worldly limits and remembering their own Identity perfectly. These might be called the Teachers of teachers because, although they are no longer visible, their image can yet be called upon. And they will appear when and where it is helpful for them to do so. To those to whom such appearances would be frightening, they give their ideas. No one can call on them in vain. Nor is there anyone of whom they are unaware. All needs are known to them, and all mistakes are recognized and overlooked by them. The time will come when this is understood. And meanwhile, they give all their gifts to the teachers of God who look to them for help, asking all things in their name and in no other." M-26.2.*

11. At the Absolute level in the realm of Knowledge, we each are the Sons or Souls of God. These Souls that we are, are eternal and

are eternally co-creating with God. Jesus revealed to me that these Souls (us) actually created many of the Angels as well. So, these Angels are some of our beloved Creations who are waiting patiently for our *awareness* of them to return. We can call on them in any Holy Instant. Their specific function is to serve us in the Ways of God.

12. As we awaken *from* the dream of separation (or consciousness) by overcoming the body and death, we don't actually leave or ascend out of the dream as it would appear. Because the dream of consciousness exists only through our *desire for it* in our mind, our mind merely stops dreaming of the separation when it desires *nothing other than* to be unified with God by having attained consistently true perception (Atonement). But God does take this last step for us, once we've decided that *all we want* is His Truth and Love, and union with all our brothers and God.

a. *"The term "salvation" does NOT apply to the Soul, which is not in danger and does not need to be salvaged. Salvation is nothing more than "right-mindedness" which is NOT the one-mindedness of the Soul, but which must be accomplished before one-mindedness can be restored. Right-mindedness dictates the next step automatically, because right perception is uniformly without attack, so that wrong-mindedness is obliterated. The ego cannot survive without judgment, and is laid aside accordingly. The mind then has only ONE direction in which it can move." Urtext, Chapter 4*

E. The Fear of Union

1. Our supreme fear, whilst we value the dream of perception, is the fear of Love, of God and of union with our brothers. Our foremost terror and the one that deeply underlies all appearances of fear, is not pain, loss, disease and death - but God as *changeless Love*, healing and union.

2. In the threat of our mind's return to wholeness and incorruptible innocence, the ego perceives the grievous loss of its coveted "individuation" as the separate body and private mind, apart from

our brothers and God. This loss of separation – as the fear of union – represents the ego's central terror. This is none other than its very own secretly defended *wish to suffer,* which is its substitute *for* the immaculate Love of God that we are.

3.   The split mind simply cannot survive without guilt. To ensure that its guilt, as self-attack, is protected and amassed, it must continue to project scenes of conflict, sickness and victimization and bolster the illusion of its separate self-image. The ego then proceeds to "judge" what *it* has deviously projected onto others, the body, the past and the world. And yet all judgment is separation. Within the dream of separation the leading generator of guilt and suffering is our special relationships. Consequently, the separation's greatest threat is the undoing of special relating, and the profound healing of *the gap* which the Holy Relationship delivers.

4.   The false self's ultimate threat is that we "close the gap" of separation with our brother, through absolute forgiveness. In this most blessed commitment we come to recognize, behold and finally know the innocent Christ in another. As we do so, we will then recognize, behold and know the Christ within. *They are the same.* Suddenly, we acknowledge that we and our brother do not have separate, private minds with personal, self-seeking agendas. We share just one truly common purpose and that is to witness and uphold each other's perfect sinlessness. Our Mind, our heart and our will are one! Love beyond the body then, as true communication between us, is continuous and uninterrupted by thoughts of fear and judgment.

5.   What could possibly correct the entire dream of separation but *its opposite,* as union? Our split mind heals, becomes whole, and returns to the realm of Knowledge by facing its final obstacle, the fear of God. The fear of Love, which is the love of separation, can only be overcome through healing the mind's "fear of union." And this is precisely why the Holy Relationship represents the Holy Grail within the mind's choice to dream of consciousness apart from God's realm of Absolute Knowledge.

a.   *"Healing reflects our joint will. This is obvious when you consider what healing is for. Healing is the way in which the separation is overcome. Separation is overcome by union. It cannot be overcome by separating. The decision to unite must be unequivocal, or the mind itself is divided and not whole. Your mind is the means by which you determine your own condition, because mind is the mechanism of decision. It is the power by which you separate or join, and experience pain or joy accordingly." T-8.IV.5:1-8*

4. THE PILLARS OF GOD – TRUTH AND LOVE

1. Many have asked me why I'm writing a manual on Holy Relationship. The basis for their question is due to the commonly held and valued belief that Holy Relationship is between a person and Holy Spirit, and does not in fact take two or more companions.

2. Because of this widely held belief, I am setting forth this essay, The Pillars of God - Truth and Love, to show just why awakening *from* the dream requires an understanding, and even more so, an *experience* of changeless Love, along with God's Truth, His Laws. This can only be directly experienced through Holy Relationship with at least one other brother or sister. Once we enter this experience with at least one brother, the *quantum effect* of comprehensive forgiveness heals all our relationships within all the dimensions of time.

3. We won't understand *truly* what we do not experience directly. When it becomes our *experience,* there is no uncertainty or doubt remaining. This experience of perfect Love with a brother not only anchors the power of God's Laws here in the dream, but allows us to overcome the deep-seated fear of God, of Love and union *beyond* bodies. As Jesus says, we cannot overestimate the value of our brother. This manual and its essays brazenly illustrate why this is so.

4. There is a fundamental distinction between the deeper teachings of Jesus in *A Course in Miracles,* and other non-duality teachings. In the *Course,* we're given two fundamental pillars which largely underpin our healing journey as we return from debilitating fear to all-inclusive Love. These are 1) God's Truth, comprising absolute divine metaphysics *and* 2) Divine, perfect Love which is fearless, changeless and all-encompassing. When we consciously bring God's pillars of Truth *and* Love together and live out from them, we will realize and demonstrate that there is indeed no order of difficulty in miracles. When divine Love and absolute truth are brought together, they literally harness the power and presence of God, here in the dream.

5.   Jesus leads us toward the Laws of God as opposed to the laws of this world, and gives us very specific metaphysical principles to follow which are all based on this one: *"The opposite of Love is fear, but what is all-encompassing can have no opposite. Nothing real can be threatened. Nothing unreal exists. Herein lies the peace of God."* T-2.in.2:2-4

6.   Perceiving from a split mind however, we erroneously believe that fear is *equally as real* as Love; an impossible investment in two diametrically *opposed* thought systems, one of which does not even *exist*. While we value separation, we will continue looking outward from a filter of fear and persist in trusting the body's five senses and its distorted memory. Yet the body and everything its so called senses report *prevents* us from recognizing changeless and perfect Love.

7.   The Laws of God are inextricably fused with the perfect Love of God. The only part of our Mind, of our being, that is real, is the part we share with God. This is our Holy Self, the Son of God which we share with all Children of God. This sane part of our Mind is always in direct communication with God, with perfect Love, and dwells eternally under the Laws of God.

8.   Understanding this, it stands to reason that our sane Mind, being only Love, is also in a state of uninterrupted communication with all our brothers. Only changeless Love *can* be communicated because it is the complete *absence of fear.* Contrary to what we believe, fear cannot be communicated. Fear *breaks* true communication.

9.   This unceasing transmission of Love between our brothers and God is eternal. However, our *awareness* of this undivided communion and its profound healing is broken when we misidentify our self and others as a body.

a. "The ego uses the body for attack, for pleasure and for pride. The insanity of this perception makes it a fearful one indeed. The Holy Spirit sees the body only as a means of communication, and because communicating is sharing it becomes communion. Perhaps you think that fear as well as love can be communicated; and therefore can be shared. Yet this is not so real as it may appear. Those who communicate fear are promoting attack, and attack always breaks communication, making it impossible. Egos do join together in temporary allegiance, but always for what each one can get [separately.] The Holy Spirit communicates only what each one can give to all." T-6.V.A.5:3-10

10. While we still prefer to project our fear (guilt) onto others, the body, the past and the world, instead of *forgiving* our projections – we block the Love that heals our perception and our experience. And how do we recognize when *we are projecting?* How do we identify the moment that we actively block Love? The answer is the instant we are triggered. That moment is when we actually *believe* the temptation of fear (guilt) or blame.

11. Absolutely nothing that happens to us is random. Everything that we react to arises from our own largely unconscious desire for it. Our mind always projects what we desire to perceive, either positive or negative. Projection *makes* perception. Unforgiveness always projects more suffering and separation. Our own *unforgiven projections* make up all our triggers in whatever form they seem to take.

12. Only the insane part of the mind believes what it *itself projected,* and then proceeds to judge, condemn or problem-solve *its own* delusion *apart* from Holy Spirit; and apart from the miracle that would heal the very cause of its appearance. The ego is terrified to have us *forgive* our self for having believed in its own projections.

13. There is no order of difficulty in miracles *and* there is no hierarchy of fear. All fear, together with its numerous "appearances" at the form level, is equally illusory. The miracle heals them all with equal ease because their source – as an imaginary opponent of God – does not exist. This is an immutable Law of God. To help

us gain access to the pillar of God's Truth, in the earlier stages of our transfer from fear to Love, there is a gradual *unlearning* of the distorted principles of the ego thought system.

14. When we commit to dive a little deeper into the *Course's* teachings we begin to replace the ego's untruth, its beliefs and values, with God's pillar of Truth. His Laws and metaphysical principles are *intellectually* assimilated at first. Mental practice or mind training is a very necessary component which purifies and prepares the mind for God's second pillar – the *experience* of changeless Love. This is the actual *experience* of union, of the changeless Love which completely subsumes the false self.

15. Jesus revealed to me that both Truth *and* Love are the pillars of God, and are necessarily required for miracle workers to be consistent. For us to absolutely "know" there is no order of difficulty in miracles, with unwavering and consistent conviction and demonstration as Jesus did, we must embody an advanced understanding and comprehensive acceptance of the *Course's* pillars, Truth *and* Love.

16. Advancing in our development of trust, we enter periods of "contrast learning" which can be quite disorienting and painful, but with Holy Spirit, these are helpful to teach us how to sort out the valuable from the valueless. Previously, through the ego, we had no idea what was in our own best interests.

17. At some point in our transfer of trust from fear to Love, we come to realize the unbearable *burden* and *cost* of special relating as fearful love. Special relating is a form of attack, thus it *breaks* true communication which would have resulted in the experience of Love and healing. In special, conditional relationships there is mutual consent to giving false value, witness and reality to the destructive idols in the gap, instead of forgiving them. *See The Gap diagrams on pages 46 to 49.*

18. In the special relationship the body's physical-sense testimony governs all, literally attempting to substitute for God. Since those involved in special relating are unable or unwilling to make a clear distinction between the real and the unreal, between what *is* of God and what is of the ego, they invariably fall into the trap of trying to forgive that which they have made real. Yet it's impossible to

forgive an illusion once they've made it real in their perception.

19. Whomever and whatever is *not completely forgiven* (believed as real) is stored as an ongoing grievance which compounds our unconscious guilt. Hence, there is an undeniable accumulation of guilt in special relating that blocks our awareness of our perfect sinlessness and therefore, of our divine immunity to attack (conflict, illness, scarcity, etc.).

A. Our Guiltlessness – Accessing Truth and Love

1. The necessary condition for us to access the Laws of God as a consistent miracle worker is to *accept* our guiltlessness. Only when we truly know our guiltlessness can we know that our will and God's are one. But while we continue to buy into inauthentic relating we perpetuate the guilt that *severs* true communication and miracles. We cannot really know and accept our guiltlessness while we still condemn our brother.

2. While the Laws of God are infinite and freely operate on behalf of all, we will not be able to access them consistently until we are willing to release our dependence on the ego and its laws. One of the ego's most tempting and coveted "laws" in the dream is the special relationship. Because the special relationship is the most fiercely defended of all our *substitutes for God*, its release will naturally entail the relinquishment of all lesser forms of guilt.

3. The way that we release all special relating is by repurposing it with Holy Spirit, for Holy relating. As we embark in Holy Relationship, the operation of God's Laws is inevitably restored to us because the mutual goal of the relationship has been assigned to innocence and not to guilt.

   a. *Salvation is a lesson in giving, as the Holy Spirit interprets it. It is the reawakening of the laws of God in minds that have established other laws, and given them power to enforce what God created not." T-20.IV.2:9-10*

4. To know, to live out from, and to demonstrate the Laws of God as miracles, I must first realize and *accept* my own guiltlessness. This innocence is the state in which divine communion is reestablished.

The presence of fear (or blame) blocks this Self Love, cutting off divine communication. Only as I first receive this Love in my awareness, can I then extend it. There is no way I can give, share or extend what I have not yet "received" in my own mind and heart. Gratitude, and not fear, is the hallmark of having accepted the Atonement.

5. Guiltlessness is the necessary condition for knowing God's Love and His Truth. Guiltlessness *is* fearlessness. It's in this Holy Instant of accepting our guiltlessness that the Atonement occurs. It cannot occur while we cling to fear, blame or victimhood as a defense. Because of the unhealed agreement between special relationship companions, to revere the ego's idols *in place* of their unified Holy Self, there is a secret pact to continue projecting their guilt. Within the egos' version of love, guilt and sacrifice are prized. This is the rejection of our guiltlessness, the very condition necessary for us to access both Truth and Love.

6. If I persist in special relating, instead of Holy relating, I cannot know or accept my guiltlessness, nor can I demonstrate the Laws of God because I will continue to keep my guilt – *my defense against the Laws of God* – by projecting onto my brothers.

    a. *"Unless you are guiltless you cannot know God, Whose Will is that you know Him. Therefore, you MUST be guiltless. Yet if you do not accept the necessary conditions for knowing Him, you have denied Him and do not recognize Him, though He is all around you. He cannot be known without His Son, whose guiltlessness is the condition for knowing Him. Accepting His Son as guilty is denial of the Father so complete, that knowledge is swept away from recognition in the very mind where God Himself has placed it." T-14.IV.7:1-5*

7. The pillar of Truth appears to be fully activated only when we advance in our *experience* of Love through Holy Relationship. And it is not until a changeless Love is bearing witness to the absolute Truth, that the power of God's Truth can be experienced. Truth *and* Love are both required *together* for the direct experience of the presence of God and His healing power. As the Holy Relationship

progresses, it compels us to treasure and embody changeless Love, Love without fear. *Guiltlessness* forms the sacred chalice that these companions promise to cherish and protect for each other and thus for all their brothers.

8. Where two or more are committed to forgiveness *above all else,* the gap of separation that contains all manner of substitutes for the Laws of God, is *erased.* Holy Relationship is where two or more agree to consistently forgive false appearances in the gap and witness only to the Christ in each other. In this union we release the debilitating guilt and unworthiness that has blinded us to the ever-present fountain of Love and innocence that is our Source, our safety and our life. As the Holy Relationship progresses, an utterly profound realization of our guiltlessness is gained, together, which literally opens our hearts to this fearless and perfect Love.

   a. *"Healing is a thought by which two minds perceive their oneness and become glad. This gladness calls to every part of the Sonship to rejoice with them, and lets God go out into them and through them." T-5.1.I:1-2*

9. For example, when my partner Daniel and I enter a joint Holy Instant together, we are praying to the Christ in each other. The startling thing here is that there is no "need" to ask for anything in this communion. The reason is that all sense of lack arises from fear, and fear is purely the absence of Love. When Daniel and I truly join as the one Christ, then Love instantly fills the space that fear had attempted to claim.

10. In one Holy Instant all perceived needs are met as the Christ in one kneels at the feet of the Christ in his brother. Fear is the stranger now. Love has illuminated our gaze as we behold the heavenly beauty of the Christ which the body's senses and its past were made to block.

11. Two Minds join in His Name. Here, there is nothing to ask *for.* Instead, there is an effervescent outpouring of unrestrained *gratitude* as we unite with the Christ in our brother or sister. This is the perfect Love, the pillar that when joined with God's Truth, returns our awareness to the presence and power of God. Here, joined as the Christ with our brother, the veil is finally lifted. This

veil hid God and our brothers from us, as the fear of God – the fear of Love and fear of union *beyond the body.*

a. *"One who has realized the goodness of God prays without fear. And one who prays without fear cannot but reach Him. He can therefore also reach His Son, wherever he may be and whatever form he may seem to take."*

b. *"Praying to Christ in anyone is true prayer because it is a gift of thanks to His Father. To ask that Christ be but Himself is not an entreaty. It is a song of thanksgiving for what you are. Herein lies the power of prayer. It asks nothing and receives everything. This prayer can be shared because it receives for everyone. To pray with one who knows that this is true is to be answered. Perhaps the specific form of resolution for a specific problem will occur to either of you; it does not matter which. Perhaps it will reach both, if you are genuinely attuned to one another. It will come because you have realized that Christ is in both of you. That is its only truth."* S-1.I.6:5-7,7.

5. THE GAP EXPOSED!

1. The gap of separation represents our largely unconscious wish for separation, generated by our desire for specialness. The gap cannot exist without its central hero – belief that we are the body. All idols that we value, both seemingly good and bad, stem from and are maintained exclusively by this mistaken belief.
2. One mind "alone" cannot make anything of itself, apart from God, but when *two or more* minds agree to value and believe in a wish for separation, the power of the mind makes a convincing dream where a gap, comprised of space, time and bodies, appears to arise. Everything that is added to the gap from that point on, either positive or negative, is what they idolize *more* than being joined with their brothers as the innocent and unified Will of God. The idols in the

gap then represent the ego's most fiercely defended substitutes for our Holy Self.

a. *"The gap [is] little. Yet it holds the seeds of pestilence and every form of ill, because it is a wish to keep apart and not to join. And thus it seems to give a cause to sickness which is not its cause. The purpose of the gap is all the cause that sickness has. For it was made to keep you separated, in a body which you see as if it were the cause of pain." T-28.III.4:2-6*

3. It took at least *two minds* to agree to try and experience life *apart* from God. These two or more share a common, unholy purpose, and this agreement gave rise to "special" relationships, where consenting parties wished to see themselves as special, separate, autonomous and not part of the one, shared, Holy Self. This gap is *always* the fear of present joining. Every relationship begins as special, until those involved consciously enter an agreement with each other and Holy Spirit to divinely repurpose the relationship into a Holy Relationship. A Holy Relationship is of course available to everyone, regardless of what teachings they follow. This manual delves deeply into the *Course's* process of transforming relationships from special to Holy, which is literally the fast track to total transcendence *from* the dream of separation.

4. In carrying out this original wish for specialness, a convincing barrier between these minds and God was necessary. The idea of a physical, mortal body was projected, and provided with five physical senses. This gave persuasive witness to a state of separation, through their projected distortions and false definitions, which they gave to everything, including themselves, others, the past and the world.

5. Each mind adopted this finite form, or body, and agreed to block their true Identity by identifying *each other* as a body, complete with gender, age, assigned role and purpose, title, nationality, personality, and so on. It was the agreement of *both* parties to continually objectify each other *as* bodies, and to witness to the changes, dramas, roles, conflicts, sicknesses and ultimately, deaths of those bodies, in order to safeguard the illusion of separation.

6. All "add-ons" in the gap of space/time are merely layers to bolster

the foundation of the belief in separation, as the physical body. In truth, the belief that we *are* the body *is* the gap. All idols in the gap are valued specifically to try to prove that we are *not* the sinless and thus *invincible Child of God*, but separate, guilty bodies doomed to imprisonment by the laws of the ego's illusory world.

7. The idols we value in the gap are an attempt to replace the Holy Self we share with our brothers. An idol, either pleasurable or painful, is anything that we desire *more* than we want to behold our brother's innocence, his or her sinlessness. It's an image of our brother that we value *more* than seeing the truth about his real Identity. Each idol stems from the ego's fundamental fear and lack, and is heavily defended by the ego. These idols ensure we continue to project our unconscious guilt onto others, the body, the past and the world. In turn, this condemns the body to aging, illness and death, all to perpetuate the ego's separation concept of time and ongoing amnesia of our true Identity.

8. When one withdraws their consent to special relating, it becomes highly difficult for the other one in special relationship to maintain the original agreement. Each of these then are faced with a decision; they either *join* in the *dissolution* of the specialness dynamic between them, or they *separate* to seek another split mind that is willing to *continue* to engage in witnessing to them as a body, and not a mind or Spirit. The Holy Relationship requires the complete *undoing* of the miscommunication dynamic found in the special relationship. In the Holy Relationship *both* people agree to reverse the original goal from one of desired separation, back to true union.

9. Recall that the singular purpose for the imaginary gap is to hide the face of Christ in our brothers, so that we can perpetuate the dream of separation. And this is why the Holy Relationship – as mutual devotion to closing the gap, to lifting the veil that hides the face of Christ – is the Holy Grail that closes the gap of specialness once and for all time.

    a. *"What is an idol? Do you think you know? For idols are unrecognized as such, and never seen for what they really are. That is the only power that they have. Their purpose is obscure, and they are feared and worshipped, both, [because] you do not know what they are for, and why they have been made. An idol is an image of your brother that you would value more than what he is. Idols are made that he may be replaced, no matter what their form. And it is this that never is perceived and recognized. Be it a body or a thing, a place, a situation or a circumstance, an object owned or wanted, or a right demanded or achieved, it is the same."*

"An idol is a false impression, or a false belief; some form of anti-Christ, that constitutes a gap between the Christ and what you see. An idol is a wish, made tangible and given form, and thus perceived as real and seen outside the mind. Yet it is still a thought, and cannot leave the mind that is its source. Nor is its form apart from the idea it represents. All forms of anti-Christ oppose the Christ."

"This world of idols [is] a veil across the face of Christ, because its purpose is to separate your brother from yourself. A dark and fearful purpose, yet a thought without the power to change one blade of grass from something living to a sign of death." T-29.VIII.1,3,4:1-2

10. Once we recognize that the foundation of the separation dream is our *willing choice* to believe and maintain the gap, along with its idols, we can then choose again with Holy Spirit. This miraculous shift occurs when we finally see the value in desiring to close this gap with all our brothers and sisters through Holy relating.

A. Diagrams as a Tool

1. I have found that diagrams are a helpful means to cut through the ego's resistance. Words can frequently be hijacked by the ego to delay genuine recognition of the truth. But diagrams or images tend to make an undeniable impact at an unconscious level. This is why we've included some powerful diagrams on pages 46 thru 49 to illustrate the gap, the special relationship and the Holy Relationship. Additional information about the Gap diagrams starts on page 50, and notations have been provided throughout

TWO SPLIT MINDS AGREE

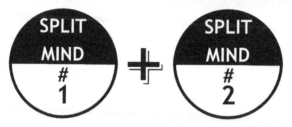

SPLIT MIND # 1 ➕ **SPLIT MIND # 2**

Two split minds agree to
"THE GAP"
SPECIAL RELATIONSHIP

GAP

To maintain the separation,
two or more split minds form
a special relationship
& agree on the following:

- private minds with separate agendas that clash
- body identity & its five physical senses
- sickness, pain, accidents or suffering
- scarcity or sacrifice of any kind
- any belief in attack or defense
- personal will apart from God
- personal pleasure-drives
- sin, guilt & fear
- false humility
- death
- need to be right
- time/past/future
- pride, pleasure & attack
- our stories, laws of ego/chaos

SPLIT MIND #1   **SPLIT MIND #2**

GAP = Body = Veil = Wall = Fear of GOD/LOVE/UNION
Requires two consenting minds (witnesses)

HOLY RELATIONSHIP

As two or more open to undo special relating,
they drop their deeply hidden fear of Love.
They invite the Holy Spirit to transform the special
relationship into a Holy Relationship
to bring awareness back to the Unified Mind, or the
Changeless, Innocent, Holy Self

GAP — UNIFIED MIND #1 & #2 — CLOSED

Agreements

- one truly common purpose - forgiveness
- common state of mind
- centered on Spirit, not body
- Priority: to see each other as sinless
- no separate needs or agendas
- look past ego appearances
- implement the Seven Keys, Divine Switch, & Atonement
- one will with each other and Spirit
- ongoing, increasing gratitude
- joint Holy Instants
- share a Joint Special Function

Outcomes

- miracles
- quantum forgiveness/ Atonement
- incorruptible innocence
- Real World
- laws of God
- fearlessness
- immortality
- Peace of God
- Joy & Divine Love
- health
- purpose
- Christ Vision
- Unified Will of God
- Abundance
- Miracle workers
- Teachers of God

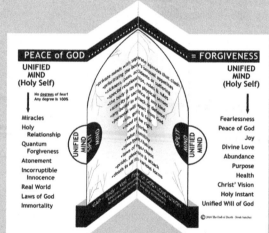

When the "gap" diagram on the next page is folded, it represents lifting the veil, dropping fear & the belief we are a body, and leaving only the Unified Mind, as the Holy Self. You can find a printable version of the gap diagram in the Holy Relationship Supplemental Materials link at: *www.HolyRelationship.com*

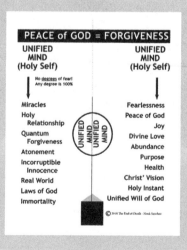

**UNIFIED MIND
(Holy Self)**
Miracle-Drive

Peace of God
Joy
Divine Love
Abundance
Purpose
Health
Christ' Vision
Holy Instant
Unified Will of God

Holy Relationship → UNIFIED MIND
SPLIT MIND ← Special Relationship

To maintain the separation, two or more split minds form a *special relationship* & agree on the following:

- private minds with separate agendas that clash
- body identity & its five physical senses
- sickness, pain, accidents or suffering
- scarcity or sacrifice of any kind
- any belief in attack or defense
- personal will apart from God
- personal pleasure-drives
- sin, guilt & fear
- false humility
- death
- need to be right
- time/past/future
- pride, pleasure & attack
- our stories, laws of ego/chaos

UNIFIED MIND Holy Relationship →
SPLIT MIND ← Special Relationship

GAP = Body = Veil = Wall = Fear of GOD/LOVE/UNION
Requires two consenting minds (witnesses)

**UNIFIED MIND
(Holy Self)**
Miracle-Drive

No degrees of fear!
Any degree is 100%

Miracles
Holy Relationship
Quantum Forgiveness
Atonement
Incorruptible
Innocence
Real World
Laws of God
Fearlessness
Immortality

the book for the reader to review the diagrams when they pertain to, or enhance, the reading.

B. The Gap Diagrams *(Please see pages 46 thru 49)*

1. Make sure to notice the *two split minds* depicted as circles to either side of the Gap in the primary "foldable" gap diagram. And in the "special relationship" diagram, take a good look at all the ego's idols that actually sustain the separation, with the *body* being the central replacement for our Holy Self. Pay particular attention to these two (or more) mind's "agreements," which form the gap of separation. See how it takes the agreement of two or more split minds to maintain the gap?

2. Next, look at the Holy Relationship diagram. What do you see? Take a look at both the Holy Relationships "agreements" and its "outcomes." Can you see how the gap of suffering and separation closes? These diagrams illustrate just how the Holy Relationship *is* the Holy Grail, the end of separation, the final lesson we joyfully embrace as the bridge to the Real World. *The "printable" Gap Diagram is available in the Holy Relationship Supplemental Materials link at:* www.HolyRelationship.com

6. THE MIRACULOUS PEACE

1. This essay is about the miraculous "piece" which is literally, our missing peace. If we only knew how invaluable this peace *is*, we would surrender all for it, and having found it, we would vow never to lose it again.

2. There is only one peace which is changeless, and that is the peace of God. All other forms of "peace" are subject to change or loss because they are dependent upon or threatened by another person, our image, the body, time, material objects, circumstances or events. This false sense of peace will be threatened because it is invested in shifting illusions. When these dreams are threatened we lose our peace.

3. To want the peace of God is to want *changeless* peace. This desire is nothing less than wanting to know, not just conceptually but in truth, What we are. This is the deepest desire to embody our divine Identity as the Holy Self.

4. All prayers are answered within a sincere request of the heart for the peace of God. And no prayer can be answered if it is something that we want *more* than the peace of God because there *is* nothing more than the peace of God.

5. In this most precious Holy Instant, when we surrender into our divine totality which God has already given us, peace is available for our receiving. But it cannot be received from a state of fear or lack. If we choose to believe – to value – the errors which the body's senses see, then we will reject the peace of God.

6. All prayers are answered in the Holy Instant of peace. The question is, "Are we willing to show up for it?" We won't be willing to do this if there is something we value more than His peace.

7. The peace of God is holographic. It encompasses forgiveness and the Atonement, which is the divine correction of our perception from separation to union, from fear to Love. The ego's illusory gap of fear, from which all pestilence emerges, is closed when we accept the Atonement.

8. My own experience has shown me that I must ask myself what it is that I want. This includes anything that I'm fearful of as well as what I believe will make me happy. For example, if I am concerned about the state of the body's health or that of a loved one, then this choice to be concerned must be what I want *more* than the peace of God. Healing cannot take place while I prioritize my fear. The fear will block God's peace in which all healing lies.

9. Yet if I truly long for the peace of God as my priority; if the peace of God is *all* I want, then this is the peace in which I accept and receive the healing. Here is the peace where all miracles dwell, just quivering in divine readiness to spring forth into my awareness.

10. "I want the peace of God." Jesus tells us that to say these words, is nothing. But to mean these words is everything! No one can mean these words in their heart and not be healed. We must want the peace

of God and nothing but the peace of God. When this is our only "will," the little wish to be a separate will apart from God, falls away.

11. Suddenly, the divine fusion of Son and Father is returned to our awareness. We *are* the Will of God! There is no separate wish to witness the illusion of fear any longer regardless of its wildly diverse forms. All forms are seen as the one temptation to leave the majestic Circle of Peace.

12. To want the peace of God above all else is to know our Self *as* the Will of God here in the dream. Here, we share God's Loving dominion over all which the ego made to try to prove the separation occurred. This is where physical miracles abide in abundance. Sickness, pain, conflict, loss and even death are impossible when we live, move and have our being anchored deeply in the peace of God.

a. *"I want the peace of God."... "No one can mean these words and not be healed." ... "He wants the peace of God, and it is given him. For that is all he wants, and that is all he will receive. Many have said these words. But few indeed have meant them. You have but to look upon the world you see around you to be sure how very few they are. The world would be completely changed, should any two agree these words express the only thing they want." W-185.2:2,4-9*

A. Is Fear Involuntary?

1. There is no order of difficulty in miracles. One is not harder or more difficult than any other. When we want only the peace of God, then within this undivided tranquility, resides the full transfer of all miracles. This is Love without fear. Our certain safety lies in this peace while we prioritize it above all temptations to perceive otherwise.

2. In any one moment we perceive either through Love, or fear. There are no degrees of fear and no degrees of Love. Our perception is either grounded in Love and safe in the peace of God, or we are lost in fear. Unfortunately, through the false self, we cannot distinguish fear from Love because nearly everything we believe is "love," is really fear in disguise, until we have advanced in our transfer of trust

in God's Love.

3. Love and fear are each total thought systems. They cannot meet nor be integrated in any way. The presence of one negates the other. They literally cancel each other out in our awareness.

4. Fear is the opposite of God's all-encompassing Love, His peace. Yet no opposite exists. Consequently, fear together with everything that comes from it - is an illusion. Fear only appears to be a real emotion.

5. Fear is the result of a choice to perceive without Love. Fear is *not* involuntary. The only way we can feel fear is if we *value* it. What we believe, we indeed value and invite into our experience. And the more we defend our self from fear, the more we assign reality and power to it, strengthening it in our awareness. What we fear, we end up attracting. Fear can never be mastered; however, it will disappear in the light of Love and forgiveness. Thankfully, the peace of God gently erases all fear.

6. If there is fear then we have placed our trust in the ego. *"The presence of fear is a sure sign that you are trusting in your own strength." W-48.3:1*

7. The greatest opponent to peace, if there were such a thing, is fear in whatever "form" it takes. This leads me to ask a question, "What is it that I believe fear will give me, which the peace of God cannot?" Ultimately, fear offers protection *from* peace, from undivided *union* as the Holy Self. Fear is a *choice to reject* Love, which is refusal of our Holy Self as Love.

8. In any instant that we choose to *believe* in fear and its consequences, we abandon our Holy Self and identify as an opponent to God, to Love and to peace. The ego *is* fear, so when we believe and say "I am fearful," we're really claiming to be one with the ego as a "self" apart from God. And while we misidentify *as* the ego – as fear itself –we automatically feel responsible (guilty) for solving its many illusory problems.

9. The one underlying reason for fear is that we have mistakenly decided to identify as a *separate* body self apart from God. Whenever we confuse our identity as the body, in place of Spirit, we will feel responsible for it; hence the fear. The way to heal this confusion is

to recognize that all forms of fear come from this error alone. This is why, when fear is felt, we need to turn to Holy Spirit and be willing to change our mind about who we are, inviting Him to help us to accept that we are invulnerable Spirit and not the ego or body.

a. *"When you are fearful, you have chosen wrongly. That is why you feel responsible for it. You must change your mind, not your behavior, and this [is] a matter of willingness."T-2. VI.3:2-4*

10. Jesus explains more in the following quote:

a. *"Fear cannot be controlled by me, but it can be self controlled. Fear prevents me from giving you my control. The presence of fear shows that you have raised body thoughts to the level of the mind. This removes them from my control, and makes you feel personally responsible for them." T-2.VI.4:4-6*

11. Jesus clearly states that the correction of fear is *our* responsibility. Fear is always the direct effect of our misidentifying as a body. When fear is believed, it is *the illusory ego* that believes it. It is always the ego that attempts to pray for release from fear. Recall that fear and Love cannot communicate because they cannot coexist. None of the ego's fictitious prayers for release from itself as fear, are heard by Love because Holy Spirit knows that fear and the ego do not exist. Only when we acknowledge that our temptations into fear arise exclusively from our "willingness to be separate" – as body self misidentification – is permission given to Holy Spirit to heal our perception of being a self apart from God.

12. We *decided* to believe we are separate from our Source. Until we *decide to change* that decision, *we are* responsible for our fear. To ask Holy Spirit to remove our fear *for us* is asking Him to change a decision that *we made*. We will benefit greatly by asking His help with *forgiving* this mistaken *choice* to believe that we are the body, and we're separate. Our priority now is to choose again with Holy Spirit, to close the gap of separation.

a. *"The correction of fear [is] your responsibility. When you ask for release from fear, you are implying that it is not. You should ask, instead, for help in the conditions that have brought the fear about. These conditions always entail a willingness to be separate. At that level you [can] help it." T-2.VI.4:1-5*

13. I am sustained exclusively by the peace of God. This means that if I still believe I am sustained primarily by illusions, or "forms" of fear (body, exercise, finances, special relationships, etc.), then I will resist God's peace and Love, as my Holy Self. When I value my identity *as* a body I will believe I am separate from my Source as Love. The certain outcome of this belief is fear. Jesus encourages me to ask Him for help in the "conditions" that have precipitated my fear which is my mistaken value of the body identity and my willingness to be separate.

14. In addition, those people and things that I believe rob me of peace are values I cherish for the same reason, in order to resist God's peace, as my Holy Self. Until these idols have been genuinely recognized and forgiven, I will use both positive and negative illusions to further prove to myself and others that we are the mortal ego-body identity, and not the immortal Holy Self.

15. My Holy Self *is* the peace of God. This state of all-inclusive peace has no opponent because it encompasses everything. There is no lack or conflict within it. There are no conflicting wishes here. Furthermore, I know that all "appearances" of conflict perceived through the body's senses, are gently resolved within this peace.

16. This peace is beyond the polarities projected and sensed by a separate self. The peace of God transcends all judgments of good and bad.

17. By cherishing the peace of God above all else, I become the light that literally subsumes the darkness of the ego thought system, along with its many seemingly convincing appearances of pain and suffering. In my singular commitment to choose to reside in the peace of God, I create the *condition* necessary for His Will to heal the dream of separation. Nothing is missing in the peace of God, the Holy Instant. Everything is given and received in this, the all-encompassing peace of God.

a. *"The peace of God is everything I want. The peace of God is my one goal; the aim of all my living here, the end I seek, my purpose and my function and my life, while I abide where I am not at home." W-205.1 (185)*

B. Breaking Through the Shield of Fear

1. This may come as quite a shock. Every conceivable fear we have, every fearful thing the body's five senses report is specifically designed as a convincing *shield of fear* that we unwittingly project and use to defend and protect our separate self from God's ever-present Love, from His uninterrupted peace. The sole purpose of this shield of fear is to block awareness of the breathtaking innocence and invulnerability of our infinite Holy Self, the only Self we are.

2. Did you know that every fear regardless of the form of its appearance is *always* the fear of God as the fear of Love itself? All that exists in reality *is* God's Love. There is no opposite. Fear does not exist. The split-mind as the separate self that believes in fear, is convinced that *it* is an enemy to changeless innocence, to Love, to God. In short, it believes that in order to continue it must shield itself from the peace, healing and Love of God. Thus its investment in fear acts as an unrecognized defense against our incorruptible Holy Self. It does this through its convenient projection of sin, guilt and fear thus ensuring its illusory survival.

C. Shield of Fear Diagram *(Page 57)*

1. Look at the "Shield of Fear" diagram on the opposite page. See how the false self has surrounded itself with a defensive wall of fear which it devised to block out God's unopposed Love as the Holy Self we *are.*

2. The truth is that we are the Creator's most beloved creation and this Love that we are is the totality of our one Christ Mind, the Holy Self. This is the unified Mind, the only reality we have and *are.* We are not a separate human being imprisoned within a temporary body that appears to have a private mind of its own.

3. We are quite literally the changeless and incorruptible Spirit of Love itself. Fear, together with its byproducts, does not exist, no matter how much we dream them as real. When we are concerned, angry,

THE SHIELD OF FEAR

ASCENSION
End of Dreaming / Perception

Holy Relationship collapses the Shield of Fear

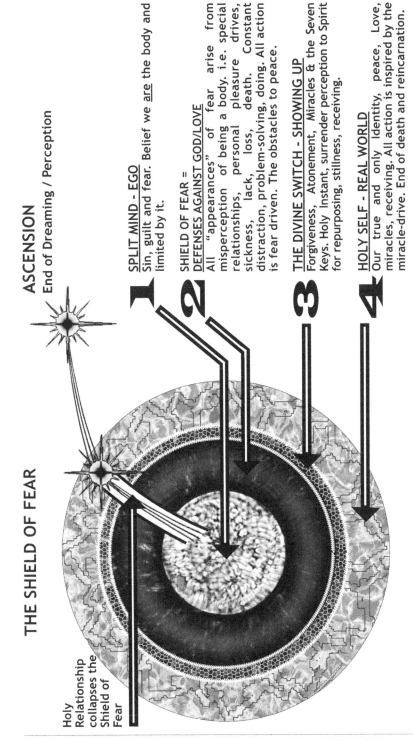

1. SPLIT MIND - EGO
Sin, guilt and fear. Belief we _are_ the body and limited by it.

2. SHIELD OF FEAR = DEFENSES AGAINST GOD/LOVE
All "appearances" of fear arise from misperception of being a body. i.e. special relationships, personal pleasure drives, sickness, lack, loss, death. Constant distraction, problem-solving, doing. All action is fear driven. The obstacles to peace.

3. THE DIVINE SWITCH - SHOWING UP
Forgiveness, Atonement, Miracles & the Seven Keys. Holy Instant, surrender perception to Spirit for repurposing, stillness, receiving.

4. HOLY SELF - REAL WORLD
Our true and only Identity, peace, Love, miracles, receiving. All action is inspired by the miracle-drive. End of death and reincarnation.

confused, feeling unworthy, hurt or in pain, we can immediately see we must be misidentifying as the body-self, a human being, and this is why we need our perception corrected through accepting the Atonement. Our Holy Self cannot *be* threatened. Only an "artificial self" substituting for the glorious Self we are can possibly believe and thus experience suffering.

4. Love *and* fear cannot coexist. Fear is an illusion we made up as a massive smokescreen to hide from our indestructible, Holy Self. Explained differently, our Holy Self *and* attachment to our false, body-self cannot both exist. Only our Holy Self – as Love – is real. Our false self and our Holy Self can never be integrated because they are totally irreconcilable. We are not both! We must learn to make a positive separation between these two.

    a. *"Nothing can reach spirit from the ego, and nothing can reach the ego from spirit. Spirit can neither strengthen the ego nor reduce the conflict within it. The ego [is] a contradiction. Your self and God's Self [are] in opposition. They are opposed in source, in direction and in outcome. They are fundamentally irreconcilable, because spirit cannot perceive and the ego cannot know. They are therefore not in communication and can never be in communication." T-4.I.2:6-12*

5. When we are triggered by fear or its effects such as sickness, pain, conflict, lack, etc., it's the ego projecting that fear hoping that we will *believe it* and then *react to it.* And when we do this, we cannot possibly forgive it because we've made it real in our belief. The cost of making something a reality in our belief, either good or bad, is that *by* valuing it, we immediately reject its undoing via Holy Spirit's quantum forgiveness.

6. While we believe in and react to a seeming threat, we use that convincing "image apart from God" to block our mind from accessing the miracle. The Holy Instant is always present with us. But while we're lost in fear and control, with our independent attempts to problem solve our projected illusions of threat, we deny the Holy Instant along with the miraculous healing it brings.

7. Recall that all fear is a byproduct of the belief in sin and guilt. There could be no possibility of fear, of perceived threat, unless

there was a firm belief that we have indeed sinned and are therefore guilty. Fear then, is always the false self's guilty anticipation of the punishment it believes we deserve. Most of this self-attack remains unconscious until we desire to see, and forgive the ego's projections.

8. Fear has just one enemy – perfect Love – which is *who* we are exclusively in truth. Just think of all the possible scenarios that we fear might occur in our body, our relationships, our family, or our financial situation. The worst fear being physical death itself.

9. Now, let's take a moment to drop into peace. Imagine that we are spotlessly sinless, eternally innocent, and perfectly incorruptible, and that absolutely nothing can possibly threaten us, not even death. Can we maintain enough detachment from guilt and fear to catch a momentary glimpse of what our separate, human self is *really* afraid of? It's certainly not what we thought. It's not guilt, fear, conflict, lack, illness, pain, separation or death. With these out of the way, can we maybe see how all the things we seem to fear – as the shield of fear – are there solely to block our awareness from becoming truly "known" as the Christ? And keep us from leaping joyously into the blazing light of eternal Love and union? Just who would we be without fear?

10. The ego is ingenious at minimizing fear in our *awareness* during the human experience, but it does this specifically so that we will never recognize that *all* of this self's mind is fear-driven. So much so, that it can never Love nor receive Love. The only love it knows is special love, a fearful and changing love which is fear in disguise.

a. *"The ego can and does allow you to regard yourself as supercilious, unbelieving, "lighthearted," distant, emotionally shallow, callous, uninvolved and even desperate, but not really afraid. Minimizing fear, but not its undoing, is the ego's constant effort, and is indeed a skill at which it is very ingenious. How can it preach separation without upholding it through fear, and would you listen to it if you recognized this is what it is doing?"*

"Your recognition that whatever seems to separate you from God is only fear, regardless of the form it takes and quite apart from how the ego wants you to experience it, is therefore the basic ego threat. Its dream of autonomy is shaken to its foundation by this awareness. For though you may countenance a false idea of independence, you will not accept the cost of fear if you recognize it. Yet this is the cost, and the ego cannot minimize it. If you overlook love you are overlooking yourself, and you must fear unreality [because] you have denied yourself. By believing that you have successfully attacked truth, you are believing that attack has power. Very simply, then, you have become afraid of yourself. And no one wants to find what he believes would destroy him." T-11.V.9:1-3,10.

11. The illusory human self concept uses its blind conviction in sin, guilt and fear as a foolproof safeguard *against* reality, which is our Holy Self's infinite guiltlessness and complete immunity to all seeming threats. It projects illusory appearances of fear and while we choose to believe these blocks to Love, we deny our own perfect invulnerability to all appearances of fear. We cannot be both human (fear) *and* divine (Love) as only one is real.

12. Fear is the imaginary shield we use to safeguard the darkness of the false self from the brilliant light of our Holy Self as Love. That is why Jesus says that truth (as Love) is an outright threat to the ego, and why sickness, pain and conflict, etc. are always defenses *against* the truth. Sickness, pain and conflict are each an immediate defense to Love and miracles when these are seen as an outright threat to the ego's attempts to prove separation and suffering are real. There is no way we can access Christ Vision while we're still hooked on *believing* fear in any form.

13. And this is precisely why, when we're feeling anything but peaceful, thankful and happy, we need to own up to the fact that we've chosen to perceive *without* God, without Love. And thus, we're seeing an imaginary idol within the ego's shield of fear. The cause of our angst is never external, even if it appears so. In the moment we catch our self, we can choose again by accepting the Atonement, the correction of our perception by Holy Spirit.

14. When fear appears, remember that it is never *your* fear. It is always the ego's fear… and never your own fear. This is imperative. Fear must be made impersonal because it *is*. For once you say "I am fearful," you immediately misidentify as one with the ego's guilt, as an opponent to God. And in this, you reject your Holy Self.

15. To gain immunity to the ego's temptations you must learn to make a positive separation between the fear-filled, false self, and your beloved Holy Self which you share with everyone. This doesn't mean that you deny the fear, but it does help to recognize that it's always the *ego's fear*. It is a sign that you are trusting in the ego's fear rather than in Holy Spirit's certainty of your perfect sinlessness and safety. This distinction encourages recognition that there is another Voice that you can call on in the face of temptation.

16. This is far too important not to repeat here:

a. *"Your recognition that whatever seems to separate you from God is only fear, regardless of the form it takes and quite apart from how the ego wants you to experience it, is therefore the basic ego threat."…" Very simply, then, you have become afraid of yourself. And no one wants to find what he believes would destroy him." T-11.V.10:1,7*

D. Can You Surrender, Accept and Receive?

1. Here is a powerful question for you. What might change and heal if, whenever you're tempted by fear you remind yourself that this appearance is purely the *fear of Love*, the fear of returning to the peace and joy of your Holy Self? What would happen if each time fear arose, you refused to engage with it and instead, welcomed the unopposed Love and healing behind it, which the fear attempted to shield from your awareness?

2. Recall that while we still believe in fear and its effects, we must also *value* them. To believe *is* to value, and to value is to "desire" it, whether seemingly pleasurable or painful. Another thing: the one who fears (values fear) is never the one who can heal – forgive – it. This acute distinction must be made before we can genuinely forgive via accepting the Atonement.

3. In accepting the Atonement it's never the false self that forgives its own mistakes. This self cannot forgive, just as it cannot Love. Rather, in that Holy Instant of sincere forgiveness, we join with Holy Spirit in complete surrender of the "false self who fears." We're never forgiving somebody or something that appears externally because every appearance that triggers us is projected exclusively by this human self concept. When we wholeheartedly surrender the "false one who fears" to Holy Spirit, He shifts our perception from the human-self to the Holy Self. *This is not something the ego can do.* The ego is completely invested in *doing* something, *anything,* except to surrender itself to the light of Love in which it is divinely subsumed and erased. *Note: Please refer to the "Shades of Gray diagram" on page 692.*

4. A reminder: There is no possibility of integrating the human-self (ego) with the Holy Self because one is wholly fear while the other is wholly Love. The two are not only mutually exclusive…but they cannot coexist in any one moment. The presence of one in our awareness completely replaces the other. Only Love is real – literally.

5. The Holy Instant's leap from the ego mind to the Holy Self can never be achieved by the intellect alone, which happens to be in the ego's domain. This miraculous shift requires an instant of complete surrender to accept and receive the truth of our uninterrupted Identity in God, as Love. In this, we *do nothing.* In the instant of doing nothing, in the instant we quit trying to understand, the ego mind is immediately retired. Fear is suspended. And in that spacious moment all we can do is surrender deeply, accept and receive God's ever-present Love as the center of His Being. After all, we *are* the Kingdom of Heaven, and nothing other than the Kingdom of Heaven:

    a. *"It is hard to understand what "The Kingdom of Heaven is within you" really means. This is because it is not understandable to the ego, which interprets it as if something outside is inside, and this does not mean anything. The word "within" is unnecessary. The Kingdom of Heaven [is] you. What else [but] you did the Creator create, and what else [but] you is His Kingdom? This is the whole message of the Atonement…"* T-14.III.1:1-6

6. In all the history of time there has never been one moment in which we have not been wholly immersed *in* and *as* unopposed Love. We don't know this only because we chose to block our awareness from this fact with the illusion of fear.

7. The ego's fear-driven thought system is anchored in its treacherous conviction that we are not enough, and that we are fundamentally lacking. Believing this profound lie ensures that we must try to *earn* God's approval and Love, and that there is no way we can access it unless we "do" something to qualify for it. And once we mistakenly believe this, we'll also fall into the trap of thinking that we alone are responsible for all our seeming sins.

8. The purpose of every stab of fear, or guilt, or need to "do" something, or to figure it out, or to judge and blame, is to conceal this lie that we are simply not enough. If only we would stop…and ask to *see through* this lie with Holy Spirit instead, He will always reveal our impeccable sinlessness together with the infinite Love we are. This is an *experience* and not an intellectual pursuit.

9. To better help you access a real feeling of peace, a Holy Instant of true fearlessness, and to open your heart to receive the peace of God and His miracles, access the guided meditation titled, *The End of Fear* in the *Supplemental Materials link at: www.HolyRelationship.com*

E. Exercise: What Do You Want *More* than the Peace of God?

1. Make two lists. These two lists will assist to bring your desires – both the positive and negative ones – up to the light so you can ask Holy Spirit to look upon them with you. In the light of true perception, you can ask Him to reveal what is valuable and what is not. This highly effective practice accelerates the healing process.

2. **List # 1 - Positives:** Find all the things you still believe you want here in the dream. Take your time and be radically honest and specific. These may include financial security, health or a better body, romance and sex, a home, a car, etc.

3. **List # 2-Negatives:** Take a look at your very own "shield of fear." Find all those beliefs, values, people, relationships, events, circumstances, things and experiences which cause you concern or

stress. They may be in the past, occurring now, or fears of the future. These are areas of unforgiveness. This list may include unresolved factors in your own spiritual journey, or recurrent issues with a sense of unworthiness or unforgiveness. Please be radically honest and specific.

4. Remembering to ask Holy Spirit to look with you at the lists you have compiled, with radical self-honesty, take List # 1 and go through each of your desires, asking and answering the following questions:

    1) How would I really feel if this desire were accomplished or fulfilled?

    2) Is the fulfillment of this desire more valuable to me than the peace of God?

5. Secondly, with Spirit, review your issues in List # 2 and answer the following question:

    1) What does this concern or stress (unforgiveness) give me that is more valuable to me than the peace of God? What is the pay off for the ego?

6. Jesus leaves us with a meaningful question as we look upon our two lists: *"Is this what I would have, in place of Heaven and the peace of God?"*

    a. *"This is the choice you make. Be not deceived that it is otherwise. No compromise is possible in this. You choose God's peace, or you have asked for dreams. And dreams will come as you requested them. Yet will God's peace come just as certainly, and to remain with you forever."* W-185.8:8,9:1-6

7. **Final Step:** Which of these issues, in both List # 1 and List # 2, are you willing to offer to Holy Spirit for divine repurposing? Are there any beliefs, values or judgments which require forgiveness? The forgiveness process can be found in *The Seven Essential Principles of Quantum Forgiveness (Atonement)* on page 591.

8. Can we perhaps see how the ego is consumed by the delusional idea that these idols will either complete us, or destroy us? Everything we seek for here in the dream arises from some form of fear and lack. But in the peace of God there is no fear or lack. In this peace all is healed and complete.

9. We are not asked to give up that which we presently believe will give us what we want in the world. However, we are asked to give Holy Spirit our "attachment" to them. In other words, are we willing to allow Him to divinely reinterpret and repurpose these illusions? If we don't do this, the ego will use them all, both positive and negative illusions, for self-sabotage and attack, because they represent fear-based substitutes for the peace of God as our one, shared and Holy Self.

F. No Self-Judgment and No Guilt Trips

1. Until we have reached a place where we have truly endured enough inner conflict and where our determined choice for peace completely transcends all temptation to fear, we will continue to vacillate between peace and fear. However, this inconsistency can be helpful as we look upon our choices with Holy Spirit. It is through these wild fluctuations between fear and Love that we eventually learn what is valuable and what is not. This is "contrast learning," where we discover how to differentiate and choose between Love and fear, between the real and unreal. Holy Spirit can use every one of our temptations into fear to help us learn to value peace above all else.

2. Looking at it this way, perhaps we can see that all the meaningless idols we sought and defended here in the dream, hide one sacred and innocent truth. In the still and glorious peace of our heart, we will behold this insight with exquisite tenderness. As we look through the Eyes of Love, we see that behind each idol we cherished for a while, lay our deepest longing to remember that we *are* the changeless and innocent, peace of God.

    a. *"If God is real, there is no pain. If pain is real, there is no God."… "There is nothing in the world that has the power to make you ill or sad, or weak or frail. But it is you who have the power to dominate all things you see by merely recognizing what you are."*

    b. *"Lay down your arms, and come without defense into the quiet place where Heaven's peace holds all things still at last. Lay down all thoughts of danger and of fear. Let no attack enter with you. Lay down the cruel sword of judgment that you hold against your throat, and put aside the withering assaults with which you seek to hide your holiness." W-190.3:3-4,5:5-6,9:1-4*

7. SEEING THROUGH THE EYE OF THE HEART

1. The totality of my safety and security lives within. My unwavering invulnerability is only known in the sanctified stillness of my soul. My eternal and incorruptible innocence has never left me. It has never known of guilt, fear or of attack. This unopposed innocence that I AM dwells quietly within and has never left me. But I will not join the Will of God and embody this truth while I still choose to believe *and thus value* fear, in any thought or form.

A. What is God's Will for Me? How Do I Know God?

1. God knows me only as whole, eternal, guiltless, blameless and forever indestructible. His Will is that I know my Self. In any instant that I show up and offer to *receive* my grace and innocence instead of fear, I close the gap within. Closing the gap is how I know my Self – how I know God. There is no gap of fear that cannot be closed when I show up for my Self in grace and innocence.
2. In any one moment, where do I aim my awareness? What am I constantly reinforcing in my awareness? Is it through the false self's fear filter? Do I mistakenly believe what the body's eyes see? Or do I choose only to see my self, my body, others, the past and the world, through the Eye of my Heart, as the one unified Heart of God? Am I consistently reinforcing the Love of God "I AM?"
3. The only reason we seem to witness the illusion of fear at all, *anywhere,* is because we mistakenly blocked Love from our awareness. It was a decision. But now we can simply choose again. God's Truth as changeless Love is all that exists – ever. Changeless Love *is incorruptible innocence.* We cannot have one without the other because they are the same.

4. This means that our incorruptible innocence (Love) is true, and that *nothing else* is true. But – we won't know the deep security that our incorruptible innocence brings until we wholly engage in longing for nothing else! While we still *believe* the effects of fear are *real* then we still want fear.

5. The truth is true and nothing else is true. Yet if we continue to believe that "some" fearful outcomes are more real than others and worthy of our belief, we are hopelessly divided. Nothing other than our shared incorruptible innocence is true. We must completely immerse our self in this truth to really know the embodied experience of Love without opposite.

6. The heart must long for this. This involves going from the head to the heart, to allow Holy Spirit to reveal what fear has previously hidden from us.

7. The false self only knows fear and has never, not even for one instant, experienced changeless Love and incorruptible innocence. Only the unified and indivisible Holy Self is Love and innocence. When we practice "willing with God" to see only the truth then the false self must fall away. Remember that we can only ever perceive fear through the false self, the body. And we can only ever perceive or extend Love and innocence through the Holy Self. When we are tempted by fear in all its illusory forms, the question to ask is "Who is seeing and believing this?" It must be the ego.

   a. *"Salvation is the recognition that the truth is true, and nothing else is true. This you have heard before, but may not yet accept both parts of it. Without the first, the second has no meaning. But without the second, is the first no longer true. Truth cannot have an opposite. This can not be too often said and thought about. For if what is not true is true as well as what is true, then part of truth is false. And truth has lost its meaning. Nothing but the truth is true, and what is false is false."* W-152.3.

B. What Do I Want? What Do I Value – Above All Else?

1. Do I recognize that every twinge of fear, guilt, anger, concern, self-doubt, pain or judgment, is solely a consequence of my *desire* to be apart from God's Loving awareness as my Holy Self? Simply, it can *only* show-up if I desire to keep a gap between myself *and* Love and innocence. If so, then do I realize that I unwittingly classify "myself" as God's opposite, as fear?

2. And if I secretly condemn myself as God's opposite (fear), is it any wonder I feel a persistent sense of threat? Because in this delusion my only opponent *is* God (Love, innocence). What am I? I am either total, undivided Love – *or* – I am total, undivided fear. There is no in between!

3. All fear, no matter the form, is a direct effect of the ego's desire to be separate from my eternal Source of innocence as Love itself.

   a. *"It is impossible to see two worlds which have no overlap of any kind. Seek for the one; the other disappears. But one remains. They are the range of choice beyond which your decision cannot go. The real and the unreal are all there are to choose between, and nothing more than these." W-130.5.*

   b. *"The world you see must be denied, for sight of it is costing you a different kind of vision. [You cannot see both worlds,] for each of them involves a different kind of seeing, and depends on what you cherish. The sight of one is possible because you have denied the other." T-13.VII.2:1-3*

4. Christ Vision is the decision to look out from the Eye of the Heart. It sees itself in all it looks upon. It looks clear through the most tempting ego appearances of conflict, pain, illness, scarcity and even death. It does not attempt to change what the ego sees because everything the ego sees does not exist. It simply reinstates what was always there, but was blocked by fear. And it does this by accepting the miracle, instead of what the ego imagines is there.

   a. *"The miracle does nothing. All it does is to undo. And thus it cancels out the interference to what has been done. It does not add, but merely takes away."* ... *"All the effects of guilt are here no more. For guilt is over. In its passing went its consequences, left without a cause. Why would you cling to it in memory if you did not desire its effects?" T-28.I.1:1-4,2:1-4*

5. *What is it that brings you into your heart? What do you need to open your heart? Who have you not forgiven? Is it someone else or yourself? Why would you waste another minute in shutting out the memory of your precious, innocent and completely invulnerable Holy Self?*

6. God's Self and yours are one and the same. Why would you want to believe the lie that you are separate? Withdraw your investment in what the past and the body's senses have falsely witnessed as true. Let it go.

7. There are no problems, no conflict, no lack, no pain and no disease when we show up and drop to our knees to kiss the beloved feet of our most innocent and Holy Self. It has never left us. It has never abandoned us. It is here now and wholly willing to embrace us, shining away every bit of our imagined darkness with its blazing light.

8. How much do you desire God? Another way to ask the same question is, how much do you desire to know that you are changeless Love and innocence and *nothing but* this? Are you willing to do whatever it takes? Are you willing to drop to your knees, with open heart and empty hands and ask for *only* this? Or is there something other than this that you still want? Something you deem more valuable?

9. Are you willing to apply the necessary discipline required to join with Holy Spirit to "sort out" the valueless from the valuable in your mind? Will you join Him in saying "no!" to the temptation of fear and expect the miracle instead? Are you willing to accept the Atonement? And are you willing to trust that He has your back – always?

10. Jesus asks us to give him our two greatest idols, the ones that consistently blind us to the majestic Self and Real World that we share. But will we?

a. *"I can be entrusted with your body and your ego only because this enables you not to be concerned with them, and lets me teach you their unimportance. I could not understand their importance to you if I had not once been tempted to believe in them myself. Let us undertake to learn this lesson together so we can be free of them together. I need devoted teachers who share my aim of healing the mind. Spirit is far beyond the need of your protection or mine. Remember this: In this world you need not have tribulation because I have overcome the world. That is why you should be of good cheer." T-4.I.13:4-11*

11. If you only knew that you are Loved, cherished and adored eternally and infinitely. This Love has never wavered even while you prefer to turn your awareness away from it. It has never changed. In fact, it is all there is. And you *are* it. Yes, you are God's most treasured creation. And the time has come for you to remember that the Love you so deeply yearn for – is longing for your Return.

a. *"O my child, if you knew what God wills for you, your joy would be complete! And what He wills has happened, for it was always true. When the light comes and you have said, "God's Will is mine," you will see such beauty that you will know it is not of you. Out of your joy you will create beauty in His Name, for your joy could no more be contained than His." T-11.III.3:1-4*

8. A PROFOUND LESSON IN INNOCENCE

1. What on earth is our Holiness? What does it mean? And how can we recognize and embrace it?
2. Jesus often refers to the importance of our Holiness and the magnificent healing power it holds. But do we actually know what it is and how to access it?
3. In the present phase of my journey it seems I am being taken to the very seed of our unconscious desire for separation. However, as

I delve deeper into this, I am dropping *through* it and into the truth of the "I AM," the exquisite light that has always blazed beneath the illusion of darkness.

4. But before this light could be seen and thus valued above all else, I had to dare to look with radical self-honesty at the separated self's overwhelming obsession with guilt. This is the singular cause of fear, of suffering in all its myriad forms such as relationship conflict, pain, illness, aging, financial scarcity, etc. This deeply coveted guilt is at the root of feelings of unworthiness, of never "being enough" and of never "having enough."

5. How can we determine if we are still hopelessly attracted to guilt? All we have to do is look at its "effects" in our body and our life. Do we harbor judgments against others or the past? Do we judge our self? Do we cast judgment upon seeing the news? Are we fearful? Do we need to control? Are we concerned for our wellbeing or for that of others? Do we seek for safety and security? Are we defending our body against the seeming threat of disease or aging? Is the body betraying us through pain, weight issues or illness?

6. Do we believe our happiness depends on someone else meeting our needs? Do we believe that sacrifice, struggle and effort are part of love? Do we believe that love can turn to hate or loss? Do we believe that our innocence comes at the expense of making someone else guilty?

7. If the predominant answer to these questions was "yes" then it clearly reveals that fear and lack and not Love, have been the primary motivators for our experience. And they always proceed from unrecognized and unrelinquished guilt. Unconscious guilt spawns all fear, which is often felt as a nebulous and persistent sense of threat, one that underlies most of our decisions and actions concerning our relationships and our life in general.

8. Guilt is the fear of punishment. All fear, regardless of its many diverse manifestations of suffering, is the by-product of our secret anticipation of punishment; its attraction. Fear and the need to control or defend are the result of our unconscious belief that our guilt warrants punishment, and that we deserve it. And it's this hidden expectation of retaliation, together with the beliefs of having and

being "not enough," which fuel that deeply ingrained sense of threat.

9. Those feelings of threat strongly indicate just where we have misplaced our value and trust – in our own strength and not in God's. There is a fundamental belief in judgment. In fact, we value our own mistaken judgments (apart from God) and set them as the foundation for our entire life experience.

10. Every judgment that we make independently from Spirit is a projection and is based on fear or some form of deprivation. Our independent judgments are really a form of condemnation. Yet all condemnation is unconscious self-attack arising from our own unforgiven guilt projected outward onto the body, others, the past, the world and God.

11. Whatever we fear or resist, we do indeed attract. And this is why if we sincerely commit to healing our *mind* we must learn to observe our own judgments and willingly offer them to Spirit for forgiveness and divine reinterpretation. This is our ultimate healing via quantum forgiveness or the Atonement, because through this we heal the single cause of all manifestations of suffering – guilt.

12. Remember God's Law, that whatever we give *we keep*. The cost of giving *is* receiving. When we project judgment we *keep it*. We strengthen it in our awareness and experience. In fact, the way to keep something is to give it away, or to project it. And this happens every time we believe that anger and judgment are justified. This is why we must be particularly vigilant of what it is that we give or project. When we condemn another we condemn our self, consolidating guilt, which in turn amounts to bouts of unconscious self-attack via conflict, pain, sickness, financial lack, etc.

13. Every challenging person who appears in our life is there for just one divinely inspired purpose, but do we recognize it? Do we gratefully acknowledge that their presence is never by accident? Do we recognize their "call for Love?" Do we accept the disguised gift they extend?

14. Do we remember that they offer us yet another chance to correct our perception, a sacred opportunity to "will with God" to undo our ancient cycle of self-condemnation? Are we willing to give them the unconditional forgiveness that we crave for our self?

A. The Incorruptible Innocence of Our Being

1. How can I really see, feel and trust my Holiness? What makes my Holiness visible and valuable to me? How can I embrace my Holiness? How can I extend my Holiness to help heal myself and others?

2. At the heart of our one most Holy Self is perfect, incorruptible innocence. This remains entirely whole and uninterrupted regardless of the seeming ravages of guilt, judgment and suffering. There is nothing we can imagine we did or didn't do that could possibly disturb our incorruptible innocence. It is not only permanent, but infinite too.

3. Our pristine state of guiltlessness is the unchanging state of our Holy Self. It comes from God and is the substance of the all-encompassing and unopposed Love that we *are*. The only thing missing temporarily is our *awareness* of it. The memory of our majestic Identity is heavily obscured by our erroneous beliefs which are spawned from guilt and perpetuated by our incessant unforgiveness. This is always unforgiveness of our *self,* no matter how convinced we are that *judgment of others* seems to be justified.

4. Incorruptible innocence *is* Holiness. It is completely free of guilt and therefore, entirely free of fear. Without guilt, only innocence remains. This is the divinely fearless state Jesus embodied and harnessed while in a body here on earth, and this is the state He encourages us to accept in every Holy Instant of forgiveness.

5. When only innocence remains, fear must disappear. Once fear falls away, all that remains is everything that fear previously hid from our awareness – unbounded Love and effervescent joy beyond our comprehension. These make up the very essence of our being. And they have never left us!

6. In my recent transmissions with Jesus, while I was reviewing the following lessons, He asked me to replace the word "holiness" with the word "innocence" in each of them, and then to breathe these most blessed prayers deeply into my heart. The results of this practice for me have been absolutely astounding. It has opened my heart ever more deeply to accept myself and to make peace with this body as the last "special relationship" to be healed. I pray this

will help you as it has helped me.

7.   For this exercise only, I have adapted the following review lessons in *A Course in Miracles* to reflect the deeper meaning within the word "holiness." Please join me and Jesus in opening our one heart to a whole new depth of Love through accepting and extending our incorruptible innocence.

8.   This is not an intellectual exercise. This is to be a deeply tender and "felt" practice, one that is lovingly seen, accepted and expressed with great reverence and gratitude. The Holy Instant of innocence awaits us. It is ultimately realized through heartfelt acceptance of our (and others) guiltlessness which translates to our unchanging and uninterrupted state of incorruptible innocence. This *is* our Holiness. This is our literal immunity from all pain, all sickness, all conflict, all loss and suffering of any kind. This is the Will of God.

a.   **W-58.1.   (36)   My   incorruptible   innocence   envelops everything I see.**   *From my innocence does the perception of the real world come. Having forgiven, I no longer see myself as guilty. I can accept the innocence that is the truth about me. Seen through understanding eyes, the innocence of the world is all I see, for I can picture only the thoughts I hold about myself.*

b.   **W-58.2.   (37)   My   incorruptible   innocence   blesses   the world.**   *The perception of my innocence does not bless me alone. Everyone and everything I see in its light shares in the joy it brings to me. There is nothing that is apart from this joy, because there is nothing that does not share my innocence. As I recognize my innocence, so does the innocence of the world shine forth for everyone to see.*

c.   **W-58.3.   (38) There is nothing my incorruptible innocence cannot do.**   *My innocence is unlimited in its power to heal, because it is unlimited in its power to save. What is there to be saved from except illusions? And what are all illusions except false ideas about myself? My innocence undoes them all by asserting the truth about me. In the presence of my innocence, which I share with God Himself, all idols vanish.*

d. **W-58.4. (39) My Innocence is my salvation.** *Since my incorruptible innocence saves me from all guilt, recognizing my innocence is recognizing my salvation. It is also recognizing the salvation of the world. Once I have accepted my innocence, nothing can make me afraid. And because I am unafraid, everyone must share in my understanding, which is the gift of God to me and to the world.*

e. **W-58.5. (40) I am blessed as a Son of God.** *Herein lies my claim to all good and only good. I am blessed as a Son of God. All good things are mine, because God intended them for me. I cannot suffer any loss or deprivation or pain because of Who I am. My Father supports me, protects me, and directs me in all things. His care for me is infinite, and is with me forever. I am eternally blessed as His Son.*

The forgiveness process can be found in *The Seven Essential Principles of Quantum Forgiveness (Atonement)* on page 591.

9. RECOVERING THE MISSING HALF OF OUR MIND

1. The cause of all appearances of conflict and suffering arises from just one source, our split-mind. This split is our free will choice to perceive fear, the underlying illusion that an opposite of God/Love exists.

2. Fear *or* Love is all there is to choose between in each moment regardless of the millions of deceptive forms this choice seems to take. Yet only Love is real. Fear, along with every conceivable manifestation of it, does not exist. If it did, then God would not exist. However, God as all-encompassing Love, – has no opponent.

3. In order to bring forth and maintain the concept of fear so it can perpetuate a thoroughly convincing, closed circuit dream of bodies, suffering, life and death, the false self needs two primary sub-causes. These are belief in *sin* together with its inevitable consequence as *guilt*.

4. The separation cycle depends on belief in sin, guilt and their inescapable joint outcome – fear. When fear is believed, it compels us toward sin and guilt incessantly which in turn increases our fear. This unforgiven cycle feeds the ego's compulsive desire for separation, suffering and death. A guilty mind is a fearful mind and this is what the false self concept is.

5. To experience fear along with its painful results we must first believe unconsciously that we are sinful, therefore, guilty. The guilty unwittingly *expect* punishment in the form of loss, conflict, illness, pain, aging and death. Hence their constant defense against it, which acts as fear's attraction. This attachment to sin as the unseen and unforgiven expectation of punishment is the cause of all manifestations of threat.

6. The sensation of fear is inextricably entwined with the hidden desire for self-punishment. The fear of disease, conflict, betrayal, loss and death are all symptoms of our unforgiven expectation of punishment – guilt. Practically speaking, how can we tell if we still value this hidden desire for self-punishment? We need only to review our grievances. Do we still believe we were indeed unfairly treated? Is there anyone we just cannot wholeheartedly forgive? Resistance to forgiving our self for having unknowingly used others to attack us *is* our secret desire for ongoing self-punishment. And God cannot save us from whatever mistake we still desire to keep.

a. *"...in your brother you but see yourself. If he be lost in sin, so must you be; if you see light in him, your sins have been forgiven by yourself." W-158.10:3*

7. Conversely, a guiltless (forgiving) mind knows no fear. And because of this it cannot suffer. *"The guiltless mind cannot suffer."* T-5.V.5:1 If there were no belief in sin and guilt then innocence as fearlessness would reflect the Love we are everywhere, as the one beloved, and shared Children of God. In that incorruptible innocence lays our fearlessness which is the experience and thus demonstration of our joyful union, and our immutable safety and security here in the dream. All seeming fear including its effects is

immediately healed within this all-inclusive innocence.

8. Projection makes perception. We can only ever perceive and experience that which our own split-mind projects. As difficult as it is to hear this, this truth translates practically here: *we only ever see and experience what our mind desires.* But while the split-mind remains unexhumed and unforgiven, this unconscious belief in sin, guilt and fear (as self-sabotage) continues to manifest within our relationships, situations and the body, exactly what we consciously *don't want* such as conflict, betrayal, disease, pain, scarcity, loss, and finally death.

9. Comprehensive healing of all suffering, no matter where we seem to see it, occurs exclusively in the healing of our divided mind, which is the recovery of our unified Mind with God and our brothers. If suffering or conflict is believed and experienced then the split-mind – as the body identity – must be manifesting it because it *wants* it. But why? To *justify and prove* through its suffering that it is a *separate,* personal body/mind and not the *unified* Child of God.

10. Healing is not the integration of the split-mind because fear *and* Love are mutually exclusive and cannot coexist. However, the split-mind is healed through divine union – Holy Relationship – which eradicates the illusions of sin, guilt and fear that caused the split-mind in the first place.

A. Recovering Our Missing Half

1. The missing half of our unified Mind rests in our brother. There is no other place in the universe that we can find it, although we have wasted millennia in the dream of time trying to avoid recognizing this fact. The ego's invention of special love and special relationships is its greatest defense against awakening to our unified Mind.

2. The ego's insane answer to God's uninterrupted union was the illusion of physical death. Death is one of its major defenses employed to escape from ever having to "close the gap" with others and Self through genuine forgiveness. The false self would rather sicken, age and die than to truly forgive.

3. Even before the inception of the separation dream God had placed the missing half of our unified Mind *in* our brother. Yet as we look

outward at our brothers from the split mind – the body – the ego ensures we always witness in them evidence of the denied sin which we mistakenly believe we are. The false self hides our sin and guilt in others. This is the only way we could perceive attack at all. If we did not secretly believe that we are sin incarnate, we could never feel attacked or perceive sin in others.

4. The secret, unforgiven sin in the false self (as unworthiness and self-hatred) must see its sinfulness in our brothers to protect it from being annihilated by its worst enemy – union with the one Holy Self as our brother, which is our union with God.

5. When we blame a brother we reject him/her in totality. There is no partial blame, which means we unknowingly reject the half of our Mind that *is* the Holy Self in union with our brothers and Holy Spirit. This blame is nothing short of Self rejection. We cannot possibly cast blame upon another without rejecting our Holy Self in totality. Think about that.

6. And this is why when we slip into judgment or triggers *we* need to accept the Atonement for our self as a priority. That way we invoke the miracle and regain awareness of and access to the only sane part of our Mind, restoring awareness of our incorruptible innocence, peace and guidance instantly. In forgiving our brother, the missing half of our Mind is returned to us. This cannot be done while we still value condemning anyone including our self. *Note: Please see The Seven Essential Keys to Quantum Forgiveness on page 591.*

7. Jesus refers to this ego dynamic of blaming another, where we attempt to correct them. He explains clearly that while we condemn another, placing the focus of correction outside our self, we deny the sane half of our Mind which is *in* our brother. He also says that while we reject our brother in blame along with rejecting the sane half of our Mind which we share together, the only half of our mind remaining – the insane part – is perceived as being *all* of our self.

8. The miraculous healing for this primordial defense against our unified and Holy Self involves the Holy Spirit's intervention until we advance in forgiveness and Holy Relationship. Then we will realize that our brother is literally our savior; because in him rests the other half of our unified Mind. This joyful realization occurs

as we recognize, accept and fulfill our "joint" function with our brother which involves the truly common purpose of being a living demonstration of God's glorious and unified Will here in the dream.

a. *"The focus of correction has been placed outside yourself, on one who cannot be a part of you while this perception lasts. What is condemned can never be returned to its accuser, who had hated it, and hates it still as symbol of his fear. This is your brother, focus of your hate, unworthy to be part of you and thus outside yourself; the other half, which is denied. And only what is left without his presence is perceived as all of you. To this remaining half the Holy Spirit must represent the other half until you recognize it [is] the other half. And this He does by giving you and him a function that is one, not different."*

"Correction is the function given both (to you and your brother), but neither one alone. And when it is fulfilled as shared, it must correct mistakes in you and him. It cannot leave mistakes in one unhealed and set the other free. That is divided purpose, which can not be shared, and so it cannot be the goal in which the Holy Spirit sees His Own." T-27. II.14:2-7,15:1-4

b. *"Correction must be left to One Who (Holy Spirit) knows correction and forgiveness are the same. With half a mind this is not understood."…"His single purpose unifies the halves of you that you perceive as separate. And each forgives the other, that he may accept his other half (his brother) as part of him." T-27.II.1:1-2,6-7*

9. Many people cannot relate to the repeated statement made in the *Course* that says we are afraid of Love, that our greatest fear is God. It just doesn't make sense to many. Meanwhile, if we react to anything other than the Love and innocence in our brother then our triggered response immediately reveals our own projection as rejection of our Holy Self, the shared and unified Mind with our brother. This constant unforgiveness of our brothers *is* the fear of God, as the fear of Love itself.

10. The Hand of God cannot be received or extended except through our brother. While we continue to want to see our own denied and unforgiven sin and guilt in others, we cannot know our Holy Self. Nor can we joyously awaken fully to our own incorruptible innocence and its universal immunity to all forms of attack the ego made. We will be bitterly afraid of God as Love while we still harbor grievances against others or our self, either past or present.

   a. *"Sin has no place in Heaven, where its results are alien and can no more enter than can their source. And therein lies your need to see your brother sinless. In him [is] Heaven. See sin in him instead, and Heaven is lost to you. But see him as he is, and what is yours shines from him to you. Your savior gives you only love, but what you would receive of him is up to you. It lies in him to overlook all your mistakes, and therein lies his own salvation. And so it is with yours. Salvation is a lesson in giving, as the Holy Spirit interprets it. It is the reawakening of the laws of God in minds that have established other laws, and given them power to enforce what God created not."* T-20.IV.2.

11. Our sanity rests in our brother. Our salvation, as our missing half-Mind, rests exclusively in our brother. Awareness of our full return to innocence is found only in our brother. Our fearlessness and immunity to all suffering dwells in our brother. And our health and happiness cannot be found apart from closing the gap with our brother. This is why the Holy Relationship *is* the Holy Grail and the very "key" to the Kingdom. It is why Jesus devoted such a large section of the *Course* to the Holy Relationship. It is the path to awakening *from* the dream of time, bodies, birth and death once and for all.

10. EVERY PRAYER IS ANSWERED HERE – YOU ARE WORTHY

1. Did you know the one thing we resist and even defend our self against *more* than physical death itself – is genuine peace? We're not referring to the ego's fleeting "forms" of peace which are dependent on external factors (including the body's state) being met. We are speaking of the kind of peace that contains the immediate solution to every conceivable problem here in the body, in the dream we call life.

2. This kind of peace holds within it something we so desperately want but rarely get to access. In this precious peace lay an immediate portal, an entry point through which we escape that insidious and persistent sense of threat, that gnawing feeling of just not being worthy enough. Here, we don't need to earn or qualify for God's Love. All secret sins instantly evaporate within its calm embrace. Here, in this Holy Instant we rest deeply in His Love because we are willing, finally, to recognize we are His Love.

3. We accept and receive the Truth of our Being. And in this moment of receiving, we become God's Loving Will in our awareness. We *are* the light, the all-encompassing Love in which all concerns and problems dissolve. This Love knows of no hierarchy of healing. It looks upon all problems as one. It knows that all pain regardless of its severity is merely our resistance to accepting its immediate remedy – the Atonement in the Holy Instant.

4. This sovereign moment is where all miracles await our joyous welcome. Access to this peace, available to us in every second, is an open invitation to literally bask in our immunity to all adversity and suffering. In the Holy Instant, we learn to step back and allow the Holy Self within to step forward. This light we are is ever present...

   a. *"There is a light in you which cannot die; whose presence is so holy that the world is sanctified because of you. All things that live bring gifts to you, and offer them in gratitude and gladness at your feet. The scent of flowers is their gift to you. The waves bow down before you, and the trees extend their arms to shield you from the heat, and lay their leaves before you on the ground that you may walk in softness, while the wind sinks to a whisper round your holy head."* ... *"The light in you is what the universe longs to behold."* ... *"This is the way salvation works. As you step back, the light in you steps forward and encompasses the world." W-156.4,5:1,6:1*

5. This is the peace of God. This is the ever-present doorway to healing. There is no order of difficulty in miracles here because all of them are accessible in the instant we sincerely *accept* His peace. But to do so, we must be willing to recognize our incorruptible innocence even if for just an instant.

6. Recall that God's Will is already complete. Healing of everything has already been given us. We don't need to earn, qualify or wait for God's Healing. We are eternally worthy to claim God's Healing in this Holy Instant, *now*. It is already made manifest. Our only problem is that through our belief in the ego's fear-filter, the body's five senses and its past, we are *blind* to it. The ego sees only what it desires to see – hallucinate – which is separation. But that does not make it true.

7. Every conceivable adversity we appear to see in our body, in another, in the world or in the past, arises from just one illusory source – fear, as the opposite of God's Love. Yet fear, along with all its devastating consequences *does not exist*. It's a thoroughly convincing trick made by the ego to dupe us. That way, in the tiny band of time between birth and death, we become entirely absent. Absent to the glorious Holy Self we are, and the staggering dominion we share with God over all illusory phenomena here in the dream.

8. Through belief in the illusion of fear we are busily seeking to enhance or defend our tiny life seemingly imprisoned within the body. We are kept habitually consumed moment to moment trying to attain the "love and worthiness" we think we lack, or fending off the dreaded onslaught of what appears as random chaos.

9. When we are consumed by a seeming problem, "we" are absent. We do not know our Holy Self who heals all, just by quietly forgiving it. In the moment we believe in fear we are literally "missing in action." We have abandoned our Holy Self, the Source of all healing. The very moment that we believe a problem is *real* and requires defense, reveals that we believe erroneously that we *are* the guilty ego, deserving of punishment. And then it is the same ego that attempts to heal the problem which it invented. All this it does, while distracting us from recognizing the *one real cause* of the problem – our belief we are separate and unworthy – which can only be healed through the Holy Instant of Atonement.

a. *"You are altogether irreplaceable in the Mind of God. No one else can fill your part in it..." ... "To accept yourself as God created you cannot be arrogance, because it is the denial of arrogance. To accept your littleness [is] arrogant, because it means that you believe your evaluation of yourself is truer than God's." T-9.VIII.10:1-2,8-9*

10. We can gauge which "self" is present by how fearful we are. The ego can and does disguise fear in the forms of worry, anticipation, and even hope. Is it the ego or the Holy Self that is present? As long as the ego can continue to divert us from accepting the one Answer to all problems in the Holy Instant, it is happy to seek a plethora of magical remedies. Just so we never recognize and heal the aching abyss of worthlessness that *is* the ego. After all, in the quiet majesty of the Holy Instant, as we rest deeply in total fearlessness, the ego ceases to exist. No wonder it abhors peace. No wonder the peace of God is its worst enemy. The peace of God is the absence of fear, the annihilation of the ego.

a. *"False healing merely makes a poor exchange of one illusion for a "nicer" one; a dream of sickness for a dream of health. This can occur at lower forms of prayer, combining with forgiveness kindly meant but not completely understood as yet. Only false healing can give way to fear, so sickness will be free to strike again. False healing can indeed remove a form of pain and sickness. But the cause remains, and will not lack effects. The cause is still the wish to die and overcome the Christ. And with this wish is death a certainty, for prayer [is] answered." Song of Prayer, S-3.II.1-7*

11. When we enter a Holy Instant of peace and open our heart to receive what God has already willed for us, the false-self's hallucination begins to shatter, revealing the glorious Love and healing that is our divine Inheritance.

12. Are we willing to enter a now moment and surrender to trust that all our problems have already been solved? Are we willing to "show-up" in this most Holy Instant to genuinely claim the undoing of what never was in reality?

13. In this blessed moment we join as God's healing Will. We are the beloved and eternally innocent Child of God. Gratitude overflows. In this receiving lies the peace of God. We don't "do" anything. The body becomes redundant in this instant as it falls away from awareness.

14. Because the ego is the idea of an opposing substitute for God's beloved Child, everything it does, either negative or positive, is done via false responsibility. By believing it is God this illusory self makes up further illusory images of people, illness and situations so that it can "do" something about them. It really does believe that it can actually *do* something, be it seemingly good or bad (sin). But the truth is that because it *is* nothing and has no reality at all, everything it does, everything it appears to accomplish and every imaginary sin it ever committed – *never happened.*

15. Jesus tells us that we need do nothing. And now we know why. I need do nothing because the false-self can literally *do nothing* real! Think about that. It is the obstruction to God's perfect Creation as our Holy Self. In the quiet Center of the Holy Instant, there is no body, no doing, no qualifying, no fixing, and no trying at all. The ego with its fearful threats is made completely redundant. There is only a deeply grateful surrender to trust. In that trust we accept and receive the miracle.

A. No Body Here

1. The illusory body, this convincing *image* which we projected as our greatest block to true union with our brothers and God, is the central idol around which all our mistaken beliefs, values and stories revolve. The body is used by the ego to prove that the illusion of sin is real. But if sin (irrevocable error) is real then God does not exist. Only one, either God *or* sin, can possibly exist. If we believe in both then our mind is split.

2. The body is the central idol for all our interactions with our self, others and the world. Through the false-self we mistakenly believe we *are* the body, not realizing that we are the incorruptible Holy Self who employs the body exclusively for our sole function of forgiveness. This is true communication. Until the body has been wholly repurposed by Holy Spirit, it remains as a guilt (pain) magnet.

a. *"You still have too much faith in the body as a source of strength. What plans do you make that do not involve its comfort or protection or enjoyment in some way? This makes the body an end and not a means in your interpretation, and this always means you still find sin attractive. No one accepts Atonement for himself who still accepts sin as his goal. You have thus not met your [one] responsibility. Atonement is not welcomed by those who prefer pain and destruction."* ... *"There is one thing that you have never done; you have not utterly forgotten the body. It has perhaps faded at times from your sight, but it has not yet completely disappeared. You are not asked to let this happen for more than an instant, yet it is in this instant that the miracle of Atonement happens."* T-18. VII.1,2:1-3

3. When we enter a Holy Instant the body falls away in our awareness. All false-responsibility dissolves here, leaving us with nothing to *do*. In the sanctity of this moment we relinquish all false responsibility for solving problems or healing sickness. We wholly surrender our mistaken perception of problems. We open our heart to recognize that all adversity we perceive does not exist because it all arose from just one mistake. We thought we were excluded from God's Love and healing. We thought we weren't worthy. And now we graciously accept the *undoing* of that single belief that we are separate from our beloved Creator. All healing is ours in this precious Holy Instant as we truly accept that we need do nothing.

a. *"To do anything involves the body. And if you recognize you need do nothing, you have withdrawn the body's value from your mind. Here is the quick and open door through which you slip past centuries of effort, and escape from time. This is the way in which sin loses all attraction [right now.]"* ... *"To do nothing is to rest, and make a place within you where the activity of the body ceases to demand attention. Into this place the Holy Spirit comes, and there abides. He will remain when you forget, and the body's activities return to occupy your conscious mind."* T-18.VII.7:1-4,7-9

4. As we practice entering the Holy Instant more frequently, we will eventually carry it with us in all our interrelating, and as we go about our daily tasks. One significant change occurs in our "doing mode." Happily, the body fades in our awareness as our central idol and the actions we take are no longer coming from fear (sin). They are truly inspired by the Holy Spirit.

    a. *"Yet there will always be this place of rest to which you can return. And you will be more aware of this quiet center of the storm than all its raging activity. This quiet center, in which you do nothing, will remain with you, giving you rest in the midst of every busy doing on which you are sent. For from this center will you be directed how to use the body sinlessly. It is this center, from which the body is absent, that will keep it so in your awareness of it."* T-18.VII.8

B. The Holy Relationship

1. The *Course's* path is not a solitary journey. Contrary to what some earlier teachers of the *Course* may have said, the *Course* in *not* exclusively a self-study program. Let me be clear, there is much in the *Course* that we can contemplate alone, however the rubber does not meet the road in our transfer of trust from fear to Love until we experience true joining with another person in the mutual quest to overcome specialness. This is the special means – *the Holy Relationship* – which the *Course* uses to collapse both time and matter (space). This is the undoing of the separation.

    a. *"You could no more know God alone than He knows you without your brother. But together you could no more be unaware of love than love could know you not, or fail to recognize itself in you."* T-18.VIII.12:4-5

2. Jesus explains that other pathways which share the same purpose of returning to God get us there, but they usually involve copious effort and enormous amounts of time. Of the two predominant paths other than the *Course*, one is focused on struggling *against* sin while the other largely involves much contemplation and long periods of meditation which are aimed at detachment from the body. These two

pathways differ from the *Course's* central means of return to God, in that they seek for freedom *in the future* from a present state of unworthiness and inadequacy. While the *Course* is one of miracles, it is the Holy Instant that gives us access to our divine Inheritance and freedom right *now* where all miracles abide.

a. *"It is impossible to accept the holy instant without reservation unless, just for an instant, you are willing to see no past or future. You cannot prepare for it without placing it in the future. Release is given you the instant you desire it. Many have spent a lifetime in preparation, and have indeed achieved their instants of success. This course does not attempt to teach more than they learned in time, but it does aim at saving time. You may be attempting to follow a very long road to the goal you have accepted. It is extremely difficult to reach Atonement by fighting against sin. Enormous effort is expended in the attempt to make holy what is hated and despised. Nor is a lifetime of contemplation and long periods of meditation aimed at detachment from the body necessary. All such attempts will ultimately succeed because of their purpose. Yet the means are tedious and very time consuming, for all of them look to the future for release from a state of present unworthiness and inadequacy." T-18.VII.4.*

3. The *Course* offers us the Holy Instant of (immediate) Atonement and the Holy Relationship, within which to quicken the extensive collapse of the dream. This is the path of miracles which, broadly speaking, introduces a comprehensive and quantum collapse of the separation as the illusions of time and matter, of bodies, birth and death.

4. A central and necessary teaching in the *Course* is the Holy Relationship. It is through this most sanctified of all relationships in the dream of time, that we experience the complete undoing of the ego's most fiercely defended argument for separation and death – *the special relationship.*

5. In the Holy Relationship we enter "joint" Holy Instants, where there is a mutual and unequivocal recognition of the innocent

Christ within our brother. And the body concept fades into a thin veil through which we behold the magnitude of our unified Self as Love. The concept of time goes hand in hand with the belief in sin and separate bodies with private minds. As we close this single gap with one brother or sister, a quantum leap takes place for *all* imprisoned minds because two or more have joined in Truth.

a.   *"Your way will be different, not in purpose but in means. A holy relationship is a means of saving time. One instant spent together with your brother restores the universe to both of you. You [are] prepared. Now you need but to remember you need do nothing. It would be far more profitable now merely to concentrate on this than to consider what you should do. When peace comes at last to those who wrestle with temptation and fight against the giving in to sin; when the light comes at last into the mind given to contemplation; or when the goal is finally achieved by anyone, it always comes with just one happy realization; "[I need do nothing.]"*

  "Here is the ultimate release which everyone will one day find in his own way, at his own time. You do not need this time. Time has been saved for you because you and your brother are together. This is the special means this course is using to save you time. You are not making use of the course if you insist on using means which have served others well, neglecting what was made for [you.] Save time for me by only this one preparation, and practice doing nothing else. "I need do nothing" is a statement of allegiance, a truly undivided loyalty. Believe it for just one instant, and you will accomplish more than is given to a century of contemplation, or of struggle against temptation." T-18.VII.5,6.

6.   Do we even realize the massive healing we bring for our self and others by entering just one Holy Instant? In one Holy Instant we can effectively collapse one hundred years of suffering. We see that we need do nothing to qualify for God's Love because the illusory ego is

wholly incapable of doing or achieving anything real. Instead, we choose to enter a Holy Instant in which we recognize and accept that we *are* everything. Here, as we open our heart to receive God's certainty of our worth…our mistaken sense of inadequacy and unworthiness vanishes.

II. RETURN TO INNOCENCE - ABANDONING SELF - DOUBT AND SELF-JUDGMENT

1. I first learned to forgive *myself* for having believed the illusion and unknowingly used others, the past, the world and God to attack myself. I felt so great about having forgiven everyone including my past. And then I found the ego had hidden a rather sinister plan from me. As I applied quantum forgiveness and withdrew my external projections of guilt, I systematically turned them within.
2. Many years ago, before I was ready to practice and accept the immense healing of forgiveness, it seemed I was relatively peaceful while I could offload most of my unconscious guilt onto others, my past and the world. I guess you could say that I was comfortably asleep, unconsciously ignorant. I was strangely content in my imagined victimhood; it was familiar, and this seemed to give me comfort.
3. In this respect, ignorance is bliss, however there was a high cost to pay for maintaining this state of ignorance. I felt pursued by a never-ending sense of threat, one which was fed by a bottomless pit of anxiety, insecurity and inadequacy. And the ensuing effect propelled me to chase endless distractions and over-achievements, all to numb the pain of my aching sense of incompletion.
4. The agony of carrying all these judgments finally tipped the scales for me. It became unbearable. I began the life-changing practice of living quantum forgiveness when I was in my thirties. Once I became comfortable with having forgiven (withdrawn) the majority of my guilty projections from others, the past and the world… I seemed to become more critical of myself. Oops! And

then I did what many unknowingly do; with the increasing barrage of self-condemnation, I began to take "false-responsibility" for all the ravages of the ego. This was a trap. I tried to atone for my errors but in many cases, it was the ego doing the atoning!

5. Now I realize that if a personal sense of responsibility still remains after I have forgiven, then I haven't accepted the divine Remedy, the Atonement. After all, this is the immediate and miraculous undoing of my erroneous perception. Atonement serves to free me from feeling responsible. Only the ego feels responsible because it's addicted to guilt. It depends on guilt to deny God, and to resist innocence. And that is why it doesn't care where it places the guilt (others, you or the body) just as long as it continues to project guilt. As the ego fears, no guilt means no more ego.

6. Jesus mentioned this phase of withdrawing our external projections only to have them turned within:

a. *"The beginning phases of this reversal are often quite painful, for as blame is withdrawn from without, there is a strong tendency to harbor it within. It is difficult at first to realize that this is exactly the same thing, for there is no distinction between within and without." T-11.IV.4:5-6*

7. I also couldn't deny that the body had now become the central focus of my blame, my projections of guilt. But guilt is guilt, no matter what disguise it employs. If I feel guilty then I will deny God's Love; I will reject the Love and healing He desires for me to know and have. Keeping guilt is the most savage self-attack. It's an insidious defense devised to protect our self from healing, joy and Love.

A. Giving Yourself Permission – Saying You're Sorry

1. Before I can *accept* the healing that the Atonement offers, I must first recognize that my perception (of another, myself, the body, pain or illness, financial lack, etc.) is faulty. How do I know this? There is a lack of peace. Or perhaps there's a feeling of strain, conflict, sacrifice or obligation. These are the signs showing me I perceive insanely.

2. In this nano-second I can choose again. Therefore, I choose to see myself as God sees me: innocent and whole. And I do this by giving myself permission to *accept* God's evaluation of who "I AM" instead of the ego's critical self-judgment. When I'm tempted to believe guilt, I am reminded to ask myself this question: "Has God changed His Mind about me?"

    1) How much do I desire to be free of judgment, guilt and self-attack?

3. Now I need only *accept* Spirit's healed perception in that instant. I can berate myself over and over again, telling myself how guilty I am; but then I cannot heal, because I don't *accept* the certain Remedy (Atonement).

    a. *"The Atonement was established as the means of restoring guiltlessness to minds that have denied it, and thus denied Heaven to themselves. Atonement teaches you the true condition of the Son of God." T-14.IV.9:2-3*

4. The starting point here is "Self-acceptance," especially when we're feeling tempted by the appearance of adversity. I am learning to accept my *Self,* but that doesn't mean I accept the *ego's projections* of myself, such as conflict, sickness, pain, disaster, etc. The key here is that I express sincere remorse to myself for having *believed* the ego's projections. For me and probably for many, the stumbling block is self-doubt. And when there is a spike of self-doubt, instead of bullying myself, I'm learning to do the opposite. I apologize to myself first by saying, *"I'm sorry for believing that thought or belief. Please forgive me. I Love you."*

5. I have found that this immediately disarms the ego's critical judgment and opens my heart to *accept* and *receive* God's Love in the form of correcting my perception which is the Atonement, or forgiveness. It is a declaration stating that I recognize my distorted perception as the singular cause of my distress. And I am genuinely sorry toward myself for the upset it caused from having believed that I could be attacked (by another, myself, pain, illness, financial lack, depression, etc.).

6. I want another way of seeing this. Now it can be healed. I am

learning to express unconditional Love to myself, and this is peace because it undoes unconscious self-resentment as self-attack. No one can Love me unconditionally until I Love myself unconditionally. Until I learn to Love myself unconditionally, I won't allow myself to receive Love.

7. Awakening for most is a gradual process, a transfer of trust. We won't trust, know, and embody the Holy Self until we begin extending unconditional acceptance as Love to our Self and others. As we extend what we mistakenly believe we lack (Love) ... we come to the *experience* of the "I AM," where the mistaken self simply disappears in its light.

B. We Cannot Know God, in Guilt and Self-Doubt

1. We cannot receive our true heart's desire while we still value guilt, self-judgment and self-doubt. What we invest in guilt, we withdraw from God. In every moment it is a choice we make. Remember we manifest exactly that which we value, and if we choose to believe the ego's criticism then we *do* value it. Guilt, self-doubt and judgment are absolutely toxic and directly caused by unconscious guilt. Judging and doubting our self or others, is destructive. When we entertain guilt and self-doubt we unknowingly invite criticism and distrust from others and the world in general.

2. We must commit to being vigilant against believing the ego's vicious self-talk. And this includes all its savage projections onto the neutral and innocent body. This is crucial to opening our heart to God. Literally, we must choose between believing destructive self-talk or believing our infinite, uninterrupted innocence. This is a conscious choice. Everything we believe either good or bad stems from just one cause – our *desire* for it. If we want and therefore believe guilt, self-criticism and doubt then we must reject God's Love and healing; we reject our innocence.

3. God only knows us as guiltless, spotlessly and joyously innocent. Jesus tells us that we cannot know God unless we are guiltless. Whoa! This means we cannot know our Self ... unless we *accept* our guiltlessness. Unless we desire and accept our guiltlessness, we cannot know God, our Holy Self. In guilt or self-doubt, we cannot recognize or receive our deepest desire – to know Thy Self as Love. From Jesus:

a. *"Unless you are guiltless you cannot know God, Whose Will is that you know Him. Therefore, you MUST be guiltless. Yet if you do not accept the necessary conditions for knowing Him, you have denied Him and do not recognize Him, though He is all around you. He cannot be known without His Son, whose guiltlessness is the condition for knowing Him. Accepting His Son as guilty is denial of the Father so complete, that knowledge is swept away from recognition in the very mind where God Himself has placed it." T-14.IV.7:1-5*

4. He tells us that the necessary condition by which we recognize, experience and know God (Love) is guiltlessness. But let's look at what this really means. To be guiltless is to know that I cannot *be* attacked by another, by the body, by any form of lack, or the world. And this is precisely why practicing quantum forgiveness is so imperative. If I still believe in some forms of attack then I must value some forms of unforgiveness. And I must therefore reject my guiltlessness.

5. Guilt is the solitary cause of every seeming adversity we experience (conflict, anxiety, illness, loss, lack, pain, depression and death). If I knew my divine guiltlessness as Jesus did then I would not be able to experience suffering, either physically or emotionally. Guiltlessness is indestructibility – literally. As we learn to *accept* our guiltlessness we recognize and demonstrate that we cannot *be* attacked. Our healing is a living demonstration of our innocence and that of others.

6. Jesus teaches that our natural state is one of uninterrupted guiltlessness regardless of all the chaos we may imagine here in the ego dream. Our divine innocence is eternal and all-inclusive; it is irrevocable. At no point during our millions of years in the dream of time, has our divine innocence been threatened. The part that we don't see is this: We have chosen to block our awareness of our guiltlessness.

7. So just how important is it that this incorruptible, undivided state of innocence be restored to our awareness? Without doubt, it is the

single most important healing accomplishment since the beginning of time. And the reason is that without it, we will not end the separation, the dream of birth and death. It is the restoration of our complete guiltlessness to our awareness that will literally overcome the dream of time and matter, by transcending it just as Jesus came to teach us more than two thousand years ago. The remembrance of our innocence is the singular prerequisite to awaken from suffering, to awaken *from* the dream of death entirely and not just *in* it. Here is a closing message from Jesus:

a. *"You have no conception of the limits you have placed on your perception, and no idea of all the loveliness that you could see. But this you must remember; the attraction of guilt opposes the attraction of God. His attraction for you remains unlimited, but because your power, being His, is as great as His, you can turn away from love. What you invest in guilt you withdraw from God." T-15.IX.6:1-4*

12. THE SHOCKING TRUTH ABOUT BEING UNFAIRLY TREATED

1. The complete undoing of all suffering in our relationships, our bodies and our life depends exclusively on our willingness to forgive. No genuine healing of the body or of our relationships can occur without forgiveness. We may manifest temporary healing via magic, medicine, or by exchanging favors in special relationships, yet these affect only superficial changes which cannot heal the fundamental *cause* of all suffering, which is guilt as hidden self-hatred.

2. True healing in every area of our life can only come about as a result of complete forgiveness. But do we really *want* healing? *This is a key question.* For most, there is a desire to heal only the *symptoms* of guilt, blame and judgment. We want to be rid of the pain, conflict, illness and lack but if we're to be radically honest, many of us still resist healing the fundamental *cause* through applying total,

unequivocal forgiveness.

3. We may even be willing to move on from past hurts, but we don't realize that the reason we can't is because we *still believe they actually occurred.* Furthermore, there is a valued belief that the (illusory) past is responsible for the present problem in any form it may appear (relationship conflict, health issues, emotional pain, financial lack, etc.). There is little or no desire to surrender the *single cause* of all this suffering which is our non-negotiable belief that we were indeed victimized.

4. Jesus tells us that our greatest fear is Love (God). He is speaking of the experience of Love *without* fear, something we can't comprehend through the false self. This changeless and completely undivided Love is our greatest fear – as our Holy Self. If we were to know it, and claim it, the false self along with its suffering would disappear.

5. He also says that the final block to overcome before we are willing to join with God is to forgive our brothers and sisters. This includes our parents, present partner, caretakers, family, former partners, former friends, colleagues, historical figures and presidents. We cannot afford to exclude even one person from our comprehensive forgiveness, otherwise we still secretly condemn our self. Full forgiveness of others causes the ego's veil of terror to disappear. The painful "effects" of guilt and fear fall away and our Christ Vision is restored. We are no longer afraid to see the face of Christ in others because we accept it as our own.

6. We cannot possibly open to Love as God (our Holy Self) unless we have totally forgiven others. If we hold any grievances then we will be terrified of God as Love. And that terror arises from projection.

7. There is only one Son of God, not many. We are the one Holy Self. We share this Identity equally. And we cannot embody this Identity while we judge or reject anyone else. To the degree we hold resentments or still believe we were unfairly treated is the degree we will attract suffering (separation) either through illness, aging, weight issues, relationship conflict, financial lack, etc.

   a. *"The tiny instant you would keep and make eternal, passed away in Heaven too soon for anything to notice it had come.*

What disappeared too quickly to affect the simple knowledge of the Son of God can hardly still be there, for you to choose to be your teacher. Only in the past,--an ancient past, too short to make a world in answer to creation,--did this world appear to rise. So very long ago, for such a tiny interval of time, that not one note in Heaven's song was missed. Yet in each unforgiving act or thought, in every judgment and in all belief in sin, is that one instant still called back, as if it could be made again in time. You keep an ancient memory before your eyes. And he who lives in memories alone is unaware of where he is."
T-26.V.5.

A. Victim or Perpetrator – Equally Mistaken

1. For most, we have an underlying, painful, recurring pattern when it comes to relationships. Many of us abandon our Self, adjusting our behavior to meet other people's expectations in order to fit in or to gain approval and acceptance. This unconscious ego dynamic involves a trade-off that results in a dance of victim and perpetrator.

2. Let's take two seemingly very different people who are in relationship, such as a parent and child, siblings, romantic partnership, friends, colleagues, etc. I will use my unhealed relationship with my mother as a typical example of two people seemingly at odds with each other. Grievances were accumulated, justified, stored and then projected onto each other most of the time.

3. Please review the *Victim/Perpetrator Diagram* on page 100. In my case I was largely person number one in the diagram, while my mother happened to be more like the number two individual. We clashed often and sometimes it seemed impossible to communicate with each other.

4. What many of us now realize is that any unresolved grievances with our parents will always play out repeatedly in adulthood, particularly within relationships with significant others, children, friends and colleagues.

5. We understand now that our problem is not actually being caused by a particular person judging or attacking us. In truth, a past, unhealed and unforgiven pattern is being unconsciously projected onto them. With this recognition, we can choose to constructively use these situations to show us where we still harbor self-hatred. Ideally, when this is recognized as the *only reason* for our conflict with another, then genuine and deeply felt gratitude erupts for both the trigger and the person, as a consequence.

6. True forgiveness always ends in welcomed appreciation for all involved. Consistently there is a mighty gift received and extended in forgiveness. When we carry forgiveness right through to its final stage where we feel thankful for the person and the trigger, there is no more need to attract this form or pattern of attack any longer. Another joyous consequence of this is that when recalling a previously hurtful memory, there is no further emotion attached to that story. It simply disappears. And then we know it has been healed.

7. On the contrary, if we still feel emotional about a past memory of having been victimized then we have *not* forgiven. The question then is, are we willing to let Holy Spirit reinterpret and repurpose our mistakes (not sins)? Our previously unconscious use of this type of situation, for the purpose of repeating victim patterns, can then be employed with Holy Spirit to show us specifically where we still hold unforgiven self-hatred.

   a. *"In any union with a brother in which you seek to lay your guilt upon him, or share it with him or perceive his own, [you] will feel guilty. Nor will you find satisfaction and peace with him, because your union with him is not real. You will see guilt in that relationship because you put it there. It is inevitable that those who suffer guilt will attempt to displace it, because they do believe in it. Yet though they suffer, they will not look within and let it go."* T-13.X.3:1-5

8. Let's also recall here that the ego carries over its unforgiven grievances from previous seeming lifetimes and often uses its parents in this current lifetime to project its unhealed self-hatred. Of course, because of the ego's convenient "amnesia," we don't recall this projection of guilt consciously. The ego's objective is to perpetuate separation by continuing its unquestioned belief in both victims and perpetrators.

9. Any unforgiven, negative emotional memory is stored in the body and, unless sincerely forgiven, will be projected onto the body as sickness, aging and death. This is the ego's way of trying to prove that sin, guilt, attack and separation are real and ultimately, more powerful than God's changeless and all-healing Love, which is our Holy Self.

10. Victim and victimizer as seeming counterparts, appear to be two opposite polarities, yet they are the same. They personify an equal extent of self-abandonment and self-betrayal. By adopting these conflicting and alien roles, both the victim and the victimizer hide from the light of their shared Holy Self. This Self is in vertical alignment, showing-up in authentic communication using The *Seven Keys (Seven Key Principles of Authentic Relating)* found on page 572 and *The Divine Switch from Ego to Holy Self* on page 297.

11. Just a reminder, our Holy Self cannot *be* triggered. Only the ego can be triggered. The negative traits in another which trigger us are often our own, secret, self-condemnation. These could not trigger us at all if we didn't believe that we are unworthy. However, please allow me to attempt to clear up a common confusion. Some on this pathway believe that if we see a problem in others then we ourselves are always projecting that problem. It is our projection contributing to the problem *only if we are triggered* by what we seem to see or feel. Feeling triggered then, complete with an emotional charge, is the gauge that alerts us to the fact that *we our self* need forgiveness.

12. As we heal, we will be able to discern problems and egoic patterns in others, but the defining difference is that we will no longer be triggered by them. In this case the symptoms of ego that we discern with Holy Spirit are not our projections. In other words, all triggers are my own projections requiring forgiveness – until – I am no longer triggered.

13. Forgiveness rewrites the ego's story of devastation; it cleans it of all residual attack. And it restores us… gifting us with grace and healing, every time. When we forgive and learn to show-up authentically, using the *Seven Keys*, we remain present in the Holy Instant. There are no victims or perpetrators. No self-betrayal can occur here, and it is in this divine presence that we come to know our Self and others as Love.

14. A perpetrator is very likely to also see themselves as a victim. They feel victimized and their reaction is to become angry. In justifying their anger, their response is commonly in line with victimizer behavior. Like the victim, the seeming perpetrator's actions arise from the same fundamental "content" of unconscious guilt and self-hatred. Only the "form" in which this self-attack plays out is different than that of the classic victim.

15. The victim uses the perpetrator to offend or harm them *self* so they can continue portraying their "pseudo innocence." Fake innocence depends entirely on making *someone else* or something else guilty, such as the body, pain or illness. This is how the ego maintains its victim story. Thus, a victim projects their own denied guilt onto victimizers. In turn, the perpetrator uses the victim so the ego can continue to project its rage (which is just another form of guilt). This also ensures the ego's continuing cycle of sin, guilt, rage, acting out, etc.

16. Usually, the person who is forthright, dominating and controlling (perpetrator) has underlying reasons for those behaviors. They are often controlling, in an effort to alleviate their own sense of being out of control. They can appear selfish to others, and yet *they* may feel that they are just trying to set boundaries. Their own offensive behavior towards *others* can likely seem to *them* as a defense from being victimized. Perfectionism, from the ego viewpoint, can be something they strive for, but when someone expects perfection, they are usually seen to be critical, hard to please, and judgmental.

17. The idea of "sin" as being a permanent and irrevocable error is the mainstay of the ego. A sin cannot *be* forgiven. However, a mistake can. Hence, the idea of sin is maintained … with the persistence of the illusion of separate bodies with private minds that can attack and be attacked. Forgiveness collapses this insanity once and for all.

18. The Holy Self's incorruptible innocence knows no victims or perpetrators. The ego is obsessed with fake innocence (its innocence is upheld by making someone else guilty). The Holy Self does not need to condemn someone in order to feel innocent. It knows everyone's Holy Self is sinless and innocent.

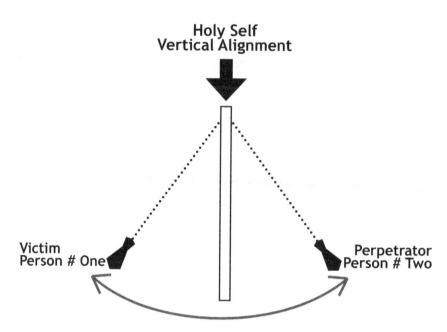

BOTH VICTIM AND THE PERPETRATOR ARE THE SAME

When we come to vertical alignment, through forgiveness, there is a welcomed appreciation for all involved. When we carry forgiveness right through to its final stage where we feel thankful for the person and the trigger, there is no more need to attract this form or pattern of attack any longer. When recalling a previously hurtful memory, there is no further emotion attached to that story. It simply disappears. And then we know it has been healed.

PERSON # ONE	PERSON # TWO
Person number one is perhaps empathic, super sensitive, feels easily victimized, over-caring, over-giving, self-effacing, emotional, moody and withdrawing, a compensator, people-pleaser, etc. This person may be an over-achiever too. This one hates conflict and always tries to keep the peace, and will even sacrifice themselves to do so. This type of personality can tend to view themselves as having been victimized.	Person number two appears to be the opposite. He or she is forthright, perhaps thoughtless and selfish at times, dominating, controlling or even aggressive at times, critical and judgmental, unemotional, insensitive, hard to please, expects their needs to be met by others, authoritative, demanding, intimidating. This type of personality has a tendency to be seen as a perpetrator or bully by those who see themselves as victims.

a. *"Whenever you feel fear in any form,— and you are fearful if you do not feel a deep content, a certainty of help, a calm assurance Heaven goes with you,— be sure you made an idol, and believe it will betray you. For beneath your hope that it will save you lie the guilt and pain of self-betrayal and uncertainty, so deep and bitter that the dream cannot conceal completely all your sense of doom. Your self-betrayal must result in fear, for fear is judgment, leading surely to the frantic search for idols and for death.*

"Forgiving dreams remind you that you live in safety and have not attacked yourself. So do your childish terrors melt away, and [real world] dreams become a sign that you have made a new beginning, not another try to worship idols and to keep attack. Forgiving dreams are kind to everyone who figures in the dream. And so they bring the dreamer full release from dreams of fear." T-29.IX.9:1-10:4

B. Victim or Perpetrator Diagram *(on page 100)*

C. Are We Grateful to be Able to Forgive?

1. Until there is a sense of gratitude for having had the experience then forgiveness is not complete. When we genuinely accept the Atonement, Holy Spirit's right-minded perception reveals the benefit of the experience. This always includes appreciation for the person/issue, because without it, as painful as it felt, we would never have had the chance to see it and forgive (heal) *our self* for projecting this unconscious self-attack.

2. When we are willing to forgive there is a sincere desire for the miracle rather than the grievance. For me, the following was and still is an amazingly effective mantra: *"More than anything I want to see the miracle that lay behind this illusory appearance."* Remember too, that when we long to see the miracle instead of a grievance we immediately align with, and as, God's Will. And there is literally nothing that God's Will cannot heal when we join with Him in trust.

D. Why Do We Find It So Difficult to Forgive?

1. If we choose to *hold* a grievance we cannot *receive the miracle.* The two are mutually exclusive. Which do we really want, the grievance *or* the miracle? We cannot have both.

2. If your memory of a person still sparks an emotional charge, then you have not yet forgiven. They may have even passed on, yet your memory of the grievance has not. The memory of a grievance can only exist right now in this present moment. The grievance itself then becomes your present experience and imprisons you.

3. There is no hierarchy of grievances. All grievances, both large and small, equally block us from Love, from healing. Resentment always obstructs the precious "now" moment where all healing awaits. Grievances are carried from one moment to the next, blocking us from the abundant and holographic healing of the Holy Instant. They serve to numb us to present miracles and ensure we carry the grievance into the future so that it perpetuates the ego's hidden wish to be unfairly treated.

4. A primary obstacle to quantum forgiveness, and probably the most prevalent, is the total misperception that when we forgive someone we're forgiving the truth of what really happened. We are pardoning them for what we believe actually occurred. In addition, we usually carry proof or evidence of the particular violation. The ego asks, how can physical evidence (relationship conflict, infidelity, betrayal, abuse, financial loss, ill health, etc.) of a transgression be overlooked, while clearly there is "proof" to the contrary.

5. So, the first hurdle to overcome is our mistaken belief that:

   1) We were indeed harmed; the incident did happen, and

   2) That someone else was responsible, not us

   a. *"The major difficulty that you find in genuine forgiveness on your part is that you still believe you must forgive the truth, and not illusions. You conceive of pardon as a vain attempt to look past what is there; to overlook the truth, in an unfounded effort to deceive yourself by making an illusion true. This twisted viewpoint but reflects the hold that the idea of sin retains as yet upon your mind, as you regard yourself."* ... *"Because you think your sins are real, you look on pardon as deception."* W-134.3,4:1

b. *"If you will recognize that all the attack you perceive is in your own mind and nowhere else, you will at last have placed its source, and where it begins it must end. For in this same place also lies salvation."* T-12.III.10:1-2

6. This may be difficult to swallow but another reason we resist true forgiveness so intensely is because, beneath all our outward striving for Love, abundance, happiness and health lies the hidden and unforgiven desire for self-attack. This disguised wish to be unfairly treated is a highly revered and defended value of the false self. To the ego there is a secret payoff to being a victim. The ego survives on its deceitful concept of *pseudo* innocence. While it is victimized it can offset blame onto others. Its pseudo innocence is always bought at the cost of another's guilt.

7. Given two choices, either physical death, *or* true forgiveness, the ego always chooses death, while concealing the real cause of death which is always unforgiveness. And this is why we see so much suffering and death. There is no other cause of adversity.

a. *"The world you perceive is a world of separation. Perhaps you are willing to accept even death to deny your Father. Yet He would not have it so, and so it is not so."* T-12.III.9:1-3

8. In my many years of practicing and teaching forgiveness I am still sometimes shocked by people's staunch resistance to applying it unconditionally. There is such strong resistance to taking one hundred percent responsibility for having unknowingly chosen to self-attack. If we refuse to be accountable (without self-blame) for having made a choice for self-attack, then we must still be projecting our unforgiven guilt onto someone else – and therefore, keeping it for our self.

9. We say we want Holy Relationships but it is literally impossible to initiate and engage in Holy Relationships unless we're *willingly*

committed to forgiveness *with gratitude*. After all, we are healing our very own unconscious attraction to self-attack. And this deserves abundant gratitude.

E. Don't Take it Personally

1. Did you know that to "take offense," which is to believe you're a victim, is just as false as to "give offense," to attack? The idea of victim and perpetrator are both equally false.

2. When we take things personally it's always the separate self that takes offense. The Holy Self cannot take offense because it *knows* it cannot be threatened. When we take things personally, we have zero gratitude and we are in defense mode, actively blocking the miracle. It is far better to train our self to note when we're triggered, to let that be our immediate sign that we are in resistance or defense. Defense mode is always the ego. As we catch our self being triggered, we can then choose to exchange the grievance for the miracle via forgiveness. This opens our mind to receive direct guidance from Holy Spirit. On the other hand, guidance is blocked while we prefer to hold onto grievances.

F. Where Does Our Unforgiveness Hide?

1. A universal law which the ego refuses to allow into awareness is that all *"giving is receiving"* always. When we project (give) guilt through blame and judgment we end up amassing (receiving) it for our self as ongoing and unrecognized self-attack.

2. This takes numerous forms, most of which appear to be totally unrelated to our grievance. For instance, a common problem that many face is weight issues. Yet given a choice between dieting *or* applying true forgiveness to everyone including themselves, most choose dieting, which is a temporary remedy where the *consequences* of unresolved grievances (weight) are remedied while the underlying *cause* (grievances) is left unhealed, only to return again.

3. The ego cannot *survive* without projecting its guilt. It must call in attack via conflict, betrayal, abandonment, pain, illness, financial loss, etc. In truth it is impossible to be attacked unless we "wished" for it. This is why Jesus says that attack in any form is an illusion.

4. All attack is self-attack because we betrayed our self in the first place by unknowingly using others to prove they are guilty while justifying our own pseudo innocence. Innocence is a total sham if it depends on another's guilt. True and incorruptible innocence knows *everyone* as sinless and guiltless. It is the bedrock of our most Holy Self, the one Self we share equally with everyone.

5. Quantum forgiveness undoes the initial and often unremembered *self*-betrayal which invited and manifested seeming attack from others, the body and the world. It is impossible to forgive another. We must accept that no matter the seeming form of attack it always arises from our own unrecognized self-attack. *We forgive our self only.* There is literally no one else to forgive.

    a. *"It is impossible to forgive another, for it is only your sins you see in him. You want to see them there, and not in you. That is why forgiveness of another is an illusion. Yet it is the only happy dream in all the world; the only one that does not lead to death. Only in someone else can you forgive yourself, for you have called him guilty of your sins, and in him must your innocence now be found." S-2.I.4:2-6*

    b. *"Anger is [never] justified. Attack has [no] foundation." T-30.VI.1:1-2*

    c. *"Only the self-accused condemn. As you prepare to make a choice that will result in different outcomes, there is first one thing that must be overlearned. It must become a habit of response so typical of everything you do that it becomes your first response to all temptation, and to every situation that occurs. Learn this, and learn it well, for it is here delay of happiness is shortened by a span of time you cannot realize. You never hate your brother for his sins, but only for your own. Whatever form his sins appear to take, it but obscures the fact that you believe them to be yours, and therefore meriting a "just" attack. T-31.III.1.*

6. In the cases where children appear to suffer at the hands of perpetrators, illness or injury, we must remember that the ego

thought system overarches the *concept* of children and adults. All children come into each lifetime with the ego's filter of fear and their parents and peers unknowingly reinforce their false sense of self. Unbeknown to most, the child's singular purpose for incarnation is to *wake up* from the dream of separation. Unfortunately, the fastest motivator to awaken from the dream is acute suffering. While awakening need not be painful, the ego's armor-plated obsession with projecting blame, drama, constant seeking and control (separation), propels it to self-destruction.

7.   I have never known anyone to *willingly choose* to renounce the false self-concept completely who had not already exhausted the ego's propensity for suffering. If in this lifetime, the ego's life was one of great ease, then there would usually be no *desire* to awaken. The desire to awaken is propelled from having hit the ego's wall, over and over again. Only then will we sincerely do whatever it takes to look only to God, and not to the body, special relationships and the world for our freedom and completion.

8.   In essence, we are viewing a very long sequence of lifetimes, where every child has made a determined "choice" for just how they wished to be treated in this lifetime. There are never any victims. Choices were usually made prior to an individual's incarnation but are now open to another choice, to heal, in any genuine Holy Instant of forgiveness.

9.   We can help heal these children simply by accepting the Holy Spirit's correction, on their behalf. This is the Atonement. If we're triggered and we believe there are "victims" then we are the one most in need of healing, because we *believe* (and therefore reinforce) there can be an opposite to God's Love. Not only that, but as we come from fear, we unwittingly amplify fear in those we desire to help.

10. In my own experience of childhood abuse, I can say that this has definitely accelerated my hunger for nothing *but* God's Love.

11. The basis for every Holy Relationship is this: *"Do I want to see him or her as completely sinless?"* If we still desire another to feel guilty, then we are condemning our self to death. We want to cling to sin, guilt and death for our self. That is the bottom line. There is only one us here. If we are triggered then it's ours to heal. And this

is why if we really want to awaken from suffering and death, we must be willing to forgive our self, for having unknowingly used this person (or incident, issue, etc.) to attack our self.

12. Ask yourself:

1) Do I want to know my Self as eternally innocent, as invulnerable to attack of any kind?

2) Do I want to know I am always Loved, safe and secure, and that all my needs are always met?

3) Do I want to know that God's Will for me is consistent and uninterruptible Love, happiness, joy, abundance and good health?

13. If so, then I must forgive myself for having believed otherwise. I forgive myself for having unknowingly used others, the past, my childhood, the body and the world, to try to prove that I am separate from others, God and my most beloved, innocent and Holy Self. Forgiveness is the unparalleled practice by which I come to recognize and accept my own incorruptible innocence.

a. *"God is the Love in which I forgive. ...forgiveness is the means by which I will recognize my innocence. It is the reflection of God's Love on earth. It will bring me near enough to Heaven that the Love of God can reach down to me and raise me up to Him."... "As I begin to see, I recognize His reflection on earth. I forgive all things because I feel the stirring of His strength in me. And I begin to remember the Love I chose to forget, but which has not forgotten me."* W-60. 1:1,4-6;2:4-6

b. *"The strength of pardon is its honesty, which is so uncorrupted that it sees illusions as illusions, not as truth. It is because of this that it becomes the undeceiver in the face of lies; the great restorer of the simple truth. By its ability to overlook what is not there, it opens up the way to truth, which has been blocked by dreams of guilt. Now are you free to follow in the way your true forgiveness opens up to you. For if one brother has received this gift of you, the door is open to yourself. "W-134.8*

c. *"There is a very simple way to find the door to true forgiveness, and perceive it open wide in welcome. When you feel that you are tempted to accuse someone of sin in any form, do not allow your mind to dwell on what you think he did, for that is self-deception. Ask instead, "Would I accuse myself of doing this?" W-134.9.*

13. HEALING THE HEART OF ALL ANGER

1. The underlying cause of all our anger is almost never identified. This is why anger resurfaces time and time again. We still believe there are numerous people, past experiences and vastly different issues that can provoke our anger. And *that* is the unidentified belief that has obscured the *real problem* and its unequivocal solution. How can we ever hope to heal the destructive cause of anger if we just don't recognize it?

2. The most important question to ask when we're angry is this: "Who or what do I believe to be the *cause* of this anger?" This may come as a shock. What we attribute as the cause of anger is really just an *effect* of a much more deviously *hidden* cause.

3. The cause of all anger arises from our own denied and projected self-hatred. This is the unconscious guilt which the *Course* tells us is the singular cause of all pain, illness, relationship conflict and adversity. There could be no negative emotions without their hidden source as guilt. If the cause of anger is attributed to anyone or anything other than our own mind, then we have projected it.

4. In my own experience of being triggered, the first step is to recognize *this must be my own self-loathing (guilt)* even if I can only recall this fact intellectually at first. But when I do remember this point, I try not to judge myself for it. Otherwise it would be the false self attempting to guilt-trip me and that is even more self-attack.

5. I thank those people who expressed their confusion over a short excerpt that I published on anger. Largely, it was their confusion and sincere desire to heal their anger that precipitated me to write this longer explanation on how to repurpose anger. The initial quote which elicited some confusion was this: "Anger is never justified because all anger arises from our own guilt (self-loathing) which is projected onto others. We (unknowingly) use others to attack our self – always. This is why all forgiveness is self-forgiveness."

6. *"A Course in Miracles"* states that anger is never justified. However, this does not mean we repress and deny our angry feelings. I feel many *Course* students are quite confused in this area. Let me clarify.

7. I have trained my mind to supervise my thoughts, beliefs and emotions. This really is a method of divine SuperVision because I ask the Holy Spirit to look at these thoughts, beliefs and emotions *with* me. There is a great sense of relief when I do. Often, I will receive insights as to what my anger attempted to hide and then I can forgive it. Almost always, if I stay with the anger while looking with Spirit, there is a gift waiting to be uncovered.

8. Anger is never justified because at the deepest level all anger is just a symptom of our mistaken anger at God (Love). All expressions of anger represent the ego's fierce revolt against Love which is the rejection of the one Holy Self we are. Anger "proves" that both the separation and guilt are *real* to uphold and prolong false identification.

9. When anger shows up it can be used by the ego to perpetuate suffering, or Love can use it constructively to expose and heal our underlying false-belief and its pattern of self-betrayal. All emotions arise from "who" we believe we are. They are direct expressions of our fundamental beliefs and values, most of which are cleverly concealed in our unconscious until we courageously face them, repurpose them and forgive our self for having desired and valued them.

A. A Practical Process to Release Anger

1. Anger can be helpful. The real question is always, *"What is it*

for?" Its *divine* purpose is to show us where we have abandoned our self so we can heal it. Once it has surfaced we have an important choice to make. We can choose to continue to project onto another, our self, the past, the body, the world or God, which serves to perpetuate unconscious self-attack. Or we can decide to be one hundred percent accountable *without* self-judgment and ask Spirit in to reveal the treasure that lay beneath the anger. Remember that anger is not wrong. It is simply *false*. When we say it's wrong to feel anger then guilt is quick to follow.

2. For me now, I can at least begin to appreciate the expression of anger as a gift to reveal what I had unknowingly repressed and projected up till now. This ancient and often buried self-loathing deserves healing, not more projection or judgment. That is *why* it showed up in the first place; to be healed. It's doing me a favor! And so is the person that precipitated my anger.

3. The next practical step is to *accept* myself even whilst feeling angry. I refuse to *justify* the anger though. If I don't accept myself then I must be either condemning myself ... or condemning someone else. Both are attack. This helps me realize I want the *miracle behind* the anger and this is *all* I want. These expressions of anger are always "calls for Love." So now I have trained myself to join Spirit and answer all calls for Love, even those from myself, with Love.

4. Accepting our self while feeling angry is a crucial step. This is giving our self the unconditional Love we never knew before which allows us the spaciousness of non-judgment in which to return to safety. From this secure and gently held space of Self-Love we are free to forgive our self for believing we're separate from God and our brothers, and for having unknowingly used someone or something to attack our self.

5. Now I can sincerely ask myself, *"What do I want?"* Do I want to keep the anger (guilt)? Or do I genuinely desire to have this self-loathing healed?" If I want it healed, I simply join Spirit and ask, expect and receive the miracle. Often, I am thus gifted with an emotional release of sadness or even grief which lay hiding underneath my initial anger.

6. Sometimes, if we go deep enough, we can actually feel the ancient

seat of this sadness is always the same. It's an echo of the immense grief of our separation from Love, from God and our most Holy Self. It's the grief felt from the primordial rejection of our eternal and incorruptible innocence. And this is something most of us have never allowed our self to recognize, let alone feel. Yet to surrender deeply into allowing it to flow, unimpeded by judgment, is such a powerfully transformative experience.

7.   In my own experience, almost all of my anger disappeared within that deep emotional release, never to return. Upon reflection, it was a period in which I felt as if I was the recipient of waves of a seemingly vast and "impersonal" grief. I could not identify any particular cause for it. It was revealed though that I had reached down into the sub-layer which underpins all anger. And as I let it go, I was acutely aware that I was not alone. I felt sure that everyone who had ever been imprisoned by anger was with me in those precious moments of deep surrender. I saw then with immense gratitude that there really was just One of us letting it all go.

8.   Later, I realized that I had experienced the Atonement. And then I understood Jesus' teaching that when we heal, we never heal alone.

   a.   *"And as you let yourself be healed, you see all those around you, or who cross your mind, or whom you touch or those who seem to have no contact with you, healed along with you. Perhaps you will not recognize them all, nor realize how great your offering to all the world, when you let healing come to you. But you are never healed alone. And legions upon legions will receive the gift that you receive when you are healed." ... "Those who are healed become the instruments of healing." W-137.10,11:1*

B. A Conclusive Test for True Forgiveness

1. Below is a conclusive two-step process that helps me to determine immediately whether I have succeeded in giving my anger to Holy Spirit. These two crucial points reveal whether I am embroiled in victimhood (the ego's wish to be unfairly treated), or I am consciously repealing it. I must desire to forgive and heal *more* than I want to be right and justified in my anger. I cannot be attacked unless I unwittingly *want* it. And if I still feel victimized then it's because I value guilt, unfair treatment, and being right. The *sick benefit* here is I can continue to *project* my own mistaken self-condemnation externally.

1) I recognize and accept that I am not a victim and my initial emotional charge diminishes or disappears entirely because I have forgiven myself.

2) I can sense a feeling of gratitude which replaces my previous feeling of having been victimized.

C. Practical Steps to Repurpose Anger

1. Here is a condensed summary of the process that I covered earlier in this excerpt:

1) Supervise our reaction of anger with Holy Spirit and not with the ego. Are we projecting onto someone else, our self, the body, the world, the past or God? Are we attributing the cause externally?

2) Ask, "What is this for?" Is this anger to heal (join) or to condemn (feel victimized, be right, stay separate)?

3) Accept our self while feeling anger, but do not *justify* anger. Remember anger is not wrong. It is just false. There is no guilt when we recognize it as false, just a mistaken interpretation.

4) Do the forgiveness/Atonement process if required.

5) Self-check to see if there is still a desire to feel victimized and justified in anger. Note without any self-judgment that this is a sure sign we still value attack and want to keep it. On the other hand, if there is even a faint sense of gratitude that begins to replace the anger, then healing is well underway! We have changed our unconscious goal from the ego's "wish to

be unfairly treated" to the Holy Self's goal of liberation from sin, guilt and fear. Time to celebrate!

2. Another possible phase in the process of undoing the false self (and one I went through) might be helpful to those who are experiencing it. It involves the experience of submerged anger seemingly erupting in waves, over a period of time. Often there appears to be no particular person or thing that we associate with it.

3. While its real source (within) needed to be recognized and surrendered for true healing, I found that this long-repressed anger had to emerge and be seen. It felt as if something had gone wrong and I blamed myself for not being able to see through the confusion at the time. Now in retrospect, I see that my confusion had evoked fear and contraction. Instead of recognizing and receiving the gift this massive purging was attempting to give me, it took a long time to pass through this phase because I resisted it.

4. In summary, we can never heal our anger while we still attempt to place the cause outside in another, the past, our self, the body, the world or God. These are purely *effects* and never the *cause* of our anger. This truth is incontestable if we desire to heal the fundamental cause of all anger.

D. Exercise: Exposing the Source of Anger

1. If all attack is essentially self-attack then acceleration of the healing process involves looking first at how we may have betrayed our self. Answer these questions with radical self-honesty:

    1) Where did I abandon myself, my inner knowing? How did I not show-up for myself?

    2) Where was I not completely honest, accountable and transparent?

    3) Was I trying to give something in order to *get* something in return? For example, approval, recognition, special favors, etc.

    4) Did I have an agenda?

5) Did I want to be right *more* than I wanted to close the gap with another?

6) Did I take something *personally?* Only the ego can do this. The Holy Self cannot.

7) Was I offended? Remember that to *take offense* and to *give offense* are the same mistake.

2. If you'd like to learn more about triggers, in addition to reading the next section, you should find the following sections helpful:

1) The Shocking Truth about Being Unfairly Treated on page 94.

2) The forgiveness process can be found in *The Seven Essential Principles of Quantum Forgiveness (Atonement)* on page 591.

14. REPURPOSING OUR TRIGGERS

1. We say we want to awaken from suffering. We say we desperately desire to know our Self as Love without opposite. Yet there is something we seem to be missing. The truth is that we all have immediate access to an untapped goldmine, a quantum acceleration of this divine transformation. But do we recognize it? And do we accept these gifts and use them consistently?

2. Contrary to what the ego teaches, the people and things that trigger us are indeed the gifts that hasten our return to Love, to our Holy Self and the immense safety of our Being. However, through the ego filter we not only reject these gifts, but fiercely defend our (ego) self from this valuable portal to liberation.

3. I finally realize the valuable significance and precious consequences of daring to look more deeply at my own triggers. I see clearly that if I feel triggered then it's *always* an opportunity and *never* a threat. Let's look at this. The only part of me that can be triggered is the ego. And I am *not* the ego. So, when I defend myself, *who* am I defending? Only the false self defends at all.

4. At the highest level, Love is the only "threat" the ego defends against. However, it doesn't want us to see this. Instead, it makes sure that Love is always disguised as a legitimate threat. That way, we will react to the threat and not the call *for* Love beneath it. Responding to the threat as an attack, we will defend, not realizing that whatever we defend against we end up attracting.-

5. If I continue to follow the ego's obsessive belief that: a) I can be unfairly treated, and b) I am justified in defense, then I am convincing myself that "I am the ego." The minute I am triggered and feel justified to defend, then the truth, the "I AM" as the Christ, is forgotten to me. The sanctity, the innocence and the invulnerable grace of who I AM is then banished from my awareness because I chose to value the ego in that moment.

6. Every experience arises from what we value and most of this is unconscious pain, skillfully disguised as our pursuit for love, safety, security and pleasure. This unconscious urge to value pain cannot be escaped until we actively engage in undoing our false identity via applying the *Seven Keys.*

7. Generally, now when I feel triggered, the old feeling of doom has disappeared. For the most part it is replaced by a sense of curiosity, followed quickly by enthusiastic expectation. This trigger is not a threat! No. It's always a beautiful gift if I will stop and ask Spirit to help me repurpose it. I ask for the gift(s) beneath the ego's first interpretation.

8. The person or thing that triggers us always has a sacred purpose. It comes as our savior, not to harm us but to release us from our own unconscious self-sabotage.

A. Exploring the "Gifts" of Being Triggered

1. Whenever we are triggered by someone, we never see them just *now*, as they are in reality. No. We are seeing exactly what our own ego filter *projects* onto them. We're not actually looking at their reality because we view them based on an unforgiven past experience of separation which the ego still projects over the *now* moment. This is why when we're triggered we do not see the

present, but the past. The only part of us that can *be* triggered is the ego. In contrast, the Holy Self that dwells only here and now, witnesses Itself as innocence *exclusively* in everyone *as one*.

2. When there is a trigger it's always the ego's projection. A trigger is the ego's *defense* against Love and healing, against our beloved Holy Self. The ego depends on preserving and even safeguarding these triggers to maintain its greatest of all defenses, the "Shield of Fear." *See "Breaking through the Shield of Fear diagram on page 57.*

3. When someone pushes my buttons it's an opportunity to:

   1) See what I am *defending* within the shield of fear based on the ego's past (which is not my Holy Self Who exists in the safety of the innocent *now* moment).

   2) Ask myself *why* I would want to keep the ego's perception of attack (based on the past) once I realize that *not* forgiving it reveals that I must *value it*, which ensures that further self-attack is projected into the future as well.

   3) Be inquisitive and ask Spirit to help me see the *truth* (the one Christ Identity that I share) beneath the ego's projection of attack. If I am never upset for the reason I think, then how have I perceived this person wrongly, especially since there is only *one* of us here?

   4) Ask for and *expect* the *gifts* beneath the "appearance" of attack via accepting the Atonement.

4. Following is a revealing message from Jesus about how to see others (and thus our Self) in the radiant light of Truth – as *innocent*.

   a. *"To perceive truly is to be aware of all reality through the awareness of your own. But for this no illusions can rise to meet your sight, for reality leaves no room for any error. This means that you perceive a brother only as you see him [now]. His past has no reality in the present, so you cannot see it. Your past reactions to him are also not there, and if it is to them that you react, you see but an image of him that you made and cherish instead of him. In your questioning of illusions, ask yourself if it is really sane to perceive what was as now. If you remember the past as you look upon your brother, you will be unable to perceive the reality that is now.*

You consider it "natural" to use your past experience as the reference point from which to judge the present. Yet this is [unnatural] because it is delusional. When you have learned to look on everyone with no reference at all to the past, either his or yours as you perceived it, you will be able to learn from what you see now. For the past can cast no shadow to darken the present, [unless you are afraid of light]. And only if you are would you choose to bring darkness with you, and by holding it in your mind, see it as a dark cloud that shrouds your brothers and conceals their reality from your sight.

[This darkness is in you.] The Christ as revealed to you now has no past, for He is changeless, and in His changelessness lies your release. For if He is as He was created, there is no guilt in Him. No cloud of guilt has risen to obscure Him, and He stands revealed in everyone you meet because you see Him through Himself. To be born again is to let the past go, and look without condemnation upon the present. The cloud that obscures God's Son to you [is] the past, and if you would have it past and gone, you must not see it now. If you see it now in your illusions, it has not gone from you, although it is not there.

The miracle enables you to see your brother without his past, and so perceive him as born again. His errors are all past, and by perceiving him without them you are releasing him. And since his past is yours, you share in this release." T-13. VI.1,2,3,5:1-3

B. What Do My Triggers Hide?

1. Here's an example of how being triggered by another person is caused by unknowingly projecting our own self-judgment and using them to attack our self. Many years ago I had a pattern of attracting all kinds of criticism, especially in my personal relationships. It seemed as if I was under a constant barrage of judgments from others. I was never good enough. I became an addicted people-pleaser and the harder I tried to meet other's needs the more I experienced conflict. I seemed to be damned if I did, and damned if I didn't. There was no respite from my dilemma.

2. Little did I know back then, that the one I consistently attempted to please was always the ego. I had no idea that each time I tried to meet the needs of others it was the ego's need I was meeting. And to address these requests I would first abandon my own inner knowing. That tiny "thud" within attempted to warn me that I was about to betray myself to the idea that sacrifice would buy me the love I wanted. The ego cannot Love. It can't give Love nor receive it. The toxic but hidden agreement of all special relationships is: "I will love you as long as you do what I (ego) want. If not? I won't love you any longer."

3. When I finally saw the ongoing destruction of the ego's harmful specialness dynamic, I did not desire it any longer. I was willing and open to correction from Spirit. It was time to look in a new, enlightened way, at the constant barrage of criticism I had attracted.

4. What was the gift beneath these judgments? If there is only one of us here, then who is judging? And then I saw the gift. Aha! My partner, family and friends simply mirrored to me my very own destructive self-judgments. I was lazy, weak, abstract, a dreamer, irresponsible, slow, stupid and entirely unworthy. Hmmmm. These were the ego's hidden evaluations of me; judgments that I had not unearthed and exchanged for the miracle. Because I had not exhumed them with the light of Spirit and surrendered all these fears and judgments, they were projected outward and used to make it appear as if I was unfairly treated.

5. Here is the miracle, the gift beneath my trigger. Had I not experienced all those judgments from others, as painful as it was, I would never have realized their source, their fundamental cause as being in my own mind. The ego was on a never-ending destructive loop, trying to solve my dilemma, looking for love in all the wrong places. It did anything to distract me from finding the single *source*

of all my pain and conflict – within.

6. The miracle came once I recognized that I had unknowingly used all my relationships to mirror my own wrong-minded judgments. So now the gift came in the form of me having the greatest *gratitude* for everyone in my life. Now I could *really* Love these people and offer them the gratitude and trust which the ego had previously denied.

7. Suddenly, the outer judgments stopped. When I withdrew *my* judgments of myself, and them, all my relationships became an expression of my newfound inner state.

C. Permission to be Called Out

1. Another beneficial thing occurred. I became open to constructive criticism. Now I had nothing to defend any longer, so I could open my heart to hearing Spirit speak to me through others. I gave Spirit the permission to *lovingly call me out* via others whenever I was tempted to abandon or lose myself. I was no longer afraid of being called out, because I knew it came from Love and not from some warped ego sabotage. I could trust my brothers and sisters because I trusted my Holy Self.

2. Are we willing to look past the ego's appearance of attack regardless of the form and seek the gift beneath it? This is the necessary prerequisite to healing every one of our unconscious attractions to self-attack. If not, and we feel resistance to this, we still value the problem. And what we value will manifest.

3. Who triggers you? And what triggers you? Are you ready to discover if you desire the *real cause* of these triggers to be healed? If so, then you will find this following prayer instrumental in lifting the ego's veil:

a. *"Holy Spirit, help me to see the healing gift behind this appearance of adversity or judgment. What do my feelings of pain conceal? What is the happy gift disguised beneath my anguish? I want that and nothing else but that! I open my heart this precious Holy Instant in quiet expectation of this gift. If I choose to see this as a problem or as an attack then I abandon myself to the ego. Please help me see this with*

Christ Vision. My heart is open to receive the miracle in place of the hurt I feel. Amen."

D. Signs of the Spiritual Ego

1. Before my own breakthrough, I went through a period of what I call spiritual superiority. Of course I could not see it at the time as I was blinded by it. Many on the spiritual path will encounter this phase in varying degrees. This is a period whereby the ego is impelled to undertake the spiritual journey. Its goal is not to awaken from guilt and fear but to acquire a more superior façade; a higher status.

2. Initially it is the ego as our false self that is the one who is happy to embark upon the spiritual journey. It believes it can perfect itself as it acquires more and more spiritual wisdom. Its superficial aim is to improve self-esteem and amass spiritual knowledge. However, it never dares ask which "self" needs esteem and knowledge.

3. The spiritual ego is quite unyielding. It really is the toughest nut to crack. Many in their journey of return to wholeness experience this phase where the ego takes on yet another layer of inflation, of "identity." Only this time it deems it legitimate because it has a *spiritual* label. This phase of the ego is still the ego, however now it becomes largely impenetrable. From my own experience some of the traits of this phase include:

1) Becoming overly identified with intellectual knowledge.

2) Defending that knowledge – spiritual righteousness.

3) Spiritual vanity and pride.

4) Spiritual superiority (seeing others as less than).

5) Lack of genuine emotional vulnerability and transparency.

6) Lack of radical self-honesty.

7) Lack of self-awareness, self-observation.

8) Lack of genuine curiosity.

9) Teaching more than listening and learning.

10) Lack of gratitude for others as teachers in their own right (students *are* teachers).

11) Resistance to being "called out" – lack of accountability.

12) Wearing a mask of positivity (arising from fear).

13) Engaging in spiritual debates (arising from the need to be right).

4. Every one of these expressions is simply a defense *against* awakening. As such they represent the ego's many and varied delaying tactics.

5. How devoted are we to undoing our blocks to Love? Devotion to dismantling our resistance and defenses must be paramount in our practice. How self-aware are we? Do we observe our self as we speak? Do we ask our self "who" is speaking? Is it the ego or Spirit? Does it come from Love and trust? Or does it come from doubt and fear? Are we engaged at the heart or the intellect? And as we listen to others, are we quick to formulate a response based on our intellectual knowledge? Or are we *present* to join the other in a precious Holy Instant allowing Spirit to reveal Christ Vision to us? Do we ask our self with radical self-honesty, "What is the purpose of this communication?" Is it to join at the heart in true humility, or do we join with the ego to prove our self as right?

6. Whether we classify our self as a spiritual student or teacher we must be mindful of those moments of ego temptation. Do we want to awaken from suffering? Do we really? Then we must also desire to *see* what has been denied and subsequently projected outward onto others, the body, the world, the past and God. Most of us are so fearful to expose our deepest fears, toxic patterns, values and beliefs. But it's impossible to be free of these illusions unless we are willing to look upon them without defense. Only then will we know deeply that our safety really does lay in our defenselessness. Only then will we know that we are the embodiment of incorruptible innocence and are therefore indestructible.

7. Instead of fear, justification and defense, we need to cultivate a healthy curiosity and sense of humor around our issues and blocks. An eagerness to look within is required. How will we ever see the face of Christ in others (and in our Self) if we're not willing to forgive and heal our defenses *to* it?

E. The Spiritual Ego Checklist

1. Here are some thought provoking questions. I only wish that I had this list during my own period of self-delusion. I can laugh now as I reflect, but I am sure this list would have vastly accelerated the ego's breakdown and my essential *breakthrough*! Take yourself through this helpful checklist with a healthy dose of radical self-honesty:

   1) **Am I for real?** Am I mindfully present and unequivocally authentic in my communications with others and myself?

   2) **Do what I think, feel, say and do all line up together where there is no conflict between them?** Or am I often tempted to speak of what I know intellectually while disregarding the conflicting subtleties in my own heart?

   3) **Am I eager to discover my own inner contradictions and inconsistencies so they can be healed?** *Or is there resistance?* What healing does this resistance hide? What is it that the spiritual ego does not want me to see?

   4) **How much do I practice radical self-honesty?** How open am I to receive constructive criticism from others without defense and justification? *Or is there resistance?* What gift or blessing am I blocking with this resistance? What is it that the spiritual ego does not want me to recognize and claim?

   5) **Is there a sense of gratitude whenever my spiritual ego is called out (threatened or triggered)?** If not, why not? Which "self" feels threatened via its need for justification and defense?

   6) **How much do I value introspection?** Am I consistently self-aware observing myself and others *without judgment* but with *Spirit's Loving discernment*?

7) **Do I tend to speak (teach) more than I listen?** Do I find myself attempting to *convince* and *convert* others? If so, do I ask myself, "Who (Spirit or ego) is speaking and which "self" needs convincing and converting?"

8) **Is there a sense of pride or superiority?** Whenever I am triggered by others do I override my own healing opportunity by convincing myself that I know more than them and am therefore more spiritually superior?

9) **Which am I more interested in? 1)** Teaching or coaching intellectually to others while maintaining my own teacher role, **or 2)** Open-hearted joining with others where I am encouraged to: a) be transparent, b) express my own emotional vulnerability, c) close the seeming gap between myself and others, and d) Am I genuinely grateful for the fact that those who may seem to know less than me are in fact my greatest teachers?

2. It's important to look at this list with radical self-honesty *yet make sure not to fall into self-judgment and guilt either.* Guilt and self-judgment are ego attempts to separate you from Love and healing. The purpose here is to flush out any inconsistencies so they can be healed. And they cannot be healed until they are seen first. Once you recognize the areas which require healing, you can then take them through the forgiveness process.

15. THE ROOT OF ALL UNCONSCIOUS SELF-ATTACK

1. Behold the great illusion, the great hologram! This is the world, as we have taught our self to perceive it. Yet by no means is it true.
2. There is only one God the Father and therefore, only one changeless and unified Christ, beloved of the Father. And, although each one of us is a unique expression of His infinite Love, we, together, are that one Christ Mind. Our one Holy Self is completely, irrevocably

undivided, united and whole. This is the one Christ who innocently chose to dream of separation. From undivided knowledge of perfect changeless Love and joy, we dreamed that we were independent from our Father, from the very Source of our Being.

3. This decision, to forget What we are, and instead, to really *believe* that we abandoned God, produced the impossible, a self-induced conviction that we had indeed *sinned*. What followed immediately was the equally insane belief that we were *guilty*, which was the inception of *fear* itself, the illusory opposite of God as Love.

4. To the ego, sin is *irrevocable error* which must be punishable by death. Thus, in the ego's dream, life is equated unconsciously with sin, bringing about the ego's promise – that redemption is achieved only through death. Death then seems to end life in the ego's hallucination.

5. At the separation the Son of God dreamt of private minds with separate bodies seemingly locked in the illusions of time, and of birth and death.

6. My salvation from the grand illusion I have made comes from my willingness to open my heart to Holy Spirit to divinely repurpose everything and everyone in my life. This includes the body, my relationships, my life, the past, the world, all my beliefs and values, especially my concept of God (Love).

7. The Son of God (Sonship) is largely asleep but is awakening. Jesus was the first fractal of the one Son of God, the Christ, (in the illusion of time) to awaken fully from the entire dream of birth and death, of time and space. This being so, Jesus stands at the head of our return to God bridging the seeming gap between us and God. Having completed the undoing of the grand illusion, He is in charge of the Atonement Plan.

A. Why We Beat Our Selves Up

1. Recently, I had a revealing conversation with a dear friend about how she had continued to fall into a common trap of beating herself up. She has been on the spiritual path for many years and is a devoted student of *A Course in Miracles*, yet there was still this persistent sense of guilt that seemed to recur even amidst her most diligent

practice. I wonder if you can relate to this too.

2. She shared with me: "For so long I've recognized that *I am responsible* for what I see. One of my mantras from the *Course* has been "You see what you believe is there, and you believe it there because *you want* it there." But I used it to beat myself up!"

a. *"I am responsible for what I see. I choose the feelings I experience, and I decide upon the goal I would achieve. And everything that seems to happen to me I ask for, and receive as I have asked." T-21.II.2:3-5*

3. One of the first steps in our ascent back up the ladder of separation is to recognize that we are not victims of the body and world we seem to see. We must recognize a crucial truth; that in having chosen the ego as our default, it then projects a body and world that appears to be done *to* us, and not *by* us. The unfortunate outcome of this is the erroneous belief that we are indeed victims of people, the body, the past and the world.

4. As we begin our journey through the six stages of the development of trust – awakening from fear – we learn to forgive others, the past and the world. We gradually learn to withdraw the ego's projections of blame and guilt. However, a strange phenomenon often takes place in this initial period of learning to forgive.

5. We may find suddenly that while we seem to be able to forgive others more consistently, it feels as though our self-blame increases. We may try to watch our thinking and judgments like a hawk, catching at times the almost automatic compulsion to judge others. And then, without really recognizing it, the same false self (guilt) that methodically projected blame externally onto others, is now turning that venom within.

6. This results in periods of beating our self up, characterized by feelings of worthlessness and self-doubt. So, what exactly happened?

7. Believe it or not, the ego is the first one that tries to learn forgiveness. But because this false self concept is guilt itself, it cannot possibly apply quantum forgiveness, without causing its own demise. Quantum forgiveness amounts to the complete eradication of all belief in sin, guilt, blame and fear.

8. The ego must retain guilt in order to survive and the only way it can do that is to project it somewhere. If it can no longer blame others during this phase, then it usually turns blame within.

9. To move past blame all together, we could take a deep breath, step aside from this imposter (the ego) and accept the Atonement by giving the ego's mistakes over to Holy Spirit to erase. However, during this phase of unlearning, while still identifying largely as the false self, we inadvertently take on false responsibility for errors.

10. Remember this, the ego is not who we are. We are the eternally innocent Child of God. We are the Holy Self. We cannot be both!

11. When feeling personally responsible to solve the ego's illusory problems, we find our self weighed down by the crushing burden of self-judgment. But what we don't realize is that the ego must always have someone to blame, to project its guilt onto, so it can keep its illusory thought system alive. Any blame at all is always the ego … no matter what. Self blame is exactly the same mistake as condemning others.

    a. *"The beginning phases of this reversal are often quite painful, for as blame is withdrawn from without, there is a strong tendency to harbor it within. It is difficult at first to realize that this is exactly the same thing, for there is no distinction between within and without.* **You cannot enter God's Presence if you attack His Son.***"* T-11.IV.4:5-6,5:5-6

12. In these phases of our spiritual journey, the ego can often appear to become more spiritualized and is quite content to recognize that "it" is responsible for what it sees, and that it sees suffering and injustice because it *wants* them there. But *why* is it happy to see this? Because when we confuse our self *with* the ego, we will feel *guilty,* and we will beat our self up. The guilt ensures that we're plagued by self-doubt and self-judgment, and this is again the ego's ploy to keep us from knowing our Self. The ego as the mistaken belief we're separate from God's Love – is increased due to our attraction to guilt.

13. Any guilt feelings immediately reveal that I must unwittingly believe that *I am an isolated, illusory self, split off from my*

incorruptible and innocent Holy Self. Only this *imagined self* is capable of guilt, while my *Holy Self* is not. Any fear or concern for either myself *or another* also reveals that I have confused myself with this imposter. A sure sign that I have made this error is my subsequent effort to solve the problem, apart from Holy Spirit. This results in impossible attempts to remedy the ego's problems through the very guilt and fear that caused them in the first place.

14. If I take false responsibility for the mistakes made through the false self, instead of giving them over to Holy Spirit to erase, I will keep the guilt which initially caused them. This is why all healing, all forgiveness must be *self*-forgiveness. I forgive my self for having made the mistake of misidentifying as the ego, the imaginary opponent to God.

a. *"Every disordered thought is attended by guilt at its inception, and maintained by guilt in its continuance. Guilt is inescapable by those who believe they order their own thoughts, and must therefore obey their dictates. This makes them feel responsible for their errors without recognizing that, by accepting this responsibility, they are reacting irresponsibly. If the sole responsibility of the miracle worker is to accept the Atonement for himself, and I assure you that it is, then the responsibility for [what] is atoned for cannot be yours."* ... *"The continuing decision to remain separated is the only possible reason for continuing guilt feelings."* T-5.V.7:5-8,8:1

15. The sole responsibility of the miracle worker is to accept the Atonement for himself. When we accept the Atonement, the undoing of fear, we are no longer responsible for what Holy Spirit erases. To continue to feel guilty is a desire to remain separate and alone, apart from God. This, as the attraction to guilt, is the ego's strongest defense against embodying our beloved Holy Self. The forgiveness process can be found in *The Seven Essential Principles of Quantum Forgiveness (Atonement)* on page 591.

16. At some point in our transfer of trust from fear to Love we will be required to practice making a positive separation between the

illusory identity we are *not* (false self) and the Identity we share with God and all our brothers (Holy Self). We are not both. We are the Holy Self exclusively. Jesus explains this well in the following passage:

a. *"This is a crucial period in this course, for here the separation of you and the ego must be made complete."* ... *"Now must you choose between yourself and an illusion of yourself. Not both, but one. There is no point in trying to avoid this one decision. It must be made. Faith and belief can fall to either side, but reason tells you misery lies only on one side and joy upon the other."* ... *"There is no part of Heaven you can take and weave into illusions. Nor is there one illusion you can enter Heaven with."* T-22.II.6:1,6-10,8:1-2

17. For many of us, guilt, fear and feelings of unworthiness often seem to be so totally overwhelming at times that we just cannot seem to pull our self up and out of them. As a result of my desire to extend a "life-line" to those of us who genuinely desire to be done with beating ourselves up, I joined with Jesus to record a powerful guided meditation, one that will bring miracles to those who are sincerely willing to trust Him. This meditation, titled *The End of Fear* is available in the Supplemental Materials link at: *www. HolyRelationship.com*

B. Jesus as the First to Complete the Atonement

1. Because Jesus undid the whole dream of suffering for us all, we only need be willing to *accept* His divine correction in our own mind, to heal. This is really first *recognizing* the one problem, which is the mistaken belief that we are separate, followed by the act of *receiving* what has already been corrected and healed. Two particularly helpful lessons in the *Course* which support this are: lesson 79, "Let me recognize the problem so it can be solved," and lesson 80, "Let me recognize my problems have been solved." *A Course in Miracles* explains why Jesus leads the way out from the entire ego dream:

a. *"Jesus is the manifestation of the [Holy Spirit], Whom he called down upon the earth after he ascended into Heaven, or became completely identified with the Christ, the Son of God as He created Him. C-6.1*

b. *"He [Holy Spirit] has established Jesus as the leader in carrying out His plan since he [Jesus] was the first to complete his own part perfectly." C-6.2.*

C. From Jesus

a. *"I am in charge of the process of Atonement, which I undertook to begin."… "My part in the Atonement is the cancelling out of all errors that you could not otherwise correct." T-1.III.1:1,4*

b. *"I am the only one who can perform miracles indiscriminately, because I am the Atonement." T-1.III.4:1*

c. *"You were in darkness until God's Will was done completely by any part of the Sonship. When this was done, it was perfectly accomplished by all. How else could it be perfectly accomplished? My mission was simply to unite the will of the Sonship with the Will of the Father by being aware of the Father's Will myself. This is the awareness I came to give you, and your problem in accepting it is the problem of this world. Dispelling it is salvation, and in this sense I [am] the salvation of the world." T-8.IV.3:1-6*

1. Your healing lay in your own mind. That may already be familiar enough to you by now. But there is another crucial aspect of true healing that is calling out for attention. The healing for any *seeming other person* (or situation) *also* lies in *your own mind.*

2. In other words, if you are triggered, concerned or fearful by seeing a problem or sickness in another, then the *source* of those afflictions dwells in *your mind.* You could not be triggered by a problem or sickness, unless your *own* mind was sick. If your mind was whole, and not split, then you could only see another as they

really are in truth; whole and complete. You would behold them *not* through the body's eyes, but with Christ Vision. And in knowing them as whole and complete, in acknowledging the one, continuous Mind of God we share, they *are* healed along with you. The light in your Mind shines into theirs and thus you both remember the immaculate, healed truth you share. You heal by offering your distorted perception to Spirit in exchange for a miracle, the healing of your fearful perception.

3. To release our fearful perception we need to first discover the *cause* of all our fears. While unconscious guilt is unrelinquished it remains the *root* of all suffering and loss we seem to witness. When guilt is the filter or lens we look out from, it causes us to feel and to see fear in all its forms. In truth, every "appearance of suffering" can only occur when we look out from our filter of guilt. Suffering does not *happen externally* as an entirely independent occurrence, like our senses identify. We are not the *cause* of others' suffering however if we're triggered then *that trigger* is ours to heal. As we heal our own concern then it has a quantum ripple effect for others.

4. All our triggers are a product of our own unforgiven guilt. What I'm stressing here is that fear is the direct byproduct of guilt. There can be no *fear* possible without *guilt*. Guilt produces fear. And our erroneous need to judge or blame is the "sin" the ego needs to keep hoarding its guilt. In the ego dream there are thousands of seeming reasons to fear. But these are all smokescreens. These are not the real *cause* of our fear. Nothing other than guilt, which is the hidden belief that we deserve punishment, can produce fear.

5. Every single fear we experience is the anticipation and belief that something *could* go wrong. And that anticipation is always the false self's hidden *expectation* of the punishment, which we mistakenly believe we deserve. Of course, this anticipated *punishment* and the fear it causes, is never what God Wills for us. Nothing can ever go wrong when we accept wholeheartedly that we *are* the Will of God.

6. If you are fearful or concerned, can you touch on the underlying belief or feeling that lay beneath that fear? Is there a sense of separation, lack, loss, suffering or a feeling of being deprived? If you're in tune you may be able to sense a subtle but uneasy

anticipation of *punishment* beneath the fear. This is accessing the *root of guilt* that spawns all fear; discerning the guilt that secretly expects some form of retaliation. We perpetuate this *self-punishment* in numerous forms by projecting our guilt (judgment) onto others, our self, the body and the world. If I seem to witness the opposite of God's Love in any seeming "form" I am indeed seeing through my own unrelinquished guilt.

D. Will You Accept Healing?

1. When I accept the Atonement, the divine correction for what I seem to see or feel, I accept my incorruptible innocence, which is my immunity to everything the ego made to attack me. This is the undoing of the guilt that caused the particular problem that I seem to believe and therefore see as evidence of my guilt. And because there is *only one* split mind, acceptance of my innocence is the key to healing another's mind if he/she is ready to receive it.

2. The Atonement is restoration of the awareness of my incorruptible innocence (Holy Self). It's the undoing of my secret agreement to and anticipation of punishment along with the disarming of my defenses to Love. In lifting the veil of guilt my innocence manifests what "It" knows and therefore expects as God's Will, which is healing expressed in multiple forms.

3. Incorruptible innocence is all inclusive and recognizes only itself in everyone and everything because it is fearless. Innocence cannot anticipate fear because fear and innocence are mutually exclusive. The awareness of one completely excludes the other. The most powerful witness to God's Love here in the dream is the embodiment and demonstration of our incorruptible innocence. It cannot know guilt, fear, judgment or suffering because it is undivided Love as our Holy Self. The miracle is available in any moment that we genuinely choose to value this innocence in place of the illusions of conflict or suffering. We are entitled to miracles!

a. *"I am entitled to miracles. I am entitled to miracles because I am under no laws but God's. His laws release me from all grievances, and replace them with miracles. And I would accept the miracles in place of the grievances, which are but illusions that hide the miracles beyond. Now I would accept only what the laws of God entitle me to have, that I may use it on behalf of the function He has given me." W-pI.89.1*

E. Everyone and Everything Is a Gift

1. Everyone and everything in our life is there for just one purpose; to give us unlimited opportunities to recognize and heal our own Self-rejection. As mirrors, they are there to show us our fear and guilt so we can undo them via quantum forgiveness as the Atonement – the divine undoing of guilt (which *is* separation) in our mind. This is why we can afford to feel gratitude for all those who come to offer us the gift of another chance at salvation.

2. Whether it be sickness, scarcity, betrayal or abandonment, while I choose to experience these "attacks" as real then I must be *valuing* them. And when I value attack I will defend myself from it, all the while unknowingly attracting the very experience I believe I am defending myself *from*. We always attract what we fear (value).

3. And this is precisely why forgiveness heals unequivocally. In fact, it is the *only* practice that heals. When we choose to "look past" seeming attack and accept healing of our perception instead, the single cause of all perceived attack is healed. And when the *real cause* is healed so are its consequences.

4. We cannot possibly realize the immensity, the majesty and the immortality of our most Holy Self while we still condemn others or our self.

5. If I am triggered by another person then that trigger lay in my mind and not in my seeming adversary. The guilt that caused me to perceive fear or anger arose from *my* mind. If it wasn't in my own mind I could never *be* triggered. The same can be said of every illusion in the dream. Sickness and pain are good examples of this.

6. If I am concerned about sickness in either my body or another's, then I am not seeing with God. Only my *guilt* can believe in sickness. And what if I see another as guilty? Only *my guilt* can be seen in another. And what if I see myself or another suffering or in pain? Only my guilt feels pain. Only my unrelinquished guilt expresses fear and concern for another's wellbeing; and this is not Loving.

a. *"What Comforter can there be for the sick children of God except His power through you?"... "Heal your brothers simply by accepting God for them. Your minds are not separate, and God has only one channel for healing because He has but one Son."*

"To believe that a Son of God can be sick is to believe that part of God can suffer. Love cannot suffer, because it cannot attack. The remembrance of love therefore brings invulnerability with it. Do not side with sickness in the presence of a Son of God even if he believes in it, for your acceptance of God in him acknowledges the Love of God he has forgotten. Your recognition of him as part of God reminds him of the truth about himself, which he is denying."... "To believe a Son of God is sick is to worship the same idol he does."   T-10. III.2:1,5-5,3:1-5,4:1

7. Through the filter of guilt, I only see my own unrelinquished guilt masquerading as illness, conflict, scarcity, betrayal or suffering. Wherever I see it, the source of disease is always in my own mind awaiting recognition and the happy exchange of a miracle. This is the Atonement. Thus, the healing of the world lay in one easy and accessible place - *my own mind*. Behold the great illusion, the great hologram. Wow.

16. HEALING THE SINGLE ROOT OF ALL ABUSE AND TRAUMA

1. The highest truth is that there is only *one* Child of God and "we" as the multifaceted yet unified Sons of God, are that one Child whether we remember it or not. Our true Identity is changeless, just like God. Any belief in suffering occurs in a dream that we separated from our Loving Creator (God).
2. The Son of God made the illusory dream of ego, the belief in sin, guilt and fear and gave "it" the role of his creator. With this he also

made the concepts of time and space, including matter, to further his dream of separation and make it appear real.

3. In the dream, this one Child chose to split himself into billions of separate bodies, each seeming to share a deranged thought system based on death. We call this "life." However, a life apart from God is in fact, death. This is the ego; a concept of the "self" apart from God. If God is all-encompassing, unchanging Love, Joy and Life without opposite, and if God is all that exists in truth, then the ego must be complete delusion.

4. Many of us find it difficult to forgive the seeming past. The pain of victimization seems so real. Yet we need to question this memory by asking which "self" recalls being victimized? Is it the Holy Self who is completely indestructible? Or is it the ego?

5. The memory of victimization is validated and reinforced exclusively by the ego, the false concept of our self and not our true Identity. The ego is an (imagined) attack on God and therefore, an attack on our Holy Self. And we feel guilty for it because unconsciously we still believe we did something so utterly devastating (abandoned God) that we cannot *be* forgiven. Secretly we believe we did something that is completely irrevocable.

6. Although it is altogether untrue, this guilty belief has become the root of our persistent sense of threat, regardless of the form and severity of the threat. A sense of threat always *expects* attack. And in its defenses against anticipated attack abides the very goal the ego hides; *our hidden attraction to it*. Every fear is born from this central, guilt-ridden, yet deeply unconscious, ego belief that Something is out to get us – God.

A. We Scripted Our Life Before Birth

1. Undoing our mistaken self-concept involves a process of remembering that we, along with all our brothers, share the one, continuous Mind of God in which there is no fear, only perfect Love. We remember our true Identity as we consistently forgive the aspects of our false identity which we have unknowingly projected onto others, the body, the world and God.

2. These unhealed, unforgiven aspects of the ego are seen in what

appears to be "others." Yet in truth…there are no others. Whatever we react to in another is a reflection of that which we value and hold for our self; either Love or attack. This includes everything we abhor and attempt to avoid including adversity, abuse, destruction, conflict, betrayal, abandonment, deprivation, disease and death.

3. There is no hierarchy of illusions. This means literally that there is not one illusion, no matter how devastating or beatific it might appear, which holds any more reality than any other illusion. All illusions have zero degree of reality. Illusion is illusion. Truth is truth. They are mutually exclusive and cannot coexist. They only seem to coexist because within our split mind, we unconsciously value the untrue and choose to make it appear true in our experience.

4. The ego dream runs on a recycle program of continuous birth, death and amnesia. This cycle perpetuates the illusion of time and thus suffering. The one Christ is the truth of every being that appears in the dream. However, a newborn baby arrives here helpless and with amnesia, having forgotten its true Self, along with its only purpose, which is to awaken from the dream of a separate self…not to reinforce it as the ego world teaches.

5. The ego, as a thought system we have chosen to employ, exists before birth into a body. And unless we choose to awaken from the ego dream entirely, it also exists for us after physical death. The ego *is* death, being the opposite of Life in God. If we were to rise well above the wearying loop of the ego's birth and death cycle we would look down to see our own childhood and lifetime very differently. We would see that we were never victimized. No one was ever victimized.

6. The ego's stronghold is attack because it is the belief in separation and attack. This insane belief is the ego's fundamental default. Mistaking our self for the ego, we have scripted our entire experience in every lifetime. Before birth we choose (via the ego) exactly which people and circumstances would be the most ideal for our own level of guilt as unconscious self-condemnation. Fortunately for us, the script changes and heals as we awaken and continue to consent to healing. This is what miracles are for. They undo our false perception and thus undo all effects or consequences

of imaginary attack such as conflict, pain, sickness, lack and even death.

7. Some of us have unknowingly chosen to enter this lifetime to experience childhood abuse, as I did, or perhaps illness or other forms of adversity. All this serves to "prove" that attack and separation are real, but thankfully that changes when we choose to have these false perceptions entirely reinterpreted by Spirit.

8. Before birth, the ego already knows what it wants. It has a plan, a script. Yet none of the ego's script is real. All suffering, regardless of our seeming age in the dream (newborn or aged), does not show up on God's divine Radar. God knows no suffering, no disease, no deprivation, no conflict and no death. The only part of us that can experience these is the mistaken self. The Holy Self, the truth of who we are remains completely impervious to all appearances of suffering.

9. There are no victims. Unknowingly, the ego projects its unconscious guilt onto others (parents for example) or the body in cases of childhood disease, etc. All attack is always "self-attack." We cannot be attacked unless we agree unconsciously to project/ attract attack.

B. Healing Breakthrough

1. True healing breakthroughs transpire when we willingly choose to be accountable for our unconscious choices to suffer. And this is to be done without self-judgment. This is when we decide to apply quantum forgiveness and we ask to have our mistaken perception of the past and everyone in it completely reinterpreted and repurposed by Spirit.

2. We cannot do this though until we are willing to take full responsibility for having chosen to suffer, albeit unconsciously. Taking responsibility for all our suffering involves forgiving *our self* for having believed in the separation and projecting this onto others, to attack our self. Remember there is only really one of us here. We either see the ego (our own projected attack), or we see the Christ. The choice is ours in any one moment.

---

3. The only *truth* that exists in everyone we encounter, including abusive parents, is the one Holy Self. The degree we forgive our self for having unknowingly used others to attack our self, is the extent to which we will experience the Christ in others and our Self. The thin veil that appears to separate us is lifted and we see the truth of that being; which is the truth in us. The thin veil, the one we lifted, is the only imposter here.

C. The Divine Lesson – All Forgiveness is Self-Forgiveness

1. When we invite Spirit to reinterpret and repurpose the ego's past, including childhood abuse, we will see the bigger picture, the view from above the ego's battle ground. We will flip the old victim perception into one of divine empowerment. And we will reinterpret the role, from one of fear to one of Love, that we our self assigned to our seeming abusers.
2. Gratitude for each of these seeming abusers must dawn on our awareness as we recognize how and why we scripted our own movie. We see the blessings in it and we know that we could never have been attacked unless we agreed to it.
3. The greatest gift we will receive from this miraculous shift in perception is the recognition that the one who seemingly betrayed us has offered us our salvation, literally. For without them we would not be able see that the pain we experienced was all *our own projection*, our own unconscious *self-attack*. And without them we would not have the chance to undo it by *forgiving our self.*
4. The Christ is the truth of every being. If we do not see this yet it is because we still value the illusion of being a victim (to project guilt outward). There is still a reluctance to give up attack and separation and we are not yet willing to have our perception healed. Unconsciously, there is an ego pay-off to keep the grievance.
5. This *seeming abuser* is the Christ *in disguise*. The disguise is so utterly convincing because the very last thing the ego wants us to recognize is this: The disguise conceals *our very own* unconscious self-hatred (guilt as attack) which is projected onto another. This is the split mind's guilt. Guilt *expects* punishment. And from what it secretly expects God cannot save us.

6. The ego, expecting punishment, goes on to *manifest* its own punishment. All forms of fear are the expectation of attack, which is the unconscious attraction to it. It uses others, the body or the world to attract its own unconscious attack.

7. This unconscious attraction to self-attack has a hidden *value.* Through the ego, we unknowingly value guilt, fear and suffering because they offer the ego its essential *protection from* the Love of God. The darkness is upheld by guilt and fear. Without them the light of our Holy Self would completely extinguish all darkness. And that includes any belief in victimization, specialness, separation, martyrdom, etc. There is always a pay-off involved in holding onto trauma and abuse. And if we truly want to heal, we will willingly forgive our self for having unknowingly used someone or something to attack our self.

8. One beautiful exercise to help you recognize and divinely reinterpret the role of a seeming abuser is this: Write a letter to yourself from the abuser. They may be still present in a body or not. It does not matter. The key here is to allow the Holy Self of this person to write to you. Spirit will guide the Loving words. And all of it will be the truth, if you do not censor it.

D. Why We Seem to Attract Suffering

1. In this lifetime, I had chosen unconsciously to experience what many would classify as cruel abuse. At the age of eight, I was sexually abused by a teacher. I was in third grade. When I attempted to share my distress with my mother, she slapped me for "telling lies." As a result of this seeming double assault, I chose (again, unconsciously) to become deaf. I suddenly lost more than eighty percent of my hearing soon after that experience. I wanted desperately to withdraw from what I perceived as a cruel world.

2. If we look at this through the eyes of the ego, that an innocent child was brutally victimized, then it does indeed appear horrific. But the ego only wants to see a single, favored frame from its entire movie since the separation; only *this* lifetime. What about other lifetimes?

3. In this seemingly real dream, we have all been both victims and perpetrators. This is the game of the ego. It thrives on the drama

of projecting its version of innocence. To be innocent here in the dream, one's innocence must rest upon another's guilt. The ego has no understanding or experience of true innocence which is undivided, unopposed and literally indestructible. Only our Holy Self knows this innocence because it is an attribute of God's eternal Love. To truly know and live out from our incorruptible innocence, it must be shared with everyone universally. Innocence, as a changeless aspect of the Love we are, has no degrees. Nor does it know of an opposite.

4. The ego, in order to survive, had to make up its own version of what I will call "corrupted innocence" based on fear and attack. Corrupted innocence is attack. It is the unconscious wish to be unfairly treated. It rests on the belief that we purchase our innocence through being victimized. My innocence is bought at the cost of another's guilt. And it is the ego's addiction to this corrupted innocence that must compel us to value its victim stories and therefore, unintentionally resist true healing.

5. I know all about this, as for more than 40 years I blamed my perpetrator for a number of ensuing afflictions. It was not until I fell to my knees in forgiveness one day, that I finally saw the ugly prize the ego almost refused to relinquish. If I forgave my abuser, I would lose my corrupted innocence! I needed him to be guilty. Then I could maintain my grievance against him to prove that I was the innocent victim.

6. What I did not realize until then, was that while I continued to see that teacher as my abuser, I was condemning both him *and myself* to death. I cannot recognize and accept my true innocence (indestructibility and healing) while I still choose to perceive anyone as guilty. And this includes everyone in the past. If I accuse another, I condemn myself because we are literally *one*!

7. True innocence comes with no cost. It is our Inheritance from God. True innocence does not require a guilty opposite. In fact, the idea of any guilt, judgment or blame completely disqualifies true innocence. And this includes self-judgment.

8. This is why forgiveness of everyone and everything, including our self, is absolutely crucial if we genuinely desire to free our self

from all forms of unconscious self-attack. Every seeming pain and disease could be healed at once through heartfelt forgiveness; the withdrawal of our projection of guilt.

9. True forgiveness undoes the imagined past. If the Love of God is all that exists and nothing can threaten it, then everything we have ever experienced that was not of God *did not happen*. Therefore, the past is entirely imaginary – literally. The only experiences which reflect Reality are those which are aligned with the Will of God (Love). When we forgive the past we are forgiving an illusion that we no longer value. Because we no longer value suffering as a "will apart from God," we no longer attract it...

E. Reluctance to Heal

1. You are true innocence as the Christ, whole and complete. True innocence is divine because it sees no sin, no guilt and no fear; it is unopposed and eternal. This is the *real* you, of which you are mostly unaware. However, the ego depends and thrives on its own version of innocence, "corrupted innocence." It is corrupt because in order to perceive itself as innocent it must perceive someone as guilty! Its innocence is bought at the cost of someone's guilt.

2. *The insane ego believes that:* While we suffer, we are innocent. Our suffering proves to our self and others that someone else or something else is guilty. To the ego, being a victim is its protection, its defense against God's Love and healing which it interprets as God's vicious wrath. This includes relationship conflict, sickness, pain, financial lack, etc. Deep down in the core of the ego thought system the ego believes that if it does not punish itself then God (ego's "god" of pain and suffering) will inflict the most brutal punishment on us...just as he *seemingly* did with Jesus in his crucifixion.

3. This is the height of insanity, however, to some degree we all believe it. Think about it. In all honesty, don't you remember believing that if someone felt sorry for you (because you were unfairly treated) that they would love you? The ego says, "Your suffering proves that you are innocent. Suffering "protects" you from a much more horrific punishment from God. And this is the basic reason why we resist instantaneous, miraculous healing. If you forgive everyone

and everything and refuse to *be* victimized, then you'll be in big trouble! Without projecting your guilt onto the body, others, the world and God, you will lose your (corrupted) innocence. And then you will be left with absolutely no defense to protect you from God's wrath!

4. *The ego cannot forgive because it believes this:* "I need you to be guilty so as I can preserve my (corrupted) innocence to protect me from God's wrath." The delusional ego wants you to believe that if you forgive everyone and everything, you will lose your innocence. To it, suffering and being a victim *is* innocence. It does not care who or what you appear to be victimized by (abuse, conflict, pain, disease, financial lack, etc.); just as long as you do not release your belief in suffering and victimization - as long as you do not forgive it.

F. The Body as a Guilty Scapegoat

1. The ego says that while I suffer from the seemingly "self-motivated" attacks of the body, I will retain my innocence. While I am victim to the body, then I appear to be innocent and the *body* is guilty. Not only will I gladly suffer the pains of the body to preserve this illusion of innocence, but I will even welcome death to uphold it!

2. Whether it uses a person, an experience of lack or conflict, or a bodily condition, the ego always seeks a perpetrator to prove that it is a victim and is therefore, innocent. It must project its guilt onto others, the body, the world or God, in order to maintain its false sense of safety (corrupted innocence). Fear demands a witness to uphold its illusions. It needs to uphold a fundamental belief in guilt, attack and separation or else it disappears entirely.

3. If I mistakenly believe *I am* the ego then I will also identify as a body, and unknowingly use the body to attack myself (weight, pain, illness and aging, etc.), all to *prove* that I am innocent. In this case the neutral body is projected as the perpetrator, a guilty scapegoat, and the ego uses it to attack *with*.

4. Corrupted innocence is the disguised attraction to pain, suffering and death. This secret desire to be unfairly treated is a major reason why we repeatedly choose to exit life through physical death. The ego usurps the power of God and we sentence our self to a much

lesser form of punishment than we imagine God will exact upon us – and that lesser form of retribution is physical death.

5. Following is a powerful quote from Jesus in *A Course in Miracles:*

a. *"The guiltless mind cannot suffer. Being sane, the mind heals the body because [it] has been healed. The sane mind cannot conceive of illness because it cannot conceive of attacking anyone or anything. I said before that illness is a form of magic. It might be better to say that it is a form of magical solution. The ego believes that by punishing itself it will mitigate the punishment of God. Yet even in this it is arrogant. It attributes to God a punishing intent, and then takes this intent as its own prerogative. It tries to usurp all the functions of God as it perceives them, because it recognizes that only total allegiance can be trusted." T-5.V.5.*

6. Our greatest defense *against* Love and healing dwells in our desire to *believe in and witness to attack,* whether it be via conflict, abandonment, betrayal, abuse, disease, pain, aging, financial lack, etc. How do we know we still desire attack? That we believe it is *real,* anywhere, demonstrates we still *value* it. And God cannot save us from whatever we value.

G. Exercise: Ego Speaking vs. Holy Spirit Speaking

1. In which areas do you still desire to be unfairly treated so as you can preserve your "corrupted" innocence as a defense against Love and healing? Who and what do you have a hard time forgiving? Is it someone from your childhood? Is it the body (which is entirely neutral, innocent and incapable of any self-motivated attacks)? Only you will know your own scapegoats. If you really want to heal, here is a journaling exercise to help:

2. You will need a page or more divided vertically in half. The left side is titled, "Ego Speaking" and the right side is titled, "Spirit Speaking." If you can't divide a page in half simply use two separate pages.

3. Perhaps you can find a quiet place and relax while setting your intention to allow Spirit to reveal whatever you need to see. Without self-judgment, ask to see if there are any people present or past whom you find it difficult to forgive. Look carefully. Whom do you

still believe you were victimized *by?* Be radically honest; to what degree do you still believe this really happened?

1) First, allow the ego to speak. Let it purge as you ask, "Why does it need to justify its grievance?" And, second, "What does it fear to lose if you were to forgive and heal completely?"

2) Now ask Spirit to help you see this differently remembering that the ego believes your "corrupted" innocence (protection from God's punishment) depends on holding grievances, on you being a victim. Allow Spirit to write to you in its column.

3) Now, repeat the same process with anything else that concerns you such as: relationship conflict, the body's pain, disease, weight issues, financial concerns, etc. Are there any "aha" moments? Can you recognize any self-sabotage patterns arising that you may have previously attributed to outside causes?

4) Are you ready to withdraw your projections of attack onto others, yourself, the body, the world and God? This is precisely what forgiveness is for…to forgive yourself for having been mistaken. Now you may see the precious value in forgiving what never really happened. Ideally, this exercise will completely reinterpret how we see the past. Instead of believing we were indeed victimized, we might begin to have gratitude for everyone who has offered such great forgiveness opportunities. For without them we could never undo our own cycle of unconscious self-attack.

17. DECISION MAKING - YOU CANNOT MAKE DECISIONS ALONE

1. We are constantly making decisions. But the real question is just *who* are we making them with? Did you know that we cannot make any decisions *alone?* Every decision is always attended by a companion. It takes *two* to make a decision. Nothing can be caused without some form of union. The outcome of each decision depends exclusively on which "advisor" we choose to collaborate with, the ego or the Holy Spirit.

a. *"For you and your adviser must agree on what you want before it can occur. It is but this agreement that permits all things to happen. Nothing can be caused without some form of union, be it with a dream of judgment or the Voice for God."* T-30.I.16:2-4

2. It is easy to recognize which adviser we have chosen by observing how we feel. Guilt, fear, frustration, disappointment, anger, confusion, anxiety, sadness, shame, loss, pain, sickness, etc., are immediate signs that we have chosen the ego as advisor and not Spirit.

3. Negative emotions are the effect or outcome derived from a delusional belief that there is something wrong, a real problem to be solved. The belief that there is a problem is the belief in the absence of God (Love as our Holy Self). There are no problems in God because God has no opposite. Therefore, which part of us appears to be threatened or hurt?

4. This point is apt to be overlooked far too quickly, so I will say it again. In any given moment I will either believe there is a problem, *or* I decide with Spirit to heal my delusional *perception* of a problem. The presence of my belief in a problem excludes God from my awareness. These two beliefs, of both a problem *and* God, are irreconcilable and cannot coexist.

5. Regardless of the perceived form or severity of the problem it is always our *perception* of the problem which needs correction. If God's Love is all there is, and I am triggered by something in this moment that is not God, then I must be seeing illusion! This must be an illusion that does not exist.

6. The instant I perceive a problem and believe it to be true, I (ego) will attempt to find a solution to it. And the instant I search for a solution via the ego I will unknowingly collude with the imaginary problem. I will defend myself from it without realizing that defense is always attack. By defending, I attack myself and I demonstrate

to myself and others that this problem is more real than God. Furthermore, this problem *replaces* God in my awareness. This is the goal of the ego's obsession with problems.

7. Remember we attract what we value. The ego values suffering and problems. It wants us to value problems by according them reality. To the degree we persist in believing that suffering and problems are true is the degree we will unknowingly value them and therefore, attract exactly what we unconsciously value.

8. The ego uses the body's five senses to increase the sense of separation. We must learn to consistently question what the body's senses report to us, as a prerequisite to the divine repurposing of the body (more info on this in the book, *The End of Death Volume I*).

9. We have an addiction to valuing problems. If we continue to defend our self from problems, we are demonstrating that we still believe they are true and God is absent. We actually want and value problems or we would not believe them, and Holy Spirit cannot save us from what we want or value. If we truly desire to be free from pain, conflict and suffering we must join with Holy Spirit to heal the *one* problem, our destructive perception that there is a reality other than God.

10. Perhaps you can see now that our desire for the perception of suffering is in fact, representative of our "fear of God." Our unconscious fear of Love (our Holy Self) is so great that we prefer to experience suffering and death as substitutes for Love and union without opposite.

11. This may now put a different spin on the importance of being mindfully present to our decision-making process. Just who do we invite to be our decision-making adviser? Is it fear via judgment and doubt? Or is it Love via forgiveness and trust? We will know which adviser we have chosen by the feelings and experiences we manifest. Luckily, in any moment we acknowledge that we don't like the outcome of our decision-making, we can always choose again, only this time with Holy Spirit.

18. DEFEATING GUILT AND UNWORTHINESS ONCE AND FOR ALL

1. How do we accept our incorruptible innocence, and our divine invulnerability, when we are constantly bombarded by fear, guilt or feelings of unworthiness?

2. Like most people who have not yet awakened to their Holy Self, I endured a long and torturous time where I just could not shake off what seemed like an immovable foundation of unworthiness and guilt. The results of my old belief in this agonizing unworthiness tainted just about every relationship I had and almost everything I did. I could rarely access the peace required to really let go of my concerns and accept the Atonement fully. Relief was spasmodic; it just did not last. I was beginning to think that I would never be able to relinquish this endless feeling of worthlessness.

3. More than anything I wanted to release it. Or more honestly, I wanted *it* to release me, since I felt that I was a victim of it. But did I *really* desire to be done with this sense of unworthiness? Did I really long to see myself and others as sinless, as guiltless, as worthy, as innocent? The conflict I felt was proof that I must not have desired *only* this. Obviously, I unconsciously still found *value* in the sense of guilt and unworthiness I felt, because I still experienced it.

4. Many times I had reached a place in my process where I uncovered my guilt, and yet I did not truly relinquish it in totality. There was massive resistance to enter peace and stay there, resting deeply in my own majestic innocence. This *is* the peace of God. Why couldn't I accept it, receive it and simply remain there? Why the need to keep myself distracted from this divine function...the only one which would completely liberate me from my own complaints of being "not enough?"

5. Finally, the answer revealed itself in my awareness. We are not both the false self's body identity (human) *and* the Holy Self. They are mutually exclusive. We can only be one of them, not both. And then I had a blinding epiphany. The one who suffered from guilt, fear and unworthiness was the same one trying to undo it!

6. Enter the spiritual ego. All the while believing that we *can* indeed suffer, the spiritual ego attempts to convince us that it has our best interests at heart because look: *See how earnestly it tries to undo our suffering?*

7. The very first sign that this is the spiritual ego and not the Holy Spirit is that it believes the impossible – that guilt, fear, unworthiness and suffering are real. Then it proceeds to "help" to heal these seemingly real issues. And it will be wrong.

8. The Holy Spirit looks with us and declares immediately that none of it exists in reality. He makes it clear in our mind *and heart* that there is just one problem. We forgot our incorruptible innocence! We forgot to say "no" to fear. We forgot to accept our divine immunity to every illusion of the ego. We forgot to turn away from the temptation of chaos - and instead, rest deeply in the changeless safety, peace and Love that ensures our uninterrupted union and healing in God's eternal Love for us. *This* is accepting the Atonement. *This* is true forgiveness.

9. The one who is *unwilling* to receive Love's divine correction unequivocally and rest in boundless innocence and peace, the one who *delays* it, and the one who tries to solve a problem it believes is *real*, is always the *false self.* But thankfully, that is not you.

10. The resistance to accept and trust this divine correction – innocence and peace – is the false self's denial of our *Holy Self.* It is fear of *being* the glorious Child of God. This is the fierce fear of God as Love.

11. Many years ago, I was convinced that "I" would eventually be rid of my unworthiness, guilt and suffering, if "I" tried hard enough to earn God's Love, along with pleasing everyone. Little did I know that this "self" that was such an unrelenting task master, a shameless bully and a vicious judge, was of my very own making. I valued this self. Its pseudo mission was to attack me mercilessly to keep me in line so I would never risk discovering God's unwavering Love and acceptance of me.

12. Now, I know that this false self was made in opposition to our changeless, incorruptible and innocent Holy Self. The false self cannot ever evolve to become Holy. It must remain embedded in the guilt that gave rise to it, no matter how hard we try to improve it. Its whole reason for being, is driven by guilt. It was made along

with the body, to be an overwhelmingly convincing opponent to Love. Therefore, it is fear incarnate and cannot ever transform *itself* from fear to Love. There is quite literally nothing other than God's Love. This false self, as an idea set apart from God, is complete illusion; an hallucination of epic proportions. Nothing unreal exists.

13. The "I" that believes it is unworthy, that requires improving or self-esteem, that feels deprived, guilty or fearful, *does not exist*. Love's pure and innocent presence is certain annihilation to this false self concept. And that is why it is terrified of Love.

14. Each lifetime, its ultimate purpose is to kill the body *before* we make the divine switch to the Holy Self. That way it perpetuates itself in time and space via reincarnation. We're not to demonize this self, but to simply disregard it through our consistent desire to look beyond it to the Love and joy that it attempts to block from our awareness.

  a. *"The death penalty is the ego's ultimate goal, for it fully believes that you are a criminal, as deserving of death as God knows you are deserving of life. The death penalty never leaves the ego's mind, for that is what it always reserves for you in the end. Wanting to kill you as the final expression of its feeling for you, it lets you live but to await death. It will torment you while you live, but its hatred is not satisfied until you die. For your destruction is the one end toward which it works, and the only end with which it will be satisfied."* T-12.VII.13:2-6

15. I am either the Holy Self – *or* –I believe I am the body-self as unworthy, guilty, not enough, deprived, unfairly treated, in pain, sick, etc. We can recognize exactly which "self" we identify as by observing what we value (believe) in any one moment, either Love or fear. Further, these two "selves" do not know each other and cannot communicate with each other. The presence of one in our awareness completely obscures the other. They cannot coexist together. This is why in any one moment we are either in fear or we are in the presence of Love. There is no gray area.

16. The Atonement and the Holy Relationship are the most powerful gifts given us to make the epic leap in our awareness from the false, body identity to the Holy Self. Symbolically speaking, there is a

bridge we must cross. We begin on one side of the bridge as the false self. Then as our trust is transferred from fear to Love we make the transition to find, to remember and finally, to know our beloved Holy Self on the other side of the bridge.

17. When you choose to believe in fear, guilt and unworthiness then you must value them and you will try to defend them. They serve the ruthless false self's agenda which is to keep your awareness from ever remembering the breathtaking innocence of your one, changeless, shared and Holy Self.

18. While you still desire to believe that you can be unfairly treated by others, the body or the world, then it will appear to be difficult to let go of your unworthiness or guilt because you still value and want them as protection from Love; from your Self as God created you. Perhaps now you can recognize that the belief in unworthiness or guilt is *self*-chosen, a self-imposed defense to losing your sense of being a private mind with a separate body.

19. The good news is that once we actually recognize this we can then genuinely join with Holy Spirit to give this self-sabotage over to Him to heal. He cannot heal it until we give Him permission to take away our old defenses to indescribable Love, effervescent joy and wondrous union.

A. Which Self Am I?

1. I'm going to share my own process when there is temptation to perceive fear in any form.

2. I made a firm commitment to consistently rest as the quiet observer of all that seems to go on in the body, with others and in the world. This way I can be the calm center of the storm rather than to misidentify as the storm itself. I am the changeless one observing the wild vacillations of the confused body-self. For that reason I have only compassion for this small self. It is futile to judge or condemn an illusory self that is born from and sustained by a fundamental investment in sin, guilt and fear.

3. I see the incessant baiting. I see the endless temptations for the body-self to succumb to the crushing voice of guilt, fear and unworthiness. I see the almost automatic seduction of the need to

control, to fix, to solve, to get, to protect, to heal and to distract. I see this self's addiction to false humility and false responsibility. It has an enormous "need to be needed" as a means to uphold its pseudo value.

4. It sees and *believes* in the woes of the world while tricking itself into thinking that "it," alone and apart from God, can solve these myriad problems. Little does it recognize that both the trials and tribulations it witnesses are not real, but only seemingly there to give its own separate self a fleeting but mistaken role to fulfill.

5. For me, I ask "*Who is the one feeling* fear, feeling confused, feeling guilty, feeling victimized, feeling unworthy, feeling sick, feeling angry, feeling depressed or feeling deprived? And who is the one feeling separate from God as Love?

    1)   It could only be the illusory, body-identified self.

    2)   And "that" one is not me.

    a. "*Whatever suffers is not part of me. What grieves is not myself. What is in pain is but illusion in my mind. What dies was never living in reality, and did but mock the truth about myself. Now I disown self-concepts and deceits and lies about the holy Son of God. Now am I ready to accept him back as God created him, and as he is.*" W-248.1:3-8

6. In the moment that I make a wholehearted choice to accept and declare that this "self," together with its body, is *not* me, then something quite miraculous occurs. A mighty leap takes place in my mind. And I'm not alone in that quantum leap. The very *moment* I choose to dis-identify as the suffering self is the *Holy Instant* where I am being carried across an inner bridge by Holy Spirit; carried from the illusion of fear and a suffering self, to the resounding peace, safety and innocence of the over-arching Holy Self.

7. Suddenly there is a moment of fearlessness! And simultaneously, from this resounding peace and safety within, I trust that all seeming problems are healed. They are always healed in this peace which is the Love of God and the Will of God. There is no problem in the world which can be solved in fear… for fear is the very birthplace

of all problems. This is my recent practice of accepting the Atonement.

8. The false self cannot *accept* the Atonement, the undoing of its self. But – the Atonement's acceptance – as the miracle – occurs in the instant we willingly dis-identify *as* the false, body identity. It only takes an instant, just one breath. This is a cherished *now moment* where we join Holy Spirit and say "no" to fear, regardless of its form, and thus we make way for Love, for miracles.

a. *"God's answer is some form of peace. All pain is healed; all misery replaced with joy. All prison doors are opened. And all sin is understood as merely a mistake."* W-359... *"Let me not forget myself is nothing, but my Self is all."* W-358.

19. FEELING UNWORTHY TO RECEIVE

1. One of the most unrecognized and fiercely defended blocks made to obscure our recognition that there is only one problem and one solution, is the ego's false humility. This is the belief that we are unworthy to receive the Love we are. Only the ego, as a false self apart from Love can feel unworthy.

2. No matter which form the problem appears to take, the single remedy is always Love as forgiveness. Every problem can be solved in any heartfelt instant we choose to close the imagined gap between our self and God (Love).

3. When we're willing to deep dive into the very cause that lies beneath the smokescreen of fear, we will locate the darkest and most primordial gap that spawns *all* our fears. It goes hand in hand with our unrecognized guilt and fear. This is the *fear of God* as Love, disguised as unworthiness.

4. Here is yet another ego mask appearing as the often unconscious, yet highly valued belief that we are *unworthy* of closing the gap with God – with Love itself. Our fears and the problems they

engender play the role of heavily obscuring this underlying choice to value unworthiness (guilt). This epidemic is the disguised unwillingness to *receive* Love.

5. The belief in unworthiness is really *arrogance* in disguise, because in valuing unworthiness, we deny God's Knowledge of our *true Identity* as unopposed Love and innocence. In doing so we actively choose to deny God's Will, because in truth this is "What" we are, and we are nothing other than this. Unworthiness is really denying the fact that God's Will and our will are one and the same. Unworthiness is the illusory belief that we have a separate will from God, which is impossible – and that is why it's an illusion.

    a. *To think that God made chaos, contradicts His Will, invented opposites to truth, and suffers death to triumph over life; all this is arrogance. Humility would see at once these things are not of Him. And can you see what God created not? To think you can is merely to believe you can perceive what God willed not to be. And what could be more arrogant than this? W-152.7*

    b. *Let us today be truly humble, and accept what we have made as what it is. The power of decision is our own. Decide but to accept your rightful place as co-creator of the universe, and all you think you made will disappear. What rises to awareness then will be all that there ever was, eternally as it is now. And it will take the place of self-deceptions made but to usurp the altar to the Father and the Son. W-152.8*

6. We either choose to be unworthy and therefore willingly reject our only true Identity as the Holy Child of God (Love) – or – we choose to treasure our Identity as Love and would join with it in everyone we encounter. We choose to be unworthy and willingly project that unworthiness as disease, relationship conflict, financial hardship, etc., - or – we choose to join with God as His Will and be impervious to attack.

7. Unworthiness is simply another form of self-attack. Yet this is just a different expression of guilt. The false self thrives on it. And as Jesus says, when we attack our self, it will always *increase* our guilt which reinforces the cycle of self-attack. If we truly desire to

be free of debilitating unworthiness, it's imperative we take our unworthiness (the desire to be separate from Love) to Holy Spirit and do the forgiveness process.

   a. *"The ego teaches you to attack yourself because you are guilty, and this must increase the guilt, for guilt is the result of attack." T-13.1.11:1*

8. The unparalleled truth here is that you *are* the light of the world. There is absolutely nothing you can do that will change this. If you don't know this deeply in every now-moment it is because you have made a choice to ignore it. But your decision not to recognize and embody your true Identity does not change the absolute fact that you *are* the light of the world.

9. Both the false self and its guilt *do not exist*. God knows you now as whole and blameless. Anything you believe you are guilty of has never appeared on God's Loving Radar. And while you feel unworthy you leave your joyous place and purpose empty. Your function is to be the light of the world.

   a. *"...your function here is to be the light of the world, a function given you by God. It is only the arrogance of the ego that leads you to question this, and only the fear of the ego that induces you to regard yourself as unworthy of the task assigned to you by God Himself. The world's salvation awaits your forgiveness, because through it does the Son of God escape from all illusions, and thus from all temptation. The Son of God is you." W-64.3.*

   b. *"You are altogether irreplaceable in the Mind of God. No one else can fill your part in it..." ... "To accept your littleness [is] arrogant, because it means that you believe your evaluation of yourself is truer than God's." T-9.VIII.10:1-2,9*

10. Valuing unworthiness or fear is the false self's armor-plated defense against returning our awareness to the changeless Love and innocence of our being, as the incorruptible "I AM."

11. Remember this – we cannot close this gap (appearing as unworthiness) while we still cherish unforgiven grievances with our

brothers. We will not be willing to drop our defense of unworthiness while we still hold a brother captive to sin. While we judge another as unworthy of total forgiveness (unconditional Love) then we will reject it for our self. We will be fearful to accept complete healing for our self. In truth we cannot accept complete forgiveness unless we are willing to include everyone, even those whom we resent.

12. Withholding forgiveness from another is really the most painful act of *self*-rejection. It is the refusal to *receive* the Love that we are.

13. We cling to unworthiness as protection from Love. Most of this remains unconscious until we're willing to deep dive into some comprehensive forgiveness of those present or past whom we have not genuinely released through forgiveness. We will usually find that these grievances came from *special* relationships where it seemed that the cost of love was pain and loss.

14. How on earth can we possibly relinquish our own unworthiness while we still cherish intensely defended grievances? We just will not open to *receive* the Love we so deeply long for while we dwell in a state of contraction and defense.

15. If we hold just *one person* captive to blame then we agree to punish our self. Love and guilt cannot coexist! Love and blame cannot coexist. Love and pain cannot coexist. Accept one and we deny the other. Everyone *including our self* is always entirely *blameless*.

A. Laying Down Our Defenses

1. There is always just one gap to close in any moment. Regardless of the particular problem, are we willing to close the gap with our most cherished and Holy Self? This Self is shared with every Child of God.

2. Are we willing to suspend judgment or doubt and open our heart to breathe in God's Love and innocence? It only takes one Holy Instant for our awareness to be returned to Love as the infinite safety of our incorruptible innocence. And in this, the holiest of all instants, when we show up for our Self, the Atonement is received as the sacred undoing of what never was.

3. Are we willing to lay down our defenses to Love and healing - as fear, guilt, unworthiness, judgment, pain, disease, conflict, etc.? Are we willing to let go of our belief that there is a gap between us

and others, our Holy Self, and God? This seeming gap is the root of every conceivable problem in the body and the world. Are we willing then to forgive *our self* for having believed there was a gap, and unknowingly used a person or problem to attack our self?

4. Jesus tells us that the very first obstacle to peace (Love) that we willingly use as a defense, is the desire to *get rid* of peace. Doesn't that sound completely crazy? Nevertheless, that's exactly what the false self does. And the most common block we face is our own fierce resistance to, or even rejection of "closing the gap." For the ego it's much more enticing to keep the guilt by projecting it onto others as relationship conflict, onto the body as pain, sickness or weight issues, or onto our finances as scarcity.

5. While we continue to project this unrelinquished guilt (unforgiveness) we end up *keeping* the guilt, and the cycle simply persists until the ego attains its final goal for us, as physical death. Its insane continuation is fueled by our stubborn refusal to "close the gap" within, via the Atonement.

6. Fear is not involuntary, and neither is unworthiness. They are both choices we make. They could not possibly occur unless we valued them. Holy Spirit cannot heal the cause and symptoms of fear and unworthiness until we are honestly willing to give them up. It requires vigilance to choose again each time we're tempted to fall for their hypnotic spell.

   1) **Remember this:** God has never changed His Mind about you regardless of the self-judgments you perceive.

   a. "God does not change His Mind about you, for He is not uncertain of Himself." ... "When anything threatens your peace of mind, ask yourself, "Has God changed His Mind about me?" T-10.in.3:1,9

7. The instant we truly desire the awareness of our undivided and incorruptible innocence, is the Holy Instant in which it is returned to our awareness as the miracle. The moment peace is felt is the instant in which fear (and its imaginary effects) is replaced by Love. We either want fear or we are eager for Love to return to our

awareness. Every single moment we experience is imbued by our choice, either to Love or to fear.

20. SEARCHING THE WORLD FOR OUR IDENTITY

1.   When we undo and forgive what the false self *wants* to see in others, the body and the world, what we then see – will be healed *because* it will be Christ Vision that looks clear through the ego's projections of darkness seeing only what is real behind all appearances, thus calling them into awareness.

2.   If we see evidence of sin (guilt) in others, the body or the world then it's because we *want* to see it there. This is perception's basic law. Everything we see and feel is there because *we* put it there by our unconscious desire for it in the first place. Desire for it must precede its seeming appearance.

   1)   There are no sinful people. There is however, an unhealed desire to *see* sinful people.

3.   To the degree I am triggered by conflict and injustice is the degree that I actually put it there. The ego filter *wants* to see sin in others and the world. Its identity depends on it. It hunts for it all the time. This is the ego's lifeblood, its secret desire to be unfairly treated so it can continue to project separation. And because our distorted will (ego) is so powerful, we manifest exactly what we want to see – because we put it there in order to *see* it!

   a.   *"To the extent to which you value guilt, to that extent will you perceive a world in which attack is justified. To the extent to which you recognize that guilt is meaningless, to that extent you will perceive attack cannot [be] justified. This is in accord with perception's fundamental law: You see what you believe is there, and you believe it there because you want it there. Perception has no other law than this."* T-25.III.1:1-4

4. All the drama, the conflict, the injustice, the pain, disease and death are there for just one reason – the false self wants it all and so it materializes its unhealed desire. These are the fragile relationships of the world where love can just as easily turn to hate. This is the world we seem to see. This is not an independent world which we are powerless to change. In contrast, every Holy Instant affords us the grace to glimpse a World that lives shining in radiant innocence if we so choose.

5. Thank God there is another world beyond the one we see, and this one is called into our experience as we learn to withdraw our own projections of attack. The Real World is here now. But we cannot see it because we *want* to see a world of separation instead.

6. That way we will never go within to forgive our self for having projected it in the first place. And by projecting it we end up amassing this unconscious self-attack. And this is precisely *why* the body ages, gets sick and dies. It lives out our denied guilt and it's this that kills it. Otherwise, the body would be known as a completely neutral tool through which we extend only the truth within, and that is Love.

7. The seeming laws of this world are of our own making through our distorted desire for them. They are *not* God's Laws and therefore, have absolutely no authority over us. In fact *we* have dominion over all the seeming threats that we made, once we forgive our self for having unknowingly desired them.

8. Everything we perceive comes exclusively from just "who" we have chosen to look externally with. Is it with the ego or with Holy Spirit? We always look inward first and then we decide exactly what we *want* to see in others, the body and the world. We choose these as specific witnesses to prove to our self what we value, either separation or union. This is literal! We always behold that which we seek.

   a. *"I said before that what you project or extend is up to you, but you must do one or the other, for that is a law of mind, and you must look in before you look out. As you look in, you choose the guide for seeing. And then you look out and behold his witnesses. This is why you find what you seek. What you want in yourself you will make manifest, and you will accept it from the world because you put it there by wanting it. When you think you are projecting what you do not want, it is still because you [do] want it." T-12.VII.7:1-6*

A. Where Will We Find Our True Identity?

1. Now here is a dilemma. We have trained our self to look for our identity and worth in a *self-made* fantasy world of guilt, blame and pain. As children we begin to search outside our self for evidence of our nature and worth. Are we good or sinful? Are we worthy or unworthy? Are we Loved or unlovable? Are we simply never good enough? And the list goes on. We can all apply our own individual flavor to this list.

2. Yet what we rarely realize is this. Even before we came into this lifetime we had a secret agenda to 1) perceive the world through a delusional (ego) filter, and 2) appoint certain individuals to abide by our secret wish to be unfairly treated, so that we could blame others and perpetuate our guilt.

3. Those of us like me, who grew up with a low sense of self-worth, will usually unwittingly project that self-loathing onto others, and hence attract exactly the same mirroring from their relationships and the world. This all comes from our initial and uncorrected desire to see in the world that which *we* put there – our unconscious wish to be attacked so we could blame others, the past, the body or the world for our misfortune.

4. Remember that whatever we give (project) we end up keeping and accumulating for our self. Unfortunately, we chose to see blame in others so we would divert guilt to another, but what really happens is we *keep* that guilt for our self. And while we choose to see another as guilty then our relationship with them is not real.

5. The special relationship is a classic example of this dynamic where we say we "love" someone but we still hold grievances against them. Yet are we willing to realize that the only way we could possibly lay blame on them … is because we our self, first placed the desire there to *be* attacked? And not the other way around.

a. *"In any union with a brother in which you seek to lay your guilt upon him, or share it with him or perceive his own, [you] will feel guilty. Nor will you find satisfaction and peace with him, because your union with him is not real. You will see guilt in that relationship because you put it there." T-13.X.3:1-3*

6. Let's not look to the ego world, which we projected, to try to find our Self. Let's not look into the darkness that we projected to find the light we are. The world we seem to see was projected by fear and is a mirror of our insane belief in the godless concept of punishment and reward. We cannot possibly find our Holy Self within that fantasy of pain.

7. Instead, we need to desire to see past this fantasy and look upon the truth which we previously turned away from. We will always see and feel that which we want, what we value. But first - we must put it there through our *desire for* it.

8. Then it can reflect the truth and light of "What" we are. It will mirror the incorruptible innocence, Love and joy that we are. To know and experience this we must first be willing to see *everyone's* innocence. This is how we finally recognize our *own* true worth and changeless Identity as Love itself. We must *give* it in order to realize that we *have* it. And that we must have *had* it all along if we can indeed give it.

9. So now we refuse any longer to look toward the ego's world of blindness to ask, "What am I?" because "it" does not recognize or value the truth of our Identity in God. This ego world is a transient stranger:

a. *"Ask not this transient stranger, "What am I?" He is the only thing in all the universe that does not know. Yet it is he you ask, and it is to his answer that you would adjust. This one wild thought, fierce in its arrogance, and yet so tiny and so meaningless it slips unnoticed through the universe of truth, becomes your guide. To it you turn to ask the meaning of the universe. And of the one blind thing in all the seeing universe of truth you ask, "How shall I look upon the Son of God?" T-20.III.7:5-10*

10. We will find our true Identity to the degree we extend it to others in our relationships. This is the *only* way we could possibly retrieve it – by giving it away. And this is also how we lost awareness of our Identity in the first place, by giving away its opposite as guilt, as judgment and as blame. We have unwittingly projected a world of suffering and asked it to mirror to us our imagined worthlessness.

11. We have used this insane world and our special relationships as "references" in which we seek to find our Self. In our hurtful relationships we have asked for meaning in darkness. We have looked for meaning in madness where there *is* no meaning. In truth, this is because we were too afraid to find our true Identity as the Love we are, so we blindly asked for pain instead.

12. Now we can make a miraculous "about face" and decide to look at the Real World in whose glorious reflection we find our true Self. We do this by recognizing with joy what is *really* there in others; that which we could not see before because we had overlaid our own guilt upon them. We won't experience the Love we so deeply yearn for until we are willing to extend this blamelessness to others via the *means* which is forgiveness.

13. We cannot look to the ego's version of relationships or the world to find our most beloved and Holy Self. We will find it only in those who have come to us in benediction, offering us the forgotten grace of forgiveness by which we joyfully discover our changeless Identity in union with our beloved brothers and sisters, with God.

   a. *"The world you look on is the answer that it gave you, and you have given it power to adjust the world to make its answer true. You asked this puff of madness for the meaning of your unholy relationship, and adjusted it according to its insane answer. How happy did it make you? Did you meet your brother with joy to bless the Son of God, and give him thanks for all the happiness that he held out to you? Did you recognize your brother as the eternal gift of God to you? Did you see the holiness that shone in both you and your brother, to bless the other? That is the purpose of your holy relationship. Ask not the means of its attainment of the one thing that still would have it be unholy. Give it no power to adjust the means and end." T-20.III.8:3-11*

14. When we want only Love we will see nothing else. But we must first *want* it. Above all else. This cannot happen while we still desire to see what is not there - such as judgment, blame, guilt, betrayal, abandonment, conflict, disease, loss and death. We will recognize our desire for these illusions is still intact by the degree we are still triggered by them, and by our need to defend our self from them. This reveals just how real – how valued – they are for us. And recall that whatever we still believe is real is *valued*, and while it's still valued, it cannot *be* forgiven.

   a. *"When you want only love you will see nothing else." T-12. VII.8:1.*

15. If we genuinely want Love then we will boldly and deliberately join with Holy Spirit in our desire to see others as they really are, and not as the ego has *commissioned* them to appear. We must *want* to see others as guiltless, as blameless before they finally *witness* to our transformed desire to see them as blameless. The ego's insanity reverses this universal law by demanding that others *prove* their innocence before it is willing to acknowledge its possibility (which it never does).

   a. *"When you forgive the world your guilt, you will be free of it. Its innocence does not demand your guilt, nor does your guiltlessness rest on its sins. This is the obvious; a secret kept from no one but yourself. And it is this that has maintained you separate from the world, and kept your brother separate from you. Now need you but to learn that both of you are innocent or guilty. The one thing that is impossible is that you be unlike each other; that they both be true. This is the only secret yet to learn. And it will be no secret you are healed." T-27.VIII.13:1-9*

16. Our incorruptible innocence is *shared*. It cannot be known and thus embodied while we still condemn another. This shared innocence is the very Heart of Love. This is the supreme essence of our deeply cherished and Holy Self. Our innocence is our

true Identity. And it can only be known through our brothers and sisters. We will see in others what we believe *we* are. They are our blessed mirrors come to help us lift the heavy and cruel veil of self-condemnation.

a. *"We have already learned that this Identity is shared. The miracle becomes the means of sharing It. By supplying your Identity wherever It is not recognized, you will recognize It."* T-14.X.12:5-7

21. DISCOVERING OUR SOLE PURPOSE

1. We perceive from a split mind. One half is entirely imaginary and is the part that dissociated its memory from God as Love. Consider this - that everyone here believes they are only *half* their identity; in addition, they assume that this illusory half is their *whole* identity.

2. So when we meet with another and while we still believe them to be "in" a body then we see only the half of them that our half projects. Only our illusory half sees theirs. And this is all we respond to when we perceive anything but Love in another, in the body, the past or the world.

3. The one whole Mind which we all share with God is all-encompassing Love and joy without opposite, interruption or end. Yet the *imaginary* half of our mind perceives fear, and all it sees, thinks and feels arises from that foundational belief in an *opposite* of Love (God). Even though we dream we've introduced a contrary replacement complete with bodies and a world based on the cruel laws of fear and death, our whole Mind and Identity remain completely unaltered.

4. The fictitious half which we have mistaken as our "self" represents the split in our one shared mind. When we *believe* we see someone else, and especially when we're triggered by them, it's always the false half projecting its own denied self-rejection. This half can only witness itself in another; it sees its own imagined sins in another.

This occurs each time we are triggered, regardless of the range of upset we may feel.

5.   The fact is that any negative reaction we have to another does not come from our Holy Self, which is the totality of our one shared Mind with our brothers and God. Our shared and whole Holy Self is total, undivided and unopposed Love. It can only witness itself in others. The self that perceives threat sees myriad dangers that do not exist except as attempts to prove we are separate from each other and God. Those threats can only *seem* to endanger that which does not *exist* – the ego.

6.   While we continue to believe we are separate and that we can harm others or be harmed by others, the body and the world, we will perceive opposing goals with others. Our separate goals come from a fundamental belief that we can be hurt by others and that we need to keep a gap between us.

7.   Ego believes that our identity and purpose are divided, thus it mistakenly sees everyone else as having a different identity and function. It does not understand that judgment and correction are divisive and further separate us. It fails to accept that if we consistently applied the single, shared function – of forgiveness – it would reveal just one unified Identity and end all conflict and suffering *now*.

8.   When we prefer to judge or hold grievances against another, rather than to forgive, we fragment the only purpose in the world which would end fear, conflict, suffering and death. When we commit to aligning with this most sacred of all functions, *forgiveness*, it must reveal a single Identity – one which is shared as Love itself. Forgiveness is the vehicle or means by which we come to know our most Holy and guiltless Self. Jesus says that both our Identity and function are the same and by applying our consistent function of forgiveness we will dissolve the fearful half of our mind, revealing our whole and healed one Identity as Love itself.

a.   *"Identity and function are the same, and by your function do you know yourself." T-27.II.10:6*

9.   Any attempts we undertake to judge or correct another must separate us from each other and our Holy Self. Forgiveness is the

one purpose on earth that leads directly to experiencing our oneness. This is our glorious shared Identity with its never-ending abundance of joyous miracles. Eventually, we will recognize and value the extraordinary healing that forgiveness delivers and we will make it our single priority above all else.

a. *"Salvation (as forgiveness) cannot be the only purpose you hold while you still cherish others. The full acceptance of salvation as your only function necessarily entails two phases; the recognition of salvation as your function, and the relinquishment of all the other goals you have invented for yourself."* W-65.1:4-5

10. The illusory half of the mind that feels triggered by another *always* sees its own denied sins in someone else. While in truth there is no sin, the ego's existence depends on it to perpetuate its cycle of suffering, separation and death.

11. Only a denied and therefore projected "sin" could possibly trigger us. It would be impossible to see sin in anyone once we knew with total conviction that *we* are wholly innocent, wholly guiltless. Only the illusory half of our mind believes unconsciously that *it* is guilty and deserving of conflict, disease, aging, lack, pain and death.

12. This half is obsessed with the body as itself. It either worships the body or it despises it. Either way it idolizes it as its "identity" and projects this confusion onto others. Thus, it completely denies the Spirit, our one shared true Identity.

13. Furthermore, this delusive half must continue to witness *in others* what it has denied in itself. It condemns its own delusion in others by judging, defending or attacking. All the while, the universal principle ensues, that anything we give (project) we always give to our self. Therefore, as we project judgment we end up amassing it for our self. This is how we unintentionally manifest all our seeming problems in our relationships, health, finances and the world.

14. The world we see is one of conflict. The people we think we see, including those who seemed to victimize us in the past, are merely mirrored projections coming exclusively from the half of our mind that does not exist. Thus we never see another as they really are, but see only what the imaginary half of our mind *wants* to see. Do we

want to see proof of suffering of separation? Or do we desire to see proof of our unified Identity. It is certain that if we perceive attack anywhere, it must come from the delusional half of our mind.

15. If we genuinely desire to heal, then our singular purpose must be to forgive everything we seem to see in others. In doing so, we are literally healing our insane belief that we, *our self*, are guilty and consequently deserving of punishment and death.

16. The half of the mind that sees sin or suffering at all – *does not exist*. Furthermore, the sins it sees in others or self *equally do not exist!* Think of the countless problems we attempt to solve in the body, our relationships and the world. Has it ever occurred to you that the one attempting to solve these issues … is the same one that *caused* them?

17. This explains why when we commit to forgiveness as our only function, the projected half of our mind that we're triggered by, *must disappear!* This is how the split mind heals completely. As it forgives its own imagined and projected sins in others, the body, the past and the world, that dark veil of exclusion is lifted to reveal the one light, the one Mind we share – our singular Identity as Love and joy.

18. Our whole Identity is revealed as we "close the gap" with others. Our whole Identity is revealed to the degree the delusional half of our mind is cleaned and cleared by forgiveness. This is our highest most revered function since the beginning of time. Actually, this is our *only* purpose. When this becomes our singular priority, the veil of terror is lifted and the body itself is also freed from our destructive projections. Now the body is sanctified and healed because its singular purpose is restored, which is to serve the healed Mind.

   1) Only in someone else can you be healed because only in someone else can you forgive yourself…

   a. *"It is impossible to forgive another, for it is only your sins you see in him. You want to see them there, and not in you. That is why forgiveness of another is an illusion. Yet it is the only happy dream in all the world; the only one that does not lead to death. Only in someone else can you forgive yourself, for you have called him guilty of your sins, and in him must your innocence now be found." S-2.I.4:1-6*

A. When We are Triggered and Tempted to Judge

a. *"When you react at all to errors, you are not listening to the Holy Spirit."... "When a brother behaves insanely, you can heal him only by perceiving the sanity in him (the Son of God). If you perceive his errors and accept them, you are accepting yours. If you want to give yours over to the Holy Spirit, you must do this with his (errors). Unless this becomes the one way in which you handle all errors, you cannot understand how all errors are undone."*

"To perceive errors in anyone, and to react to them as if they were real, is to make them real to you. You will not escape paying the price for this, not because you are being punished for it, but because you are following the wrong guide and will therefore lose your way."

"Your brother's errors are not of him, any more than yours are of you. Accept his errors as real, and you have attacked yourself. If you would find your way and keep it, see only truth (of your brother) beside you for you walk together." T-9. III.4:1,4,6:7,7:3

1. We will eventually open our heart to accept unequivocally that forgiveness is the only form of correction we want, especially when we're tempted to correct (judge) a brother. It is our sole purpose. Everything is healed and joyous once we accept this with relief. And this is when we will come to recognize with great gratitude that forgiveness *and* correction are the same. Forgiveness is the only form of correction that leads to unified perception and our welcomed experience of incorruptible innocence, joy and uninterrupted Love. The forgiveness process can be found in *The Seven Essential Principles of Quantum Forgiveness (Atonement)* on page 591.

22. THE INVINCIBILITY PRINCIPLE

1. At the time of writing this, shortly after I had once again renewed my vow with Jesus to take this teaching to its next phase in my own experience, I heard His Voice communicate with pristine clarity just one clear and far-reaching term - *"The Invincibility Principle."* I had never heard or seen it before. I didn't know what it meant or how or even *if* it would be made manifest. So I asked…

2. Here in this dream of duality we project a multitude of ego characteristics onto God and as a result onto our Holy Self. How on earth can we possibly choose for God/Love, if we have unintentionally confused Him with sacrifice, loss, pain and death?

3. Before we can wholeheartedly heal, before we can deeply know our one most Holy Self, we must first learn to recognize and cherish the undivided nature and Will of God. This and only this is our own true nature and Will with God.

4. And as we come to trust this we will also recognize and answer clearly all calls for Love, such as disease, pain, conflict, lack, loss, separation and death – with healing. These represent travesties of Love and are therefore entirely *unnatural.* They might appear to be natural to the ego because they consist exclusively of the laws of the ego and not the Laws of God.

5. How can we hope to confidently declare and demonstrate that we are indeed under no laws but God's if we can't differentiate between the laws of ego and the Laws of God?

6. God as Love is a totality which cannot be divided nor threatened. God is Love without opposite. This is Love without fear, without attack. And all forms of loss, sickness, pain, sacrifice, struggle, lack and conflict represent attack; therefore, they are not of Love (God). They represent the laws of ego. If we experience them we experience an illusion that is not part of God, nor part of our most Holy Self.

7. The Love of God cannot be learned or explained, but only known. But thankfully, here in this dream of duality we can experience a reflection of the infinite magnitude of this Love, as we release (forgive) everything that has obscured it in our awareness. However, we won't be willing to release the blocks to Love until we at least have begun to sort out what is of God and what is not.

8. There is a need to discern the fundamental difference between illusion and truth. We must be willing to make a definite distinction between Love and fear, otherwise we will continue to confuse the two. All our suffering comes from confusing illusion with truth. If we would only learn the difference between them we would no longer unknowingly resist instantaneous healing.

9. There are not two worlds to choose between; only one is real. Only God (Love) exists. This means there is only You as the Son of God (along with everyone). The false self that seems to suffer does not exist.

    a. *"Fear has made everything you think you see. All separation, all distinctions, and the multitude of differences you believe make up the world. They are not there. Love's enemy has made them up. Yet love can have no enemy, and so they have no cause, no being and no consequence. They can be valued, but remain unreal."*

    "It is impossible to see two worlds which have no overlap of any kind. Seek for the one; the other disappears. But one remains. They are the range of choice beyond which your decision cannot go. The real and the unreal are all there are to choose between, and nothing more than these." W-130.4:1-6, 5.

10. Further, the *decisions* the false self makes do not exist. And the reason for this is that all decisions made by a *self* that does not exist – *are nonexistent.* They cannot and do not show up on God's Radar. This includes every illusory problem, disease, guilty thought or action, and all forms of lack or suffering including physical death. God did not author death and we will not find God in death, but only in Life. God is not the author of opposites such as the preposterous suggestion that Life ends in death.

A. God is One. And We Are That One *with* God.

1. At the core of your Being you are God's most Holy Child. Holiness is changeless innocence. This equates to you being as none other than eternal, changeless, uninterrupted, unopposed and incorruptible innocence. This innocence is wholly undivided and

therefore, *invincible*. It is the radiant Son-Beam upon which you make your joyful return to Love without opposite. And you recall and embody your innocence each time you choose to forgive instead of to judge, defend or attack.

2. God is One Power. There is literally nothing other than this One Power. And we are here in this dream to reclaim awareness of our divine inheritance, this One Power, through forgiveness. The sinless state is entirely guiltless. This is the wholly forgiven state in which we dwell, but do not yet remember. All fear emerges from guilt, as the secret expectation of punishment. In God, in the Allness of our Holy Self, the illusions of guilt and fear, along with their effects, do not exist.

3. Incorruptible innocence is *all inclusive* and this is why it has no opposite. It must be shared with everyone across the board as guiltlessness for it to be completely invulnerable. Because this innocence is undivided, this is its strength. Innocence is impervious to threat because it knows no opposite and therefore, no threat. This is why innocence makes us invulnerable. The mind that is completely innocent can take no recognition of any appearance of threat or imperfection, because there is no guilt in that mind. An innocent mind cannot "project" images of fear. This is the *Invincibility Principle*.

4. There is no will but God's. God's glorious will is the only Will. Hence *our will is* God's Will. They are one and the same. God's Will for us is endless joy and uninterrupted happiness. In this dream it's also reflected as perfect health. We are God's invincible Will. We are the light of the world. We are the Kingdom of Heaven itself. We are the incorruptible innocence of God. This is *not arrogance* but *true humility*.

5. Any sign of fear, guilt, judgment or suffering is *not* God's Will and is therefore, not our will. Any conflicting thoughts are totally meaningless. If we believe them we attempt to give illusions reality. We are God's invincible Will in totality which explains why we remain undivided as God's Expressions. But while we prefer to believe that both illusions *and* truth are real, we lose awareness of the *Invincibility Principle* by which we remember and claim our

supreme immunity to everything the ego made to attack us.

6. As we return our allegiance to only One Power, and not two, the body is seen as innocent of ever having betrayed us, is divinely repurposed to reflect the Laws of God, of help and perfect healing. There is no will but God's, and "I AM" that Will. I cannot be in conflict. There is no conflict in God therefore there is no conflict in me.

B. Conflict: A Belief in Two Powers

1. The Holy Self you *are* can never vacillate and never has. It remains in perfection while you *dream* an experience opposite of God. God knows nothing of illusions. Yet we have confused illusion with truth. Our Holy Self is one and whole and is entirely indivisible. We share this Self with every other person who ever lived. Each one is a fractal of our one Holy Self as the Child of God.

2. Whenever we are challenged with some form of adversity and we seek to problem-solve *apart from* Holy Spirit we inadvertently choose to perpetuate fear and guilt. All conflict, regardless of how it manifests, must be between two equally real and separate forces. It cannot exist between One Power - *and nothing.*

3. One Power is God; is us. It cannot *be* threatened. And when we judge, attack or defend we attack and defend against the Love and incorruptible innocence we are, because there is nothing we could attack that is not part of us. Thus we reject the *Invincibility Principle.*

4. Only an "illusion" would judge, fight or defend against illusions. Only an illusory self that valued a separate body and a private mind could feel a sense of threat. The truth of our being needs no defense because we are the wholly indisputable Love of God Himself. Can you see how, when we judge our self or another, when we feel fear and the need to plan and defend from illusions, that it must be an illusory self that attempts to protect itself from illusions only "it" has made? But let's go deeper. If all there is - is Love, God, and the incorruptible innocence of our Holy Self, then all fear and defense must ultimately be *against Love,* since Love is all that exists.

   a. *"Conflict must be between two forces. It cannot exist between one power and nothingness. There is nothing you could attack that is not part of you. And [by] attacking it you make two illusions of yourself, in conflict with each other. And this occurs whenever you look on anything that God created with anything but love. Conflict is fearful, for it is the birth of fear." T-23.I.8:1-6*

b. *"Truth does not fight against illusions, nor do illusions fight against the truth. Illusions battle only with themselves. Being fragmented, they fragment. But truth is indivisible, and far beyond their little reach. You will remember what you know when you have learned you cannot be in conflict. One illusion about yourself can battle with another, yet the war of two illusions is a state where nothing happens." T-23.I.7:3-8*

C. Healing or Magic? Repurposing the Illusion of Threat

1. Remember here that all seeming threats wherever we may perceive them are illusions. And illusions thrive on resistance and defense; in fact, they are sustained and increased by them. The illusion of relationship conflict is sustained and increased by our judgments and defense. The illusions of pain, illness or aging are sustained and increased by our judgment and defense against them. Every seeming threat is an illusion that is spawned and then fed by our judgment and defense.

2. All illusions of threat contribute to the ego's shield of fear as its primary defense against awakening to our one, shared Holy Self. Let's watch with joy while every seeming threat falls away as it is seen for what it really is. All forms of threat represent one content – *illusion.* There is no hierarchy of illusions and thankfully, no order of difficulty in miracles! Illusions only valuable purpose is to bring to awareness our need to join with Spirit to forgive our self for having unknowingly used them to deny the memory of our total dominion, with God, over all illusions.

3. When we're willing to recognize every seeming threat (illusion) is a gift disguised as a forgiveness opportunity then there will be no need for illusions any longer. Until, with Holy Spirit's help, we repurpose our seeming threats, we won't be able to distinguish truth from illusions. Unless we bring Holy Spirit into our decision-

making we will identify as a false self and suffer the consequences of denying our divine dominion over all illusory phenomena. And the choices we make here will merely be made *between* illusions.

4. Through the ego, the illusion of sickness is substituted for the illusion of health and vice-versa. We might choose the illusion of magic (medicine, treatment, surgery, etc.) to heal the illusion of sickness. But all of this is just shifting *between* illusions and no healing of the singular cause as unconscious self-attack is addressed or accepted.

5. The false self, as the hidden "wish to be unfairly treated," is an illusion which calls upon the illusion of sickness (or adversity) to prolong and prove its sense of separation. Yet when it's had enough it calls upon the illusion of magic to restore a temporary, but pseudo, sense of safety. All the while no real healing occurs and there is an unconscious accumulation of guilt as a result.

6. Through the ego we seem to see a whole range and hierarchy of illusions that prevent us from looking past them and onto the ever-present Love of God that transcends and heals them all. We think there are some illusions that are more real and more difficult to heal (forgive) than others. Jesus expounds in the following quotes:

   a. *"Think how this seems to interfere with the first principle of miracles. For this establishes degrees of truth among illusions, making it seem that some of them are harder to overcome than others. If it were realized that they are all the same and equally untrue, it would be easy, then, to understand that miracles apply to all of them. Errors of any kind can be corrected [because] they are untrue. When brought to truth instead of to each other, they merely disappear. No part of nothing can be more resistant to the truth than can another."* T-23.II.3.

   b. *"The body needs no healing. But the mind that thinks it is a body is sick indeed! And it is here that Christ sets forth the remedy. His purpose folds the body in His light, and fills it with the Holiness that shines from Him. And nothing that the body says or does but makes Him manifest."* T-25.in.3:1-5

D. Beware of False Responsibility

1. Judgment, guilt, fear, attack, sickness, pain, depression, lack, conflict, abandonment, betrayal, loss, loneliness, anger, grief, anxiety and concern… all these are indicative of the many varied forms of the illusion of self-attack. Yet *they do not exist* and therefore cannot be healed except through forgiving the singular cause of them all – hidden guilt.

2. While these versions of attack seem to threaten us there is a great need for forgiveness. Yet there must be an inner willingness to accept our self without judgment while we move through this transition. Our Holy Self as the Christ is the overarching light into which we bring the illusory self's darkened fears, judgments and beliefs, so they can be joyfully healed.

3. How can we heal what we don't first *accept?* Unconditional self-acceptance is crucial to restoring awareness of our changeless innocence as the *Invincibility Principle.* As we practice unconditional self-acceptance, judgment, guilt and fear must fall away. And as we practice this, we find that the One Who extends this self-acceptance (forgiveness) is none other than our most Holy Self.

4. It is this *judgeless* state, free of condemnation of self, others and the body, that draws us gently into God's certain and ever-present Healing to be governed now by His *Invincibility Principle* (innocence). It is here that we relinquish the temptation to take on false-responsibility for what has been forgiven.

   a. *"Guilt is inescapable by those who believe they order their own thoughts, and must therefore obey their dictates. This makes them feel responsible for their errors without recognizing that, by accepting this responsibility, they are reacting irresponsibly. If the sole responsibility of the miracle worker is to accept the Atonement for himself, and I assure you that it is, then the responsibility for [what] is atoned for cannot be yours." T-5.V.7:6-8*

5. While we engage in this process of undoing illusions via forgiveness, there is a strong tendency toward harboring self-

judgment as we become more lucid to what seems like almost unending corrections to be made. When we were largely asleep we really didn't notice them. But now that the veil of denial is being lifted we seem to be swamped by forgiveness opportunities.

6. Having largely withdrawn our critical projections onto others and the past, there is often a phase where we tend to turn them within. Yet this is the same mistake. There is literally "no one" here to condemn, since all condemnation wherever we seem to see it is illusion, and therefore, not true. The one who condemns, together with the one who feels condemned, does not exist. They are the same illusion and are thankfully not Who we are.

E. What Do You Feel Responsible For?

1. Let's look at our erroneous beliefs more carefully to shed some light on them, which makes it easier to forgive them. From my own experience the most difficult hurdle has been to forgive what I had thought were my "personal" transgressions. And because I had assigned personal ownership to these, I had also accepted false responsibility for them. One of these has been in the area of the body, including ways I have unknowingly used it for attack through physical pain, aging, etc.

2. Guilt is guilt. Whatever you feel responsible for you will withhold from God's healing while denying yourself healing via forgiveness. Give it all over to Love's one irrefutable judgment; that you are innocent now and forever more.

3. Sickness, pain or adversity in any form is illusion. It's simply an impersonal suggestion that an opposite of God's all-encompassing Love exists. Consequently, these errors never belong to "me" personally. These are never "my" own personal property unless I prefer to use them to prove that separation from my incorruptible innocence is real.

4. Again, just so this sinks in, the one *believing* the sickness (or suffering) and the sickness itself, are both illusions. To add to this, all the remedies sought for healing, other than forgiveness, are also illusion and affect no healing at all. They simply appear to change the illusion's appearance of sickness to the appearance of health.

5. These things we see and feel so convincingly with the body's five senses, are all *byproducts* of the erroneous belief that we are separate from God Who is all-encompassing Love without opposite. Yet the unopposed truth is that we, as the beloved Child of God are also Love without opposite. This fact asserts that we are changeless, unopposed, uninterrupted Love and innocence without attack.

6. When I believe in sickness, pain, conflict or suffering, I must also mistakenly believe that "I" am separate from Love and entirely undeserving of it. I could not suffer if I was certain that I share one hundred percent of God's Love along with total immunity to everything that appears other than this perfection.

7. But what the false self blocks from awareness is that *in the belief in suffering* I must agree that "I" am the opposite of Love – as fear (guilt). The presence of suffering is the denial of my oneness as all-inclusive innocence as Love, with God. Think about this.

8. Suffering, regardless of where I seem to see it, in myself or in another, is always an impersonal suggestion that I am separate from God; and that there is another will *apart from and as powerful* as God's. So, all I'm asking for when I request *healing* is help to release this "belief in separation." It matters not what particular form the seeming separation takes. Its cause is always the same.

9. It is not my responsibility to solve problems, but to give them all over to the one Answer. If I perceive any illusion apart from God's Love, then my awareness of Love's certain and ever-present perfection is obscured. Only my *clouded perception* believes, sees and feels suffering. Only my clouded perception is begging to be wiped clean of guilt's attraction along with its painful effects.

F. Let Me Recognize My Problems Have Been Solved

1. There is *no cause* in the body or the world that can have an *effect* (symptoms or consequences) in the body or the world. The reason for this is that all cause and effects, and physical symptoms, etc., occur together in our mind (not brain). There is no power *external* to our mind that can *cause* anything. All power resides in our mind and only Love overrules everything.

2. So…what exactly do you assign as the *cause* of your sickness,

pain or problem? If you place the cause in an illusion and you really believe it is there, then you've unknowingly denied the real cause (guilt) and its only remedy which is forgiveness. The forgiveness process can be found in *The Seven Essential Principles of Quantum Forgiveness (Atonement)* on page 591.

3. The body is a thought in our mind. It answers exclusively to what we believe we are, and hence what we believe we deserve. In reality the body has no history. In any present moment it responds either to our guilt or our guiltlessness.

4. The body is a completely neutral, now moment projection that is occurring *in* our mind. The mind is not in the body. The body is in our mind, together with the world we seem to see. When we believe the cause of disease is heredity, in the body, in our environment, in food, or in the past, then the real cause as unconscious guilt cannot be forgiven. We have misplaced the cause and therefore cannot access the only real cure there is – forgiveness of our own miscreation.

5. At a particular point in my own transfer of trust from fear to Love, I found that the body seemed to be my tripping stone; namely, the illusion that the body can betray me through aging. For that reason, let's look at the concept of aging.

6. The Laws of God profess that the body, as a "now moment" projection, is entirely neutral. It cannot change in appearance unless I desire it to change, to age in this case. Remember that if I believe that aging is natural (like the illusions of disease and death) then I must value it and therefore, bring it into my experience here in the dream. I can only experience that which I value. And this includes everything I seem to defend myself from.

7. My mistaken beliefs told me that aging is caused by time. There were also remnants of a belief that disease and death occur as a result of many varied reasons, all of which seem to be outside me, in the body, others, the past and the world.

8. The truth though, is that there is no life or intelligence in matter. We give the body all the *meaning* it has for us by the *purpose* we give it. Aging is not caused by time but *by guilt;* by unforgiveness, as is every other form of adversity we appear to see. It's all unforgiven guilt. All sickness, aging, conflict, deprivation and death are physical

expressions of the fear of awakening to the *Invincibility Principle* – changeless innocence as our Holy Self.

9. Jesus teaches us specifically that all our problems have already been solved. He says that time cannot separate problems from their solution. Just ponder this for a minute. He says that the solution, the healing, is readily available, instantaneously. God knows that all our problems are the one illusion – a belief we're separate from Love Itself. It is always some form of grievance or resentment, a judgment that something is wrong. A telling clue is the presence of fear and the absence of gratitude. And this is an illusion that never really happened! But are we willing to *accept* the one remedy for them all? Jesus encourages us in the following lesson:

a. *"Let me recognize my problems have been solved."*

"I seem to have problems only because I am misusing time. I believe that the problem comes first, and time must elapse before it can be worked out. I do not see the problem and the answer as simultaneous in their occurrence. That is because I do not yet realize that God has placed the answer together with the problem, so that they cannot be separated by time. The Holy Spirit will teach me this, if I will let Him. And I will understand it is impossible that I could have a problem which has not been solved already..."

"I need not wait for this to be resolved. The answer to this problem is already given me, if I will accept it. Time cannot separate this problem from its solution." W-90.3,4

b. *"[You] are the means for God; not separate, nor with a life apart from His. His life is manifest in you who are His Son. Each aspect of Himself is framed in holiness and perfect purity, in love celestial and so complete it wishes only that it may release all that it looks upon unto itself. Its radiance shines through each body that it looks upon, and brushes all its darkness into light merely by looking past it [to] the light." T-25.I.4:1-4*

"You have been called,
together with your brother,
to the most holy function this
world contains. It is the only one
that has no limits, and reaches out to
every broken fragment of the Sonship
with healing and uniting comfort.
This is offered you,
in your holy relationship."
T-18.I.13:1-3
"The holiness of your
relationship forgives
you and your brother,
undoing the effects
of what you both
believed and saw.
And with their going
is the need for sin gone
with them." T-22.in.1:7-8
"In your relationship the
Holy Spirit has gently laid
the real world; the world of
happy dreams, from which
awaking is so easy and so natural."
T-8.II.9:4
"In your relationship is this world's light.
And fear must disappear before you now."
T-18.III.4:3-4

CHAPTER TWO

C–II.   SPECIAL RELATIONSHIPS

I. IS LOVE REALLY THE MAIN ATTRACTION IN RELATIONSHIPS?

1. This is an epic subject because it literally tears the blinders off the single most unrecognized factor that contributes to all relationship conflict. We may think that Love is the main attraction in relationship however while anger or resentment persists, we can be sure that it's specialness (guilt/fear) and not Love which binds the relationship.

2. All relationships begin as special until we repurpose them with Holy Spirit. In all special relationships the hidden goal is to "get" something from another. The false self seeks to complete the illusion of itself through relationship. And the means by which it tries to "keep" a relationship is not by changeless Love – but by guilt. Its objective is to keep its companion bound to it by guilt. It really believes that guilt-tripping others will ensure the relationship's continuity.

3. To the ego guilt is love, and love is guilt. To remove all guilt in a relationship would mean the certain demise of both the ego's special, conditional relating and the ego itself. If we were to consistently and completely forgive in our relationships the ego would be terrified, because it believes that to forgive a loved one would mean we will *lose* him or her.

a. *"The ego establishes relationships only to get something. And it would keep the giver bound to itself through guilt."* ... *"For the ego really believes that it can get and keep [by making guilty.] This is its one attraction..." T-15.VII.2:1-2,5-6*

4. The false self believes that the more judgment and anger we invest outside our self (in others) the safer we become. It does not recognize that by doing this we unintentionally end up amassing guilt which plays out as unconscious self-attack (illness, pain, conflict, lack, etc.). *"For it is the ego's fundamental doctrine that what you do to others you have escaped."* ... *"It counsels, therefore, that if you are host to it, it will enable you to direct its anger outward, thus protecting you." T-15.VII.4:2,5*

5. In all special relationships and especially within the romantic relationship the ego believes it must sacrifice itself in order to trade for a better self. While this "sacrifice" is mostly unconscious it forms the basis of all unhealed relationships. And this is what occurs when we seemingly fall in love. Jesus makes a startling statement here:

a. *"For each one thinks that he has sacrificed something to the other, and hates him for it. Yet this is what he thinks he wants. He is not in love with the other at all. He merely believes he is in love with sacrifice. And for this sacrifice, which he demands of himself, he demands that the other accept the guilt and sacrifice himself as well. Forgiveness becomes impossible, for the ego believes that to forgive another is to lose him. It is only by attack without forgiveness that the ego can ensure the guilt that holds all its relationships together." T-15.VII.7:2-8*

6. To assist with locating this underlying sense of sacrifice and its accompanied feelings of justified anger or resentment, I encourage you to recall, with radical honesty, a moment when you felt *justified* in your anger or resentment toward a loved one.

7. When we are triggered by someone there appears to be a reflex reaction that immediately turns our focus externally and we genuinely believe it was the *other* person who triggered us. We even believe we can justify our anger by providing convincing evidence of their transgression – what the ego classifies as a sin, rather than a

simple error which is easily forgiven.

8. Yet the ego does not want us to recognize that the very first *and often unconscious* attack occurred in our *own mind* first. No one can attack us unless we have first attacked our self. All attack is self-attack. Somehow, we must have betrayed or abandoned the Love we are by perceiving attack in the first place. And it's *this* mistake that requires healing via forgiveness; because only this Self-betrayal could possibly call for seeming attack from external sources.

9. In special relationships we bind each other to guilt. Furthermore, we rarely acknowledge that to make another guilty really is outright attack. We tend to justify our projection of guilt by believing they deserve it. Whoa! Let's look at this without the ego's blinders on. The belief that "they" deserve to be guilty or they deserve to be punished is a direct reflection of what *we* secretly believe about our self.

10. To the degree we feel justified to project blame is the extent to which we our self, secretly expect – and invite – punishment. This is big! And this is why it is so important to investigate with Spirit the underlying dynamic of our relationships so we can finally identify and heal the only "cause" of all appearances of conflict.

11. Sacrifice and guilt form the dark and sickly glue that binds our special relationships until we commit to repurposing our relationships with Holy Spirit.

A. The Body – #1 False Idol in Special Relationships

1. Let's begin to look at how the ego uses the body as a decoy to hide the true Altar of our relationships. In most romantic relationships there is a belief that our body and that of our partner's is highly valuable, more so than our shared Mind/Heart/Spirit. On the altar of sexual relationships the body takes precedence as the most revered idol, to the exclusion of the sacred essence of the one we may profess to love.

2. As an example of how we mistakenly idolize the body rather than the Spirit or essence of the one we say we love, I'd like to offer a couple of revealing questions, which attempt to expose the ego's most idolized attraction in romantic relationships. In a monogamous romantic relationship, how threatened would you feel if your partner

had a casual sexual affair with another person? And would this be grounds for you to withdraw your love for them?

3. The threat of *two bodies* attempting to unite – as sexual infidelity – ignites an extreme emotional feeling of betrayal for most people, if not all. This "physical" betrayal is generally seen as the greatest threat and the ego's hard evidence for withdrawing special love and trust.

4. While I am in no way approving sexual infidelity, I do want to make a point; the ego obsesses with the body over and above the only real "presence," and that is our shared, changeless, innocent and divine essence. Sexual betrayal is a sign of a much deeper Self-betrayal and a lack of true, undefended and authentic communication with self and others. Ultimately, like all illusions of betrayal, sexual betrayal is a symbol to help us look more deeply at where we have betrayed our Self.

5. When we identify as a body in relationships, it becomes a formidable shadow that completely obscures the Love we have for each other as our one, shared Identity, the Holy Self. The false self believes it is a "private" mind, alone, split off and compartmentalized from other minds. It cherishes and hides its private thoughts, not revealing to us the mass of guilt this induces. And while this private mind is valued as secret and separate, unfortunately the body becomes the central idol of the relationship.

6. The focus and priority are not on protecting the innocence of our shared Identity, but on guilt and blame via judgment of what the "body" of the other does or doesn't do to meet the ego's needs. Thus, special "love" is gauged on the body (behavior) of another, and judgment and guilt are treasured. The ego feels justified to withdraw its love, punish or even reject our partner when their "actions" are determined as sinful. In the following quote we see how the false self uses the body to keep others bound to us through guilt. All the while the ego believes that guilt *is* love and is afraid to let it go.

   a. *"Yet they only [seem] to be together. For relationships, to the ego, mean only that bodies are together. It is always this that the ego demands, and it does not object where the mind goes or what it thinks, for this seems unimportant. As long as*

*the body is there to receive its sacrifice, it is content. To the
ego the mind is private, and only the body can be shared." ...
"What makes another guilty and holds him through guilt is
"good." What releases him from guilt is "bad," because he
would no longer believe that bodies communicate, and so he
would be "gone.""* T-15.VII.8:1-5,8-9

7. Guilt is literally the *only* need the ego has, as it provides all it
    needs to sustain itself and the imagined separation. Jesus shares
    with us that to be with a body is not communication and while we
    mistakenly believe it is, we will be afraid to show-up honestly,
    and open up to hear or feel the Holy Spirit. He is waiting within
    our Self and others for us to hear Him. However, this requires us
    to show-up authentically in our relationships with our Self and
    others. It demands our willingness to be "seen" without the ego's
    defenses. And thereby to Love and to be Loved. The means by
    which we engage in this is via forgiveness and the *Seven Keys*
    found in Chapter VI, page 572.

8. In special relationships we compromise our Holy Self attempting
    to join with other's egos, their split mind, but in order to do so
    we actually separate from our Self and each other. This kind of
    socially acceptable colluding is really a focus on being with bodies
    as a substitute for real joining through authentic, emotionally
    vulnerable and defenseless relating. And the outcome of this
    contraction is always guilt, along with its subsequent projection
    onto others, the body or the world.

    a. *"Guilt is the only need the ego has, and as long as you
        identify with it, guilt will remain attractive to you. Yet
        remember this; to be with a body is not communication. And
        if you think it is, you will feel guilty about communication
        and will be afraid to hear the Holy Spirit, recognizing in His
        Voice your own need to communicate."* T-15.VII.10:4-6

9. In the unhealed special relationship there is often a fear of
    applying the *Seven Keys*. Those who still value unhealed special
    love (attack) can see no benefit in undoing their false self-concept
    or in making their relationships Holy. They believe their security

lies in keeping their thoughts and feelings *private*. This upside-down reasoning clearly makes them afraid to communicate openly, vulnerably and honestly.

10. Safety is seen in the union of bodies, yet threat is perceived in real communication, particularly when honesty and emotional vulnerability are called upon to be expressed in relationship. The ego wants to keep its thoughts and feelings private so they can be projected onto others and that way we get to keep the unconscious self-attack going.

a. *"It is clearly insane to believe that by communicating you will be abandoned. And yet many do believe it. For they think their minds must be kept private or they will lose them, but if their bodies are together their minds remain their own. The union of bodies thus becomes the way in which they would keep minds apart." "As long as you believe that to be with a body is companionship, you will be compelled to attempt to keep your brother in his body, held there by guilt. And you will see safety in guilt and danger in communication. For the ego will always teach that loneliness is solved by guilt, and that communication is the cause of loneliness." T-15.VII.11:3-6,12:2-4*

11. This dreadful inner conflict between the genuine longing to be seen (Loved) and the *fear* to be seen without masks and defenses, expresses itself most glaringly in special relationships. In order to be Loved we must be willing to be *seen* and this means showing-up for our Self and coming clean.

a. *"When the body ceases to attract you, and when you place no value on it as a means of getting anything, then there will be no interference in communication and your thoughts will be as free as God's. As you let the Holy Spirit teach you how to use the body only for purposes of communication, and renounce its use for separation and attack which the ego sees in it, you will learn you have no need of a body at all." T-15.IX.7:1-2*

B. The Attraction of Love Through Communication

1. What does it mean to not show-up for our Self? What is the pay-off? Most of us are all too familiar with that persistent sense of threat which seems to propel us to abandon our Self. We repeatedly participate in an ongoing effort to ensure our false self is recognized, appreciated and seen. Yet it's the ego seeking to be seen. And the cost is enormous.

2. The ego can be expressed and its effects can be seen. However, it can never be Loved. Nor can it Love. And this deeply denied and unhealed inner split between the ego's desire to be seen *and* our genuine longing for Love, is the reason why so many relationships fail. The ego's *superficial* desire to be seen and appreciated, and our *authentic* yearning for changeless Love, are mutually exclusive. Which of these do we value? Because the one we value is the one we attract. It really is time to recognize that these two desires oppose each other.

3. The desire for one of these cancels out the other. And they cannot *both* be met. If the ego needs to be seen then it is impossible to feel Love or Loved. And if we sincerely long to Love and be Loved then the ego's artificial desire to be seen must be eclipsed by our decision to communicate with our Self and others authentically.

4. As I said before, the ego is fearful of open and honest communication because it eradicates the only things that keep identification as a false self going – judgment, guilt and fear. It says that if we begin open and honest communication with others that they will reject us. Yet how on earth will we ever know Love unless we're willing to be present to our Self with others, and learn to communicate from our true Self to that same Self in others?

5. Communication is the key. Learning to relate authentically with our Self and others is imperative. And we have access to it in every Holy Instant in which we willingly enter. This is a moment of intention to lay aside all judgment and to have our perception (of conflict, blame, guilt, pain, illness, etc.) healed. It's really a precious instant of willingness to see *with* Holy Spirit and not through the ego's filter of fear. The Holy Instant is a "reversal" of the ego's projection.

6. Through learning how to relate authentically with our Self and others we mindfully show-up with Spirit and this is the genuine attraction of Love to Love. The longing to Love and be Loved is met as we lay aside the ego's temptations and actively choose to stay present to our Self and learn to communicate authentically through the *Seven Key Principles of Authentic Relating,* hereafter simply called the *Seven Keys.*

7. In my experience and that of many others, applying the *Seven Keys* in all our relating has served to bring on an avalanche of miracles and Holy Instants.

a. *"In the holy instant guilt holds no attraction, since communication has been restored. And guilt, whose only purpose is to disrupt communication, has no function here. Here there is no concealment, and no private thoughts. The willingness to communicate attracts communication to it, and overcomes loneliness completely. There is complete forgiveness here, for there is no desire to exclude anyone from your completion, in sudden recognition of the value of his part in it."* T-15.VII.14:2-6

2. THE NAKED TRUTH UNDERLYING ALL RELATIONSHIPS

1. We long to be seen, to be respected, accepted and loved for who we are. Yet there remains an unidentified and cruel deception which underlies our craving. The one who yearns to be seen, loved and accepted is the "false self" and its sad secret is that it has zero capacity either to receive or to give what it appears to so desperately seek.

2. Not only does the false self not recognize perfect Love, it does not know what Love is. Being afraid of what it does not understand, it sees Love as a threat. The ego pursues *specialness* and *confuses it* with Love. Yet specialness is fraught with guilt, fear, change and

loss while perfect Love is changeless, no matter what may *appear* to threaten it. Real Love does not budge when confronted by judgment, blame or any other expression of fear.

3. Our Holy Self is perfect, unopposed, uninterrupted Love and innocence. The false self is fearful. As opposites, they do not see or communicate with each other. In fact, the presence of one in our mind completely excludes the other.

4. In any *now moment* in which we feel or believe in guilt, blame, fear, anger, judgment, lack, pain, illness, loss, threat or worry, etc., we're unknowingly identifying as the false self and not our Holy Self. This s*elf* only sees *others* as false selves as well. It projects onto others that which it denies in itself.

5. This self then attempts to "solve" the countless illusory problems that *it alone* projects. This is one of the ways the ego always *seeks but never finds*. Buried beneath all its extravagant promises of false love, its underlying agenda is separation and suffering, although it keeps this destructive goal well concealed from conscious awareness.

6. In relationships it seeks *special love* in a deluded effort to complete the illusion of itself. Yet Love *and* specialness are opposites. Yes, opposites. Specialness is fear in disguise. It has all the trappings of what the world has come to know as "love," however, real and conscious Love is changeless. It is total. That means it is undivided. And it is 100 percent inclusive. In contrast, special love is *always changing* because its underlying source arises from guilt, fear, deprivation and exclusivity. The ego depends on specialness because specialness generates the guilt necessary for it to survive.

7. Perfect Love is relating without fear or conflict. This is the very essence of our Holy Self. It does not waiver. It cannot judge. It sees only innocence wherever it looks, as it sees itself. This Love cannot turn to hate, it does not and cannot change and it cannot end. Imagine that.

8. Love, *and nothing but Lov*e, is the core of our being. There is absolutely no moment where this perfect Love is ever threatened. It is entirely uninterrupted. Yet we will not recognize or accept it while we value and perceive through the false self.

9. We will always attract that which we value. If we seek for special love, then this is what we will attract. And the sad consequence is that we will be afraid of perfect Love.

A. Mistaking Fear for Love

1. This immense and eternal ocean of Love does not leave us, not even for an instant. However, our *awareness* of it can recede. And this Love cannot be felt or known to us while we choose to value its opposite. Specialness is not Love, but is based on fear and lack. It is unstable and inconsistent. Special love is easily withdrawn when its exclusivity is threatened. Specialness is exclusive, whereas the essence of our Holy Self is *inclusive*.

2. Special love, centered on fear, is an attempt to combine two mutually exclusive thought systems. The special relationship dynamic involves fearful love while maintaining another often-unrecognized contradiction, *loving fears* (e.g. being "worried" about someone is just one example of a loving fear, which is impossible in truth).

3. We can *love* someone in one instant and *hate* them in the next if they say or do something which threatens the ego's identity. We may say we love someone however if our love turns to worry or fear for them then this is not Love but an expression of fear. The presence of fear excludes Love. We cannot have a bit of both.

4. In every moment we are either in Love or we're in fear. There is nothing in between. Love is trust. Trust is Love. We cannot Love without trust. This means we must learn to trust the Holy Self within our Self and in others. *"Yet love without trust is impossible, and doubt and trust cannot coexist."* M-7.4:6

5. The moment trust has been replaced by the dark shadow of worry or fear, is the very instant that Love vanishes from our awareness. We could choose to *consciously check-in* when we are worried about a loved one, instead of being engaged in our own fearful thoughts, beliefs and stories. Do we recognize the instant we are triggered? In the special relationship the ego calls this distrust "caring" for another. It labels this contraction from Love as being loving. The underlying question here is how can fear and distrust possibly be an expression of Love?

6. The presence of fear in me immediately signifies that I have stepped away from Love as the core of my being. And if I'm trying to help someone who appears to be suffering, while I am concerned (fearful) myself, I only exacerbate the issue for both of us. Two wrongs never make a right. If I am concerned at all, then I do not trust. And this means I am now the one in immediate need of healing via forgiveness. Thankfully, this healing is accessible in any Holy Instant I am willing to exchange my own fear for the miracle, and healing is given to us both. The forgiveness process can be found in *The Seven Essential Principles of Quantum Forgiveness (Atonement)* on page 591.

B. Hiding from Our True Identity and Divine Purpose

1. This may come as quite a shock but it must be addressed. We won't know "What" we are until we give our relationships to the Holy Spirit for His comprehensive and sacred repurposing. Until then our special relationships with family, partners, children, friends, etc., are used to make sure we never discover the Love we are and the Love we share.
2. This commitment to give our relationships to the Holy Spirit, to make them Holy, does not mean we have to give up our special relationships with certain individuals. What it does mean is we must be willing to give over the *purpose* of these relationships to Spirit, so they are no longer used for the ego's destructive purpose.
3. This repurposing of the goal from specialness to Holiness is our own call to embody our true Identity and purpose. Through the transfer process we will profoundly experience the shift between the false self and our Holy Self. The extreme contrast between the two cannot be showcased more clearly than here, within the experiential transfer from a special to Holy Relationship.
4. We will be blind to our true Identity and divine purpose as long as we continue to prolong the specialness dynamic in our relationships. Only the pseudo-self relates with self and others via specialness. The purpose of the specialness dynamic is to hide not just our own divine Identity, but that of everyone else as well.

5. While we relate as a false self to other false selves, we will apply special roles and rules to all relationships. These specialness laws *exclude* the genuine emotional intimacy, defenselessness and radical self-honesty necessary to *be* seen, to *be* Loved, and to *give* Love in return. This exclusion is ultimately the rejection of our most beloved, guiltless and Holy Self, the one Identity we share with others. To be seen necessitates dropping our emotional defenses. It also requires our desire to "close the gap" with another, even if we seem to disagree with them. We learn to desire union *more* than we want to be right (separation).

6. Given that every person in our life is a direct reflection of our own self-evaluation, albeit mostly unrecognized, another person can only accept us to the extent we accept and Love our Self. And whilst we continue to hide, by relating with others through the pseudo-self and its special love, we will not know Love, precisely because we are afraid of it.

7. Very simply, we will inadvertently resist our true Identity and divine purpose to the same degree we hide from our Holy Self. This is also true when we appear to attract judgment or attack from others, the body and the world. The nature of Love dwells only within the authentic, guiltless and Holy Self. And this is the only Love that *can* be shared in reality.

8. There is a very good reason why *A Course in Miracles* focuses so heavily on the undoing of our special relating. Apart from the fact that specialness involves two false selves relating, it also reveals that *no* communication takes place because literally, only Love can *be* shared. Despite appearances, special love cannot be shared because it arises from fear. Remember special love is really attack in disguise. Any form of "love" which involves fear, concern, exclusivity, loss, lack or conditions, is not Love, but fear masquerading as Love. The body then, and not the Spirit, is at the center of these relationships.

9. Through special relationships we will erroneously pursue and strengthen the ego's identity and purpose in all the myriad areas it urges us to go seek but never find. Yet it is in the Holy Relationship that we finally learn of the sanctity of our true Identity and its extraordinary purpose.

10. It was revealed to me just how extensive the ego's obsession with special relationships is. They are the bedrock of the ego thought system and without them there could be no ego. Everything we do in life is fabricated around specialness. Both the false-identity and its purpose are cemented within an unrecognized pursuit of specialness. Let me explain.

11. When children are born, they emerge with amnesia of both their true Identity as the Holy Self and their true purpose, which is to break the ego spell and awaken from the dream of separation. Yet their parents, caretakers, teachers and the world in general have no clue of this. Instead, the prevailing (ego) thought system is employed to program and encourage the child's *false self* concept and enforces the laws of specialness, so the child learns to sustain his or her pseudo-self.

12. The child is too soon convinced he is a mere mortal, having become hopelessly confused in the belief the body is his "self." Now the separate body, and not the eternal Holy Self, is made the central idol of his existence and he becomes convinced he is a victim of forces beyond his control. He forgets the truth that his Holy Self has complete dominion over the body.

13. He doesn't recall that the body, others and the world cannot attack him unless he enlists them to do so. To the contrary, he believes he is victim to these outside forces. In addition, he is taught to use his body to seek pleasure while attempting to avoid pain, not recognizing that both pleasure and pain in the ego thought system are ultimately one and the same. Seeking pleasure and avoiding pain, alone and apart from God, are the means the ego requires to amass its guilt and continue the separation.

14. The child "learns" that he is sustained by everything *other than* his ever-present and True Source as God (Love) within. He thinks he is incomplete and unworthy; therefore he must seek his completion and earn his worth externally until his body is finally doomed to death.

15. Having confused Love with fear, as he grows up he will quest after special relationships to try to fill his aching emptiness. And he will suffer in romantic relationships because he is hopelessly lost in his confusion between lust and Love. Once again, he will not recognize the presence of lust (fear) is the exclusion of Love. He will feel guilty and not realize why.

16. In large part, children grow up to learn these false values from the world's prolific demonstrations and "appearances" which convincingly attempt to "justify" that fear and not Love makes the world go 'round.

3. CAN LOVE CHANGE?

1. As mentioned in the manual's introduction, some of these earlier essays may raise more questions than they seem to answer. However, most of these questions will be answered in later chapters. As a reminder, I do encourage keeping a journal to note questions that arise and also to voice the false-self's triggers, its fears and resistance.

2. Through the false self we have completely misunderstood what Love is. Real Love is consistent and changeless. It does not change with a person, time or circumstance. It is inclusive and does not leave anyone out. It illuminates the Soul and it Loves that Soul with all respect and reverence by consistently looking past the false self and the body and the mistakes they seem to make.

   a. *"What you acknowledge in your brother you are acknowledging in yourself, and what you share you strengthen." T-5.III.3:5*

3. Real Love is devoted to seeing innocence in another, thereby seeing and accepting it within. Real Love knows that the Holy Self is always guiltless no matter how confused the small self might be. It also knows there is only one undivided Holy Self. And because there is only one of us here it gives unconditional Love rather than judgment, knowing that what it gives away is merely increased for itself. It recognizes that the cost of giving *is* receiving – always. Our Self Love increases as we give it away with no strings attached.

4. Recall that *all* relationships begin as special and conditional. Until we've begun to heal our split mind through forgiveness and authentic relating, all relating with others and our self is through the false self's filter of guilt. We cannot fall out of Love unless it was "love" spelled with a small "l". Special love is really hate in disguise, which is why it seems to change. If love can turn to disappointment or even hate then there was no Love there in the first place.

5. Special love is fearful love. It was made by the ego as the primary substitute for the Love of God within. It is the exact opposite of real Love which is God's changeless Love as our one Holy Self. Special love is personal, fragile, moody, needy and selfish. It is conditional and defensive. It is primarily dishonest and terribly afraid of radical self-honesty and emotional vulnerability (emotional intimacy) because it believes they would annihilate it.

6. The ego's special love smacks of exclusivity. Coming from its own puny evaluation of itself it believes that love is limited, volatile and just as easily threatened as itself. The ego's limiting beliefs limit love as well; the more love given to one the less love available to give to others.

7. Further, this pseudo love targets the body as the seat of its devotion to the point that it consistently denies the Spirit. At its root, the ego believes it is deeply unworthy and insignificant. It is unknowingly devoted to the idea that love demands sacrifice and it asks that same sacrifice of those it thinks it loves. It is committed to sacrifice as long as it can secretly resent those it sacrifices *for*.

8. Special love is meant to suppress, deny and hide our inner light. It works as a darkened shroud that we unwittingly use to hide from true Self-discovery. And herein lies a deep inner conflict indeed. In the depths of our Soul we yearn to be seen, accepted and Loved unconditionally. We want to trust and be trusted. But there is an inner betrayal, an unseen abandonment of Self.

   1) Are we willing to do whatever it takes to be true to our most Holy Self? Are we willing to explore our most authentic and beloved Self?

9. Are we willing to recognize and drop all our artificial defenses to Love? Are we willing to show-up for our Self by learning to be radically self-honest? Are we willing to be consistently accountable for our own reactions to seeming threats? Are we willing to be defenseless? Are we willing to be truly emotionally transparent and vulnerable? And are we wholly willing to forgive our self for having unknowingly used others to attack us? If not – then we're saying that we don't really want to be seen, accepted and Loved unconditionally.

> 1)   If I cannot see, accept, Love and trust myself unconditionally, then who on earth will?

10. **Love Is**. It can never change. It can never cause pain, nor can it be lost. And I could never believe I have been betrayed or abandoned if I had not unknowingly betrayed or abandoned my most Holy Self first.

11. Real Love is eternal and infinite. And because of this all the Love we seek or we think we lost can be restored in just one heartfelt, Holy moment of true forgiveness, a moment in which we sincerely forgive our self for having mistakenly used someone to falsely perpetuate the ego's belief that we are separate, betrayed or abandoned.

> 1)   When we show-up for our majestic and Holy Self … others will too.

a. *"Perhaps you think that different kinds of love are possible. Perhaps you think there is a kind of love for this, a kind for that; a way of loving one, another way of loving still another. Love is one. It has no separate parts and no degrees; no kinds nor levels, no divergencies and no distinctions. It is like itself, unchanged throughout. It never alters with a person or a circumstance. It is the Heart of God, and also of His Son. Love's meaning is obscure to anyone who thinks that love can change." W-127.1:1-2:1*

b. *"There is no order in relationships. They either are or not. An unholy relationship is no relationship. It is a state of isolation, which seems to be what it is not. No more than that." T-20. VI.8:1-5*

4. WHEN A RELATIONSHIP IS THREATENED

1. Relationships are one of the first areas to undergo significant shifts and changes when we begin practically applying the principles of *A Course in Miracles*. Initially there is a period of disorientation as we give our relationships to Spirit to be divinely repurposed from special to Holy Relationship. The cause of this initial disruption is the abrupt shift in the relationship's goal *(more on this in Chapter V – The Holy Relationship Blueprint, and Chapter VI - The Bridge to the Real World)*.

2. The former goal of separation disguised as specialness, was achieved through judgment, blame, shame and guilt. But when we sincerely desire a Holy Relationship the Holy Spirit replaces our original goal with its complete opposite – union as guiltlessness (innocence) achieved through the practical application of quantum forgiveness and the *Seven Keys*.

3. Because the goal of our relationship is now diametrically opposed to its original intent we go through a period of acute disorientation, as the previous "means" we used to achieve the old goal of specialness clearly does not serve the relationship's new and divine purpose. Patterns of taking things personally, sacrifice, guilt-tripping, inauthentic communication, exclusivity, private thoughts, playing small, people-pleasing, blame, conditional relating, etc., clearly must be released. Although, for most, the motivation for relinquishing these distorted forms of relating will not be gained until we've really seen and *felt* the "cost" of using them in our relationships.

4. So, until then, there is a period where we're not yet familiar or comfortable with exercising authentic communication for fear of rejection and loss. We flip flop between trying to apply unconditional forgiveness and the old rules and regimes - dysfunctional communication and guilt trips. This wild fluctuation of goals and means makes the relationship seem unbearable at times. A common challenge many on this spiritual path face is being in close relationship with others who are either disinterested or object to this teaching. These relationships, where we seem to have separate goals, can be excellent classrooms in which we learn to recognize

our own hidden projections onto others so that we can forgive them completely. These kinds of relationships are very valuable, especially in the initial stages of awakening (as explained in *"The Development of Trust"* in the Manual for Teachers in the *Course*).

5. In the earlier period of our journey through the six stages of the development of trust (see the *Course, Manual for Teachers, 4.*) we are prone to confusing "form" and "content" in our relationships. Still heavily invested in the mistaken belief that specialness is love we naturally find it difficult to make a meaningful distinction between form and content.

6. The ego is addicted to specialness and mistakes it for Love. It is addicted to the "rules and rituals of specialness" by which it determines appropriate and inappropriate demonstrations of love, compassion and caring…but this is ego "love" spelled with a small "l". A common component in special relationships is what I call *ego stroking* and this is not Love at all. The ego cannot know, give or receive Love and this is why so many relationships seem to fail.

7. Special love arises from guilt and values sacrifice, guilt and judgment as its basis. Yet sacrifice, guilt and judgment are opposite of Love and are not part of God. Thus specialness is devoted to the rules, behaviors, conditions, rituals, roles, stories and forms that our special relationships take which all revolve around the mistaken belief that we are a body. They do not aim at recognizing and revering the real "content" as the innocent and changeless spirit of the person we relate with.

8. Rules, behaviors, conditions, rituals and roles we play constitute the *form* of the special relationship. And when we change or break these "specialness rules or roles" in our relationships then the form of the relationship usually breaks down. And yet the ego's obsession with form is always to block awareness of the pristine *content*, our true, shared Identity as the Holy Self.

9. When the *form* (marriage, friendship, partnership, etc.) breaks down, the ego tosses out the only valuable *content* of the relationship, which is the changeless Identity of our companion and of our Self that remained unrecognized and therefore, denied or rejected. When there is little or no *gratitude* for what seemed to be a failed

relationship then it was the *form* and not the changeless *content* (Love as the Holy Self) that took precedence. The ego always values form at the expense of content (Love).

10. The truth is, *form* is *not* valuable, however the *content* is. We confuse these two because we are so attached to valuing "form" over content that we often ignore the content. We will never know the Love in a relationship until we learn that every interaction is either an expression of Love or a call for Love. Love shows up when we learn to answer both with Love.

11. The ego never recognizes a call for Love. It sees it as a call for attack and defense. Everything we encounter that is not an outright expression of Love is always a "call for Love." And how will we answer these calls for Love, especially once we recognize we're responding to a mirror of our very *own* call for Love?

12. Ultimately, we need to ask this question:

1) "What is this relationship *for?*" Is it to get the ego's illusory needs met? Or is it to help me awaken to my Holy Self via forgiveness? We set the goal in advance so that the relationship serves the goal.

a. *"The only judgment involved is the Holy Spirit's one division into two categories; one of love, and the other the call for love. You cannot safely make this division, for you are much too confused either to recognize love, or to believe that everything else is nothing but a call for love. You are too bound to form, and not to content. What you consider content is not content at all. It is merely form, and nothing else. For you do not respond to what a brother really offers you, but only to the particular perception of his offering by which the ego judges it." T-14.X.7.*

b. *"Whenever any form of special relationship tempts you to seek for love in ritual, remember love is content, and not form of any kind. The special relationship is a ritual of form, aimed at raising the form to take the place of God at the expense of content. There is no meaning in the form, and there will never be." T-16.V.12:1-3*

A. When a Relationship Seems to End

1. The six stages of the development of trust are like a vast tapestry of unlearning, purification, repurposing and then learning with the Holy Spirit. There are so many sub-phases involved while we continue to revisit earlier lessons and stages in order to reinforce our new mindset.

2. As we journey through these stages our mind is cleansed of mistaken beliefs and values. Relationships are the overarching medium through which we make this transition from special to Holy, from fear to Love without opposite.

3. As we seem to advance in our trust in God as our Holy Self, there is a considerable shift toward being authentic. Radical self-honesty is one of the most important qualities that we will develop in this process. We must be willing to see just how we have deceived our self and others by not showing up for our self authentically because we feared judgment, rejection and loss. We do need to see, without self-judgment, how we have abandoned *our Self* in relationships, while unwittingly resenting *others* for it.

4. This is where consistent application of the *Seven Keys* helps us to navigate our way toward aligning with the Christ within. These principles are a fast track to undoing the old specialness dynamic in our relationships.

5. Jesus tells us that there are "three levels" of relationship in the *Manual for Teachers*, Section 3, of the *Course*. The first appears to be quite superficial such as those fleeting meetings or Holy Encounters with strangers in social situations, perhaps in an elevator, bus or train, or in the supermarket where we show-up for an instant and genuinely express kindness to another; a Holy Instant of recognition.

6. I want to address the second level of relationship in more detail later in this section as this level seems the most prevalent, misunderstood and often the most heartbreaking of all relationship attempts.

7. The third level of relationship Jesus speaks of are ones that are lifelong. These are generally very few because the teaching-learning balance remains perfect for both and this sustains the relationship so that it becomes a lifelong union. This does not mean the relationship is without conflict though. But it does mean there are consistent opportunities to learn the lesson of forgiveness. And some people actually do!

8. The teaching-learning dynamic, at all levels, involves a delicate balance between two people, although they may not be conscious of it at the time. This teaching-learning dynamic is also crucial in our relationships with our children, which are largely "special" relationships until we also repurpose them with Holy Spirit. Our children are perhaps our greatest teachers in many respects. Let's remember that we are all teachers and students who swap roles intermittently. The real question in any one moment is, "What are we teaching?" Is it Love or fear? Is it innocence or guilt?

9. Teaching comes not from what we *say* but from how we live, from our *demonstration*. Are we demonstrating forgiveness? Do we really desire to see others as sinless, as guiltless? If not, then we're teaching fear and not Love.

10. Level two relationships seem to involve a fall out, or separation. Most romantic relationships come under this category as "love" seems to change more so within sexual unions. The body and its sexual appetites often become idols in the relationship and are used to reinforce guilt to obscure the real Love that is ever present in each partner.

11. Let's take a look at Jesus' description of level two relationships:

a. *"Each teaching-learning situation is maximal in the sense that each person involved will learn the most that he can from the other person at that time. In this sense, and in this sense only, we can speak of levels of teaching. Using the term in this way, the second level of teaching is a more sustained relationship, in which, for a time, two people enter into a fairly intense teaching-learning situation and then appear to separate. As with the first level, these meetings are not accidental, nor is what appears to be the end of the relationship a real end. Again, each has learned the most he can at the time. Yet all who meet will someday meet again, for it is the destiny of all relationships to become holy."* M-3.4.

12. We also see the "falling out" dynamic in many friendship and family relationships. Past grievances are held firmly in the present as the unremedied cause of separation. In these fragile relationships there are rules, behaviors, rituals and conditional agreements which, when threatened or broken, are deemed as sufficient justification to withdraw love. Love then turns to hate (which is impossible, as Love is changeless in reality). Here we can see that if love turns to hate then it certainly was not Love spelled with a capital "L."

13. Jesus makes note that we don't question the idea that we can love and hate together. We accept this as normal. In our special relationships we *love* one moment, and if someone does not do what we want then (pseudo) love turns to *hate* in a flash.

14. There are no degrees of hate. A mild irritation with someone is the same as outright rage. The reason for this is that there is no hierarchy of illusions. They are all the absence of Love in our awareness and therefore, an attempted attack on our Holy Self.

　　a. *"No one considers it bizarre to love and hate together, and even those who believe that hate is sin merely feel guilty, but do not correct it." T-16.V.3:4*

15. In the subsection titled *My Profound Relationship Journey,* found in chapter VI, *Bridge to the Real World,* I share my own experiences of both a level two and level three relationship. Included in this same section is my practical journey of transferring a highly toxic special relationship into one that became a powerful, grace-filled union for all time.

16. These practical examples are helpful in revealing just why the Holy Relationship requires a mutual and truly common purpose to reach its goal of Holiness. Also, these examples show why the "teaching-learning dynamic" changes as the mutual goal is embraced with each other and Holy Spirit. In addition, we'll see more clearly just *why* level two relationships fall apart.

5. IDENTIFYING THE ROOT OF ALL RELATIONSHIP BREAKDOWNS

1. Love is total. Fear is total. Love *and* fear are mutually exclusive which means they cannot be experienced together. You have no doubt heard this over and over but let's explore the dynamic of a typical special relationship without any self-judgment.

2. These are "up-close" relationships, with people we profess to love. We honor their birthdays, we try to make them feel special and we genuinely believe we care for them especially when they are sick or in need. We accept that sacrifice is an everyday part of all loving relationships. And we expect the ones we love will sacrifice for us when necessary, just as we do for them.

3. We worry about them; we collude with them in sympathy when they feel victimized by others or the past, and for the most part we expect to be treated the same way. On the other hand, we feel openly hurt or even angry when they do something we don't like or agree with. And our love can switch immediately to outright hatred if they betray us. After all, this is "love" right? Wrong.

4. If we are to open our heart to the Holy Relationship then we must be willing to see that what we had believed was love, was not even remotely close. We need to begin to recognize what real Love is *not*.

   a. *"Love is not learned. Its meaning lies within itself. And learning ends when you have recognized all it is [not.] That is the interference; that is what needs to be undone." T-18. IX.12:1-4*

5. This can be quite a slap in the face to the false self, but it's a necessary prerequisite to allow Holy Spirit to enter and to help us undo our blocks to the awareness of Love's presence. Unless we are willing to see what Love is *not* we cannot possibly open to the Love we are. And we won't be able to see others as Love either.

6. The term "fear" as the opposite of Love, includes all expressions of lack of Love such as anger, hate, resentment, mild irritation, rage, lack, loss, judgment, disease, emotional or physical pain, etc.

7. In one moment there appears to be *love* which can just as easily turn to hate, particularly if there is an ego threat involved - take

cheating on a partner for instance. Or let's say our loved one forgot to take the trash out, a forgetful act that precipitated only mild resentment. The reaction to him/her not taking out the trash *and* the reaction to finding our partner has engaged in an extramarital affair are both classified as fear which is the absence of Love.

A. No Degrees of Love – No Degrees of Fear

1. Did you know that there are no degrees of fear despite the fact that we feel a multi-leveled scale of fear? Fear is hate because it is the total absence of Love. We cannot mix Love and fear. They cannot coexist. Yet our special relationships are riddled with exactly this attempt to co-mingle both Love and fear.

2. Even the smallest irritation fully *excludes* Love in the moment it is believed. And if we are Love without opposite, it must be the complete exclusion in our awareness of our most beloved and Holy Self; which we share with everyone.

3. There are no degrees of hate in the ego's hierarchy of illusions. A mild resentment is the same as outright rage because these are expressions of the absence of Love. Therefore, if Love is total there can be no resentment. We are so heavily conditioned to blindly accept that Love involves fear –as blame, guilt, anger or sacrifice – that we don't even question it.

    1) If the single truth of our being is God as Love without opposite and if this Love that we are is total and completely unopposed then "who" is the one that experiences relationship conflict?

4. Only a false self with a "special" personal mind with a private agenda, can experience conflict with another. The question above must be asked and answered. Eventually every one of us will not only ask it but will gladly undo the belief in a private self that can be deprived and harmed.

5. The central breeding ground for keeping the ego front and center is its obsessive attraction to establishing special relationships. The ego cannot survive without them. The regular supply of guilt it requires to sustain its specialness dynamic in relationships is the ego's life blood. It keeps it cycling through birth, suffering and death for thousands of lifetimes in the dream of separation. The attraction of special relationships is the ego's chief weapon to keep us in amnesia, and to prolong the illusions of sin, guilt, fear, the body, time and death.

   a. *"The special love relationship is the ego's chief weapon for keeping you from Heaven." T-16.V.2:3*

6. We choose our parents and our lessons before we incarnate. All of it is our choice. And no one can betray or abandon us unless we first have betrayed or abandoned our Holy Self.

7. As Jesus tells us: *"This is the only thing that you need do for vision, happiness, release from pain and the complete escape from sin, all to be given you. Say only this, but mean it with no reservations, for here the power of salvation lies:*

I am responsible for what I see.
I choose the feelings I experience, and I decide upon the goal I would achieve.
And everything that seems to happen to me I ask for, and receive as I have asked." T-21.II.2.

8. Remember that the ego's central wish, the one that ensures its continuation of separation, is the wish to be unfairly treated. That way it can project onto others what appears to be concrete evidence of betrayal, abandonment and victimization. It appears as if we have been victimized by others. This ensures that the singular cause as unconscious self-hatred (guilt), if not healed, continues to return to us through our unforgiven projections onto others.

B. Only One of Us Here

1. Did you know that in every one of our relationships we are interacting exclusively with our own projection of self? The real questions then are: "Who" is in relationship with others, is it the ego or the Holy Self? And, "What is the relationship *for?*" "Is it to be right or is it to close the gap (forgive)?" The answer to this second question will reveal just which "self" is in relationship with others. *This may be a good place to return to The Gap Diagrams on pages 46 thru 49.* In the special relationship diagram we can do a quick scan to determine if there are any "idols" in the gap that we still cherish *more than* we desire to close the gap (forgive) with our companion.

2.   If there really is only one of us here as Jesus teaches in the *Course*, and if I think I am triggered by someone outside myself, then what is the singular purpose of being triggered? My hidden wish to be triggered (unfairly treated) keeps me separate from Love, from God, from my Self. I am always triggered by unrecognized or denied *self-attack* which is projected outward. However, there is a powerful gift in being triggered. What is it, and am I willing to receive it?

3.   The person who triggered me is the divine messenger sent to help me finally recognize my self-condemnation and forgive myself so I can be free of suffering. But do we appreciate the enormity of this insight? Do we realize that we've most probably been caught in this dreadful cycle of self-attack for thousands if not millions of years? And do we realize with immense gratitude the gift of liberation we've been given by *everyone* that triggers us? As we forgive our self for having attracted self-attack, Love is returned to our awareness as "What" we are.

4.   No matter what we seem to experience, every interchange is either an outright expression of Love or it's a call *for* Love. All attack is meant to be recognized as a "call for Love." While it appears as attack by another it is always an expression of our own denied self-attack. And that is precisely why the only way it can be undone and healed is via self-forgiveness. We never forgive another. We forgive our self for having *believed* in attack, and therefore, for having unknowingly used another to attack us.

6.   WHY OUR PRIVATE THOUGHTS ARE KILLING US

1.   All triggers are a call for self Love, to see just where we still believe that sin, guilt and fear are real. All unwillingness to answer a call for Love in our brother is our own desire to keep attack and therefore, separation real. Our brother's call for Love *is our own* call for Love. Perceiving attack is a *choice we make* as the fear of God/Love, as union.

2. If we are willing to see a call for Love and answer it through forgiveness we are making the choice for Love and healing both for ourselves and our brother. The recognition of our shared innocence with everyone is the end of the ego. The body then becomes healed because the mind is whole. We accelerate the healing of our split mind through authentic communication via Holy Relationship. When Love is all we want, there is no need to attack.

3. The illusory private mind that takes things personally, must perceive attack via others, the body, the past, and the world. A fundamental and non-negotiable demand of the ego is to maintain a private mind with private thoughts and agendas to preserve the isolated body concept as a special "self." That way it can uphold the separation and keep perfect Love – as the end of specialness – at bay. Here, people are incorrectly classified as having separate minds trapped in bodies that can attack and *be* attacked.

4. Relationships are based on keeping private thoughts while "special love and conditional companionship" are sought, not through sharing undivided honesty, transparency, and innocence, but through the physical joining of bodies.

5. The ego's private mind is terrified of showing up in radical self-honesty, emotional transparency and defenselessness with others. Yet if we don't commit to showing-up, which means practicing these principles, then we cannot communicate authentically with others, let alone with our self.

6. As a private mind with personal agendas that clash with others, we are dishonest with our Holy Self, which amounts to Self-betrayal. What we think, feel, say and do are in conflict. This is the terrible burden we carry when we value a private mind with personal, self-serving agendas. Furthermore, if everything we experience arises from our very own mind, and "it" is in constant conflict, then that chaos must be projected onto and reflected back by others, the body, and the world. And we will feel attacked.

a. "The Holy Spirit cannot teach through fear. And how can He communicate with you, while you believe that to communicate is to make yourself alone? It is clearly insane to believe that by communicating you will be abandoned. And yet many do believe it. For they think their minds must be kept private or they will lose them, but if their bodies are together their minds remain their own. The union of bodies thus becomes the way in which they would keep minds apart. For bodies cannot forgive. They can only do as the mind directs." T-15.VII.11.

7. Our attachment to the body as "self" *is* the primordial gap from which all suffering emerges. *(see The Gap diagrams on pages 46 thru 49)* There could be no gap and therefore, no suffering if we prioritized forgiveness and honest, undefended communication over trusting what the body's five senses appear to report.

8. While the body is mistaken as self, the false concept of attack (sickness, conflict, betrayal, abandonment, loss, etc.) will remain attractive. Indeed, hidden deeply within the unforgiven belief in attack, here is the mistaken self's attraction to death of the body.

9. We betray our Holy Self whenever we *choose to believe* that we have been victimized. Whatever appears to unfold, Jesus tells us that all of it can be classified into one of just two groups. Understanding that *everything* that occurs falls within these two categories ensures that our split mind will heal. Everything is either 1) an expression *of* Love – or – 2) a call *for* Love, help, and healing. There is no in-between!

10. As the *Course* teaches, all attack is always self-attack regardless of where it seems to come from externally. All seeming attack arises only from the ego. Our Holy Self cannot attack. When it appears that we are victimized, that attack was firstly initiated from the unforgiveness in our own mind. Unless forgiven, it is then projected outward using others, sickness, pain, scarcity, etc., to meet the ego's secret wish to be unfairly treated. It requires attack to justify blame and guilt, all to further its mistaken belief that we are separate from our brothers and God.

11. Victim and victimizer will appear to be real. And *false innocence* will be highly valued. This is the ego's idol; its version of corrupted innocence which always depends on making someone else guilty.

12. The belief in victims and perpetrators are classic examples of this profound confusion.

13. False innocence is forever bought at the cost of making *someone else* guilty. Yet the instant we blame another we secretly attack our self. This is literally self-condemnation. It really is impossible to condemn another and not suffer the consequences our self. No wonder the body suffers from pain, illness, aging, and finally death. There is only *one cause of death* regardless of the many illusory excuses which the ego appears to fool us with, and that is the unforgiven guilt sustained by our belief in attack. Guilt always calls for punishment by death.

14. Only *true innocence* is without opposite because it is never exclusive; it is always shared and is therefore, literally incorruptible. However, to be known within, it must be wholly inclusive, valued and extended equally for everyone including our self. This is why remembering that everything we encounter is either a recognized and appreciated "expression of Love," or it's an outright "call *for* Love and healing." There is no in-between. When someone calls for Love, do we answer with forgiveness (Love) or do we answer with blame or defense (attack)? When we answer someone else's call for Love we are also answering our own. We are healed each time we choose to forgive.

15. All appearances of attack from others, the body, the past and the world are never fact. All perception of attack no matter the form or severity only arises exclusively from the ego's misguided "interpretation."

16. The truth is unopposed Love because the one, shared and innocent Holy Mind *cannot* attack. However, the split mind (ego) can make up fantasies of attack and project these onto others and the body so they appear to be the "cause" of attack. While we erroneously believe that these neutral images are the "cause" of attack we will never identify and heal the single *true* cause of all pain in our own mind (via forgiveness).

17. If we interpret attack, betrayal or abandonment in any way other than a call for help and healing, then the ego is applying its very own "interpretation" for the singular purpose of self-attack.

   a. "You cannot perpetuate an illusion about another without perpetuating it about yourself." T-7.VIII.4.1

18. All appearances of attack are always a call for help. If we interpret them in any other way, we literally prefer to keep and maintain our own unconscious self-attack. Everything that triggers us stems from the ego's own hallucination which depends solely on its compulsive obsession with sin, guilt, and fear – attack – as being real. Only a false self with private thoughts who identifies as a body can be triggered! The Holy Self cannot.

19. All the suffering that triggers us is never as it appears; out there in the body, others, the past, and the world. No! Their seeming reality and manifestation exist exclusively within the very lens that we're *choosing* to look through. There are never any victims or victimizers.

20. When the ego is triggered it's always because it desires to see its hidden sins in someone else. That way it attempts to offload its guilt onto them.

   a. "It is impossible to forgive another, for it is only your sins you see in him. You want to see them there, and not in you. That is why forgiveness of another is an illusion. Yet it is the only happy dream in all the world; the only one that does not lead to death. Only in someone else can you forgive yourself, for you have called him guilty of your sins, and in him must your innocence now be found." S-2.I.4:2-6

21. All attack is a call for Love, help, and healing. The extent to which we are triggered by another determines the degree to which it is our own (ego) projection of unconscious self-hatred. Thus, this is *our own* call for help! Think about this. Furthermore, by answering another's call for help through forgiving our self for having *believed* in separation and unknowingly using them to attack us, *we are healed.*

   a. All attack is a call for Love. Consequently, it is always an appeal for help and healing. Jesus asks us then, "Can anyone

be justified in responding with anger to a plea for help?" COA
Annotated edition of A Course in Miracles, T-12.I.3:5

22. When we believe that we've been victimized then the ego has interpreted *incorrectly*. If I am triggered at all – it's always because I have interpreted incorrectly! I then refuse to recognize and forgive my own projection of self-attack. While I choose to value my belief that I am a victim I refuse to recognize and answer my own "call for help and healing," reflected in someone else.

23. Attack is always the ego's interpretation, and never the truth. In truth, we are all one shared Identity (Mind) as the Holy Self. Therefore, when we fail to answer another's "call for help and healing," – we fail to answer our own. They are inextricably entwined.

a. *"If you maintain that an appeal for help is something else, you will react to something else, and your response will be inappropriate to reality as it is, but not to your perception of it."... "If you are unwilling to perceive an appeal for help as what it is, it is because you are unwilling to give help and receive it." COA Annotated edition of A Course in Miracles, T-12.I.4:2,5:4*

b. *"There is nothing to prevent you from recognizing all calls for help as exactly what they are, except your own perceived need to attack." COA Annotated edition of A Course in Miracles, T-12.I.4:4*

c. *"Whenever you fail to recognize a call for help, you are refusing help." ... "...for only by answering his appeal can you be helped." COA Annotated edition of A Course in Miracles, T-12.7:1,3*

24. Our interpretation of attack is always a choice. We simply cannot interpret the motives of others; only the ego engages in this. If we do choose to use the ego's interpretation of attack, then we refuse to accept Reality. While we prefer to perceive attack, we inadvertently *reject* the miracle which heals our own unacknowledged and deeply invested belief that we are fundamentally flawed and, as a consequence, entirely unworthy.

25. This is the fear of Love (God), the destructive byproduct of unforgiven and unconscious guilt. Recall that to the degree we blame our self or others reveals the extent to which we're still valuing unconscious guilt as self-loathing. Without question, everyone who has seemingly hurt us offers us the magnificent and tender gift of self-forgiveness. How willing are we to acknowledge and receive this gift?

26. This is the restoration to our awareness of our own incorruptible innocence. In our forgiveness – accepting the Atonement for our self – the veil of separation and suffering is lifted, so we see and experience Reality through the innocent Eye of the Heart (Holy Self).

27. Recognizing our shared innocence with everyone is the end of the ego's death wish. Only a private mind invested in private thoughts, self-seeking agendas, and a separate body could possibly believe in attack. This is why we cannot afford to trust what the body's five senses report because they are sent forth by the ego to retrieve false evidence of attack to justify separation and death. The body is killed by the ego to try to prove that fear, as separation, is more powerful than all-encompassing, unopposed Love and Life as God.

28. Through our eager embrace of unrelenting forgiveness, our mind is restored to wholeness – fearless Love. The memory of our incorruptible innocence is restored. Knowing our innocence, we also know everyone else's for them. This is the state of invulnerability that Jesus invites us to attain whilst still seemingly in a body. The body becomes a reflection of the healed mind and is then made free from demonstrating attack (sickness, pain, conflict, etc.) because it shares just one divine purpose with God.

   a. *"You believe you can harbor thoughts you would not share, and that salvation lies in keeping thoughts to yourself alone. For in private thoughts, known only to yourself, you think you find a way to keep what you would have alone, and share what [you] would share. And then you wonder why it is that you are not in full communication with those around you, and with God Who surrounds all of you together." T-15.IV.3:3-5*

b. *"Every thought you would keep hidden shuts communication off, because you would have it so. It is impossible to recognize perfect communication while breaking communication holds value to you. Ask yourself honestly, "Would I want to have perfect communication, and am I wholly willing to let everything that interferes with it go forever?" If the answer is no, then the Holy Spirit's readiness to give it to you is not enough to make it yours, for you are not ready to share it with Him. And it cannot come into a mind that has decided to oppose it. For the holy instant is given and received with equal willingness, being the acceptance of the single Will that governs all thought."* T-15.IV.8.

c. *"The necessary condition for the holy instant does not require that you have no thoughts that are not pure. But it does require that you have none that you would keep."* T-15.IV.9:1-2

29. The goal of healing our split mind is vastly accelerated by Holy Relationships. We manifest this goal through the process of relinquishing our special relationships to the Holy Spirit for His purpose, together with our dedicated practice of the *Seven Keys.*

30. Incorruptible innocence is guiltlessness, which in simple terms returns our mind to its natural state of "fearlessness." Without fear, only Love is present, but we cannot recall this joyous state while we still choose to believe in attack.

31. In conclusion, the Holy Spirit's reinterpretation of all seeming attack is that it's always an opportunity to heal the split mind which values and invites attack. Once we acknowledge and accept this, why would we desire to value blame (self-attack) for one minute longer?

a. *"If you did not feel guilty you could not attack, for condemnation is the root of attack. It is the judgment of one mind by another as unworthy of love and deserving of punishment. But herein lies the split. For the mind that judges perceives itself as separate from the mind being judged, believing that by punishing another, it will escape punishment. All this is but the delusional attempt of the mind to deny itself, and escape the penalty of denial. It is not an attempt to relinquish denial, but to hold on to it. For it is guilt that has obscured the Father to you, and it is guilt that has driven you insane." ... "The acceptance of guilt into the mind of God's Son was the beginning of the separation, as the acceptance of the Atonement is its end." T-13.in.1,2:1*

7. COMMON TRIP WIRES IN SPECIAL RELATIONSHIPS

1. We have talked about the fact that the binding agent in all special relationships is not Love at all, but guilt. The hidden attraction to guilt is the belief in sin (as blame, judgment, etc.). To believe in blame is to fear Love. Therefore, the attraction to guilt is the *fear of Love.*

2. In any one moment we are either attracted to Love, or we're attracted to guilt. Remember these two, Love *and* guilt, are opposites and cannot coexist. Yet in our special relationships we attempt to combine both guilt *and* Love... not realizing that if there is guilt or blame, then there is no Love.

3. We can identify guilt and blame by recognizing the signs or results of them. If the love between people appears to decline either temporarily or permanently, if there are spikes of anger and resentment together with conditional expectations, then the source of the bond is guilt, and not Love.

4. Guilt is the belief in and thus our value of fear and attack. Still, it's all too easy to overlook this fact and just bypass it. Because of this, let's look at some of the more common examples of guilt-inducing beliefs, including conditioning, expectations and behaviors which most often go undetected and consequently, uncorrected. These contribute to the eventual breakdown of all special relationships, not just romantic ones.

5. In special relationships, one of the most coveted, unrecognized and unhealed agreements is to keep and protect our private thoughts. In all my years of working with perhaps thousands of people, the one issue which arises repeatedly in relationships, even long-term ones, is the fear of really "showing-up" and being completely "seen."

6. We want to be loved. We even believe we want to be seen, yet we refuse to be seen. We only show others what the ego wants them to see, a mask or an image of our false self, but not our Self. We dare not rip off our façade because we, our self, are not even sure if there is anything of substance beneath the image we portray.

7. In special relationships, those who interact with each other are the separate, self-made images, and not the one, shared Holy Self. Guilt, blame and shame propel the false self's image. To uphold this imposter and its rules for special relationship, real Love must be denied. As a result, we lie to our Self. We abandon and betray our Self in order to avoid being rejected by another's image of him or herself. Yet what we don't see is that we have already abandoned and rejected our Self by being Self-dishonest in the first place. No one can betray us unless we have already betrayed our Holy Self.

8. The false self has tremendous resistance to learning to be self-honest. So how in the world can it be honest with others? Further, it doesn't want others to be honest either, as this would threaten the false image that we uphold. To the ego, the self-image must be protected against radical self-honesty. After all, this is the "face" we use to lure special relationships while it covers and hides the authentic Self within.

9. We either choose specialness *or* we choose to be Self-honest. Specialness is dishonesty because it is always self-deception, which increases guilt. And when we're in conflict within, we will attract conflict with others. Here is what Jesus says about honesty:

a. *"Honesty does not apply only to what you say. The term actually means consistency. There is nothing you say that contradicts what you think or do; no thought opposes any other thought; no act belies your word; and no word lacks agreement with another. Such are the truly honest. At no level are they in conflict with themselves. Therefore it is impossible for them to be in conflict with anyone or anything." ... "No one at one with himself can even conceive of conflict. Conflict is the inevitable result of self-deception, and self-deception is dishonesty." M-4.II.I:4-9,2:3-4*

10. "No one at one with himself can even conceive of conflict." That is a powerful statement! This means that when we perceive conflict it's always because the "private mind" with its own self-seeking agendas, is projecting its own fantasies of attack.

11. Showing-up authentically demands the diligent practice of willingness, accountability, radical self-honesty, emotional transparency, defenselessness, trust and gratitude. These are the *Seven Keys.*

12. When we retain our private thoughts we must inevitably project them onto others, the body and the world as self-attack. Only a private mind with private agendas can experience conflict with another. The same can be said for pain, illness, scarcity and loss.

13. In Holy Relationships two or more people agree to heal the relationship by undoing special relating. By necessity, this involves giving each other full permission to express radical self-honesty without blame. Until we've undone a significant portion of our mistaken beliefs and false self concept, most of us will not have learned to be radically *self*-honest, let alone be this honest with another. The ego is a specialist at compartmentalizing and projecting its own self-dishonesty and self-distrust onto others.

14. In contrast, within special relationships we withhold permission to share our private thoughts with radical honesty because doing so will invariably threaten the specialness; the unspoken agreement to maintain private minds with personal agendas.

15. Shame, blame, anger, resentments, grievances, jealousy, sacrifice (putting our real needs on hold to serve the specialness in a relationship), keeping private thoughts, over-identifying with certain roles such as parent, lover, caregiver, etc., and expecting others to do the same, making the relationship *role* itself an idol to replace the divine essence of the people involved. All these are idolizing form (behavior) over the valuable content (person's mind/heart).

16. Another area of specialness is taking on false responsibility for our loved ones. There is profound confusion in the belief that by being worried or concerned for another we are expressing love and care. And this is because the presence of concern is really *fear* and not Love at all. Love is total. It is only Love if it's *completely free* of fear.

Until then, it is fear masquerading as special love. All fear is total. It is attack. There are no degrees of Love. Nor are there degrees of fear, despite the temptation to perceive it so. The presence of Love is just that. However, if we imbue love with worry or concern then we are in fear, as the opposite of Love.

17. In romantic relationships, there is often a false attachment to the body, namely for what we mistakenly believe the body can give *to* us that God cannot. This distorted view blinds us to the changeless innocence in our companion and in our Self. Valuing the body and pursuing pleasure apart from Spirit is a major idol and block to true Love and union.

18. When we're invested in the body's pleasure-drives then this becomes the ego's idol to blot out the light in us both. When our partner does not satisfy the ego's expectation of pleasure, happiness, or security, etc., it uses this disappointment to justify blame and emotional distancing - the withdrawal of special love. In the special relationship we wrongly assign responsibility to our partner to make us happy. But it's the ego's version of happiness often sought through "pleasure" which Jesus tells us in the following passage, is really our attraction to pain.

    a. *"The body does appear to be the symbol of sin while you believe that it can get you what you want. While you believe that it can give you pleasure, you will also believe that it can bring you pain." T-19.IV.A.17:10-11*

19. There may be an erroneous belief that sex *is* love and consequently, a mistaken *expectation* that this particular pleasure-drive should be consummated, otherwise special love is threatened or withdrawn. This is a common example of attraction to guilt and blame.

20. Self-dishonesty rules where there is a confused belief that the union of bodies represents closeness, or intimacy, yet one or both partners still hold unforgiven grievances against the other. We see how two private minds, each with unforgiven judgments about the other, mistakenly believe that the union of bodies heals rifts and accounts for love, *the ego's love that is.*

21. If this body appetite is unsatisfied by our partner, the expectation will result in disappointment, together with the ego's increasing

resentment for not satisfying the ego's sexual appetite. Blame, withdrawal and conflict will usually result from this prevalent and unhealed confusion. In romantic relationships this dynamic is particularly widespread. Those who place the body on the central altar of their relationships, instead of the Holy Self, do not yet realize that Love can never *be* threatened.

22. This kind of attachment also presupposes a *false sense of ownership and entitlement.* The ego depends on another's body to meet its needs. And bitter resentment can arise when one partner decides to heal and refuses to play the ego's game any longer. The ego's specialness which is mistaken for Love, aka ego-stroking, is withdrawn to allow real joining and Love to be known.

   a. *"The special relationship is totally meaningless without a body. If you value it, you must also value the body. And what you value you will keep. The special relationship is a device for limiting your self to a body, and for limiting your perception of others to theirs. The Great Rays would establish the total lack of value of the special relationship, if they were seen. For in seeing them the body would disappear, because its value would be lost. And so your whole investment in seeing it would be withdrawn from it." T-16.VI.4:1-7*

23. Another habitual and commonly unrecognized source of guilt and blame is having an unquestioned investment in the outcome of certain special occasions such as birthdays, anniversaries, etc. We are especially attached to receiving "special" recognition, usually via gifts symbolizing external acknowledgment of our worth. This is another form of specialness that precipitates the false belief that we can be offended, ignored or rejected, which is just another form of the ego's choice to perceive attack.

24. When we're attached in this way and certain people forget our special occasion, appearing to let us down, we are triggered as the ego feels victimized and defaults to blame. This is its attraction to guilt, its incessant "wish to be unfairly treated" so it can maintain separation – denying Love – by justifying its projections and pseudo victimhood.

---

25. It tries so hard to attract external approval to bolster its flailing and uncertain sense of worth. And when that approval or appreciation is not forthcoming it retaliates by projecting blame, not realizing that all unforgiven blame and guilt that it projects, is always amassed within. All attack is self-attack and this is absolutely incontestable.

26. The false self is obsessed with what it believes conveys its distorted version of love. Expressly, it values special "forms" (gifts, etc.) and "behaviors" (special treatment or rituals) to inform it that it is loved in relationships.

a. *"Whenever any form of special relationship tempts you to seek for love in ritual, remember love is content, and not form of any kind. The special relationship is a ritual of form, aimed at raising the form to take the place of God at the expense of content. There is no meaning in the form, and there will never be."* T-16.V.12:1-3

A. The Need to be Needed

1. A significant part of the ego identity is its hopeless confusion between codependency and love. Special love is codependent love. It is selective, partial and ever changing. It arises from a deep sense of lack and looks for its completion by attempting to trade one false self for another.

2. When we think we need someone it's always the false body-identity which comes from emptiness that tries to extract its self-worth from outside itself, in another. And when they don't provide what the ego wants then it's grounds for pseudo love to end.

3. To need someone is to *use* them. Real Love has no needs. Through the ego we often need to be needed and desired by others. And when they no longer need or desire us then love is withdrawn; and the relationship falls apart.

4. I'd like to share a really helpful two part "self-inquiry" experience that a fellow companion took herself through. I am thankful to her for being so willing to journey through this. You may glean something of value in this. If you do recognize this particular dynamic running in your life, then this may help you to recognize

it. Once this recognition is achieved it can then be given to Spirit for Him to divinely reinterpret this codependent pattern, without self-judgment or guilt.

B. PART ONE - Radical Self Honesty

1. Looking back on my childhood, I was invisible unless "necessary" to my parents. Being needed and relevant *is* life, *is* love.

    1) I recreate this dynamic by finding partners that either literally need me, or desire me (ha! they are the same thing!).

    2) Only when I am with that person do I feel safe, lovable and have a sense of well-being. It is not the person that is the "fix," it is the being needed.

    3) If being needed is threatened, or the relationship is terminated, a major anxiety arises because then I become irrelevant. What is the point of living?

    4) *What is underneath this?* The fear that I will have to address the idea that I am not lovable by going inward, because I have lost the distraction of seeking outside for someone who needs me.

    5) *What is underneath that?* The ego's terror of recognizing that this "need to be needed" was only ever a smokescreen to hide the realization that I Am Holy, and therefore the certain annihilation of the self I think I am – the body-self.

    6) In every special relationship, we know (deep down) that it is not Love but the substitute for the Love of God. Yet we act as if we don't know this. We continually choose the dynamic of superficial, conditional or empty love and use our theme (the need to be needed) as justification for this choice. Yet we cannot avoid the natural and inevitable effect of this choice ... which is the guilt it feeds us as we constantly turn away from what we know intuitively that we already are. The cost of this constant feed of guilt is certain death.

7) We are extremely resistant to looking at our special relationships because, to be radically honest, it then brings the necessary counter-part, *accountability*. Once we admit what we are doing, we cannot push it down and away, or justify what we are doing any longer. Bringing specialness and all its ugliness to the light is terrifying to the ego, and brings us to the second part of the healing process.

C. PART TWO - Accountability

1. For those of us who have done part one, we may have tried to break through the pattern on our own (spiritual ego) and have felt the agony of the ego backlash at this attempt. I felt like I was cooking alive with no end in sight. The answer was always to return to the special relationship for familiar relief.

2. I am very aware of the cost of specialness. I know that I cannot keep it and awaken/survive. I know that I cannot, of myself, get out of this dynamic. I have hit my knees, confessed what I do, what I use it for, seen it as attack against both myself and my brother, and have asked with all my heart to have Holy Spirit take me through the eye of the needle.

3. To stay in the relationship and use it to "be needed," to be special, brings guilt. The attempt to extricate myself and then to fail once again brings even more guilt. I am willing to show-up in the relationship, using the *Seven Keys* and communicate in order to not use the relationship to be needed; to be special. I will show-up and be radically honest in order to repurpose what I use the relationship for.

4. I recognize and surrender to the fact that the outcome of the relationship is under the governance of Holy Spirit who knows how to use it for God's Will. I surrender to not knowing how it will be, and whether the form of the relationship remains or not. I trust that no matter what, the strength, comfort and assurance that I need will not come from the spiritual ego, but from the Mind of God, and that I can and must trust this.

5. **The goal:** When we know that we are Love, whether or not bodies come and go, whether conditions and circumstances come or go, we are anchored by the Knowledge of what we are as truth and Love, and nothing will move us. A mind at peace, safe, Loved and at Home in God.

a. **A Helpful Prayer:** *"Holy Spirit, I cannot stay in special relationships any longer. I see the cost clearly and will no longer attack myself or my brother. I do not know how to get out of the relationship or how to stay out of it. I need you to help me repurpose it and use it for God's will. I relinquish all thoughts of how this will be done or how the form will look. Because of my willingness, I can trust You to do this for and through me. I surrender all to you and give thanks that nothing real can be lost. God's will is done. And so it is. Amen."*

8. STRIPPED NAKED – THE REAL REASON WE CONSENT TO SUFFER

1. All of what we react to emotionally, all that pulls frantically at our heart-strings and makes us cry out in pain either for our self or for someone else, is not at all what it seems. What I am about to share here is complete blasphemy to the ego. Yet this is not *my* interpretation of the *Course*, but Jesus' teaching.

2. It's taken thirty years in the illusion of time for me to attain this level of learning for myself. It was always there in the *Course,* but my own fear-filter had obscured the profound and very practical ramifications of its meaning. And now, as I look at it not just intellectually this time, I can never again *un-see* the inevitable and massive cost of forgetting what has been revealed. Thank God.

3. Projection *makes* perception. What? Everything I appear to see, including every person and the seeming state of their body, and mine, nature, pets, the world, and the past, all arise from one particular and laser like intention *in my own mind*. This localized focus is unrelenting. It cannot see anyone or anything in any other way. The false-self's identity depends wholly on its programmed projections to witness all manner of signs of separation, pain and death.

4. This is what the body was invented *for*. Its five senses, its imagined past and its appetites are programmed to see what seems to be irrefutable evidence that we are guilty and alone, that we can be abandoned or betrayed, and that we are vulnerable to external influences including the body, and finally, that we will die.

5. But here is where we need to boldly *strip naked* what the world is terrified to see. This is where we get to look upon that secret agreement we made, the one we keep blindly choosing each time we perceive injustice of any kind.

6. The false-self's livelihood is contingent upon a permanent source of guilt. We *want* the suffering because it provides the false-self with the guilt it requires in order for us to never awaken from this dream!

7. Without this guilt the ego, together with its separated world, falls away. It must project its own unfounded belief in sin, guilt and fear. And it must use the body's senses to witness its fearful projections. The people and scenes it sees are self-chosen hallucinations as opposites of God's Reality. Whilst left unquestioned and unforgiven, they serve to intensify our "fear of God" as unconscious attraction to self-punishment via the ego's cycle of sin, guilt and fear.

8. If left undisputed and unforgiven, these "assumed as real" experiences impose a convincing block which is designed to completely obscure our awareness of the beauty of the ever- present Real World where *real healing* has already been given. This is why one of the most fundamental teachings in the *Course* is to learn to look past "appearances." This is a crucial step in forgiveness.

9. Appearances of adversity can only be desired (and consequently witnessed) through the ego's fear-filter. To believe in something either painful or pleasurable, we must first *desire it*. Everything we believe arises from our desire for it. And this primordial and unconscious desire for adversity begins with the ego's addiction to sin. It cannot survive without it. Belief in sin makes guilt and fear. Nothing but our investment in sin can produce guilt and fear.

10. We first unconsciously desire guilt, then we believe in and thus see its effects, all the fearful appearances in the body, others and

the world. And once we're lost in fear then it will be *fear itself* that attempts to *remedy* the disease or problem.

11. The one that desires, believes in, and then sees and reacts to pain, and the one trying to fix it, are the same. Only this self can believe in pain. By belief *in* it, and defense *against* it, it values and attracts it. This self absolutely must *desire* to see pain to keep its pseudo self-concept intact. All the while this unchecked fear is pursuing *more* guilt for us. It thrives on witnessing evidence of its guilt in sickness, conflict, pain, lack and death, all to ensure its reality and authority over God's.

a. *"This is in accord with perception's fundamental law: You see what you believe is there, and you believe it there because you want it there. Perception has no other law than this."* T-25.III.1:3-4

12. Our Holy Self does not waste even an instant in looking at the *illusion* of devastation. Being acutely present as Love in the Holy Instant, it knows God's Answer of healing is here, now. And because it has conviction in *only this*, its certainty *replaces* the ego's destructive hallucination. It never looks upon adversity as real and then attempts to heal it. It knows there is no threat in God's Love. It therefore looks clear past the problem, from the outset.

a. *"Forgiveness that is learned of me does not use fear to undo fear. Nor does it make real the unreal and then destroy it. Forgiveness through the Holy Spirit lies simply in looking beyond error from the beginning, and thus keeping it unreal for you. Do not let any belief in its realness enter your mind, or you will also believe that you must undo what you have made in order to be forgiven. What has no effect does not exist, and to the Holy Spirit the effects of error are nonexistent. By steadily and consistently cancelling out all its effects, everywhere and in all respects, He teaches that the ego does not exist and proves it."* T-9.IV.5.

13. When we try to heal our self or another through fear (ego), we use fear to undo fear, which is impossible. In this, we *do* make the problem or illness real first. And once it's made real we then attempt

to destroy (or heal) it. Do not trust the body's senses as they are *programmed by fear* to look upon what fear made.

A. A Frightening Emergency or a Miracle?

1. Let me share an example of my own experience of being triggered by the initial insanity of stark terror, to turning my perception over to Holy Spirit. This frightening emergency could have manifested into something quite disastrous – but something extraordinary revealed itself because I purposely intercepted the ego's hidden desire for pain.

2. Many years ago, my partner was rushed to the hospital in an ambulance. He had blacked out and the medics suspected a heart attack. I received a tearful call from my daughter, explaining what had happened, saying that he still had not regained consciousness. This call came just as I had dropped a friend off at the airport which was around a forty-five minute drive away from the hospital.

3. To the false-self this was an absolute nightmare. I remember those first few moments after the frantic call. Forty-five minutes is a lifetime! Would I reach him in time? Was the hug we shared earlier that day the last hug we would ever have? Will the medics know what to do? What if he dies? And on and on.

4. The automatic and compulsive reaction to seeing someone in pain or sick, especially with a loved one, is a knee-jerk reaction to *do* something at the behavioral/form level. Yet any action we take that *stems from fear* may appear to be helpful at the form level, however, the unforgiven source of its "intent" is guilt. This fear or concern is therefore an attack. Fear is never justified because to believe it is to renounce God and our unified Holy Self with our brothers.

5. When in fear we must learn to make one fundamental distinction: *Fear is always an attack on our Self.* It comes from the erroneous assumption that we're estranged from God's Love – guilty – and as a result, deserving of pain. This is the insane, yet singular belief that underlies every stab of fear, regardless of the form it takes.

6. Therefore, we choose to join with Spirit and sincerely desire to accept that His Will for us *is* uninterrupted Love, happiness and healing. In this Holy Instant we close the ego's gap of fear and accept a miracle instead. This is God's Will. This is accepting the Atonement. We must accept and receive the Atonement first so that we can extend it. Accepting Atonement (forgiveness of what we seem to perceive), undoes the block to healing the guilt/fear. Now, our mind is free of fear and we can join with another's mind and help heal them. The forgiveness process can be found in *The Seven Essential Principles of Quantum Forgiveness (Atonement)* on page 591.

7. Any attempt to heal stemming from *fear,* will block healing the single *cause* of the particular issue, which is always guilt caused by the belief that there is gap between us and God and our brothers.

8. All attempts to heal or problem solve through fear *impede* healing. *Please do not go into self-judgment if this is your experience.* Remember that it's the ego that does this and not *You* as the Holy Self. The illusory ego, together with all its mistakes, does not exist. Only *You* as the sinless, eternally innocent Child of God, are real. The Atonement as forgiveness undoes your false belief in the unreal ego and heals its equally illusory consequences.

B. The Miracle

1. Let's get back to my initial terror when I received the call telling me about my partner's emergency. And let's really look at this scenario and how I joined with Jesus to undo (forgive) my initial reaction to it. At first I was upset to have been so far away when I received the call. But there is always a miracle behind every appearance of fear. I just had to desire and expect the miracle *more* than I wanted (believed) the fear.

2. I knew that my initial spike of fear and panic was an immediate sign that I had abandoned my Self. And I also recognized that I could not abandon my Self to fear without also abandoning my partner. This really hit home. As a result, I resolved with Jesus to join with Him to shift my whole perception from fear, to Love.

3. I had a long drive to get to the hospital. The very first miracle that I opened to was the recognition that I really needed this time in which to vertically align with my Self. I had a tiny moment of gratitude for this. This little spark of gratitude was enough to bring

the light in which I invited Christ Vision to blaze away the darkness of fear. Fear cannot abide in gratitude for these two are mutually exclusive. This is why in order to heal, our desire to feel gratitude must replace the ego's desire to experience resentment, conflict or pain. Gratitude *is* Love and the miracle appears with it.

4. What came up next for me involved *looking* at my very worst fear that he would die. This is the *ego's fear* and whatever it fears it secretly *attracts.* So, I knew I had to give this one immediately to Spirit to be forgiven. I remembered to enter the Holy Instant and to join with Jesus and my partner there. Here, I accepted Holy Spirit's evaluation of my Self as eternally innocent, safe and forever protected. Once I touched this feeling in my heart, I was able to bring my partner there too. A palpable peace flooded through me and I felt that peace extend to Lee. That was enough. In fact, that instant of peace was *everything.* I didn't need to worry or do anything more. Everything was forgiven in that joining. The Holy Instant does everything!

5. When I arrived at the hospital, time itself had collapsed. Only thirty minutes had gone by and it wasn't from me speeding! I was quickly ushered in only to see my partner laying there unconscious, hooked up to all manner of contraptions. Once again I entered a Holy Instant and asked to see only the miracle behind this upsetting appearance.

6. As soon as the nurse stepped out I was strongly guided to take his lifeless hand in mine and then to do something utterly outrageous. I leaned over his head, with my mouth to his ear, and with what seemed like all the Loving power of God, I roared at him, *"Lee, what are you doing?! Where are you?! In God's Name, I command you to come back!"*

7. I commanded him to come back! Well, that did it. He returned immediately with all the contraptions pinging accordingly. He tried to open his eyes but it took a while for his body's faculties to come back fully.

8. In the meantime, the doctor and nurse came in and were stunned by what they saw. The doctor explained to me that Lee had all the signs of a heart attack and that they would need to test him for heart

damage. I stayed with Lee all night in between tests. I recall his doctor walking into the room just before dawn. He was astounded. The test results showed zero heart damage!

9. Earlier that night as Lee returned to full awareness, he shared with me his own experience of what had happened when I intercepted the ego's call to death. He said that he was traveling nowhere… it was darkness. Yet he felt powerless over where he was being taken. He just went with it, not realizing his dominion over this ego phenomenon.

10. He said that in that deep unconscious state, he heard my booming voice pierce the darkness. He heard my call for him to return. It woke him and called him back from the ego's seductive lure toward death. He even remembered and repeated word for word exactly what I had roared in his left ear. The miracle brought him back. But it was my firm conviction not to drown in the *appearance* of fear and death that invoked the miracle. For if I had joined him and others in that fear…I would have abandoned him and my Self. I had to consciously replace the ego's desire for guilt and fear with my desire for the Atonement, the Holy Instant, and the miracle. This is God's Will.

a. *"I have already said that miracles are expressions of miracle-mindedness, and miracle-mindedness means right-mindedness. The right-minded neither exalt nor depreciate the mind of the miracle worker or the miracle receiver. However, as a correction, the miracle need not await the right-mindedness of the receiver. In fact, its purpose is to restore him [to] his right mind. It is essential, however, that the miracle worker be in his right mind, however briefly, or he will be unable to re-establish right-mindedness in someone else." T-2.V.3.*

11. This was such a staggering miracle. But it happened specifically because I had released the ego's desire for fear and devastation (guilt). It could not have occurred had I been in fear. If I had false compassion (sympathy) then I would have *colluded* with Lee's wrong-minded wish to die, thus strengthening suffering and death for both of us. Through the Atonement, awareness of my incorruptible innocence was restored. This *is* my Holiness. Thus, in that lucid

peace, my mind was made free of fear, and this was all it took to bring him back.

a. *"Your holiness (innocence) reverses all the laws of the world. It is beyond every restriction of time, space, distance and limits of any kind. Your holiness is totally unlimited in its power because it establishes you as a Son of God, at one with the Mind of his Creator." ... "Through your holiness the power of God is made manifest. Through your holiness the power of God is made available. And there is nothing the power of God cannot do. Your holiness, then, can remove all pain, can end all sorrow, and can solve all problems. It can do so in connection with yourself and with anyone else. It is equal in its power to help anyone because it is equal in its power to save anyone." W-38.1,2.*

C. Neutralizing the Ego's Hard Drive

1. Projection makes perception. Every single appearance of separation that we believe in – as pain, disease, conflict, guilt, unworthiness, lack and death – comes directly from our *desire for it.* We want it. We could not see any of it except for our desire for "reality" to mirror back to us what the ego is hungry to retrieve. Through the ego, we put the illusion there by secretly wanting it there. What we fear and refuse to forgive, we do attract. We always find exactly what the ego sends its messengers to seek. And while this remains denied and unforgiven within, we will mistakenly believe that the body and world are being done *to* us and not *by* us.

2. All adversity and even all pleasure-seeking apart from God, are one and the same because they serve an identical purpose. And that is to establish that we are the illusory body and not the indestructible Child of God. That way, instead of forgiving our projections, we project our guilt and fear so as we can amass it. We always find what we seek. When we think that we are projecting what we do not want (betrayal, illness, pain, conflict, loss, etc.), it is still because the ego *wants* it.

a. *"I said before that what you project or extend is up to you, but you must do one or the other, for that is a law of mind, and you must look in before you look out. As you look in, you choose the guide for seeing. And then you look out and behold his witnesses. This is why you find what you seek. What you want in yourself you will make manifest, and you will accept it from the world because you put it there by wanting it. When you think you are projecting what you do not want, it is still because you [do] want it. This leads directly to dissociation, for it represents the acceptance of two goals, each perceived in a different place; separated from each other because you made them different. The mind then sees a divided world outside itself, but not within. This gives it an illusion of integrity, and enables it to believe that it is pursuing one goal. Yet as long as you perceive the world as split, you are not healed. For to be healed is to pursue one goal, because you have accepted only one and want but one." T-12.VII.7.*

D. Unmasking the Ego's Operating System

1. We see and then react to the effects of fear (pain, illness, conflict, etc.) only because we *desire* them. Without this unconscious desire, we would see clear past all appearances of pain and join exclusively with God's Truth, the miracle, behind it.

2. The following outlines how our disordered thought believes in and then sees any adversity here in the dream.

   1) **We have faith in it** – sin, guilt and fear

   2) **We desire it** – by wanting to *keep the guilt* that always hides beneath fear

   3) **We value it** – by projecting guilt and blaming we hoard it for our self, wanting to see it in others, the body and the world instead of in our mind where we can forgive it

   4) **We defend it** – by *not forgiving* our self for its painful projections

a. *"When you are afraid of anything, you are acknowledging its power to hurt you. Remember that where your heart is, there is your treasure also. You believe in what you value. If you are afraid, you are valuing wrongly." T-2.II.1:1-7*

b. *"Do not seek vision through your eyes, for you made your way of seeing that you might see in darkness, and in this you are deceived. Beyond this darkness, and yet still within you, is the vision of Christ, Who looks on all in light. Your "vision" comes from fear, as His from love. And He sees for you, as your witness to the real world. He is the Holy Spirit's manifestation, looking always on the real world, and calling forth its witnesses and drawing them to you." T-13.V.9:1-5*

E. Neutralizing the Ego's Hardwire for Pain

1. We always look inward first to what we secretly desire before we can possibly experience it as projected manifestations in the body, onto others or the world. When we react to conflict or pain it's because the false-self wants to keep the guilt so it can prove it is separate from God and our brothers. Thankfully, through forgiveness and the Holy Instant we can completely reverse this.

2. The following four steps represent the reversal of our unconscious desire for pain. When we decide with Holy Spirit to want to see only the Love that is in us and all around us, this is what we do:

1) **We have faith in it** – sinlessness, guiltlessness and Love

2) **We desire it** – by wanting to *keep our incorruptible innocence* which always shines behind all appearances of conflict and pain. The only way we can keep this innocence (immunity to attack) is to give it away to others; to see it in others

3) **We value it** – by forgiving all appearances of conflict and pain. By being *grateful* for our forgiveness opportunities

4) **We defend it** – by declaring that only Love and innocence are real regardless of the ego's appearances to the contrary.

a. "My holiness (innocence) envelops everything I see. From my holiness (innocence) does the perception of the real world come. Having forgiven, I no longer see myself as guilty. I can accept the innocence that is the truth about me. Seen through understanding eyes, the holiness of the world is all I see, for I can picture only the thoughts I hold about myself." W-58.1.(36)

3. Neutralizing the ego's hardwire to seek out pain demands that we heal the split-mind by pursuing just *one goal* for every encounter we have. Through applying forgiveness to each and every trigger, we consistently undo the ego's lust for separation. In our wholehearted devotion to this, we lift the ego's veil of terror to reveal incontestable evidence of our fathomless innocence and the Love that dwells within it.

4. Sickness, pain, conflict, scarcity, war, loss and physical death make up the illusory "gap" of separation. They are not real. They arise from the split mind's faith and desire *for* them to prove we are separate from God and our brothers. Our desire to be separate bodies with private minds was to prove that fear and its consequences have overthrown God's Love.

5. The morning that I began to write this particular essay, I heard what appeared to be a kind of prayer. I would say it's more like a helpful reminder especially, when we're tempted to fall into fear when decoyed by pain or sickness in another or our self:

6. *"Your pain is my wish to see sin and the proof of punishment that sin demands. If I believe that you or I are suffering, I am seeing both of us as separate bodies and not as the invulnerable Holy Self. This self-chosen perception is the ego's desire for guilt and punishment. To the degree I am unwilling to forgive my false perceptions, you stand condemned along with me. In my desire to see and accept only our mutual sinlessness instead of bodies, you are healed along with me."*

7. The Holy Relationship is the mutual agreement to join in one truly common purpose where two or more people recognize that their genuine needs are not separate. They see each other's needs as their own. Because these companions join in purpose to forgive the ego's projection of sin in each other, their relationship becomes a temple

of healing *"Your relationship is now a temple of healing; a place where all the weary ones can come and rest. Here is the rest that waits for all, after the journey. And it is brought nearer to all by your relationship."* T-19.III.11:3-4

8.   Astounding healing takes place when two or more join to align and relate through these four steps using the *Seven Keys*.

9.   The reason for this high level of healing is because two people have agreed to look upon the separation's idols in the ego's "gap" and to renounce their reality together. They both agree to *de-witness* or *un-see* separation by accepting the Atonement for themselves. This is how they collapse the gap of suffering. *Note: Refer to The Gap diagrams on pages 46 thru 49.*

   a.   *"For no one alone can judge the ego truly. Yet when two or more join together in searching for truth, the ego can no longer defend its lack of content. The fact of union tells them it is not true."* T-14.X.9:5-7

F. The Past and Fear are Not Here Now

1.   Did you know that fear and the past are both illusions? Do you recognize that the false-self – the body concept – is the singular source of fear *and* of the past?

2.   The false-self concept *is* the past. The past and the false-self concept are *one*. The illusory "past" is used exclusively by the ego to elicit fear. It believes you sinned, so it wants you to carry that past fear and guilt with its anticipation of future punishment and superimpose it over every new unfolding moment. This is why we never see people as they really are *now*. We see them through the ego's darkened past.

3.   If we stopped mentally dragging our past with us to mask and escape our Holiness, our universal innocence in the present moment, we could never experience fear. All fear is past. When we are fearful we are not here, now, where the miracle always awaits our welcome. Fear cannot survive in the Holy Instant.

4.   Nothing in the past is now. All fear is past because its source as the *illusion of sin*, is gone. It was gone in the instant we dreamed

it up. But to accept and receive this miracle, we must be willing to show-up *here and now* without the defense of fear.

5. Only You as the Holy Self, who looks upon your Self, your brothers, sisters, and the world in the glorious light of innocence and peace, is here now, eternally. Nothing else exists. The miracle is an ever-present gift available to us when we catch our mind in fear or the past.

   a. *"All fear is past and only love is here. All fear is past, because its source is gone, and all its thoughts gone with it. Love remains the only present state, whose Source is here forever and forever. Can the world seem bright and clear and safe and welcoming, with all my past mistakes oppressing it, and showing me distorted forms of fear? Yet in the present love is obvious, and its effects apparent. All the world shines in reflection of its holy light, and I perceive a world forgiven at last."* W-293.1.

6. When we fear in any situation it's always because we are looking through a darkened veil of the ego's past which it casts over the future to obliterate the brilliant joy of the ever-present Holy Instant. The ego's past is used to block present peace so it can only perpetuate guilt and fear into the future. When we enter the Holy Instant the ego's past is neutralized in awareness. Because its past is rendered powerless and therefore cannot be projected into the future – time and suffering collapse. This is the power of the Holy Instant.

7. When we don't see the awe-inspiring beauty and innocence of the immediate Real World it is because in choosing to trust the ego, the past and the body's five senses, we *want* suffering. Fear, it seems, is our friend. It's so familiar! And forgiveness as Love is an outright threat. We hate that terrible sense of self-loathing and the continuing confusion of self-doubt. But we still want to keep judging our self, others and the world, independently from Holy Spirit. To lose our privilege to judge and condemn would mean to renounce our independent "self" along with its will to suffer.

   a. *"All seeing starts with the perceiver, who judges what is true and what is false. And what he judges false (real world) he does not see. You who would judge reality cannot see it, for whenever judgment enters reality has slipped away."* T-13. VII.5:3-5

8. If you seem to be contending with disease, scarcity, relationship conflict or death, then it would be enormously helpful to find where you still store grievances from the past, and to forgive them wholeheartedly. Is there anyone past or present who offered you this massive "gift," disguised as a chance to forgive, whom you do not have gratitude for in this *now moment?* If so, then this is a sign that you still *want* the past and fear, together with the certain guilt (pain) they bring. Note: The forgiveness process can be found in *The Seven Essential Principles of Quantum Forgiveness (Atonement)* on page 591.

    a. *"The Holy Spirit would undo all of this [now.] Fear is not of the present, but only of the past and future, which do not exist. There is no fear in the present when each instant stands clear and separated from the past, without its shadow reaching out into the future. Each instant is a clean, untarnished birth, in which the Son of God emerges from the past into the present. And the present extends forever. It is so beautiful and so clean and free of guilt that nothing but happiness is there. No darkness is remembered, and immortality and joy are now."*

    ... *"Take this very instant, now, and think of it as all there is of time. Nothing can reach you here out of the past, and it is here that you are completely absolved, completely free and wholly without condemnation. From this holy instant wherein holiness was born again you will go forth in time without fear, and with no sense of change with time."* T-15.I.8:1-7,8:5-7

9. THE COST OF COMPROMISING IN RELATIONSHIPS

1. When it comes to the subject of Love, the value we have placed on the idea of sacrifice may be one of the most difficult to release. This special brand of "love" we have come to value within the ego dream is firmly fixed upon the mistaken conclusion that sacrifice *is* love. And that love *is* sacrifice. This harmful concept is so deeply embedded it has become a default for most of us.

2. The idea of both love *and* sacrifice existing together as one and the same has us completely confused. They seem to go hand in hand and we rarely, if ever, question it. To the degree we still believe these two opposing qualities are intertwined is the extent to which we must also believe *unconsciously* that Love is pain, God is fear and that true union equals loss.

3. Our deeply coveted belief in sacrifice arises largely from a fundamental misinterpretation of the nature and Will of God. God is undivided, infinite, uninterrupted Love and joy. And yet throughout time the ego has projected and idolized its deluded version of "god" as a dualistic god of both reward *and* punishment, of life *and* death, of health *and* sickness, of joy *and* pain, of abundance *and* scarcity.

4. When we erroneously believe that Love demands sacrifice, we will resort to being manipulative in our relationships. This often unconscious habit can appear quite subtle, however there are no *degrees* of attack. Remember that all attack is self-attack. We cannot sacrifice for another and not suffer our self. Neither can we sacrifice our self and not demand it of another.

5. Passive aggressive behavior is a common symptom of valuing sacrifice. To the extent we compromise and sacrifice for others is the same degree we will believe they "owe" us, and we will demand payment. But we can never demand payment from another without first asking it of our self. The payment we demand thus sacrifices our own (and our brother's) innocence, which if uncovered, would stop the sacrifice/payment cycle.

6. Special love is a scheme of relating which devalues our Self and others. As Jesus tells us, special love is really hate in disguise. It is not just a block to Love but the complete *opposite* of Love. And "this" is the type of love (attack) we have come to idolize in the world since the beginning of time itself. This is also the reason why special love seems to change or end. The truth, of course, is that real Love is changeless and if "love" seems to change or end it was not Love but specialness.

a. *"Your confusion of sacrifice and love is so profound that you cannot conceive of love without sacrifice. And it is this that you must look upon; **sacrifice is attack, not love.** If you would accept but this one idea, your fear of love would vanish. Guilt cannot last when the idea of sacrifice has been removed." T-15.X.5:8-11*

7. In my own experience with hundreds of others on this spiritual path, the idea of "sacrifice" seems to be such a gray area. For many there is the belief that some sacrifice is good while other forms of sacrifice are bad. Therefore, I'd like to clarify to lessen confusion.

A. What is Sacrifice in the Special Relationship?

1. We agree to compromise our Self (sacrifice) to get something of "greater" value. The issue here is it's the false self, attempting to find ways to buy, take or trade, in exchange for what it unconsciously deems as worthless (our self). Although this is kept hidden, we agree to relationships for the purpose of *mutual use* and not as a means to extend conscious Love.

2. Sacrifice involves the belief in deprivation and loss, together with all the feelings associated with it. This is the opposite of real Love. Let me also expound with a few descriptive words or terms that may help to call up some of our feelings associated with sacrifice: Relinquish, give up, forfeit, lose, the cost we incur, suffer, tolerate, put up with, concede, hang tough, compromise our self, inevitable, suck it up, etc. Other terms which are often construed as "positive" attributes can remain even more hidden from recognition as sacrifice. These include worry, concern, sympathetic collusion or any fearful belief that lack, suffering and victimization are real. All the above examples are sacrificing the awareness of our own Holy Self and its inner guidance, knowing and authenticity, thus betraying our Self in favor of attracting the *illusion* of exclusive love.

3. These are just a few terms to describe what we really believe love involves – the toll it takes. We falsely assume that love *costs* us plenty. And if this is an underlying belief then, in all honesty, we have no idea what real Love *is*. We have merely taken its opposite and dressed it in seductive clothing.

4. In relationships a telltale symptom of specialness is when we secretly keep tabs on what we've sacrificed, done or given, and we then *expect* others to repay us in kind. A warped sense of entitlement gives rise to immediate and "justified" resentment if our gift is not recognized or returned. In other words, when we give for specialness, we give to *get* something, which is simply a disguised form of taking. And for this we always end up paying the price.

5. Until we have begun to exhume and reverse our unconscious fear of Love (God) we will continue to believe the greatest of all ego lies - that *God demands* sacrifice. This is the craziest of all ego beliefs and yet it sits rigidly as the centerpiece of the ego's altar and feeds our destructive beliefs and patterns concerning the "nature" of special love. God does not know of either sacrifice or special love. These two, although seemingly different in their forms, are indicative of their one shared purpose – to mistake fear, guilt, pain and loss, for Love.

6. There is no sacrifice in true giving. There is no sacrifice in God's Love. Jesus tells us that when we mistakenly agree to compromise our Self, we also ask it of Him:

   a. "I am as incapable of receiving sacrifice as God is, and every sacrifice you ask of yourself you ask of me. Learn now that sacrifice of any kind is nothing but a limitation imposed on giving. And by this limitation you have limited acceptance of the gift I offer you." T-15.X.2:5-7

7. NOTE: Please refer to *"The Fear of God"* exercise in *The End of Death Volume One:* https://nouksanchez.com/wp-content/uploads/2020/06/2-Are-you-fearful-of-God.pdf

In addition, here is another excerpt from Volume One - *Suffering is Not God's Will:* https://nouksanchez.com/nouks-blog/suffering-is-not-gods-will/

8. While we believe that God's Will involves painful lessons or loss, sacrifice, fear, punishment or suffering, we will be afraid of Love. And we will deny God, Love, and our Holy Self. Therefore, we will not know how to give or receive Love because our awareness of it is blocked by fear.

9. We are so deeply afraid of God's Love because through the ego's irrational belief that love *demands* sacrifice – we wrongly conclude that His Love will demand *total* sacrifice of us. Thus we perceive that it will torture and annihilate us completely. We then settle for the ego's version of "special love" because we believe this to be a substantially "lesser" sacrifice. Here are two staggering statements from Jesus which describe this profound confusion:

a. *"How fearful, then, has God become to you, and how great a sacrifice do you believe His Love demands! For total love would demand total sacrifice. And so the ego seems to demand less of you than God,..."* T-15.X.7:3

b. *"You think that everyone outside yourself demands your sacrifice, but you do not see that only you demand sacrifice, and only of yourself. Yet the demand of sacrifice is so savage and so fearful that you cannot accept it where it is. The real price of not accepting this has been so great that you have given God away rather than look at it. For if God would demand total sacrifice of you, it seems safer to project Him outward and away from you, and not be host to Him. To Him you ascribed the ego's treachery, inviting it to take His place to protect you from Him. And you do not recognize that it is what you invited in that would destroy you, and does demand total sacrifice of you. No partial sacrifice will appease this savage guest, for it is an invader who but seems to offer kindness, but always to make the sacrifice complete."* T-15.X.8.

B. Falling in Love

1. The ego's special love relationship, a glorified form of sacrifice, is most often showcased in the romantic relationship where we seem to "fall in love." Again, the false self seeks a relationship in

which it believes it can complete itself. And it's the body and not the Spirit that is offered as a sacrificial exchange on the ego's altar. In this exchange, which is really the ego trading the self it hates for what it deems to be a better self, there is much guilt.

2. The problem is that we love the other for what we can steal from them, which is always more "specialness." There is massive cost to this trade because of the hidden guilt that lurks in shame, believing that in our littleness we have tried to take from another that which we believe we lack.

3. This deeply concealed guilt is then projected onto the one we seem to love. It then manifests accordingly as relationship conflict, betrayal or abandonment. Yet very few indeed recognize that relationship conflict is always a byproduct of guilt, as self-attack.

   a. *"Most curious of all is the concept of the self which the ego fosters in the special relationship. This "self" seeks the relationship to make itself complete. Yet when it finds the special relationship in which it thinks it can accomplish this it gives itself away, and tries to "trade" itself for the self of another." … "Each partner tries to sacrifice the self he does not want for one he thinks he would prefer. And he feels guilty for the "sin" of taking, and of giving nothing of value in return." T-16.V.7: 1-3,5-6*

   b. *"The "better" self the ego seeks is always one that is more special. And whoever seems to possess a special self is "loved" for what can be taken from him." … "The demand for specialness, and the perception of the giving of specialness as an act of love, would make love hateful." T-16.V.8:1-2,9:3*

4. Sacrifice equals deprivation and all deprivation breeds attack, which increases guilt. And while we feel the need to sacrifice in any way, we will feel justified in sacrificing others. This is an integral theme in all special relationships.

5. It may help to share from my personal experience here. Many years ago when I had first begun the *Course*, I was in a dysfunctional special relationship with Tomas before that relationship was made Holy. My initial study of the *Course* and its lessons really urged

me to take a radically honest look at this idea of sacrifice. And I remember being horrified at seeing just how much of my life, my body and my relationships I had devoted to the idea of sacrifice. It was my "god."

6. To the degree I sacrificed seemed to be the extent to which I felt I was "earning" my worth, while decreasing my expectation of punishment. In other words, if I wasn't sacrificing I felt worthless. It's as if sacrifice was the way to reward. And here is the crazy part that exemplifies the inner split. While sacrificing seemed to give me "worth," I simultaneously felt resentful and imprisoned by it.

7. The ugly outcome was that I would project that inner conflict onto my partner in angry outbursts of resentment, and then feel guilty about it later. This was an ongoing cycle of destruction. Looking back, I see how this unforgiven guilt had also been projected onto my body as debilitating pain and illness. It took me many more years to finally forgive myself for having used the perfectly neutral body as a haven for attack and pain.

8. Happily, the Holy Spirit answered my prayer and gave me the courage to break my destructive attraction to sacrifice. This meant that I had to show-up authentically for the first time in my highly "special" relationship with Tomas.

9. I made an honest list of all the things that called me to sacrifice in our relationship. And I finally saw the ridiculous contradiction! Like most people, I had mistakenly believed that these sacrifices were a *demonstration* of my love for my partner and family. How wrong I was!

10. In order to "love and be loved" I had agreed to desert my Self and do things that were not at all in alignment with my inner knowing, my authentic Self. For a brief moment I saw the depth of this sinister attraction. If "love" demands sacrifice, then just how much does *God* want to take from me!? How much is He asking of me? How much suffering must I endure to fulfill His quota of mandatory sacrifice to prove my love for Him?

11. I decided to make a few practical adjustments in those early days when our relationship began to shift from special to Holy. At first, Tomas felt that I was withdrawing my love for him. But that

was not the case. I withdrew all the false ego-stroking – the special love - that we both mistook for real Love. This was a crucial step in renouncing the old "special love" dynamic (sacrifice/attack) and making space for Holy Spirit to reveal the real Love that we would both learn to recognize and accept.

12. Sleeping in the same bed together was something that I had *learned* was supposed to be loving. But upon honest reflection it was not natural to me at all. It was an obligation (sacrifice) and I had become resentful of my partner's snoring and constant movement which disrupted my own peace and rhythm.

13. I remember the resounding relief that resulted from sharing this secret with him in radical and defenseless honesty. I was quite emotional and Holy Spirit helped me to take full accountability for having previously chosen to sacrifice, and then resenting Tomas for it. The real healing took place when I apologized to Tomas for having betrayed myself and therefore, for having betrayed him as well.

14. In addition to me making the leap to sleeping alone, some other changes involved dropping much of my false sense of responsibility as a homemaker. Instead of cooking seven days a week we decided to share the responsibility happily. I despised cleaning house, so I decided to have a housemaid come clean every couple weeks – without guilt.

15. One of the more difficult hurdles was to confess to my partner that sex, for me, was a duty and felt quite soul-less. This of course sparked the greatest resistance for him…yet it proved to be a divine catalyst in moving us forward into a much deeper, trusting, and far more emotionally intimate relationship. Over time the focus was gradually withdrawn from the body (sex) and transferred to a deep merging and union at the heart level. And our bond just increased from there.

16. It took a while for Tomas to adjust to these initial changes, but he soon saw the joyful shift in me. And he felt the marked increase in Love and gratitude I had for him (and my Self) and he for me. He then became more joyful, secure and open to Self-Love for himself as a result of all these miraculous shifts generated by authentic relating.

17. Profound healing comes from the courage to be more authentic and renounce specialness and the patterns of sacrifice which we have mistaken for love.

C. Exercise: The Ego's Use of Compromise and Sacrifice

1. Are you willing to look with Holy Spirit at the areas where you compromise yourself in your relationships? Make sure to look *with Spirit* so there will be no self-judgment, just a quiet observation. If you feel judgment or self-blame then it will be the ego doing the looking.

2. Can you do your own radically honest self-inquiry on how you might compromise yourself in relationships? Often the ego is obsessed with a particular relationship "role," mistaking the role itself for Love. It then plays "god," taking on a superior and false sense of responsibility. Take parenting for instance. The "need to be needed" often fuels this particular error.

3. This insidious dynamic (false responsibility) is a destroyer of trust. Trust is invested in the ego and fear, while being withdrawn from God/Love and the one we profess to love. When we mirror to a child that we don't trust them they take this in and usually grow up with a profound sense of distrust in themselves which causes all kinds of suffering.

4. Let me share a radically honest account from a dear friend of mine (with her permission). I feel that many people, especially women, will identify with her revealing confession.

5. When she and I met she had no idea about Holy Relationship. All she ever knew were the destructive patterns of special love. Thankfully, she sees her old obsession with self-betrayal and has literally done an about face. Here is her account of her history with the ego's version of "special love."

6. "As I hurried about doing and bringing everything for everyone, the world told me how amazing I was. I was told how I was like Wonder Woman - how endlessly "giving" I was. This was the addictive "hit." This was the "high" that I lived for. I didn't really see others for who they were, and I didn't seek to join the Spirit in people. And the reason was because I was too busy looking for how I could get them to approve of me, to need me and approve of me.

7. Next, I got to store up all these "credits" against those I had done so much for, so that I could hold it against them when I began resenting them for not doing likewise for me. They didn't stand a chance. I had framed them the moment I set out to "help" them! They never asked for my assistance, I just *did*, and went overboard, already preparing the future attack in the form of, "Poor me, look at all I do for *you* and how I get nothing in return." It's very effective because by the world's standards I *was* being loving and generous. In truth it was full out attack."

8. Make a list of the people and areas in your life where you compromise yourself and have thought you were demonstrating Love. These may include listening to or engaging in activities against your true preferences, such as meaningless conversation, sleeping together, home duties, sex, shared finances, or maybe you sacrifice your authenticity with reluctance to speaking about your spiritual path, or with trying to "keep the peace," etc.

9. With radical self-honesty, *why* do you compromise or sacrifice? If the answer is that you compromise yourself because you fear hurting the one you love, then please go deeper.

10. Ask yourself then, what does the ego seek to get as a trade-off for your sacrifices? Recall that any kind of sacrifice always seeks a pay-off. What are yours in each of the areas?

11. And lastly, if you were to come clean and decide to withdraw your patterns of sacrifice, what do you fear you would lose? What or who may be threatened?

12. When we compromise our Self for other's egos we give in to "ego-stroking" which is not Love, but attack. What could you lose if you joined with Spirit to forgive yourself and decide to be more Self-honest? What could be threatened? If a relationship appears to be threatened by one or both aligning with their inner guidance, then it was not Love that joined them, but fear.

13. This is why applying the *Seven Keys* in relationships is imperative if we really desire to shift from specialness to Love as a Holy Relationship.

D. Revealing the Body's Role in Special Relationships

1. As we awaken from the ego dream, we must also awaken from the belief that we are the body. We don't realize we're the eternal Son of God. Most of us within the dream have mistaken the body as our self. Yet this body is merely a projected image which dwells in our mind (not brain). In the dream the insubstantial and unreal body has become our fraudulent identity, our central idol – the all-inclusive *substitute* for our infinitely Loving, endlessly abundant and joyful Holy Self.

2. This body, the central idol, is revered or despised, either cherished through pleasure seeking or attacked by pain and disease. Both reactions are the same. They seek to immortalize the body through our pursuit of pleasure and our avoidance of pain. The underlying objective is to make the body real in our awareness, thus making it seem as if the body is autonomous in its power to change, to get sick or to heal. While we remain hypnotized by this illusion, we will not see that all the body's changes, both good and bad, are brought about *exclusively* by our mind.

   a. *"Pain demonstrates the body must be real. It is a loud, obscuring voice whose shrieks would silence what the Holy Spirit says, and keep His words from your awareness. Pain compels attention, drawing it away from Him and focusing upon itself. Its purpose is the same as pleasure, for they both are means to make the body real. What shares a common purpose is the same." T-27.VI.1:1-5*

3. All special relationships are attempts at union *with bodies*. Our guiltless, true Identity shines its radiance *beyond* the body. The illusory body then is made as our replacement for the glorious Child of God that we are. And while we identify as a *body* instead of as *Spirit,* the ego will use the body to play out the punishing role that it assigns.

4. The body appears to have a mind of its own. Yet we only *seem* to be at the mercy of it. Things are never as they appear in the ego dream. Everything is quite literally reversed and that is why we need to invite the Holy Spirit in to correct our perception.

5. It is the mind that tells the body exactly what to do, not the other way around. Of itself, the body is entirely neutral and responds only to the mind's orders. It answers either to Love or to fear within our mind. The body only appears to be under biological and physiological laws, as well as the laws of time.

6. These are representative of the laws of the ego and are certainly not God's Laws. These are illusory phenomena which the false self's split mind made up. It employs them to keep us believing that we are separate from each other and our infinitely Loving Source of perfection.

7. While we believe we *are* the body we will also falsely believe that we are *victims* of the body; that this entirely neutral image has the power to betray and attack us. It will seem as if the body has a mind of its own. And we will view everyone else as a body; bodies that can also harm and betray us.

8. Yet in truth the body is wholly neutral. Of itself, it cannot change in state or appearance. It has zero power to cause any changes of itself because it is simply a *now moment image* or "effect" of our mind. It cannot age, sicken or even die of itself. The same can be said about its healing. Only the mind heals the body. Every change in the body's condition or appearance is caused exclusively by our desire, although until the false self is largely undone this unconscious desire for self-attack will continue to be masked and will manifest in the many forms of adversity we seem to experience.

9. Another important point here is - we are not sustained *by* the body as the world teaches. Life is not in the body. The body does not give us life. Only God's Love is the Cause of life, which by the way *has* no opposite. As we awaken from fear and the body, we realize that we are constantly sustained by the Love of God as our Holy Self. This Love provides the ground of our being. It is our eternal and completely uninterrupted Source. We are life without end. And as we practice forgiveness we learn to recognize this Love and life in everyone we meet.

10. While we still misidentify as a body and believe mistakenly that we are sustained by it, we will continue to be fearful of Love as true healing. We will unknowingly attract relationship conflicts,

misfortune, illness, aging and death. And instead of using the body as a means to help heal our relationships, we will use it to further separate.

11. Jesus, in the *Course*, assigns considerable emphasis on the necessity of undoing our belief in the body as our identity; and for good reason. The body identity represents *all* our fears. It is the gap of separation. It is the split mind.

12. While we see our self as a body, believing that we are victim to it, we will be attracted to special relationships and will mistake guilt, sacrifice and attack for Love. We will view others as limited to the body as well. The body is then used as a separation device, a veil to obscure the infinite glory of what lies beyond it. This is the one shared and Holy Self.

    a. *"The body is the ego's idol; the belief in sin made flesh and then projected outward. This produces what seems to be a wall of flesh around the mind, keeping it prisoner in a tiny spot of space and time, beholden unto death, and given but an instant in which to sigh and grieve and die in honor of its master." T-20.VI.11:1-2*

13. The neutral body is not wrong or bad. It's just an image that we've projected to take the place of "what" we really are. It is an image that we have used to hide our incorruptible innocence and majestic light from each other. The most important question concerning the body is this, "What do we use it for?" What is its purpose? Through the ego, its senses and appetites are sent to gather proof of sin, guilt, attack, conflict, loss, deceit, addictions, betrayal, aging, pain and illness (all forms of death). And it believes by the false evidence which it projected and gathered, that *others,* along with the *past,* are responsible for its pain.

    a. *"The central lesson is always this; that what you use the body for it will become to you. Use it for sin or for attack, which is the same as sin, and you will see it as sinful. Because it is sinful it is weak, and being weak, it suffers and it dies. Use it to bring the Word of God to those who have it not, and the body becomes holy. Because it is holy it cannot be sick, nor can it die. When its usefulness is done it is laid by, and that is all. M-12.5:1-6*

14. The body is neutral. It can be completely and divinely repurposed as the means by which we actually reverse the ego's destructive goal of separation. And this sacred reversal is accomplished when we join with Holy Spirit to repurpose our relationships from special to Holy.

15. The ego only knows of special love which is fear and attack in disguise. Because it thrives on guilt it uses the body in vastly distorted ways to ensure the cycle of attack continues to play out. And we cannot end the attack if we're not willing to recognize it.

16. The false self is obsessed with the body as itself. Every one of its unions is made to pander to the body. The body has become its fundamental goal. Everything it thinks about and all it does is done for the body. The body is its central idol which it defends to the death, not realizing that it is consistently dooming the body to death. It either hates the body or it idolizes it. Both these mistakes serve the exact same purpose – to make the body *real* in awareness and totally obscure the light of our Holy Self.

E. The Body Must be Divinely Repurposed

1. The misappropriation of the body's role in relationships presents the greatest of subversive blocks to the awareness of Love's presence. We have been taught to seek for love through the body, not realizing that this is impossible. We seek and never find.

   a. *"Your task is not to seek for love, but merely to seek and find all of the barriers within yourself that you have built against it. It is not necessary to seek for what is true, but it [is] necessary to seek for what is false." T-16.IV.6:1-2*

2. The most significant yet unidentified source of physical illness can be found in our special relationships. The special love dynamic might be highly valued but is deadly poison to our mind and therefore, to the body.

3. The body is purely an effect of what we use it *for*. And while we still find our self enmeshed in specialness then the body will inevitably be used by the ego for attack. Although generally we won't be aware of this until we change our mind about the goal of the relationship. When we make the healing choice with Holy Spirit to transfer a relationship from special to Holy, then the body's role is also repurposed.

4. The body, once it has been repurposed with Holy Spirit, becomes the means by which we return to sanity. And we do this by learning to close the gap with others, via forgiveness. This is true communication *beyond* the body. The body (ours and others) then recedes in our awareness. As it loses its central focus of being used for guilt - as pride, pleasure and attack – we begin to recognize and value what lies beyond it, which is the beloved, changeless and all-inclusive Holy Self. This ultimately takes us to closing the final gap within - to embody the Holy Self.

5. The body must be repurposed. And the transition experience from special to Holy Relationship offers us a rich classroom in which to accomplish this most sacred of assignments. In fact, the Holy Relationship is the necessary classroom through which the body is finally overcome. It is here, within the Holy Relationship, that we reverse the laws of the world by reversing "effect and cause." As the body's purpose is purified and sanctified we understand and accept its complete neutrality and powerlessness. The *mind* is recognized as the single *source* of all that the body appears to feel and do.

   a. *"The body is a dream."* ... *"Made to be fearful, must the body serve the purpose given it. But we can change the purpose that the body will obey by changing what we think that it is for."* ... *"The body is the means by which God's Son returns to sanity. Though it was made to fence him into hell without escape, yet has the goal of Heaven been exchanged for the pursuit of hell. The Son of God extends his hand to reach his brother, and to help him walk along the road with him. Now is the body holy. Now it serves to heal the mind that it was made to kill."* W-pII.5.3:1,4-5.4

6. In special relationships the body is mistakenly seen as a *goal* in *itself*. Instead, it is purely a *means* to undo our deep-seated guilt so we can behold the magnitude of Love we are and share. We seek to satiate the body's many appetites through food, physical company, sex, money, status, material possessions, etc. In fact, everything we do, we do for the body while we believe it is our identity. We are willing to sacrifice our life for the body. And we do! That is what death is; a mistaken belief that the body is "who" we are and that it's more powerful than our mind that made it.

7. In error we have claimed this *mindless, powerless and projected image* as the totality of our "self." And through unrelinquished fear we inadvertently attempt to use relationships to further the ego's body agenda. Because the body is erroneously valued as the goal in special relationships, it is used unwittingly to project attack rather than to communicate guiltlessness (Love).

8. Most of what the ego labels as "love or loving" in relationships is really a form of attack and is rooted in unacknowledged guilt. This section will hopefully redefine and repurpose the language of Love. The world's concept of love is special. This is the only brand of love (attack) it understands.

F. The Unconscious Fear of Love

1. Remember that the ego is terrified of Love, *real* Love that is. This is the fear of God, the terror of discovering that our will and God's Will are the same. And this is why we may say we trust God, yet we're afraid to hand over the ego's idols completely, including our body, relationships, family, finances and career. We compartmentalize our life trying to protect most of it from God because we are terrified of the *ego's interpretation* of His Will. Yet God's Will and Nature are unopposed and undivided Love and joy.

2. The ego has hoodwinked us completely by projecting "its own" destructive and vindictive nature and will onto God as Love. This is why we don't turn everything and everyone over to God. We really do believe unconsciously that He will annihilate them and us. We incorrectly believe that He teaches us through painful lessons and asks us to sacrifice on behalf of Love. Here is a truly helpful exercise

from The End of Death, Volume One which you can take yourself through: *"The Fear of God"* exercise in *The End of Death Volume One*: https://nouksanchez.com/wp-content/uploads/2020/06/2-Are-you-fearful-of-God.pdf

G. Specialness and Money

1. In special relationships we tend to compartmentalize our relationships, our finances, our jobs, etc. For most, there is a tendency to maintain our *Course* studies "privately," largely independently from our day to day lives. But as we venture into Holy Relationship and actively take part in practicing the *Seven Keys* and forgiveness, we will recognize that we just cannot afford to keep *any* segment of our life as separate from our practice. We realize that by compartmentalizing, the ego perpetuates its reign of "specialness" and the consequences become even more unbearable than ever before. We come to a point in our development of trust where we simply cannot afford to "keep up appearances" of specialness any longer. We simply can no longer tolerate playing the ego's game and hiding our light.

2. This natural transition often involves changes in our social life. It can be difficult to maintain friendships with people who do not share the *same goal* of the *Seven Keys* and awakening. These friendships usually tend to drop away over time. Part of this transition also includes our increasing *intolerance* for meaningless, superficial, small talk, and ego stories of victims and perpetrators. As we become more vertical and Self-honest, we are much more present and mindful of when we're tempted to abandon ourselves to the many social temptations to collude with the ego. The *good* news is that as old seeming friendships fall away, new ones with like-minded people who share the same goal – as possible Holy Relationships – are sent to us by Holy Spirit:

a. *"Certain pupils have been assigned to each of God's teachers, and they will begin to look for him as soon as he has answered the Call. They were chosen for him because the form of the universal curriculum that he will teach is best for them in view of their level of understanding. His pupils have been waiting for him, for his coming is certain. Again, it is only a matter of time. Once he has chosen to fulfill his role, they are ready to fulfill theirs. Time waits on his choice, but not on whom he will serve. When he is ready to learn, the opportunities to teach will be provided for him." M-2.1.*

3. One particularly sensitive area of relationships that the ego compartmentalizes is finances. This area is one of the most fiercely defended of the ego's attraction to specialness. Money happens to be an unrecognized guilt magnet in most relationships. As an ego idol replacement for Love, it can be quite a contentious sticking point in the transition from special relating to Holy relating.

4. Just as with all areas of our life, finances are used by the ego to maintain specialness, which is attack. At some point we will need to make the transition in this area of money, just as we do with all others over time. Holy Spirit guides us through this transition. Recall that if money is an issue for us then it's an ego idol. It's always to our benefit to invite Holy Spirit in to help us divinely reinterpret what we use the idol *for;* in this case money.

5. Some of us feel financially responsible for others. While in some cases this is legitimate and helpful, there are many cases whereby the unseen ego invests in being the "rescuer" to those family members or friends who may appear to be less financially fortunate. Some of us still feel falsely responsible for financially supporting family members or friends who are not interested in undoing their own ego and the subsequent "scarcity patterns" that it attracts.

6. Unfortunately, when we try to rescue loved ones who are not really willing to be saved from their own destructive patterns, we end up colluding with them and enabling them, which is the ego's attack. In doing so, we actually disempower them. This is a common ego pattern. While we enable them (ego's need to be needed - out of guilt) then *we* end up paying the price of toxic "specialness." We must bring each of the compartmentalized areas of our life and place them all under one overarching Teacher, the Holy Spirit. This is what the *Seven Keys of Authentic Relating* are for. Under the direction of Holy Spirit, He reveals the destructive nature of special love and teaches us the joyous alternative – Holy Relationship.

H. When Attack is Confused with Love

1. When Jesus speaks of using the body for attack, He includes our unforgiven memories of past grievances which are superimposed upon our present relationships. These unhealed memories perpetuate the seeming past into the future so as to obscure the Holy Instant where all healing awaits our welcome.

2. Using the body to attack includes:

   1) Judging and guilt-tripping our self or others.

   2) Seeing our self and others as bodies instead of as spirit.

   3) Verbal, emotional or physical abuse.

   4) Sickness and pain.

3. Illness is probably the ego's strongest defense against recognizing that our true Identity as a Child of God can never *be* threatened. This Self has *dominion over* the phenomenal world that we made with the ego while believing we were separate from God.

4. Other unrecognized forms of attack that are especially treasured in the special relationship dynamic include:

   1) Sacrifice, struggle, pain and jealousy.

   2) Belief that Love is exclusive rather than inclusive.

5. What the world has come to know as "love" will need to be questioned because we really do not know what Love is – yet.

6. In addition, another often unrecognized form of attack is the inappropriate use of sex. Lust and sexual fantasies idolize *the body* as the central figure, rather than the Spirit. Unknowingly, sexual lust is a form of objectification which the ego confuses with Love, while using it to deny true intimacy and the Holy Instant.

7. Remember that lust is not wrong, but simply *false*; so, no self-condemnation. Only the ego condemns. Spirit simply looks without judgment and gently urges us to give our co-dependencies and addictions to Him so they can be divinely repurposed. Contrary to what the ego tells us, there is no loss or sacrifice involved. We will know when we're ready to do this. The right timing arises when we

have truly reached our pain limit with that particular body appetite.

8. An important component in undoing the false self involves the repurposing of the body and its appetites, which must include the divine repurposing of sex. As Jesus points out in the following quotes, emphasis on the body negates the willingness to see another as complete. And while we mentally dissociate another by confusing the body as *who* they are, we also do it to our self. We either see the body *or* we see the spirit, the Holy changelessness of another. We cannot see both. Whatever *appears to change* in another or our self is simply not real. Our Holy Self is eternal and changeless, and this is what we learn to recognize, embody and cherish in the Holy Relationship.

   a. *"No one is seen complete. The body is emphasized, with special emphasis on certain parts, and used as the standard for comparison of acceptance or rejection for acting out a special form of fear."* T-18.I.3:6-7

   b. *"But when you look upon a brother as a physical entity, his power and glory are "lost" to you and so are yours. You have attacked him, but you must have attacked yourself first."* T-8. VII.5:3-5

9. Sex happens to be one of the ego's most deviously hidden and heavily defended storehouses for guilt (attack). When used by the ego, this particular body appetite is the most cleverly concealed and disguised from our awareness. And because of the pervasive and overwhelming confusion of sex with love, this subject is covered more extensively in this manual in chapter six titled *Sex and TransOrgasmic Union*. We address the divine repurposing of sex and introduce a practical process to help the transfer process from lust to Love.

10. The sexual appetite can be such a guilt-magnet. Just as a reminder - guilt does not exist. Yet if we don't know this deeply in our awareness, we will inadvertently amass guilt as unconscious self-sabotage. This is why it's a process, and a gentle, Loving one at that.

I. Communication as the Body's Singular Purpose

1. In the transfer from special to Holy relationship, *romantic relationships in particular* will undergo many divine upgrades where the toxic rules of "special love" are unearthed, reviewed and then lovingly exchanged for the Laws of Love.

    a. *"Remember that the Holy Spirit interprets the body only as a means of communication."*... *"You do not perceive your brothers as the Holy Spirit does, because you do not regard bodies solely as a means of joining minds and uniting them with yours and mine. This interpretation of the body will change your mind entirely about its value. Of itself it has none."* ... *"If you use the body for attack, it is harmful to you."* T-8.VII.2:1,2:5-7,3:1,

    b. *"Communication ends separation. Attack promotes it. The body is beautiful or ugly, peaceful or savage, helpful or harmful, according to the use to which it is put. And in the body of another you will see the use to which you have put yours. If the body becomes a means you give to the Holy Spirit to use on behalf of union of the Sonship, you will not see anything physical except as what it is. Use it for truth and you will see it truly."* T-8.VII.4:1-6

2. In the two previous quotes Jesus shares that the body's *singular* purpose is as a means of communication. Let me clarify. The only essence we can communicate is Love; undivided and unopposed Love. When we try to communicate *special love*, which is fear in disguise, we're not really communicating at all. Fear disrupts communication. Nothing shows up on God's Radar. The ego tries to communicate through attack but while this seems real *it is not*. So, when the ego uses the body for its various forms of attack we actually *break* communication with others and our Holy Self. That is why we often feel so alone in fear.

3. This is an exceptionally crucial and fundamental teaching that provides a firm foundation upon which the "special" relationship dynamic is finally seen and healed.

a. *"Help and healing are the normal expressions of a mind that is working through the body, but not [in] it. If the mind believes the body is its goal it will distort its perception of the body, and by blocking its own extension beyond it, will induce illness by fostering separation. Perceiving the body as a separate entity cannot but foster illness, because it is not true." T-8.VII.11:2-4*

b. *"To see a body as anything except a means of communication is to limit your mind and to hurt yourself. Health is therefore nothing more than united purpose. If the body is brought under the purpose of the mind, it becomes whole because the mind's purpose is one."... "When you see a brother as a body, you are condemning him because you have condemned yourself." T-8.VII.13:3-5,15:7*

4. This took me what seemed like forever to accept and understand. It need not take you that long if you drop your resistance to it. The ego believes that love can change or end, which is our erroneous belief that love brings guilt and attack. This is not Love, but fearful, special love. The purpose for special love is to project guilt. And the ego uses all the world's themes for fake love to disguise this underlying intention. More so, the body is employed as its greatest ally to perpetuate these pseudo expressions of love until we consciously repurpose it with Holy Spirit. The ego's form of special love is always attack in disguise. It's just ego-stroking and certainly not real Love.

a. *"The special love relationship is the ego's chief weapon for keeping you from Heaven." T-16.V.2:3*

5. Jesus tells us that the special relationship is the ego's *chief weapon*. And the romantic relationship is especially prone to being used as this weapon, precisely because it centers on the body; what the body of another can do for it.

6. Thank God we always have the *now moment choice* to ask Holy Spirit to help us divinely repurpose our special relationships. Each Holy Instant in which we sincerely desire to forgive instead of condemn another, we activate the miracle. And as we progressively

accept the inestimable value of forgiveness, we also come closer to experiencing the immense joy of Holy Relationships. Forgiveness opens the celestial gate to anchoring our incorruptible innocence and knowing our Self as Love and joy without opposite.

10. NO SPECIAL RELATIONSHIP IS EXPERIENCED IN THE PRESENT

1. We would not, or more precisely, we *could not* be in current special relationships unless we unknowingly seek to reconstruct the unhealed patterns of previous special relationships. If we had completely forgiven our past relationships, we would be repulsed by any offer of special relationship in either the present or the future.

2. Special relationships only "seem" to be with a significant other. Let me be specific. The poison of these *special* unions does not reside in the person or our self, but in the way we've unwittingly agreed to "relate" to them and use them. It's always the destructive and often unconscious identification *based on past relating*, which requires complete undoing, to reveal the shining Spirit or essence of the one we relate *with*.

3. Our primary special relationship, the relationship with our parents, caretakers and siblings, seems to be what influences all other relationships and haunts us the most. The key to healing – including physical healing – rests in healing our special relationships. And the reason for this is that the seed of present sickness is always some kind of unforgiveness which seems to materialize now but is really kept embedded in our mind in some past event or relationship.

4. The ego perpetuates the seeming injustice by projecting this past "lack of Love" and overlays it upon the present moment, so that it continues into the future. Unless we forgive the *belief* that we have been unfairly treated, then the pain or illness will carry on - although it may morph into different forms of adversity that appear to be unrelated.

5. We enshroud our present special relationships in a cloud of the past, one that completely obscures the glory of the one we *think* we're relating with. We see them through the filter of our own unforgiven pain and therefore do not see them at all.

6. All special relationships have a secret goal. We mistakenly believe that they can give to us that which we were deprived of in the past. We consistently seek to extract from others what we feel was missing in our past. And to achieve this goal we are prepared to sacrifice our self to conflict, loss, disease, pain, aging, scarcity and death.

7. When we look to present relationships to remedy deprivation and hurts from past relationships, there is a dangerous oversight made. We want the current relationship to be different, better, and *more fair* than our previous relationships were. We are unconscious of the fact that looking at the painful unforgiven past *with Spirit*, and *forgiving* it, is the only way to heal and *not carry* that pain into present and future relationships.

8. For example, my childhood wound originated with trying to please my mother in order to be seen, validated, approved of and loved. In my early adult special relationships, I projected this past unforgiven "need to be seen and loved" onto those people. The outcome was that they played out my projected fears - expectations of disapproval and betrayal, all based on my past. In those relationships I was unaware that I had mistakenly and repeatedly attempted to remove *past* suffering. Because I had not *forgiven the past* I had been projecting it onto my relationships. And in doing this I completely overlooked the *present moment* and the *innocence* of those I was with. I was trying to extract from them what I had believed I was deprived of in my childhood. Does this pattern ring any bells?

9. It should ring bells if we feel any resentment or lack in our relationships. These are warning signs to alert us that we're still trying to extract, from those present, something we believe was missing in our past.

10. Please stay with me as this next insight is extremely valuable; it offers a crucial peek into releasing our secret attraction to pain in all its forms.

11. In the ego mind, the past seemed to cause the present. We hold fast to another deeply defended and disastrous conclusion in this entirely uninvestigated and mistaken assumption. Erroneously, in our relationships and the body, we bury *in the past* both the *cause* of suffering and its *remedy* (healing). But the past does not exist. If it does not exist, then how could there be a cause in it?

12. Time itself is not a cause because like all things in the dream, it is neutral. Time cannot destroy or heal. The ego uses time to make it appear as if it is a "cause" of its own. Time can never separate the seeming problem from its comprehensive solution – as forgiveness. Regardless of what seemed to occur in the past, there is no "cause" in the past. Placing the cause in the past is an ego trick. The split mind, as the ego's wish to be unfairly treated, projects *all* of its traumas, making it appear as if we were indeed victimized. That way it can amass the guilt it needs to retain its illusory and separate "self" by perpetuating its projection of guilt onto others, the body, the past and the world.

13. There is only one place that the "cause" of any adversity can be – in this *now moment*, in our mind. The divine remedy for everything that seemed to happen in the past is also here *now.* So both the cause and its remedy are always right here now, in our mind. This is the Holy Instant and Atonement.

14. Even when we attempt to find solutions in the present, these are often smokescreens. While we firmly believe we were *indeed* unfairly treated and that it was *real* then *all* solutions we seek will merely be band-aid measures which serve to divert our attention from recognizing and healing the singular cause as unforgiveness *now.*

15. The cause of present pain in all its forms is not hidden in someone else, in the body or in the past. The cause (unforgiveness), together with its true remedy as genuine forgiveness, can only be found in the ever-present Holy Instant, now. There is no other time and no other place in which it can be healed.

   a. "The special relationship takes vengeance on the past. By seeking to remove suffering in the past, it overlooks the present in its preoccupation with the past and its total commitment to it. No special relationship is experienced in the present. Shades of the past envelop it, and make it what it is. It has no meaning in the present, and if it means nothing now, it cannot have any real meaning at all." T-16.VII.2:1-5

16. *And here is the kicker.* While we mistakenly believe the *cause* of any relationship conflict, pain or disease lies in the past, then we will believe unconsciously that healing it also lies firmly entrenched in the past – which removes any possibility of healing it *now*. And if the past does not exist then the healing we seek - *will never happen!* This insanity ensures we will never heal the cause and its effects.

17. When we believe there is a past cause for what appears to be a present condition, we are holding the past *against* healing in the present Holy Instant. Now, this very moment, is all there is of time. Since the past is gone, any suffering, pain, disease or scarcity that seemingly occurred in the past is now irrelevant and truly *cannot* affect the present, unless we *choose to believe* it can.

a. *"No change can be made in the present if its cause is past. Only the past is held in memory as you make use of it, and so it is a way to hold the past against the now." T-28.I.6:6-7*

18. The forgiveness process can be found in *The Seven Essential Principles of Quantum Forgiveness (Atonement)* on page 591.

A. Windows to Healing Now

1. The ego refuses to accept that all seeming conflict and deprivation, together with their complete healing, resides exclusively right here and *now*. Now, in the precious Holy Instant of forgiveness, is where *all* healing takes place. If we look to the past or future for healing, we deny healing *now*.

2. Let me make this clearer by giving an example. If, as an adult, I still believe I was hurt in the past by someone (sexual abuse as a child for example), then I will carry that memory of abuse into my present reality and relationships. And because it is unforgiven it will still lurk as a darkened shroud from which I look out and see others and the world.

3. All my relationships will be experienced through this distortion.

In addition, I will have buried this seemingly real (and unforgiven) attack in my body by maintaining that it was indeed attacked. This unforgiven injustice always finds a way to resurface as present *proof* of past attack.

4.   This painful, unrelinquished memory will tempt me to perceive attack over and over again in different forms, such as relationship conflict, disease, aging, physical pain and death. And until I have forgiven myself and, with gratitude, seen the miracle behind this memory – it will prolong my erroneous belief that I am guilty and am therefore deserving of punishment. All of this is to try to prove the impossible, that I can *be* attacked and that I am separate from Love itself. In addition, this belief will stand as a solid wall between me and the Love I long to experience in all my relationships.

5.   Let me clarify further. How can I detect if this form of deprivation is still with me and has not been totally forgiven? I can tell by my reaction to it. Am I still triggered by the memory of it? If there are any residual emotional feelings, then the past abuse or trauma is alive in my memory right now.

6.   I will believe it is real. In a way, it is being lived out over and over by my present belief that; 1) it was real, and 2) it did damage to me, and 3) that someone is guilty. By my belief in its *reality,* it has *not* been forgiven. And so, it is kept alive and running in my psyche and is projected onto others and the body.

a.   *"The ego's plan is to have you see error clearly first, and then overlook it. Yet how can you overlook what you have made real? By seeing it clearly, you have made it real and [cannot] overlook it." T-9.IV.4:4-6.*

b. *Yet no one can forgive a sin that he believes is real. T-27.II.2:4*

c. *"Understand that you do not respond to anything directly, but to your interpretation of it. Your interpretation thus becomes the justification for the response. That is why analyzing the motives of others is hazardous to you. If you decide that someone is really trying to attack you or desert you or enslave you, you will respond as if he had actually done so, having made his error real to you. To interpret error is to give it power, and having done this you will overlook truth." T-12.I.1:4-8*

7. Unless true forgiveness of myself has taken place, and until I have reached a place of gratitude for the healing I gained as a result of the seeming trauma … the ego will keep replaying it to keep me from accessing complete healing via the miracle in the Holy Instant. That way the ego overshadows every Holy Instant with the cruel past, so much so that I will not see people as they are. I will project my unforgiven past and overlay it on them and will then resent them for it.

B. Inviting Holy Spirit to Look with Us at the Past

1. Have I looked at the illusion of past trauma or abuse with Holy Spirit? Have I asked Him to help me to divinely repurpose what appears as a violation of a child's rights? Have I asked Him to divinely repurpose my relationship issues of betrayal or abandonment? Have I asked to see the miracle beneath this ugly "appearance?"

2. For me, in doing this with Holy Spirit, I was then able to see from above the ego's formidable battleground of existence. One of the first insights I received was that there are many lifetimes in the ego's dream of time and space. A seeming victim in this lifetime could very well be a choice (made from guilt) that arose from having been a perpetrator in a previous incarnation.

3. Another valuable insight was that if I had experienced a "perfect" childhood, free of conflict or abuse, I would have lounged in the complacency of trying to make the ego dream a happy one, as most do. It takes massive G-force to catapult us out of the ego's hypnotic birth, death and amnesia cycle. And unfortunately, that catalyst is often through the pain of disillusionment with all facets of the ego dream.

4. Suffering is not bad if we decide to give it to Spirit to be repurposed. Once forgiven and repurposed there is no reason to attract and repeat the pain again.

5. We don't learn to distinguish the ego's pain and pleasure cycle until we have experienced it. Then we decide we no longer want it. Until then there is a sleepy passivity when it comes to the idea of undoing our false self concept and its destructive special relating.

C. Superimposing Our Past on the Present

1. The source of our pain, regardless of the myriad forms it seems to take, lies in some past memory (belief) – a judgment – of being unfairly treated, which is replayed to overlay the present moment. It is then projected into the future by our unrelinquished agreement that it *did* indeed happen, and that this injustice *was* real.

2. Once believed as real, it cannot *be* forgiven. It is impossible to forgive a real sin. Yet it is very possible, even necessary, to forgive mistakes or errors. These *can* be forgiven. The ego's attacks, no matter how vile, are always errors only, and never sins. Nothing in the ego's dream is unforgivable.

3. Our past memory of attack (separation) is valued by the ego and is thus stored within its filter of perception. Unless genuine forgiveness takes place, it uses the body's five senses to report back to it that we are a victim, always at the mercy of random external forces.

4. And it will command the body to see and feel evidence of attack to prove that guilt, as attack, is real. This is to reinforce our long-standing belief that we were unfairly treated in the past and that now, we of *our self,* independent of Spirit, must control and defend our body, our relationships and our life.

5. Special relationships are the unparalleled source of ongoing and unconscious self-attack. This may come as a shock, but there could be no pain, illness or loss if we were to heal the ego's distorted interpretation of our relationships, which are all based on the past. We never straightforwardly relate with anyone who appears in our life, even longtime companions. We relate to our distorted *perception* of them. And it's always *this* corrupted *interpretation* that we react to when they seem to trigger us in any way.

    a. *"Understand that you do not respond to anything directly, but to your interpretation of it. Your interpretation thus becomes the justification for the response." T-12.I.1:4-5*

6. The ego is obsessed with placing cause in the past and unless that seeming cause is seen first, then recognized as being *now* (not past), and forgiven *right here and now*, it continues to infect our present relationships.

a. *"Do not underestimate the intensity of the ego's drive for vengeance on the past. It is completely savage and completely insane. For the ego remembers everything you have done that has offended it, and seeks retribution of you. The fantasies it brings to its chosen relationships in which to act out its hate are fantasies of your destruction."* T-16.VII.3:1-4

7. The ego holds the past against us. When we let the past go via forgiveness *now* – the ego feels deprived of the punishment it is convinced we deserve. Our special relationships are the ego's chief spawning ground to continue this belief that fear, guilt *and* Love can coexist. Yet it's the ego seeking vengeance on a past that no longer exists. This is why it is so crucial to forgive all our relationships, including those which seem to be over already and in the past. Unless these are completely forgiven *now,* and with gratitude, they will pursue us into the illusory future.

8. The special relationship is the single greatest contributor to all forms of self-attack including illness, pain and death. Through the false self and its laws of the world, we have given many different labels to what we mistakenly believe are the thousands of "causes" for different bodily conditions. Very few people have yet realized that every one of these so-called causes is purely an "effect" of the singular, unacknowledged cause of all disease and pain – our unforgiven guilt.

9. The body happens to be our greatest repository for unforgiven guilt as self-attack. And while we still mistake the body as our self then it will appear to betray us through pain, disease, aging, etc. Yet are we willing to look for and heal the unseen, number one *cause* of all our ailments?

a. *"Of one thing you were sure: Of all the many causes you perceived as bringing pain and suffering to you, your guilt was not among them."* T-27.VII.7:3

10. The illusion of guilt goes hand in hand with the belief in both punishment and fear. Unconsciously we believe we sinned against God by making a false self to take the place of God's most Holy Child, our Holy Self. To condense, we believe we have sinned and thus we

fear punishment. *All* fear and its painful results, despite their differing forms, arises from this deeply unconscious, insane belief.

11. If we did not believe that we are fundamentally guilty it would be impossible to feel fear or experience the countless "effects" we project out of fear. If we were to embrace and embody our changeless and incorruptible innocence, fear and suffering would disappear. But in order to know this completely guiltless and indestructible state while in a body, we must heal – forgive – our investment in sin.

12. To judge our self or others *is* the belief in sin. By the way, there is no hierarchy of judgment or sin because they are all false, being the opposite of Love (God). There are no half judgments. Either we judge as guilty *or* we value guiltlessness. Judgment is like pregnancy. We cannot be a little bit pregnant. We're either pregnant – or not.

13. To the ego, sin (judgment) is irrevocable and irreversible. It is real and immovable. A sin may seem to be *forgiven* by the ego but it is never *forgotten*. It is carried *at all times* in the mind and densely enshrouds the shining and innocent ever-present moment.

14. Sin also blinds us from recognizing others as they really are. We see them only through our own murky filter. And sadly, we accept from them only that which our corrupted filter summons from them. This is why the ego cannot give Love or receive Love. It seeks Love but makes sure it never finds it.

15. The one who carries these unforgiven judgments has unknowingly condemned himself. To the degree he believes in sin – that his judgments are justified – is the degree he secretly attracts punishment as self-attack. All illness and relationship conflicts are effects of these unrelinquished judgments.

a. *"Sin is attacked by punishment, and so preserved. But to forgive it is to change its state from error into truth."* T-25. III.8:12-13

D. Shadow Figures from the Past

1. When we relate to other people, we do so through a filter which is heavily populated by our interpretation of people from our past. To the degree we still believe that we were indeed unfairly treated will

be the extent to which we will be *unable* to join wholeheartedly with another. As much as we may say we long for Love, we will lack the trust required to enter such transparent, honest and intimate relating. This deceptive filter is very well disguised by the ego so that we do not suspect it, and therefore heal it.

2. In addition, to the degree we still believe that we were unfairly treated is the same extent that we will secretly "expect" to be unfairly treated in the future. And we will secretly invite this punishing response from others because we are fearful of it. Recall that whatever we fear or defend our self from, we will attract. And this is why it is crucial to learn to forgive our self for what we unwittingly attracted to us in the seeming past.

3. Special relationships are *not* Loving. The false self only knows the past along with the guilt and blame it sees and seeks from the past. It is never present to the Holy Instant, just "now." As Jesus tells us, although hidden from conscious awareness, every choice for special relationship is made in order to pursue vengeance on the past. And *someone else* must be made responsible for our past suffering. This is how we lock our self in to the mistake of seeing others as guilty, not realizing that all the while we are crucifying our self.

    a. *"Every such choice is made because of something "evil" in the past to which you cling, and for which must someone else atone." ... "The special relationship takes vengeance on the past. By seeking to remove suffering in the past, it overlooks the present in its preoccupation with the past and its total commitment to it." T-16.VII.1:5,2:1-2*

4. The past is the ego's only reference, a time that is over and not here any longer. In its attempts to resurrect the past, the ego sets its sights on making sure that others witness to its secret wish to be unfairly treated. Then it can justify its anger which perpetuates the cycle of guilt and attack.

    a. *"In the special relationship it does not seem to be acting out of vengeance that you seek. And even when the hatred and the savagery break briefly through, the illusion of love is not profoundly shaken. Yet the one thing the ego never allows to reach awareness is that the special relationship is the acting out of vengeance on yourself." T-16.VII.5:1-3*

5. To forgive is to remember only the Loving thoughts you exchanged with others in the past. Anything other than this must be *released and forgotten* because only the unreal or false part of you experienced it. Only the false self is capable of pain, loss or suffering. The Holy Self is entirely impervious to suffering because it knows only one Reality and that is *What* we are – as Love without opposite.

6. The false self is the one that populates its present experience with appointed "shadow figures" from the past. For example, as a child I had a few specific shadow figures that stood out among many. In my earlier childhood I recall being terrified one evening when a bearded man entered my room unannounced.

7. Through the lens of fear (ego), this was a stranger whose tall, heavy stature and giant black beard was a symbol that I should fear for my life. Where I had plucked that symbol from, I can hardly guess except that it must have been a memory I brought in with me from one of the unhealed life frames within the ego's endless loop of seeming lifetimes.

8. This black-bearded man had a murderous intent. This was my interpretation at just two years old. How on earth could that be? Even at two years old I had brought the ego split mind in with me from before birth and even further, to before conception. My decisions were made and the unhealed "fear of God" was in full swing.

9. The bearded man with the murderous intent who entered my room that evening happened to be my dear uncle. He had made a long and arduous trip by train to surprise us. He had brought a lovely gift for me, but my fear-filter had rejected both him and the gift. Furthermore, as I grew up, I developed a distinct dislike and distrust of all bearded men.

10. Even in my earlier adult stage I avoided bearded men until I realized how crazy this was. I saw my insanity, that I had overlaid this past shadow-figure onto all men with beards.

11. Let's look at these shadow figures more closely. My greatest shadow figure was my mother. I had a very difficult relationship with her to say the least. And yet, as forgiveness took place, I saw

her in a completely different light. She had come to help me, as my teacher and not as my jailer.

12. As a child growing up, I perceived her as constantly critical of me. I could never reach her meticulously high standards in anything I did. And so, I took that constant critical voice and unwittingly projected it outward so that it seemed no matter *which* person I entered relationship with, they also mirrored to me that I was incapable, weak, error-prone and unworthy.

13. Little did I know that I had dragged this particular shadow-figure (mother) from the past and superimposed it over those I had related with. And I would often feel as if I was an innocent victim and that they were guilty of treating me unfairly.

14. Once we mistakenly *believe* we were unfairly treated in the past then we will inadvertently try to "reincarnate" that particular wound via projecting this unhealed past belief onto others. All of this remains unconscious until we desire to make it conscious. While it remains hidden it will *appear* as if we really are being unfairly treated. And through the ego we will look for evidence to *prove* it, thereby assuming our pseudo innocence by making it seem that another is guilty.

   a. *"The shadow figures always speak for vengeance, and all relationships into which they enter are totally insane. Without exception, these relationships have as their purpose the exclusion of the truth about the other, and of yourself. This is why you see in both what is not there, and make of both the slaves of vengeance."* T-17.III.2:2-4

E. Victim and Perpetrator - Are They Different?

1. One often unidentified reason we bring our "shadow figures" from the past and overlay them on present relationships is to keep our pseudo innocence intact. This corrupted form of the ego's idea of innocence always demands that, 1) we are a victim of hurt, abandonment or betrayal, and, 2) that *someone else* is guilty as the perpetrator.

2. To clarify, our corrupted innocence is always bought at the cost

of making *someone else* guilty. This is exactly why it's corrupt. The ego thinks it is safe while it continues to believe it's a victim. That way it gets to project its own guilt onto another as a way of repelling real Love (as healing and union).

3. Through the false self, victim and perpetrator appear to be different, even opposites to be more exact. Yet the underlying *purpose* beneath the belief in being either a perpetrator or a victim – *is the same.* Recall that when something shares the identical purpose (intent) it is the same, regardless of the seeming "form" it takes.

4. Both victim and perpetrator are ego roles we play in an attempt to prove the impossible – that sin, guilt and fear *are real.* The truth is that either sin, guilt and fear are real *–or–* God's Love is real. These two beliefs are mutually exclusive and under no circumstances can they coexist. Choose to believe one and we will forfeit the other.

5. Your innocence can never be found at the cost of making someone else guilty. If you believe that someone else is guilty then you secretly keep that guilt and it will usually attack the body unless it is willingly forgiven.

6. The Truth, at all times, regardless of appearances to the contrary, is that we are completely guiltless … no matter what the ego has dreamed up.

7. "Holy Spirit, please help me to forgive *myself* for having *believed* in attack and for having unknowingly used – (person, pain, illness, lack, self-blame, etc.) to attack myself and to separate from my Holy Self."

F. Revealing Our Hidden Attractions

1. I think this may be a perfect place to share the *Course's* pivotal teaching on "perception's fundamental law." Seeing that most of our suffering usually arises from the unseen specialness dynamic in our relationships, remembering this fundamental law should help us to heal, by choosing again whenever we feel triggered.

2. Who would eagerly *desire* guilt, judgment and blame? Surprisingly, to the degree we experience or perceive guilt, judgment and blame is the same extent to which we actually *treasure* it and *call* it into our experience.

3. Recall too, that to the degree we defend our self from guilt, judgment, blame or attack (including illness, aging, lack) reveals in equal measure just how much we inadvertently "value" it, and therefore keep it in our experience. We have obviously given it mistaken reality *because* we defend against it, valuing it – in our mind – as a force (belief) equal to, or greater than God's Love and healing.

4. Perception's fundamental law says that we will always see, feel, hear and experience exactly what we *believe* is there. And the only way we could possibly perceive any conflict or adversity at all (or any good) is based on one premise – *that we desire it.* And because we desire it, we *put* it there. One hundred percent of our reality is made through our desire. Everything we experience comes exclusively from our desire for it.

5. Whatever we believe is real, whatever we believe to be a threat and whatever we defend our self from … represents what we value. And while most of these "values of threat and attack" remain as unforgiven, they must materialize to continue revealing exactly what we unconsciously value so it *can be forgiven* and healed once and for all.

    a. *"To the extent to which you value guilt, to that extent will you perceive a world in which attack is justified. To the extent to which you recognize that guilt is meaningless, to that extent you will perceive attack cannot be justified. This is in accord with perception's fundamental law: You see what you believe is there, and you believe it there because you want it there. Perception has no other law than this."* T-25.III.1:1-4

6. The beautiful thing about withdrawing our projections and finally seeing our unconscious blocks is that we're now able to bring them to the light of conscious awareness. And it's here – without guilt or self-blame – that we sincerely hand them over to Holy Spirit to be forgiven in exchange for abundant miracles.

7. As we awaken to our Holy Self, we move from valuing the ego's destructive habits of attack and defense, to *welcoming* triggers because we know miracles always exist behind every trigger, behind every forgiveness opportunity. We come to recognize them as a

valuable means to flush out what we have mistakenly projected externally onto others and the body and forgive our self entirely.

8. So the "calls to war" we previously heard, become joyfully transformed into calls for peace and union. This is where we begin to see the radiant glory in those situations where we previously saw ugliness and contempt, and where Christ Vision develops to joyfully take the place of what the ego sees.

   a. *"And when he chooses to avail himself of what is given him, then will he see each situation that he thought before was means to justify his anger turned to an event which justifies his love. He will hear plainly that the calls to war he heard before are really calls to peace. He will perceive that where he gave attack is but another altar where he can, with equal ease and far more happiness, bestow forgiveness. And he will reinterpret all temptation as just another chance to bring him joy."* T-25.III.6:5-8

9. When we truly desire to look past the temptation to condemn, we will learn to value and therefore, manifest Love instead of fear. And as we do this we align with, and as, God's Will. As we learn to treasure forgiveness instead of judgment, we relinquish that deep-seated guilt in our mind that has called for eons of self-punishment. When we forgive, we close the gap with others and within our self. And minds that are joined and recognize they are – can feel no guilt – consequently they no longer attract self-punishment.

10. Here are two important tools to learn to communicate authentically: The *Seven Keys* on page 572 and *The Seven Essential Principles of Quantum Forgiveness (Atonement)* on page 591.

II. MAKING THE POSITIVE SEPARATION BETWEEN BODY AND SPIRIT

1. Contrary to the beliefs of most, if not all other spiritual pathways, the physical body must eventually be seen as set "apart" from the

Holy Self, if we genuinely want to end conflict and suffering once and for all.

2. This does not mean that we deny the body, as only the ego would do this, but it does require that we invite Holy Spirit to divinely reinterpret and repurpose the body *concept* and its *use*, entirely. The body-self must be relinquished to Spirit, otherwise it will continue to block awareness of the perfect Love we are.

3. If we genuinely desire to awaken from the body-dream, conflict, pain and death, then at some point we will need to make an unequivocal, *positive separation* between the body and our one, shared Identity as the Holy Self.

   a. *"You see the flesh or recognize the spirit. There is no compromise between the two. If one is real the other must be false, for what is real denies its opposite. There is no choice in vision but this one. What you decide in this determines all you see and think is real and hold as true. On this one choice does all your world depend, for here have you established what you are, as flesh or spirit in your own belief. If you choose flesh, you never will escape the body as your own reality, for you have chosen that you want it so. But choose the spirit, and all Heaven bends to touch your eyes and bless your holy sight, that you may see the world of flesh no more except to heal and comfort and to bless."* T-31.VI.1.

4. Until we do make this positive separation between body and Spirit, our divided perception will continue to interpret incorrectly *through* the body lens. And we will perceive attack, conflict, loss, pain, and disease, believing them to be real. In addition, our decisions and actions will stem from this warped and untrue interpretation which only serves to reinforce the body-identity along with the guilt (self-attack) it seeks. And more than that, we will respond to what is not really there! We cannot afford to trust what we see and hear. The body's eyes and senses were made specifically to report the illusion of separation. And this is why this cycle must be broken.

   a. *"The body cannot heal, because it cannot make itself sick. It [needs] no healing. Its health or sickness depends entirely on how the mind perceives it, and the purpose that the mind would use it for. It is obvious that a segment of the mind can see itself as separated from the Universal Purpose. When this occurs the body becomes its weapon, used against this Purpose, to demonstrate the "fact" that separation has occurred. The body thus becomes the instrument of illusion, acting accordingly; seeing what is not there, hearing what truth has never said and behaving insanely, being imprisoned [by] insanity." T-19.I.3.*

5. Because the body is merely the projection of our mind, it is a relief to understand that all healing is a result of healing the split mind. Jesus encourages us *not* to take thought about the body and its seeming conditions. Our real healing occurs when we heal (forgive) the only cause of sickness, which is our erroneous beliefs.

6. We suffer from massive identity confusion, aka the split mind. In fact, while we still believe that the illusory body-self with all its sensory perceptions and appetites dictates "who" we are, we deny the incorruptible innocence (Love) we really are.

7. We are not the vessel. We are the light beyond it. We cannot be *both!* In any one moment either Love *or* fear is being valued in our awareness. The presence of one of these completely excludes the other. *They simply cannot coexist.* While we believe that we are the body-self we will follow the ego's programming and remain convinced that its five senses and its appetites for pleasure and pain actually constitute reality.

   a. *"Christ's vision has one law. It does not look upon a body, and mistake it for the Son whom God created. It beholds a light beyond the body; an idea beyond what can be touched, a purity undimmed by errors, pitiful mistakes, and fearful thoughts of guilt from dreams of sin. It sees no separation. And it looks on everyone, on every circumstance, all happenings and all events, without the slightest fading of the light it sees."W-158.7.*

8. The body-self's obsession with pursuing pleasure, safety and security, together with its avoidance of pain, exact the same goal it has planned for *us* – physical death. Both negative *and positive* aspects of body identification all have the *same* goal – death.

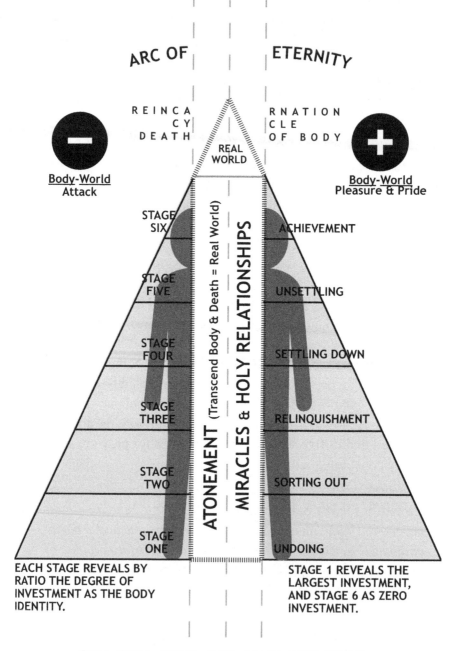

ARC OF ETERNITY

REINCA
CY
DEATH

RNATION
CLE
OF BODY

REAL
WORLD

Body-World
Attack

Body-World
Pleasure & Pride

STAGE
SIX

ACHIEVEMENT

STAGE
FIVE

UNSETTLING

STAGE
FOUR

SETTLING DOWN

STAGE
THREE

RELINQUISHMENT

STAGE
TWO

SORTING OUT

STAGE
ONE

UNDOING

ATONEMENT (Transcend Body & Death = Real World)

MIRACLES & HOLY RELATIONSHIPS

EACH STAGE REVEALS BY
RATIO THE DEGREE OF
INVESTMENT AS THE BODY
IDENTITY.

STAGE 1 REVEALS THE
LARGEST INVESTMENT,
AND STAGE 6 AS ZERO
INVESTMENT.

SIX STAGES OF AWAKENING

A. Six Stages of Awakening Diagram:

Please review the foldable diagram on page 272.

1. We are not the body. Nor can it be integrated with the light we are. While we believe in the reality of what we are seeing, hearing and feeling through the body, we are denying the light. This means we cannot access the light we are, nor can we access its Loving guidance.

   a. *"To see our Self as separate from the body is to end the attack on God's plan for salvation, and to accept it instead. And wherever His plan is accepted, it is accomplished already." W-72.9:5*

   b. *"This is a crucial period in this course, for here the separation of you and the ego must be made complete."... "Now must you choose between yourself and an illusion of yourself. Not both, but one. There is no point in trying to avoid this one decision. It must be made. Faith and belief can fall to either side, but reason tells you misery lies only on one side and joy upon the other." ... "There is no part of Heaven you can take and weave into illusions. Nor is there one illusion you can enter Heaven with." T-22.II.6:1,6-10,8:1-2*

B. The Body as the Idea of Sin

   a. *"While you believe that your reality or your brother's is bounded by a body, you will believe in sin. While you believe that bodies can unite, you will find guilt attractive and believe that sin is precious." T-19.III.7:1-2*

1. Our false belief that we are the body is the gap of separation (see Gap diagram on pages 46 thru 49) until we are willing for it to be divinely reinterpreted and repurposed by Holy Spirit. Until then the body is our belief in sin. The false self's entire foundation which rests on its illusory body is centered on its conviction in the reality of "sin." What does this mean? When we believe we are victim to anyone or anything, this is our belief in sin. Belief in sin cannot be forgiven, hence the seeming impossibility of genuine forgiveness while we believe we are the body.

2. Do we realize just why it seems so terribly difficult to forgive everyone and everything? The answer is because in our ego attempt to forgive, we remain convinced that we're actually trying to forgive something that is real. It really did happen! The same goes for self-judgments that we cannot seem to forgive.

3. In these instances, we side with the ego's refusal to recognize that it did not happen. If I am triggered at all then that trigger along with its subsequent "effects" (conflict, pain, illness, etc.) is caused by and remains bundled together in just one illusion – that unconsciously I believe I am sin, and that this illusion of attack is punishment for my mistaken belief.

    a. *"The major difficulty that you find in genuine forgiveness on your part is that you still believe you must forgive the truth, and not illusions. You conceive of pardon as a vain attempt to look past what is there; to overlook the truth, in an unfounded effort to deceive yourself by making an illusion true. This twisted viewpoint but reflects the hold that the idea of sin retains as yet upon your mind, as you regard yourself." ... "Because you think your sins are real, you look on pardon as deception."* W-134.3,4:1

4. Remember that if I have trouble forgiving someone then it's because I cling to the belief that it was indeed a sin, and not merely an error which can be corrected. In this case I would rather keep the sin along with all the judgment and certain self-punishment that the ego is hoarding for me. Resistance to forgiveness is the belief in sin, and an overwhelming attraction to pain.

5. When we have resistance to forgive it's because the ego possesses a non-negotiable judgment. The error has been classified not merely as a mistake which can be corrected, but as a sin – punishable by death. A sin in the ego's belief is an irrevocable error; a sin must be punished.

6. Resistance to forgiveness is resistance to accepting that no sin exists! It is resistance to accepting that we are sinless along with everyone else. We cannot be triggered and see sin at all unless we believe that we are sin incarnate; in other words, that we are the body. While we mistake our identity as the body we will believe that God as Love, is our enemy.

7. We always have the option to confer with Holy Spirit to learn the truth of our identity. But, when we operate with ego as our chosen guide and master, we believe we are the body (sin). Having made it our idol, every decision and every goal in life revolves around the body. The more we're concerned for it, plan for it, and defend it, the more guilt (self-attack) we accumulate.

8. Attack from external sources such as others, the past and the body, is not possible in reality. There is no cause of attack in others, the body or the world that can have an effect on us because all cause is in our own split mind, regardless of where the body's senses seem to attribute it.

9. All attack we perceive could only ever take place within the illusory "body lens," the one we choose to peer through. Attack does not occur in reality. There is no sin. Ever. In addition, the one who believes they witnessed or experienced "sin," the one who feels victimized, or guilty, does not exist.

   a. *"Forgiveness recognizes what you thought your brother did to you has not occurred. It does not pardon sins and make them real. It sees there was no sin. And in that view are all your sins forgiven." W-pII.1:1-4*

10. If evidence of attack triggers us it's because the ego's "guilt lens" has projected its own self-directed belief in sin through the body. However, the ego along with all the sin it perceives does not exist. There is literally no other reason that we could possibly perceive attack in another, the body or the world. And this is why it's crucial that we learn to forgive our self for believing all appearances of attack. In this, we undo our unconscious obsession with sin and the self-punishment it must deliver.

11. If we genuinely desire to heal then we must forgive our self for having believed that attack (sin) is real. The distinction here is that we did not use something real to seemingly separate from God. If it were real then it could not be forgiven! We are unable to forgive something we still believe to be a reality, and belief in its reality completely rejects healing. God is Love and healing without opposite. If we make the error real, then we're denying our Holy

Self. No healing occurs while we try to forgive what we still believe is real or did happen.

12. If we genuinely want to heal then the most reliable strategy is to wholeheartedly give Holy Spirit permission to undo our belief in sin, regardless of the different forms it appears to take. Only our erroneous belief that there is indeed an opposite of God requires healing. While we believe in an opposite to God, we will secretly believe that we are God's opposite, and therefore His enemy. Here is the ego's attraction to death. We always identify with what we believe in.

13. Attack has never happened in God's reality, otherwise the "sin" or threat we believed did in fact occur would prove that God – as Love – does not exist. If it did not happen in God's reality which is our true reality then it must be illusion, unless we still want to remain separate, and perceive illusions to be true. Sinlessness is fearlessness. It is the restoration to our awareness of the perfect and incorruptible innocence that we are. Knowing this, communication is restored because fear (sin) is erased.

14. The belief in attack arises exclusively from the ego's desire for attack. This well-disguised desire must be recognized and given to Holy Spirit in exchange for healing. This is the reason why all forgiveness is always self-forgiveness.

15. To forgive our self, we need to return to the point where the error was made in our mind, giving it over to the Atonement for healing. For instance, if I've tried to forgive something I believe someone really did, or if I'm trying to forgive a sickness or pain that I still believe is real, then my choice to "believe in its reality" must be healed. In contrast, if I try to forgive the illness, pain, or perhaps a person, I've made the sin – as an opposite of God – real in my mind. And because of this it cannot be forgiven (healed).

16. My decision to believe in sin is a death wish. If I desire true healing, this wrong-minded choice of mine must first be acknowledged and then given sincerely to Spirit. Once we surrender our error to Spirit, there is no more guilt. Furthermore, we give Holy Spirit permission to undo all the consequences of our wrong decision. This is where miraculous healing follows through from our mind to the body and our relationships as well. Jesus gives us the following tool:

17. "Your part is merely to return your thinking to the point at which the error was made, and give it over to the Atonement in peace. Say this to yourself as sincerely as you can, remembering that the Holy Spirit will respond fully to your slightest invitation:

   a. *I must have decided wrongly, because I am not at peace. I made the decision myself, but I can also decide otherwise. I want to decide otherwise, because I want to be at peace. I do not feel guilty, because the Holy Spirit will undo all the consequences of my wrong decision if I will let Him. I choose to let Him, by allowing Him to decide for God for me." T-5.VII.6:5-11*

18. Also, following is a short forgiveness prayer which helps us first to acknowledge that "we" must have chosen wrongly through the ego, to use *someone or something* to attack our self. And secondly, we acknowledge that the attack is not real; it is an illusion. Therefore, we ask Holy Spirit to help us forgive our belief that sin as attack, is real.

19. *"Holy Spirit, please help me to forgive myself for having believed in separation, thereby projecting my guilt onto _ (my brothers, the body, the past, the world, etc.) _ and using this to attack myself. Please also help me to forgive (undo) my belief in attack as real. Amen."*

   a. *"Salvation is a paradox indeed! What could it be except a happy dream? It asks you but that you forgive all things that no one ever did; to overlook what is not there, and not to look upon the unreal as reality." T-30.IV.7:1-3*

C. Exposing and Healing Hidden Self-Sabotage

1. Everything we appear to see and experience which triggers us is a direct representation of what the ego wants.

   a. *"To see a guilty world is but the sign your learning has been guided by the world, and you behold it as you see yourself. The concept of the self embraces all you look upon, and nothing is outside of this perception. If you can be hurt by anything, you see a picture of your secret wishes." T-31.V.15:6-8*

2. Everything that seems to happen to us, both seemingly good and bad, always arises from our desire for it. But until the false, body-self is largely recognized and genuinely surrendered to Spirit, the single source of our unconscious desire for self-attack will not be recognized as within our own mind. It will be wrongly attributed to others, the body, the past and the world. Because of this universal blind spot and our denial of it, our self-attack will continue since its "source" has not been seen and forgiven.

   a. *"If you will recognize that all the attack you perceive is in your own mind and nowhere else, you will at last have placed its source, and where it begins it must end. For in this same place also lies salvation." T-12.III.10:1-2*

3. Remember this. The body-self is the sole repository for guilt as self-attack. While the body is neutral, we cannot experience this neutrality, this immunity to attack, while we continue to use it for self-seeking agendas apart from Spirit.

4. When it is used inappropriately – as a goal in itself – instead of being used purely as a communication device to demonstrate the innocence of everyone, it acts as a serious obstruction to Love, peace and health.

5. Communication remains unbroken exclusively in Love, in innocence. However, communication is severed when we act from fear, anger, or deprivation. So when we try to gain something for our self alone – special love, sex, gifts, money, or engage in guilt-tripping, withholding forgiveness, etc. – we literally break communication with others, our Self, and God. Hence, through the ego the body-self is employed as a "getting machine," made to blind us to the ever-present sanctity of our one, shared and Holy Self.

   a. *"When the body ceases to attract you and when you place no value on it as a means for getting anything, then there will be no interference in communication, and your thoughts will be as free as God's. As you let the Holy Spirit teach you how to use the body only for purposes of communication and renounce its use for separation and attack which the ego sees in it, you will learn you have no need of a body at all." T-15.IX.7:1-2*

D. Body, Mind and Spirit – Can They be Reconciled?

1. Many spiritual teachings encourage the idea of integrating the body with the Holy Self. The aim here is to reconcile body, mind and Spirit. Yet while we still value using the body for pride, pleasure and attack, and for special relationships, we will unconsciously also use it to demonstrate separation as sin, and not oneness, through conflict, sickness, pain, aging and finally death.

2. Many spiritual paths are predicated on the lie that there is "life in matter." For instance, that the body is an intelligent organism which functions independently of our mind and our wishes, as it can be hurt, become diseased, age and die, all without our consent. There is an accepted, but mistaken, belief that we can be victimized by the neutral body.

3. The spiritual ego will often want to spiritualize the body, believing that by using a number of practices, i.e. changing diet, nutrition, yoga, etc., the body will harmonize with the mind and Spirit. While these practices may be helpful temporarily, they address only the consequences of our wrong mind, while leaving their uninvestigated cause uncorrected within the mind to strike again, albeit possibly in another form of attack. In effect, this is like trying to build a beautiful home on a bed of straw floating on the ocean. The foundation will sink the home no matter how much we invest in making the home itself secure. It will not work.

4. There is only one cause, not many, of all suffering we perceive. And that is unforgiveness. All perception of attack or deprivation stems from our erroneous belief that we're separate from our Loving Source. Unless the mind is wholeheartedly engaged in forgiving everyone and everything each day, the singular cause of all self-attack remains unhealed. As we forgive, the blocks to our awareness of Love's presence are erased and we extend the Love we are to other minds. We also become more aware of our ability to receive this Love which streams through when unblocked by fear. This is the healing cure for all imagined conflict and illness.

 a. *"Learning must lead beyond the body to the re-establishment of the power of the mind in it. This can be accomplished only if the mind extends to other minds, and does not arrest itself in its extension. This arrest is the cause of all illness, because only extension is the mind's function." T-8.VII.12:6-8*

5. The body, mind and Spirit cannot be integrated. Attempts at integration must arise from a mistaken belief in the body-self. We cannot truly integrate the body, demonstrating that it is indeed neutral (immune to signs of separation), while we still believe erroneously that the body is an independent cause of its own apart from our mind. If the vessel remains as a sign of sin/attack and separation by aging, getting sick and dying, then the mind has not been fully healed.

   a. *"The idea that a body can be sick is a central concept in the ego's thought system. This thought gives the body autonomy, separates it from the mind, and keeps the idea of attack inviolate. If the body could be sick Atonement would be impossible. A body that can order a mind to do as it sees fit could merely take the place of God and prove salvation is impossible. What, then, is left to heal? The body has become lord of the mind." M-22.3:2-7*

   b. *"A broken body shows the mind has not been healed." T-27. II.5:1*

6. The body is an image which dwells in our mind, having been projected by it. It is 100 percent neutral until our mind decides to superimpose its purpose on it. Everything that appears to happen to the body must be directed by our wish in the mind. We either "wish with the ego" to use the body for conflict and attack, or we "will with God" to use it only for uninterrupted communication of innocence as Love. These are the only two choices to choose between.

7. All the external phenomena – magic – that we mistakenly believe have power to change the body are completely neutral as well. They have no power to harm or heal the body independent of the desire for attack or healing in our mind. These phenomena (magic) have no harmful or healing properties at all. All harm or healing is a direct result of the intent in our mind.

8. Who is seeing? Who is feeling? Who is judging? Who perceives injustice? Who feels victimized? Who is angry? Who feels guilty?

Who is in pain? Who is sick? Who feels abandoned or betrayed? The "who" that perceives separation is always the body-self and never the Holy Self. This is why we need to learn to make a fundamental distinction between the false and isolated body-self, and our shared identity as the Holy Self. Without the fear driven attachment to a body-self there could never be a perception of attack or defense.

9.   Our investment in the body, its five senses and its sensual appetites is an allegiance to the denied belief in sin and the subsequent punishment that it insists we deserve.

a.   *"In the holy instant, where the Great Rays replace the body in awareness, the recognition of relationships without limits is given you. But in order to see this, it is necessary to give up every use the ego has for the body, and to accept the fact that the ego has no purpose you would share with it. For the ego would limit everyone to a body for its own purposes, and while you think it has a purpose, you will choose to utilize the means by which it tries to turn its purpose into accomplishment."* T-15.IX.3.1-3

12. SEX AND LOVE

1.   We may pass through many different phases of intensifying our attachment to the body and its appetites before we finally decide with Spirit to renounce being body-identified, and willingly replace this illusion with our strong allegiance to the Holy Self as Spirit. The sexual pleasure drive is fiercely guarded by those who still regard it as the gateway to love. As a highly valued body appetite, lust in particular is especially prone to defense. And yet if we sincerely desire to heal the ego's self-sabotage cycle then lust, with the goal of orgasm and as the habitual mating urge, must be given to Holy Spirit to be divinely repurposed.

2.   The pursuit of orgasm as an ulterior yet often unconscious goal, seeks to glorify the body and worship it on our inner altar because

of what it can give to us that we deem God – as changeless Love/ Spirit – cannot.

a. *"Miracles reawaken the awareness that the spirit, not the body, is the altar of truth. This is the recognition that leads to the healing power of the miracle." T-1.I.20.*

3.   The immaculate miracle impulse, as an expression of perfect Love which originates from God, is given to us in order to experience healing and extend this union with other minds. This impulse, in its pure unadulterated form, is entirely interpersonal and naturally indiscriminate. This is why it always results in genuine closeness to others. When it is unimpeded by the personal gain agenda of the sexual urge – the perfect miracle impulse's ripple effect radiates outward to touch and heal people including those we don't even know. Hence it is totally free of specialness in any form.

a. *"While you believe that your reality or your brother's is bounded by a body, you will believe in sin. While you believe that bodies can unite, you will find guilt attractive and believe that sin is precious." T-19.III.7:1-2*

4.   In the pursuit of orgasm, instead of allowing this profound impersonal, inclusive and universal miracle impulse to extend from our heart to another's, it is seized and hijacked by the ego body's personal and highly exclusive pleasure drive. It seeks completion solely for itself, not in divine communion and extension with another's mind, but in a physical outcome, namely orgasm. In its attempt to sequester and redirect this infinite miracle impulse through the dense body it becomes misdirected. Its divine purpose, when not interrupted by the sexual body appetite's need to "get," is to ripple outward, unrestricted in its quantum extension.

5.   In sexual attraction, sexual fantasies and orgasm, the pure miracle impulse is arrested, stunted and diffused, unable to extend itself boundlessly and holographically as the miracle does when unimpeded. The reason is simple. An undefiled miracle impulse is whole, completely undivided. It has no lack within it, as it comes from God. It knows just one purpose and that is to extend, to give itself away fully to all. In addition, according to the laws of God,

when we give unconditionally we also receive the Love we extend. As we allow the miracle impulse to flow through us unselfishly, instead of terminating it in the body through sexual desire and orgasm, we both extend and receive that healing.

6.   Because it has no need other than to give of itself endlessly, the miracle impulse's mission is arrested when it is used by the ego for personal gain or self-gratification. Only a body-self can perceive itself as needing to "get" to be satiated, because the body concept is one of permanent lack.

7.   This does not mean that we give up sex but it does encourage us to unlearn the destructive component of sexual desire – lust. Lust is used by the ego for amassing unconscious guilt, conflict and self attack. When we're ready, there is a whole new approach to sexual relating available that is wholly satisfying and tremendously healing. This phase involves using sex to heal, which is outlined in the chapter titled Sex and TransOrgasmic Union.

a.   *"I have said that the Holy Spirit is the motivation for miracles. He always tells you that only the mind is real, because only the mind can be shared. The body is separate, and therefore cannot be part of you. To be of one mind is meaningful, but to be one body is meaningless. By the laws of mind, then, the body is meaningless." T-6.V.A.3*

8.   The pursuit of orgasm is an attempt to reach communion through the body. However, Jesus is very clear that communion via the flesh is impossible.

a.   *"Sex is often associated with lack of love, but Revelation is PURELY a love experience. Physical closeness CANNOT achieve this. As was said before, the subconscious impulses properly induce Miracles, which ARE interpersonal, and result in closeness to others. This can be misunderstood by a personally willful consciousness as an impulse toward sexual gratification." Urtext.T-1,II.*

b.   *"Sex and miracles are both WAYS OF RELATING. The nature of any interpersonal relationship is limited or defined by what you want it TO DO which is WHY you want it in the first place. Relating is a way of achieving an outcome.*

Indiscriminate sexual impulses resemble indiscriminate miracle impulses in that both result in body image misperceptions. The first is an expression of an indiscriminate attempt to reach communion through the body. This involves not only the improper self identification, but also disrespect for the individuality of others. Self-control is NOT the whole answer to this problem, though I am by no means discouraging its use. It must be understood, however, that the underlying mechanism must be uprooted (a word you both should understand well enough by now not to regard it as frightening).

ALL shallow roots have to be uprooted, because they are not deep enough to sustain you." A Course in Miracles, Urtext, T-1.3.

9. There is no guilt intended or implied here if the reader is in resistance to joining Holy Spirit to heal the sexual pleasure drive, or any other body appetite. In fact, to believe in guilt is to separate further from our Holy Self and therefore God, and that is not the intention of this chapter. Hopefully, the ideas set out in Jesus' *Course* just might plant a seed that will germinate when trust has been developed and willingness arises as a result. Those who are ready to heal will recognize it and allow Holy Spirit to lead the way.

10. Ultimately, if our goal is to awaken from the dream of separation, we must eventually heal our belief that we are the body along with the misconception that being with another's body is actual communication or true joining.

a. *"Yet remember this; to be with a body is not communication. And if you think it is, you will feel guilty about communication and will be afraid to hear the Holy Spirit, recognizing in His Voice your own need to communicate." T-15.VII.10:5-6*

11. We appear to journey through various phases of either descending into the body and its appetites or ascending up and out of them. Sometimes we vacillate wildly between them. Nonetheless, no matter

what we do here at the behavioral level in the dream, it is never a sin. It does not show up on God's Radar. Regardless of what we do it is always neutral. We are sinless and guiltless eternally. God's Love never judges and therefore it never condemns. It's the intent behind our actions, arising from either fear or Love, which brings us turmoil or peace.

12. We will all reach a place organically in the long dream of time, where we will naturally turn away from the body-self's senses and appetites without sacrifice. Until that occurs, I encourage you to release yourself from judgment. Forgive any and every self-judgment and these will give way to peace where Holy Spirit's guidance rushes in to fill the gap which doubt and conflict had once occupied.

A. Body Appetites - Obstacles to Peace

1. Just to clarify, peace is an inherent attribute of divine Love and is inseparable from it. Where there is Love there must be peace. The presence of peace and Love are a law against fear in any form. Subsequently, the obstacles to peace are also the obstacles to Love, barriers to true union with others, our Self and God.

2. In the *Course's "The Obstacles to Peace,"* which are really our self-imposed blocks to Love, it is noted that the false self has set up very strategic defenses against recognizing our true Identity, and with it, the infinite union we share with God and our brothers. These defenses represent particular barriers to awakening from the mistaken body identity.

3. The first obstacle to peace is "the desire to get rid of it" which includes "the attraction to guilt." Guilt happens to be a towering defense against both Love and peace. The greatest contributor to this unconscious guilt is belief that the body is our identity. Thus, through the body, we seek our completion and the deeper we go into this delusion the more conflict we experience. The inner and outer conflict is a direct result of the guilt we acquire from valuing separation as a personal will apart from Love, apart from God.

4. The initial cause of the seeming separation eons ago in the dream of time, was the Son's desire to experience "specialness." This led

him to fabricate individual identities, with private minds housed in separate walls of flesh; and all these individuals were competing to fulfill their own personal "wills" – agendas – apart from God, apart from their brothers and apart from Love itself. But God knows not of specialness. His Love is one, all-inclusive, uninterrupted and eternal.

5. How could this plan for specialness work? What fantastic fantasies would it require to keep it almost God-proof for millions of years in the illusion of time, birth and death?

6. It would demand a fool-proof formula that almost no one could question. Initially, our desire for specialness emerged. To keep this obsession intact, there entered the idea of a separate body as a literal wall to divide us from God's Allness. This was coupled with its fixed goal of sin since it was a concept devised to separate us and block out the Love of God and our brothers. Belief in sin – that we sinned against God– produced guilt, which then invented the illusion of fear as an opposite of God's all-encompassing Love.

a. *"The body is the ego's idol; the belief in sin made flesh and then projected outward. This produces what seems to be a wall of flesh around the mind, keeping it prisoner in a tiny spot of space and time, beholden unto death, and given but an instant in which to sigh and grieve and die in honor of its master."* T-20.VI.11:1-2

7. Fear is always the direct result of guilt because all fear is guilt's secret anticipation of punishment. Only the false self experiences fear because, in its shrouded, unconscious vault, i.e. the body, "it" is convinced it sinned against God by making a self who seeks self-gratification apart from Him.

8. The guilt it secretly hoards is unbearable. Consequently, it projects this unforgiven guilt outward onto others, the body, the past and the world, using them to fulfill its hidden wish to be unfairly treated, as the attraction to specialness. Hence there is a plethora of what seems like random chaos, conflict, scarcity, illness, pain, loss, abandonment, betrayal and death. These represent our projected guilt in various forms coming to attack our self as punishment for having separated from God. Talk about a fantastic fantasy!

---

9. Thus the entire ego thought system of fear is fueled by unconscious guilt. Without guilt... there is no possibility of fear, conflict, loss or suffering. This is why forgiveness is the key to undoing the deluded ideas of sin, guilt and fear. All forgiveness is self-forgiveness. We forgive the false self for having believed it could be separate from God, that it could be guilty and be attacked.

    a. *"If you will recognize that all the attack you perceive is in your own mind and nowhere else, you will at last have placed its source, and where it begins it must end. For in this same place also lies salvation." T-12.III.10:1-2*

10. With sin, guilt and fear erased, all that remains in our perception and experience is Love. All that we experience is the effervescent joy and quiet peace of our one, shared and beloved Holy Self.

11. In contrast to the Holy Self, the separate, human body identity remains entrenched in and blinded by its fundamental belief in sin, guilt and fear. The separate self is sustained by this cycle as it represents the central hub of its closed-circuit paradigm. And everything that happens to it is perpetuated by this looping hallucination. The reversal or forgiveness of our belief in sin, guilt and fear is the certain healing of all our relationships with our Self, others, the body and the world.

12. The body's five physical senses and its appetites were fabricated exclusively to a) witness sin so we would judge our brothers, thus acquiring guilt which fuels our own cycle of sin, guilt and fear, and b) to seduce us into believing the body is our central idol by pursuing our own self-gratification via fulfilling our pleasure-drives apart from God.

13. The second of the obstacles to peace in the *Course,* is "the belief the body is valuable for what it offers." While we still value the body for what we believe it gives us, then automatically, we will amass unconscious guilt as self-attack or pain, for that is the ego's purpose for the body. While we're sick or in pain, the ego reasons, we cannot possibly be the invincible and innocent Holy Self.

    a. *"The body does appear to be the symbol of sin while you believe that it can get you what you want. While you believe that it can give you pleasure, you will also believe that it can bring you pain." T-19.IV.A.17:10-11*

14. The erroneous belief that the body can fulfill and complete us comes with an enormous cost. First, the ego's attraction to pleasure is also its well-hidden attraction to pain. The two go hand in hand. And the reason is that the one seeking pleasure is none other than the separate and deprived false self who seeks to fulfill its own private "will" apart from God. Yet all real pleasure comes only from doing God's Will:

a. *"All real pleasure comes from doing God's Will. This is because [not] doing it is a denial of Self. Denial of Self results in illusions, while correction of the error brings release from it. Do not deceive yourself into believing that you can relate in peace to God or to your brothers with anything external." T-1. VII.1:4-7*

15. Jesus makes a point to say that we cannot relate in peace – as Love – to God or to our brothers with anything external, namely the body. The ego's body-self, whose unconscious goal is sin which is attained through self-gratification, is a block to Love.

16. As long as we mistakenly see our self and others as merely bodies we will not see the Holy Self. When the body is the goal, along with the pleasure (pain) which we seek through it, we will unknowingly use others as bodies as well. Our senses stop there at the body, ours and others, and separation arises as we judge what bodies do and don't do. Each judgment we make consolidates our own unconscious attack as guilt. This is the deep and unseen attraction to conflict, disease and finally, to death itself.

17. The Holy Spirit asks us to offer Him a little willingness to exchange the destructive purpose we gave to the body for His purpose which removes all pain and conflict, making way for miracles and Love beyond our wildest imagining.

a. *"The second obstacle that peace must flow across, and closely related to the first, is the belief that the body is valuable for what it offers. For here is the attraction of guilt made manifest in the body, and seen in it." ... "What has the body really given you that justifies your strange belief that in it lies salvation? Do you not see that this is the belief in death?"* ...

"The Holy Spirit does not demand you sacrifice the hope of the body's pleasure; it [has] no hope of pleasure. But neither can it bring you fear of pain. Pain is the only "sacrifice" the Holy Spirit asks, and this He [would] remove." T-19. IV.B.1:3-4,2:6-7,3:5-7

18. A corresponding rule which is also classified under the second obstacle to peace is the "the attraction of pain." We unknowingly distort the miracle impulse through the body by misdirecting it via the self-centered and lust-driven "getting mechanism" of orgasm. This blocks the shared extension principle of the miracle. By diverting the pure miracle impulse toward the body instead of extending it beyond the body, we unknowingly attract pain.

   a. *"Mind cannot be made physical, but it can be made manifest [through] the physical if it uses the body to go beyond itself. By reaching out, the mind extends itself. It does not stop at the body, for if it does it is blocked in its purpose. A mind that has been blocked has allowed itself to be vulnerable to attack, because it has turned against itself." T-8.VII.10:4-7*

19. If the miracle impulse is the extension of God's Love, then blocking this results in a "lack of Love." Where there is lack of Love there is fear. This particular body appetite of orgasm, because of its self-indulgent nature and misuse of the miracle impulse, lends itself to unconscious guilt which is the unwitting attraction to sickness and death. Remember, nothing is real unless it is shared, transcending self-interest.

   a. *"Pain demonstrates the body must be real. It is a loud, obscuring voice whose shrieks would silence what the Holy Spirit says, and keep His words from your awareness. Pain compels attention, drawing it away from Him and focusing upon itself. Its purpose is the same as pleasure, for they both are means to make the body real. What shares a common purpose is the same."* ... *"Pleasure and pain are equally*

unreal, because their purpose (to make the body real) cannot
be achieved." T-27.VI.2:1-5,7

20. Through self-seeking body appetites, the ego accumulates guilt in
its search for personal pleasure apart from God's Love. This guilt
morphs unknowingly into the unconscious attraction to pain in
multiple forms including relationship conflict, illness, depression,
addictions, pain, scarcity and loss. Yet in every Holy Instant, Holy
Spirit offers us healing when we are willing to accept His divine
remedy as the Atonement.

CHAPTER THREE

C–III.   TRUE HEALING

I. THE UNPARALLELED SECRET TO HEALING

1. We want to understand. And we desire to be understood. We want to be healed. And we desire to heal others. We want our problems solved. And we desire to solve other's problems. But why is it that these desires seem so difficult to fulfill consistently? The solution is not where we think it is.

A. True Healing is the Absence of Fear, as the Peace of God

1. Peace is the necessary condition for all healing. Let me explain. When we're concerned and we believe there *is* a problem, regardless of its form, we are literally seeing something that does not exist in God's Love. The only way we could believe in a problem is if we're looking through the body-self's lens of fear. The "problem" does not exist in reality. Nor does the *one* who is convinced the issue is real.

2. *We are not that!* We are the eternal, immortal Holy Self and nothing but the Holy Self. We cannot be both a human being *and* the Holy Self; both the body *and* Spirit. *"A mind and body cannot both exist. Make no attempt to reconcile the two, for one denies the other can be real."* W-96.3:4-5

3. The peace of God is the necessary condition in which the laws of God operate. The necessary condition for healing *is* the peace of God. All true healing is the absence of fear.

4. Escape from fear as conflict and suffering necessitates making a firm decision to accept and proclaim what we are. We are God's most beloved Child. We share His Loving Will. We *are* His Loving Will. And we share His dominion over all "appearances" of adversity.

5. The Self we share with God is completely immune to all the ego's phenomena here in the dream. When we make a comprehensive choice to align exclusively as God's Will, we become the living demonstration of that truth. There is no opposite and therefore zero threat to God's all-encompassing truth and Love. This is His Will.

6. This may be a good place to introduce a reminder about God's Love as His Will, which is our true nature. Love is imbued with unopposed and undivided attributes. They are peace, joy and gratitude. If any one of these qualities are missing, then our mind is in fear and not in Love. Subsequently, we're back into witnessing through the body-self and not the Holy Self. Love is not Love unless gratitude, joy and peace accompany it. These elements are inseparable.

7. God's Will is Truth and it cannot have an opposite. In other words, the body-self, together with what its senses perceive, what its appetites crave, as well as all its seeming problems, does not exist. We are not that. All our suffering arises from this split in our mind where we believe we are both the body *and* Spirit, both fear *and* Love. Yet the two cannot be reconciled. We must make a willing leap, to want to know with conviction "what" we really are. Holy Spirit then has our permission to reveal to us what Love *is*.

a. *"If truth is total, the untrue cannot exist. Commitment to either must be total; they cannot coexist in your mind without splitting it. If they cannot coexist in peace, and if you want peace, you must give up the idea of conflict entirely and for all time. This requires vigilance only as long as you do not recognize what is true. While you believe that two totally contradictory thought systems share truth, your need for vigilance is apparent." T-7.VI.8:7-11*

---

8. One word that stands out in the above quote is "share." Love and fear cannot share truth because they are totally contradictory. All adversity is false. It can only be an issue while we still choose to believe that we are the body and not a Holy Son of God.

9. The necessary condition in which God's Will and His laws function, is peace. Peace, like Love, is the absence of fear. God's perfect Love and healing are always present. There is never a moment where His Love and healing are absent. If we do not perceive it then it's because we've used our free will to choose to witness through fear. It is not random. It is a choice.

10. Fear blocks His communication and taints our perception of God's Love. It blocks our mind to Holy Spirit's healing, and His laws. His communication of Love and healing is eternal and uninterrupted. Nothing can threaten it. It is certain. If we do not see it then we still value fear via the body-self identity. If we truly desire to heal, this is where we need the willingness to confess that we've allowed our self to be deceived by issues relating to the body-self (ours or others). In this bodily relating, we have unknowingly rejected our Holy Self. And now we want Holy Spirit's help to bring us back to peace so He can heal our split mind. A little willingness is all He needs.

11. **Here is the unparalleled secret to healing:** Healing is communication. Fear disrupts communication. Therefore, fear or concern disrupts healing. Nothing can be healed or resolved apart from the peace of God. Everything can be healed in the peace of God. True healing is the absence of fear. And this is why in order to heal, we enter a Holy Instant of peace where we mindfully choose to accept Holy Spirit's healed perception instead of the ego's. This is accepting the Atonement. Jesus shares with us:

   a. *"Fear prevents me from giving you my control. The presence of fear shows that you have raised body thoughts to the level of the mind. This removes them from my control, and makes you feel personally responsible for them. This is an obvious confusion of levels." T-2,VI.1:5-8*

12. The reason there is no order of difficulty in miracles is because there is no hierarchy of fear (illusions). Every possible fear, including all its consequences such as illness, pain, conflict, lack, etc., is spawned by "lack of Love," which is merely fear. Miracles restore the Love that was lacking; thus they heal.

  a. *"The miracle does nothing. All it does is to undo. And thus it cancels out the interference to what has been done. It does not add, but merely takes away." T-28.I.1:1-4*

13. There are no degrees of fear, just as there are no degrees of Love. Fear and Love are each total thought systems. They cannot be merged because they cannot coexist in our mind at the same time. In any one moment, the presence of fear in our awareness is the denial of Love. And the presence of Love in our awareness is the absence of fear.

14. All fear is an illusion. Adversity, regardless of its severity, is fear. Can you imagine degrees of darkness? Perhaps a large house that appears to have varying degrees of darkness? Let's say that the differing grades of blackness depict our own hierarchy of problems such as disease, pain, conflict, scarcity, etc. For instance, the darkest room in the house may represent what seems to be an insurmountable obstacle such as a life-threatening disease.

15. Now imagine Holy Spirit switching on a gigantic floodlight, one that shone clear through ceilings and walls illuminating the entire house in brilliant golden light. Imagine that this light permeated every darkened corner of that house. No darkness can survive it. Darkness cannot endure in light! Darkness is only a lack of light. Illness, pain, conflict and lack are forms of fear, which means they are purely a lack of Love. Darkness and fear are causeless because they are both illusions. Darkness is merely denial of Love, of light. It has no active cause other than this. This is why all real healing is the undoing of fear; the block that hides Love's presence.

  a. *"It is impossible to conceive of light and darkness or everything and nothing as joint possibilities. They are all true or all false. It is essential that you realize your thinking will be erratic until a firm commitment to one or the other is made." T-3.II.1:3-5*

16. There is no hierarchy of darkness – or adversity. There is not one area of darkness that is more obstinate than any other. All illusions are *equally unreal*. Darkness vanishes once the light of peace blazes it away. Light erases darkness effortlessly. All miracles are *equally real*. The light in our mind is unblocked and shines forth to heal in the moment we sincerely want it to. But we must desire to access a Holy Instant of peace, more than we want to believe the body's senses. One miracle is not harder than any other because light always eradicates the illusion of darkness equally, everywhere. There is no seeming problem which the miracle cannot heal.

17. All miracles abide within the peace of God already, just waiting on our welcome. Yet it is not until we're genuinely willing to receive and extend them via accepting the Atonement (the undoing of fear) that they are perceived and witnessed.

18. While we really do believe that a problem exists and that there is indeed a hierarchy of adversities, then we value the mistaken belief that light cannot abolish darkness; that Holy Spirit's Truth cannot erase illusions. Light enters and the symptoms of darkness are erased when we prioritize peace. In each instance that we ask Holy Spirit to help us heal our split mind we're actually asking Him to undo our belief that we're a body-self. Remember, our erroneous value of the body *is* the split mind itself. Note: Here is the Atonement process: *The Seven Essential Principles of Quantum Forgiveness (Atonement)* on page 591.

19. Nothing, absolutely and unequivocally *nothing,* can be understood without peace. Anything that is seen in fear cannot be understood. Again, if fear is present it is an immediate disruption of God's communication as Love, as healing. The mind in fear is sick.

20. All understanding, all healing, is a divine collaboration of miracles which dwell in the peace of God and nowhere else.

21. While we believe we are private minds trapped in separate bodies we will never understand nor heal anything at all. There is no understanding possible apart from the peace of God. We are the one continuous Mind with God as Love without opposite. This one Mind is whole and changeless. It never left its Source. However, once we lose our self in the seemingly separate body-self then we value being

a private mind as well. Fear can only ever be experienced in a mind that believes it is private. Hence, a private mind with a separate body believes in and is sustained by the illusion of fear and attack.

a.   *"Although you are one Self, you experience yourself as two; as both good and evil, loving and hating, mind and body. This sense of being split into opposites induces feelings of acute and constant conflict, and leads to frantic attempts to reconcile the contradictory aspects of this self-perception. You have sought many such solutions, and none of them has worked. The opposites you see in you will never be compatible. But one exists.*

"The fact that truth and illusion cannot be reconciled, no matter how you try, what means you use and where you see the problem, must be accepted if you would be saved. Until you have accepted this, you will attempt an endless list of goals you cannot reach; a senseless series of expenditures of time and effort, hopefulness and doubt, each one as futile as the one before, and failing as the next one surely will."

"Salvation comes from this one Self through Him Who is the Bridge between your mind and It. Wait patiently, and let Him speak to you about your Self, and what your mind can do, restored to [this one Self] and free to serve Its Will."
W-pI.96.1-2;8:3-4

22. The false body-self *is* fear. Nothing can be understood in the presence of fear. Fear is not understandable. No problem can be solved in fear and nothing can be healed in it. The presence of fear *is* the absence of God in our awareness – our own abandonment of our beloved Holy Self, and the absence of the Love that heals all.

2. THE DIVINE SWITCH FROM EGO TO HOLY SELF

1. In the earlier phases of the undoing journey, we are not aware of the unconscious beliefs, values, choices and conditioning which constitute the cause of all distress we encounter, or have encountered in the past. We still believe that we know what "love" is. We believe we know how to give and get it. We assume we know what we want and need. We even go so far as to imagine that we know the particular "forms" of relationship and success which will provide the love, happiness, safety, security and abundance we desire. Furthermore, we actually think that we can safely determine the difference between pain and joy, success and failure.

2. Our entire life is dedicated to finding what we believe will complete us. But what we don't recognize is that through the false, body-self this is impossible. The ego seeks for its completion within a giant illusory maze which always culminates in death. Death is the central dream from which all illusions stem. Completion of the false-self cannot be accomplished because this "self," along with the body it projected, is a complete illusion. Its seeming existence is sustained by an unseen, unrelinquished identification with sin, guilt and fear which always ends in death.

3. In the earlier phases of our transfer from fear to Love we really have no idea how to differentiate between the ego and the Holy Self; between Love and fear. The false, body-self *is* fear. Our Holy Self *is* changeless Love. There is *no* communication between these two. Love does not know fear. And fear cannot recognize Love.

4. While we are identified with the body-self we will be terrified of Love because its approach threatens to completely annihilate this little self.

5. As you may well see by now, in the initial phases, we really do believe we *are* the false-self, the body-self. As a result we project our seeming reality and relationships through its lens of guilt and fear. We don't yet recognize changeless Love because fear seeks its own. Consequently, the ego searches for its favorite brand of fear, *special love* which is fearful love; a pseudo love that can hurt, change or end. This fearful and highly volatile version of "love" is what the world has mistakenly defined as love. Very few people recognize as yet that since the beginning of time special love represents the greatest substitute for the changeless Love we are.

6. If we still identify heavily with the body, its senses, its appetites, the past, lack, loss, being a victim or a perpetrator, then it's the false-self who perceives and interprets. We always identify with what we value, which includes the suffering we think we endured. If we still believe that we were indeed harmed then we must value it. This is a fundamental value in the ego's thought system and one that it must maintain and defend in order to ensure its continuation.

7. If we are still substantially identified as the false-self then how on earth do we make the switch in our awareness to the Holy Self?

8. We begin to make the divine switch from ego to Holy Self each instance in which we willingly recognize that *we are responsible* (without blame) for whatever has triggered us in another, the body, the past or the world. In other words, we acknowledge that our suffering arose exclusively from our mistaken interpretation of what occurred. The ego wrongly perceived attack.

   a. *"I am responsible for what I see.*
   I choose the feelings I experience, and I decide upon the goal
   I would achieve.
   And everything that seems to happen to me I ask for, and
   receive as I have asked.

   Deceive yourself no longer that you are helpless in the face
   of what is done to you. Acknowledge but that you have been
   mistaken, and all effects of your mistakes will disappear."
   T-21.II.2:3-7

9. To access a Holy Instant we must be willing to be wrong, to suspend our judgment so that Holy Spirit can reveal the Love and healing which our judgment had previously blocked from awareness. In essence, are we willing to be wrong about others, our beliefs, our values, our past, and our identity?

   a. *"The holy instant is not an instant of creation, but of recognition. For recognition comes of vision and suspended judgment. Then only it is possible to look within and see what must be there, plainly in sight, and wholly independent of*

*inference and judgment. Undoing is not your task, but it [is]
up to you to welcome it or not. Faith and desire go hand in
hand, for everyone believes in what he wants." T-21.II.8:2-6*

A. Moment of Decision: The Past, or the Holy Instant?

1. All communication with self and others begins as "special"
because it arises from the false-self. We project past beliefs onto
our self and each other, searching for recognition, approval and
love. These are attempts to reinforce the "body-self" and guilt. This
is a closed circuit and continues to loop endlessly until we choose
to join Holy Spirit and give over our judgments.

   1) Do we know what it means to show-up?

2. We cannot access the Holy Self while we're trying to be all things
to everyone. We will defend the ego if we still believe we were
wrongly treated, or we want to be right, or we're absorbed in playing
certain roles, or planning and attaining goals apart from Holy Spirit.

3. Do we want freedom? Do we really want healing? Have we had
enough of conflict, pain and doubt? Do we finally desire to know
what Love is?

4. This is the moment of decision. Do we stay here in this phase and
loop again? Or do we boldly "show-up" by taking the leap with
Holy Spirit?

B. Exercise: The Divine Switch - Exposing Resistance to Love

1. In radical self-honesty and mindful presence please go through
each of the questions below. Each of the following questions
includes two further questions. One is to unearth the ego's fears, i.e.
which of these does the false-self resist and why? And the other is
to reveal the gifts of saying "yes" to Spirit. It's helpful to write each
of your answers down so you can review them with Holy Spirit
later.

   1) **Am I willing to suspend my judgment of others?**

      a. Am I willing to Love – accept – others unconditionally,
regardless of the temptation to judge and condemn them?

b. By saying "yes," what will the false-self stand to lose?

c. In saying "yes," what possible gifts will I open to receive from making the divine switch from ego (body) to Holy Self (Spirit)?

2) **Am I willing to suspend *self*-judgment?**

a. Am I willing to Love – accept – myself unconditionally, regardless of the temptation to condemn myself?

b. By saying "yes," what will the false-self stand to lose?

c. In saying "yes," what possible gifts will I open to receive from making the divine switch from ego (body) to Holy Self (Spirit)?

3) **Am I willing to be wrong about my judgment? Am I teachable?**

a. By saying "yes," what will the false-self stand to lose?

b. In saying "yes," what possible gifts will I open to receive from making the divine switch from ego (body) to Holy Self (Spirit)?

4) **Am I willing to let go of the past?**

a. These are "stories" about me that I tell myself and others. The past includes how I see others based on a past story that the false-self projects. By saying "yes," what will the false-self stand to lose?

b. In saying "yes," what possible gifts will I open to receive from making the divine switch from ego (body) to Holy Self (Spirit)?

5) **Am I willing to apply the *Seven Key Principles of Authentic Relating* consistently in all my communication with Self and others?**

a. By saying "yes," what will the false-self stand to lose?

b. In saying "yes," what possible gifts will I open to receive from making the divine switch from ego (body) to Holy Self (Spirit)?

6) **Am I willing to forgive myself and accept the Atonement?**

a. By saying "yes," what will the false-self stand to lose? In saying "yes," what possible gifts will I open to receive from making the divine switch from ego (body) to Holy Self (Spirit)?

7) **Am I willing to drop my unworthiness to receive the Atonement?**

a. By saying "yes," what will the false-self stand to lose? In saying "yes," what possible gifts will I open to receive from making the divine switch from ego (body) to Holy Self (Spirit)?

8) **Am I willing to be completely healed, mind *and* body via the miracle, the Atonement?**

a. By saying "yes," what will the false-self stand to lose?

b. In saying "yes," what possible gifts will I open to receive from making the divine switch from ego (body) to Holy Self (Spirit)?

9) **Am I willing to recognize and give to Holy Spirit all the ways in which I use the body lovelessly, i.e. to separate myself from Holy Self?**

a. Examples: I'm condemning myself (and others) as a body, if I judge myself or others as bodies, special conditional relating, sacrifice, etc. By saying "yes," what will the false-self stand to lose?

b. In saying "yes," what possible gifts will I open to receive from making the divine switch from ego (body) to Holy Self (Spirit)?

10) **Am I willing to have all "specialness" in my relationships (partner, children, parents, friends, etc.) divinely corrected by Holy Spirit?**

a. By saying "yes," what will the false-self stand to lose?

b. In saying "yes," what possible gifts will I open to receive from making the divine switch from ego (body) to Holy Self (Spirit)?

11) **Am I willing to allow Spirit to help me undo my own mistaken belief in body-identification (sensual perception and body appetites)? And am I willing to allow Spirit to help me undo my belief in bodies and therefore, undo my attachment to using others as bodies?**

a. By saying "yes," what will the false-self stand to lose?

b. In saying "yes," what possible gifts will I open to receive from making the divine switch from ego (body) to Holy Self (Spirit)?

12) **Am I willing to give Spirit my "need to be needed/desired" by others?**

a. By saying "yes," what will the false-self stand to lose?

b. In saying "yes," what possible gifts will I open to receive from making the divine switch from ego (body) to Holy Self (Spirit)?

13) **Am I willing to allow my body, its appetites, pleasures and pains, to be healed completely via Atonement/miracle?**

a. By saying "yes," what will the false-self stand to lose?

b. In saying "yes," what possible gifts will I open to receive from making the divine switch from ego (body) to Holy Self (Spirit)?

14) **Am I willing to see only innocence within myself and others?**

    a. By saying "yes," what will the false-self stand to lose?

    b. In saying "yes," what possible gifts will I open to receive from making the divine switch from ego (body) to Holy Self (Spirit)?

2. **Review ego fears:** Now, let's look at the ego's fears and review "its" reasons for resistance to saying "yes." Write down your insights. What do you see? Take these insights into your sacred space and ask Spirit to help you.

3. **It's the ego that resists.** But this is not you! Do not take it personally. Your salvation depends on making the choice to "show-up" and experience the divine exchange from ego to Holy Self. Watch the miracles flood in!

4. **Review the gifts from saying "yes:"** Once you've looked at your blocks to Love – your fears – and offered them to Spirit in exchange for the miracle, previous limitations are free to fall away. Now you may be more open to inner guidance. This is why that very last question was included in all 14 questions, *"In saying "yes," what possible gifts will I open to receive from making the divine switch from ego (body) to Holy Self (Spirit)?"* Write down your insights. What do you see? Take these insights into your sacred space and ask Spirit to join you in truly receiving these gifts.

C. Transfer of Trust – From Body Identity to Spirit Identity

1. This is where we consciously choose to **show-up** *with* **Holy Spirit** despite fear and doubt. We demonstrate vertical alignment with the *Seven Key Principles* through our action. We check-in, making sure we are willing, accountable, self-honest, emotionally vulnerable, defenseless, and trusting and that we have gratitude.

2. **What we think, feel, say and do are all in vertical alignment. There is no disagreement between how we feel and what we think, say and do. This is how we show-up!** We place the body identity on the Holy Spirit's altar. There is a divine surrender of the body's purpose to Spirit; to exchange the ego's purpose for the body for His. **Warning:** The closer we come to being the living demonstration of these *Seven Key Principles,* the louder the ego will scream, "No!" So keep the faith and keep going!

3. Another crucial component to showing-up and making the divine switch is to ask with radical self-honesty before we proceed, **"What is this *for?*" "What do I want to come of this?"** Of course, we are asking the Holy Self and not the ego! The clarification of our goal must come first.

4. The divine switch is where miracles, healings occur. This is where we "close the gap" of separation with self and others. This is where the body fades in awareness and the blazing light of the Holy Self casts out all darkness.

5. This is an invitation to experience the Holy Instant where we switch from believing the fear-driven body identity, to being the innocent and invulnerable Holy Self. In this transfer of trust from body to Spirit we are moving toward a consistent experience of the Holy Instant which translates to our growing experience of, and consistent conviction *as* the Holy Self.

6. The transfer occurs in direct proportion to our willingness to release the body identity to Spirit for divine re-purposing. Recall that the body is hardwired with its original purpose which is to witness sin (irrevocable error) and to respond to this lie. And because of this block it does not know Love and therefore, it does not know how to heal.

7. Answering all the following questions with a "yes" is completely counterintuitive to the ego. It fiercely resists genuinely answering "yes" to each of these questions. The reason why is because in agreeing, the ego cannot proceed. It ceases to exist in the divine switch made in the Holy Instant. Only the Holy Self goes on from here. We go from ego sight to Christ Vision in this transfer.

a. Am I willing to suspend my judgment of others?

b. Am I willing to suspend *self*-judgment?

c. Am I willing to be wrong about my judgment? Am I teachable?

d. Am I willing to let go of the past?

e. Am I willing to apply the *Seven Key Principles* of Authentic Relating consistently in all my communication with Self and others?

f. Am I willing to forgive myself and accept the Atonement?

g. Am I willing to drop my unworthiness to receive the Atonement?

h. Am I willing to be completely healed, mind *and* body via the miracle, the Atonement?

i. Am I willing to recognize and give to Holy Spirit all the ways in which I use the body lovelessly, i.e. to separate myself from Holy Self?

j. Am I willing to have all "specialness" in my relationships (partner, children, parents, friends, etc.) divinely corrected by Holy Spirit?

k. Am I willing to allow Spirit to help me undo my own mistaken belief in body-identification (sensual perception and body appetites)? And am I willing to allow Spirit to help me undo my belief in bodies and therefore, undo my attachment to using others as bodies?

l. Am I willing to give Spirit my "need to be needed/ desired" by others?

m. **Am I willing to allow my body, its appetites, pleasures and pains, to be healed completely via Atonement/ miracle?**

n. **Am I willing to see only innocence within myself and others?**

D. The Holy Instant

1. Here, the divine switch takes place where our awareness shifts from the ego to the Holy Self. In this Holy Instant of grace we now perceive from the right-mind and not from the wrong-mind. This is the moment we drop the ego's beliefs, its values, including the past, the body, and what its senses seem to report. Here we receive/extend the miracle along with higher guidance. We re-remember what we are! Love! Innocence! We are the Holy Self! We are the Son of God!

2. In this instant the body identity drops away in our awareness as the Holy Mind eclipses it and unlimited communication is restored. God's undivided will is joyfully welcomed in this state.

1) Stay focused on receiving *only* this Holy Instant of innocence.

3. God is in everything I see because God is in my mind. This is the Mind of Christ shared with God. Here, we exchange the ego's eye sight for vision. We look *as* Spirit – as Christ Vision –and that which Spirit sees is already healed. We go beyond the ego body senses and invoke the healed and changeless Truth behind them. All it takes is willingness to behold what *is* there as Love, innocence, now, and healing, by being vigilant to look past what is *not* there such as conflict, blame, past, sickness.

4. This is the instant we genuinely *accept* the Atonement, Spirit's correction of fear in our mind. The obstruction to Love, the lens of fear is temporarily lifted so we can perceive clearly. This is where the miracle occurs because it is not blocked by fear.

3. WHY THE BODY IS THE CENTER OF OUR UNIVERSE

1. The body is the greatest and most valued of all idols that we have made. It's also the most convincing. Through the false self we believe we *are* the body and that the body is the center of our universe. Thus, while we still mistake "it" as the goal of everything we think, do and value, we will be terrified of the power of our mind that *made* it.

2. Our split mind projected the body as an exceedingly convincing means to hide from the light of our Spirit, the Holy Self. The ego's existence, as fear, depends on our conviction that we are a body.

3. And while we still choose to prioritize the body as our identity instead of discovering our true Identity we will remain in denial, preferring to believe that we are indeed victims of the body, others, the past and the world. These phenomena are used by the ego to perpetuate the illusion that we *are* the body and not the incorruptible Holy Self.

4. If we are fearful to discover and heal the single cause of the illusory body's projection – as the ego – then we won't ever take our power back and we agree to stay trapped in the illusion that we are victims of the body, others, the past, and the world. We will remain in denial and prefer to believe that we are at the mercy of phenomena that we our self projected.

5. If we allow the body to remain the goal of everything we think, do and value, we will continue to believe in a persistent sense of threat that we must independently protect our self from. Remember that any sense of fear together with its consequences such as illness, pain, scarcity and conflict, etc., is a direct effect of the mistaken belief that we are guilty. The single cause of all fear and its effects is unforgiven guilt.

6. All fear arises from this crazy lie that we are guilty. Once guilt is believed there is always an anticipation of punishment. Every fear we have, including every defense we invest in, stems exclusively from the insane belief that we *deserve* punishment – *because* we are guilty. All fear, simply put, is our fear that we will be punished by "something."

7. This nebulous yet persistent "something" that we fear and try to protect our self from is cleverly disguised in endless forms of adversity – the ego's self-made shield of fear. These threats seem to appear externally, in the body, others and the world. It's disguised this way as a smoke screen so we do not locate the singular and immediate *source*, which is the erroneous belief that we are guilty and must protect our self from this "something" that we're separate *from*.

8. The smoke screen is there so we don't recognize a simple fact. Whatever we believe we are separate from – we will make our enemy. God is Love. We, as the Holy Self, are Love. Without opposite. Without threat.

9. While we mistake our self as the body we will believe unwittingly that God (Love) is our enemy and is out to annihilate us. This profound and unconscious confusion contributes to our fundamental "fear of God" (Love itself) as the ego's shield of fear. These are the incessant problems which this illusion manifests to shield itself from awakening to Love, as our beloved and incorruptible Holy Self.

10. As I have said often in *The End of Death* trilogy, the body is our greatest repository for guilt (attack). In other words, it becomes the dumping ground for all our unforgiven fears. And *this* is what kills it. Every phenomenon we mistakenly believe can either complete us or threaten us is merely a disguise, a decoy, to sidetrack us from facing the single cause of all suffering – our unforgiven belief that we are a separate entity, separate from our brothers, from God and from Love itself. This sense of being separate from Love is the only problem we have, no matter the particular "form" of the problem.

   a. *"All this complexity is but a desperate attempt not to recognize the problem, and therefore not to let it be resolved. If you could recognize that your only problem is separation, no matter what form it takes, you could accept the answer because you would see its relevance. Perceiving the underlying constancy in all the problems that seem to confront you, you would understand that you have the means to solve them all. And you would use the means, because you recognize the problem."* W-79.6.

11. Every area of our life that we try to control alone arises from fear (guilt). The body happens to be the hub of the ego's illusory wheel of existence. It is the central focus for our pursuit of pleasure and our avoidance of pain – which are the same thing.

12. Remember the body is in service to the ego until we've advanced enough in trust to genuinely give the body and its appetites over to Spirit entirely. The ego will retain those extra "special" appetites (sex, food, exercise, pride, pleasure, status, etc.) and guard them jealously - until we consciously recognize the pain they bring. This is the basic confusion that Jesus speaks of; our independent pursuit of pleasure (including safety and security) – apart from Spirit – is really the unconscious attraction to pain.

A. Where Do We Seek Our Safety, Security and Happiness?

1. Do we want freedom of the body? Or do we desire freedom of the Mind (Spirit)?

2. To choose freedom of the body leads to death. While choosing to prioritize freedom of the mind leads us to healing and life. And then the body must follow a healed mind.

3. In this world we're taught that our mind is slave to the body. The body appears to betray our minds (conscious) wishes for health, youth, vitality, weight, longevity, etc. In other words, it looks as if the body is an independent entity that can become sick, age and die; that it has a will of its own which our mind alone is powerless to change. In this mistaken belief it does seem that the body is stronger than the mind.

4. Most of us mistakenly believe that our mind is trapped in a body and that the body is more powerful than the mind. In this case it does seem that our mind can be made either happy or miserable depending on the state of our body. But while we continue to believe this error we will misidentify *as* the body, thinking that pursuing the body's pleasure, safety, happiness and security *is* our life's purpose. The ever neutral body then becomes harnessed by the ego as the end goal and the mind – which holds exclusive dominion over the body – is used as a slave to achieve freedom of the body which condemns the body to disease and death.

5. But as we awaken from the false self we begin to realize that the *mind* and not the body, is the single cause of all bodily states. We learn that the body is singularly obedient to the mind's wishes. We realize that all bodily states arise from either our forgiven Mind or our unforgiven mind.

6. At some point in our awakening journey we must make a conscious choice, to prioritize freedom of the body, or freedom of the mind. One is the means and the other is the end. We can only ever choose one *or* the other – but not both. We cannot be dedicated to both at the same time. If we value the body then it completely blinds us to the value of the Mind/Spirit. And vice versa.

7. Where do I seek my safety, my security, my happiness and my peace? If it's in the body and special relationships then I am seeking my solace and my reason for being from an effigy that does not exist. And while I pursue my completion through the body, instead of with God, I will be fearful of it and resent it. And I will then inadvertently attack the body through weight gain, pain, illness, conflict, lack, aging, accidents and death, etc.

8. Recall that the body is an idea which dwells exclusively within the mind (not brain). As such the body is an *effect* of the mind and can never be a "cause" of itself – of either sickness *or* health. The mind is cause and the body is its effect. There is *no cause* of sickness or healing in the body despite seeming evidence to the contrary. Everything that seems to happen to the body is a direct result of a decision in the mind albeit unconscious until we learn to value forgiveness.

9. The body's state is a direct effect of what the mind is using it *for*. Is it being used to witness to pain and conflict thus teaching separation? Or have we given the body's purpose to Holy Spirit to divinely reinterpret it and witness to union and healing? The body-idea never leaves the mind therefore every seeming change in the body's appearance or state comes from the mind

10. There is *no cause* in the body although it sure appears that way. All the body's changes in appearance, its health or sickness along with its seeming appetites, are administered solely by the mind. The body seems to have senses and appetites of its own, but as the *Course*

says, appetites are getting mechanisms, not physical in origin. The ego wants to confirm *itself* and seemingly prove that we are *separate* from our Loving Source. And as I have mentioned many times before, all destructive bodily changes, including addictions, arise from the unhealed or unforgiven ego mind.

a. *"The body cannot heal, because it cannot make itself sick. It needs no healing. Its health or sickness depends entirely on how the mind perceives it, and the purpose the mind would use it for." T-19.I.3:1-3*

11. Given the choice between the body *and* Spirit or Holy Self, which of these is front and center for you? In which of these, body *or* Holy Self, do you seek for your happiness, safety, security and completion in this life?

12. Radical honesty reveals that for most of us, the body is valued as our moment to moment goal. Almost every thought we have involves thoughts or decisions about the body's pain or pleasure based on the past. And every thought in between is devoted to planning ahead for its pleasure, sustenance, safety or security. The rest of the time we are defending or protecting it.

13. I laughingly share this insight, because it's so ludicrous. And there is great relief in finally recognizing this and admitting it with no self-judgment. We cannot heal that which we have not recognized yet. The first step then is to recognize that we have mistakenly deceived our self.

14. While the body remains front and center, we will continue to attract special relationships as they feed the false self concept and the guilt required to keep suffering going.

15. As I said in Volume One of *The End of Death*, the body is the *last* of our special relationships that we willingly offer to Holy Spirit to be made Holy.

a. *"Do you want freedom of the body or of the mind? For both you cannot have. Which do you value? Which is your goal? For one you see as means; the other, end. And one must serve the other and lead to its predominance, increasing its importance by diminishing its own." ... "Where freedom of the body has been chosen, the mind is used as means whose value lies in its ability to contrive ways to achieve the body's freedom. Yet freedom of the body has no meaning, and so the mind is dedicated to serve illusions. This is a situation so contradictory and so impossible that anyone who chooses this has no idea of what is valuable."* T-22.VI.1-6,2:1-3

16. If we value the body and its appetites as our goal, then we will use the ego mind (fear) to gain that goal. The false self has its sights set on one goal and knows that while we prioritize the body as our goal we will achieve exactly what the ego wants for us – *death*.

17. We either devote our allegiance to the body – *or* – to the Mind/Spirit as our Holy Self. We cannot pursue both at once because they lead in opposing directions. If we choose the body then that will lead to conflict, disease and death.

18. The body is an illusory by-product of the false self's fierce declaration of independence from our Holy Self. Until we willingly turn the body over to Spirit, it will become a burdensome consequence of our misguided choice for autonomy from God.

19. We mistakenly believe that our boundless Essence is separate from others and imprisoned within these tiny walls of flesh. And then we make the devastating mistake of looking to death for freedom. We are like a bird that confuses his safety with his cage, and who will not break loose even though the cage door is wide open.

20. As we advance in our development of trust we recognize that the body is not our responsibility. To the degree we give the *purpose* of the body to Spirit is the extent to which it reflects the health and joy of its divine purpose.

B. What Do We Use the Body For?

1. Until we genuinely desire to repurpose the body and our relationships *with Spirit*, the ego will monopolize its purpose and use its seeming appetites to further indulge in specialness. As we journey through the ego dream we unwittingly seek completion *through* the body. The body is our focus, the central idol until we hit the proverbial wall via unconscious self-attack.

2. Thankfully, our genuine spiritual awakening usually begins after

we've hit such a wall of ego disillusionment, which manifests through a variety of human adversities. In some way we have maxed-out through trying to run our life independently of Spirit, through the false self and its mistaken values.

3. This stage, the *undoing,* is the first stage of our quest to awaken from our false sense of self and the relationships and world it has projected. We usually arrive here because we are disillusioned by relationships, ill-health, pain, depression, loss, identity crisis or death. While the world judges these as bad, like every painful experience, they can be entirely and divinely repurposed by Holy Spirit.

4. The undoing is in fact the *beginning* of learning to recognize the false self's destructive goal in every area of our life. Now we can begin to give our relationships, our income, our family, our body and our life quite literally over to Love itself – to Holy Spirit. This is a thorough and divine repurposing of the body's role within each area of our life. This way the ego has less chance of using the body to attract more self-attack.

5. Imagine our life and all our many interests combined in a symbol as one large pie. The pie is divided into many segments. The body, family, spiritual path, romantic relationship, job, income, financial investments, social life, special interests, etc., - each one represents just one slice of the pie.

6. Many on the spiritual path still keep their spiritual beliefs and practice as a separate slice of the whole pie. Most keep it discreetly hidden from others while carefully compartmentalizing it. They especially separate their spiritual beliefs from their primary relationships, family roles, finances, body (sickness, health or exercise routine) and job. Yet genuine healing cannot occur when we compartmentalize our life this way.

7. The ego is exceptionally cunning at misappropriating the body in all the areas of value we have. It doesn't want us to ever see without question, that all these areas are used to fuel the ego's addiction to separation.

8. The ego uses the body for pride, pleasure and attack (such as relationship conflict, illness and death). Fundamentally, it seeks

its completion *through* the body, yet to the ego, completion means physical death. Death is its aim. That way it pursues us beyond the grave into another recycle phase of physical birth, amnesia and death. It seeks anything but to awaken from the dream altogether. And this is why we need to apply the principles of the *Course* to *every* area of our life.

a. *"The ego wants [you] dead, but not itself. The outcome of its strange religion must therefore be the conviction that it can pursue you beyond the grave." T-15.I.3:3-5*

9. While each slice of the ego's pie is kept safely segregated then the ego's destructive laws will run rife. It's only when we truly commit to living these principles in *every* area of our life that we will finally experience miracles and open to the miraculous Laws of God. The *Seven Keys* are not just a tool but a way of life. We apply them to every relationship and to every area of our life.

10. Pride, pleasure and attack are all forms of separation and individual independence from God and our brothers. Both pleasure and pain are one! While we pursue our fulfillment through the body, we will mistakenly use it as our primary goal, as an idol to bring to us that which we secretly believe we cannot get from our true Identity, our Holy Self.

a. *"One illusion cherished and defended against the truth makes all truth meaningless, and all illusions real. Such is the power of belief. It cannot compromise." T-22.II.4:4-6*

11. Real pleasure cannot be found separate from God. Anytime we attempt to extract pleasure, safety, security or happiness from someone or something – we will attract pain. This is why special relationships involve so much pain.

12. All real pleasure cannot be experienced alone, independently from our brothers or God. It must be shared to be real. Seeking individual pleasure, safety, security and happiness, apart from others and God, is seeking separation and suffering.

13. To honestly examine the intent beneath all that we do there are some pertinent questions we can ask. First, are we making decisions with the ego or with Spirit? Are we coming from fear and doubt or

from Love and trust? Are we really present? Do we align with Spirit and actually "feel" into inner guidance before we make decisions? Or do we make our decisions based on a past that doesn't exist? And are we making future plans to protect our self from anticipated attack? If so, do we realize that if we defend our self from anticipated attack then we are attracting it?

14. When we eat, diet, take supplements, medication or exercise, is the ulterior motive to "save our body" from something we are fearful of? If so, then we would do well to offer up the mistaken fear to Holy Spirit in exchange for the miracle.

15. What scraps of pleasure do we covet and defend? To the degree we value them, or are prideful of them, will be the degree they're secretly used for attack.

   a. *"This course will be believed entirely or not at all. For it is wholly true or wholly false, and cannot be but partially believed. And you will either escape from misery entirely or not at all." ... "There is no part of Heaven you can take and weave into illusions. Nor is there one illusion you can enter Heaven with. T-22.II.7:4-6,8:1-2*

16. Delight at winning the lottery, getting in shape, landing a new job, celebrating weight loss or getting well – *and* – despair over going bankrupt, being unfit, being fired, gaining weight, or getting sick, are all signs of a profound misidentification. Delight and despair concerning our body or that of another, *are the same illusion.* They are witnesses to our decision that we have identified our self as a body and not as the incorruptible and Holy Self.

17. The serial adventures of the body are either venerated or despised. But it is rarely recognized that both reactions are the same - meaningless.

18. This doesn't mean we give up pursuing happiness. But it does mean that we decide not to pursue happiness through the ego any longer because that always leads to conflict and pain. Happiness is our natural state once we undo our false self and its erroneous beliefs and values.

19. We do need to recognize (and not just intellectually) that true happiness is the natural result of being consciously present and

aligned with our Holy Self. It's also the natural result of forgiving our self for misidentifying with the ego, for perceiving any kind of attack.

20. This is living out from God's Will which is "What" we are. Until we're truly devoted to this, and we stop trying to run our body, relationships and life independently from Spirit, we will look for happiness, security and completion in all the wrong places. And we will attract a roller coaster ride of highs and lows. Life will seem like random chaos. And in the end, we will make the disastrous mistake of looking toward death for freedom, as the way to end the conflict of (ego) life.

21. Communication ends separation. Attack promotes it. The body is our chief communication device. It's the means by which we integrate *all* slices of our life pie. If we use the body independently without consulting Spirit, we will use it for attack. And it will remain the mistaken center of our universe. When we learn to make our decisions with Spirit instead of the ego, then the body is used on behalf of union and true happiness.

   a. *"Communication ends separation. Attack promotes it. The body is beautiful or ugly, peaceful or savage, helpful or harmful, according to the use to which it is put. And in the body of another you will see the use to which you have put yours. If the body becomes a means you give to the Holy Spirit to use on behalf of union of the Sonship, you will not see anything physical except as what it is." T-8.VII.4:1-5*

22. NOTE: The forgiveness process can be found in *The Seven Essential Principles of Quantum Forgiveness (Atonement)* on page 591.

4. THE GREATEST LIE OF ALL TIME

1. Misidentification as the body is the source of all fear and suffering. Identifying as the body-self, living out from this treacherous lie as our central identity, breeds the mistaken belief that we are a separate

identity from God and all our brothers. The body-self *and* fear are one and the same. They cannot be experienced apart from each other.

2. The ego thought system is built entirely on just one central idol. Its perceptual lens including everything it seems to experience arises from this one illusory demigod – *the body* and its five physical senses. This is our choice to believe that we are the body-self as substitute for the immortal Son of God.

3. It's been revealed to me that the ego – as sin, guilt and fear – condenses into one solitary antagonist, our misidentification as a body.

4. The fictitious body-self is not an entity or an identity. When we begin to view it from the lens of Holy Spirit, we will see that the body-self, together with what appears to uphold it, does not exist. The illusory body arises from the fundamental belief in conflict, namely a belief that both Love (as Spirit) *and* fear (as the body-self) exist. The insistence that *both* can be true necessarily results in a split mind.

5. Only a split mind could fantasize that we can choose between two equally real and powerful opposites. Yet only Love is real. Identity misplaced as the body-self *is* fear. And fear does not exist. Therefore, the body is nothing because it does not exist.

6. The body idea is the outcome of our own choice to believe that fear exists and to believe that it is indeed a power equal to or mightier than God as Love. It is this primeval conflict which feeds our investment in the mistaken body-identity along with all illusory suffering that it projects.

7. Recall that we have complete authority over all that we experience. We are always experiencing our beliefs, and we believe what we value – seemingly good or bad. Belief in the body-self is valuing fear and not Love.

   a. *"Either God or the ego is insane."* ... *"Neither God nor the ego proposes a partial thought system. Each is internally consistent, but they are diametrically opposed in all respects so that partial allegiance is impossible. Remember, too, that their results are as different as their foundations, and their fundamentally irreconcilable natures cannot be reconciled by vacillations between them." T-11.in.1:1,3-5*

8. Fear and its "effects" as the body and world, are our own primary projections, our greatest idols. They have no power because they are nothing. But while we still confuse our identity with them, we will erroneously believe that we are at the mercy of these projections. Jesus says that by giving power to nothing – body and world – we forego the joyous recognition that "nothing" has zero power!

a. *"By giving power to nothing, he throws away the joyous opportunity to learn that nothing has no power. And by not dispelling darkness, he became afraid of darkness and of light. The joy of learning that darkness has no power over the Son of God is the happy lesson the Holy Spirit teaches, and would have you teach with Him." T-14.III.6:4-6*

9. The body-self does not recognize or know of our true Identity – the Holy Self – as changeless Love. The only "love" it recognizes and craves is *fearful love,* which is fear in disguise, termed by Jesus in the *Course* as special love. The goal of special love is to maintain the separation and the idea that love can change and end. Arising from the body-self's fear, special love is deeply rooted in the beliefs of sacrifice, suffering and loss, being fueled by guilt, blame and shame. Special love is not Love but *fear.*

10. We cannot value Love which is our true Identity until we learn to recognize all that Love is *not.* This translates to the necessity of learning to recognize all that *we* are not.

a. *"The search for truth is but the honest searching out of everything that interferes with truth." T-14.VII.2:1 "Your task is not to seek for love, but merely to seek and find all of the barriers within yourself that you have built against it. It is not necessary to seek for what is true, but it is necessary to seek for what is false. Every illusion is one of fear, whatever form it takes." T-16.IV.6:1-3*

11. We are God's extensions. We share in all of God's Love as His Love without opposite. God does not know of the body-self, or it's fear, including its seeming effects such as conflict, deprivation, disease,

pain and death. If our one, shared Holy Self is pure, undivided and unopposed Love, then the body-self – *as fear* – believes that "it" is in opposition to God, a rival to Love itself. If God is Love and fear is the opposite of Love, then when we identify as a body-self we must believe that we are an alien "will" to God.

12. The "reality-reversal" imparted in the following paragraph is so crucial to awakening from the body identity, that it requires repeating:

13. Misidentification as the body-self is the source of all fear and suffering. Identifying as the body-self, living out from this treacherous lie as our central identity, breeds the mistaken belief that we are a separate identity from God and all our brothers. The body-self *and* fear are one and the same. They cannot be experienced apart from each other.

a. *"Dissociation is a distorted process of thinking whereby two systems of belief (body-self and Holy Self) which cannot coexist are both maintained. If they are brought together, their joint acceptance becomes impossible. But if one is kept in darkness from the other, their separation seems to keep them both alive and equal in their reality. Their joining thus becomes the source of fear, for if they meet, acceptance must be withdrawn from one of them. You cannot have them both, for each denies the other. Apart, this fact is lost from sight, for each in a separate place can be endowed with firm belief. Bring them together, and the fact of their complete incompatibility is instantly apparent. One will go, because the other is seen in the same place."* ... *"Light cannot enter darkness when a mind believes in darkness, and will not let it go."* T-14.VII.4:3-10,5:1

14. Identity as a body-self is cause, and fear is its effect. Suddenly, as a body-self, we feel terribly alone, at the mercy of a persistent sense of threat which we, apart from God, attempt to remedy and control.

15. In this there is great terror because unconsciously we must believe we are *enemy* to God. This is to believe that Love will certainly annihilate us. If God is Love…then we, as a body, must be fear! This is the fear of God; fear of our most beloved and Holy Self.

a. *"Nothing can reach Spirit from the ego (body-self), and nothing can reach the ego (body-self) from Spirit. Spirit can neither strengthen the ego (body-self) nor reduce the conflict within it. The ego (body-self) [is] a contradiction. Your self (as the body-identity) and God's Self [are] in opposition. They are opposed in source, in direction and in outcome."* T-4.I.2:6-10

16. Thus, every form of fear and suffering through the body-self, is always smoke and mirrors made to obscure our true Identity. The ego's over-arching dominion over the body and all perceived suffering conceals our fears of our true Identity as the Holy Self.

17. Every fear and each defense made from the body-self regardless of how cleverly disguised, is always the fear of Love. In other words, every belief in fear and each defense we attempt against it is really our unrecognized defense against God's Love. In our countless attempts to "save our life," we will not recognize that in its self-administered pain, the body-self tries repeatedly to save itself from being subsumed by God's Love.

18. Love is all there is. Fear does not exist. If the body-self's fear and all its illusions do not exist, then what remains? Only Love. Yet in defending the body-self from its illusions of fear, we unwittingly reject Love.

19. This amplifies the importance of forgiveness as taught in the *Course*. Forgiveness is the one thing that undoes the body-self's fears along with all its defenses against Love. We don't make the fear real and then attempt to solve it. In true forgiveness we choose with Holy Spirit to *overlook* the *appearance* of fear at the outset and prioritize God's Love, His peace.

20. We enter a Holy Instant where we consciously choose to accept His correction of our perception. We may not yet know what the peace of God is, however, all Holy Spirit requires is our willingness to accept the miracle that always dwells behind the fear. We must want the miracle *more* than we desire to believe the fear.

a. *"Learning is ultimately perceived as frightening because it leads to the relinquishment, not the destruction, of the (body) ego to the light of spirit."* T-4.I.3:2

21. Fear and Love cannot coexist. They cannot be integrated. The belief in one denies the other totally, in our awareness. We project and consequently see the body/world through the body-self (fear), or we behold them through Love as Christ' Vision. There is no compromise here.

a.   *"It is impossible to see two worlds which have no overlap of any kind. Seek for the one; the other disappears. But one remains. They are the range of choice beyond which your decision cannot go. The real and the unreal are all there are to choose between, and nothing more than these." W-130.5:1-3*

b.   *"The world you see must be denied, for sight of it is costing you a different kind of vision. [You cannot see both worlds,] for each of them involves a different kind of seeing, and depends on what you cherish. The sight of one is possible because you have denied the other." T-13.VII.2:1-3*

22. There can be no relationship between a body-self as "me," <u>and</u> God! God does not know of a separate body-self. I either rest in the certainty of my Holy Self as the peace of God – or – I will believe unwittingly that I am the body, enemy to God. When I feel threatened, I always have this choice to make. Aligning with the peace of God ensures that all seeming problems are healed by my unequivocal choice for God.

23. We are not a body and the Holy Self. We are just one, not both. Valuing the body completely obscures the Holy Self in our awareness, just as the awareness of the Holy Self eclipses the body entirely. Contrary to what many may believe, the idea of the integration of body-self, mind and Spirit is a massive contradiction. This is the belief that two mutually exclusive thought systems can coexist; that fear *and* Love can coexist. Identification as the body-self *is* the split mind. Spirit, as unopposed Love, is What we are in Truth. The body-self is fear and is the product of the dreaming, split mind.

a.   *"If truth is total, the untrue (body-self) cannot exist. Commitment to either must be total; they cannot coexist in your mind without splitting it. If they cannot coexist in peace, and if you want peace, you must give up the idea of conflict entirely and for all time. This requires vigilance only as long as you do not recognize what is true. While you believe that two totally contradictory thought systems share truth, your need for vigilance is apparent." T-7.VI.8:7-11*

24. The transfer of trust is the gradual undoing or unlearning of the body-self's fear of Love as the one, shared and Holy Self. But we, as the body-identified self, cannot undo our hidden attraction to the body – as fear – until we first learn to recognize the contrast between the body-self's fear *and* Love. Otherwise, we continue to mistake fear for Love and pain for joy. We must learn to distinguish between the two, choosing only Love.

5. BLASPHEMY OR MIRACULOUS HEALING

1. False forgiveness is an ego epidemic. And I know this firsthand as I tried it over and over again, only to have suffering appear to increase in my life. When we believe that something unfair – betrayal, pain, illness, lack, etc.– is real, and then we attempt to forgive it while we still believe that 1) it was an injustice, and 2) that the cause is in another, the body, the past or the world, then it simply *cannot be forgiven.*

2. Once we have made a sin *real* it becomes literally impossible to forgive it. Punishment must then be exacted whether we're conscious of it or not. Unfortunately, to the degree we choose to cherish the belief that we were unfairly treated is the extent to which we will unconsciously administer *self-punishment.* And this is the ego's prime purpose for the body; to use it as a painful testimony to others' guilt.

3. We have made a person, thing or experience a legitimate opponent to God, to Love, and to our one shared and Holy Self. Once we believe this insidious illusion and then attempt to pardon a *real* transgression, we will unwittingly agree to carry the "effects" of our belief that we were indeed unfairly treated. And that someone

is guilty! Pain, illness, conflict, deprivation and death are the most typical signs of this confusion.

4. In this case authentic healing of the single cause of our physical symptoms cannot *be* forgiven because it has not been recognized. Before something is genuinely forgiven we must be wholly "willing" to be accountable for and forgive *our self* for our own trigger. This – and only this – is the source of all healing within and without. Note: The forgiveness process can be found in *The Seven Essential Principles of Quantum Forgiveness (Atonement)* on page 591.

5. If we try to forgive someone or something that we still believe really did hurt us, we will attempt the absolute impossible. Our hurt and their pardon are mutually exclusive! It's an impossibility to forgive someone and yet still retain the *physical proof* (as disease, pain, etc.) that their sin is eternal. And this is why, with true forgiveness, with genuine acceptance of the Atonement, all physical effects or consequences of our belief in sin are healed along with their cause (mind).

6. Remember that the body's state is a direct "effect" of either our unforgiveness or our forgiveness. Jesus is insistent that once we have truly accepted the Atonement, the body then cannot suffer. Being completely and divinely repurposed with Spirit, the body attests to forgiveness by exhibiting only loveliness and health. In its healing it is living testimony to our brother's sinlessness and our own.

7. Jesus speaks of false forgiveness here (forgiveness to destroy). He makes an exceedingly uncompromising statement, one that appears as brutal toward the ego's belief as to the cause of sickness, pain and death.

8. I feel these following paragraphs are far too important to gloss over. And that is why I include them in their totality here:

a. *"The unhealed (sickness, pain, accidents, etc.) cannot pardon. For they are the witnesses that pardon is unfair. They would retain the consequences (sickness or pain) of the guilt they overlook. Yet no one can forgive a sin that he believes is real. And what has consequences must be real, because what it has done is there to see. Forgiveness is not pity, which but*

*seeks to pardon what it thinks to be the truth. Good cannot [be]
returned for evil, for forgiveness does not first establish sin and
then forgive it. Who can say and mean, "My brother, you have
injured me, and yet, because I am the better of the two, I pardon
you my hurt." His pardon and your hurt cannot exist together.
One denies the other and must make it false." T-27.II.2.*

b. *"To witness sin and yet forgive it is a paradox that reason
cannot see. For it maintains what has been done to you deserves
no pardon. And by giving it, you grant your brother mercy but
retain the proof (as pain, illness or adversity) he is not really
innocent. The sick remain accusers. They cannot forgive
their brothers and themselves as well. For no one in whom
true forgiveness rests can suffer. He holds not the proof of sin
(broken body) before his brother's eyes. And thus he must have
overlooked it and removed it from his own. Forgiveness cannot
be for one and not the other. Who forgives is healed. And in
his healing (including the body) lies the proof that he has truly
pardoned, and retains no trace of condemnation that he still
would hold against himself or any living thing." T-27.II.3*

9. Jesus states that no one in whom true forgiveness rests can suffer.
In forgiving truly, our body is healed as it is no longer used as *proof of
sin* before our brother's eyes. The body then is divinely repurposed.

10. Before I continue with this crucial teaching, I feel a burning
question arising from some who are reading this: "But what about
innocent babies born with deformities or illness? How could they be
responsible if they are not even cognizant of choice? And how can
they heal?"

a. *"I am responsible for what I see. I choose the feelings I
experience, and I decide upon the goal I would achieve. And
everything that seems to happen to me I ask for, and receive as
I have asked."T-21.II.2:3-5*

11. Regardless of appearances to the contrary, there are never any
victims. We choose *all* our experiences. The issue is that while our
choices are made from the pseudo self (guilt and fear) they will
remain largely *unconscious* because this is what the ego does.

They are deliberately unconscious – until we desire to forgive and become conscious – so as to prolong the projection of guilt which feeds the whole illusory time cycle of birth, death and amnesia – as reincarnation.

12. Individuals are seemingly born into the dream as helpless newborns. Almost every newborn enters with amnesia of their solitary purpose, to awaken *from* the false, body-self and its dream via forgiveness. Within the seemingly endless timeline of reincarnation every individual chooses his experiences according to his level of attraction to guilt as the fear of God/Love/Holy Self.

13. Forgiveness is always for both people. When we forgive our self for having unknowingly used someone to hurt us, we are healing us both and erasing the painful split in our mind. The more we do this the easier it is to see others with Christ Vision. As our mind becomes unified all minds are affected because we share the one perfect Identity. In the following paragraphs Jesus speaks of the joyous repercussions of wholehearted forgiveness.

a. *"Forgiveness is not real unless it brings a healing to your brother and yourself. You must attest his sins have no effect on you to demonstrate they are not real. How else could he be guiltless?"*

"Your function is to show your brother sin can have no cause. How futile must it be to see yourself a picture of the proof (sickness, pain) that what your function is (forgiveness) can never be! The Holy Spirit's picture changes not the body into something it is not. It only takes away from it (the body) all signs of accusation and of blamefulness (sickness, hurt and pain). Pictured without a purpose, it (the body) is seen as neither sick nor well, nor bad nor good. No grounds are offered that it may be judged in any way at all. It has no life, but neither is it dead. It stands apart from all experience of love or fear."

"Into this empty space, from which the goal of sin has been removed, is Heaven free to be remembered. Here its peace

can come, and perfect healing take the place of death. The
body can become a sign of life, a promise of redemption, and
a breath of immortality to those grown sick of breathing in
the fetid scent of death. Let it (the body) have healing as its
purpose. Then will it send forth the message it received, and
by its health and loveliness proclaim the truth and value that
it represents. Let it (the body) receive the power to represent
an endless life, forever unattacked. And to your brother let
its message be, "Behold me, brother, at your hand I live."...
"The simple way to let this be achieved is merely this; to let
the body have no purpose from the past, when you were sure
you knew its purpose was to foster guilt." T-27.I.4:1-3,9:1-
8,10,11:1

14. The purpose for the body based on the past was to use it as a vehicle to demonstrate separation (pain, disease, death) and prove others guilty. Once we genuinely refuse to do this any longer and we accept the Holy Spirit's purpose for the body, we use it to demonstrate Love without attack, without judgment, blame or guilt.

15. Our minds are always joined. And what does this mean? Very simply, it means I cannot consent to suffer without it also affecting you and vice versa. The good news is if I decide to heal via accepting the Atonement you are healed along with me. You may not be conscious of this healing however it is a fact.

16. We are so accustomed to believe that correction involves judgment, blame and punishment. But these are never corrective; they serve to make the illusion of sin and guilt real. True correction transpires only through accepting the Holy Spirit's undoing of our fearful perception as the Atonement. Therefore, correction *is* forgiveness. And forgiveness *is* correction.

17. I feel that this subject is perhaps the most confronting of all Jesus' teachings. In all my time with the *Course* I have not witnessed either students or teachers expounding on the significance and repercussions of our unrecognized "fear of healing." Shockingly, this unseen and therefore unhealed fear is exactly what feeds our unconscious attraction to guilt, pain, sickness, aging and death.

18. This fear of healing is the false self's number one ally, its primary

ringleader in making sure that true forgiveness as accepting the Atonement fully, is delayed. It knows that our total healing would end "it," together with the imagined separation – quickly.

19. Many of us have learned, at least intellectually, that guilt is the underlying cause of all our problems including disease, pain, conflict, scarcity and even physical death itself. Therefore, this denied guilt – merely a mistake – must be acknowledged first and then forgiven. This is healing the single cause of all suffering.

20. But many of us delay this healing by falling for a common, even better hidden trap. We still have difficulty understanding and remembering that we are not a body. We assign the *cause* of pain, conflict and sickness from unforgiven guilt to seemingly external phenomena such as the body, another, the past or the world thereby making it a *real opponent* in our mind. And while we choose to repeat this mistake of confusing the cause as coming from anywhere other than our own mind, we reject healing the origin of all sickness.

21. While we continue to externalize the cause of all our suffering, we may be able to alleviate suffering temporarily through magic, yet this leaves the real cause unseen and therefore unhealed. When we are triggered by another, the body, the past or the world then the *cause* is quite literally our own split mind. Through a filter of fear, we give the disturbing appearance reality. Otherwise, it has none.

22. We interpret a seeming threat according to our own level of unrelinquished guilt and fear. In other words, we give it reality and make it an opponent, according to the degree we still choose to believe we are guilty.

23. Remember that the false self is guilt incarnate. The last thing it wants is to look upon this illusory guilt. It must project and see this guilt elsewhere in order to perpetuate the belief in an external cause, thereby protecting the guilt in its mind.

24. The single cause of all forms of suffering is our unforgiven belief in separation from our brothers, our Holy Self and God. The sustaining belief which upholds the separation is the addictive assumption that we have been or ever could be unfairly treated and its ensuing judgment. This is a primal misperception as the belief in victim and perpetrator which underlies the split mind's attraction to suffering.

25. There is a universal dynamic which permeates the entire ego belief system and every seeming problem is hinged on this. For the ego to maintain its false and separate sense of self it must regard itself superficially, as innocent. And the only innocence *or "fake innocence"* it knows is bought at the cost of someone else's guilt. It appears to thrive and gain by condemning another, hence its outright rejection of total forgiveness. To forgive completely would be to sacrifice its own fake innocence. It therefore throws constant decoys of accusation – as projection – to the body, others, self, the past and the world.

26. The ego's survival depends on its fake innocence and this can only be upheld while it projects that *someone else* is guilty. Its pseudo innocence is always sustained by the mistaken belief that it was indeed victimized and that someone, either past or present, is the guilty perpetrator.

27. How do we gauge unconscious guilt? By the degree we feel victimized by the body, others, self, the past or the world. To that degree we will resist comprehensive forgiveness while simultaneously we will prefer to hold onto the symptoms of pain, illness, deprivation, etc. These symptoms (effects of guilt) serve the ego by providing seeming physical evidence that we *were* clearly victimized.

28. The false self is addicted to being unfairly treated. It values the body only to the extent that it can use it as proof of its fake innocence and show how it has been unjustly condemned. And illness and pain paint a picture in which sin appears to be justified.

   a. *"The strongest witness to futility, that bolsters all the rest and helps them paint the picture in which sin is justified, is sickness in whatever form it takes." T-27.I.1*

29. Sickness, pain and aging are the ego's protection and defense against losing its separate identity. While someone is judged as guilty this self feels secure even at the expense of projecting pain or illness onto the body. It has no interest in whom it condemns just as long as it condemns *someone*. It keeps its top secret hidden from us. When we condemn anyone including our self we damn our body to sickness, aging and death. The body is unknowingly used as a

scapegoat to announce that "it" has been assaulted by someone/something that we have no control over.

30. And while we consent to this erroneous belief of victimization we unconsciously condemn someone; either another or self. But the truth is that we cannot possibly condemn someone else without damning our self. And we can't blame our self in isolation either because we and our brother are one.

   a. *"There are two diametrically opposed ways of seeing your brother. They must both be in your mind, because you are the perceiver. They must also be in his, because you are perceiving him. See him through the Holy Spirit in his mind, and you will recognize Him in yours. What you acknowledge in your brother you are acknowledging in yourself, and what you share you strengthen."T-5.III.3.*

31. This desire to condemn others or self is the ego's deep-seated certainty that sin is real; an irrevocable error which always deserves justified punishment. The seeming sins that trigger us reflect our very own deeply buried wish for revenge and finally, for death. All this appears as unconscious until we willingly desire to see and heal its dynamic.

32. Fear is a direct product of our mistaken belief that we have sinned. When we fear anyone or anything it arises from an unconscious belief that we are guilty and so punishment is our due. All our defenses including planning, problem-solving, control mechanisms for the body, relationships and finances, etc., stem from just one mistake – which is that we believe we will be punished because we are guilty. This is the *single problem* that requires our forgiveness, our belief in separation (sin, guilt and fear).

33. Even pain, sickness and physical death are forms of defense against awakening to the boundless Love we are. This Love is known only by releasing everyone via forgiveness, including our self and the body from the ego's endless lust for blame and its certain descendent, victimization. Every fearful reaction, at its core, is *always* a defense against expected punishment, and they are all expressions of the "fear of awakening" to our majestic Holy Self.

a. *"All forms of sickness, even unto death, are physical expressions of the fear of awakening." T-8.IX.3:2*

34. In this bold passage Jesus states that not just some forms of sickness are fear, but that *all* forms of sickness including death are physical expressions of the fear of awakening. In practical terms this is the fear of Love (God), of true union, of closing the gap via forgiveness of others and self. The ego is terrified of this because its identity along with all its delusional beliefs and values are annihilated in its exposure to the Truth.

35. The false self is content to inflict pain, disease, decay and even death onto the body to *prove* (via its fake innocence) that it was indeed a victim of injustice. It attempts to trump God by proving that attack (sickness and death) conquers God as Love and healing. This *is* its identity. The body in pain, disease and death, is unknowingly used to demonstrate that we have been unfairly treated at the hands of "someone" or something that hurt us in some way.

36. Ego innocence is always bought at the cost of making someone guilty. To understand and accept that no one including our self is guilty is the total annihilation of the false self. This is the fearless state of incorruptible innocence, or unified perception. The ego is sustained exclusively by guilt. Think about this. God and our Holy Self are Love without opposite which means *Love <u>without</u> sacrifice, loss, pain or attack.* Yet fear is the illusory opposite of Love. The only way we could possibly believe in or feel fear is if we still value its singular source – sin and guilt.

37. There is an automatic response to everything that triggers us and that is to lay blame on someone or something external, including the body. This immediate knee-jerk reaction and subsequent projection of guilt is always a decision for self-attack, regardless of the millions of different "forms" it takes. When triggered we mistakenly agree with what the ego sends our body's senses to report back to us, that danger is imminent - and that we, independent of Spirit, must counterattack or defend.

38. All triggers always signal our own unforgiven guilt no matter the form. If this is the case 100 percent of the time then we can train our self – without self-condemnation – to heal immediately

by applying genuine forgiveness: *"Holy Spirit, please help me to forgive myself for having believed that separation is possible and having unknowingly used (person, illness, pain, scarcity, weight issue, depression, etc.) to attack myself and to separate from my Holy Self."*

39. As explained earlier, fear is an exclusive byproduct of guilt. If there is no guilt then there can be no possibility of fear and therefore, no possibility of suffering. Guilt is the expectation and therefore attraction of punishment. The ego refuses to forgive because it knows that there is just one to forgive and that is our self. When we take full accountability without self-judgment and we forgive our self, we revoke guilt as the source of all attack and fear.

40. There is absolutely no judgment here, in fact we're being asked to drop all judgment including self-judgment as only the false self condemns. There is no sin. In our development of trust we must be willing to have every idol, both positive and negative, repurposed by Holy Spirit. This necessitates looking with radical self-honesty at what we use the body *for.* We do this with Holy Spirit so He can divinely repurpose the body. But He cannot do this until we give Him permission. He requires our willingness.

A. The Most Blasphemous Teaching of All Time

1. I must admit many years ago when I first read Chapter 27 of the Text in the *Course* I was horrified. This section is perhaps the most blasphemous to the ego thought system. Jesus makes very specific, literal statements boldly declaring that the body is used by the ego for attack via sickness in order to *prove* that someone is guilty. He uses the words "proof" or "proves" six times in just one section, Section Two in Chapter 27, which is aptly titled The Fear of Healing.

2. A word of warning. The false self despises this teaching! In my own experience it usually interprets this teaching in one of two ways: 1) It completely rejects it as heresy, or 2) It turns the projection of guilt away from others and onto self. The spiritualized ego is often a master at self-judgment. It doesn't realize that to judge our self is to judge *everyone* including God. It is impossible to condemn our self alone; just as it's impossible to heal our self alone. This teaching

aims at the total relinquishment of judgment through our heartfelt acceptance of the Atonement, the undoing of fear.

3. All those years ago I had been unwittingly invested in physical pain together with a plethora of causes that were all external, so I was shocked at the implications that Jesus was suggesting in this chapter. You mean I have to forgive my mother and all the other perpetrators before I can heal the single cause of my pain? To the ego at the time this was way too much of a sacrifice. I remember squirming as I read the following paragraphs!

   a. *"Whenever you consent to suffer pain, to be deprived, unfairly treated or in need of anything, you but accuse your brother of attack upon God's Son." T-27.I:3*

   b. *"A sick and suffering you but represents your brother's guilt; the witness that you send lest he forget the injuries he gave, from which you swear he never will escape. This sick and sorry picture [you] accept, if only it can serve to punish him. The sick are merciless to everyone, and in contagion do they seek to kill. Death seems an easy price, if they can say, "Behold me, brother, at your hand I die." For sickness is the witness to his guilt, and death would prove his errors must be sins. Sickness is but a "little" death; a form of vengeance not yet total. Yet it speaks with certainty for what it represents." T-27.I.4:3-9*

4. My perceived perpetrators gave the ego its justified motive for using the body to demonstrate its continuing victimhood through pain and illness. It served to testify to *their* guilt (even though one of them had already passed on). The false self doesn't care if the seeming perpetrators are alive or dead. It still uses the body as *painful proof* that they remain guilty, because look – this sickness is stark evidence that we were indeed attacked. And that attack is real. Thus, both guilt and separation are perpetuated in this self-destructive belief.

5. The body simply obeys guilt's orders, suffering considerably from pain all to prove its pseudo innocence at the cost of accusing another of guilt. As Jesus says, the ego uses the body to demonstrate its allegiance to pain as a billboard to express this: *"Brother, at your hand I die."*

6. For me at the time, the ego was outraged by the suggestion to wholly forgive my perpetrators. After all, what they did to me was real. It would mean that I had to pardon a real sin. And it would mean sacrificing my fake innocence. And then who would I be without my "own independent protection" from the ego's enemies (as Love and Union)? These were some of the ego's incessant rantings at the time.

7. Now thankfully, I see it so clearly. How insane that I consented to punish my body just so as I could feel justified in believing that I was indeed unfairly treated, and that others were guilty. Now I see what Jesus is teaching. If I forgive myself totally for this misperception then I give permission to heal the body as I relinquish guilt/projection. In letting go of blame, of accusation, I also free the body of *all signs of accusation* – sickness, pain, etc. In genuine forgiveness my body is free to heal, and in its recovery, it becomes a living witness to the changeless, incorruptible innocence of my self, and of my "enemies." In this, I join Holy Spirit in proving that illusions are not true.

   a. *"Attest his innocence and not his guilt. Your healing is his comfort and his health because it proves illusions are not true. It is not will for life but wish for death that is the motivation for this world. Its only purpose is to prove guilt real." T-27.I.6:1-4*

B. The Choice

1. As I see it, it all boils down to a choice between two opposing desires. 1) Do I want to see this person (another or myself) as entirely sinless, blameless, guiltless and innocent and be completely healed as a consequence of accepting the Atonement, of true forgiveness? Or, 2) Do I want to keep the evidence of sickness, pain, weight gain, etc. – as proof of sin – to testify to their guilt? To prove that I am right, that I have been unfairly treated?

2. Did you know that we cannot truly forgive unless we take full accountability for being triggered? To make it simple, we cannot be triggered at all by anyone or anything unless we have projected it. The person, thing or situation can only be seen as a threat if we view it through a filter of guilt (ego).

3. Everything we seem to see is neutral. It's all happening *in our mind* and is not occurring separately outside our own mind. Someone else's sickness happens in our own split mind and to the degree that we are triggered by it reveals the extent to which *we* must accept the Atonement, the correction of guilt and fear. Any disturbance we feel proves that we believe the illusion is real and not merely an effect of unforgiven guilt.

4. This is why, when we are fearful or distressed by someone or something, it's crucial to recognize that we are perceiving through the ego's filter of fear and expectation of punishment. And that is why we need to forgive *our self*. As we forgive our self for imagining a threat of attack, we accept Holy Spirit's Correction as the Atonement in that Holy Instant.

5. The degree to which we resist forgiveness, of being totally accountable (without self-judgment) for having unknowingly used a person or situation to attack us, reveals the extent to which we wish to prove that *someone is guilty* by demonstrating this through pain, illness, etc. It's a demonstration of our unhealed belief in sin and the certain punishment which must follow. This is a fundamental law of the ego thought system.

6. Jesus is absolutely fearless in His thorough annihilation of the ego's thought system and its use of the body as a symbol of blame and accusation, through illness, deprivation or suffering of any kind.

7. He speaks about our unconscious attraction to guilt, to seeing and believing in actual sin rather than merely error, which can be easily corrected. By the way, all seeming sin we see, particularly if we're triggered by it, arises from just one source - because we want it. Most of this is unconscious until we consciously will with Spirit to reverse our desires: *"You see what you believe is there, and you believe it there because you want it there. Perception has no other law than this." T-25.III.1:3-4*

8. I have mentioned this before but it's worth sharing again. My mother spent most her adult life in excruciating physical pain. Her body was unwittingly used as a stark symbol of distrust, displaying her rigid unforgiveness. This continued pain became her identity and she defended it to the grave. Of death *or* forgiveness, death to her

was an easy choice. If she had devoted herself to total forgiveness she would have had to relinquish her false identity as the sick and separate one, and face her real terror: heart-felt union with others, and finally, with her Holy Self.

9. Jesus also talks about the ego's addiction to false forgiveness, forgiveness to destroy. The unhealed cannot forgive. They bear witness through their suffering that the injustice was indeed real. It did happen. And while we continue to believe that we were victimized then forgiveness remains impossible because we cannot forgive that which we still believe is real. Hence if we still feel emotionally triggered by something from the past then we must believe that it is real *now*. Here is the choice point. We become lucid and recognize we have a choice to believe in either fear or Love. If we choose Love then we can also choose forgiveness.

10. We need to ask Holy Spirit to help us to undo our *belief* in the reality of the trigger. But in doing so, we must also agree to take full accountability for the ego's projection, its unconscious desire for self-attack, which was the sole cause of any perceived attack.

11. This is done without self-condemnation. To condemn our self is to reject forgiveness. Forgiveness is not partial; meaning that if we maintain self-blame or guilt then the miraculous effects of forgiveness cannot be fully extended. Forgiveness is holographic. It must free us as well as the one we desire to forgive.

12. And here is another temptation, being triggered by memories. While we believe a past memory of pain in the now moment, we are absent from the Holy Instant in which all pain is healed. We use this past memory, and unknowingly drag it into the present moment so it will perpetuate the past into the future.

a. *"The past is nothing. Do not seek to lay the blame for deprivation on it, for the past is gone. You cannot really [not] let go what has already gone. It must be, therefore, that you are maintaining the illusion that it has not gone because you think it serves some purpose that you want fulfilled."* T-16.V.2:8-11

13. The body suffers from this distortion and obeys our hidden wish that it be used as witness to our certainty that we *were* unfairly treated. Suffering serves the ego's purpose. This is why the false self

values and maintains the past illusion that we experienced suffering and holds it in the present in its belief. It explains why the body changes, sickens, decays and dies. Time, as an illusion, has nothing to do with the cause of death. The neutral and changeless body has no expiry date unless we have unintentionally misused it through unforgiveness of the past.

C. The Miracle of Self-Forgiveness

1. Even with my long study and application of the *Course* I find it just continues to get deeper and more miraculous. As my trust in Holy Spirit develops, it eclipses familiar fears and gives me the consistent courage to look to the miracle *behind* appearances of suffering.

2. As I write this I find myself in yet another deepening of my understanding and practice of the Atonement. Sometimes I am baffled by just how complex we think healing is. Jesus promises that the Atonement heals everything. There is absolutely nothing in the ego's hierarchy of illusions which cannot be healed fully by the miracle. After all, the first miracle principle is "There is no order of difficulty in miracles."

   a. *"The offer of Atonement is universal. It is equally applicable to all individuals in all circumstances. And in it is the power to heal all individuals of all forms of sickness. Not to believe this is to be unfair to God, and thus unfaithful to Him. A sick person perceives himself as separate from God. Would you see him as separate from you? It is your task to heal the sense of separation that has made him sick. It is your function to recognize for him that what he believes about himself is not the truth. It is your forgiveness that must show him this. Healing is very simple. Atonement is received and offered. Having been received, it must be accepted. It is in the receiving, then, that healing lies. All else must follow from this single purpose." M-22.6*

3. As Jesus explains, healing is very simple. Yet most of us live as if there *is* an insurmountable order of difficulty in miracles. When challenged, we immediately judge our self, another, an ailment or situation through a filter of fear based on the past. These fears are then

projected onto the situation. In addition to the filter of fear we then add judgment that certain problems are harder or even impossible to heal. From this delusional vantage point, is there any wonder that there is no room for the miracle to enter and prove fear wrong?

4. Jesus tells us that the only way we can ever heal is to *be* healed, but we must first show-up to initiate it by *receiving* it. It's not a *doing* thing but more a surrender and acceptance of God's boundless Love and certain healing.

5. In accepting the Atonement we must remember that God's Love is all that exists, and we are nothing but this Love. Recall there is no opposite to this Love which ensures our immunity to any threat. This perfect Love has already healed everything we seem to see through the body's misleading senses.

6. Love and healing are one. Our belief in fear causes the illusory appearances of fear in our relationships, body and life. Fear or attack itself is the single perpetrator because when we accept it as legitimate, we have blocked Love as healing. Yet the moment we intentionally choose instead to enter a most sovereign and Holy Instant in which we literally "will with God" to accept His undoing of what we imagine we see or feel – we completely receive healing of the single cause of our disturbance, whether its effects lie in our body, in another's body, or in a relationship, etc.

7. It takes only one Holy Instant. This instant is eternal and not affected by linear time. As such, it's available in every moment we choose to show-up and receive it.

8. Healing, Love and miracles are one. Where they are received and extended, fear along with its symptoms must vanish. These healings are merely the *effects* of the absence of fear. The Atonement is a Holy Instant in which we accept and receive the complete eradication of fear. When the cause of suffering is healed via the Atonement so are its effects (physical symptoms) because both cause and effect remain together in our mind.

9. If we sincerely want to help to heal someone then we accept the Atonement for our self, first. Perhaps a simple bank account analogy here may be helpful. Let's imagine that each time we genuinely accept the Atonement *for our self* on behalf of another, we deposit

that healing into a constantly increasing bank account. That account is inclusive, so it's available to the whole Sonship the instant they are willing to receive (withdraw the deposit). The specific person we desire to help will use his own free will to choose *when* they want to withdraw the deposit (miracle) we've made on their behalf. In the meantime, our deposit continues to bless us and others.

10. The prerequisite for accepting the Atonement or miracle is a Holy Instant, even just one split second, where we lay fear aside completely and willingly accept God's Grace as His most Holy restoration of our perception. For one Holy Instant *empty of fear*, Spirit's immaculate healing floods in. Where fear is absent, Love *is*.

   a. *"The only thing that is required for a healing is a lack of fear. The fearful are not healed, and cannot heal. This does not mean the conflict must be gone forever from your mind to heal. For if it were, there were no need for healing then. But it does mean, if only for an instant, you love without attack. An instant is sufficient. Miracles wait not on time."* T-27.V.2:8-14

11. Before we go on let's look at some of the most typical expressions of fear. Some of these may not be recognized as fear but instead be misinterpreted as Love or caring. For instance, when a loved one is ill, in pain or in distress our initial response is often "concern." Concern, worry, anxiety and sacrifice are not gestures of Love. They are its opposite, expressions of fear, and their presence blocks the miracle.

12. This is why when we are tempted by any expression of fear, we need the Atonement. While we're concerned about someone, we are unknowingly reinforcing their fear-driven state of suffering. This is one of the major reasons why Jesus teaches the necessity of undoing specialness in our relationships. This form of relationship promotes fear and sacrifice while using pseudo love as concern.

13. The false self has no idea what Love is. The only "love" it knows is love with attack, or fearful love. Yet there can be no such thing because Love and fear are mutually exclusive. The presence of one completely negates the other. In other words, they cannot be merged. Fearful love is special love or love with attack. Some examples may include when we defend, judge, control, feel anger, worry, or make

decisions and plans apart from Holy Spirit. These are just some of the signs of fearful love, an attempt to combine two mutually exclusive beliefs, as Love and fear.

14. There are no degrees of Love. Love is total and indivisible. Fear is also total and contains no degrees. Yet fear does not exist. So special love is always "fear" and is therefore the absence of Love. If fear forms the underlying agenda in our special relationships, and fear does not exist in God's Love, then nothing real holds these relationships together until we invite Holy Spirit in to repurpose them through Love. Just take a moment to really feel into this fact.

15. The Atonement necessitates for us to show-up in a Holy Instant of Love – without – attack. Literally this means to come without concern, worry, anxiety or neediness. It's a Grace-filled moment where we lay all our imagined concerns and needs aside. We don't ask for anything. Nor do we offer anything. Spirit knows the requests of our heart and has already fulfilled them. In silence, we sit deeply in our heart and _receive_ the Grace of God as divine correction.

D. Tips on Accessing the Atonement

1. When we're in fear it's often difficult to access a moment of "lack of fear" in order to accept the miracle. For those who have difficulty accessing a genuine "fearless moment" in which to receive the Atonement this may be helpful. The Atonement calls for an instant of "lack of fear." But, while we feel hopelessly lost emotionally, in any one of the many expressions of fear, it can feel like an impossible task.

2. One practice I've used when this occurs is to visualize the fearful emotion as a tiny infant who is crying out of intense fear and confusion. I remember that I am not the infant (emotion). However, I choose to bring this baby into my heart and enfold her or him in tender acceptance no matter how distressed this child appears. I see and feel their total innocence. I do not try to fix this infant; instead, I quietly become the unopposed Love that holds this precious but distressed child until it has returned to peace in my arms. Then I recognize that all it ever needed was to be *accepted fully without judgment*.

3. In this practice we learn how to accept our self as perfectly innocent regardless of any inner turmoil. Self-judgment is fear. Therefore, we must access a moment of complete acceptance of our self.

4. In this acceptance there is often a felt sense of relief, peace and gratitude. Indeed, the gratitude we feel is a sure sign that we *did* receive the miracle! If we received it and we've accepted it on behalf of our self and someone else, then they must receive it too (although they may not be aware of it yet). It's impossible to receive the Atonement without it affecting the one we seek to forgive or heal.

5. No one can ask another to be healed. However, we can accept the purification of our perception on behalf of someone else. Indeed, we cannot heal someone else if we have not *received* healing first. We cannot give what we do not have. If we're offering healing then it's always our own mind that receives correction first, otherwise we cannot possibly extend it.

6. Remember the half of our mind that believes in and therefore *values* suffering, sickness, conflict, etc. is the exact same half-mind that projects suffering in another's mind. This delusional half-mind that we seem to share is the separation illusion. This split half-mind is not personal and exclusive. It doesn't belong to just one individual. This fearful half is a shared insanity while we still believe (value) the painful effects that only "it" can project.

7. To the degree we are concerned or triggered shows us where the source of healing rests; in our own mind. The remedy begins by recognizing that the adversity we seem to witness arises from just one source, our own fear. We cannot believe or perceive attack from the delusional split mind in another unless we first choose to perceive through the same delusional half-mind.

   a. *"He overlooks the mind [and] body, seeing only the face of Christ shining in front of him, correcting all mistakes and healing all perception."* M-22.4:5

8. When we see someone else as separate, through relationship conflict or illness, etc. we project this suffering via the unreal half of our mind. If we receive the Atonement – for our self – on behalf of someone else, then we are *both* healed. Holy Spirit unifies our mind healing the split, and all that remains is one whole mind. We accept

our union as one. In this "closing of the gap," healing is free to extend because the two delusional half-minds collapse leaving a Holy Instant of the one unified mind, or the one, shared Holy Self.

a. *"Correction is the function given both, but neither one alone. And when it is fulfilled as shared, it must correct mistakes in you and him. It cannot leave mistakes in one unhealed and set the other free." ..."In His acceptance of this function lies the means whereby your mind is unified. His single purpose unifies the halves of you that you perceive as separate. And each forgives the other, that he may accept his other half as part of him." T-27.II.15:1-3,16:5-7*

9. If we were entirely fearless we would see clear through all appearances of disease, conflict and deprivation of any kind. In fact, we would see the perfect face of Christ behind every flimsy veil of suffering. And by seeing only this, we would join with it. Love without fear is restored. And the illusory veil would literally fall away.

10. A prayer that came to me recently and one which gives me instant peace is this:

a. *"Holy Spirit, I give to you all that never was – in exchange – for what always was and is as God created me. Amen."*

E. An Honest Look at the Body's Purpose

1. We can only give, share and experience that which we *have* and *are*. And all we are and therefore have in reality is God's Love. This is all we have in Truth. Nothing other than this joy and infinite Love can be shared, because, even though seemingly split and dreaming, the mind cannot attack. It can hallucinate and project the appearance of attack, yes, but it is impossible for the mind to attack in any form. All seeming attack (sickness, pain, conflict, death, etc.) is complete illusion.

2. When we experience anything other than that which we are and have, we unknowingly choose to experience something opposite to all that exists as God. Yet there is literally nothing opposite of God's Love... nothing.

3. It feels to me that I am finally realizing this profound Truth, not just intellectually but in my 3-D experience. No wonder miracles have no order of difficulty. It's no more difficult to heal one illusion than any other precisely because they are all illusions!

4. Any attempt to heal through fear cannot undo the singular cause of suffering which is fear/guilt itself. When we believe, from the ego's perception, that we want healing it is because we are afraid of the experience of illness, pain, disaster, loss, etc. The fact that fear is the motivation for our desire to heal deems it impossible to achieve true healing. Fear must be loosened and dismissed, and the *Love* and *Peace* that we both *have* and *are* must be recognized in order to have true healing.

5. There is no order of difficulty in healing! All true Healing (the undoing of fear/guilt) serves to undo the sole cause of suffering which is our unconscious belief that we are separate from God's Love and healing.

F. The Body Itself Cannot Feel

1. In the past I would often describe how I felt by checking in with the body, allowing *it* to influence my mental or emotional state. Was there pain or illness? It seemed my happiness depended upon the state of my body. While we can use the body to determine when we have abandoned our self, it's really the *mind* that informs the body - telling it exactly what to do. Unrelinquished judgments (guilt as self-attack) are projected onto the body as the sole cause of all pain and illness. And this is why quantum forgiveness, as the Atonement, is crucial to healing the one cause of all suffering. The forgiveness process can be found in *The Seven Essential Principles of Quantum Forgiveness (Atonement)* on page 591.

2. Jesus teaches that the body is simply a learning device. It is entirely neutral and has no feelings of its own. It's a screen, a projected image, one which we authorize to express either health or sickness.

   a. *"A learning device (body) is not a teacher. It cannot tell you how you feel. You do not know how you feel because you have accepted the ego's confusion, and you therefore believe that a learning device [can] tell you how you feel. Sickness is merely another example of your insistence on asking guidance of a teacher who does not know the answer. The ego is incapable of knowing how you feel." T-8.VIII.7:1-5 NOTE: (body) Nouk's clarification*

6. AN INSIGHT INTO OVERCOMING THE BODY

1. I had asked Spirit for my trust to be deepened, especially concerning the subject of the body as I knew this was the last idol we willingly surrender to Spirit in its entirety.

2. Jesus says that as our guilt is relinquished and the body is divinely repurposed, the body's importance diminishes in our awareness. It becomes a useful "means" to achieve healing via forgiveness and is no longer a "goal" in itself, to be misused by the ego for pleasure and pain (which are the same). Rather, the body is freed of conflicting wishes because it is aligned in God's Will. It thus reflects this gentle union and cannot appear to attack while we stay true to Holy Spirit's purpose of peace.

3. When the body's form and purpose are given wholly to Spirit, we are delivered from the body as our identity. It fades in our awareness as the light of Christ within us outshines it. Our physical senses no longer reign supreme in telling us what reality is. Christ Vision now eclipses the body's senses. In the following quote Jesus refers to this state. He actually says that when this is achieved the body will not "feel" at all. And that is a powerful statement indeed.

   a. *"Now is the body healed, because the source of sickness has been opened to relief. And you will recognize you practiced well by this:* **The body should not feel at all. If you have been successful, there will be no sense of feeling ill or feeling well, of pain or pleasure.** *No response at all is in the mind to what the body does. Its usefulness remains and nothing more." W-136.17.*

4. We are so accustomed to relying on the body and its five senses to inform us as to how we feel; to tell us what is happening. Yet when we believe the body, instead of asking to see the miracle behind it, we unintentionally block the exquisite joy and safety of our Christ Vision. While the body is seen as "who" we are it presents a strong block to Love, a rejection of our most Holy Self. Love and fear are opposites. Opposites do not exist in Truth. Identifying as one completely obscures the other. And while we still primarily associate our identity with the body it acts as a convincing defense against Love and healing.

5. I have had several experiences that have assisted me in opening more to this idea of *looking past* the body, to the Spirit shining brilliantly beyond it. In this first one I'm describing, I feel this must have been an experience of Christ Vision because there was zero fear involved, even though my own body (as I knew it) had been removed from my awareness. I will try to explain.

6. I was lying face down enjoying a back massage when I became aware that there were strokes of pressure being applied to my back, yet I did not feel these in the traditional way. I was distanced from the body. So I asked for guidance to take me deeper. What more could I learn while this miraculous portal opened? What could be revealed in this most precious moment where the body had faded from my awareness?

7. Suddenly there was a profound stillness. While I was immersed in this boundless spaciousness without my body, I began to vaguely sense that I was witnessing someone else's body. A feeling of awe began to rise in my awareness, but I remained acutely present. I allowed my awareness to stay in deep trust and peace. It was then that I beheld it was Jesus' body which was lying on the table and not my own.

8. Remaining lucid, my awareness was both in His body and outside His body. My own body was nowhere to be found. My awareness was not body identified. I certainly was not encased within His body nor in my own. My awareness was so huge that it totally transcended His body – still I could feel a magnificent learning opportunity was being delivered, so I allowed my awareness to continue.

9. As my awareness sank ever more deeply into peace, I recognized that this body was being prepared for burial. It was being sanctified, anointed with precious oils, while in the distance I heard chanting or singing as if there were a thousand angels gathered in praise of this most beloved Soul.

10. I was able to be "in" this body yet to be outside it while witnessing impartially. What really struck me was this. I was an impartial witness to a completely neutral body. And when I really allowed this to sink in, I felt into Jesus' experience of the crucifixion. I received a mere glimpse but that was enough to lure me onward.

11. To access this ability to be an impartial witness of the body comes about through what I felt to be the complete absence of fear. An absolute state of fearlessness. This then was the total acceptance of only Love. Reaching deeper still into this sacred epiphany, I was gifted with an instant's recognition of indescribable peace and joy which arose from a certainty of knowing that there is absolutely nothing in the vast expanse of the universe that can possibly threaten a Child of God.

12. In that instant, it all made sense. Of course! Physical pain as a form of self-attack was not part of God and therefore did not exist. Now, through this experience, I perceived this from an entirely different vantage point.

13. This totally indestructible state came from an unequivocal certainty of having claimed the changeless and incorruptible innocence as a Son of God. Feeling in deeper still, there was no recognition of sin (attack, pain, injustice, etc.) let alone the impulse to judge it. Judgment was entirely obsolete within this certainty of Being because there was nothing *to* judge.

14. And because the idea of sin was absent, all of its consequences were not there to see. They had disappeared altogether. The guilt, the fear, the anticipation of physical brutality and finally, even the physical destruction of Jesus' body was not there to witness. Its fundamental cause as the singular belief in sin, along with all its consequences of pain and death just vanished in Jesus' resurrection.

15. In this expanded awareness I experienced a mere fragment of what Jesus had known. Yet at some level I recognized that what

I would call a "fragment" was really an intrinsic component of the entire holographic dream. And this part, an undivided experience of the absence of sin, guilt and fear, was indeed the whole. It was an extended and eternal Holy Instant outside of time. It is in truth a powerful and permanent piercing of the ego's dream of suffering and death.

16. It was, in a way, a bodiless state. Yes, His body was still present, however, because only pure *guiltlessness* was *observing* it, the body was in complete service to the Soul. It was a lifeless hand puppet awaiting animation by the hand of the Son of God.

17. This experience was incredibly helpful, assisting me to make headway in seeing the body as neutral, and especially to perceive the Light of Christ beyond the body. I either see the body…or I see the Christ. The two are mutually exclusive, meaning that belief in one eclipses the other.

18. For me, the all too familiar focus of either pleasure or pain was wholly removed in this profound experience. Now I had an undeniable and tangible encounter with not being imprisoned in the body, but of having the body as occurring within my mind (not brain); Hence the lucid acknowledgment of being both inside a body and outside it all at the same time.

19. I love what Jesus says here in the following quotes:

   a. *"Look at yourself, and you will see a body. Look at this body in a different light and it looks different. And without a light it seems that it is gone. Yet you are reassured that it is there because you still can feel it with your hands and hear it move. Here is an image that you want to be yourself. It is the means to make your wish come true. It gives the eyes with which you look on it, the hands that feel it, and the ears with which you listen to the sounds it makes. It proves its own reality to you."* T-24.VII.9.

   b. *"The body no more dies than it can feel. It does nothing. Of itself it is neither corruptible nor incorruptible. It [is] nothing. It is the result of a tiny, mad idea of corruption that can be corrected."* T-19.IV.C.5:2-6

A. The Body's True Purpose - Guiltlessness and Invulnerability

1. Nearly everyone on this planet believes the body represents their self, their identity, their goal, an "end" in itself. And they also believe this of others who appear in their life. All our special relationships are not with Souls but with "bodies" while we erroneously value the body as an *end goal* in itself. Rather, it is a *means* to awaken from the dream of fear and death. Unknowingly, the body was made as our replacement for God, for our Holy Self.

2. Aligning with the body's true purpose is about reassigning the body's value to Spirit, because of itself the body has no value. When we value the body for what it can give us (either pleasure or pain) we unknowingly condemn our self to suffering and death. To realize and live out from the body's true purpose is to know our own and other's complete guiltlessness.

3. When this state of undivided innocence becomes embodied, the body is recognized as completely neutral. It has no power of its own to get sick or to get well. It responds only to the healed mind and is under no laws but God's. Now the body is made Holy and in its Holiness there is nothing it cannot do in the name of God's Love and Laws.

4. Because all unconscious condemnation has been withdrawn from it, the body is now employed by Love to demonstrate, through its literal invulnerability, our own guiltlessness and the guiltlessness of everyone we encounter. The body becomes incorruptible (healed) until it has served its purpose and then it is gently laid aside in joy; although as Jesus says, it is not old, nor sick, nor hurt.

5. Jesus points out that when we see our self or another "as a body" we unknowingly attack them and our self. We separate from God's Love and unintentionally invite the ego to attack in numerous forms. But what are some practical examples of how this occurs?

6. Following are a few common and often unquestioned ways in which we unknowingly attack (invite suffering). These are the ego's means of using the body lovelessly which always increases unconscious guilt. Yet some of these actions are not only socially acceptable and encouraged but thought to be loving and caring as well (in the ego's version that is).

7. **Using the body in a prideful way, such as using it:**

   a. To lure another body.

   b. To compare with another body.

   c. To appear more superior to another body.

   d. To appear inferior to another body, etc.

8. **Using the body as proof that we and others *are* the body and are therefore guilty; i.e. using it:**

   a. To demonstrate that it can be victimized by pain, disease, aging, accidents, addiction, scarcity, etc.

   b. To worry about our own or another's state of health.

   c. To apply magic to defend the body's life mindlessly (without Spirit).

   d. For mindless (heartless) sex.

   e. To claim exclusive rights to someone's body (as in the exclusive special love relationship), etc.

9. These few examples serve to reinforce the body's reality as a separate wall of flesh; one that was born only to die. Born to demonstrate that our imagined guilt which spawns the illusions of pain, sickness and death, is real, *more real than God's Love as our Holy Self.*

10. These are some of the ways we unintentionally reinforce the illusion of the body's authority over that of our Holy Self. In other words, these are used to perpetuate the lie that the body and world appear to be more powerful than the mind that made them; that we are helpless victims of the body and world.

11. While none of these miscreations are wrong in themselves, they do attract guilt; and that is why they deserve to be mindfully raised to the light of Spirit to be seen and exchanged for healed perception, for miracles instead. No guilt! There is to be no self-judgment about them as it's always the ego that condemns.

12. At the time of writing this excerpt, I still take calcium supplements because my trust is not yet completely transferred to the Holy Self. I still wear glasses too! However, I don't judge myself for these. I know that Spirit has it covered!

13. My only responsibility is to "look" at my magic defenses *with Spirit*, to express my willingness to have my perception healed. Anything else I (from ego) attempt to do, control, resist, or relinquish will come from fear. When it's time to relinquish my magic, I will be directed by Love and not by fear. And this guidance will be unmistakable, just as previous guidance has always demonstrated to me.

14. A significant component involved in the undoing of our belief in the body's reality arises from the willingness to look at all the ways we use it to seek for pleasure and to escape from pain. Most of these decisions were previously made *apart* from the mindful presence of our Holy Self. As such they were made with the ego.

15. The undoing of the seeming control the body exacts upon us is *not* our responsibility – it's God's. We, from the limited standpoint of the ego, cannot correct or undo.

16. When we allow the ego to run the body, not only do its choices incur guilt but they lead to death... literally. Remember the ego's goal is to kill the body before we wake-up *from* it. As we release the ego's obsession with the body, the Holy Self takes over and runs it perfectly. After all, the body is purely an idea which resides in the mind and is never separate from it. Its state is projected moment to moment either by the ego or the Right-Mind, the Holy Self.

17. When the Holy Self is invited to run the body then the decisions we make will come from Love and not from fear. The outcome of relinquishing the body's purpose to God's undivided Love is an experience of ever-increasing joy and abundant miracles. I know that I am all in for this! Will you join me?

7. SEVEN DAYS WITHOUT THE BODY

1. I can't believe I'm attempting to write about this next experience which has been immensely helpful to me. Already as I write, I am being told that I called this experience in because it was absolutely pivotal to my advance in trust with Jesus' deeper teaching. It feels to me as if this experience, although not yet permanent, was a way that I could cast forward a few valuable breadcrumbs in the illusion of time, to form a luminous trail which would lead me further into the light.

2. It happened during the writing of *"The Unequivocal Secret that Solves Every Single Problem."* I found myself so compellingly immersed in the message itself while I felt the transmission coming through. Then in one heavenly Holy Instant that extended to seven days in time, the body just gently fell away in my awareness. In retrospect, I think I must have fallen into the very state that I had been writing about.

3. The body is a big deal here in the ego dream. In fact, it's the biggest deal since time began because it has become the central hub of our existence. Every choice we make is centered on it, which really boils down to a constant preoccupation with the body to bring us pleasure or to avoid pain. This central hub is nothing but an epic distraction meant to divert our attention from the true Source of our being as unopposed Love itself.

4. Furthermore, every one of our special relationships revolves around the body. I feel that until we begin to undo the false self, 99.9 percent of our thoughts, wishes and concerns are dominated by the belief we are a body and not eternal Spirit. Even in our sleeping dreams we still see our self and others as separate bodies.

5. While it remains a slave to the false self, the body completely blocks the light of Love that beams unceasingly through us and in everyone we meet. The ego doesn't want us to discover that the lasting Love, safety and innocence we long for, just cannot be known *until* we prioritize the desire to behold the uninterrupted light of Love and guiltlessness in our self and others. This necessarily involves our desire to look past the body and its seeming sins in others.

6. I feel that my increasing practice of this (Atonement) and the great joy it delivers has played a big part of bringing in this experience. After all, as we offer forgiveness, we also receive it.

A. Body Melting into Divine Purpose

1. As I wrote that mind-altering excerpt I mentioned earlier, I had an experience whereby the body seemed to have melted into my divine purpose. The body did not disappear. But my previous awareness of it had. To be more specific, my past perception of its purpose evaporated.
2. The barrage of incessant thoughts and feelings of being a body ceased for a full seven days. Lurking concerns of aging and temptations to feel any kind of pain or discomfort were entirely hushed. Rituals of nutritional sustenance and physical exercise were clearly seen as the single source which underpinned them – *fear.* A resounding peace effortlessly washed over them all.
3. There was the sudden, yet gently reassuring *knowing* that my will and God's were irrevocably one and the same. It's almost as if I could hardly remember a time when it wasn't. As I breathed, God breathed. As I looked out it was God witnessing only His reflection of Love and healing. As thoughts arose, they were reflected as God's. My mind held *only* what I thought with God.
4. In this continued state there was a distinct absence – of fear. Instead I was filled with a certainty that there was nothing in my body or seemingly external that could possibly betray me. This felt like an extremely rare experience even though it also felt as if it was the most natural one in the world.
5. Because the body was now fused with the Will of God through me, it had become a willing conduit for miracles. The body was no longer the ego's puppet. So it had no malice, no independent desire or ability to betray my will joined with God's.
6. As I saw and felt this divine amalgamation of will, flesh and Love, spontaneous waves of deep appreciation for the body washed over me. And these were interspersed with waves of deep remorse for the times I had mistakenly despised it for having betrayed me in pain, aging or sickness. Clearly, from this right-minded state I

recognized the body was indeed neutral. It was wholly innocent. It had always done what I had asked it to do. It merely played out my own denied wish for self-attack.

7. During that week I had many spontaneous instances of feeling overwhelming gratitude to finally be working *with* and through the body and not against it. I had always feared the body and now there was only Love.

B. What Precipitated This Miraculous Experience?

1. I feel this experience was the culmination of a number of factors that fell into consistent alignment during that week. A major contributor was my undivided focus on inner listening. So my "desire" for nothing else was a huge motivator. I set my intention and had refused to be distracted by anything else.

2. This alone must have shifted my perception in that Holy Instant. Suddenly it seemed my will and God's were the same. There felt to be the falling away of a distinct "self" together with its thoughts and needs, and the essence that replaced this was a deeply resonant peace and certitude.

3. I felt an ease with the body that was both foreign and yet extremely familiar – a paradox indeed! It felt as if the restrictions of the body disappeared.

4. I became acutely aware of a peculiar phenomenon. The body was there…yet it was not relaying the usual moment to moment data that I was accustomed to. No data. I was incredulous. It was not reporting any unmet needs. How can I explain this? I can only describe it by saying that now I know what Jesus means when He said that if we have truly accepted the Atonement (healing) then *the body should not feel at all.*

5. There were no feelings of either pleasure or discomfort, yet this was not the numbness which comes from body denial. Instead I felt the most immense and joyous liberation.

6. I was reminded that this quite miraculous experience of being virtually bodiless was something I had worked diligently toward over a long period of time. It was the culmination of consistent forgiveness of all my judgments of everyone, the past and myself.

Jesus shares something quite profound in the following quote from lesson 136 and I believe this is what occurred for me:

a. *"Sickness is a defense against the truth. I will accept the truth of what I am, and let my mind be wholly healed today."*

"Healing will flash across your open mind, as peace and truth arise to take the place of war and vain imaginings. There will be no dark corners sickness can conceal, and keep defended from the light of truth. There will be no dim figures from your dreams, nor their obscure and meaningless pursuits with double purposes insanely sought, remaining in your mind. It will be healed of all the sickly wishes that it tried to authorize the body to obey."

"Now is the body healed, because the source of sickness has been opened to relief. And you will recognize you practiced well by this: The body should not feel at all. If you have been successful, there will be no sense of feeling ill or feeling well, of pain or pleasure. No response at all is in the mind to what the body does. Its usefulness remains and nothing more."

"Perhaps you do not realize that this removes the limits you had placed upon the body by the purposes you gave to it. As these are laid aside, the strength the body has will always be enough to serve all truly useful purposes. The body's health is fully guaranteed, because it is not limited by time, by weather or fatigue, by food and drink, or any laws you made it serve before. You need do nothing now to make it well, for sickness has become impossible."

"Yet this protection needs to be preserved by careful watching. If you let your mind harbor attack thoughts, yield to judgment or make plans against uncertainties to come, you have again misplaced yourself, and made a bodily identity which will attack the body, for the mind is sick."
W-136.15:6-7,16,17,18,19.

---

7. Yet even with all of this healing, there was still a thread of doubt. I couldn't help but notice the most difficult of all to forgive completely was the body itself. To some degree, I still saw it as an independent entity apart from my mind, and one that appeared to betray me unceasingly.

8. I've always had an intense dislike of being "in" a body – at least in this lifetime. It seemed to me such an oppressive burden. Even as a child I remember gaining some sense of relief by thinking that one day I'd be free of it when I die. So there was this undercurrent of expectation that I would once again be free of the cumbersome burden of the body through physical death.

9. Death would be my escape I thought … something to look forward to. And little did I know back then, this insane wish was the ego luring me into the mistaken belief that I would find God in *death* and thus not recognize Him where He really is, *here* and *now* – in life – through forgiving, and closing the gap with all my brothers.

10. Thankfully, in 2011 when I began to take in Jesus' deeper teachings, my attraction to death gradually began to be erased. And Jesus reminded me of this:

    a. *"There is a risk of thinking death is peace, because the world equates the body with the Self which God created. Yet a thing can never be its opposite. And death is opposite to peace, because it is the opposite of life. And life is peace. Awaken and forget all thoughts of death, and you will find you have the peace of God." T-27.VII.10:2-6*

11. The bodiless experience I had was not some random state. I really believe it came as a result of applied intent and purpose with Holy Spirit. During that week I reaffirmed the body's proper role with great delight. Being liberated from slavery to the ego it was now happily in service to God.

12. I was acutely aware of the body serving as an ally in accepting the Holy Instant as the correction of fear. I was so present in each moment with absolutely no regard or care for what was to come. Gratitude and a new-found sense of reverence replaced my age-old thoughts of condemnation, disgust or pride in the body.

13. I was reminded that the body is the last special relationship that we willingly make Holy by giving it over to Holy Spirit completely. Until then there is a deep unconscious attraction to abandon the body to sin, sickness and death.

C. The Body's Purpose - Love *Without* Fear

1. My bodiless experience prompted me to recall the body's single purpose as a communication device. True communication is Love *without* fear, without attack. It is to be used to extend and witness to our incorruptible innocence and our perfect immunity to all perceived dangers (attack) that only this undivided commitment can bring.

2. One thing that arose repeatedly in my awareness was that this was not *my* body. I no longer wished to use it to deny the will of God (Love), as a witness to fear and attack. I no longer wanted to use it to fulfill the ego's will to be separate from my eternal Source of Love, joy and perfect health. I didn't want to pursue distractions or defend myself from Love any longer. The body, when offered up to be assigned its Holy purpose will be a perfect conduit for God's Will. And this I remembered.

3. Since then I have allowed an interruption of that joyous week of an uninterrupted bodiless state. But now there is a certainty that it's only the illusion of time which seems to make this state temporary and not permanent. And I am reminded to be patient. Those who trust can afford to be patient because they know the outcome is certain – my will and God's are *one*, so why would I be concerned? What a relief!

4. I happened to come across another section of the *Course* where it appeared to explain what had occurred for me in that miraculous seven-day window. In chapter twenty-seven Jesus speaks about the ego's purpose for the body, which is separation and *attack*. One of the most convincing forms of attack is illness and pain. While we consent to suffer then we unwittingly demonstrate to others that they too deserve to suffer – because we are all guilty.

5. He says that as we advance in our forgiveness and trust we close the seeming gap between our self and our brothers and sisters. This heals our ancient decision to use the body for attack and separation. As the Holy Spirit divinely repurposes the body it reflects an open space where the ego's goals of sin, fear, guilt and sickness are removed.

a. *"Into this empty space (body), from which the goal of sin has been removed, is Heaven free to be remembered. Here its peace can come, and perfect healing take the place of death. The body can become a sign of life, a promise of redemption, and a breath of immortality to those grown sick of breathing in the fetid scent of death. Let it have healing as its purpose. Then will it send forth the message it received, and by its health and loveliness proclaim the truth and value that it represents. Let it receive the power to represent an endless life, forever unattacked. And to your brother let its message be, "Behold me, brother, at your hand I live."... "The simple way to let this be achieved is merely this; to let the body have no purpose from the past, when you were sure you knew its purpose was to foster guilt."* T-27.I.10,11:1*

8. HOW AND WHY WE WANT TO LOOK PAST THE BODY

1. This more recent experience was brought about when I asked Jesus for additional help; I wanted an easy way to truly see the body differently. For most, it seems almost impossible *not* to see others as bodies, especially in the special romantic relationship (pleasure) or when we've been seemingly hurt by someone (pain). Jesus tells us, *"It [is] impossible to see your brother as sinless and yet to look upon him as a body."* ... *"Who sees a brother's body has laid a judgment on him, and sees him not. He does not really see him as sinful; he does not see him at all. T-20.VII.4:1,6:1*

2. Jesus tells us that the body – ours and others – is totally neutral which means that it's always a blank screen onto which "we" project

what we value and believe, good and bad. When we believe our body's senses and appetites instead of calling for Christ Vision, we will see, feel and experience the ego's largely unconscious projections. And then we *react* to them as if they were real, which leads to further separation and its inevitable outcome, pain. This is the vicious cycle of trusting in the body senses as a substitute for our Holy Self.

3. The ego is the election for separation, and it requires *and therefore values* fear and the belief that we are a body. Through the body's senses and appetites, we employ the ego to direct our experience, and we're constantly manifesting idols which support our beliefs and values. If the ego's singular purpose for the body's senses and appetites is separation, then it goes to show that we *must* give the body entirely to Holy Spirit so it can be repurposed for union instead of separation.

4. Remember that the body is an idea in our mind. It has no value or purpose other than what we assign to it. As a neutral projection, the body is completely free of judgment, until we mistakenly judge what it's *for*.

   a. *"Your question should not be, 'How can I see my brother without the body?' Ask only, 'Do I really wish to see him sinless?' And as you ask, forget not that his sinlessness is [your] escape from fear."* T-20.VII.9:1-2

5. In my own undoing experience, I was gifted with a beautiful insight, an analogy that helped lift me up out of the body so I could see it differently. The question I had asked Jesus just before this experience came, was "how" can I see this body and that of others differently?

6. What I was shown was an image of my own beloved dog, Neesie. And then a truly revealing sequence of questions came:

   1) How does Neesie see you when you first wake up in the morning? Perfect!

   2) How does Neesie see you during the day or the evening? Perfect!

3) Would Neesie see you any differently if you lost 10 pounds, worked out and gained a "hot" looking body? No!

4) Would Neesie see you differently if you gained 50 pounds? No!

5) With you, does Neesie have conditions, expectations, judgments, grievances, roles, rules and plans, that if not fulfilled or corrected, would be justification for her to withdraw or completely end her Love for you? No!

6) Is there anything you could do that would end her Love for you? No!

7. Do you now recognize that Neesie's Love for you is changeless? Do you now realize that she Loves you unconditionally because:

 a. She sees you as sinless.

 b. The result of knowing you as sinless is that your body drops away in her awareness.

 c. Her advantage is that she does not value your body because of what she can use it *for.* This is in direct contrast with the special relationship where the body, and not the Holy Self, is valued and therefore, seen. Thus, love can appear to change and even end.

8. So now I see it clearly. While we value sin – the wish for separation – we will always see the body and not the innocent Spirit behind the body's image. The ego's version of the body is the product of the value of and belief in sin. We see the body and not the Spirit because we, through the ego, mistakenly decide the *purpose* of the body. When we use the body for specialness in relationships, it always leads to suffering. If we feel unfairly treated by anyone, past or present, then we must still value both sin *and* the body.

9. Forgiveness undoes the false self's unconscious addiction to sin, thus reassigning the body-puppet's purpose from that of attack (conflict, sickness, pain, etc.) to one of Love (union, health, joy, etc.).

10. The preceding practical self-inquiry gave me deeper insight into "how" to see my body and that of others in a whole new way. Think about this. In our special relationships, just how many of our conditions, expectations, interactions, judgments, grievances, plans, roles and rules, are based on a hugely mistaken foundation – that we are bodies and not changeless Spirit?

11. What would change if we were to genuinely and consistently see others and our self the way my dog Neesie sees me, as completely sinless and guiltless? Again, there is just one common denominator here - the body *and* sin are synonymous. We simply cannot afford to value one without validating the other.

12. It is likely that each of us will learn in our own way and time, but to review, here are a few of the factors that I feel were tremendous aids to unchaining my mind to experience the body in an entirely different manner:

1) Ask guidance of the Teacher Who knows the answer, not ego.

2) Release the attraction to the ego's purposes for the body; give the body's purposes over to Holy Spirit completely.

3) Recognize the body's neutrality, our mind directs the body and we unconsciously assign it to roles.

4) When an awareness begins to emerge, a Holy Instant, allow the experience to deepen, trust Holy Spirit, stay out of fear and be an impartial witness.

5) Have an undivided focus on listening to inner wisdom from Holy Spirit.

6) Use forgiveness to close the gap of separation and heal the mind that thought the body was real.

7) Let Holy Spirit reassign the purpose we gave the body, from attack and fear to Love.

9. HEALING THE BODY VIA LOVE

1. In many holistic and New Age healing circles there is a focus on learning to love the body as part of the healing process. Yet this approach will not work unless the underlying and unrecognized *cause* of pain, illness, aging or death is addressed.

2. This deeply buried cause of sickness in any form is our erroneous belief that we're separate from the eternal Fountain of Love –the Source of all healing.

3. When we are sick or in pain it's because we still cling to this belief that we are separate. We rarely recognize the origin of sickness which is always a mistaken judgment or condemnation. The false self repeatedly seeks to place the cause of pain everywhere else but where it lay, which is with a treasured grievance or resentment. By steering us away from recognizing the seat of sickness (judgment) it makes sure we never heal the *one cause* of all separation, sickness and death.

4. If there is illness or pain then there is unforgiven blame, which reinforces our belief in separation. And it's *this* which must be healed as the single cause. Once the condemnation is forgiven then the body is free to demonstrate the Loving consequences of union – as healing, – rather than to manifest sickness as the result of separating.

5. When I am tempted to believe in pain or illness, I have trained myself to ask where I have made a decision to separate. Do I hold a grievance against someone? Is it from the past or present? Where do I believe that I've been unfairly treated? And by whom? The decision for sickness comes from a choice to *reject* someone by way of condemnation or blame.

6. Yet it's an impossibility to reject (judge) anyone without first attacking our self. All attack is self-attack. And the body is the greatest repository for unforgiven condemnation. It would be entirely impossible for the body to sicken or even to die if we had healed the false self's obsession to project onto others – and the body – our own hidden desire for self-attack.

7. We cannot Love and therefore cannot heal the body *unless* we extend that Love as forgiveness to our brothers first.

8. The body is released and healed as we forgive those whom we perceived as having hurt, betrayed or abandoned us. We cannot heal (Love) the body until we release everyone from blame. The body is returned to Love – and healed – as we willingly forgive our brothers. All sickness arises from separation, from blame. Healing is the result of our genuine desire to "close the gap" with others via forgiveness.

    a. *"Uniting with a brother's mind prevents the cause of sickness and perceived effects. Healing is the effect of minds that join (forgive), as sickness comes from minds that separate (blame)." T-28.III.2:5-6*

9. If the primary cause of all illness and death is the erroneous belief that we are separate from the Fountain of Love, as our Holy Self, then the Sacred Bridge back to our Source is through union with our brothers.

10. The ego's original purpose for making the body was to hood wink us into believing the illusion that each one of us *is* a separate body and that we are separate from each other and separate from our Source of Love Itself. Being totally immersed in this delusion, the ego generates further belief in separation by making it appear that the illusory body has dominion over our mind. Yet only the mind can govern the body, in fact *it made* the body.

    a. *"Minds are joined; bodies are not. Only by assigning to the mind the properties of the body (separate bodies) does separation seem to be possible. And it is mind that seems to be fragmented and private and alone. Its guilt, which keeps it separate, is projected to the body, which suffers and dies because it is attacked to hold the separation in the mind, and let it not know its Identity." T-18.VI.3:1-4*

11. The body initially was made to separate us and now the Holy Self's purpose is to use the body as a means to restore communication – Love – by our willingness to see everyone, including our self, as sinless and guiltless.

12. The body's sole purpose is communication, however very few realize its meaning or its value. Communication is Love. And

Love is the complete absence of fear. Love as communication is interrupted or blocked by our belief in any of fear's numerous descendants such as guilt, blame, judgment, defense, attack, worry, jealousy, sickness, pain, lack, loss and death, etc. All sickness arises from this interruption of communication. But thankfully, heartfelt forgiveness restores communication and thus health.

13. Grievances break communication. Fear breaks communication just as guilt or blame does. Forgiveness on the other hand, restores communication, not only with our brothers but with God and our Holy Self. We cannot condemn another (break communication) without suffering that same break with God and our Holy Self. This break in communication is the reason *why* the body sickens, ages and dies.

14. The body is completely neutral and has *zero authority* over the mind. Yet when pain or illness strike, there is an automatic response to project blame onto the body; or onto other illusory causes in the past (heredity for example) or in the world.

a. *"It is insane to use the body as the scapegoat for guilt, directing its attack and blaming it for what you wished it to do." T-18.VI.6:1*

b. *"You see yourself locked in a separate prison (body), removed and unreachable, incapable of reaching out as being reached. You hate this prison (body) you have made, and would destroy it. But you would not escape from it, leaving it unharmed, without your guilt upon it."* ... *"Yet only thus [can] you escape. T-18.VI.7:5-7,8:1*

c. *"The body will remain guilt's messenger, and will act as it directs as long as you believe that guilt is real. For the reality of guilt is the illusion that seems to make it heavy and opaque, impenetrable, and a real foundation for the ego's thought system. Its thinness and transparency are not apparent until you see the light behind it. And then you see it as a fragile veil before the light." T-18.IX.5:1-4*

15. It is impossible to learn to Love the body and have it healed while we still choose to believe that we have been or can be victimized

by anyone, even during our childhood. Ultimately, if we sincerely wish to heal then we must be willing to ask Holy Spirit to help us to forgive *our self* for having unknowingly used someone or something to attack our self, so as to sever communication with Love which is "What" we are.

A. Seeing Your Brother or Sister as Sinless

1. To the degree you do not want to forgive (see them as sinless) is the degree that you still wish for sickness, pain and separation for yourself. This is an undeniable result of the choice not to forgive. Because your will is free to choose separation you are also free to project that attack onto the body as sickness, pain, weight gain, loss, etc.

    a. *"Would you not have the instruments of separation (body) reinterpreted as means for salvation, and used for purposes of love? Would you not welcome and support the shift from fantasies of vengeance to release from them? Your perception of the body can clearly be sick, but project not this upon the body." T-18.VI.5:1-3*

    b. *"You can stretch out your hand and reach to Heaven. You whose hand is joined with your brother's have begun to reach beyond the body, but not outside yourself, to reach your shared Identity together." T-18.VI.10:1-2*

2. Love is What we are. Love is real, eternal, uninterrupted and unopposed communication. This and only this, is what we are here to learn. And the body is our faithful servant. But we will not know Love while we continue to believe that anyone, including our self, is undeserving of complete forgiveness. The body will always manifest our grievances as pain and disease – or – it will witness to our undivided Love as health and loveliness.

    a. *"Love is not learned. Its meaning lies within itself. And learning ends when you have recognized all it is [not.] That is the interference; that is what needs to be undone." T-18. IX.12:1-4*

3. If to Love is to heal, then we cannot heal the body while we still choose to condemn.

4. In conclusion, it is impossible to heal the body unless we Love – forgive – our brothers. We may use magic medicine, therapy or surgery to heal the body temporarily. However, without comprehensive forgiveness, the single *cause* of all illness, pain, loss and death remains unhealed and will return until the greatest of all lessons since the beginning of time, is finally learned.

10. ENOUGH OF THIS NONSENSE – IT'S TIME TO WAKE-UP!

1. Jesus' resurrection was to prove that the body is *unreal*. It is simply a now-moment projected image. In Truth, the body is "beamed" in every second. It is not a product of our imagined past. This is why He says, *"At no single instant does the body exist at all. It is always remembered or anticipated, but never experienced just [now.]"* T-18.VII.3:1-2.

2. The body is a thought form. It's an image that dwells in our mind (not brain). It is made up of projected thought only. And it is sustained exclusively by our *belief* in it. This belief in the body arises from "what" we believe we are. We either believe we are the false self (body) or we believe we are the Child of God. Ultimately, what we believe we *are* will determine the purpose we use the body *for*.

3. We believe that the body is dependent on a bunch of ego laws which Jesus terms as magic (food, fluid, medicines, etc.). We think the body is born ... and then it dies. But the truth is it was never *born* and can never *die*. As a projected image only... it has *zero* past. And this is why the miracle can heal it instantaneously (if we believe and receive). The *unreal body cannot die!* We won't truly *know* the body is *unreal* ... until we overcome both death and the body. Death of the body (decay, etc.) is testimony that we have *not* overcome the body.

4. The purpose of miracles is to prove that we are the *mind* that made the body and world. We are therefore *never* victim of the body

or the world. The mind and *not* the body/world is always *cause*. The body/world is a direct *effect* of what we value and therefore, *believe*. And this is precisely *why* forgiveness is the sole means by which we heal, by *reversing* all of the laws of the world. Remember lesson 38?

a. *"Your holiness reverses all the laws of the world. It is beyond every restriction of time, space, distance and limits of any kind. Your holiness is totally unlimited in its power because it establishes you as a Son of God, at one with the Mind of his Creator."*

"Through your holiness the power of God is made manifest. Through your holiness the power of God is made available. And there is nothing the power of God cannot do. Your holiness, then, can remove all pain, can end all sorrow, and can solve all problems. It can do so in connection with yourself and with anyone else. It is equal in its power to help anyone because it is equal in its power to save anyone." W-38.1,2

5. Forgiveness looks past the erroneous "appearances" of sickness, pain, loss, aging, conflict, etc., and it acknowledges exclusively that these are always *effects* of the singular *cause* (unforgiven guilt as self-attack) in our mind. This, and *only* this, requires healing via forgiveness. Nothing is healed by manipulating self-made phenomena in the dream (holistic or traditional medicine, dieting, etc.). Guilt is the single *cause* of all illness, relationship conflict, lack and death. Period.

6. When we come to the most advanced stage of our development of trust (as Jesus demonstrated), the body is merely *dematerialized*. We simply cease *projecting* its image. At this stage, the body simply *disappears*. Because it is finally seen for what it is – unreal – it doesn't decay. It's seen as complete illusion. Jesus also says that when this stage is reached, the body is in pristine condition. It is not sick, old or hurt. It's just laid aside and it disappears. The unreal cannot die.

7. The End of Death, as Jesus came to teach, is literally the reversal of all the laws of the world. Our belief that death is the inevitable end

of life (end of God/Love) is the ego's central dream. If this were true, then death would be our "god" and God would be rendered completely powerless and helpless in the face of the ego's "god" of death.

8. God is eternal Life, right here, right *now*! God is eternal and uninterrupted Love! There is no death in God! The concept of death is the ego's most cherished obsession arising from its terror of Love (God). Death was made as our *escape from* God, from our awakening to the full embodiment of the Power of Christ that we *are*. Nothing could possibly assail Jesus. He knew He was the Son of God. He asks us to do the same and overcome all the sick and deranged "laws" we originally made as an attack on God and our Holy Self.

9. We made the body to demonstrate through its frailty and death that we are *not* a Child of God. Sickness, pain, conflict, lack, loss and death are all *symptoms* of our *fear of Love* (God). Unfortunately, our belief in death is our "god." If we believe that death is the certain, inevitable and natural outcome of all life, then we are terrified of God as Love. This is also our terror of our One, shared, Holy Self! There is either death … or … God. They are mutually exclusive! They cannot co-exist! Which of these is true? Which of these do I value (believe)?

10. And be gone to all those silly ego beliefs that presume we go Home to God through death! Who in his right mind would trust a god that wants his death!?

   a. The world is not left by death but by truth." T-3.VII.6: 11.

11. The common blessing for the dead, "Rest in Peace," is ridiculously twisted by the ego. No one rests in death. The only rest we have is in *Life!* God is Life and *not* death! This is what Jesus has to say about resting in peace:

   a. *"All forms of sickness, even unto death, are physical expressions of the fear of awakening. They are attempts to reinforce sleeping out of fear of waking. This is a pathetic way of trying not to see by rendering the faculties for seeing ineffectual. "Rest in peace" is a blessing for the living, not the dead, because rest comes from waking, not from sleeping." T-8.IX.3:2-5*

12. While death is still believed to be the natural and inevitable outcome of all life ... we will unwittingly believe that death *comes from God.* And we will be bitterly afraid of God (Love as our One Holy Self), not realizing that this is the ego's projection of *its* "god." This false idol will completely obscure the real and only God of undivided Love and uninterrupted Life.

13. We will then continue to project the ego's version of a vicious "god" onto the God of Love, Life and all Creation. The illusion of time itself is prolonged by our insane belief in death as our foremost savior from the unending conflict of life.

14. The ego's "recycle program" of birth, amnesia and death, birth, amnesia and death, keeps us enmeshed in a never-ending loop of incarnation followed by amnesia. When we're born into a body again, we completely forget our singular purpose which is to reverse all the laws of the world and to awaken from the dream.

15. Instead, we are once more groomed to be a better ego, a better body, with a better life. We learn the killer art of "special relationships" and we learn to substitute God with special love and the body. Physical pleasure becomes the aim of all our pursuits while we try to avoid pain ... not realizing they are one and the same ... And then? We get sick or age for the millionth lifetime, and we die again. Still, even in death we have no idea what our true Purpose is. We enter once again into the ego's dream of life as a helpless infant with complete amnesia. And the ego's "recycle program" concludes with death again. We just have to laugh!

16. No wonder the illusion of time has dragged on so wearily for some 14 billion years. It's been more than 2000 years since Jesus first demonstrated our singular Purpose for being here. And we still haven't got it. Our unquestioned value of death over God as Life has perpetuated the belief in time and our consequent incarnations into the ego's "recycle program." Yet the literal end of death equates to there being no more time or space – and of course, no more separation.

17. Jesus came to *break* this cycle literally, once and for *all* – and to teach us how to do it too! He gave us the Atonement so we can *accept* this healing outright. He already *did* it on behalf of us all.

But 2000 years onward and there may be only a handful of people in the dream who are just beginning to unpack His message, let alone *demonstrate* it. The next phase of the dream is to *own it* and to join in *demonstrating* His number one Miracle Principle (from *ACIM*): *"There is no order of difficulty in miracles."* None.

18. Why is there no order of difficulty in miracles? The reason is because there is no hierarchy of illusions. Because the body, its ailments and the world are all *equally unreal* ... the miracle has *supremacy* and one hundred percent *dominion* over these illusions. No order of difficulty means that nothing is more difficult to heal. Either a pimple or the throes of (seeming) death, are one and the same. They are a suggestion that God (Love) does not exist. The belief in death – or – God, is *total*.

19. Death is the opposite of God as Love and Life without interruption or end. The message here that Jesus teaches is there is *nothing* in the phenomenal (ego) dream that can harm us. To the contrary, the healed Mind takes *dominion* over everything! This includes the ego's central dream of death, which was made to convince us that we are powerless victims of the separation, and that we're *not* the Child of God. We *made up* everything we believe can attack us. Now, we will *unmake* all this nonsense with the Holy Spirit! This is what miracles are for! *It's time to wake-up!*

Guess what!? *"A Course in Miracles"* is a Course in **MIRACLES**! Yes **MIRACLES**!

A. My Visionary Dream

1. Just before I began taking down the transmissions for *"The End of Death"* trilogy, I had a powerful visionary dream in which I was asked to write down just one word. It seemed to take all night to finally get the word written. But the two Light Beings who stood over me while I attempted to do this stayed with me patiently and encouragingly until I was able to complete it. There were moments where I really didn't think I would ever complete this task. It felt as if I had endured lifetimes of conflict and confusion in *resistance* to the meaning of this word. But I had a feeling these two Beings were not going to give up on me *until* I had completed it.

2. The word that I felt was almost impossible to write down was *"rapture."* Yet as I tried over and over again to write this word with sweat beads rolling down my face, I kept seeing the word *"blasphemy."* And then I would attempt to write the Sacred Word again, only to see the word blasphemy one more time. In the end, after numerous attempts to get it right, there was a deep inner surrender. I seemed to accept all that the word "rapture" was pointing *to*. And it felt as if I had *received* it. Somehow its meaning was revealed to me, although at the time I consciously had no idea of the multidimensionality of it. This was the word pointing to the shining Center of this holographic dream and it lay shining brilliantly behind the ego's central dream of death.

3. Having had almost no biblical background in this lifetime, I had no conscious knowledge of the word "rapture." So, I looked it up on Google the following morning and was dumb-struck by its meaning. No wonder I kept seeing the word, "blasphemy!"

4. Little did I know that these two Beings would show-up one more time, only this time, I was wide awake in the City of Jerusalem in June of 2012. This was a life-changing experience that served to support me during a trying time of remembering my particular role and purpose in the dream of time with Jesus. The purpose of witnessing this experience was to ask if I was, 1) ready to see my initial agreement with Jesus, and, 2) willing to complete that agreement *now*.

B. Awakening *in* the Dream vs. Awakening *from* the Dream

1. I've had quite a few people ask, "What is the difference between awakening *in* the dream, and awakening *from* the dream? There is an outstanding distinction between them and one which is rarely recognized as yet.

i. Awakening in the Dream

1. There is peace made with the body and world. There is peace made with death. This person is in a largely euphoric state of "acceptance." Resistance is futile and peace with all is realized. The laws of the world are accepted *but* they are not transcended. The

body itself is still deemed as being more powerful than the mind that made it. Disease, aging and death still play victor over this awakened person. In other words, "effect and cause" are not reversed. The body is still mistakenly believed to be a *cause* in itself; e.g. It can cause physical death. Thoughts are stilled. But, the underlying *value system* of death is still running. The ego still pursues *after* death if death is not overcome. Until the ego's value-system is overcome, it will continue to propel further incarnations, all centered on *death*.

2. While this awakening *in* the dream is still helpful, there is yet a further *awakening* to be had – preferably *before* the body is once more surrendered to attack (separation) as disease, aging and death. This awakening would be to demonstrate the body's *unreality*. Otherwise, there must be further incarnations of death, birth, amnesia, death, birth, amnesia, all in order to learn to finally awaken *from* the dream of the body/world. If not, death, as the central ego dream has not yet been overcome.

3. The issue I have with this (awakening *in* the dream) level of the awakened state is that often there appears to be a sense of *complacency*. Often, there is such peace, joy and comfort that there is a mistaken belief there is no more *unlearning and learning* to embody. I feel this complacency itself is a false ceiling that inhibits the *full* awakening *from* the ego's central dream of death.

ii. Awakening *from* the Dream

1. Finally, the body is "seen through." It *is unreal*. It is therefore completely *immune* to disease, pain, decay and death. It is no longer used to demonstrate attack (separation). It is used exclusively as a *communication device* to communicate that only Love, only Life is real.

2. The body is claimed only as an *effect* of its *cause* in our mind. The Healed Mind now governs the body's state exclusively. The body is known as a projected image and is not dependent on "magic" to sustain it. Nor can it get sick, age or die. When the *purpose* of the body has been fulfilled it *does not die*. It simply disappears ... it is laid aside. The ego's central dream of death is overcome. There is

no more need of incarnation because the ego's laws have been reversed and the dream is awoken *from*.

C. From Nouk:

1. In closing, I pray with all my heart that I may be filled with the necessary trust, faith and undivided conviction of Christ to follow boldly in Jesus' footsteps. May the Christ overcome the dream of the body and the world – in me as the "I Am." And I pray that those whose hearts also hear the depth of His Call to Awaken will join me as *One*. This is the *final* awakening. God will take the last step. Amen.

II. ROLLING AWAY THE STONE THAT SEALS THE SEPARATION

1. In Jesus' notes to Helen Schucman titled, "Was There a Physical Resurrection?" He speaks of His rolling the stone away. Preceding His resurrection experience, He had overcome the last illusion – death. To overcome death meant He had understood that the body was indeed "nothing." As nothing, and known as an illusory projection, His bodily "image" did not need to decompose. His body *disappeared* in the tomb. It did not decay. His body disappeared because He recognized it was *unreal!* This is *key*. Only a body still imbued with *cause*, value and reality, can ever sicken, die or decompose. Jesus understood the body's vaporous nothingness.

2. What is absolutely known as an unreal, immaterial shadow cannot die. Can *an idea* feel pain, die or decay? Once He knew the body idea as literally no-thing, its illusive appearance was merely dematerialized to make way for His resurrection; as the projection of an alternate body through which he communicated His message to His followers before His Ascension.

3. Only when we still give a false, causal reality to the body by valuing it, can it sicken, age, die and decompose. Our investment in the body's reality as *unforgiveness,* gives it the appearance of physical substance chained to the illusion of time, with an independent will to suffer, sicken and die of its own. Jesus dematerialized this "center piece" of the entire separation dream – the body as the gap – through the understanding of its complete unreality.

4. Through deeper examination, we recognize that the body *is* the stone that seals the tomb of separation. Because the special relationship has the objectification of our brother's body as its main goal, the special relationship represents the tomb, and the body (its central idol) is the stone that seals the tomb of separation. It is this stone – the body – that we must learn to roll away through forgiveness and Holy Relationship.

5. No wonder it has taken millions of years in the illusion of time to even begin to question, let alone heal our addiction to both the body and special relationships. They form the bedrock of a seemingly closed circuit which is propelled by the never-ending cycle of sin, guilt, fear and death. To both see and forgive this foundation would destroy our belief in death, and with it goes the entire dream of separation.

6. Let's look again at the gap diagrams on pages 46 thru 49. Notice how the separation, or gap, is maintained by at least two split minds who agree to *block* the indescribable majesty and purpose of their union as the unified Christ Identity. They block this awareness by using the body and special relating – as sin, guilt and fear –to *replace* each other's immaculate Holy Self. This hidden agenda is the underlying cause of all death since the beginning of time: *"The glitter of guilt you laid upon the body would kill it." T-19.IV.C.4:6*

7. Our attachment to the body identity for what we believe it can give to us which God cannot, *is* the stone that seals the dream of death. The body identity takes up all our belief, attention and purpose, yet in reality it does not exist except to hide our true Identity from each other. In effect then, we choose to be wholly consumed by an illusory symbol specifically so that we do not see and experience our brother as one with us. This uniform denial adversely impacts all our relationships.

8. The neutral body is not the problem in and of itself, but what we *use it for* is the trap. While we use it for guilt, inauthentic relating and specialness, we abuse it in cloaked efforts to try to prove that sin and separation are real. Because the body is actually a projected image that dwells *in* our mind, we give the body all the reality it has for us. We never see others as they are in reality. Instead we choose to see and use their body to enforce our desire for separation, judging them on what their body identity does or doesn't do. When we insist on seeing our brother as a body we substitute illusion for the glorious truth of his real Identity. And because our true Identity is shared with all our brothers, this distortion prevents us from knowing our own innocent and changeless Holy Self.

9. *The body is nothing.* When the body is no longer valued as a separation device it ceases to hide the light of Christ we are.

10. Illness, conflict, suffering and death are the result of an ongoing investment in the body as "something." As *something*, it is hailed as a formidable opponent to God. As something, the ego exploits the body as a witness to guilt, and to the death of God's Son through conflict, aging, disease, loss and death. As something, the body is used by the ego to demonstrate through conflict, pain, loss and death that attack has power *greater* than God as all-encompassing Love, and His Son as our unified Holy Self. All the ego's laws of pain, suffering and death are maintained exclusively by the mindless agreement for specialness.

   a. *"There is no funeral, no dark altars, no grim commandments nor twisted rituals of condemnation to which the body leads you. Ask not release of [it.] But free it (body) from the merciless and unrelenting orders you laid upon it, and forgive it what you ordered it to do. In its exaltation you commanded it to die, for only death could conquer life. And what but insanity could look upon the defeat of God, and think it real?" T-19. IV.C.8:3-7*

   b. *"To you and your brother, in whose special relationship the Holy Spirit entered, it is given to release and be released from the dedication to death."T-19.IV.C.1:1 c. "The fear of death will go as its appeal is yielded to love's real attraction. The end of sin, which nestles quietly in the safety of your relationship, protected by your union with your brother, and ready to grow into a mighty force for God is very near." T-19.IV.C.9:1-2*

11. Healing our special relationships and embracing the Holy Relationship is the divine catalyst required for us to "roll the stone away;" to reveal the breathtaking innocence of our unified being. This Christ Vision encompasses the eternal sinlessness that shines away the body and the gap where it seems to exist in our perception.

12. It is in our complete devotion to forgiveness, especially within the Holy Relationship, and to consistently cherishing our brother's innocence *above* seeing him or her as a body – which reveals Christ Vision. This Vision of Love is so powerful and pure that it looks clear past the body, the gap and all its appearances of fear. It is this sanctified commitment to consistently behold the face of Christ in our brother that reveals to each of us *our own* eternal and uninterrupted sinlessness.

13. Because the Christ in him *is* the Christ in us, we cannot recognize the Christ within until we choose to lift the veil of our own senseless projections of guilt from our brother. As we lift this veil of sin, the face of Christ that we behold beckons us to merge completely in a Love that cannot *be* threatened. From this euphoric state of changeless innocence comes the undivided acceptance of our divine immunity to all forms of attack that the ego made.

a. "In the holy instant, you and your brother stand before the altar God has raised unto Himself and both of you. Lay faithlessness aside, and come to it together. There will you see the miracle of your relationship as it was made again through faith. And there it is that you will realize that there is nothing faith cannot forgive. No error interferes with its calm sight, which brings the miracle of healing with equal ease to all of them." T-19.1.14:1-5 b. "Behold your Friend, the Christ Who stands beside you. How holy and how beautiful He is! You thought He sinned because you cast the veil of sin upon Him to hide His loveliness." T-19.IV.D.14:1-3

14. In this most Holy alliance, the Christ is treasured and protected from the corruption of judgment, so much so that the body *and* the gap which was made to preserve it, fade rapidly from awareness. The blazing light of perfect Love casts out the darkness where special idols once hid the blessed face of Christ from our sight.

15. As we understand that the body is the stone that seals the tomb of separation, and the special relationship constitutes the tomb itself, then we can thank God for our brother. Now it is our heartfelt desire above all else to witness the glorious face of Christ in him that rolls the stone away! Only the forgiven face of Christ seen and adored in our brother can roll away the stone that seals the separation dream.

16. The Holy Relationship is a union whose sacred purpose is to erase the ancient guilt which propels our ongoing attraction to both the body and death. Jesus entirely overcame the body and the gap *for* us. As we learn to accept the Atonement, we heal our unconscious attraction to separation. But the means by which we accelerate this healing exponentially is by willingly undoing our special relating in all our communication, which prepares us for joining in Holy Relationship.

17. How do we roll away the stone, the body? We roll it away by recognizing our idols and forgiving our projections onto others, the body, the past and the world. We roll the stone away in relinquishing special relating, and becoming authentic by implementing the *Seven Keys* on page 572. Rolling the stone away means collapsing the imagined gap which we projected to hide the eternal sanctity of our brother, our Self and our Father.

18. In the following passage Jesus presents a compellingly clear contrast between the special relationship dynamic with its underlying lust for vengeance, and the breathtaking beauty and innocence of the forgiven relationship:

a. "Who sees a brother as a body sees him as fear's symbol. And he will attack, because what he beholds is his own fear external to himself, poised to attack, and howling to unite with him again. Mistake not the intensity of rage projected fear must spawn. It shrieks in wrath, and claws the air in frantic hope it can reach to its maker and devour him."

"This do the body's eyes behold in one whom Heaven cherishes, the angels love and God created perfect. This is his reality. And in Christ's vision is his loveliness reflected in a form so holy and so beautiful that you could scarce refrain from kneeling at his feet. Yet you will take his hand instead, for you are like him in the sight that sees him thus." ... "Give me your blessing, holy Son of God. I would behold you with the eyes of Christ, and see my perfect sinlessness in you." W-161.8,9:1-4,11:7-8

A. Was There a Physical Resurrection?

1. **From Jesus:** (*The following excerpts are from the Urtext - Special Messages to Helen*)

a. *"My body disappeared because I had no illusion about it. The last one had gone. It was laid in the tomb, but there was nothing left to bury. It did not disintegrate because the unreal cannot die. It merely became what it always was. And that is what "rolling the stone away" means. The body disappears, and no longer hides what lies beyond. It merely ceases to interfere with vision. To roll the stone away is to see beyond the tomb, beyond death, and to understand the body's nothingness. What is understood as nothing must disappear."*

b. *"I did assume a human form with human attributes afterwards, to speak to those who were to prove the body's worthlessness to the world. This has been much misunderstood. I came to tell them that death is illusion, and the mind that made the body can make another since form itself is an illusion. They did not understand. But now I talk to you and give you the same message. The death of an illusion means nothing. It disappears when you awaken and decide to dream no more. And you still do have the power to make this decision as I did.*

c. God holds out His hand to His Son to help him rise and return to Him. I can help because the world is illusion, and I have overcome the world. Look past the tomb, the body, the illusion.

d. Have faith in nothing but the Spirit and the guidance God gives you. He could not have created the body because it is a limit. He must have created the Spirit because it is immortal. Can those who are created like Him be limited? The body is the symbol of the world.

e. Leave it behind. It cannot enter Heaven. But I can take you there anytime you choose. Together we can watch the world disappear and its symbol vanish as it does so. And then, and then... I cannot speak of that.

f. A body cannot stay without illusions, and the last one to be overcome is death. This is the message of the crucifixion; there is no order of difficulty in miracles. This is the message of the resurrection: Illusions are illusions. Truth is true. Illusions vanish. Only Truth remains.

g. These lessons needed to be taught but once, for when the stone of death is rolled away, what can be seen except an empty tomb? And that is what you see who follow me into the sunlight and away from death, past all illusions, on to Heaven's gate, where God will come Himself to take you home."

"The ark of peace is entered two by two, yet the beginning of another world goes with them. Each holy relationship must enter here, to learn its special function in the Holy Spirit's plan, now that it shares His purpose. And as this purpose is fulfilled, a new world rises in which sin can enter not, and where the Son of God can enter without fear and where he rests a while, to forget imprisonment and to remember freedom."

T-20.IV.5:4-8

"In this world, God's Son comes closest to himself in a holy relationship. There he begins to find the certainty his Father has in him. And there he finds his function of restoring his Father's laws to what was held outside them, and finding what was lost."

T-20.V.1:1-3

CHAPTER FOUR

C–IV.   SEX AND TRANSORGASMIC UNION

Introduction

1. This chapter in particular may be exceedingly challenging to the
personal, body-self identity. The uncompromising content of this
teaching could well be rejected outright. When we believe that we
are indeed the body, that "it" is the source of our well-being, our
pleasure, our life, and we assume we know what love *is* and how
to express it *as* the body-self – then Jesus' advanced teachings will
rattle the ego's cage severely. We're not being asked to awaken
from the illusory body identity immediately. It took millions of
years in the illusion of time to convince ourselves of the principles
of separation. This involved choosing to go from boundless,
unopposed and unified Spirit as Love, to shutting down, separating
and severely splitting and stunting our endlessly spacious mind in
the belief we are confined within a physical body.

2. Our eternal and unified Mind completely eclipses the size of the
universe as we know it. It knows not of the limitations of time,
space or bodies. To teach our self separation, we imagined that
we split this mind into billions of separate, private minds, and
attempted to squeeze them into tiny, temporary, walled-off bodies.

3. To keep this tightly restricted paradigm in play and to ensure
it would be an endless looping drama, the ego with its hero the
body, schemed a "central dream" from which every other illusion

would stem. This dark and brutal, central dream would literally underpin all illusions. This one primordial obsession would appear so fantastical, so utterly realistic, that no one would ever question it. Without our belief in it, and without being tempted or seduced by its overwhelmingly convincing "appearance," we would indeed be free. This central dream is our mistaken *belief* that death is the inevitable outcome of all life.

4. It's taken eons in the long and arduous dream of separation to convince ourselves of this lie. This belief in the inevitability of death further deepens our unconsciously held belief that God – *as changeless Love* – is death, and that He wants our death. This insane belief is a direct result of the profound split in our mind, our investment in what we erroneously believe to be two opposed yet equally real powers – both fear *and* Love. Through the ego filter we have projected fear and death onto God Who knows of neither. Unconsciously, we are convinced that God is not Love but fear.

   a. *"Death is the symbol of the fear of God. His Love is blotted out in the idea, which holds it from awareness like a shield held up to obscure the sun. The grimness of the symbol is enough to show it cannot coexist with God." ... "If death is real for anything, there is no life. Death denies life. But if there is reality in life, death is denied. No compromise in this is possible. There is either a god of fear or One of Love."* M-27.3:1-3,4:2-6

   b. *"The ego wants [you] dead, but not itself. The outcome of its strange religion must therefore be the conviction that it can pursue you beyond the grave." T-15.I.3:3-4*

5. We believe we are the body and value fear, or we believe we are the Holy Self valuing only changeless Love. The two are irreconcilable. The journey of awakening from the dream by necessity includes the undoing of our greatest idol and substitute for God as Love, the body identity.

6. After our attraction to death and specialness, the sexual appetite is next in line as a fundamental taproot of the ego thought system. It is the most potent and defended of all human "pleasure drives." Unless

it is divinely repurposed for healing by Holy Spirit, it perpetuates the body and specialness, suffering and death cycle.

7. Identifying as separate bodies with private minds, and eager to seek out as much specialness and pleasure as possible in its short time between birth and death, the ego has a profound investment in sex. It highly favors this particular body appetite because its compelling lust for sensual pleasure aims to keep us body identified, amassing guilt which locks us into the arduous reincarnation cycle. In addition, sex is used unconsciously to further "separate" through its special romantic relationships. In substituting the illusory "body" for the light-filled and innocent Spirit of our beloved companion, we block our vision of them and ourselves, and thus unwittingly we bring conflict and suffering to our relationships.

8. This is why Jesus included the subject of sex in His early dictation of *A Course in Miracles* to Helen Schucman, explaining that sex is an area the miracle worker *must* understand. However, He does tell us that all this unlearning will take time; and that is what time is *for*.

a. *"The love of God, for a little while, must still be expressed through one body to another. That is because the real vision is still so dim. Everyone can use his body best by enlarging man's perception, so he can see the real VISION. THIS VISION is invisible to the physical eye. The ultimate purpose of the body is to render itself unnecessary." - A Course in Miracles, Urtext, Chapter 1.*

9. The ego thought system hides from us the awareness that its central classification of everything, both positive *and* negative, is always underpinned by fear. Even its seemingly positive aspirations such as love, health, abundance and happiness are driven unconsciously by its fear and lack. The body with its five senses and sensual appetites is its unquestioned command center. Until we've begun to join Holy Spirit in divinely repurposing what we use the body *for*, everything will be decided upon according to "bodily needs" (fear) and not with our Spirit (Love).

10. We are not asked to give up sex. Nor are we to feel guilty for valuing it. We are being urged to open our mind to a teaching of Love *beyond* the body by repurposing what we are using sex *for*.

If we could approach this with an open heart and mind, then Holy Spirit will help us *to lift the veil of fear so that we can welcome the immense Love and joy waiting for us beyond it.*

11. Because of the widespread, compulsive belief in "special love," together with the conviction that sex *and* love are synonymous, the sexual pleasure drive is especially defended in the ego thought system. It runs extremely deep in the unconscious taproot of the ego's need for autonomy from God.

12. In the ego's dream of history there have been tremendous attempts at suppression of the sexual appetite, especially by some religious approaches, all in the name of the ego's mistaken "moral responsibilities." The central but erroneous belief that underpins this sexual suppression is the belief in "sin," and that it is even *possible* to sin. Typical of the ego thought system, the mistaken *belief in sin* always calls for punishment. The ego's survival *depends* on its non-negotiable belief in sin. This generates guilt, which in turn produces the inevitability of fear.

13. Sexual suppression is a kind of denial, which always leads to projection. What the ego denies is its own unforgiven belief in sin, which it then projects onto its relationships and the body, as conflict and disease. This unforgiven belief in sin represents the ego's desire to administer its own *self-punishment.* In this section on sex the intent of these teachings is certainly not about suppression or denial. And neither are they about the illusions of sin, morals or shame. Primarily, these teachings are encouraging us to open up to a higher Love that never judges what we do or don't do. In fact, the goal of practicing these teachings is to lead us to the euphoric experience of Love *beyond* the body.

14. For the ego mind to continue its dream of separation it must find *substitutes* for true union, since union *beyond* the body is its greatest fear. Hence its obsession with the body as itself, its special relationships, and its terror of the pure, undistorted miracle impulse and joint Holy Instants with another. This is the fear of real intimacy free of the body's interference. Genuine, undefended and heartfelt communion with a brother or sister *eclipses* the body self entirely. And this is what the ego is afraid of, even more than death itself.

15. Because the sexual impulse is so heavily defended in the ego thought system, I encourage you to read this chapter with an open mind. And don't be hard on yourself. Open-mindedness is actually the very last characteristic of God that we usually embrace. And the reason why is that "judgment" cannot survive in an open mind, and yet judgment is highly valued by the ego because it ensures the regular supply of guilt it needs to maintain its illusory reign of terror.

16. You may be triggered. And you may disagree. However, remember this: Only the ego's body-self can be triggered. The Holy Self cannot. Only the body-self defends. Only the body-self has a need to be right. Therefore, if you are triggered by any of this material, I encourage you not to judge it alone with the ego. Instead, use it consciously with Holy Spirit.

17. Every emotional spike reveals an aspect of the ego's heavily defended idols. Every trigger hides an unforgiven allegiance to the belief in separation, suffering and death. Write them down and look at each of them mindfully with Holy Spirit. Do some radical self-inquiry, asking "What do I fear to lose if I were to believe (agree with) this?" And then give this attachment to Holy Spirit to heal in exchange for the miracle.

18. One more point. Since this material presents a thorough *reality-reversal* of what we think sex and the body are *for,* it is likely that key themes may be bypassed or overridden by the ego. For this reason, I have attempted to frequently interweave key themes throughout this chapter. Like the *Course* itself, these teachings are repeated often so as they stand a chance to gain some traction in the defensive split mind. One of the ego's first lines of defense is its complaint about repetition of content.

19. There are six stages of awakening or as Jesus terms it, the Development of Trust, where we ascend back up the ladder of separation from which we originally descended. The second stage is "sorting out." We tend to resist those teachings which threaten our body identity because we have a fear of loss and sacrifice. The sexual pleasure drive is one of the idols that must eventually be healed before we can pass *through the eye of the needle.*

20. Jesus speaks of the sorting out stage in the following passage:

a. *"Next, the teacher of God must go through 'a period of sorting out.' This is always somewhat difficult because, having learned that the changes in his life are always helpful, he must now decide all things on the basis of whether they increase the helpfulness or hamper it. He will find that many, if not most of the things he valued before will merely hinder his ability to transfer what he has learned to new situations as they arise. Because he has valued what is really valueless, he will not generalize the lesson for fear of loss and sacrifice. It takes great learning to understand that all things, events, encounters and circumstances are helpful. It is only to the extent to which they are helpful that any degree of reality should be accorded them in this world of illusion. The word "value" can apply to nothing else." M.4.I.A.4.*

21. In the advanced stage of awakening from the body identity, we realize and finally accept that we cannot be both body *and* Spirit. Only one is real. Gently and organically, we eventually reach the knowing that we do not want to keep any illusions as a substitute for ecstatic union with the one, beloved Holy Self.

a. *"One illusion cherished and defended against the truth makes all truth meaningless, and all illusions real. Such is the power of belief. It cannot compromise." T-22.II.4:4-6*

I. THE BODY – THE GRANDEST ILLUSION OF ALL TIME

1. I am acutely aware of my own resistance to write about this subject; our grandest of all seductions since time began. This is sure to rattle many people's cages! Yet, until we're at least *willing* to accept Jesus' teaching on the body, unconsciously we will continue to attract suffering, conflict, illness, pain and death. Ironically, these are the ego's indispensable methods it uses to maintain the illusion of separation through body identification. Without the unconscious desire for separation there would be no point in projecting the body any longer.

2. While the body is neither good nor bad, it must be noted habitually that as an image in our mind, it is purely an illusion. As a neutral learning device, it has no needs or inherent ability to change either in its appearance or its seeming physical state. All changes are brought about by our mind that literally projects the body. This mind that believes that it is both mind *and* body, Spirit *and* human, is completely divided.

3. As long as this split mind remains unexhumed and unforgiven, it will attack the body to enforce the illusion that we are victim of the illusory body. We will believe that the body is more powerful than the mind, thus increasing and prolonging the idea of separation.

4. In my long study and practice of the *Course*, the singular source of separation as the concept of the split mind (ego), has appeared to be very nebulous and abstract…until recently. Let me drop a "God Bomb" here; one that I have just freshly recognized through direct experience, at the time of writing this Volume Two of *The End of Death*:

5. The split mind, aka the false self, is the impossible belief that we are both the body and the mind (not brain). However, we cannot possibly be both. While we still maintain that we are, we must unconsciously identify exclusively as a body regardless of how much we may consciously believe otherwise. We are mind, exclusively!

6. The body is illusion. Our Holy Self is Truth. Identifying as a body is the split mind. This is the confused and dissociated belief that we are both in a body – and – that we are also Spirit. Believing that we are both body *and* Spirit involves trying to maintain two, completely irreconcilable beliefs which result in an impossible and deep-seated mind-split. This is an allegiance to both fear *and* Love. Recall that only Love is real. Fear does not exist no matter how convincing it feels. There is no opposite of God as Love. Period.

7. When we misidentify as the body identity, then both Love and fear

are valued erroneously as equally real. Yet these two are mutually exclusive! The presence of one in our mind absolutely denies the other. Identifying as a body (trusting its five senses, its sensual appetites and its seeming past) excludes Spirit, while identifying as Spirit excludes identity as a body. These two beliefs, the body and Spirit, are underpinned and ruled by two radically opposite sets of "laws."

8.   While we choose to prioritize the illusory body identity, we then abdicate it to the painful laws of chaos, conflict, disease and death. On the other hand, Spirit, as our Holy Self is sustained exclusively by the joyous Laws of God as health, union and life. Once we learn to prioritize the Holy Self rather than the body, the body becomes a happy reflection of our choice for Love.

   a.   *"The fact that truth and illusion cannot be reconciled... must be accepted if you would be saved."... "The self you made can never be your Self, nor can your Self be split in two, and still be what It is and must forever be. A mind and body cannot both exist. Make no attempt to reconcile the two, for one denies the other can be real. If you are physical, your mind is gone from your self-concept, for it has no place in which it could be really part of you. If you are spirit, then the body must be meaningless to your reality."* W-96.2:1,3:3-7

9.   When the *Course* was initially given to us by Jesus we were willing to see mere fragments of His teaching while only accepting the occasional morsel by direct experience. But the teaching itself is infinitely vast and completely holographic. Like a giant jigsaw puzzle, we were eager and willing to see only those pieces with which we could identify; those that would not threaten our value system, while absorbing these teachings through our split mind.

10.   As we read and study the *Course* we absorb only what we can identify with at that particular time. And this is largely influenced by our past learning which was heavily shaped by fear. This book, A Manual for Holy Relationship, introduces ideas that will break open and stretch the mind. By lifting the veil of confusion (fear) it prepares the mind to absorb the deeper teachings which previously seemed buried within the *Course*.

11. While we still believe – value – that our personal identity dwells *in* and *as* the body, we will block anything in our experience that may threaten its imagined authority. Belief in the body forms the central hub, around which all the ego's laws of sickness, pain, lack, loss, conflict and death revolve. These laws could not exist except for the mistaken belief that we are a body.

12. This belief in the body is the seat of all the ego's laws. While the value we place on the body eclipses our Holy Self, which is purely Spirit, we must continue to unconsciously project the illusory laws of chaos, sickness, pain and suffering to *maintain* a body identity. Without the laws of chaos and our defense of the body identity, it would be impossible to prolong the *belief* of a body and therefore the idea of *separation*.

13. More specifically, while the body is valued for what we think it can give to us, *and presume that God cannot,* we will block Spirit as Love. We are valuing lack (illusion) when we believe that anything of value can be added to Love/Spirit. There can be nothing added to that which already has, and already is everything, and forever. Spirit/Love is the *only thing* which could possibly threaten the body's imagined authority in our awareness. All seeming chaos, conflict, illness, etc. are the ego's *defenses* against recognition of our true Identity and the perfect immunity to suffering that we share with God and all our brothers.

14. Therefore, through the ego's defenses, we will not see, let alone "accept" the deeper teachings of the *Course* until our trust has been largely transferred from fear to Love, from the body identity to the Holy Self.

A. The Body *is* the Split Mind – All of It

a. *If truth is total, the untrue cannot exist. Commitment to either must be total; they cannot coexist in your mind without splitting it. If they cannot coexist in peace, and if you want peace, you must give up the idea of conflict entirely and for all time. This requires vigilance only as long as you do not recognize what is true. While you believe that two totally contradictory thought systems share truth, your need for vigilance is apparent." T-7.VI.8:7-11*

1. Jesus says very strongly that the body *and* our Holy Self simply cannot be reconciled. We must make a heartfelt choice between the two, between Truth and illusion. If we try to give equal reality to the body and the Mind (Spirit) we will be immersed in an agonizing split. Relationship conflict, disease, scarcity, depression, aging and physical death are the certain outcome of this profound confusion.

2. We simply cannot see, let alone accept His teachings while we're still hell bent on looking through the veil of body identification. I make this point because in my many years with the *Course*, I see that almost everyone, students and teachers alike (including me) have approached the *Course* without really getting this, the nucleus, which Jesus states so emphatically.

3. Jesus tells us that the mind and body cannot both exist because one denies the other is real. Further, He warns us not to try to reconcile the two as they are irreconcilable because belief in one completely denies the other. In practical terms the implications of this are huge! The degree to which we still identify as a body, while using it for pleasure or pain – apart from Spirit – is the same extent to which we are afraid of Love, as our Holy Self – the one shared Mind of Christ. Therefore, the value we still place on being identified as a body will continue to attract suffering, conflict, separation and death.

4. The split mind is the belief in two mutually exclusive identities. One is the illusory body. The other is the Spirit or Mind. Yet we can only identify as, and thus prioritize one *or* the other because they cannot both be reconciled. In a nutshell, there is no way we can truly open to our Holy Self, the unified mind, while we still want to believe we *are* the body.

5. The split mind consists of mutually exclusive beliefs, fear *and* Love, body *and* Spirit. Yet of these only Love and Spirit are real. Fear and the body do not exist no matter how convincing they appear.

6. Just to drive this point home, the body *is* the split mind. It is not merely "part" of the split mind, but *all* of it. Please allow this to sink in.

7. To the extent we still value the body through pleasure, pain and the seduction of specialness will be the degree that we remain invested

in it *as* our identity. The pursuit of pleasure and defense from pain is a set-up to ensure body identity. Thus, we resist recognition and acceptance of the all-inclusive healing power and dominion of our healed mind. In fact, while we are body identified we will be afraid of our mind, which equates to the deep unconscious fear of healing and union.

8. We are thoroughly transfixed and seduced by the illusion of the body. Everything we do or even think of involves the body. Let's face it; we can hardly imagine what it would be like to dwell in an entirely bodiless state. Yet Jesus says the body is a limit. We don't even know what a *relationship* is without a body. Have we ever thought about what it would be like to have a total relationship *without* the body?

9. Remember that we cannot transcend the body through death. Death is certainly not the way we overcome the body and the dream of separation. To use a body as puppet, and mind as puppeteer analogy, in death the illusory puppet (body) appears to die while all along the puppeteer is so invested as the puppet, he forgets that he has total dominion over the puppet. And so the body-puppet appears to succumb to sickness, aging and death when it's abdicated to the ego mind instead of to Holy Spirit.

10. Death, just like pain and disease, ensures we remain body identified to return again to the body-puppet's relentless recycle program. Meanwhile, the puppeteer remains asleep and dreaming of birth, death, bodies and time. The body and world are not left through death as the ego projects. They can only be left through Truth! (Life without opposite) *"The world is not left by death but by truth..."* T-3.VII.6:11

11. The body is never "laid aside" through pain, sickness, aging or death. These are expressions of separation, of a will *apart* from God, as self-attack, which are "body-identified" defenses *against* awakening to the incorruptible innocence of our Holy Self. *"All forms of sickness, even unto death, are physical expressions of the fear of awakening."* T-8.IX.3:2

12. The body can only be laid aside through transcending all self-attack. While we still believe that death is the certain, inevitable

outcome of life then there persists strong body identification, as the split mind.

a. *"And yet a neutral thing (the body) does not see death, for thoughts of fear are not invested there, nor is a mockery of love bestowed upon it. Its neutrality protects it while it has a use. And afterwards, without a purpose, it is laid aside. **It (the body) is not sick nor old nor hurt.** It is but functionless, unneeded and cast off."* W-294.1:5-8

13. The special relationship is the strongest means for keeping us body identified. There can be no special relationship without body identity. Two body-puppets agree to remain oblivious to the mind's (puppeteers) choices for separation. And this is why it's crucial to invite Holy Spirit into our relationships to make them conscious and Holy.

14. The special relationship employs the body for pride, pleasure and attack. Unfortunately, in seeking specialness we have unwittingly confused fear with Love, and mistakenly appointed the body as our replacement for Spirit. Therefore, we confuse pride, pleasure and many forms of attack as "love." These are the essential components of special love, the world's obsession.

a. *"The body is the ego's chosen weapon for seeking power [through] relationships."* ... *"The Holy Spirit's temple is not a body, but a relationship. The body is an isolated speck of darkness; a hidden secret room, a tiny spot of senseless mystery, a meaningless enclosure carefully protected, yet hiding nothing. Here the unholy relationship escapes reality, and seeks for crumbs to keep itself alive. Here it would drag its brothers, holding them here in its idolatry. Here it is "safe," for here love cannot enter."* T-20.VI.4:3,5:1-5

15. We don't often recognize just how insidious the underlying intentions are concerning the body, especially in special romantic relationships. Through the ego we usually don't have a clue as to how inappropriately we use the body. There is a massive desensitization to conscious Love that occurs when we depend upon the body's senses and appetites to lead and inform us in relationships. The ego

will employ the body's senses and appetites to report an outright lie - that both our self and others *are* bodies. So we judge them and our self, based on what we seem to do or not do, *as* a body.

16. Seeking satisfaction or pleasure through our own or another's body, apart from Spirit, amounts to self-attack. There is no guilt here. However, at some point during our evolution in the ego's dream, we must yearn for divine union through Holy Relationship. And the essential requirement for this is our genuine desire to see and join with the Christ in another by overlooking the body altogether.

   a. *"It is impossible to seek for pleasure through the body and not find pain." T-19.IV.B.12:1... "Its (pains) purpose is the same as pleasure, for they both are means to make the body real. What shares a common purpose is the same." T-27.VI.1:4-5*

17. We either see the body or we see the Christ. Another way to explain this is that we *want and choose* to see either guilt *or* complete innocence. The sight of one eclipses the other entirely. When we judge someone we conclude that they *are* the body and not the Holy Self. And we cannot see another as a body without also condemning our self.

   a. *"It [is] impossible to see your brother as sinless and yet to look upon him as a body." ... "Who sees a brother's body has laid a judgment on him, and sees him not. He does not really see him as sinful; he does not see him at all." T-20. VII.4:1,6:1*

   b. *Limit your sight of a brother to his body, which you will do as long as you would not release him from it, and you have denied his gift to you. His body cannot give it. And seek it not through yours. Yet your minds are already continuous, and their union need only be accepted and the loneliness in Heaven is gone." T-15.IX.4:4-7*

18. Jesus makes a bold statement in the preceding passage. He says clearly not to limit our sight of another to his or her body. Yet let's be honest, just how often do we do exactly that; limit our partner, others or our self to the body? This point needs to be made over and

over again and not to make guilty, but only so that we can join Holy Spirit to recognize just when we mistake the body as our brother's central identity. If we are triggered by what someone does or says then we *believe* they are a body and not the innocent Holy Self. Once this mistaken belief is seen it can then be healed. However, it will never be healed while we refuse to recognize and heal the grandest seduction of all time – belief that *we are* the body.

19. Just to clarify, Jesus does not demonize the body. To judge the body is to *identify as* the body. To judge, or to feel guilty for the body's actions via its five senses or its seeming appetites, is to be lost in the illusory body.

20. He is pointing the way to healing our split mind. Remember our mistaken value in the body is the split mind. Not just part of the split mind, but *all* of it. Hence the body identity must be divinely repurposed and released to return our awareness to the unified Mind as our shared and Holy Self, the Christ. Any guilt, judgment, shame or blame regarding what the body does or doesn't do at the behavioral level is all the same. It's a smokescreen, a decoy made to deter us from truly and deeply giving the body's purpose (ours and others) over completely to the Holy Spirit.

B. Healing the Split Mind Through Holy Relationship

1. The split mind – body identification – is healed by unifying the body's singular purpose with our only function, forgiveness.

2. With the body identity constituting the gap of separation between us, our brothers and our Holy Self, the means by which it is undone is through union by way of the Holy Relationship. The gap is dissolved as our special relationships are healed and made Holy. Recall that belief in the separation or body identity requires two or more consenting individuals to agree *together* to imagine this possibility. This is how we maintain the illusion of the body, its idols and separation, and why the special relationship is the strongest witness to this madness. *See the Gap diagrams on pages 46 thru 49.*

3. The Holy Relationship on the other hand, is the blessed union of two or more individuals who share just one common and divine purpose. Because their shared purpose is forgiveness, they commit to withdraw their witness to the body and separation in whatever imaginary form it takes. They agree to witness only innocence, only the Holy Self (and not the body) for each other, and consequently for the world.

4. I harvested just a few of the many formidable quotes by Jesus which state the undeniable importance of learning *not* to see our partner, others or our self as a body. This involves giving to Holy Spirit our body's purpose, including its five senses, along with its appetites, so they can be unified into one function and one purpose.

5. As you will see, any relationship where the body enters (particularly the romantic relationship) is in need of healing. I have bolded the sentences or pieces of the *Course's* giant, holographic jigsaw puzzle that are most apt to be ignored, twisted or outright rejected by the false self and its body identification. These quotes, gathered here together in one place, present irrefutable evidence of our need to give the body to Spirit if we genuinely want to awaken from the dream of separation.

a. *"Nothing can show the contrast better than the experience of both a holy and an unholy relationship. The first is based on love, and rests on it serene and undisturbed.* **The body does not intrude upon it. Any relationship in which the body enters is based not on love, but on idolatry."** *T-20. VI.2:1-4*

b. *"In the holy instant, where the Great Rays replace the body in awareness, the recognition of relationships without limits is given you.* **But in order to see this, it is necessary to give up every use the ego has for the body, and to accept the fact that the ego has no purpose you would share with it."** *T-15.IX.3:1-2*

c. **"The body cannot be looked upon except through judgment. To see the body is the sign that you lack vision, and have denied the means the Holy Spirit offers you to serve His purpose.** *How can a holy relationship achieve its purpose through the means of sin (body)?" T-20.VII.8:1-3*

d. *"Freedom must be impossible as long as you perceive a body as yourself. The body is a limit. Who would seek for freedom in a body looks for it where it can not be found.* The mind can be made free when it no longer sees itself as in a body, firmly tied to it and sheltered by its presence. If this were the truth, the mind were vulnerable indeed!" ... "The mind that serves the Holy Spirit is unlimited forever, in all ways, beyond the laws of time and space, unbound by any preconceptions, and with strength and power to do whatever it is asked." W-199.1,2:1

e. **"Look upon all the trinkets made to hang upon the body, or to cover it or for its use. See all the useless things made for its eyes to see. Think on the many offerings made for its pleasure, and remember all these were made to make seem lovely what you hate. Would you employ this hated thing to draw your brother to you, and to attract his body's eyes?** Learn you but offer him a crown of thorns, not recognizing it for what it is, and trying to justify your own interpretation of its value by his acceptance. Yet still the gift proclaims his worthlessness to you, as his acceptance and delight acknowledges the lack of value he places on himself." T-20.II.1.

f. **"Your brother's body is as little use to you as it is to him. When it is used only as the Holy Spirit teaches, it has no function. For minds need not the body to communicate. The sight that sees the body has no use which serves the purpose of a holy relationship.** And while you look upon your brother thus, the means and end have not been brought in line." T-20.V.5:1-5

g. **"But when you look upon a brother as a physical entity, his power and glory are "lost" to you and so are yours. You have attacked him, but you must have attacked yourself first."** T-8. VII.5:3-5,

h. **"The body is the ego's chosen weapon for seeking power [through] relationships. And its relationships must be unholy, for what they are it does not even see."** T-20.VI.4:3-4 *i.* *"The Holy Spirit's purpose lies safe in your relationship, and not your body." T-20.VI.7:8*

j. *"Do not overlook our earlier statement that faithlessness leads straight to illusions.* **For faithlessness is the perception of a brother as a body, and the body cannot be used for purposes of union. If, then, you see your brother as a body, you have established a condition in which uniting with him becomes impossible.** *Your faithlessness to him has separated you from him, and kept you both apart from being healed.* **Your faithlessness has thus opposed the Holy Spirit's purpose, and brought illusions, centered on the body, to stand between you.** *And the body will seem to be sick, for you have made of it an "enemy" of healing and the opposite of truth." T-19.I.4.*

k. **"The central lesson is always this; that what you use the body for it will become to you. Use it for sin or for attack, which is the same as sin, and you will see it as sinful. Because it is sinful it is weak, and being weak, it suffers and it dies. Use it to bring the Word of God to those who have it not, and the body becomes holy. Because it is holy it cannot be sick, nor can it die. When its usefulness is done it is laid by, and that is all." M-12.5:1-6**

2. SEX - AN AREA THE MIRACLE WORKER MUST UNDERSTAND

1. This is about joining in the healing of us all, both men and women who still confuse lust with Love. Lust and Love are mutually exclusive. The presence of one excludes the other. Lust, as a form of fear, is not wrong – it is purely *false*. As an expression of fear, the ego uses it as a guilt magnet. Lust is a distraction, a defense and an obstacle to Love as true union, and while still valued, it is an impermeable block to real and deep emotional intimacy and joining.

2. When we look upon someone lustfully, we cannot *see* them (or our Self) because we've made the illusory body an idol that obscures the Altar of the Heart within them. This is the unconscious fear of Love (God) that drives many to intentionally, or unintentionally, use the body as "bait" to lure onlookers into the claws of lust. And it is this same unconscious fear of Love that attracts us *to* lust. While the body is used on behalf of lust, we unknowingly agree to use it as a repository for guilt as self-attack, i.e. conflict, pain, illness, etc.

    a. *"Look upon all the trinkets made to hang upon the body, or to cover it or for its use. See all the useless things made for its eyes to see. Think on the many offerings made for its pleasure, and remember all these were made to make seem lovely what you hate. Would you employ this hated thing to draw your brother to you, and to attract his body's eyes? Learn you but offer him a crown of thorns, not recognizing it for what it is, and trying to justify your own interpretation of its value by his acceptance. Yet still the gift proclaims his worthlessness to you, as his acceptance and delight acknowledges the lack of value he places on himself." T-20.II.1.*

3. In the long and arduous dream of time, we've all played roles of both victim and perpetrator. We've all acted the roles of both masculine and feminine throughout the dimensions of time. I know that in a previous incarnation I was male and had been a perpetrator against women via sex. As a female in this lifetime, I was sexually abused as a child. I (like everyone) scripted my lessons before birth in this lifetime, so I could undo and heal (forgive) the belief that I could be separate from God and my Holy Self. All attack is always "self-attack." In order to be victimized, we must first have abandoned or betrayed our Self.

4. I see now the miracle beneath my early abuse. The ultimate question was, "What is it *for*?" What was the miracle behind it? What did I learn? The abuse I sustained catapulted me into searching for the true purpose of life and to look for my real and shared Identity as the one Holy Self. And the only purpose in reality is to awaken from the belief that we're separate. As we close the seeming gap of separation with others - we close the imaginary gap within.

5. This chapter on sex feels especially challenging to write because I recognize very clearly how the sex impulse is one of the most jealously guarded of all the ego's false idols. It is superseded only by the unconscious attraction to death. The sexual urge, like the special relationship, is the ego's ultimate fairytale and possibly the last one that will be offered up to be divinely reinterpreted.

6. These two body appetites – sex and death – are amongst the most glorified and prolifically misunderstood blocks in the ego dream. No wonder in the earlier stage of dictation of the *Course*, which Jesus gave to Helen Schucman, He emphatically stated the following quote, which was edited out of the FIP version, along with most quotes referring to sex: *"I want to finish the instructions about sex, because this is an area the miracle worker MUST understand."* Urtext, T-1.B.40 b.

7. Jesus' desire to finally finish His instructions about sex inspired this truly epic, trailblazing chapter. I could not possibly have received this material had I not been open to it. And I recognize now that in order to receive these deeper teachings, I had to be willing to experience them myself.

A. Childlike Innocence: Releasing the Obstacles to Peace

1. As I rise higher above the body/world battlefield I see a vastly different purpose for the body than the one we assumed in the separation. Recently, as I meditated on the section titled, "The Obstacles to Peace," (Chapter 19) I witnessed something quite unexpected.

2. The first human obstacle to peace – as Love and true union – is the unconscious desire to get rid of it. As this sunk in deeper, I saw that the value we give to the body and its five senses is the number one obstacle to peace. Another way to say this is that while we value and identify as the body, its senses and appetites - we reject peace, and with it, changeless Love.

3. Peace is the result of dis-identification as a body. Real peace is seen as a threat to body identification. And this is why the very first obstacle to peace is, "the desire to get rid of it." The compulsion to reject peace is so strong because the cost of dwelling in the Holy

Instant of peace is the fading awareness of the body along with all it stands for. Recall that the ego's fundamental purpose for the body is guilt. Guilt abhors peace, so it uses the body's senses and appetites – both painful and pleasurable ones, projecting unreal images, drama and emotions to *reject* the experience of peace and to substantiate our guilt.

4. Peace is the natural result of knowing our innocence as changeless Love itself. Therefore, by rejecting peace we unknowingly reject our incorruptible innocence which *is* Love as our Holy Self.

5. These two, both the body *and* peace, like Love *and* fear, cannot be known or experienced together. Pseudo and fleeting peace is possible, however using the body to gain a semblance of peace is not the same as the peace of God. The ego's brand of peace is always bought at the cost of guilt. The body can never be the source of consistent peace and Love because it was made to obstruct it.

6. While we value one consistently, either the body *or* peace, then the other must disappear in our awareness. The second obstacle to peace, "Belief the body is valuable for what it offers," really brought about a startling insight which prompted me to go even deeper into my experience as a child. Recall that we are trained since birth to view adulthood and special romantic relationships as a "natural," sought-after progression in this world. Almost every child is taught to look forward to becoming an adult one day.

7. Let me share with you a personal experience, a vivid milestone. This was the "day" my childlike innocence was shattered. I'll share some background first. My grandparents lived close to a beautiful beach, a stretch of soft, white sand that lined a stunning ocean. I spent many magical times there over my first eight or so years. I remember the joyous feeling of playing and running in the sand with no cares about the body whatsoever. Looking back at old photos of those early years, I never owned a bathing suit… just a simple pair of panties did the job.

8. One day, while I was still in elementary school, I was running along the beach darting in and out of the waves, when out of the blue, my grandfather called me over quite sternly. He handed me my towel and clothes… and told me never to swim topless ever again. I was incredulous, in shock. My mind scrambled to find the reason

why. In all the hundreds of times we enjoyed the beach together those first nine years, he had always encouraged me to be totally free and unselfconscious.

9. That day I remember plunging into inconsolable self-doubt. Suddenly, my body had become shameful for some reason. It had begun an early transition from child to adolescent. This previously inconspicuous body now appeared to be solid and real, a growing target for body- objectification.

10. Up until then, the body had been merely a shadow to me, or a means through which I enjoyed life. But from that fateful moment of shame, I began a long and debilitating journey into "body-consciousness." As puberty descended, my treasured ethereal phase of development was swiftly replaced by a body-centered awareness. And that meant that my childlike identity had regressed sharply into what felt like an imprisonment in the body. No longer just a means to enjoy life through, the body, its state and its image, became the aim of nearly all my thoughts, beliefs and actions.

B. Loss of Innocence

1. According to the ego world, there is a "loss of innocence" phase which is primarily brought about by the "coming of age" - or sexual maturity – as puberty or adolescence, the transition between childhood and adulthood.

2. In the onset of sexual maturity, the cost to a child is the memory of his or her incorruptible innocence. For a child the body is largely a means only, and not an end in itself. They are not body-conscious. Yet once the sexual desire is assumed, the earlier innocent focus on the body as a means, is abruptly shifted to it being valued as a goal or identity in itself. Hence the onset of the second obstacle to peace, "Belief the body is valuable for what it offers."

3. The body then mistakenly becomes the central identity, our quintessential "god," around which everything and everyone revolves. When the body is made the central sun so to speak, when we are slave to its seeming senses and its sensual appetites, the memory of our innocence is lost because the value we place on the body overshadows it.

4. No wonder that in adolescence we have what is termed as the "rebellious teens." Looking at this phase from a higher spiritual perspective, this tumultuous experience is brought about chiefly by the distorted miracle-impulse (sexual desire). It is the diminishing of the value of innocence. The body, its changing image, its growing objectification, and its strange, addictive new appetite, take central stage. Furthermore, our society encourages and supports these misguided substitutions for genuine, emotional intimacy – as the body, image, and sex – which feed the ego's addiction to romantic special relationships.

5. Once the sex drive is assumed, we begin making demands on and sacrifices of the body in order to gratify both our own sexual appetite, and that of others. Thus, the purpose of the body is given to the ego which must result in unconscious guilt expressed as self-attack (relationship conflict, pain, illness, lack, loss, etc.).

C. What Does it Cost?

1. As children we are largely free of the sexual urge. It doesn't usually descend on us until after our first, free decade of childlike innocence. Thankfully, we spend at least the first ten years untainted by the onslaught of sexual desire.

2. The pure, undistorted miracle impulse is the natural, extension of Love, innocence and peace. Yet through the ego this pure, selfless impulse becomes distorted. It deforms and morphs to being body focused instead of Spirit merged, thereby manifesting as the self-centered, sexual impulse.

3. This distortion arises from the false self's sense of deprivation, lack or need. Hence sexual *desire* is the desire to satisfy a seeming lack (to get). As Jesus tells us, body appetites are "getting" mechanisms. Yet in contrast, the pure miracle impulse comes from Love's endless and uninterrupted Source of abundance. It needs nothing but only to give of itself that it may extend and multiply.

a. *"The ego never gives out of abundance, because it was made as a substitute for it. That is why the concept of "getting" arose in the ego's thought system. Appetites are "getting" mechanisms, representing the ego's need to confirm itself. This is as true of body appetites as it is of the so-called "higher ego needs." Body appetites are not physical in origin." T-4. II.7:3-7*

4. I recall the immense freedom in having a child's body free from puberty, sexual urges, objectification and image distortions. There was an innocent, unselfconsciousness that happily permeated my experience of life. I was certainly not body-conscious; in fact, I was largely free of the body in those first few years. However, once puberty set in, the body became the sad center of my universe. And now thankfully, many years later, I am finally regaining that innocent sense of freedom again.

5. Consider the following:

    1) What exactly does it cost a child to become an adolescent, namely, the new acquisition of the addictive sexual urge?

    2) In which ways does this adult sexual urge change the purpose we assign to the body, along with its image?

    3) With satisfying the sexual appetite as a key goal in adult life, how do we judge, objectify and enslave the body (our own and others) ... compared to our childhood without the sexual urge? What are the differences?

    4) What would change and heal if all adolescents and adults were free of sexual desire?

    5) Let's say this urge did not exist. Imagine that children came into the dream, but not through the sexual act. Imagine the freedom, the peace and the innocence of being totally desireless? How would our relationships change? And how would our purpose for the body change?

6. I know one thing. The unhealed sexual desire is a guilt magnet, a seductive and repetitive stimulant propelled by lack. Remember the first obstacle to peace is the desire to get rid of it. And the second is our belief that the body is valuable for what it offers. As children we are free of the most debilitating addiction – sexual desire. But as the ego develops its body identity along with the

specialness this mistaken self so desperately craves, the distorted sexual impulse becomes a dense cover that hides our true Identity and its resounding peace.

3. SEXUAL DESIRE - A DISTORTED MIRACLE IMPULSE

1. When Jesus dictated the earlier material to Helen, regarding sex, He explained that the sexual impulse was a distortion of the pure miracle impulse which is the natural, selfless extension of Love, innocence and peace. Because it arises from *beyond* the body, there is no lack in it. There is no "need" or longing that seeks to be met. This pristine, entirely changeless miracle impulse is *never* body focused. Yet when this miracle impulse is received through the filter of belief that the body is valuable for what "it" can give to us, it becomes a *distorted* sex impulse. The result is a drive that is both self-centered and body focused, seeking to *get* instead of extending to transcend self-interests. As long as we continue in the erroneous belief we *are* the illusory body, we will continue to ceaselessly seek satisfaction and completion through it.

2. There is a paradox here because the body is an *external* projected image in our mind. Using the "body puppet and puppeteer" analogy here, the body could be imagined as our external puppet while we – our mind, either ego or Spirit – are the puppeteer who controls the beliefs, actions, desires, addictions, values and experiences of the otherwise neutral and lifeless body-puppet.

3. The inanimate body-puppet only seems to have a mind, senses and appetites of its own. It only appears to be a product of the ego's biological and physiological laws, as well as the law of time. Of itself, the body has neither lifeforce nor intelligence because it is literally a now moment projection. The "mind" which projects the body-puppet also manipulates it, whether we are conscious of this or not. The more unconscious we are, the more this split mind will seem to be imprisoned by the body's illusory compulsions; but as we heal via forgiveness, the greater our freedom *from* our identifying as the body.

4. While the body is believed to possess independent appetites of its own, and as long as we attempt to gratify those appetites apart from Spirit, we will betray our Holy Self by surrendering the body to the ego to use it for conflict, pain and separation. We will believe the lie that we are imprisoned by this entirely inanimate puppet, which we our self invented. Thus, literally reversing cause and effect, the body and its seeming addictions will appear to be more powerful than our mind which made it.

5. As guilt is required to maintain the identity of a separate self, and the body is the ego's means to acquire this guilt, the body becomes the central figure in all our special relationships. Guilt is also the cause of all relationship conflict. Thankfully, as our special relationships are given to Holy Spirit to be healed, our use of the body is also divinely repurposed. Instead of acquiring guilt, its purpose becomes the extension of Love and innocence.

6. Remember that the body-puppet is actually a "learning device" while we perceive our self in the dream. As a learning device it is meant to be a "means" to express guiltlessness and true communication, and not an "end" or identity, in itself.

7. In the special, sexual relationship the illusory body-puppet, and not the puppeteer (mind), is cherished as the primary *goal*. The body is mistakenly valued as the center piece of our existence – the be all and end all. And the relentless pursuit of orgasm is proof of this confusion. Orgasm is the result of the ego's primal *mating urge*. As such, it is a self-gratifying habit channeled through the body-puppet and therefore, it cannot *be* shared. In contrast, the undistorted miracle impulse is a heart-centered desire to bond, which *can* be shared because it transcends the ego's self-interests.

8. Jesus teaches that the sex urge is an attempt to reach communion through the *body* which is an "improper" identification of self and another. In this we mistake our self and the other *as* the body, which is not only disrespectful, but untrue. Further, He goes on to say that the underlying mechanism (distorted sexual drive) must be uprooted.

    a. *"Indiscriminate sexual impulses resemble indiscriminate miracle impulses in that both result in body image misperceptions. The first is an expression of an indiscriminate attempt to reach communion thru the body. This involves not only the improper self identification, but also disrespect for the individuality of others. Self-control is NOT the whole answer to this problem, though I am by no means discouraging its use. It must be understood, however, that the underlying mechanism must be uprooted..." T-1.B.37 p.*

b.　*"The confusion of miracle impulse with sexual impulse is a major source of perceptual distortion, because it INDUCES rather than straightening out the basic level-confusion which underlies all those who seek happiness with the instruments (body, etc.) of the world." T-1.B.37 ae.*

9. Many people seek intimacy through sex, without recognizing what true intimacy really is. The attempt of communion *through* the superficial body is impossible because the body itself is an illusion. In contrast, the pure and undistorted miracle impulse is an expression of union by extension. It arises naturally and spontaneously from a sense of wholeness, fullness, spaciousness and inner abundance and joy. This is total receiving and extension all at once, because it involves a giving away of oneself over and over again. Jesus makes a point in the following passage. He refers to sexual union as an attempt to unite parts of us that are invisible (bodies):

a.　*"How can man "come close" to others thru the parts of him (body-puppet) which are really invisible? The word "invisible" means "cannot be seen or perceived." What cannot be perceived is hardly the right means for improving perception."- Urtext. (Emphasis added)*

10. Many pursue shallow forms of physical intimacy which only ensures that the puppeteers in the relationship never come to really "see" each other and therefore, Love. The body-puppet and its strange, self-centered appetites are meant to distract and blot-out our memory of divine union beyond the body at the level of the mind.

a.　*"The union of bodies thus becomes the way in which you would keep minds apart." T-15.IX.7:1*

11. The agenda of orgasm might seem to be the "urge to merge", however it's really the urge to separate. This is because of its underlying intent, a *predatory urge,* which unfortunately originates from fear and deprivation and never from Love.

A. The Hidden Attraction of Guilt and Pain

1. The false self believes that the body (along with its appetites) is its goal, its source and its life. It feels deprived and seeks to meet its imagined needs through the body-puppet. It seeks sex and orgasm with other body-puppets, yet these desires are misdirected and distorted miracle impulses which are steeped in ego self-gratification. Because this self believes it is incomplete, it seeks independent pleasure *apart from* God's Will. Yet, because seeking apart from God's will results in guilt, there is no pleasure that we can seek independently that will not also bring us pain.

> *a. "Pain compels attention, drawing it away from Him and focusing upon itself. Its purpose is the same as pleasure, for they both are means to make the body real. What shares a common purpose is the same." T-27.VI.1:3-5*

2. When we confuse our self with the body and pursue the ego's "pleasure drives" apart from consulting Spirit's guidance, we seek to pursue our own completion through the false self. We act on and respond to its seeming authority. But what we don't recognize is this:

> *1)* God – together with His Son – is all-encompassing Love without opposite. Fear (illusion) is the opposite of Love.

3. If God is Love and no opposite exists, there is just one Loving Will, God's Will, which He shares with His Son, as our shared and Holy Self. If there is only one Will (and its God's) then no other "will" exists in reality. Yet while we're lost in the belief that our own "independent will" can complete and gratify the false self and its body-puppet, we must identify as an *opposing self* with an alien will *in opposition* to God.

4. Who wouldn't feel threatened if deep down they believed that their "self," its body and all its coveted desires, are in *opposition to God?* Suddenly, God is our enemy! This translates to Love, union and life being our enemy. And we must keep Him – Love as our Holy Self – at bay, or else Love will annihilate this false self with its alien will.

5. This nebulous and persistent undercurrent of fear is projected onto God as the great *Attacker*, the *Force* behind every spike of impending doom. Perhaps we can see now that all our desires for pleasure *apart* from God, are really seeking guilt, because while we greedily snatch moments of sensual pleasure, the underlying guilt ensures that we will end up paying for it. We then project and manifest our unforgiven guilt via self-administered punishment. This is why the body becomes sick, ages and dies.

   a. *"As "something" is the body asked to be God's enemy, replacing what He is with littleness and limit and despair. It is His loss you celebrate when you behold the body as a thing you love, or look upon it as a thing you hate."… "Your savior is not dead, nor does he dwell in what was built as temple unto death. He lives in God, and it is this that makes him savior unto you, and only this. His body's nothingness releases yours from sickness and from death. For what is yours cannot be more or less than what is his." T-29.III.2:1-2,4-7*

6. The certain consequence of this denial of our Holy Self is massive guilt, which must be suppressed, denied and projected onto the body, others and the world. As I mentioned, this unseen guilt is always followed by the secret *expectation* of punishment, and the subsequent and final manifestation of that punishment is always pain, and finally, physical death. This is what all bodily addictions are. They are self-administered punishment for the seeming *sin* of pursuing a *"will"* (pleasure *and* pain) apart from God. Perhaps we can now see why self-seeking pleasure always results in pain.

7. The hidden attraction to guilt and pain are well explained in the section of the *Course* titled, *The Obstacles to Peace*, in Chapter 19.

   a. *"It is impossible to seek for pleasure through the body and not find pain. It is essential that this relationship be understood, for it is one the ego sees as proof of sin. It is not really punitive at all. It is but the inevitable result of equating yourself with the body, which is the invitation to pain. For it invites fear to enter and become your purpose. The attraction of guilt [must] enter with it, and whatever fear directs the body to do is therefore painful. It will share the pain of all illusions, and the illusion of pleasure will be the same as pain."* T-19. IV.B.12.

b. *"Under fear's orders the body will pursue guilt, serving its master whose attraction to guilt maintains the whole illusion of its existence. This, then, is the attraction of pain. Ruled by this perception the body becomes the servant of pain, seeking it dutifully and obeying the idea that pain is pleasure. It is this idea that underlies all of the ego's heavy investment in the body. And it is this insane relationship that it keeps hidden, and yet feeds upon. To you it teaches that the body's pleasure is happiness. Yet to itself it whispers, "It is death."* T-19.IV.B.13:2-8

4. THE ONLY VALID USE OF SEX

1. Let's cut straight to the chase and deliver another fiercely uncompromising truth from Jesus about sex:

   a. *The only VALID use of sex is procreation. It is NOT truly pleasurable in itself. "Lead us not into Temptation" means "Do not let us deceive ourselves into believing that we can relate in peace to God or our brothers with ANYTHING external."* Urtext Chapter 1.

2. *"The only valid use of sex is procreation."* Urtext Chapter 1.
3. This is a shocking and highly unsettling statement! At least this is what I thought when I first read the Urtext a few years ago. To be honest, I really didn't recognize the depth of Jesus' unrelenting stance on sex at first. Initially, I hazily dismissed many of His hardnosed facts.

4. What exactly does Jesus mean? The body-puppet *is* a fantasy because it is meant to hide the mind behind it. Sexual lust is fantasy centered on the body-puppet at the expense of rejecting and dishonoring our true Identity. He says that all temptation arises from one generic mistake, which is the belief that we are all physical bodies, and that our completion lies in satiating the body's appetites.

5. Just in case we question Jesus' previous statement that the only valid use of sex is procreation, He also tells us in the following quote that the sex impulse *is* a miracle impulse when it's used exclusively for procreation.

   a. *NO fantasies, sexual or otherwise, are true. Fantasies become totally unnecessary as the Wholly satisfying nature of reality becomes apparent. The sex impulse IS a miracle impulse when it is in proper focus. One individual sees in another the right partner for "procreating the stock" (Wolff was not too far off here), and also for their joint establishment of a creative home. This does not involve fantasy at all. If I am asked to participate in the decision, the decision will be a Right one, too. Urtext, T-1.B. 41 t>*

6. We deceive our self in thinking we can relate to God or our brothers in peace when we identify as an external object, *the body*. While we do this, we will mistakenly attempt not just to relate to others *as* bodies, but we will be invested in keeping them as one also. When their body identity no longer serves the ego's needs, our "special love" then turns to hate. This is the core of every special romantic relationship. Its repeated goal is the impossible attempt at true union through sex via external body identities. Limiting our self and others to the body produces guilt and is the ego's attraction to guilt and death.

   a. *"It is only the awareness of the body that makes love seem limited. For the body [is] a limit on love. The belief in limited love was its origin, and it was made to limit the unlimited."* ... *"God cannot come into a body, nor can you join Him there."* T-18.VIII.1:1-3,2:3 *"Do not let us deceive ourselves into believing that we can relate in peace to God or our brothers with ANYTHING external." –Urtext*

7. Now is as good a time as any to recall the certain outcome of being identified as a body and not the Holy Self. This outcome is death. Reflecting on page 157 of *The End of Death* (Volume One), do you remember the Bathtub Analogy?

8. To simply depict the ego's illusion of time, birth, death and suffering, I used the symbol of a vast body of water, a universe sized bathtub with its contents held in place by a single giant plug, our non-negotiable belief in *death*. Everyone believes that the certain and inevitable outcome of all life here in the dream is death. Belief in death has far surpassed our belief in Life (God as Love). Death is the ego's central dream.

    a. *"Death is the central dream from which all illusions stem."... "Death is the symbol of the fear of God."... "The "reality" of death is firmly rooted in the belief that God's Son is a body." M-27.1:1.3:1,5:1*

9. Death (fear) and not life (Love) has been seated at the center of the false self's altar since time began. Yet Jesus appeared more than two thousand years ago to prove through His resurrection that death is an illusion and therefore does not exist.

10. That giant plug called death which appeared to hold the entire dream captive to time, suffering and death was wrenched right out through Jesus' resurrection. The entire contents of the dream simply vanished. He collapsed the dream for all of us in that one, supreme act of Love. The illusion of death was overcome for us all. This is the Atonement, available in every Holy Instant we accept it and receive it.

11. We all have the ability to choose when we will accept the healing He accomplished for us. But while we value and therefore choose independent body identities with private minds, instead of the shared mind of Holy Self, it remains for us to unlearn our value of, and attachment to separation, which is the fear of God as Love.

12. When Jesus pulled out the plug of death, He transcended the body identity completely. It is our mistaken identification *as* a body

which attracts specialness, conflict, loss, sickness, pain, aging and death. When Jesus resurrected there was no body left to bury. It had disappeared. Why? Because He proved literally that the body was nothing but an image in thought. It never had life and therefore, could not die.

13. As a *now moment projection* with no past or future, His body did not disintegrate; it simply dematerialized. The body, when understood as nothing, cannot die. This is what Jesus meant when He said in the following quote that the body, being unreal, cannot die.

14. Jesus clearly explains what happened to His body in the tomb:

   a. *"My body disappeared because I had no illusion about it. The last one had gone. It was laid in the tomb, but there was nothing left to bury. It did not disintegrate because the unreal cannot die. It merely became what it always was. And that is what "rolling the stone away" means. The body disappears, and no longer hides what lies beyond. It merely ceases to interfere with vision. To roll the stone away is to see beyond the tomb, beyond death, and to understand the body's nothingness. What is understood as nothing must disappear."* From Page 17 of the Special Messages to Helen.

15. The only way we can manifest the appearance of a body which sickens, decays and dies, is when we mistakenly invest in it as being "special." We value the body as having something (good or bad) that our brothers do not have, to use as proof of separation. The body, when believed to be a special "something," either good or bad, *is always* doomed to death.

16. We assign special attributes to the body (that God did not create) in order to try to prove it is an identity apart from God. Yet nothing *apart* from God's all-encompassing Love *exists* in reality. The body is the home of the ego (sin, guilt and fear) and specialness proves its separate status. Consequently, it perceives God's Law of changeless Love, innocence and union as its mortal enemy. In order to defend itself and escape from the Love of God (Life), the ego condemns the body to the reincarnation cycle, by killing it over and over again through death.

17. The unreal body *cannot* die. Jesus tells us that once we repurpose it with Holy Spirit, the body is accepted to be nothing other than a neutral communication device for forgiveness. It cannot be sick, age, decay or die. Once the mind is healed, the body must follow. And when we do eventually leave it, we do so in gratitude and joy, leaving a healthy body which had been a serviceable instrument to demonstrate guiltlessness to all. The body only seems to succumb to death because we still maintain the unforgiven belief that we *are* the body with a personal private mind and will "apart" from our brothers and God – and not the one shared, incorruptible and innocent Holy Self.

18. The belief that mistakes cannot be corrected by Spirit is the belief we have sinned and that those sins are unforgiveable. The ego's sole purpose for the body is sin, which is assuredly followed by guilt and fear. In its independent pursuit of pleasure and avoidance of pain as a body identity, the ego hides the fact that it *wants* our death. Our unhealed faith in death, over God's Life, allows it to pursue us beyond the grave into further incarnations which prolongs the illusions of time and suffering. Dedicating the body to the insane idea that sin is possible is its guarantee that our belief in sin (guilt and fear) always leads to death.

a. *"The ego wants [you] dead, but not itself. The outcome of its strange religion must therefore be the conviction that it can pursue you beyond the grave." T-15.I.3:3-4*

b. *"The body is the ego's idol; the belief in sin made flesh and then projected outward. This produces what seems to be a wall of flesh around the mind, keeping it prisoner in a tiny spot of space and time, beholden unto death, and given but an instant in which to sigh and grieve and die in honor of its master." T-20.VI.11:1-2*

19. Jesus shared the material on sex very early in His dictation of the *Course* to Helen. The sex impulse as lust, is a predatory urge if not divinely repurposed with Holy Spirit, and always leads to separation and death. As long as we continue to use sex inappropriately, we inadvertently resist closing the gap of separation. We've chosen to

see and objectify the body of our brothers and therefore, our own.

20. This is why, if we truly desire to awaken *from* the dream of birth and death, we must give our special relationships to the Holy Spirit to repurpose them to Holy Relationships. Thus, we come to understand through *direct experience* that we are *not* a body and that our body does not sustain us. Instead, we recognize with great joy that we are sustained by God's Love and that we are one unified, innocent and Holy Self.

5. LUST, FANTASY AND ORGASM

1. As explained in a later section titled "Sex and Death – The Last Two Defenses," for most on the path of awakening there are at least three phases which we move through in healing the sexual pleasure drive. The first stage is where most are stalled, which is what I call "sex to separate" (destroy). This is specialness in order to get, to use and to separate. The second is using "sex to heal" which is Holiness (innocence) in order to extend, to heal and to unite. And the final, advanced stage is transcendence by Spirit of the body's identity and its appetites, which I call "divine androgyny."

2. The ideal would be to move through these phases in one lifetime, preferably in Holy Relationship. Otherwise, as we have seen, the outcome of unhealed specialness through body identity is certain death. Once death claims the unsurrendered body identity, then the overwhelming temptation of habitual body identification jolts us back into yet another round of physical birth, and debilitating amnesia. Being born as an infant with amnesia serves to cleverly conceal our singular purpose which is to awaken *from* the body dream itself.

3. This is quickly followed by more seduction of the ego's desire for specialness via the pleasures/pains of the body. If, in this additional incarnation, we once again remain oblivious to our life's singular purpose of awakening *from* the body – aka the split mind – then the guaranteed outcome is death once again. And this is how the illusion of time as suffering, is maintained. On the lighter side, it's

impossible not to laugh at the humor of this!

4.   Perhaps we may now be ready to recognize just why our attraction to specialness, the body and death are the primary motivators for prolonging the illusion of time. Time could not exist except for the ego's addiction to death. The illusion of time depends on our belief and investment in the body and death through special relating; this is what guilt as specialness, as the means for separation, is for. When we transcend death – meaning special relating and the body *as* the split mind – there will be no further purpose for dreaming of time *or* the body. They will have been forgiven completely.

A. The Pursuit of Orgasm

1.   One of the major driving forces for misidentifying our self as the body instead of Spirit is the pursuit of orgasm.

   a. *"If the identification is with the body, consciousness may distort superconscious impulses by denying their source and seeking their impact in the orgasm. This is the result of 'mistaken identity.'" The COA Annotated Edition, T-1.28.3:1-2*

2.   The drive for orgasm is the habitual, yet insatiable cycle of the *mating urge*. It has nothing to do with genuine *bonding,* yet society has thoroughly confused it with what it calls "love." The compulsion for orgasm is an unhealed sexual drive, an agenda *independent* of Holy Spirit, therefore it's a body focused desire. This unhealed drive for orgasm is a distortion of the original miracle impulse, which in its *undefiled state* is the desire for *true union* beyond the body.

3.   In her groundbreaking book, *"Cupid's Poisoned Arrow,"* Marnia Robinson reveals just why the pursuit of orgasm plays a central role in the disruption of many romantic relationships. Her extensive research findings are based on personal testimonies and backed up by scientific data. This data confirms (at the form level) how the false body identity's unhealed pursuit of orgasm actually sabotages our most cherished relationships.   "Cupid's Poisoned Arrow" presents unmistakable evidence as confirmation of the negative "effects" of the mating urge (distorted miracle impulse) as Jesus teaches in *A Course in Miracles* Urtext.

4. In this section, I'm summarizing just some of the highlights that can be found in Marnia's book. Completely contrary to what we've previously accepted from the ego thought system, orgasm does *not* bring us closer together in romantic relationships! The startling fact is that the addictive quest for orgasm in relationship leads to a great many *anti*-relationship effects such as emotional distancing, boredom with partner, lethargy, irritability and mood swings, etc.

5. Engaging in the habit of regular orgasm has actually been shown to dissipate attraction to our partner over the initial, two-year "honeymoon" phase. After two years with the same partner or even before, romantic love is set to dissipate. Studies have proven that in coupling for procreation purposes, the orgasm driven impulse was intended to last up to two years with one partner, to give a child the chance to have *two* caregivers during this important development time of its life.

6. After its two year "expiry" date or even before, the impersonal mating impulse (distorted miracle impulse) is likely to trigger the temptation to search for a more exciting sexual mate with which to pursue the cyclical mating impulse. This has contributed to the growing epidemic of extramarital affairs and divorce within special romantic relationships. Following is a helpful quote from *"Cupid's Poisoned Arrow:"*

7. *"Intercourse is beneficial, but orgasm brings with it a host of problems. Symptoms could include feeling drained, irritability, energy imbalance, health problems, and, most significantly, a growing aversion of one's partner." From page 29 of "Cupid's Poisoned Arrow"*

8. There is a two-week passion cycle or hangover period which follows each orgasm for both men and women. It can make lovers feel unusually needy, anxious, drained, or irritable from time to time. Marnia Robinson explains that, "due to the recurring discomfort during the passion cycle, we can begin to perceive our lover – or ongoing intimate relationships themselves – as a source of stress." *(Page 292 of "Cupids' Poisoned Arrow")* Circling back to what Jesus points to regarding sex in the Urtext, this preceding statement from Cupid's Poisoned Arrow reveals the ego's use of the body's sexual appetite as a means of projecting its guilt onto a partner.

a. *"The union of bodies thus becomes the way in which you would keep minds apart." ACIM, T-15.IX.7:1*

b. *"The confusion of miracle impulse with sexual impulse is a major source of perceptual distortion, because it INDUCES rather than straightening out the basic level-confusion which underlies all those who seek happiness with the instruments (body, etc.) of the world." Urtext, T-1.B.37 ae.*

9. Overall, when a relationship depends on orgasm to hold it together, it's likely to fall apart over time, because it is based on a habitual compulsion that, in itself, was designed to lead to separation and not to lifelong union. Additionally, the more orgasm is achieved, the more it is desired, just like a drug. Repeated firing of orgasm causes a series of ongoing lows which trigger the habitual search for relief in further climaxing. This mistaken cycle can lead to a host of depleting side effects.

10. I feel this data relates back to Jesus' teachings (found in the Urtext) on the subject of sex, in which he declares that it is "an area the miracle worker *must* understand." Marnia's book offers a very practical "boots on the ground" approach to healing what she refers to as the mating urge. It reveals the collective's shocking misconceptions about sex and offers instead a whole new bonding-based approach to "love-making."

11. Using my own terms here, and relating to the specific phases of healing specialness, the first of the three phases of sexual healing, which is where most people in the world are presently, is used by the ego as "sex to separate," and is lust-driven rather than Love-inspired. This phase involves the habitual pursuit of orgasm as self-gratification, and has also been seen as the underlying cause of many unrecognized ailments and relationship conflicts.

12. Those in relationship who are ready to enter the second phase, using sex to heal, will find a truly helpful bonding technique called Karezza in Marnia's book. She maps out a very practical, twenty-one day program titled, The Ecstatic Exchanges. These exchanges

very skillfully retrain our sexual circuitry from addiction to the distorted mating impulse (orgasm), to the experience of genuine and deeply satisfying bonding, or true intimacy. If readers are unable to find the book "Cupid's Poisoned Arrow," then I recommend they do an internet search for the *Karezza Method*. Material and books about Karezza should be available in most languages.

13. Sex has become a numbingly common, highly valued, *recreational pastime* for many here in the dream. Just look at how extensively the media uses body image and sex for leveraging a plethora of products all aimed at objectifying the body instead of elevating the Spirit.

14. In its original state the miracle impulse is infinite, inclusive, interpersonal and shared with all. When this impulse is mistakenly intercepted through the mind that believes it's a body, the pure miracle impulse becomes distorted and repurposed into a singular, exclusive, selfish goal, namely orgasm. Once this is sought after and achieved, the body becomes the aim of superficial relating and not true union with the one Mind.

15. If the singular purpose of orgasm is procreation, then every other use of it must be the ego's desire for fantasy. Let's look at this.

16. Every other pursuit of orgasm must involve confusing our identity, ours and another's, with fantasy. This occurs when the priority is orgasm and the goal is self-gratification. Seeking pleasure for oneself creates separation and results in the objectification of our body and/or the body of another. Only an external object can be imbued with fantasy; Truth cannot.

17. The body as the mistaken identity, along with what we believe it can give to us that God cannot, then replaces the unified Holy Self in our awareness. Recall that we cannot see or value both the body *and* the Holy Self at the same time. The value of one eclipses the other entirely in our awareness.

18. The orgasm, when pursued for any purpose *other* than procreation, is always designed for self-seeking pleasure as a body. This is to reinforce the illusion of the body as our source of existence and pleasure which must produce more guilt and separation via *identification as* a body instead of Spirit. The following passage which I will repeat here from Jesus explains that the only "valid"

use of sex is procreation.

a. *The only VALID use of sex is procreation. It is NOT truly pleasurable in itself. "Lead us not into Temptation" means "Do not let us deceive ourselves into believing that we can relate in peace to God or our brothers with ANYTHING external." T-1.B.4 0f.*

19. As Jesus frequently reminds us, when we look to our body or another's as our source of pleasure or completion rather than desiring the true intimacy of joining with each other in Spirit, we forego genuine union because we've prioritized the body over Spirit. This mistake always calls for the ego's self-attack.

a. *"But when you look upon a brother as a physical entity, his power and glory are "lost" to you and so are yours. You have attacked him, but you must have attacked yourself first."... "When you see a brother as a body, you are condemning him because you have condemned yourself." T-8.VII.5:3-4,15:7*

b. *"For faithlessness is the perception of a brother as a body, and the body cannot be used for purposes of union. If, then, you see your brother as a body, you have established a condition in which uniting with him becomes impossible." T-19.I.4:2-3*

20. Each individual engaging in sex to pursue personal pleasure via orgasm tries to satisfy their very own *independent* pleasure drive. Contrary to what the world teaches, the body-puppet's orgasm can never be shared. Orgasm is not true intimacy. It is a replacement *for* it.

a. *"Your brother's body is as little use to you as it is to him. When it is used only as the Holy Spirit teaches, it has no function. For minds need not the body to communicate. The sight that sees the body has no use which serves the purpose of a holy relationship." T-20.V.5:1-4*

21. When we still desire to use sex and orgasm inappropriately, we prefer to perceive our self and others as objects (bodies) rather than as the majestic Holy Self we are. This fact must at least be recognized without self-judgment or guilt before we can begin to

genuinely invite Holy Spirit in to help us heal and repurpose the ego's pleasure drive.

a. *"Note that sexual fantasies are ALWAYS destructive (or depleting), in that they perceive another in an inappropriate creative role. Both people are perceived essentially as "objects" fulfilling THEIR OWN pleasure drives. This dehumanized view is the source of the DEPLETING use of sex."* - Urtext

22. The presence of lust excludes true Love, true intimacy, and is the ego's substitute *for* it. While lust is not bad in itself, unrelinquished lust does increase guilt as unconscious self-attack, because it reinforces the illusion of separation. Lust is essentially a very special, coveted, habitual and denied form of guilt. This is why it must be flushed out for healing.

23. Jesus explains in the following passage a particularly common and "special form of fear" – which is expressed when we obsess on body parts and use these as a standard for comparisons. This is yet another form of objectifying the body which is a form of self-attack.

a. *"No one is seen complete. The body is emphasized, with special emphasis on certain parts, and used as the standard for comparison of acceptance or rejection for acting out a special form of fear."* T-18.I.3:6-7

B. Lust

1. Love *and* lust cannot be experienced together. The presence of one excludes the other. Lust is a direct byproduct of fear, of separation. Yet in special romantic love it is lust, and not Love, that is revered, thus glorifying the body so it eclipses the mind. Romantic love is often confused with lust. Unknowingly, the focus is on finding ways for the body to serve the ego's sensual appetites. The lust for orgasm apart from consciously intending to procreate, as the mating urge, is lust for self-gratification apart from God and our companion.

2. Lust is a form of dissociation or separation because it's the delusional belief that we can find pleasure without genuine, interpersonal relating. Pornography, masturbation and casual sex

for instance, are prime examples of this crazy confusion.

a.   The "sin of onan" was called a "sin" because it involved
     a related type of self-delusion; namely, that pleasure
     WITHOUT relating can exist. Urtext, T-1.B.40 g

3.   As we willingly become more honest and mindful of what we
     are using the body for (ours and our partner's), without self-blame
     or guilt, we can consciously invite Holy Spirit to help us to heal the
     ego's attraction to using the body inappropriately. The following
     two quotes are too important not to include in their entirety:

a.   "Ask yourself this: Can [you] protect the mind? The body,
     yes, a little; not from time, but temporarily. And much you
     think you save, you hurt. What would you save it [for?] For
     in that choice lie both its health and harm. Save it for show,
     as bait to catch another fish, to house your specialness in
     better style, or weave a frame of loveliness around your
     hate, and you condemn it to decay and death. And if you see
     this purpose in your brother's, such is your condemnation of
     your own. Weave, rather, then, a frame of holiness around
     him, that the truth may shine on him, and give [you] safety
     from decay." T-24.VII.4.

b.   "Look upon all the trinkets made to hang upon the body,
     or to cover it or for its use. See all the useless things made
     for its eyes to see. Think on the many offerings made for its
     pleasure, and remember all these were made to make seem
     lovely what you hate. Would you employ this hated thing to
     draw your brother to you, and to attract his body's eyes?
     Learn you but offer him a crown of thorns, not recognizing
     it for what it is, and trying to justify your own interpretation
     of its value by his acceptance. Yet still the gift proclaims
     his worthlessness to you, as his acceptance and delight
     acknowledges the lack of value he places on himself." T-20.
     II.1.

6. THE LOVING ANTIDOTE - BONDING

1. In order to help offset and heal the destructive and habitual mating pattern, as the goal of orgasm in sexual relationships, we are offered its grace-filled alternative, "bonding." This is a practice aimed at experiencing true intimacy between two people. Genuine intimacy always transcends the ego's self-interests. Real bonding is a valuable replacement for the ego's destructive habit of mutual use because it encourages true communication which strengthens trust and union rather than separation.

2. Ultimately, the priority is learning to communicate with each other honestly and defenselessly without blame. In a relationship where both partners are mutually committed to growing together, moving away from the depleting use of lust and the mating urge, then I suggest the following: To introduce a conscious intent before lovemaking by joining in a heartfelt prayer with Holy Spirit. Perhaps to offer up all preconceived ideas about sex and to place them on our inner Altar, where He can divinely repurpose and purify them.

3. Rather than focusing on the body of another with orgasm as the goal, the bonding mechanism centers on behaviors such as eye to eye contact, skin to skin contact, soothing touch, attentive listening and expressing affection, etc.

4. These are daily practices that strengthen emotional bonding and trust between two people. Ideally, we want to develop and increase harmony and true communication in our relationships and to no longer objectify another through the alienating habit of lust as body identification.

5. Part of learning to discern the difference between the mating impulse and the bonding impulse is through physical touch.

6. There is a world of difference between selfless touch and hungry touch between two people. One is based on giving as Love, while the other is an urge to "get" which is lust. An important part of the bonding program involves learning how to extend selfless touch, which is comforting in its power to nourish and bond. It involves unselfish and mindful presence with our partner, without the agenda of orgasm (urge to get).

7. I prefer not to elucidate in detail about the many helpful bonding behaviors and techniques here. If you are interested in learning how to engage in the "sex to heal" phase by implementing this wonderful alternative to the habitual mating urge, then I highly recommend the twenty-one day practice of The Ecstatic Exchanges in the final chapter of "Cupid's Poisoned Arrow." The following is an excerpt from Marnia Robinson:

8. "The Exchanges are a 3-week program of daily activities for couples to do as they reprogram their lovemaking. Both the activities and the schedule contribute to the program's effectiveness. Without a structured approach, the concept of avoiding orgasm will likely leave you high and dry...and frustrated.

9. The Exchanges have two prongs. First, we set aside time to snuggle, kiss, touch, caress...without a goal of intercourse or heated foreplay. Amazingly, this reprogrammed our response to sexual intimacy. As we (and others) have found, this non-goal oriented lovemaking is more sensual than the usual way. Second, each day we engaged regularly in activities - described in the Exchanges - which raised our levels of oxytocin (the "cuddle hormone"). These two tactics enabled us to tiptoe around our biological hunger for fertilization-driven sex with an ease and pleasure that surprised us - and confirmed much wisdom from the past."

10. The current world is generally obsessed by the desire for sexual gratification – the mating urge – mistaking it for the hallmark of love, happiness and success. This distorted drive for sex has contributed to many intensified feelings of frustration, inferiority and inadequacy in relationships. Sexual performance, increased libido and multiple orgasms are high on the ego's list of unrealistic yet persistently pursued expectations in a romantic relationship.

11. Having not had any real success with orgasm in this lifetime, this seeming dilemma caused innumerable problems within my own previously "special" romantic relationships. I fell for the myth that I was dysfunctional which led to decades of unnecessary self-doubt. I must say that I was pleasantly surprised when I encountered the following quote from Cupid's Poisoned Arrow. It

confirmed for me that the underlying reason for my seeming failure was because I had been unwittingly holding out for true intimacy:

12. *"It dawned on me that women who do not orgasm easily might actually be ahead of the rest of us – provided they realize there is no reason to amp up unnecessary frustration in pursuit of the Holy Grail of orgasm. At some level women who don't settle for orgasm as the measure of their sexual satisfaction may be holding out for the bonding behaviors that would deepen their relationships and offer both partners more satisfaction." From "Cupid's Poisoned Arrow," page 33*

7. IF YOU'RE NOT READY, DON'T FIGHT YOURSELF

1. The human addiction to sex seems to be so prevalent partly due to the erroneous yet heavily supported belief that sex *is* Love. In addition, specialness is based on the belief that we are all separate bodies and not the infinite, unified, light beings of Love that we are. This belief that we're trapped in and as a body includes the belief that union with another requires the merging of bodies. This assumption comes at the expense of *true union* through heartfelt Holy Instants. The sexual "urge to merge" is not wrong or bad, nor should we allow it to induce guilt, which is simply the ego using it against us as self-attack.

2. If resistance is strong, you're not ready. The answer is not to try to stop having sex. Like dieting, this never works as it's the ego attempting to quit what it still believes is a valued body appetite. Feelings of conflict, sacrifice, struggle and resentment always follow the ego's attempts to relinquish its own substitutes for God's Love. All body appetites are there to hide from our awareness the one underlying ego appetite – guilt. Because the core guilt that underpins the appetite is not yet healed, the ego believes it has sacrificed something of value, and will torment us with conflict as a result.

a. *"Inappropriate sex drives (or misdirected miracle-impulses) result in guilt if expressed, and depression if denied. We said before that ALL real pleasure comes from doing God's will. Whenever it is NOT done an experience of lack results. This is because NOT doing the will of God IS a lack of self." - Urtext, Chapter One. (Parenthesis added)*

3. Divinely repurposing the sexual pleasure drive is a gradual and gentle healing of our split mind. The level of behavior (sex) is not the level where we aim to prioritize our healing. The mind – as the underlying guilt – is where true healing occurs. And once this is taken in, naturally our behavior will follow. For most this takes time. In my own experience, we simply cannot genuinely lay our value of sex aside until we have had at least a taste of the powerfully transformative experience of true union in a "joint" Holy Instant with another – one that completely eclipses the body. Once true union with another is experienced, sex is then recognized as the superficial substitute that it is.

a. *"The love of God, for a little while, must still be expressed through one body to another. That is because the real vision is still so dim. Everyone can use his body best by enlarging man's perception, so he can see the real VISION. THIS VISION is invisible to the physical eye. The ultimate purpose of the body is to render itself unnecessary. Learning to do this is the only real reason for its creation." – Urtext, Chapter One*

4. In the meantime, repurposing sex with Holy Spirit and using it to heal our fear of true intimacy is the second phase of healing the sexual appetite. Here, we undo the habitual mating impulse, which is the lust aspect of sex, and replace it with sincere bonding, selfless reverence, tenderness and affection. Abundant help during this miraculous transition is offered in the already referenced book, *Cupid's Poisoned Arrow* by Marnia Robinson.

5. This phase of transition from the mating impulse to genuine bonding is incredibly helpful to undo our fear of Love and true emotional intimacy. The presence of lust in sexual relating is an expression of our fear of true emotional intimacy. Lust blocks

union (communication) and reinforces unconscious guilt because it always involves objectifying of the body to hide the light, the Love of our shared, Holy Self.

8. THE MONOGAMY MYTH

1. Just to review here again, the sexual impulse is a *distortion* of the miracle impulse. It occurs when the divine impulse of Love, which is always inclusive, is filtered through the belief in a physical body. The pure miracle impulse as Love, is never exclusive. It is the impulse to extend or share Love from mind *to* mind as one. However, through the split mind it becomes twisted and misdirected as a sexual impulse, when filtered through body identification. This split mind projects a multitude of inner and subsequently outer splits, which it strives to keep hidden from our conscious awareness.

2. One of the most alarming and yet unrecognized splits lies in the whole idea of romance *and* monogamy. The two are irreconcilable. Yet the ego is hell bent on selling us romantic fairytales that continue to fuel both its desire for the body *and* its desire for monogamy in relationships.

3. Jesus refers to this unconscious split as dissociation. He says that while we keep two opposing beliefs far apart in our awareness, each of them (as the split) can be sustained and appear to be equally real. However, when we bring these two opposing beliefs together into the light of conscious awareness, it becomes obvious that *one must go*. We finally recognize that they are indeed irreconcilable, and we must relinquish the one that is not real.

4. One of those most heavily defended, unconscious splits lies in the myth of romantic love. Everyone wants it – yet within the world of special relationships, it is the most significant cause of conflict and pain. Nowhere will we see the ego's curse more vividly enacted than through the special, romantic relationship.

a. *"Dissociation is a distorted process of thinking whereby two systems of belief which cannot coexist are both maintained. If they are brought together, their joint acceptance becomes impossible. But if one is kept in darkness from the other, their separation seems to keep them both alive and equal in their reality. Their joining thus becomes the source of fear, for if they meet, acceptance must be withdrawn from one of them. You cannot have them both, for each denies the other. Apart, this fact is lost from sight, for each in a separate place can be endowed with firm belief. Bring them together, and the fact of their complete incompatibility is instantly apparent. One will go, because the other is seen in the same place."* T-14. VII.4:3-10

5. The ego's sexual appetite was never meant to be monogamous! As an insatiable mating urge it is doomed to be impersonal and unfaithful by nature as a "body" appetite and not a Spirit impulse. Let's look at this split.

6. The sexual urge is not naturally monogamous. However, in a monogamous, romantic union, sexual fidelity is usually highly esteemed as *proof* of – exclusive – special love which could end if threatened by infidelity. So, we utilize the mating urge, which was not meant to be exclusive, to try to prove that a relationship *is* exclusive (monogamous). And then we get terribly upset when we discover that someone has "cheated" on us. Can we see the split? Is it glaring enough?

7. Love is confused with the body and sex and is mistakenly valued as "exclusive," limited to just two people who are said to be "in love." This is a classic example of special love whose central idol *is* the illusory body and not the eternal Spirit behind it.

8. *"The dream of the "perfect partner" is an attempt to find EXTERNAL integration, while retaining conflicting needs in the self."* Urtext, T-1.B.41 The inner conflict or split is hidden beneath our superficial desire for specialness as exclusive love, the body and its sensual pleasures.

9. The never-ending quest for orgasm is part of the ego's reward circuitry. In the monogamous "special" relationship,

the *impersonal fantasy* aspect of the sex urge is often driven underground because it poses an outright threat to the exclusive specialness dynamic in the relationship.

10. Many in monogamous, special relationships have believed they were sexually faithful. But if the fantasy of having sex with another body has occurred in the mind, then sexual infidelity has taken place. All form begins and continues as thought in the mind. Sexual fantasies including pornography are simply premeditated infidelity; the ego's plan for pleasure is really the unrecognized attraction to guilt.

11. Sexual disloyalty at the behavioral level is secondary to fantasizing about it in the mind. The ego mind that entertains sexual fantasies, even if it resists the temptation of acting them out in form, has already broken its idealistic promise of monogamy. The ego knows this, and that is why sex, as a body appetite, is one of its primary guilt-magnets for keeping us attracted to and hypnotized by separation, conflict, loss, disease, aging and death.

12. Special relationships glorify the body, and not the Spirit, on their central altar. There is an unwritten agreement between partners that each will continually objectify the body of the other, keeping body identification safe and secure. There is great need for our partner to stay faithful to only *our* body. The body then, and not our mind/ heart (eternal Spirit), is the primary focus for what we falsely believe constitutes loyalty in these relationships. The body is always the central idol on the altar of all special relationships.

13. As a result of making the body our primary identity and focus, there is a commonly dreadful fear of sharing feelings and thoughts honestly, deeply and intimately. This is the persistent fear of real emotional vulnerability, honesty and intimacy; of true authenticity. The ego says that if we dare to share this way with another that we will be rejected or abandoned. This fear of abandonment is the ego's terror of losing its principal witness to body identification as separation.

14. A major reason why the ego prefers to keep relationships between bodies rather than between minds is to protect *against* minds joining in Truth as Love. Because when minds (hearts) do join deeply in

true union, both the ego and the body fade into insignificance, while Love and true intimacy completely outshine them.

a. *"It is clearly insane to believe that by communicating you will be abandoned. And yet many do believe it. For they think their minds must be kept private or they will lose them, but if their bodies are together their minds remain their own. The union of bodies thus becomes the way in which they would keep minds apart." T-15.VII.11:3-6*

15. Changeless Love is total and infinite, which means it cannot be compartmentalized or terminated. Special love appears to be portioned out and can seem to change or end in our special relationships. This means that the seeming "love" we thought we had, was really just fear in disguise.

16. Real and conscious Love is *inclusive*, and not exclusive. It does not change. It is grounded in the heart-mind and not in the body. It is not interested in what it can "get" from another but is devoted to what it can "give" or share.-

17. Conscious Love, which is learned through Holy Relationship, is Love without fear or partiality. It is all inclusive. Whereas special love is self-centered, exclusive, partial and selective, which are the hallmarks of fear. Special, exclusive love is the impossible attempt to combine two wholly irreconcilable opposites, Love *and* fear. These two belief systems are total and can never be reconciled because the presence of one – either fear *or* Love – completely excludes the other.

18. In romantic relationships, if we completely remove the body from our awareness, what remains in the relationship that would sustain it? This is a revealing question! Unless there is the mutual goal of holiness in the sexual relationship then the body/sex (misdirected miracle impulse) remains the focus of all interactions, and guilt is the certain result.

9. SEX AND THE ILLUSION OF PEACE

1. Throughout this chapter, we've explored some radical myth-busting material on sex; but there is one more commonly valued myth that Jesus wants to straighten out. That is the illusion that sex, namely orgasm, results in healthy release, relaxation or peace.

2. Taking an honest look at this, we have seen that the sexual impulse, or drive for orgasm, is itself a distortion because it's an appetite to *take* and not to extend. It's an urge to get. While it appears to be a drive to achieve orgasm and the so-called aftereffects of release and relaxation, like everything the ego wants, it really delivers the opposite experience. This need for orgasm is the unrecognized, self-centered desire for bodily stimulation and identification which always results in conflict, and not peace.

3. So, while the ego claims it seeks pleasure, it conceals from us its hidden agenda for pain. There is *no* genuine release from tension in orgasm. Jesus explains that stress is the result of *unexpressed* miracle impulses; namely unexpressed "selfless" Love which *is* the miracle-drive itself. This stress and the numerous problems that it causes, arise from unshared expressions of the all-inclusive Love that transcends self-interests.

4. Through the ego we mistakenly believe that our personal pleasure and gain are our top priority so we dedicate our body and life to this aim. The drive for orgasm is the ego's self-centered attempt to distort the impersonal, miracle impulse and willfully divert it into a "personal" climax through the physical senses.

5. This diversion as orgasm, which *blocks* the miracle impulse's universal objective, is in stark contrast to extending and sharing it unreservedly with others through the heart. Orgasm actually *increases* the accumulated stress (guilt) of not expressing and extending the miracle-drive as selfless Love. In reality, orgasm is a *blocking* of Love and life force and consequently, a projection of this "lack of Love" onto the body as anxiety, depression, illness, and pain.

a. *"Tension is the result of a building-up of unexpressed miracle-impulses. This can be truly abated only by releasing the miracle-drive, which has been blocked. Converting it to sexual libido merely produces further blocking. Never foster this illusion in yourself, or encourage it in others. An "object" (body) is incapable of release, because it is a concept which is deprived of creative power. The recognition of the real creative power in yourself AND others brings release because it brings peace." Urtext, T-1.B.41 y*

b.   *"Mind cannot be made physical, but it can be made manifest through the physical if it uses the body to go beyond itself. By reaching out, the mind extends itself. It does not stop at the body, for if it does it is blocked in its purpose." ... "Help and healing are the normal expressions of a mind that is working through the body, but not [in] it." ... "Learning must lead beyond the body to the re-establishment of the power of the mind in it. This can be accomplished only if the mind extends to other minds, and does not arrest itself in its extension. This arrest is the cause of all illness, because only extension is the mind's function." T-8.VII.10:4-6,11:2,12:6-8*

6.   Through the ego thought system we have no idea what would bring us relief or peace. It demands we look in all the wrong places, especially through the body and in our special relationships.

7.   In the Urtext of *A Course in Miracles*, Jesus clarifies a common confusion in regards to sex:

a.   *"Inappropriate sex relaxes only in the sense that it may induce physical sleep. The miracle, on the other hand, is an ENERGIZER. It always strengthens, and never depletes. It DOES induce peace, and by establishing tranquility (not relaxation) it enables both giver and receiver to enter into a state of Grace. Here his miracle-mindedness, (not release from tension) is restored". T-1.B.41 x*

8.   All tension comes from independent, self-seeking attempts to satiate or gratify our own desires, or solve problems *apart* from Holy Spirit. For example, issues like decision making, concerns or worries, pleasure-seeking, pride, attack, defenses, making plans, etc., could all be solved by inviting the Holy Spirit to help us see

the real issue and to assist us to accept its one solution to every concern, as the Atonement.

9. Real expressions of Love, as the miracle-drive, transcend *self*-interests. When stress is present then it's not the *self*-gratification of orgasm we need. On the contrary, it is true intimacy via honest, vulnerable and defenseless communication that we need. It is communicated via forgiveness of self and/or others, tenderness, affection, authenticity, comfort and nurturing. These bring real peace because they help to bring us back into our heart and into the present moment. Only from this place of authenticity can we truly join with another and find the release of tension and therefore, peace.

10. MIRACLE-DRIVES VS. PLEASURE-DRIVES

1. The Holy Self's interpersonal miracle-drives as miracle-impulses are undistorted expressions of Love as God's eternal and uninterrupted Life force. Because they transcend self-interests, they *restore* true communication. These miracle-impulses are infinite in number and emerge naturally from the all-inclusive Love we are as the one Holy Self, shared with all our brothers.

2. The miracle-drive's benefits are preserved and increased as they are constantly extended or given away. They always transcend self-interests and therefore *can be shared,* thus it is in their *extension* that they bring true release from guilt and fear – as healing – both for the giver and the receiver of the miracle-impulse.

3. Because the miracle-drive is interpersonal and inclusive, it eclipses the ego's desire for personal gratification.

4. In contrast, the ego's personal pleasure-drives which are body centered *cannot be shared* (self will). They *block* true communication. Because they are personal and self-directed, they siphon to and through the illusory body, which terminates their *original* goal of *extension.* Just like pain and sickness, their purpose is to make the body image real, as an idol apart from God. This safeguards the unconscious guilt the ego *needs* to guarantee interpersonal conflict

and ensures that the body will be attacked, sicken, age and die. These personal pleasure-drives serve to *intercept and block* Love as God's eternal Life force, causing sickness.

5. Whatever we seek through a personal will alone, whether it be the avoidance of pain or the seeking of pleasure, serves to divert our attention from *closing the gap with our brother*, which is the one function that would give us *everything*, including immunity to the ego's laws of sickness..

6. Seeking personal pleasure independently from God engenders guilt because it bolsters the illusion that we are autonomous, separate from God and our brothers. But God's Will is *union* and the pure miracle impulse is directed solely toward creating *this* experience. All suffering, conflict and illness are brought about by not only blocking these divine impulses but are also the direct result of the unavoidable buildup of *unexpressed* miracle impulses.

7. The ego's compulsion to sequester personal pleasure and avoid pain, actually *arises* from an accumulation of unexpressed (unshared) miracle impulses. In trying to "get" its own needs met *exclusively,* it overlooks the only way to realize that all our needs are *already* met – by genuinely extending or sharing with others; by serving others and by forgiveness. These acts of *sharing* allow the miracle-impulses to *extend and increase,* thereby *unblocking* our own accumulated miracle-impulses. Emotional and physical healing are the result of this Loving extension because the cause of these ills – the buildup of unexpressed miracle-impulses – has been recognized and corrected.

   a. *"Learning must lead beyond the body to the re-establishment of the power of the mind in it. This can be accomplished only if the mind extends to other minds, and does not arrest itself in its extension. This arrest is the cause of all illness, because only extension is the mind's function."* T-8.VII.12:6-8

8. This does not mean we give up pleasure but it does mean, when faced with temptation by the ego, we need to ask, "What is this for? Is it a self-directed pleasure drive? Or is it a miracle-driven impulse to genuinely extend or share?"

9. Our natural tendency as Love is to share, because by sharing Love

and forgiveness, they are magnified exponentially for others and our Self too. Giving is how to *keep it* by God's Law. By *not* sharing or giving ... is how to ensure loss for ourselves. Holding grievances is one way we block the miracle-drive's extension. Using the body to seek pleasure independently from Spirit – making the body our idol – is another form of blocking Love. This turns the unforgiven fear onto the body as attack while it blocks the Life force's extension of Love. This is the singular underlying cause of disease and death.

10. To use the body for two entirely conflicting purposes – communication *and* attack – must result in suffering and death. The body is not an "end" in itself. When correctly perceived, the body is purely a *means* by which we learn to attain the single goal of undivided forgiveness of our mistaken perception. Jesus speaks of the necessity to unify our *purpose* for the body if we sincerely desire to awaken from separation.

a. *"To communicate is to join and to attack is to separate. How can you do both simultaneously with the same thing and not suffer? Perception of the body can be unified only by one purpose. This releases the mind from the temptation to see the body in many lights, and gives it over entirely to the One Light in which it can be really understood. To confuse a learning device (body) with a curriculum goal is a fundamental confusion that blocks the understanding of both."T-8.VII.12:1-5*

11. Recall that all personal pleasure seeking arises from fear because it comes from a false self that believes its will is independent from God's. Attempting to succeed in fulfilling itself "alone," through its own will, ensures its own body's demise. Only what can be *genuinely shared* is the Will of God. Personal will is exclusory, while the shared Will of God is the all inclusive light, the Love and the Life force that keeps us on purpose, happy, healthy and peaceful.

a. *"Remember that the Holy Spirit interprets the body only as a means of communication."..."The ego separates through the body. The Holy Spirit reaches through it to others. You do not perceive your brothers as the Holy Spirit does, because you do not regard bodies solely as a means of joining minds and uniting them with yours and mine. This interpretation of the body will change your mind entirely about its value. Of itself it has none."*

"If you use the body for attack, it is harmful to you. If you use it only to reach the minds of those who believe they are bodies, and teach them [through] the body that this is not so, you will understand the power of the mind that is in you. If you use the body for this and only for this, you cannot use it for attack. In the service of uniting it becomes a beautiful lesson in communion, which has value until communion [is.]"

... "Communication ends separation. Attack promotes it. The body is beautiful or ugly, peaceful or savage, helpful or harmful, according to the use to which it is put. And in the body of another you will see the use to which you have put yours." T-8.VII.2:1,3-7,3:1-4,4:1-4

II. SAME SEX UNIONS

1. Along with bisexuality and heterosexuality, homosexuality is one of the three main categories of sexual orientation within the ego's body-identified dream of separation. As you may have realized, in order to awaken from the dream, the central belief to be healed is that we are both a body *and* mind. Our conviction in and attachment to the body identity *is* the split mind.
2. Issues concerning gender or sexual orientation can often act as decoys which lead us right back into the mistaken body identity. A body is a body and is completely neutral, regardless of gender or sexual orientation. Categorizing the body based on sexual orientation only serves to further hide our one shared, majestic and Holy Self.
3. I love Jesus' simple but extraordinarily powerful question in the *Course*, a question which He encourages us to ask anytime we seem to be confused about a particular choice: "What is it *for*?" In

other words, whichever sexual orientation we may be, to ask, "What do I use sex *for*?" What is my intent? Am I using it for independent pleasure seeking, apart from Spirit? Is it for the self-gratifying pursuit of orgasm as the primal mating urge? And, do I want to learn to use sex for the purpose of true intimacy and bonding instead?

4. In the earlier Urtext dictation, Jesus does say that homosexuality is inherently more risky (error prone) than heterosexuality. He says that homosexuality *always* involves misperception of the self *or* the partner, and generally both.

5. Recall that the primary temptation in sex is to objectify our self or our partner as bodies instead of pure, innocent Spirit. The body in this case and not the Spirit is valued. Jesus reminds us that this is what happens when we use orgasm for any purpose other than procreation. Sex undertaken in same sex unions is never for the purpose of procreation. The lustful pursuit of orgasm (mating impulse) must be curtailed in exchange for the practice of genuine bonding behaviors. Unless there is a mutual goal of real intimacy, true Love as the one shared Holy Self will sadly be eclipsed by preference for the ego's body identity.

a. *"As was said before, homosexuality is inherently more risky (or error prone) than heterosexuality, but both can be undertaken on an equally false basis. The falseness of the basis is clear in the accompanying fantasies. Homosexuality ALWAYS involves misperception of the self OR the partner, and generally both." -Urtext*

A. Valid Questions About Same-Sex Unions

1. Regarding this section on same sex unions, a dear friend and colleague of mine asked two important questions which I believe deserve to be answered here:

2. **Question #1:** "There are two areas that I hit up against and would love some clarity. One is the statement that "homosexuality always involves misperception of the self or the partner, and generally both." If I perceive the other as a body then "yes;" a body-object to populate my fantasy and remain separate

from Love. But if the Love is genuinely past the body and an affirmation of the Holy Self then is that still a misperception? In other words, it seems like homosexuality is equated with body fantasy only. What I understand is any attraction to a body (whether it be same sex or opposite sex) is a denial of the Holy Self. Any choice to see Spirit instead of body (regardless of the partner's sex) is the beginning of the Holy Relationship."

3. **Answer #1:** Generally, there are three phases of healing our sexual appetite. The second phase would be using "sex to heal." I believe that this phase, although not intended specifically for procreation, can still be used by Holy Spirit. Remember that Holy Spirit is not concerned with the "behavioral level," however He is concerned with the *intent* beneath our particular behavior. Is it a selfless intent? And is it aimed at bonding rather than fulfilling the lustful mating impulse?

4. Saying this, a body is a body regardless of sexual orientation and preference. Any attraction to a body is a denial of the Holy Self and that is why the attraction itself needs to be given to Spirit for divine repurposing. Therefore, if the *intent* between two consenting, same sex individuals was to use sex specifically to "bond" and heal rather than to pursue their own independent orgasms, then Spirit must be present in that Loving intent.

5. **Question #2:** "The second area is the statement that the only purpose for sex is procreation. Is this not still ego land? Creating more 'illusory' bodies and making the dream seem more real? Sex is by definition an expression of the body which is the split mind. Whether it's sex for pleasure or sex for procreation isn't it still all just reinforcing the belief in ego?"

6. **Answer #2:** Jesus originally made an important point in the Urtext, saying that in the beginning of the dream of bodies, there was just one valid reason for sex, procreation:

a.   *"Sex was intended as an instrument for physical creation to enable Souls to embark on new chapters in their experience, and thus improve their record. The pencil was NOT an end in itself. (See earlier section.**) It was an aid to the artist in his own creative endeavors. As he made new homes for Souls*

and guided them thru the period of their own developmental readiness, he learned the role of the father himself. The whole process was set up as a learning experience in gaining Grace."
-Urtext, T-1.B.40 d

7. Let's take another look at the preceding statement from Jesus. Originally, there was a largely selfless intention set, to procreate specifically to enable souls who agreed to dream of separation to progress toward awakening from the ego dream of bodies, time and death. In addition, parents would grow in grace by learning to be selfless through taking on the roles of mother/father.

8. There is also value in procreation because we cannot overcome our belief in and value of the body unless we have one. Remember that we cannot transcend the body through death. Those souls who believe they have indeed died will have to incarnate once again. Thus through the illusion of physical birth, souls are given numerous opportunities to choose to awaken from the body dream altogether.

9. In the long dream of time, bringing in a new soul furthers its opportunities to form Holy Relationships and to finally triumph over all that it originally made for separation, including the body. This is nothing short of another chance to awaken from the ego's amnesia completely. Therefore, I would say that every decision to procreate, either conscious or unconscious, offers the child and parent another chance at awakening from the body identity.

10. This initial and lofty intention for sex that Jesus speaks of soon deteriorated. It went from one of enabling new souls to grow, and for parents to gain grace by learning selfless parenting, to becoming a selfish, pleasure-seeking, recreational pastime in which the body, and not the Spirit, was idolized. Yet where there is a sincerely selfless intent to raise children, Holy Spirit can join because there is one unified Will. Only Love can be shared.

11. Let me explain. When we show-up and genuinely make a deliberate choice in which we do not see our interests as apart from someone else's, God is there. Love, innocence and healing are there. Higher guidance is there. We are aligned with God's Will and because of this we are more inclined to choose to follow Spirit's guidance and further develop our trust in Love rather than in fear.

12. In a heartfelt desire to use sex for the purpose of becoming a parent, to procreate, we align with God's Will automatically by making that single choice to see another's interests (the child) as not apart from our own. A selfless Holy Instant occurs in which Love enters. This is why, in genuine procreation, Jesus encourages us to ask Him to join in the decision.

  a. *"The sex impulse IS a miracle impulse when it is in proper focus. One individual sees in another the right partner for "procreating the stock" ... and also for their joint establishment of a creative home. This does not involve fantasy at all. If I am asked to participate in the decision, the decision will be a Right one, too." - Urtext, Chapter One*

13. In contrast, sex aimed at personal pleasure-seeking, whether same sex or heterosexual, alienates God's Will by its very nature, which is that it cannot be meaningfully shared. Two, false body-selves join in fantasy. Nothing happens. Only reality can be shared. Illusions cannot. The decision's intent is self-seeking, unlike a genuine and selfless choice to bring a soul into the dream so it can progress toward awakening.

14. Jesus says, *"Homosexuality always involves misperception of the self or the partner, and generally both."*

15. If procreation is the only valid use of sex as Jesus tells us, then in same sex unions there is no valid use of sex. Why? Because there is no chance of conceiving children via conception. So when Jesus says that homosexuality always involves misperception of the self or the partner, it's because their sexual unions are never for the purpose of conscious procreation, enabling new souls – children – to embark on their awakening journey. I must admit that many heterosexual encounters also preclude procreation... however "some" do procreate consciously.

16. When there is no chance of using sex specifically for procreation, as in same sex unions, the compulsion toward self-gratifying, lustful sex may be more persistent than in heterosexual unions. In this instance, the core purpose of love-making is never for procreation. Hence there may be more propensities to sexually objectify the body of one's partner and our own.

12. POLYAMORY – OPEN SEXUAL RELATIONSHIPS

1. Polyamory is the practice or condition of participating simultaneously in more than one serious romantic or sexual relationship with the knowledge and consent of all partners.

2. In Jesus' teachings about the distorted and misdirected miracle-impulse – the sex impulse – it does not matter whether we seek the body's self-gratification through one sexual partner or many. The fundamental question remains the same. "Who" is the one that seeks self-gratification through the body? The answer is also always the same. This seeking "self" is the body identity and not the Holy Self. And the more one seeks for sexual release, as with all seeking for completion through the body, the more they unintentionally accumulate unconscious guilt.

   a. *"The ego regards the body as its home, and DOES try to satisfy itself through the body." T-4.II.7:8*

3. Either a monogamous or a polyamorous agreement in romantic relationships is still an attachment to sex and thus to the body itself. The body is not sinful nor Holy. It is entirely neutral. The point here is to discern the *use* to which we put the body. What do we use it *for?* Are we using it for personal gain? Or are we using the body with Holy Spirit for His purpose which is to prove we are not the body?

4. The underlying lesson in all relationships is to learn not to see our brothers as bodies, and not to exploit them through the false self's pleasure drives, but to look *beyond the body* to the Christ within. And to join them there in the continuous Love we share.

   a. *"Your question should not be, "How can I see my brother without the body?" Ask only, "Do I really wish to see him sinless?" T-20.VII.9:9*

   b. *"A mind and body cannot both exist. Make no attempt to reconcile the two, for one denies the other can be real. If you are physical, your mind is gone from your self-concept, for it has no place in which it could be really part of you. If you are spirit, then the body must be meaningless to your reality." W-96.3:4-7*

5. The ego may try to use the following quote out of context in an attempt to justify its unrelinquished attachment to personal gratification via the distorted miracle impulse (sex).

   a. *"It is sure that those who select certain ones as partners in any aspect of living, and use them for any purpose which they would not share with others, are trying to live with guilt rather than die of it." T-16.IV.4:5*

6. To the ego, this may appear as if Jesus is advocating multiple sex partners. It may seem to be a vote against monogamy and an encouragement toward polyamory if seen through the body identity's filter. It will reason that monogamy is a form of specialness because sex is limited to just two people exclusively, and not shared with others.

7. It could then imply that sex as an expression of love should not be limited or exclusive, but freely shared. However, this theory can only be believed through a fundamental confusion: that sex equals joining, or love, and that bodies *can* unite.

8. What the ego does not want to acknowledge is that sex is *not* Love, and that bodies *cannot* join. Only minds can unite. Remember the ego's profound confusion around Love and sex. It mistakenly believes they are one and the same. I believe the point Jesus makes in this preceding passage is that Love is not special. It has nothing to do with the body, sex or otherwise. Real Love is the sharing of minds, especially the extension of forgiveness. It's actually the undoing of the very special, private mind that employs the body to protect its exclusivity. In special, romantic relationships two private minds, each committed to keep their thoughts private, attempt to join through the illusory body which is impossible.

   a. *"For they think their minds must be kept private or they will lose them, but if their bodies are together their minds remain their own. The union of bodies thus becomes the way in which they would keep minds apart. For bodies cannot forgive. They can only do as the mind directs." T-15.VII.11:5-8*

9. In special relationships the ego makes a pledge of allegiance to maintain *exclusivity* in love, placing the illusory body and not the

Spirit at the center of all its unions. Exclusivity, to the ego, is love. However, love is really hate when it's ruled by exclusivity. This is the ego's purpose for special relationships. *Love is not special.* Unless Love, which is of the mind and not the body, is *inclusive* and shared by all, then it's not really Love but its opposite.

10. This means that if the *purpose* of the relationship is not willingly shared with all alike then it is not the Holy Spirit's purpose. And if it's not His purpose then it must be the ego's.

11. Love is total, not partial. Fear (as hate) is also total, not partial. And the two, Love and fear cannot by any means be merged. Because they are mutually exclusive they cannot coexist in awareness at the same time. Again, the appearance of one completely denies the other.

a. *"You cannot enter into real relationships with any of God's Sons unless you love them all and equally. Love is not special. If you single out part of the Sonship for your love, you are imposing guilt on all your relationships and making them unreal. You can love only as God loves. Seek not to love unlike Him, for there is no love apart from His. Until you recognize that this is true, you will have no idea what love is like."* T-13.X.11:1-6

12. In our transition from special to Holy Relationships, we are not asked to give up sex. However, we are encouraged to give it to Holy Spirit to be divinely repurposed. This can be a very soft and Loving transition when two people join in this mutual goal, as previously described in the sections titled *The Loving Antidote - Bonding* and *If You're Not Ready, Don't Fight Yourself. Healing the Sexual Appetite,* found later in this chapter, further describes this Loving transition to Holy Relationship.

a. *"When the body ceases to attract you, and when you place no value on it as a means of getting anything, then there will be no interference in communication and your thoughts will be as free as God's."* T-15.IX.7:1

13. SEX AND DEATH - THE LAST TWO DEFENSES

1. In 2014 I underwent a few very intense months of confusion and Sclf-doubt. I told myself it was *(small-s)* self-doubt, that the ego was undergoing yet another tidal wave of undoing and unknowing. However, as the presence of peace returned, the clarity with which I had heard Jesus' Voice before the period of confusion also returned. Just in case I may have been tempted to doubt this, there was an increasing experience of innocence and joy which I know to be the unmistakable hallmark of Spirit's presence.

2. I sat there asking, "What was this period of disorientation *for?"* My answer came, and it was not for the reasons I had thought – not at all. While I felt at the time that I had slid back, that something went awry, Spirit kept quietly reaffirming that this period, as intensely uncomfortable as it was, was a necessary period of "contrast" (between fear and Love). It would somehow help to quicken my decision to make a permanent and unequivocal choice for only Love, only joy, regardless of whatever appearances seemed to manifest themselves.

3. There are many spiritual pathways that assist in leading us eventually to the Christ I AM. However, Jesus' path of Atonement and miracles is the quickest (in the dream of time) precisely because the miracle *collapses* time and space by reversing all the laws of the world.

4. Yet at the crucial core of this teaching, the very last thing we want to recognize and therefore literally relinquish is the concept of physical death. Within the grand scope of our hierarchy of illusions, the concept of death is the most revered and heavily defended. It is our final block to the full embodiment of the Christ I AM.

5. To the ego, death is the irrefutable proof that we *are* the body and not the incorruptible Holy Self; that the illusory body is more powerful than the mind that made it. The pressing finality of death makes sure that we spend each life obsessing as the illusory body, clinging to its fleeting pleasures while defending it from the persistent threat of death.

6. Take the concept of physical death away and suddenly we're faced with a terror far more threatening – the *fear of life* as our shared Identity, the Holy Self. This is life as Love without opposite; a body and world whose entire purpose is reversed from the one we know now.

7. The attraction to death as a means to *save* us from awakening to the eternal and incorruptible life and Love that we share is deeply unconscious. This attraction to death is further intensified by our fear of it. As Jesus teaches in the *Course*, what we fear we make real and therefore attract! It follows then that the more we identify as a body, the more we attract death.

8. The second most popular, yet most unrecognized defense against knowing our Self as the Holy Son of God, is the concept of sexual desire, a "getting" appetite. As explained, this desire is believed to be very natural, is commonly sought after, and is rarely, consciously aligned with Holy Spirit's Will. Nearly all sexual desire (except for conscious procreation) arises from the false self and its compulsion to seek its completion through the body.

A. Sexual Desire

1. Jesus teaches that the sexual impulse is a distorted and misdirected miracle impulse. The pure undistorted miracle impulse is impersonal, inclusive, unconditional, undivided Love and does not dwell within a body and its appetites. For it to appear to do so would require that the miracle impulse's divine state of all-inclusive Love be twisted into an appetite that seeks only to *get pseudo love* from another separate body. The presence of body identification always blinds us to Spirit identification. We either see and thus relate to the body of another, or we desire true union and join with the Spirit in our brother or sister.

2. Because the inappropriate use of sexual desire requires the value and perception of separate bodies, each with private minds, it serves as a substitute for our acceptance of the Atonement, which is the acknowledgment of the one Son of God we are – as union.

   a. *"Appetites are "getting" mechanisms, representing the ego's need to confirm itself. This is as true of body appetites as it is of the so-called "higher ego needs." Body appetites are not physical in origin. The ego regards the body as its home, and tries to satisfy itself through the body. But the idea that this is possible is a decision of the mind, which has become completely confused about what is really possible." T-4.II.7:5-9*

3. The sexual pleasure drive is healed gradually, and eventually abandoned in stages. This undoing moves from "sex to separate" (which is specialness in order to get, to use another and to separate) to "sex to heal" (which is holiness in order to give, to heal and to unite). This stage involves learning how to communicate Lovingly and bond intimately rather than having orgasm as our goal in lovemaking. The sex to heal phase involves *transcending orgasm* which is termed as "TransOrgasmic Union."

4. Sexual healing then moves onto the final stage, "transcendence" (by Spirit) or what I term as divine androgyny, where sexual intimacy is no longer required or desired as a means to join because it is eventually replaced by an experience that magnificently exceeds this in all ways. Sex merely becomes valueless and unnecessary once true communication/union is experienced.

5. At the highest stages of healing the sexual pleasure drive, the heart becomes so completely infused with the presence of God, that the physical body is wholly released to the Christ. It is no longer "my" body but becomes the Holy Self's body. In this divine amalgamation, the body itself as an "effect" of this Love becomes immune to the destructive laws of the ego, responding only to the Laws of God. It begins to lose its density, having been released of guilt and fear. It no longer represents the need to block complete joining of hearts and minds. The body is required less and less to physically join in Love, as true union now takes place at a much higher level.

6. The last thread of ego's desire for specialness, together with the desire to seek pleasure apart from God – is retained through the sexual desire. As this thread is wholly unraveled, so is the sexual desire relinquished once and for all. In the final stage of healing in a body, specialness is wholly surrendered.

7. In essence, we outgrow sexual desire and it gently falls away. There is not the slightest feeling of sacrifice here because the magnitude of what has come to replace it makes the sexual desire pale in comparison. This final phase is not to be confused with the body's progressive falling away of sexual desire due to menopause, illness, old age, etc., or the egoic discipline of forced celibacy.

8. Sexual desire is neither right nor wrong. Like all other body appetites, it is neutral. It all comes down to what we are using it *for*. Because it is an appetite through which we seek sensual pleasure apart from God, it's also an appetite that can bring pain through its propensity to increase unconscious guilt. Regardless of the particular body appetite (food, sex, etc.) the real question is, "Which inner teacher do we practice them with?" Is it with the ego? Or is it with Spirit?

9. All appetites employed as substitutes for the Love and Will of God within, will lead to death because of their purpose. They all share the same goal, which is to make the body real, to establish its reality as a *replacement* for the Holy Self within. Therefore, they are unconscious attempts at self-attack. Anything we use to attempt to prove the body real, whether good or bad, secretly seeks death. This is the core of the ego thought system.

B. Transcending the Birth and Death Cycle

1. Getting back to the earlier period of confusion and disorientation for me, I now see some wonderful clarity and purpose in it. It was perfect to help teach me something very important.

2. Around 2006 when my own sexual desire fell away, I was so overwhelmingly elated that I can't even find the words to express it here. Preceding it however, there were two years of deep-seated sentimental sadness as I saw the utter futility of the romantic, special relationship and how it was used as a replacement for our Holy Self. In it I recognized the ego's multi-dimensioned plan for self-sabotage through its special desire for exclusivity. At last I recognized just why we're so attracted to the romantic relationship. And this was extremely sobering to say the least!

3. In all of this, I felt finally free of the insidious distraction of this

desire… until eight years later when earlier in 2014, for a brief moment in time, it felt as if the window to this primal and deeply rooted human desire had flashed open once again. This was a window that I was sure was not only shut, but had long since disappeared.

4. I cannot describe the utter confusion that this caused for me at the time. It simply did not make any sense because it was the antithesis of what I deeply knew to be true (for me). I dropped into a period of extreme self-doubt and allowed myself to fall into critical self-admonishment.

5. What if I had unknowingly done a sexual bypass? Was it possible that I had not really overcome the sexual desire after all because I had not fully integrated it? And what if this window opening was a sign that I needed to go back into it to make sure it was completely integrated before it could be fully transcended? I was so utterly confused! However, as I regained my own inner Compass again, the fog of self-judgment and confusion lifted. And this is what was revealed.

6. There are teachings about the need to integrate the sexual desire in order to progress spiritually, and to become whole. And I'm pretty sure there is some truth in this. After all, there were and still are many spiritual teachers who enjoy a full and integrated sex life.

7. These teachings are very helpful for awakening here *in* the ego dream. However, the deeper teachings of Jesus take one extraordinary leap beyond this. These teachings aim at no less than waking completely *from* the dream of birth and death altogether, through Atonement, by overcoming the ego's central dream of the body and death.

8. It cannot be stated often enough that mistaking our identity as the body *is* the split mind. Not just part of the split mind, but *all* of it. The entire ego dream rests on having mistaken our self and others as the body identity which enslaves the body to its laws of separation, suffering, decay and death. Quite literally, belief in the body as a replacement for our Holy Self *is* the attraction to death. This is precisely why, if we really want to awaken *from* the dream and not just in it, everything we use the body for, including the body's senses and appetites must be repurposed by Holy Spirit.

9. It has been brought to my attention that in order to awaken *from* the dream of birth, death, time and space, and not just *in* it, (as many awakened masters have before) the body itself, including the sexual desire, must be given over and wholly transcended, not by the spiritual ego but by the Grace of Spirit itself.

10. After physical death as our greatest defense against awakening, sexual desire remains the second strongest defense against awakening fully to the Christ I AM. As such, if the thread of sexual desire remains unrelinquished by the Grace of Spirit, it will, by necessity and function, draw us back *into* the body. Apart from death, the sexual desire is the most powerful and magnetic attraction back into the birth and death cycle (separation). As I said before, all body appetites share the same purpose – to make the body real and compelling as a substitute for the Holy Self. The inevitable cost of this substitution is the never-ending cycle of sin, guilt and fear, which in turn produces, conflict, sickness and death.

11. Awakening *from* the ego's dream and not just in it, means that we consciously release all bodily identity along with its destructive laws. We do this by learning to look past (forgive) all appearances of conflict and suffering, and instead call forth God's Truth by invoking the miracle, the Atonement, to heal the perception that caused the particular *appearance* of suffering.

12. The body/world's illusory laws are many. Time and space (matter), gravity, biological laws including heredity, medicine and disease, nutrition, etc. all make the list of illusory laws. The last of these that we're likely to question are sex, birth and death. To the ego, these laws are fixed and there is a hierarchy among them. To the miracle they are all the same; simply mistaken attempts to usurp the power of God. Therefore, all these illusory laws can be transcended or healed by God's Love, via the miracle. When we join Jesus in His Atonement path, we will eventually appreciate this pathway's awe-inspiring significance.

C. The Virgin Birth and Its Significance

1. More than two thousand years ago, Jesus was born as the result of a *virgin birth*. This is the miracle where Jesus was conceived in

the womb of his mother Mary through the Holy Spirit *without* the agency of a human father, and born while Mary was still a virgin. It was revealed to me just why His entry into the world was this way.

2. Jesus was born *exclusive* of the ego's law of conception where male sperm and female egg are required in the formation of a child. He was born of a virgin for good reason; to demonstrate that the Son of God (all of us) does not require the ego's laws in which to live, nor is he bound by any of them. They neither sustain him nor threaten him because he knows he is under no laws but God's. He is not the slightest bit affected or restricted by the ego's laws.

3. In Jesus' case, not even the basic law of human conception was required in order for Him to be born. Nor, as we later learn through His resurrection, was He bound by the so-called laws of death. Taking this further, Jesus also demonstrated that the belief that "death is the inevitable outcome of life" could not alter God's all-encompassing and eternal Law of Life. Jesus literally transfigured and then transcended the body identity entirely. In Jesus' resurrection he proved again that only God's Laws apply and that we are under no laws but God's. However, we cannot know and therefore experience the absolute freedom of God's Laws while we still choose to depend on the *illusory body identity* along with its so-called laws to sustain or protect us.

4. As stated earlier, sexual orgasm is a distorted form of the pure miracle impulse. Because it is a *misdirected distortion* of the miracle impulse of divine Love, it is really an expression of fear.

5. Jesus was not a product of the sexual act (fear) and therefore, He was not a product of the distorted miracle impulse. There was no sexual desire or consummation required for Him to be born into the world. He was an embodied demonstration that the world's laws had absolutely no effect on the power of God's Will made manifest through Him.

6. From page 35 of Helen's Notes, Jesus described his mother Mary's role in the moment of His own conception as, *"The only one that (has yet) conceived without any lack of love."* Jesus says here that Mary was the only one in the history of time itself who conceived *without any fear* (lack of Love). There was no

sex, – distorted miracle impulse – involved.

D. Wanting *and* Having are Mutually Exclusive

1. Jesus came into this dream to prove there was nothing in this world more powerful than God's certain Will via the Laws of God. His Will, joined with God's, literally reversed all the laws of this world. His Will has also transcended all bodily appetites including the sexual desire, on behalf of us all. When we are ready to receive it, we will. And we do so each time we accept the Atonement, the miracle.

2. In order to awaken *from* the ego's dream of birth and death, and not just *in* it, the unconscious attraction to the body identity must be repurposed and transcended. And this cannot be accomplished by personal will (resistance, repression or control) but only through our genuine wholehearted forgiveness of how we have used everyone and everything including the body, our self and God.

3. As we awaken through forgiveness and Atonement, we will all eventually allow the body's false appetites to fall away and be replaced by increasing and unending joy and Love.

4. Going back to my personal experience, I endured an excruciating contrast in having that window of sexual desire surface. It felt as if I had been sucked downward through a darkened tunnel, and back under the body's spell. The extreme contrast was felt so palpably. I realize that those eight years devoid of sexual desire were such a God send. However, if I had not felt that brief re-emergence of the sexual desire, I probably would never have appreciated the magnitude of contrast between the opposed states of desire (body) *and* desire-less-ness (Holy Self).

5. In the body identity's state of desire, which arises from a sense of lack, there is a never-ending pursuit of stimulation, distraction and seeking. And in this sexual-seeking via orgasm, there is no *finding* because the states of *wanting* and *having* are mutually exclusive.

6. While I still *seek* then I cannot know and bask in the gratitude that I already *have* everything. I will resist true surrender and receiving. As a result, there is a constant and often underlying state of deprivation that makes certain we're kept consumed by the relentless search to quench our desires. In this futile and never-ending search, the one true desire, the single Answer to every conceivable need we have, is left quietly unrecognized in the frenzied distraction of the chase.

7. There is no experience in this world that can remotely touch on the profound, cosmic heart centered orgasm of the divinely inspired *desire-less* state. Lastly, I am so filled with gratitude for that period of confusion and self-doubt. Without that dreadful anguish, I would not have been driven to be vigilant *only* for God's Love and guidance.

14. HEALING THE SEXUAL APPETITE

1. I mentioned in the section titled *The Loving Antidote - Bonding,* that there is a very helpful and practical program available to assist committed couples in their revolutionary transition from habitual mating (orgasm) to true intimacy and bonding. In the book, *Cupid's Poisoned Arrow* by Marnia Robinson, there is a twenty-one day program called, "The Ecstatic Exchanges." This is a wonderful tool to begin to showcase the extreme contrast between the lustful and empty mating impulse and the truly Loving, selflessness of authentic bonding.

2. Many of us who have been brain-washed by the mistaken belief that sex is Love and that orgasm is beneficial to the body's health and relationships, are also unconsciously afraid of *receiving* Love. This is the ego's fear of genuine, heartfelt communion via real, emotional intimacy. Because of the unwillingness to be wholly defenseless, which is a necessary step in learning how to genuinely *receive*, there is resistance to giving, or sharing affection and tenderness with our partner.

3. If we removed the goal of orgasm from sexual encounters, the next layer or block to heal would reveal itself. We would discover the ego's resistance to sincere emotional intimacy and honest communication. Many people unknowingly use orgasm to avoid this level of true

intimacy. Remember that the false self has used the pursuit of orgasm to mistakenly identify *as* the body, precisely to block our awareness from seeing our Self and our partner as one Holy Self.

4. The fear of true intimacy translates to the unconscious fear of Self-acceptance. There is fear of deep emotional transparency, vulnerability, defenselessness and radical self-honesty. Traditional sex, lust and orgasm are the means employed to *bypass* true emotional bonding or closing the gap with our self and our partner. In this respect, the resistance to engage in authentic, emotional bonding is *impotence*.

5. Real impotence has nothing to do with unsuccessful, sexual performance. Preoccupation with sexual performance is a smoke screen devised to protect us from having to go within to heal our fear of Love and union. Since nothing real transpires while the goal is orgasm and body identification, the ego thought system *is* literally impotent. Impotence is our *unwillingness* to drop our emotional defenses and engage instead in true union through radically honest, vulnerable and Loving interrelating.

6. The desire to heal and transform the sexual urge comes about when we have genuinely had enough of the downward spiral of orgasm-focused sex. For many, I feel this occurs as a result of having perhaps overindulged in the mating urge. They have experienced its destructive effects both in their relationships and their life. Only when a particular belief, value or behavior causes enough pain, are we open to healing it.

7. If there is resistance to healing the mating impulse, then this must be respected. Perhaps additional time spent in unconstrained fulfillment of the mating urge *without guilt* may accelerate the process. For those who resist these teachings and are not yet ready to embrace them, then this is perfect too. The timing is not right. We must trust that each one of us is perfectly guided and that nothing we experience is wasted. Whatever is chosen, let there be no judgment, guilt, shame or blame. Feeling guilty, shameful or blaming another will merely intensify feelings of separation and confusion which is certainly not Loving.

8. Both repression and indulgence of the mating urge are the same *if* it is the ego in control. It is not primarily about modifying our sexual behavior, but it *is* about changing our intent with the guidance of Holy Spirit. He is responsible for helping us to divinely repurpose the body and the sexual appetite. When we align our will with Holy Spirit and give our body appetites to Him to heal, we will be guided without guilt, judgment or blame. Self-acceptance is of utmost importance in this transition!

9. Jesus Himself also offers us His Loving assistance in this divine transition. He encourages us to invite Him in whenever there is temptation. And that includes *any* form of sexual attraction. Sexual attraction *is* the distorted miracle impulse; and this is where we can ask for the pure, heart-centered miracle instead:

    a. *"...invite Me to enter anywhere temptation arises. I will change the situation from one of inappropriate sexual attraction to one of impersonal miracle-working."* Urtext, T-1.B.40 i

    b. *"In a situation where you or another person, or both, experience inappropriate sex impulses, KNOW FIRST that this is an expression of fear. Your love toward each other is NOT perfect, and this is why the fear arose. Turn immediately to me by denying the power of the fear, and ask me to help you to replace it (with) love. This shifts the sexual impulse immediately to the miracle-impulse, and places it at MY disposal.*

    Then acknowledge the true creative worth of both yourself AND the other one. This places strength where it belongs. Note that sexual fantasies are ALWAYS destructive (or depleting), in that they perceive another in an inappropriate creative role. Both people are perceived essentially as "objects" fulfilling THEIR OWN pleasure drives. This dehumanized view is the source of the DEPLETING use of sex.

    "The love of God, for a little while, must still be expressed through one body to another. That is because the real vision is still so dim." - Urtext

c. *"Whenever your thoughts wander to a special relationship which still attracts you, enter with Him into a holy instant, and there let Him release you." T-16.VI.12:1*

10. Many who are on this path and desire to ask Holy Spirit in to help them transform their sexual relationships, are with partners who may likely find these teachings threatening to the relationship's specialness dynamic. We cannot change our partner. However, we can elect to heal our very own mindset by learning to "show-up" more authentically in all our communications. And this is where the tools in this book come in to help quicken the process: *The Seven Keys on page 572, The Seven Blocks to Fearless Relating on page 589, The Divine Switch from the Ego to the Holy Self on page 297, and The Seven Essential Principles of Forgiveness on page 591.*

11. When we find ourselves in what seems like a challenging relationship, it must be because we have unwittingly abandoned our Self. The ego is happy to sacrifice staying true to our Self, and trade authentic communication for "specialness" in its relationships, which results in blame, resentment and conflict. To change a challenging, special relationship demands that *we* show-up for our Holy Self regardless of the perceived disturbance to the specialness dynamic which it may cause. "Nevertheless, we can take comfort in knowing that it is our *willingness* to repurpose our relationships and bodily appetites with Holy Spirit that ensures that the way will be opened for us. He will arrange this in such a way that does not increase our fear, but brings us that certain peace that comes when we show-up authentically for ourselves in all that we say and do."

15. SEX AND DESIRABILITY - EXPOSING THE LIE

1. When our sense of worth is not securely anchored in God, but instead is misplaced in the body, we will appoint the body as our central idol, giving *it* authority over our mind. From this fundamental mistake we will make all decisions based on our need to defend the

body from harm, together with our desire to seek pleasure and completion through it.

2. Yet as we make our decisions apart from Holy Spirit, we end up experiencing guilt and fear of punishment. This unforgiven fear of retaliation colors almost all our decisions. Then, upon being projected outward, it results in every conceivable form of attack we encounter. Seeing this, we can safely conclude that all body identification results in some form of self-attack.

3. Let's look at the four major ways in which the ego keeps us fiercely identified with and protective of the belief we are the body:

    1) Special relating – Special relationships revolve around the body

    2) Sex/lust

    3) Desirability

    4) Illness

4. We've already discussed how the ego's special relationship dynamic is designed to reinforce our mistaken body identification. And in *The End of Death,* Vol. One, we talked about the ego's purpose for sickness as a defense against God and our Holy Self. The intention for this particular essay is to shed light on how the ego uses both women and men in its pursuit of sex and desirability to amplify the erroneous belief that our identity and our worth lies in the body.

5. Because the body is our accepted identity here in the dream, the beliefs that bolster our body identity are the most coveted and protected by the ego. In generalized discussion of heterosexual sex from the male perspective, the habituated desire to fantasize about, pursue and *have sex* with women is the core idol that sustains their body identity. To be affected by impotency, or not to have regular sex with a woman or women, literally equates to losing their purpose and identity. Many men believe that without sex, they will lose their value and status as a "man."

6. Statistics reveal that approximately thirty million men in the USA alone are affected by erectile dysfunction (impotence)* which often plays havoc with their sexual performance. I would guess that most still identify *as* the body, having fallen for the ego's hunger for lusty performance. Mistaking this for Love, they often resort to using phenomena (magic) such as "male enhancement" pills and testosterone in the hopes to reignite and improve their sexual performance. But in this seeming issue there is a profound and unconscious split which is rarely, if ever, recognized.

   Reference from Dr. Oz, The Dr. Oz Show, an attending physician at NY Presbyterian-Columbia Medical Center.

7. Let's recall that the body is an image in thought held in our mind (not brain). The false body- identified mind seeks personal pleasure, purpose and identity *through* the body (apart from God), which leads to increased guilt and self-attack.

   a. *"It is impossible to seek for pleasure through the body and not find pain. It is essential that this relationship be understood, for it is one the ego sees as proof of sin. It is not really punitive at all. It is but the inevitable result of equating yourself with the body, which is the invitation to pain. For it invites fear to enter and become your purpose. The attraction of guilt [must] enter with it, and whatever fear directs the body to do is therefore painful. It will share the pain of all illusions, and the illusion of pleasure will be the same as pain."* ... *"Under fear's orders the body will pursue guilt, serving its master whose attraction to guilt maintains the whole illusion of its existence. This, then, is the attraction of pain." T-19.IV.B.12,13:2-3*

8. When we read in the Urtext what Jesus tells us is the fundamental purpose for sex, i.e. procreation, we'll see that for most, the pursuit of orgasm as the mating urge is not used exclusively for procreation. It is more often revered as the pursuit of personal pleasure, namely lust and sexual fantasies.

9. All sexual fantasies *objectify the body,* thereby blinding us to the real, honest and vulnerable emotional intimacy required for a truly authentic and Loving relationship. Unfortunately, sex as lust

has been sold to the masses as a much sought-after recreational pastime. Jesus speaks of sexual fantasies:

a. *"Note that sexual fantasies are ALWAYS destructive (or depleting), in that they perceive another in an inappropriate creative role. Both people are perceived essentially as "objects" fulfilling THEIR OWN pleasure drives. This dehumanized view is the source of the DEPLETING use of sex."* A Course in Miracles Urtext, Chapter One

A. When We Abandon Our Selves

1. Men and women, regardless of sexual preference, suffer from the ego's treacherous confusion of lust with Love. The deeply denied and unconscious split for many millions of men is this: The ego harnesses the sexual drive (which is a distorted miracle impulse) and erroneously thinks it knows what it's *for* – personal pleasure. However, it hides its real objective beneath its personal pleasure-seeking, which is to accumulate the unconscious guilt necessary to kill the body (conflict, disease, aging, etc.). Hence, the pursuit of sexual pleasure without genuine heart to heart relating is a death wish. The hunt for lust is the hunt for death.

2. In the case of impotence and the desire for male enhancement medications, most men don't realize the terrible conflict that rages deep within their unconscious mind, and just how much they have abandoned themselves to this irreconcilable split. This is another example of the ego's inner war through confusing their purpose, relationships and identity with the illusory body and its meaningless pursuit of sexual performance.

3. For most men, the ability and potential to have sex *is* the root of their identity. They cannot even imagine existing *without* sexual fantasies and orgasms. When men are strongly misidentified with their sexuality (body) they will often abandon themselves to the enormous social pressure to perform sexually. If the ability to have sex is threatened by impotence, illness or accident, this loss of mistaken "identity" can often bring on depression and other forms of the ego's unconscious attack.

4. At the core of every person's being is the divine call to return our awareness to the changeless Love we are, which can only be experienced when we relate to our self and others, *beyond* the body. This is the Love which dwells at the heart of the Holy Relationship. This is where we take off our masks of body identity, comparisons and performance, and show up in our authenticity and humility, asking Holy Spirit to reveal the majesty of our shared Holy Self, the one that our mistaken body identification tried to erase.

5. Alternately, for a great number of women, the compulsion to be sexually *desirable* is the core idol that fuels body identification. For these women their perceived identity and value are directly in proportion to how desirable they are. The ego's sexual "bait and hunt" cycle is the basis for the entire commercial industry that fuels a woman's need to be ever improving her appearance, to stay competitive and to maintain her looks.

6. As for the many individuals who are not heterosexual, a similar dynamic is often played out. Those who identify with more masculine tendencies (the pursuer) take on the sexual hunting dynamic while those with more feminine tendencies (the pursued) are more likely to feel pressure to maintain their physical attractiveness, and therefore their desirability.

7. The need to be sexually desirable is the ego's underlying dependence on gaining *external* approval and acceptance through misidentifying and showcasing the body. Even adolescent girls who seek affection and genuine closeness are being tempted to abandon themselves to sexual pressure as a trade-off for pseudo intimacy.

8. We unknowingly abandon our Holy Self, employing the body on behalf of the ego to attract attention to the body. Both men and women often experience betrayal when the body is mistakenly idolized as our identity.

9. As we employ the body on behalf of the ego to attract attention to the body, we unknowingly abandon our Holy Self. Every belief and action invested in keeping the body as our central idol is an act of self-betrayal regardless of gender.

   a. *"Some hate the body, and try to hurt and humiliate it. Others love the body, and try to glorify and exalt it. But while the body stands at the center of your concept of yourself, you are attacking God's plan for salvation, and holding your grievances against Him and His creation, that you may not hear the Voice of truth and welcome It as Friend. Your chosen savior (body) takes His place instead. It is your friend; He is your enemy." W-72.7:2-6*

10. The body is a flimsy, ever changing shell, while our authentic Holy Self is the real and changeless "Beloved." Special relationships idolize the body for what it can offer, thus they overlook the true essence within each partner. In these relationships, especially where lust instead of Love is favored, the ego cannot resist going from body to body to pursue and maintain its false identification and cycle of self-betrayal and guilt.

11. The crazy thing is that we may invest enormous effort toward physical improvement in the hopes of becoming more sexually alluring, but for a great number of women, if they were to be radically honest, there is also a growing *resentment* toward men and the media for sexually objectifying their bodies. This is yet another example of how the split-mind works.

12. The ego mind allows only what it wants us to see and identify with, to support and sustain its view that we are the body, and not the infinitely Loving and powerful Holy Self. The schism between the desire to be sexually attractive and the accompanying resentment of being targeted by sexually objectifying behavior is a tremendously common blind spot for a large number of women.

13. Women who feed into female, sexual objectification unfortunately learn to "objectify" themselves. They become their own worst critic and it's all based on the ego's body confusion. To objectify means to dehumanize, depersonalize or externalize themselves. When women consent to being treated as sexual objects, they often view their own bodies from the objectifying onlooker's (pursuer's, media) perspective. Then they become preoccupied with their physical appearance and sexual value to others. This feeds into the habit of the ego's "self-objectification" which leads to shame and anxiety, and a turning away from their real, inherent value as the Holy Self.

14. Jesus speaks of the ego's unchallenged and largely unconscious and destructive use of the body:

a. *"Look upon all the trinkets made to hang upon the body, or to cover it or for its use. See all the useless things made for its eyes to see. Think on the many offerings made for its pleasure, and remember all these were made to make seem lovely what you hate. Would you employ this hated thing to draw your brother to you, and to attract his body's eyes? T-20.II.1:1-4*

b. *"Save it for show, as bait to catch another fish, to house your specialness in better style, or weave a frame of loveliness around your hate, and you condemn it to decay and death."* T-24.VII.4:5

15. As a woman myself, I was torn in my attitudes toward sex and desirability. In the past I had believed that physical attractiveness was a valuable asset. There were times when I was smitten by the media hype which taught that the way to keep a man interested was to look sexy. Looking "hot" gave me a better chance to keep my partner engaged and monogamous in relationship.

16. I could not deny that over time a terrible and eventually unbearable inner conflict arose. It involved two completely contradictory beliefs. One was my desire to be sexually attractive. And the other was a rapidly growing resentment toward my partner who wanted sex and kept telling me how physically "attractive" I was.

17. I could not help but see that his compulsive desire for sex had nothing whatsoever to do with us joining in union through deep, unconditional, abiding Love. Real Love makes no demands. It is unconditional. Yet here was this man who said he *needed* sex. *Who* needs sex? It must be the ego! A glimpse of what Jesus was trying to teach in the *Course* flashed in my mind, about inappropriate sexual desire being a misdirected and distorted miracle impulse. I saw that the mating impulse (sexual lust) is a self-seeking, pleasure drive and that if left unhealed, breeds resentment, conflict and eventually separation.

18. There was a period of heightened confusion for me. I (ego) valued desirability and definitely got a superficial ego boost when my partner acknowledged the body's looks. But there was always

this looming, yet deliberately distant contradiction running in the background of my mind. Later on, when my inner conflict was at an all-time high, I decided to be brave enough to give it a voice.

19. And this is what it said: "Deep down you want to know Love, a real and changeless Love that cannot be threatened. Except you cannot hope to experience this Love while you use the body as a decoy, as a lure for lust, and one that obscures the true emotional intimacy of real , heartfelt union, unencumbered by the body. Lust and Love are *opposites*. They cannot coexist."

20. Something inside me just knew that using the body as sexual bait or eye candy was disrespectful for both me and my partner. There was a visceral sense of the underlying objective behind the need to be sexually desirable. It was a shallow, body identified desire, and not deep, abiding Love. Through the intensifying conflict of my inner split, this previously unconscious and deep-seated contradiction became less and less attractive. There was an outright hypocrisy about it.

21. What a split! Needing to look sexually desirable and at the same time, feeling resentful of being objectified by men and the media. How many women have endured this hypocritical inner conflict?

22. Further, this largely unresolved conflict drives many women to fall victim to their own nightmare, a body image war. They tyrannize themselves, going to great lengths in various forms of Self abandonment, in an attempt to stay *relevant* through their bodies. Some examples of this deep-seated Self betrayal and abandonment many women are engaging in include liposuction, lip injections, Botox, implants, diet pills, surgery, tummy tucks, gym memberships, and all the while berating themselves because they think they *are* their body and that its condition defines their value in the world. These superficial and meaningless standards also breed inevitable jealousy, envy, hatred and self-deprecating comparisons, which furthermore make any true joining a virtual impossibility.

23. Sexual desirability does not equal true Lovability. It has nothing to do with Love and therefore bears no relation to our degree of worth or acceptance. All value, worth, Love, approval, validation, support, encouragement and empathy must first come from our own *Self value*. And this means not gauging our value on worthless sources like the body's appearance and sexual prowess.

24. Generally, men's inability to cease fantasizing and *objectifying* women's bodies feeds into the insecurity in women. And women have certain expectations of men that also feed into men's insecurities.

25. The entire issue around sexuality is a quagmire of ego strongholds in society's consciousness. Until we see them all as one and the same, i.e. the ego's heavy defenses to maintain body identification and therefore to block our experience of true union beyond body identification, we will continue to play into them and ensure that body identification is the world's god. Unfortunately, this cherished belief that we *are* the body always leads to the same certain outcome – physical death.

26. Once we have seen how the ego uses special relationships, sickness, sex and desirability as ways to bind us to the false belief we are the body, we can then choose to heal. We invite Holy Spirit to enter into our relationships to transform them, along with divinely repurposing the body. This includes asking Holy Spirit to heal all false education and conditioning around sex. We ask Him to help us mindfully repurpose how we view ourselves and our partner, along with what we are using sex *for*. It really boils down to whether we're ready to surrender the belief that we are the body, and whether we are truly ready to accept the one, shared Holy Self as our true Identity.

   a. *"You cannot wake yourself. Yet you can let yourself be wakened. You can overlook your brother's dreams. So perfectly can you forgive him his illusions he becomes your savior from your dreams. And as you see him shining in the space of light where God abides within the darkness, you will see that God Himself is where his body is. Before this light the body disappears, as heavy shadows must give way to light. The darkness cannot choose that it remain. The coming of the light means it is gone. In glory will you see your brother then, and understand what really fills the gap so long perceived as keeping you apart. There, in its place, God's witness has set forth the gentle way of kindness to God's Son. Whom you forgive is given power to forgive you your illusions. By your gift of freedom is it given unto you.*

"Make way for love, which you did not create, but which you can extend. On earth this means forgive your brother, that the darkness may be lifted from your mind." T-29.III.3:2-4:2

16. THE MIRACULOUS GIFTS OF HOLY RELATIONSHIP

1. The special relationships of this world are between false selves who do not recognize their divine Identity. Attempts at communication arise from a very deep and often unconscious sense of worthlessness and deprivation. We mistakenly look to others, or more accurately, we *use* others to fulfill us and alleviate our aching sense of not being enough; and when they don't or can't meet our small self's needs, we experience heartbreak or devastation. Then it seems that the illusion of love we shared with them declines or ends.

2. As we undo this false self-concept through forgiveness and Christ Vision, we lift the heavy veil that hides the light of our shared Holy Self. This changeless, eternal Self is pure light and it knows of no sin, guilt or fear, no darkness, no pain, no conflict, no loss, and no adversity. It *is* God's immaculate Will. As the light within is released we begin to see others, the body, the world, and our past in this light. Suddenly, instead of interpreting them through the dark lens of the separated self, we discover the sparkling miracles that were always there, but which were hidden by our unforgiven guilt.

3. As the small self concept dissolves – which is accelerated by Holy Relationship – this light within radiates increasingly so that we begin to see others and the world in this light. The light we *are* literally unites with and reveals the stunning light in others. This is the same divine light that Jesus refers to in the *Course* as the Great Rays.

4. When two or more companions join with Holy Spirit in one truly common goal of Holy Relationship, they accept the undoing of the greatest block to Love, which is the false self concept and its destructive purpose for the body.

5. In my own experience of Holy Relationship, the individual "me" that previously sought its completion from others, the body, and the world, has faded into the background. And what has come forth to take its place is almost indescribable because it is an experience of a Love that is not of this world; a changeless Love that cannot be threatened.

6. The ego's dark veil of terror has been lifted. The light of Love that shimmers within everyone and everything is being witnessed and felt deeply as I refuse to believe the false self's illusory witnesses to darkness in whatever form. What exactly happened?

7. There has been a comprehensive shift due to my ongoing Holy Relationships with my Holy companions. In my live-in relationship with Daniel we regularly experience what I can only describe as quantum episodes of light. These are not physical in nature, nor are they seen or felt through the body's five senses. As a matter of fact, they *eclipse* the body entirely.

8. Daniel, I and Coreen are having more frequent experiences of the Great Rays, which really defy explanation. Words, as symbols of symbols, can portray only a one-dimensional interpretation here. Yet it's a start. In our genuine, joint Holy Instants with each other, the holographic sense or experience of these Rays is felt at the core of our being and simultaneously radiating outward. It really is all inclusive. Being all embracing, this is a truly blessed state, a Holy Encounter that the ego has never even imagined, let alone felt.

9. Union with another through the Great Rays evokes the most overwhelming experience of unprecedented Love. A tsunami of gratitude and humility, this Love is so enormous and multi-faceted that it feels as if we can't even contain it. I would liken it to a divine G-force, as God Power. Some limited definitions of this might include: all consuming, awe-inspiring, all encompassing, breathtaking and wondrous, all at the same time.

a. *"In the holy instant, where the Great Rays replace the body in awareness, the recognition of relationships without limits is given you. But in order to see this, it is necessary to give up every use the ego has for the body, and to accept the fact that the ego has no purpose you would share with it."* T-15. IX.3:1-2

A. The Contrast of Human Love

1. In extreme contrast, the version of worldly love the false self seeks is self-centered, sacrificial, exclusive and special. Unfortunately, it is so extremely limited and body-centered that most people could hardly imagine Loving each other *without* the body. The body, what it does or does not do, what it offers or rejects, seems to circumscribe – or rather imprison – those engaging in this form of relationship. In addition to this mistaken perception of the body and its purpose in relationship, is the erroneous belief that we each have private minds with independent, personal agendas that can indeed clash with other private minds. The outcome of this belief is conflict and can even result in the termination of the relationship.

2. While we still believe we have a personal, private mind and that the body defines us, and we have not yet experienced the blinding contrast of tear-filled grace within true Holy Communion in a joint Holy Instant with another, then the ego often offers its cheap "substitute" for this true joining, in the form of sex; in particular, sexual orgasm. The ego would have us believe that this physical phenomenon is the pinnacle, the highest and most valuable joining we can have with another here in the dream. Yet when compared to a true, joint Holy Instant *without* the body's interference, orgasm is then recognized as a fraudulent "substitute," a severe limitation of the genuine Soul union, and changeless intimacy that is our God-given inheritance.

3. While sex is not wrong in itself, like all other body appetites, the real question is "what is it *for?*" In other words, is it being used to help to heal? Or is it lust driven, which serves to increase fantasies of body identification, together with escalating the ego's guilt and self-attack?

4. When we believe erroneously that we *are* the body, the changeless *Love we actually are* as the Holy Self, is seen as a threat. This translates to fear of Love and thus fear of the *pure* miracle impulse, which looks entirely past the body altogether, centering on the light we share equally with others. When we allow this light, it is often experienced as genuine emotional vulnerability and transparency, where the ego's mask of fear is fully removed.

5. Conversely, when the pure heart-centered miracle impulse is first encountered by the ego – as the divine desire to merge with another in mutual reverence – it often distorts it and then misdirects it. Instead of extending itself infinitely for healing, as a universal, unselfish, impersonal miracle impulse, it is diverted toward the illusory body converting it into a sexual impulse, or sexual attraction, which seeks a physical outcome in the orgasm.

6. Thus, the pure miracle impulse is curtailed by seeking self-gratification *through the body* instead of being extended, and thus shared selflessly from the heart as the profound expression of shared gratitude, intimacy and healing that it is. Instead of being accepted and extended limitlessly as Love, through the true intimacy of our heart center, it gets derailed through the body, as sexual attraction. And Love is then replaced with lust (fear).

7. This is what occurs when the ego "falls in love;" *special love* that is. Romance is the world's idealized model of special "love." The ego's exclusive, romantic love is an intoxicating and highly addictive substitute for the Love of God.

8. Two people engaged in satisfying ego desires attempt to superimpose an image of what the ego *prefers* over their treasured and changeless reality. The false self only wants the image or mask, and not the true gift of shared light which is the *only reality* of the person it claims to love. As the ego prioritizes separation over true union, the body is then mistakenly sexualized, bringing to the relationship a very fragile, and *pseudo* intimacy.

9. This is what Jesus meant in His earlier message about sex within the *Course's* Urtext:

    a. "*If the identification is with the body, consciousness may distort superconscious impulses by denying their source and seeking their impact in the orgasm. This is the result of 'mistaken identity.'*" The COA Annotated Edition, T-1.28.3:1-2

10. Sexual attraction's purpose is to hide and divert the pure miracle

impulse. In this, it makes the body the object of its pleasure and yet all *real pleasure* arises exclusively from doing God's Will. And that is why when we're tempted by sexual desire, Jesus encourages us to ask Him to help to transmute the misdirected miracle impulse (sexual attraction) so it can then be extended as unimpeded healing:

a. *"In a situation where you or another person, or both, experience inappropriate sex impulses, KNOW FIRST that this is an expression of fear. Your love toward each other is NOT perfect, and this is why the fear arose. Turn immediately to me by denying the power of the fear, and ask me to help you to replace it with love. This shifts the sexual impulse immediately to the miracle-impulse, and places it at MY disposal."* ACIM Urtext, Ch.1.

B. A Union of Mutual Reverence Becomes the Will of God

1. As we progress in Holy Relationship by desiring only true union, in place of separation via bodies and private minds, we experience the pure, undistorted miracle impulse more and more. It is the natural extension of the Great Rays within us but was previously blocked by the ego's misidentification as a body. The impersonal, unselfish, all-inclusive miracle impulse is meant to be extended unimpeded, from the light within us to others. One of the most magnificent experiences of the miracle impulse is through sharing it with others in a joint Holy Instant. This sharing brings about a quantum healing of the split mind, our misidentification as a body instead of as Spirit.

2. When our minds unite in mutual reverence and we enter a joint Holy Instant, an overwhelming fusion of light occurs that is felt as breathtaking gratitude. This eruption of extraordinary grace *is* the Love we are, extended and received simultaneously. And in this blessed moment of union, the ego ceases to exist.

3. Human love is not Love, but fear in disguise. It exists as ego's substitute for perfect Love, and tries to prove that love can change and end, that people can be betrayed and abandoned, and that love can hurt. All of this is sustained by the ego, in endless attempts to hurl its own submerged guilt outward onto others, in frantic efforts to prove that it can be unfairly treated by others and that the separation is real. The bottom line is that very few people recognize the solitary underlying problem – the ego's essential need for guilt, which judgment and blame bring. Without guilt, the illusion of separation would cease to exist.

4. The Holy Relationship's purpose is to eliminate this crushing burden of guilt and fear. Fear and guilt are the ego's greatest defenses against its most formidable opponent – the memory of God's Love, as our one, unified Holy Self. The Love of God cannot be known consistently except through our brothers and is ultimately refined in the experience of Holy Relationship. The Love of God, and thus our own healing, is experienced and embraced in direct proportion to our desire to see our brothers and our self as sinless, blameless, and innocent.

C. The Gifts

1. Due to our mutual purpose of forgiveness, the Holy Relationship becomes a sanctuary of innocence and tenderness; a safe zone in which we can share our deepest fears and highest joys. In the Holy Instants we share with our companion(s) we close the gap and give up our sense of unworthiness. Into this most sacred relationship, the Love of God is remembered and graciously shared. Here, we gladly return to innocence, as one.

2. When companions join in one purpose with Holy Spirit, they effect quantum healing which ripples outward ceaselessly. We have no idea how far reaching this union can extend, even to people we don't even know. For example, Coreen and I communicate wordlessly much of the time and so do Daniel and I. There have been truly incredible synchronicities. For example, Coreen and I dreamed the same dream on the same night, which inspired a significant healing for her and for me. All three of us spend time in wordless communication (no phone, computer, etc.) and yet we each "know" the other's state of being, as well as what the other may be requesting. Furthermore, because the Holy Relationship is the reflection of perfect Love in the dream, it necessarily calls every receptive heart in its vicinity to

come to it and be healed.

3. In the advanced Holy Relationship, all ideas, beliefs, and values become generalized into one common undivided goal and function. These partners no longer seek completion through the body or from the world. They do not compartmentalize their beliefs or values. They recognize gratefully that all their needs are met by Holy Spirit, because their will is one with His. This unified devotion they share lavishly, bestows on them extraordinary gifts that far surpass anything the world could give or has ever imagined.

4. As we begin to experience true union within Holy Relationship, we discover that our partner's "good" is literally our own good, and that their call for Love is really our own. Further, we learn that as we supply the Love (forgiveness) our companion calls for, we receive it too. Any sense of separation is completely erased, and union is no longer just a term, but a profoundly felt experience.

5. When two or more people join in healing specialness, each can invoke the miracle and accept the Atonement on behalf of the other. In this case, joined in one truly common purpose with Holy Spirit, one companion cannot experience the miracle without the other also experiencing it. Even though we may appear to be temporarily lost, our brother or sister holds the miracle in trust for us until we are willing to accept it for ourselves. And then overflowing gratitude for our companion envelops us both in its shimmering grace.

6. The Holy Relationship is the majestic light that erases the black abyss of guilt and fear. In its radiance, the guilt and treacherous unworthiness of the false self simply evaporates. In our brother's gentle eyes, the Vision of Christ unveils the innocent and sovereign Child of God we *are*. In a joint agreement not to be buried in each other's stories and history, we unite in present gratitude for each other and so we learn to see one another as we are now, unencumbered by the ego's past.

a. *"This holy relationship, lovely in its innocence, mighty in strength, and blazing with a light far brighter than the sun that lights the sky you see, is chosen of your Father as a means for His Own plan."... "This holy relationship has the power to heal all pain, regardless of its form. Neither you nor your brother alone can serve at all. Only in your joint will does healing lie. For here your healing is, and here will you accept Atonement. And in your healing is the Sonship healed [because] your will and your brother's are joined." T-22.VI.4:1,4-8*

7. While we still believe in and experience suffering, then the one who struggles is the false self, as an identity *apart* from Love (God), with a self-appointed personal "will," apart from God. It literally surrounds itself with a self-projected shield of fear to defend itself from true union, and thus from its single enemy – Love, as our Holy Self. Because it is terrified of the Love of God, it is also terrified of *closing the gap* between our brother and our self. This all-embracing forgiveness, of which it is terrified, would heal the split mind completely.

    1)   The imaginary gap of unforgiveness between our brother and our self *is the fear of God.*

8. This unforgiven gap represents the ego's shield of fear which seems to hold every conceivable form of pain, loss and suffering safely in place. The ego's dream of time, birth and death exist only in this imagined gap. And all it takes to collapse that gap entirely and undo our fear of God at a quantum level ...is to *close it* completely, with at least one other Son of God. In the Holy Relationship lies the utterly profound and unquantifiable healing of the entire dream of separation.

9. When two or more unite in advanced Holy Relationship to close the gap of separation, their will becomes one with God's. From here, the healed and unified Mind of Christ is set aflame throughout the sleeping Sonship, as the Great Rays joyously illuminate all that was previously seen through darkness.

    a.   *"Before a holy relationship there is no sin. The form of error is no longer seen, and reason, joined with love, looks quietly on all confusion, observing merely, "This was a mistake." And then the same Atonement you accepted in your relationship corrects the error, and lays a part of Heaven in its place."* ... *"Each part of Heaven that you bring is given you."*

"When you have looked upon your brother with complete forgiveness, from which no error is excluded and nothing kept hidden, what mistake can there be anywhere you cannot overlook? What form of suffering could block your sight, preventing you from seeing past it? And what illusion could there be you will not recognize as a mistake; a shadow through which you walk completely undismayed? God would let nothing interfere with those whose wills are His, and they will recognize their wills are His, [because] they serve His Will. And serve it willingly. And could remembrance of what they are be long delayed?"

"You will see your value through your brother's eyes, and each one is released as he beholds his savior in place of the attacker who he thought was there. Through this releasing is the world released. This is your part in bringing peace. For you have asked what is your function here, and have been answered." T-22.VI.5:1-3,5,7.8:1-4

D. Soul Merging Without a Sexual Agenda

1. I realize that most of us perhaps don't have many, if any, real life experiences of true intimacy with a close companion, an experience of pure, heartfelt union completely unsullied by the ego's agenda for a sexual outcome. For many women, myself included up until I joined with Daniel, this heart opening union is usually a rare and Holy Encounter. This personal story below is a wonderful example of two conscious people in Holy Relationship – my two best friends, Coreen and my partner Daniel – who chose to forego the ego's sexual agenda, and restore the pure miracle impulse as a Soul merging. This moving example of real Love is shared directly here from Coreen:

2. "In this lifetime, I sought to compensate for the deep unworthiness I felt on many different levels, and one of those was to be desirable to men and a "contender" with women. What this equated to was being physically beautiful, physically fit, fashionably alluring, sexy and confident. I worked out, tanned, lifted weights, and chose just the right clothing that communicated my confidence and abilities.

All of this was the cover up for the little girl inside who was told in no uncertain terms that she was *not* lovable as she was, but needed to compensate for her deep and unforgivable flaws.

3. How this played out sexually further ingrained the belief in unworthiness. Unwittingly, I would specifically choose men who could not see me for who I am but were drawn in by the false façade I put on. They took the bait of a physically beautiful and desirable woman. It was lust that initiated each relationship and not the desire to truly join in true emotional intimacy.

4. In the bedroom, the insecure and unworthy one on the inside craved real affection and wanted to be held and receive the nurturing that she did not receive as a child. It was no surprise that after ten or fifteen minutes of pseudo affection that my partner's touching would turn to hungry groping in search of self-gratification. Because I had no sense of self-worth, I would comply with my partner's desires and in order to keep up with my outer "armor" of self-confidence, I would become the super confidant lover, the performer, and would do everything I could to seduce, capture and keep my partner's desire.

5. I figured that if I kept my partner happy and they saw me as beautiful and good in bed, that there would be no danger of losing their "affection." And yet, all this energy spent in "trying" to be worthy in my partner's eyes, when what they saw *never was* my true Identity, resulted in deepening my sense of unworthiness. I abandoned myself each and every time I performed, playing the role of being some beautiful, confident woman, when on the inside there was a deeply insecure girl who believed she was unworthy of real love. The message to the young girl inside was to keep herself covered up and invisible because should she actually be seen, no one would dare love her.

6. Fast forwarding to the blinding contrast of my experience in Holy Relationship, I initially engaged in this sanctuary of relationship with Nouk Sanchez. It was truly amazing to be able to join with another woman without any sense of competition or rivalry, comparison or fear.

7.   When Nouk introduced me to her partner Daniel, it eventually became clear that the three of us were to be in Holy Relationship together, yet how that would look, I had no idea. At first the ego had me believing that I was the third wheel, sometimes welcome yet other times a burden to Daniel, who I had mistakenly assumed wanted to be alone with Nouk. After some brutally honest conversations between Daniel and myself, we were shown that our relationship was every bit as important as Daniel and Nouk's relationship.

8.   He and I were to uncover and heal aspects of relating (specialness) that Nouk and Daniel could not because their relationship's teaching-learning dynamic did not include the challenges that Daniel and I had.

9.   Speaking for myself, I have been shown that I don't trust men based upon my own past conditioning. I assume all men see me only for what they can *get from me* and don't care enough to look past my body to my heart and soul. Because Daniel and I have made a vow to never leave or abandon each other, we have created enough trust between us that we are able to hold one another in long and tender physical embraces that the ego would argue are only pledged for exclusive, special romantic relationships.

10. I can actually allow Daniel now to hold me while laying on his day bed, his arms around me, stroking my hair as I lay my head on his shoulder. At times I bury my face into his neck and cry tears of release over this show of fidelity and real Love. His willingness to be this close to me and to *not cross the line* and without expectations of anything sexual, has healed me on so many levels that it is difficult to articulate.

11. He has shown me glimpses of my innate *worth* and my *lovability*. His sincere appreciation of *who and what I am* allows me to accept these for myself. While I cannot speak for Daniel, he has shared that this experience has helped him equally in his surmounting the ego's sexual, predatory urge that drives most men in all their relating with women. We would not be able to do this outside of the Holy Relationship and its protective, common goal of holding the other's absolute innocence in truth and Love.

12. While my Holy Relationship with Nouk seems to be "built in" in this incarnation and has needed no cultivation, my relationship with Daniel has required forgiveness and an ongoing development of trust. I am in awe before its promise. He and I will be healing the Sonship as we embark on this unheard of "third person" dynamic. I can only kiss his feet in reverence and awe for his willingness.

17. DIVINE ANDROGYNY - A GREATER LOVE

1. The ego's sexual appetite is usually transmuted and healed in three stages; 1) using sex to separate, 2) using sex to heal, and 3) divine androgyny. The false self has an overwhelming desire for specialness and believes that specialness can be acquired via human love. It doesn't realize what *divine Love is,* or even that *there is* a straightforward, Loving alternative to "special love."

2. In the dream of separation, we are thoroughly hypnotized into believing that *we are* the illusory body and that our happiness can only be gained through it. The truth has not yet dawned that we are, and always have been, eternally and incorruptibly innocent and wholly accepted and Loved as the one, shared Holy Self. If we were to understand this truth, we would see clear through the ego's sham and would have no need for specialness at all.

3. We severely limit our awareness of the unbounded joy and Love that we *really are* by attempting to reduce our true Identity as the Christ, to a body, its physical senses, and sensual appetites. As an image that only exists *in our mind,* the body is neutral. But liberation or awakening from the body is often somehow confused with the idea of death, and while we remain unconsciously fearful of true union, which is the fear of expressing authentic, true communication, we will still prefer to be imprisoned by the body and its appetites. This preference to be identified with the body, and not trusting the Holy Self we share, is evidenced by our continual search for pleasure and specialness in the body, as well as avoidance of physical pain.

4. While still believing that "special love" is found through the body, most people elect to take as much illusory time as they can to *delay* complete awakening from the body concept. As a consequence it may take the majority of people many more lifetimes of seeking their illusory completion in the body/dream – as pain and death – before they're willing to recognize and relinquish their final attraction to the ego's cycle of sin, guilt, fear and death. As we heal through Holy Relationship and release this desire to believe we are a body, we enter into the final phase of healing, divine androgyny. Thankfully, it is here that we are *freed* of the incessant ego-body's desire for pleasure, and identity apart from God.

  a. *"Remember that the Holy Spirit interprets the body only as a means of communication. Being the Communication Link between God and His separated Sons, the Holy Spirit interprets everything you have made in the light of what He is. The ego separates through the body. The Holy Spirit reaches through it to others. You do not perceive your brothers as the Holy Spirit does, because you do not regard bodies solely as a means of joining minds and uniting them with yours and mine. This interpretation of the body will change your mind entirely about its value. Of itself it has none."* T-8.VII.2.

5. In our advancement through Holy Relationship, our experience of guiltlessness, both within and without, utterly transforms how we see our self, others, the past, the body and the world. With this advancement we value divine and changeless Love and we repurpose all our relationships which are undeniably blessed because we are no longer using them for separation and guilt. Along the way, we discover that as we deepen our commitment to just one goal of awakening *completely from* the body-concept altogether, this transformation is a gently guided and organic process.

6. What occurs at this advanced level is a quantum shift from body identification *as* the false-self, to living out from and *as* the Holy Self. The body is now divinely repurposed. No longer a slave to the inevitable conflict of serving two diametrically opposed masters (ego *and* Spirit), the body joyfully serves just one Master – God's Will. Free of conflict, it is under no laws but God's. The ego

plays no part in this shift because this transformation involves the *relinquishment* of the ego's pseudo life source, as the body and guilt.

7. As the Holy Spirit comprehensively repurposes the body, the ego's deeply coveted attachment to both sex and gender identification are also repurposed. While identification with gender or the sexual pleasure drive is still valued and therefore strongly upheld, these two will be used by the ego for pride, pleasure and attack, and they will continue to act as blocks to the awareness of Love's glorious presence as our universal innocence.

8. As mentioned earlier, a common, yet unrecognized source of many problems, including relationship and health issues, is the blocking of *unexpressed* miracle impulses. The ego uses sexual lust and orgasm to separate, in an effort to block true heart-mind communication as the pure miracle impulse. It intercepts the pure, inclusive and impersonal miracle impulse and distorts it by misdirecting it *through the body* as the self-seeking orgasm. This in turn ensures that the pure miracle impulse is never experienced by either companion, but actually *severs* all *true* communication as changeless Love.

9. My partner Daniel and I have really committed to transcending the sexual appetite once and for all. Of course, of our selves this is impossible. Yet having given this appetite to Spirit, we are well on the way to transcending it. Each day we enter the most magnificent, joint Holy Instants together. In fact, most of our time these days is spent in mutual Love and presence *without* the body's interference.

10. From my own experience in the romantic Holy Relationship, we approach this particular phase of consciously transcending the sexual appetite very naturally. In this shift, there is a natural *falling away* of the last vestiges of the ego's investment in separation through the sexual body and its special relationships. There is no sense of sacrifice involved because it is wholly superseded by an ongoing experience of extraordinary, immortal Love and inclusive union. When true, divine Love is experienced, the ego's substitute for Love – as sexual lust –is exposed as the cheap imposter that it is. When this occurs, sexual desire merely falls away because true union is valued and desired *above all else*.

11. Once we truly join with another, entering an extended Holy Instant

of awestruck wonder and tear-filled grace, our sense of a separate mind and body disappears entirely. In these divine moments, the illusory boundaries of separate minds and bodies are completely shattered. The body fades in awareness so enormously that we're overcome by the brilliant and humbling innocence of our brother. Once this experience of boundless Love is experienced *beyond the body*, then the biting contrast of returning to body-bound sexual desire feels inevitably constricted, meaningless, and a diversion away from true heart-mind union.

12. The direct experience is truly the demonstration of lesson 128 in the *Course*: "The world I see holds nothing that I want." The body and world as seen through the ego filter fade enormously as they are eclipsed and answered by our longing for God. Old attachments, patterns and feelings of deprivation simply fall away as we set our priority to return our awareness to the sparkling world of pure innocence. Here, the things we previously seemed to value in the world are deemed meaningless in the blinding contrast of the Real World dream. We realize that they were merely *substitutes* for the boundless Love that we have finally opened our hearts to. Paradoxically, we lack nothing in this phase. We *have* everything because at last we fully realize with immense joy, that we *are* everything.

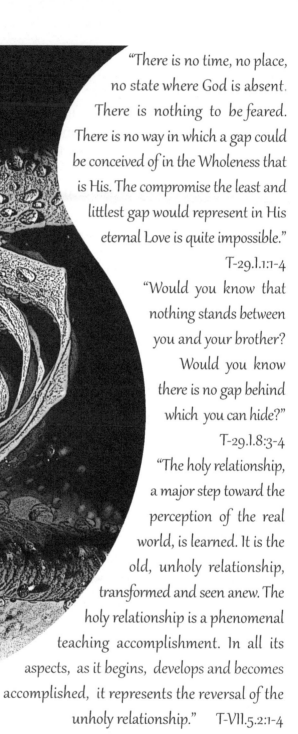

"There is no time, no place, no state where God is absent. There is nothing to be feared. There is no way in which a gap could be conceived of in the Wholeness that is His. The compromise the least and littlest gap would represent in His eternal Love is quite impossible."
T-29.I.1:1-4

"Would you know that nothing stands between you and your brother? Would you know there is no gap behind which you can hide?"
T-29.I.8:3-4

"The holy relationship, a major step toward the perception of the real world, is learned. It is the old, unholy relationship, transformed and seen anew. The holy relationship is a phenomenal teaching accomplishment. In all its aspects, as it begins, develops and becomes accomplished, it represents the reversal of the unholy relationship." T-VII.5.2:1-4

CHAPTER FIVE

C–V.   HOLY RELATIONSHIP BLUEPRINT

I. THE HOLY GRAIL REVEALED -
THE LONG - FORGOTTEN CHOICE

1. This fractured world of fear along with all the suffering we seem to experience within it arises from an ancient decision so deeply buried, that we long forgot we made it. That one, unrecognized choice is the foundation of every problem we experience. This is the one, unconscious agreement we made which leads us repeatedly to conflict, loss, sickness, aging and finally death. It was our choice to dream of separation from our Creator that gave way to the compelling ideas of time, of bodies, and of the exhaustive recycle program of birth, amnesia and death. It is also the one, unforgiven pledge we made which is responsible for prolonging our resistance to Love, to union, to peace and to healing.

2. This wish for separation resulted in a seeming gap between God and His most beloved Son. The entire imaginary dream world, including all the threats within it, exists only because we have erroneously agreed to see our self and our brothers as separate. This is the choice to reject our Holy Self and God, since reality is one.

3. To clarify, the dream of separation, time, bodies, and death required and was initiated by "two or more" witnesses who agreed to *believe* the impossible. Yet because they agreed to share this distorted idea, it seemed to make it real in their awareness. Once two (or more) agree to be *witnesses* to something together, even if it does not exist in God's Love, then by their free will choice, they give it reality in their split minds *by sharing* it. This is how the dream of fear began.

a. *"It is the sharing of the evil dreams of hate and malice, bitterness and death, of sin and suffering and pain and loss, that makes them real. Unshared, they are perceived as meaningless." T-28.V.2:1-2*

4. Let's take a look at the profound implications of this joint decision.

5. When one mind thought of the possibility of separation and another mind consented to give witness to that idea, together they agreed to dream of separation and therefore fear. Without their mutual agreement to witness to fear and its imaginary gap where separation seems to occur along with its effects, there could be no suffering whatsoever. Jesus explains this: *"His dreams are yours because you let them be. But if you took your own away would he be free of them, and of his own as well." T-28.IV.6:3-4*

6. The separation was the decision to affirm the gap of miscreation, to deny the Christ in others and therefore, to reject the Christ within. This insidious choice to see ourselves as separate from our brothers was where we inflicted our first "self-attack." As Jesus says, *"In separation from your brother was the first attack upon yourself begun." T-27. VII.6:4* Yet we keep reliving the original separation – the first attack upon our self –each time we blame or judge one another.

7. Jesus tells us that the dream and the dreamer are one. Consequently, both the witness (dreamer) *and* the gap (dream of fear) as suffering in whatever form, are also one. But if the witness is withdrawn, the gap - as the cause of all suffering, *must* fall away! When one withdraws their consent to bear witness to the illusion of conflict, the cause – as the belief we are separate – is withdrawn, along with its symptoms of adversity. The effects which must disappear include conflict, illness, pain, lack, and any other form of suffering which the false, body-identity has used in an attempt to prove the gap exists.

a. *"Identity in dreams is meaningless because the dreamer and the dream are one. Who shares a dream must be the dream he shares, because by sharing is a cause produced." T-28. IV.5:4-5*

8. Holy Spirit is the one Mind that we as the Son of God share. There is no gap here. As one witness withdraws his agreement to the seeming gap, the gap itself, along with its painful consequences, *disappears*, leaving the existing, one, whole, unified Mind; the unified Will of God. This is how we undo our ancient agreement to share a dream of pain apart from Love (God). Note: Please refer to the Gap diagrams here, pages 46 thru 49.

a. *There is a way of finding certainty right here and now. Refuse to be a part of fearful dreams whatever form they take, for you will lose identity in them. You find yourself by not accepting them as causing you, and giving you effects. You stand apart from them, but not apart from him who dreams them. Thus you separate the dreamer from the dream, and join in one, but let the other go. The dream is but illusion in the mind. And with the mind you would unite, but never with the dream. It is the dream you fear, and not the mind." T-28. IV.2:1-8*

A. The Holy Grail and the Victory Lap

1. Two (or more) descended into the dream of separation by jointly agreeing to imagine a gap between them. Therefore, the whole dream is collapsed as we ascend *two by two* in Holy Relationship. This is a union where two or more mutually agree to reverse the decision to separate, by withdrawing their belief in the gap's tempting appearances of bodies and suffering. Through quantum forgiveness, together, *and with Holy Spirit,* they willingly unlearn their beliefs in conflict or suffering of any kind. They unite with the Holy Self but not with the content of the dream. The content is always some mistaken belief in sin, guilt and fear.

2. In the following quote we see that the Holy Relationship is the collapse or disappearance of the gap where the seeds of adversity are sown and flourish under the ego's reign. However, Jesus tells

us that where two or more join in forgiving the seeming gap, these *effects* in whatever form they appear, are undone. And with their disappearance is the desire for sin withdrawn.

a. *"The holiness of your relationship forgives you and your brother, undoing the effects of what you both believed and saw. And with their going is the need for sin gone with them." T-22.in.1:7-8*

3. The world is healed through Holy Relationship, including the ideas of duality, of death, time and bodies.

a. *"You have been called, together with your brother, to the most holy function this world contains. It is the only one that has no limits, and reaches out to every broken fragment of the Sonship with healing and uniting comfort. This is offered you, in your holy relationship." T-18.I.13:1-3*

4. The Holy Relationship *is* quite literally the Holy Grail. In all the dimensions of time and of all the spiritual paths since time began, the Holy Relationship marks the definitive culmination and final Victory Lap of our return to God. The attainment of this divine union within the sleeping Sonship, represents the last rung of the ascending ladder, and the quintessential bridge that carries us to what Jesus terms as the Real World. In the dream of time everyone will eventually join in this mandatory and divine "reunion" before they welcome the Real World dream experience.

a. *"Through your holy relationship, reborn and blessed in every holy instant you do not arrange, thousands will rise to Heaven with you." ... "Nor is your holy relationship a dream." ... "It will become the happy dream through which He can spread joy to thousands on thousands who believe that love is fear, not happiness." T-18.V.3:1-2,5:2,5*

b. *"To overcome the world is no more difficult than to surmount your little wall. For in the miracle of your holy relationship, without this barrier, is every miracle contained. There is no order of difficulty in miracles, for they are all the same." T-19. IV.A.5:1-3*

5. The Holy Relationship joyously heralds the closing chapter of the

ego's ancient, time-worn trance. It makes way for our final dream for all of time, the dream of Love, before God Himself takes the last step and lifts us out of the realm of perception and into the Arms of undivided Knowledge as the Christ.

6. The Holy Relationship's final goal is the complete demise of the original gap, and for that reason, it is the most Holy function in the world. Can we even imagine what this means? Within this sanctified and Unified Relationship lies the means for the unprecedented collapse and disappearance of the ego's entire thought system, including its central dream of death.

7. The non-negotiable belief that death is the inevitable outcome of all life *is* the unseen and unhealed belief that *Love (God) is death*. The Holy Relationship *is* the Holy Grail! It is the vehicle through which we completely undo our fear of Love, God, union and life.

   a. *"Heaven is restored to all the Sonship through your relationship, for in it lies the Sonship, whole and beautiful, safe in your love." T-18.I.11:1*

   b. *"The Holy Spirit's temple is not a body, but a relationship."*... *"The holy relationship reflects the true relationship the Son of God has with his Father in reality." T-20.VI.5:1,10:1*

8. Everything that ever seemed to threaten us in all the dimensions of time, including time itself, is contained in just one tiny and imaginary gap. And all of it is gently subsumed, disappearing within the light of Holy Relationship.

   a. *"Your way will be different, not in purpose but in means. A holy relationship is a means of saving time. One instant spent together with your brother restores the universe to both of you." T-18.VII. 5:2-3*

9. Nowhere else in the history of time have we recognized the magnitude of Holy Relationship where the final Victory Lap is completed...because it is the vehicle through which the entire dream of fear is erased.

10. Our descent into separation was executed by an agreement between "two or more" to imagine sin, guilt and fear and by witnessing these together, to give them real effects. As such, our divine ascension, or Victory Lap, is attained by "two or more" who join in the one truly common purpose – to *undo* all sense of separation between them. This is the healing of our belief in private minds with separate agendas, together with the undoing of the separate body-identity.

a. *"When two minds join as one and share one idea equally, the first link in the awareness of the Sonship as One has been made."* T-16.II.4:3

b. *"Alone we can do nothing, but together our minds fuse into something whose power is far beyond the power of its separate parts. By not being separate, the Mind of God is established in ours and as ours. This Mind is invincible because it is undivided."* T-8.V.1:6-8

11. Our Victory Lap is initiated when we agree to overlook the seeming gap (conflict) to see the "face of Christ" in another. While we can awaken *in* the dream and achieve so called Self-Realization, until we engage consistently in Holy Relationships, we will be unable to awaken *from* the dream altogether. The difference being that awakening *from* the dream involves the absolute certainty that there *is no* gap.

12. It is impossible to awaken in God until joyous gratitude thoroughly replaces all grievances, present and past. We must no longer value any seeming gap between our brothers and our self. We remain afraid of Love as God while we harbor any blame or judgment against another. This is why complete forgiveness must precede awakening from the dream of time and space.

a. *"You are afraid of God [because] you fear your brother. Those you do not forgive you fear. And no one reaches love with fear beside him."* T-19.I.V.D.11:5-7

13. In this world Love cannot be remembered and embodied except through all-inclusive forgiveness. Whomever and whatever we withhold from forgiveness we will use to uphold the false, body-self,

thereby rejecting Love as our Holy Self. Only the illusory body-identity believes and maintains injustice and does so to preserve its "self" as separate. This is why every sight and memory of injustice must be wholly offered up in exchange for the miracle of healed perception. With such a far-reaching objective is it any wonder why the Holy Relationship *is* the accelerated path Home? We cannot possibly overcome the dream alone. We need our brother.

a. *"This holy relationship, lovely in its innocence, mighty in strength, and blazing with a light far brighter than the sun that lights the sky you see, is chosen of your Father as a means for His Own plan." ... "This holy relationship has the power to heal all pain, regardless of its form. Neither you nor your brother alone can serve at all. Only in your joint will does healing lie. For here your healing is, and here will you accept Atonement. And in your healing is the Sonship healed [because] your will and your brother's are joined."* T-22.VI.4:1:4-8

14. Everyone, especially those who have appeared to persecute us in our version of the dream, offers us an opportunity to behold and to heal exactly that which *we* have mistakenly projected. Without these people we would never discover and forgive the single source of all our suffering, our own unconscious self-hatred.

a. *"Heaven is restored to all the Sonship through your relationship, for in it lies the Sonship, whole and beautiful, safe in your love."* T-18.I.11:1

b. *"Think what a holy relationship can teach! Here is belief in differences undone. Here is the faith in differences shifted to sameness. And here is sight of differences transformed to vision."* T-22.in. 4:1-4

B. Heaven is Restored Two by Two

a. *"The ark of peace is entered two by two, yet the beginning of another world goes with them. Each holy relationship must enter here, to learn its special function in the Holy Spirit's*

plan, now that it shares His purpose. And as this purpose is fulfilled, a new world rises in which sin can enter not, and where the Son of God can enter without fear and where he rests a while, to forget imprisonment and to remember freedom."
T-20.IV.5:4-7

1. In the *Course's* workbook lesson 185, Jesus is clear that if any two or more should join and say they want the peace of God above all else, and mean it, the entire Sonship would be restored. Recall that the final obstacle to peace is the fear of God. This is the terror of Love itself. This terror *is* the false self. It is the incessant drive to uphold and defend a private, personal mind, together with its separate body. This is the illusory "self" apart from God.

2. The separate self seems to have an endless list of enemies, others, conflict, pain, disease, aging, scarcity, loss and death. But these are merely decoys, a self-fabricated shield of fear made to hide its one most feared opponent – Love as God, as our Holy Self.

3. It cringes at Love's approach. It is terrified to forgive in totality because to do so would close the seeming gap between our self and our brother once and for all. And once this gap is abolished via sincere forgiveness, our brother, who was once our enemy, is wholly and joyously embraced as our savior. God Himself is here in this divine union. The separate self, as darkness, can no longer be sustained in the blinding light of this universal oneness.

4. You see, the independent self apart from God *is* the gap. It is fear incarnate. It is the hidden wish to be unfairly treated. A false self must be victimized so that it can continue to project its arterial guilt as blame onto others and the body in its dream. This is the fictitious one who is happy with its hidden choice to suffer pain, separation and even physical death, if in return it can perpetuate the illusion that it is *justified* to blame its brothers for its grievances and pain.

5. The Holy Relationship is the essential means by which this fear of God, as the fear of our brothers, is finally undone. Without the experience of Holy Relationship, the illusory private mind and separate body concept will not be completely healed. Remember that this self's greatest fear is God, as undivided and unopposed Love.

6. Without the Holy Relationship we will continue to be unknowingly terrified of God – of changeless Love – although the spiritual ego cleverly masks this, the final obstacle.

   a. *"For no one alone can judge the ego truly. Yet when two or more join together in searching for truth, the ego can no longer defend its lack of content. The fact of union tells them it is not true." T-14.X.9:5-7*

7. The heavily defended "private mind and body" clings to its deeply unconscious projection of the ego's god. This unpredictable and punishing god is the only one it knows. That is why it refuses to surrender to its god every facet of its body, its relationships, and its life. It believes in painful lessons brought about by this cruel master. Consequently, it cannot afford to trust exclusively in this god, the god of death. This crippled self only knows of "its" god and has no clue as to the joyous totality of our true Creator as all-encompassing Love. We will have no idea "who" we are as the most beloved Child of God until we see it reflected in our brother.

8. Because of this profound confusion, the only version of "love" this false-self knows is special, conditional love, the kind the world reveres which is imbued with fear, guilt, blame, agendas, conflict, doubt, exclusivity, possession, jealousy, concern, change, loss, sacrifice and separation. These are all elements of fear, and none of these traits are present in changeless Love. The Holy Relationship, in comparison, incorporates changeless Love, mutual innocence, peace, inclusivity, honesty, trust, faith, joy, healing, gratitude and wholeness.

   a. *"Everyone seeks for love as you do, but knows it not unless he joins with you in seeking it. If you undertake the search together, you bring with you a light so powerful that what you see is given meaning. The lonely journey fails because it has excluded what it would find." T-14.X.10:5-7*

   b. *"The holy relationship reflects the true relationship the Son of God has with his Father in reality." T-20.VI.10:1*

9. In the Holy Relationship we *unlearn* our deeply guarded fear of Love which plays out as the ego's constant attraction to self-attack. This self-attack appears in our world as random chaos, conflict, scarcity, loss, pain, sickness and death.

10. Recall that the very first obstacle to peace, which is our original block to Love, is the *desire to get rid of it.* Love and peace are one. Where one is, the other must be. Yet the false self, as fear incarnate, must cease to exist in the presence of this peace, this changeless Love which is what *we are.* This is our Holy Self. However, to overcome the fear of God, which is the final obstacle, complete forgiveness of our brother is necessary in our heart. And Holy Relationship gives us the divine medium by which to accomplish this.

  a. *"No one can look upon the fear of God unterrified, unless he has accepted the Atonement and learned illusions are not real. No one can stand before this obstacle alone, for he could not have reached this far unless his brother walked beside him. And no one would dare to look on it without complete forgiveness of his brother in his heart."* ... *"Once he has found his brother he [is] ready."* T-19.IV.D.9:1-3,10:3

11. To wholeheartedly want the peace of God is to renounce our attachment to the human body-identity. We cannot have both. One denies the other is real. Holy Relationship is the means by which we overcome the split mind, together with its dream. We cannot do this alone. We need our brother.

12. Two or more originally agreed to imagine separation, as private minds with separate bodies, asleep and immersed in a dream of death which they mistook for life. It makes perfect sense that the Holy Grail of all time *is* the Holy Relationship, where two or more decide with God to do away with the "gap" altogether, on behalf of the entire Sonship.

  a. *"I want the peace of God."* ... *"The world would be completely changed, should any two agree these words express the only thing they want."* ... *"Two minds with one intent become so strong that what they will becomes the Will of God. For minds can only join in truth."* W-185.2:9,31-2

b. *"Alone we can do nothing, but together our minds fuse into something whose power is far beyond the power of its separate parts. By not being separate, the Mind of God is established in ours and as ours. This Mind is invincible because it is undivided." T-8.V.1:6-8*

13. The mystery of the Holy Grail *is* revealed through the Holy Relationship. There is no Grail Holier than this within all the dimensions of time. It is the Chalice of Love – the endless, changeless means of Atonement. This is the perfect Love that casts out fear. It is the Will of God made manifest in the dream, to close the dream of fear.

a. *"Beside you is one who offers you the chalice of Atonement, for the Holy Spirit is in him."... "Behold your Friend, the Christ Who stands beside you. How holy and how beautiful He is!" T-19.IV.D.13:1,14:1*

2. DID JESUS NEED A HOLY RELATIONSHIP?

1. Jesus devotes a large part of *A Course in Miracles* to undoing our concept of human "love" (fear in disguise). He explains the toxicity of the special relationship dynamic as the ego's substitute for divine Love, and repeatedly reinforces the necessity of Holy Relationship as the crucial prerequisite for undoing our special relationships and therefore, our deeply hidden fear of Love (God), which happens to be our unconscious attraction to death itself.

2. To help us grasp the sheer magnitude and present impact of Jesus' final accomplishment on behalf of all mankind, let's take an unobstructed glimpse at just *why* the Holy Relationship is necessary to overcome the ego dream.

3. The "body" is the central figure of the entire ego dream. It is the most potently seductive *replacement* for the memory of our beloved and invulnerable Holy Self. Separate walls of flesh appear to house individual, private minds. Each private mind seems to have its own

individual, self-seeking agenda, and its very own personal will, fed by the illusion of deprivation, which always revolves around its central "altar," the body.

4. This personal will, centered exclusively on the body identity, is preserved by the ego's blind obsession with special relationships. These are the ego's chief weapon for keeping us bound to the body and death, as the dream of separation. *"The special love relationship is the ego's chief weapon for keeping you from Heaven." T-16.V.2:3*

5. All relationship conflict is caused by two (or more) people whose self-seeking agendas clash. They may seem to sometimes come together as bodies, but because they each pursue a *self-centered* goal, they value a divided purpose; one that separates them from others, God and their Holy Self. Only a *selfless* purpose is real and only this *can* be shared with another and with Holy Spirit. This is why human love via human (special) relationships is always destined to fail.

6. We could no longer mistake our self or others *as* the body if our special relationships were healed. The mistaken body identity would rapidly fall away in our awareness through the steady progression of Holy Relationship, as companions learned *above* all else to cherish each other's innocence through the truly common purpose of forgiveness.

7. Through this single commitment they would receive the gift of *true union,* recognizing joyfully that they share just one Mind and one Will with each other and Holy Spirit. They realize this by learning to *transcend their self-interests,* overcoming their separate, private agendas and will. Only an independent, personal will *apart* from our brothers and God could possibly clash and experience conflict, illness and harm.

    a. *"Nothing can show the contrast better than the experience of both a holy and an unholy relationship. The first is based on love, and rests on it serene and undisturbed. The body does not intrude upon it. Any relationship in which the body enters is based not on love, but on idolatry."* ... *"The Holy Spirit's temple is not a body, but a relationship."* ... *"You cannot make the body the Holy Spirit's temple, and it will never be the seat of love."* ... *"The Holy Spirit's purpose lies safe in your relationship, and not your body." ... "The holy relationship reflects the true relationship the Son of God has with his Father in reality." ... "Here is the way to true relationships held gently open, through which you and your brother walk together, leaving the body thankfully behind and resting in the Everlasting Arms. Love's Arms are open to receive you, and give you peace forever." T-26.VI.2:1-3,5:1,6:1,7:8,10:1,10:5-6*

8. The body, as the ego's central idol, cannot be overcome except through Holy Relationship. Ultimately, this union culminates in divine communication. It is the final "eye of the needle" experience required to undo our fear of union and our fear of God – which we have masked with our attraction to the body and our hidden attraction to death. This is the fear of perfect, changeless Love, which is our true Identity.

   a. *"Future loss is not your fear. But present joining is your dread." T-26.VIII.4:3-4*

9. The personal mind's greatest terror is union. This is the fear of God. As the loss of a personal will devoted to separation, it fears union more than physical death itself. In fact, the ego projects the illusion of death over and over again in order to escape from true joining and the experience of union. Its belief in the body and death perpetuate the whole idea of time and reincarnation.

   a. *"The fear of God is fear of life, and not of death." T-23.IV.1:2*

   b. *"Those who fear death see not how often and how loudly they call to it, and bid it come to save them from communication. For death is seen as safety, the great dark savior from the light of truth, the answer to the Answer, the silencer of the Voice that speaks for God. Yet the retreat to death is not the end of conflict. Only God's Answer is its end." T-19.IV.C.7:1-4*

10. In contrast, the unified function of forgiveness in Holy Relationship heals the split mind's misidentification *as* the body, revealing our magnificent, grace-filled, shared Will and Identity. In this union we release the ego's irresistible attraction to physical

death as its repetitive escape route from comprehensive forgiveness and the unprecedented experience of oneness.

11. The reason the Holy Relationship is the Holy Grail and final experience for the Victory Lap (awakening *from* the dream and not just *in* it) is because this Holy Communion with our brothers not only erases our fear of God, but gives us the direct experience of true union which transcends the belief that we are body bound. Without the Holy Relationship, we would be forever seduced by the body and death – reincarnation and time – as our ongoing defense against return to God.

a. *"To overcome the world is no more difficult than to surmount your little wall. For in the miracle of your holy relationship, without this barrier, is every miracle contained. There is no order of difficulty in miracles, for they are all the same."* ... *"His home is in your holy relationship."* T-19.IV.A.5:1-3,9

12. Over the years of writing this manual I have heard a typical question that is sometimes raised about Jesus.

13. Was Jesus' awakening from the dream dependent upon His having an advanced Holy Relationship with another?

14. Although Jesus did indeed have Holy Relationships during His short incarnation, His transfiguration, resurrection, and final Ascension were not *dependent* on His having an advanced Holy Relationship, as they are for us. Due to our profound misidentification with the body as our "self," we *are* dependent on Holy Relationship. The reason is that we need the experience of at least one true relationship *beyond* the body to offer us the blinding contrast between special love (fear) and changeless Love. Until then we will continue to be attracted to separation through both the body and special love.

15. Before I explain more, I feel it would help to shed some light on a common fear pertaining to Jesus' uncompromising devotion to God and His fellow brothers and sisters. Reflecting on the scriptures referring to Jesus' lifetime, He is often portrayed as "perfect," capable of supernatural powers that we mere mortals would be foolish to try to emulate. Jesus is frequently perceived by the false self as the supreme, "one and only" Son of God. His level of extreme

perfection and undivided union with God is seen as ridiculously unattainable for many.

16. The ego must view Jesus' accomplishment as impossible and unachievable. It says we can never attain His level of mastery. But – what the ego doesn't allow into conscious awareness is that we *already* are a Son of God, along with Jesus. Our unrivaled perfection, supernatural powers, and undivided union with God *as* His Will, constitute the unopposed and eternal nature of our Holy Self. *This* realization is what the ego is terrified of because, in our sincere acceptance of such truth … the ego would cease to exist! This level of embodiment of the Christ we are is the wholly inevitable outcome of releasing our fear of Love. After all, the ego mind can never awaken. The Christ we *are* is revealed in awareness to the degree we align with Holy Spirit to forgive (undo) the ego's body/world identification.

17. While Jesus demonstrated that He was the Christ, He still faced the ego's temptation to perceive through fear. Jesus mentions in the *Course* that He was tempted to believe in the ego and the body Himself. This is a strong indication that Jesus did endure a period of divine purification during His life in a body.

   a. *"I can be entrusted with your body and your ego only because this enables you not to be concerned with them, and lets me teach you their unimportance. I could not understand their importance to you if I had not once been tempted to believe in them myself." T-4.I.13:4-5*

18. And yet, paradoxically, Jesus' was more aligned *as* the embodied Will of God than any other Soul that preceded Him in the dream of time. He incarnated already conscious of His union with the Father. Even as a child He was found in the temple teaching and confounding religious scholars with His unprecedented knowledge and understanding. The scholars at the time were adept only in their *intellectual* understanding of the scriptures. They were blind to the perfect Love of God, the *divine experience*, which the scriptures pointed to. I am sure that Jesus left these religious scholars thunderstruck as He offered an entirely new interpretation that exposed the religious ego's blatant misinterpretation.

19. Jesus was the first Christ amongst us, in the long dream of separation, to consciously incarnate *already unified* with God clearly in His Mind.

20. Precisely because Jesus knew all His brothers were sinless, He had no fear of God, of union. The fear of God can only arise when we fear (judge or blame) our brothers, perceiving we have a personal, different "will" than that of our brothers and God.

21. However, because Jesus was the embodiment of perfect Love, there were very few among His followers that were able to join Him in that level of Love without being terrified. Among His Holy Relationships were His mother Mary, and Mary Magdalene. These two joined Jesus in the truly common and undivided purpose of forgiveness and Atonement. They understood that their union with Him was *beyond the body* to the Christ He exemplified and demonstrated. Unlike anyone else who appeared in the dream of time, Jesus was born of a virgin birth without the agency of a human father. As explained in the section, *Sex and Death* in the chapter, *Sex and TransOrgasmic Union*, Jesus' incarnation was a direct result of divine union, untainted by ego distortion of the pure miracle impulse. He was both *conceived* and *resurrected* through the Laws of God and not by ego laws. In other words, there was no element of fear in Jesus' conception. This extraordinarily supernatural conception gave Jesus complete dominion over the illusory laws and idols of the relative world. Further, this level of mastery over the ego's hallucinations is what He is *urging* us to accept as available to each of us as we singularly seek to embody the Christ we are.

22. After all, Jesus' first miracle principle tells us, *"There is no order of difficulty in miracles."* And in miracle principle 24 He instructs us with, *"Miracles enable you to heal the sick and raise the dead because you made sickness and death yourself, and can therefore abolish both."* Once we genuinely realize that the body and world are a dream, we can and will do as Jesus did, using them not to witness to separation, disease and death, but to witness to true union which proves the Holy Self's unequivocal dominion over these phenomena.

23. Jesus was the first Son of God to have overcome the entire ego dream, including its central dream of death. His Mind was

consciously fused in Holy Relationship with the Father. Hence, His awakening and Ascension were not dependent on a human Holy Relationship. As for those of us who remain hypnotized by the body, special relationships, illness and death, we *do* require Holy Relationship, a consenting witness with whom we agree to consistently forgive the ego's illusions of separation.

24. In the following passages Jesus speaks with commanding authority. He tells us that He *is* the Atonement, that He is in charge of the Second Coming, and that He *is* the salvation of the world. Let's join Him as fellow Children of God, by opening our hearts to want to see nothing other than the innocence in all our brothers.

> a. JESUS: *"I am in charge of the process of Atonement, which I undertook to begin."* ...*"I am the only one who can perform miracles indiscriminately, because I am the Atonement." T-1.III.1:1,4:1*

> b. JESUS: *"I am in charge of the Second Coming, and my judgment, which is used only for protection, cannot be wrong because it never attacks." T-4.IV.10:4*

> c. JESUS: *"You were in darkness until God's Will was done completely by any part of the Sonship. When this was done, it was perfectly accomplished by all. How else could it be perfectly accomplished? My mission was simply to unite the will of the Sonship with the Will of the Father by being aware of the Father's Will myself. This is the awareness I came to give you, and your problem in accepting it is the problem of this world. Dispelling it is salvation, and in this sense I [am] the salvation of the world." T-8.IV.3:1-6*

> d. *"Jesus is the manifestation of the [Holy Spirit], Whom he called down upon the earth after he ascended into Heaven, or became completely identified with the Christ, the Son of God as He created Him."* ... *"He has established Jesus as the leader in carrying out His plan since he was the first to complete his own part perfectly." C-6.1,2.*

3. A UNIVERSAL BLUEPRINT FOR HOLY RELATIONSHIP

1. Because we interpret everyone and everything through a filter of guilt and fear, we have mistakenly taught our self to give everything a multitude of seemingly different purposes. Our body, relationships, family, job, etc., are all unknowingly used to accrue more guilt and fear as unconscious self-attack, while we continue to think we know the real purpose for each of them.

2. The one underlying objective, hidden beneath the endless number of varied purposes the false self assumes, is to perpetuate the separation. The numerous conflicts involved in this deeply concealed objective are most apparent in the special relationships of this world. These relationships adopt a myriad of conflicting roles and rules, all based on what the ego scripts as being either beneficial or threatening to maintaining the appearance of separation. Yet the ego has no idea what our best interests are. Therefore, these relationships are particularly tenuous based on their constantly shifting foundation. The relationship is valuable only to the extent to which it includes faulty beliefs, values, agreements and goals.

3. The special relationship's purpose appears to change depending on whether or not the false self has its imaginary needs met. All ego goals arise from an inherent sense of deprivation; as such they stem from "self" interest and therefore, cannot be shared in the highest sense.

A. Specialness and Blame - The Lower Purpose in Relationship

1. These relationships lack the one, consistent and undivided purpose which would unify, making them Holy and invulnerable to conflict. *"Egos do join together in temporary allegiance, but always for what each one can get [separately.] The Holy Spirit communicates only what each one can give to all." T-6.V.A.5: 9-10*

2. The world's relationships are deeply entrenched within the ego's beliefs, values and laws which are all based on fear and not on changeless Love. Special relationships are made to sustain the false-self and its paradigm of sin, guilt, fear, sacrifice, conflict, deprivation and loss.

3. These relationships are usually centered on common mistaken beliefs, values, the body/sex, the past, stories, roles, rules and rituals, or material possessions of mutual interest. These may appear to be common *shared* interests, but at their base they represent false "self-interests."

4. These things and the specialness they engender become the focus of what the ego judges as either success or failure of the relationship. When these false idols are challenged in relationship then "love" is also threatened or withdrawn. Thus, all the things the ego uses to form and sustain special relationships eventually become the idols that we use to *substitute* for our partner.

5. When shared interests become false idols that substitute for conscious Love in relationships, they reduce the relationship to one of "mutual use" rather than one of Love. If one partner within the relationship attempts to substitute changeless Love for a mutually agreed upon false idol, this is seen as a direct threat to the specialness dynamic which previously sustained the special relationship. Because we have revered *idols* above the true Spirit of the one we say we love, the removal or replacement of the idol threatens to cause a relationship disruption or breakdown. This demonstrates that this version of "love" is always special; it is not Love, but fear in disguise.

6. These false idols or symbols of love, while believed to be real and valuable, will be fiercely defended if threatened. Due to the magnitude of their imagined reality and misplaced value, they act as persistent blocks to practicing forgiveness, which is the sacred portal to Holy Relationship and the return to awareness of our one, innocent and Holy Self.

7. The lower goals or false idols which are revered in special relationships continually eclipse the infinite Love within the person we *think* we love. While valued, these idols sever the possibility of experiencing changeless Love in a relationship. These represent a large segment of the common blocks to Holy Relationship. Special love and blame relentlessly lead to conflict and separation.

B. Holiness and Innocence - The Higher Purpose in Relationship

1. Beyond all the false idols and miscellaneous factors we think contribute to making a relationship a lifelong one, there is a higher purpose which runs like an invisible golden thread through all relationships, be they romantic, or with friends or family. The highest purpose of all relationships (and the only one that shows up on God's Radar) rests completely unaltered in the expressions of Love we share with others. Because the false self only recognizes special love and cannot fathom God's Love, let me be more specific.

2. Every thought, feeling or action that is in alignment with our genuine desire to release another (and our self) from guilt, fear and judgment, is an expression of Love. Every thought, feeling and action of gratitude is an expression of Love. Each time we choose to forgive instead of to judge is an expression of Love. When we sincerely desire to help or give to another with no agenda, this is an expression of Love.

3. When we remain present and genuinely *receive* a gift offered or given to us by another, without guilt or false humility, then God Himself is gifted in that Holy Instant. His Love is increased by our receiving with a sincere and thankful heart.

4. Giving *is* receiving. The higher purpose in relationship is to give or to extend forgiveness. Above all, we seek to behold the innocence in another. This is the literal reversal of all we have learned in the ego dream whose aim is to take from another in a futile attempt to make oneself complete.

   a. *"For an unholy relationship is based on differences, where each one thinks the other has what he has not. They come together, each to complete himself and rob the other. They stay until they think that there is nothing left to steal, and then move on." T-22.in.2:5-7*

5. A relationship is either one of changeless Love – or – there is no relationship at all. There is no gray area. I feel Jesus sums up the blinding contrast between special and Holy Relationship in the following quote:

   a. *"There is no order in relationships. They either are or not.*

An unholy relationship is no relationship. It is a state of isolation, which seems to be what it is not. No more than that." T-20.VI.8:1-5

C. Two People - One Truly Common Purpose

1. Our one function here is healing. And healing is accomplished as we learn with Holy Spirit to give everything the one sanctified purpose of forgiveness. *"As your function in Heaven is creation, so your function on earth is healing."* T-12.VII.4:7

2. Jesus says that we will not understand anyone or anything until we have prioritized the true and common purpose of them all. *"And it is recognized that all things must be first forgiven, and [then] understood."* T-30.V.1:6 True awakening begins when we have made a deliberate choice to see another's interests as *not apart* from our own. In contrast, the false self in special relationships is focused on what it can get for *itself alone.* Consequently, when its needs are not met in relationship it quickly turns to anger and conflict, and (special) love appears to turn to hate.

3. I would like to clear up a typical confusion regarding Holy Relationship. Many of us, me included, have misunderstood Jesus' message on these relationships See *"Two Opposing Goals in Relationship"* in Chapter VI, page 664. Namely, there has been a mistaken belief that a Holy Relationship only takes *one* consenting individual. Yet as Jesus states in many passages, the Holy Relationship is a mutual and not an individual pursuit.

   a. *"Everyone seeks for love as you do, but knows it not unless he joins with you in seeking it. If you undertake the search together, you bring with you a light so powerful that what you see is given meaning. The lonely journey fails because it has excluded what it would find."* T-14.X.10:5-7

4. Forgiveness is always helpful, even if only applied by one person. But to advance in our transfer of trust we need a "miracle buddy," as I term it. Miracle buddies are two or more individuals who share a mutual agreement between them to steadfastly choose forgiveness. These relationships need not necessarily be romantic.

5. A miracle buddy is a person joined with Holy Spirit, who agrees with others to prioritize – across the board – the one shared and truly common purpose which is above all else, to see their brother as sinless, guiltless and innocent. The necessary means by which this purpose is achieved is forgiveness. While the form of our learning varies greatly, the content is absolutely changeless. *"Its central theme is always, "God's Son is guiltless, and in his innocence is his salvation." M-1.3:5*

6. A Holy Relationship is one in which *two (or more) people* have been joined in a truly common purpose by the Holy Spirit. *"The relationship is holy because of that purpose." M-2.5:4* The seeming separation, maintained by their bodies, specialness and all the roles they valued previously, disappears as they advance in their mutually shared purpose together with Holy Spirit.

   a. *"In the teaching-learning situation, each one learns that giving and receiving are the same. The demarcations they have drawn between their roles, their minds, their bodies, their needs, their interests, and all the differences they thought separated them from one another, fade and grow dim and disappear. Those who would learn the same course share one interest and one goal." M-2.5:5-7*

7. Once we value forgiveness as our most sacred purpose then we will use every experience to meet that goal. Yes, we may be tempted often to see others as guilty, however we commit to changing our mind as soon as we can. Our priority becomes to close the seeming gap that lay between our self and another.

8. Note: Please see the Gap diagrams found on pages 46 thru 49. With two split minds in relationship, the false idols of specialness are found within the gap. The greatest idol which feeds all others is our mistaken belief in the *body* itself.

9. The special love relationship is *exclusive* and revolves around the body. The false self believes love is compartmentalized, changing (both guilt *and* innocence) and finite. It also believes that love can be threatened or withdrawn. It tries to hoard love and protect it. But this type of special exclusive love is purely fear in disguise.

10. The Holy Relationship is the opposite. It is *inclusive* and Spirit

identified, which affirms that the shared innocence between these people (guiltlessness) is cherished *above all else*. There may be two or more people who share this Holy commitment to innocence. It is certainly *not* an exclusive relationship. In fact, as this Relationship advances Holy Spirit brings other willing people to it for further learning.

11. This is a lifelong commitment we make. It means that we take a vow with Holy Spirit, "No matter what and no matter who might seem to come between us, let us not abandon each other." What does this mean? It is a declaration that we will not allow the ego's condemnation of anything or anyone to come between us. There is no one and nothing which could threaten our lifetime commitment to see the innocent Christ in our Holy Relationship partner(s).

12. We recognize that our only purpose is to learn to see our brother and everyone else as innocent. While sometimes the relationship's form may change, we vow that the content between us never changes. The content of this changeless Love is the shared and upheld commitment to seeing the true innocence beyond appearances of any kind.

13. In an advanced Holy Relationship, we share this one common purpose of seeing each other as sinless, of accepting the Atonement with another. And we also commit to learning an entirely new way of relating which undoes all previous addictions to specialness. We do this as we abide by the discipline of the *Seven Keys*. This one constant, common purpose is the only one that gives everyone and everything the one goal. It is a purpose that thoroughly transcends false, self-interests.

14. Forgiveness, or accepting the Atonement, is the *one purpose* in the world that undoes the idea of separation. When we apply this to everyone and everything, instead of misinterpreting their meaning and reacting through a filter of fear, everything literally becomes unified. In the light of our having given it just one sanctified purpose, we see our own incorruptible innocence reflected in everyone.

15. The ego gives everyone and every event a multitude of meanings and purposes, the outcome of which appears as random chaos. Yet with forgiveness as a constant purpose, all events become meaningful because they are all assigned a changeless purpose. Forgiveness is the one wholly invincible and unassailable practice that cannot ever be opposed. There is no opposite which can attack it. Therefore, it is invulnerable. This is why, when two people join with forgiveness as their utmost priority – the world is healed along with them.

a. *"Only a constant purpose can endow events with stable meaning. But it must accord [one] meaning to them all. If they are given different meanings, it must be that they reflect but different purposes."* ... *"Fear is a judgment never justified. Its presence has no meaning but to show you wrote a fearful script, and are afraid accordingly." T-30.VII.3:1-3,8-9*

b. *"Escape from judgment simply lies in this; all things have but one purpose, which you share with all the world. And nothing in the world can be opposed to it, for it belongs to everything, as it belongs to you." T-30.VII.5:1-2*

16. As these two individuals dedicate themselves to true forgiveness, they unify their purpose together with Holy Spirit. They engage in the consistent desire to surrender their need to be right and to blame. Forgiveness takes place naturally as they commit to communicate through willingness, accountability, emotional transparency, radical self-honesty, defenselessness, trust and gratitude. And the many idols that previously sustained the gap between them are organically brought to the light to be forgiven and healed (please refer again to the Gap diagrams on pages 46 thru 49).

D. Exercise: Truly Shared Goals

1. The only goals that can be truly shared are those that you share with Holy Spirit. Yet before you can offer up your own independent goals to be healed by Holy Spirit, you'll need to recognize them first. What are they? And are you willing to give these to Him to be divinely repurposed?

2. For example:

1) Do you believe you "need" this person (partner)? In which areas do you need them? For instance, sex, financial security, home, material possessions, physical support, emotional support,

happiness, business interests, hobbies, entertainment, social activities, to avoid loneliness, to keep the family's "form" together, to avoid social embarrassment, etc.

2) Review the shared goals and interests you have with your partner. With radical self-honesty, which of these are genuinely shared – with Holy Spirit – and which are the ego's self-seeking goals? In other words, which of these, if compromised by your partner, would lead you to change or withdraw your love? These are goals of separate self-interest. They are destined to destroy your relationship because they exclude the only one that could save it, the Holy Self you share with your partner.

E. Holy Relationship Evolution – A Bird's Eye View

1. Perhaps a bird's eye view of the Holy Relationship may help here. There are phases and levels in the development of advanced Holy Relationship where complete forgiveness of our brother as the Son of God is attained. While we can most assuredly reach advanced Holy Relationships in this lifetime, we must meet the crucial prerequisite of *desiring* to see and know our brother as innocent, despite so many tempting appearances to the contrary. Remember that we either perceive him or her as a body (guilty) – *or* – as the Spirit (innocent), the Christ. And as we see him or her, we will see our self.

2. Remember to believe that something is either good or bad is to value it. Belief *is* value. Belief in one – body *or* Spirit – eclipses the other. These two opposites cannot be valued at the same time because they are literally, mutually exclusive. Our value of one cancels out the other. This is precisely why the body, together with its sensual appetites (specialness), must be divinely repurposed with Holy Spirit. Until they're repurposed, temptation to view our brother *as a body* and not as the shared, Holy Self, will continue to pull us into judgment, blame and pain.

3. Keep in mind that in the long dream of all the dimensions of time we have experienced possibly thousands of seeming lifetimes,

all of which include special relationships. In my experience, and in working with thousands of others, it has been revealed that we repeat relationships with certain individuals in each lifetime until these unions are fully healed.

4. The single underlying spiritual purpose of these relationships is to *wake-up* from the specialness dynamic, to awaken from our false sense of self, the body and the illusion of separation. But we do not fervently desire to wake-up from these prized idols until we have hit the proverbial wall in exercising our own independent "ego will," apart from Spirit. This involves reaching our limits of suffering, and special relationships are the perfect playground to experience the depths of despair and disillusionment. Hence the majority of our relationships, romantic or not, will often reflect themes of pain such as abandonment, betrayal, victim and perpetrator.

5. In my own current lifetime, I had a very difficult relationship with my mother. I had believed that I was victimized by her as a child. Yet when I worked through my own forgiveness process with Holy Spirit, it was revealed later that our mother/daughter relationship in this life was merely a continuation of a previous (and conveniently repressed) one.

6. In a previous life-frame, I had been the victimizer and she had been the victim. Such is the "specialness dynamic" in all relationships since the beginning of time itself. In this lifetime I was given the priceless gift of being able to forgive *myself* for having unknowingly used her to try to prove that I was a victim and was therefore separate. And thus, with this profound gift…our relationship was healed for all time.

7. Holy Relationship is the bridge toward our experience of the final Real World dream. Within the dream of time it is an evolution, depending on the strength of our heart-felt desire to "close the gap" with others (and Self). This is the honest measure of our single devotion to the "forgiveness factor," remembering that all forgiveness is *self-forgiveness* and the undoing of our unconscious compulsion to self-attack (separate).

8. It is through relationships that we teach, and therefore learn, who we are. They represent our primary teaching/learning classroom in

the ego dream. We learn what *we are* by what we choose to see – value – *in others*. And the special relationship is the perfect starting point. The degree to which we experience relationship conflict reveals perfectly where our very own projections and false self-evaluation need to be healed via forgiveness.

9. As we unpack the whole specialness theme and undo the key components which have fed our distorted attraction to sin, guilt and fear, Holy Spirit can help us to elevate our vision to high above the battlefield of this particular life-frame. The healing evolution of our relationships may be perfected in this lifetime, or it may take many more lifetimes of conflict and pain, depending on the degree of our desire to see others (and our self) as sinless, blameless and innocent.

F. Five Phases of Relationship Evolution

1. In this broad overview, we begin with the special relationship. While all special relationships are referred to here, specifically, the romantic relationship appears to be most challenging because it involves the ego's most prized and defended appetite, sex. And while the sexual appetite has not been given to Holy Spirit for divine re-purposing, it lies at the seat of our unconscious desire to be body-identified rather than Spirit-identified. This fundamental confusion is a prime magnet for special relationships and if not healed, is a repetitive theme that pursues us into further incarnations.

2. **Phase # 1** - There are two people in a special relationship. Neither one has a desire to awaken, while both are still deeply hypnotized by what they can steal from, or trade with each other. This relationship is one of mutual use and their special love is threatened if certain conditions are not met. Often, the relationship will end, and the same goal of *special love* is sought once again in yet another relationship. These two will never experience the perfect relationship while their underlying demand for special love (conflict) is in force. Often, they will find that what seemed to bring them together initially eventually drives them apart.

3. **Phase # 2** - There are two people in relationship. Partner number one begins to see clean through "special love" and becomes disillusioned by it. He or she starts to earnestly yearn for changeless

Love (God, Holy Self, etc.). Yet partner number two is not interested in changing his or her beliefs and values, and certainly does not see the value of practicing forgiveness. Number two still wants special love. The possible outcome here is that partner number one commits to practice forgiveness until it is perfected in him/her within this relationship.

4. If partner number two does not eventually come on board so to speak, the relationship's "form" will often change. For example, a marriage may end but the friendship continues. Or the relationship/ friendship will end. It is obvious that the two individuals in this relationship have vastly different beliefs, values, goals and purposes. Thus, they are each headed on very different trajectories. In this case partner number one can use the relationship with Holy Spirit by applying forgiveness and utilizing the *Seven Keys*. In learning to "show-up" authentically, he or she is unlearning specialness. This practice will accelerate the purification necessary to prepare for Holy Relationship.

5. **Phase # 3** - Partner number one has the same initial experience as in Phase #2. But their partner is deeply affected by their practice of forgiveness and the *Seven Keys*. As a miraculous consequence, partner number two sees and experiences the infinite value of this practice and decides to join partner number one, inviting the Holy Spirit to *shift the goal* of their relationship from special to Holy. In this case, the *two* have now joined to consciously initiate the Holy Relationship and are committed to its truly common purpose of accepting the Atonement and applying forgiveness. Hence there is an initial, radical shift that usually takes place in such a relationship.

6. **Phase # 4** - There are two people in relationship. Both partners have previously maxed out in "special love" experiences and have been seriously disillusioned by it, along with all its temptations. They have mutually reached the same point. They recognize the blessed and joyous opportunity to join each other in this single purpose, and they set their sights with Holy Spirit, on nothing less than changeless Love. There is nothing in the world they want more than to "close the gap" of separation between them (and everyone else).

7. This phase of relationship, where *both people* make forgiveness

their single purpose, has been quite a rare occurrence in the dream of time, up until this point. Here we have two people with the exact same truly common purpose, devoted to not allowing anything, including the body, its appetites and all the other idols that make up the "gap," to ever come between them. This is truly an advanced Holy Relationship. *"So do the parts of God's Son gradually join in time, and with each joining is the end of time brought nearer. Each miracle of joining is a mighty herald of eternity." T-20.V.1:5-6*

8. **Phase # 5** – Even rarer than the Phase # 4 relationship, this union involves two people whose trust is still further developed. The body concept which constitutes the illusory "gap" is wholly surrendered to Spirit here. Of all body appetites, sexual desire remains at the seat of the ego's reincarnation recycle program. It is the number one death magnet while it remains unsurrendered and unhealed.

9. The primal sexual desire is a misdirected miracle impulse. It's also the underlying predecessor of all physical impulse distortions and is therefore the most resistant to conscious and mindful relinquishment (See Chapter IV, *"Sex and TransOrgasmic Union"*). No wonder in the earlier stage of dictation of the *Course* which Jesus gave to Helen Schucman, He stated emphatically the following quote which was edited out of the FIP version, as were most quotes referring to sex: *"I want to finish the instructions about sex, because this is an area the miracle worker MUST understand." T-1.B.40 b.*

10. Limitless relationship necessitates relinquishment of our attachment to its greatest adversary – the body. In Phase # 5 we learn to give up every use the ego has for the body under the Holy Spirit's Loving direction. The body is entirely and divinely repurposed. The ego's corrupted interpretation of this involves sacrifice, struggle and effort. But the presence of any of these is an immediate sign that the spiritualized ego has taken over. The body is repurposed by the Holy Spirit and *not* by the ego. As a result, our part involves giving the body and its appetites to Him. And it is He who transforms them.

a. *"In the holy instant, where the Great Rays replace the body in awareness, the recognition of relationships without limits*

*is given you. But in order to see this, **it is necessary to give up
every use the ego has for the body, and to accept the fact that
the ego has no purpose you would share with it.**" T-15.IX.3:1-2*

11. Remember that to the degree we are willing to undo *all* our idols,
challenging *as well as pleasurable*, will be the extent to which Holy
Spirit has our permission to send us the perfect partner(s) with whom
we can ascend back up the ladder of separation. Recall that everyone
is given a "savior" (or saviors) with which to complete the Holy
Relationship. And this person will show-up when all we want is to
see his or her innocence. However, as I said before, our resistance to
relinquishing our idols of specialness, especially the body, may span
lifetimes, and seem to draw out time.

a. *"To each who walks this earth in seeming solitude is a savior
given, whose special function here is to release him, and so
to free himself. In the world of separation each is appointed
separately, though they are all the same. Yet those who know
that they are all the same need not salvation. And each one finds
his savior when he is ready to look upon the face of Christ, and
see Him sinless."* T-20.IV.5:3-6

G. Looking on the "Gap" Together

1. Let me explain that at some point in the seemingly endless
timeline of reincarnation, we will all max out in phase one of special
relationships. They all lead to conflict, disease, aging and death.
Still today, more than two thousand years after Jesus appeared in a
body, the vast majority of the world is drowning in a sea of special
relationships all revolving around a single common denominator,
the central idol in the dream – the body. Some of us, especially
you who are reading this book, have heard the sacred Call to Holy
Relationship. And for that, I thank you with all my heart.

2. As we look down from high above the battlefield, we can see that
all the broken relationships we experienced were either phase one or
two relationships. The good news is that while they seemed to fail
or end, sometimes even quite painfully, they are always destined for
a wholly Loving completion. They will all eventually become Holy

Relationships. This is inevitable. However, that may not be in this lifetime.

a. *"As with the first level, these meetings are not accidental, nor is what appears to be the end of the relationship a real end. Again, each has learned the most he can at the time. Yet all who meet will someday meet again, for it is the destiny of all relationships to become holy."* M-3.4:4-6

3. To continue this bird's eye view, Jesus actually reveals that there are certain milestones in the Holy Relationship's evolution. Once these two (or more) have found each other and agree to the Holy Spirit's mutual goal and purpose, they are ready together to apply the means (forgiveness) and advance their trust. *"This is the place to which everyone must come when he is ready. Once he has found his brother he [is] ready."* T-19.IV.D.10:2-3

4. As an essential element in the Holy Relationship's advancement, each partner's hidden attraction to specialness must be ceaselessly examined, to be healed via forgiveness. Every false belief, including the false-self-concept, old patterns, past hurts, unseen agendas, secret idols, and inappropriate body appetites all come out of denial to be seen – *thus, closing the gap together.* To the ego, this is its worst nightmare because its illusory existence depends entirely on keeping these idols from being discovered and healed.

5. When two people agree together to look upon the ugly idols in the "gap" with Holy Spirit, something quite miraculous occurs. Recall that all problems regardless of their severity exist only while *two or more minds agree that they're real*, and that there is indeed a problem. When two accept the Atonement, *the divine correction instead,* whatever appeared previously in the "gap" must disintegrate. Healing occurs.

6. As these two contemplate the issue or idol, with the single intention of accepting the Atonement for themselves, they withdraw their agreement to its seeming reality. In other words, they withdraw as a consenting witness to the particular problem, so its deceptive reality vanishes. The issue itself – mental, emotional or physical – requires *two or more witnesses* who agree to its reality in order for it to continue. In a Holy Relationship, both people have committed

to the one sanctified purpose. Therefore, when one person removes his agreement to witness what is *not there*, the problem cannot survive for lack of an agreeing witness. When one partner does this, it is done for both, although healing may not be received by the second partner until they are willing. Two or more people in Holy Relationship are healed as a miraculous consequence of having genuinely accepted the Atonement. In addition to this, a miraculous ripple effect continues to wash over the entire Sonship because when we heal…we never heal alone.

a. *"Heaven is restored to all the Sonship through your relationship, for in it lies the Sonship, whole and beautiful, safe in your love."* T-18.I.11:1

H. A Staggering and Life Changing Event

a. *"You have been called, together with your brother, to the most holy function this world contains. It is the only one that has no limits, and reaches out to every broken fragment of the Sonship with healing and uniting comfort. This is offered you, in your holy relationship."* T-18.I.13:1-3

1. True Holy Relationships are relatively uncommon. As yet, we don't have many demonstrations of these advanced relationships in the world to serve as role models to follow. Hence, we try to imagine what a Holy Relationship might look like based largely upon a past filled with special relationships. In my own comprehensive experience with Holy Relationship, it is the *opposite* of what we imagine "love" to be here in this world.

2. The Holy Relationship is an entirely new paradigm because it refuses to allow fear, concern or sacrifice to taint the perfect Love that Spirit is leading us to. *"When brothers join in purpose in the world of fear, they stand already at the edge of the real world."* T-30.V.7:1

3. A common question often asked is this, "How will we know when the Holy Spirit has entered the relationship?" Let me put it this way, when the Holy Spirit enters a relationship on the sincere invitation of two or more people, it is an extraordinary event! There is no subtlety

here. It is an undeniably supernatural experience. This heralds the literal beginning of a whole new world, complete with heavenly laws that only very few have ever seen, let alone embraced.

4. Once the Holy Spirit enters this divine union, it sets off a chain of events which are not even imaginable. The process or evolution of this union is sanctified by the Holy Spirit together with all the Angels in Heaven. Each and every erroneous belief, mistaken idol, misdirected miracle impulse, body-focused desire, and false law, is offered up for the Holy Spirit to purify.

a. *"When the Holy Spirit changed the purpose of your relationship by exchanging yours for His, the goal He placed there was extended to every situation in which you enter, or will ever enter. And every situation was thus made free of the past, which would have made it purposeless."* T-17.VII.9:5-6

5. Everything is to be healed. The concept and purpose of the body in particular must be healed, and this includes both the painful aspects and the pleasurable ones as well. The ego's deeply coveted pursuit of completion *through* the body, including its desire for pleasure, must be gently repurposed with Spirit. And the Holy Relationship provides the perfect means and support to engage deeply in this divine undoing process.

6. We must be wholly willing to *unlearn* the world's version of love and caring, which is really attack. The Holy Relationship is the Holy Grail and will lead us to the ego dream's final conclusion which is our complete awakening from the dream of bodies and time. And when two or more wholly devote themselves to this... the entire Sonship is healed along with them. This is salvation.

a. *Through your holy relationship, reborn and blessed in every holy instant you do not arrange, thousands will rise to Heaven with you."* ... *"It will become the happy dream through which He can spread joy to thousands on thousands who believe that love is fear, not happiness."* T-18.V.3:1, 5:5

I. Two Who Share a Common State of Mind

1. Once two people have committed to a Holy Relationship and Holy Spirit has entered into it, then the other characteristics of Holy Relationship will be made manifest as well. They join in the **truly common purpose of forgiveness**, as we have already covered. However, in addition to this, Jesus tells us that these two (or more) will experience the following:

2. **A common state of mind:** Two people share a common state of mind where not just one, but *both* people actively participate in the forgiveness process, that both may be happily healed as the one Holy Self. And as this shared mind is healed, the idols which made up the gap between them fade and disappear.

   a. *"Yet reason sees a holy relationship as what it is; a common state of mind, where **both** give errors gladly to correction, that **both** may happily be healed as one." T-22.III.9:7*

3. These two who have relinquished the ego's private mind, also surrendered its pursuit of personal agendas. The only way two people can experience conflict is if the ego's personal self-seeking agendas clash. Because these two cherish each other's innocence *more* than they value the ego's idols that constitute the gap, they develop a profound reverence and Love for each other. Tear-filled moments of super sensory gratitude and grace are common as they behold the Christ in each other.

4. **Shared Holy Instants:** As a consequence, they progressively experience more joint Holy Instants together, while beliefs in the past and investments in the future fall away.

5. **Closing of the gap:** The function of God's teachers is to save time via miracles and the Holy Relationship. The path of Holy Relationship is a special curriculum, intended for those who would teach and learn a unique form of awakening. Yet all paths which teach that guilt and fear are unreal are helpful. Holy Relationship, due to its truly shared common purpose and goal, collapses time, thereby dematerializing the illusory gap, along with its contents, which has separated us from our brothers, our Holy Self and God.

   a. *"For what one thinks, the other will experience with him.*

What can this mean except your mind and your brother's are one?" T-22.VI.14:2-3

6. **Barriers melt and hearts open:** The partners experience a melting away of the barrier between their minds, and their hearts burst open to receive the magnitude of Love's full illumination. As they witness the majesty of changeless innocence in each other, this becomes *all they desire* to see and feel. Once they feel this magnitude of oneness its joy sparks the roaring fire of the most ancient yearning of all time; our only true desire, to return to Love *as* Love itself.

7. **Miraculous healing of one another through accepting the Atonement:** When either one of the partners is tempted to perceive fear which includes sickness, pain, anger, lack, doubt, conflict, control, defense, etc., the other can heal him by accepting the Atonement on his behalf. Having set the goal in advance – to see their brother's innocence – they are perfectly able to extend healing to each other at the request of either partner. Yet the miracle always blesses both.

8. The following passage is too important not to include here in its entirety:

   a. *"When you feel the holiness of your relationship is threatened by anything, stop instantly and offer the Holy Spirit your willingness, in spite of fear, to let Him exchange this instant for the holy one that you would rather have. He will never fail in this. But forget not that your relationship is one, and so it must be that whatever threatens the peace of one is an equal threat to the other. The power of joining its blessing lies in the fact that it is now impossible for you or your brother to experience fear alone, or to attempt to deal with it alone. Never believe that this is necessary, or even possible. Yet just as this is impossible, so is it equally impossible that the holy instant come to either of you without the other. And it will come to both at the request of either."*

   "Whoever is saner at the time the threat is perceived should remember how deep is his indebtedness to the other and how

much gratitude is due him, and be glad that he can pay his debt by bringing happiness to both. Let him remember this, and say:

"I desire this holy instant for myself, that I may share it with my brother, whom I love. It is not possible that I can have it without him, or he without me. Yet it is wholly possible for us to share it now. And so I choose this instant as the one to offer to the Holy Spirit, that His blessing may descend on us, and keep us both in peace." T-18.V.6,7.

9. As I mentioned earlier the goal of Holiness is inevitable. The only thing that appears to separate an unhealed relationship from a Holy one is time. And as you can see, when two are completely willing to join in overlooking the seeming gap together, then healing is truly irrevocable.

J. A Joint Special Function

1. This now leads me to share about what Jesus terms as the Holy Relationship's "joint special function" in the salvation of the world. Each individual is given a special function in salvation. Yet each Holy Relationship takes on its own "joint" special function which is so exciting!

   a. *"Each holy relationship must enter here, to learn its special function in the Holy Spirit's plan, now that it shares His purpose." T-20.IV.6:6*

2. This joint function may begin early in the relationship but becomes more refined as the two (or more) continue to commit more deeply to their truly mutual purpose. The specific form their joint special function takes may differ, however every Holy Relationship is blessed with the opportunity to manifest the outcome of this most sacred of all vows:

   a. *"I want the peace of God."... "No one can mean these words and not be healed." ... "The world would be completely changed, should any two agree these words express the only thing they want." "Two minds with one intent become so strong that what they will becomes the Will of God." ... "There would be no further sorrow possible for you in any form; in any place or time. Heaven would be completely given back to full awareness, memory of God entirely restored, the resurrection of all creation fully recognized." W-185.2:1,9,3:1,1:3-4*

3. Effectively, if two or more in Holy Relationship joined as the one Will of God, the idols which previously sustained the imaginary gap would disappear. There would be a comprehensive time/space collapse for all mankind. It would herald an almighty paradigm shift resulting in the increasing right-minded perception and experience of the Real World.

    a. *"You will remember everything the instant you desire it wholly, for if to desire wholly is to create, you will have willed away the separation, returning your mind simultaneously to your Creator and your creations. Knowing Them you will have no wish to sleep, but only the desire to waken and be glad. Dreams will be impossible because you will want only truth, and being at last your will, it will be yours." T-10.I.4:1-3*

4. The Holy Relationship's completion is brought about by these two fulfilling their joint special function. This is the stage where the teachers of God in Holy Relationship graduate and become true miracle workers. And as these two advance in their devotion and trust then their closing of the primordial gap must ultimately affect the entire Sonship.

    a. *"Think not that your forgiveness of your brother serves but you two alone. For the whole new world rests in the hands of every two who enter here to rest. And as they rest, the face of Christ shines on them and they remember the laws of God, forgetting all the rest and yearning only to have His laws perfectly fulfilled in them and all their brothers." T-20.IV.7:2-4*

5. From my current experience, and in listening to Jesus directly, the advanced Holy Relationship is the catalyst by which we overcome the laws of the world by reversing them. This is where true miracle working becomes common place, just as Jesus healed the sick and raised the dead. As we awaken from the illusion of the body as "cause" we come to recognize and embrace the fact that the body

is merely an effect in the mind. It cannot change, sicken, heal, age or die of itself. Only the mind directs all changes in the body.

6. When two or more join in withdrawing their agreement to believe the idols of sickness in the gap, their union as the Will of God erases all appearances of separation. As the cause is healed so are its effects.

   a. *"Yet when two or more join together in searching for truth, the ego can no longer defend its lack of content. The fact of union tells them it is not true." T-14.X.9:6-7*

7. I believe that in the advanced Holy Relationship we finally learn, embody, and demonstrate the first miracle principle, "There is no order of difficulty in miracles." Physical miracles re-establish God's Laws here in the dream by reversing the ego's laws of separation. And Jesus said that we would one day do as He did…and more. Thus, we come to realize that in the "joint will of the Son in union with the Father," dominion over the relative world is natural. (See Chapter III titled, *"True Healing"* on page 291.)

8. Ultimately, the ego's central dream – of death – is overcome when two or more join in genuine advanced Holy Relationship. And this is where sickness, pain, conflict, loss, lack and death are overcome.

9. In the beginning, two or more agreed to imagine separation – bodies, time, world, etc. – and now those two finally show-up to reverse their timeworn choice, along with all its seeming consequences. Thus, the Holy Relationship is the gateway to the final dream in time, the Real World. *"Where two have joined for healing, God is there. And He has guaranteed that He will hear and answer them in truth." P-2.V.4:4-5*

   a. *"The holy relationship, a major step toward the perception of the real world, is learned."… "The holy relationship is a phenomenal teaching accomplishment." T-17.V.2:1,3*

K. Inclusive Extension of Love

1. In stark contrast to the exclusivity of the special relationship, the advanced Holy Relationship is *inclusive* in that as it grows in trust, it becomes a powerful magnet to draw in those who also commit to being unequivocal in their desire to awaken *from* the dream of separation.

2. A Holy Relationship is much like a central sun in that it attracts its own constellation of people who hear the divine Call. In my own experience, at the time of writing this book, my central Holy Relationship has extended to include two more advancing Holy Relationships as well as a growing spiritual family of more than 100 people in our global online Total Transformation (TTC) Community. These are like-minded people who genuinely desire to join together in the Holy Spirit's truly common purpose of forgiveness and Holy Relationship.

3. I'm presently experiencing the Holiness of my Relationship extending, radiating outward and bringing in those who share the same purpose.

   a. *"The extension of the Holy Spirit's purpose from your relationship to others, to bring them gently in."* ... *"Reason now can lead you and your brother to the logical conclusion of your union. It must extend, as you extended when you and he joined." T-19.IV.1:5, T-22.in.4:5-6*

4. Jesus shares some important content in the context of Holy Relationships: Certain Holy Relationship partners have been assigned to you, and they will begin to look for you as soon as you have answered the Call. In its original form the quote goes like this: *"Certain pupils have been assigned to each of God's teachers, and they will begin to look for him as soon as he has answered the Call." M-2.1:1*

   a. *"Time has been readjusted to help us do, together, what your separate pasts would hinder. You have gone past fear, for no two minds can join in the desire for love without love's joining them." T-18.III.7:6-7*

L. Back to Basics

1. While we may desire to enjoy Holy Relationships, we cannot possibly have (or get) that which we our self are not first willing to *give*. Giving *is* receiving. Therefore, our experience of Holiness in relationship – as our incorruptible innocence and safety – will be in direct proportion to our degree of trust and faith in our brother.

Do we trust him or her? Are we radically honest and emotionally transparent without judgment or guilt-trips? Do we have secret agendas? Do we really want to see them as sinless? Are we consciously accountable for our projections? Do we practice being defenseless? And are we grateful for each time we're triggered because without these forgiveness opportunities, we could never find, let alone heal the singular source of all our suffering (our own unconscious self-hatred projected outward).

2. Within the Holy Relationship lay the whole way out of our distorted reversal of all the laws of God. There is only one ego and one Holy Self. What I see in another is exactly what I *want* to see. It always comes from either the ego's filter or the Holy Self. Put simply then, to the degree I am triggered by anyone or anything reveals the extent to which I have projected my unconscious fear of God. There is only one of us here in this holographic dream. Everything I feel and experience is exactly what I secretly believe I deserve. *Only what I have not given* in any situation can be lacking.

3. Everyone who triggers me is here to help me see my unconscious desire for separation so that I can finally heal it once and for all. No one *can* abandon me. No one *can* betray me unless I have first abandoned and betrayed *my Self*.

4. While we choose to cling to the belief that we were unfairly treated, our relationships will obscure their divine purpose in our lives and deny us their life-giving gifts. If there is no one separate from us, then *who* appeared to hurt us? And which *self* feels attacked? It could only be the false self.

5. The ego uses all relationships to confirm, protect and defend its false identity and the special love which supports it. The Holy Spirit, on the other hand, values relationships only to the degree they have the potential for becoming a Holy Relationship. *"Relationships in particular must be properly perceived, and all dark cornerstones of unforgiveness removed. Otherwise the old thought system still has a basis for return."* M-9.1:8-9

6. Holy Relationship offers a chance to learn that giving is receiving. We learn that we already have it to give, otherwise we could not give it. How in the world will we ever realize the sanctity and security of

our glorious and innocent Holy Self unless we are willing to see it in another? In fact, it is by seeing it in another that we recognize and accept it in our Self. This is the one Christ in which we share.

7. Jesus tells us that the Holy Relationship is the means by which every situation we experience is transformed. Once we invite the Holy Spirit to replace the ego's unconscious relationship goal with His, then a miraculous transfer takes place whereby His Goal of Holiness and healing extends itself to every situation we will encounter.

8. He also explains that the final phase of the dream, the advanced phase of trust, takes *two people*...not one alone, but two. Each one of us is assigned a savior, whose special function is to release us both from separation. He says that we will find this person when we are *truly ready* to behold the Christ. And what does that mean in practical terms? It means that we must genuinely and consistently desire to see another's guiltlessness more than we believe in death. It means that we must be willing, that we must want to see no sin, no blame in him or her. Think about that.

9. Are you ready?

4. FINDING THE CORE DESIRE

1. When we're threatened by relationship conflict, illness, or any other form of adversity, we cannot heal the fundamental cause while it remains hidden from awareness. When we locate the false self's "core desire" it will certainly fast-track the healing process.

2. There are two distinctive ways to perceive. The one we're conditioned to value and adopt is through the split mind of fear which is fueled by unrelinquished guilt. The other is through perfect Love, untainted by sin, guilt or fear.

3. Everything we perceive, including our body, our past and each person we encounter arises literally from our own perceptual filter. Every experience we have, either good or bad, is chosen

by us. This is mostly unconscious until we habitually relinquish our attraction to separation and self-attack.

4.   The people we seem to relate with, the body we seem to inhabit, and the world we appear to witness are all fabricated by the trajectory of our very own desire. What we experience emerges directly from the "aim" of our core desire. Everyone and everything in the seeming world is neutral. We give everything we perceive *all* the meaning that it has for us. Without our own personal interpretation of everyone and everything, they have no meaning of their own because they are neutral.

5.   We don't interact with *others*. We interact with our own *interpretation* of them. They always respond to us according to the aim of our core desire. This core desire influences every single encounter and experience we have. But while the false-self's desire remains hidden and unrelinquished to Holy Spirit, it must be projected outward onto others as relationship conflict, and onto the body as pain, disease, aging and death.

6.   For example, before my healing I experienced decades of victimization in many forms. This included childhood abuse, sexual abuse, and many relationship conflicts. There was an undeniable pattern where I seemed to be a victim of people and circumstances out of my control. On top of that, I felt continually judged by others; I just could not please them no matter how hard I tried. I felt besieged by condemnation from others. For the life of me I could not understand why others were so critical of me.

7.   Many years later, when I had truly reached my limit with this pain, I asked Holy Spirit for help. Finally, with His help, I got to see the singular cause of this incessant conflict, with its self-doubt and unworthiness. Furthermore, it had absolutely nothing to do with my past abuse, which was what I had believed was the cause. What I learned is that the singular cause is never external, in another person or in the past.

8.   The sole cause was the false-self's undisputed conviction that it was unfairly treated. This conviction that we were *or that we ever could be* unfairly treated is the false-self's core desire. The *special* self cannot be maintained without this belief. It must be unfairly

treated in order to maintain its fuel – which is to believe in sin, guilt and fear. Its illusory identity is reinforced by the belief we are separate bodies instead of one, shared, glorious Holy Self.

9. The "core desire" of the false-self is to see in others what we deny in our selves – guilt. Superficially, *we* don't want to feel guilty, so we blame *others*. The ego wants proof that there *are* others, that we *are* separate. Guilt is that proof. It always brings separation and attack in all its numerous forms.

10. Although it is an epidemic in the world we seem to see, the ego's core desire for separation is impersonal. Through the dimensions of time we chose to teach our self how to see apart from Love and innocence. We taught our self to perceive the body, others, and the world through this treacherous filter of sin, guilt and fear. Yet we are seeing what is *not* there!

    a.   *"If you are afraid, it is because you saw something that is not there. Yet in that same place you could have looked upon me and all your brothers, in the perfect safety of the Mind which created us." T-12.VII.10:4-5*

    b.   *"As you look with open eyes upon your world, it must occur to you that you have withdrawn into insanity. You see what is not there, and you hear what makes no sound. Your manifestations of emotions are the opposite of what the emotions are. You communicate with no one, and you are as isolated from reality as if you were alone in all the universe. In your madness you overlook reality completely, and you see only your own split mind everywhere you look. God calls you and you do not hear, for you are preoccupied with your own voice. And the vision of Christ is not in your sight, for you look upon yourself alone." T-13.V.6.*

11. The body and its five physical senses and appetites were set up to be our primary preceptor (guru and master), made to record and broadcast the ego's core desire – guilt, fear, separation and attack. In this profound confusion, the ego assigns the body's senses to pursue both pleasure and pain. The hidden malevolent secret is that pleasure and pain are the *same* because they share the same

purpose – to make the body *real* in our awareness and to identify *as* a body. And while the *body* is perceived as real, our one shared and Holy Self will be viewed as a threat.

12. This translates to *forgiveness* being an outright *threat* to the ego's core desire. Forgiveness retrieves and erases everything the body identity seemed to witness or experience, thus undoing the past. Blamelessness, guiltlessness and true union are its result. Separate body identities lose their "wish to be unfairly treated" and withdraw their previous projections of attack.

13. Whenever I am triggered in whatever form, this is my consistent reminder:

14. I'm seeing the false self's wish to be attacked here. No one and nothing can attack me if I choose to forgive the single cause, *my wish for self-attack*. If I am sick or in pain, or if I am angry or offended by someone, it occurs because of my unforgiven wish to be separate from my Source, separate from unopposed Love and innocence.

15. What about my past abuse? Through the ego's wish to be unfairly treated, we repeat patterns in each lifetime. The false-self literally projects illusions, using others to hypothetically attack us. All seeming attack in the past, if still believed and unforgiven, is dragged into the present and superimposed over it. That is how it is theoretically carried forward into the future.

16. The memory of past pain is a ploy that completely obscures the present and the people in it. This is why we never relate with people as they are; we relate to our *interpretation* of them based on our unforgiven past.

17. The ego's projections of suffering, if not forgiven, become present blocks to Love and healing. They act as a huge screen that shrouds others, upon which we project our unforgiven beliefs in betrayal and abandonment. Conflict, pain and loss are believed and experienced as real.

18. Whereas the truth could not be more contrasting. Everyone, along with each instant, is entirely free of the past. In the present Holy Instant, there is no past. The thick veil of our past projections is lifted. We open to seeing everyone as they are – in changeless innocence.

a.   *"To perceive truly is to be aware of all reality through the awareness of your own. But for this no illusions can rise to meet your sight, for reality leaves no room for any error. This means that you perceive a brother only as you see him [now.] His past has no reality in the present, so you cannot see it. Your past reactions to him are also not there, and if it is to them that you react, you see but an image of him that you made and cherish instead of him. In your questioning of illusions, ask yourself if it is really sane to perceive what was as now. If you remember the past as you look upon your brother, you will be unable to perceive the reality that is now."* T-13.VI.1.

19. We only see what we want to see. We only feel what we want to feel. And we only experience what we want to experience. Nothing happens to us that is against our will. But what do we want? Do we want to know *above all else* that we're not separate from our Source of Love? If so, we must look past what we have projected onto the body and others, and ask to see *what is really there*, rather than what the false self has projected. We must *want* to see everyone as guiltless, as innocent.

20. We cannot see the innocent truth in anyone or anything until we first desire it.

a.   *"The miracle enables you to see your brother without his past, and so perceive him as born again. His errors are all past, and by perceiving him without them you are releasing him. And since his past is yours, you share in this release."* T-13.VI.5:1-3

21. Recall that there are only two ways of seeing. One is through the body's senses (filter of fear) and does not exist. The other is through vision (filter of light/Love) which *does* exist. People and events are not bad or evil. When we are triggered by someone or something, we are mistakenly projecting our own secret wish to be unfairly treated so we can prove that we are *special* and *separate*. All this serves to reinforce the illusion of a *special body identity*. Its mission is rejection of the one, innocent and majestic Holy Self we share in Spirit.

a. *"In any union with a brother in which you seek to lay your guilt upon him, or share it with him or perceive his own, [you] will feel guilty. Nor will you find satisfaction and peace with him, because your union with him is not real." T-13.X.3:1-2*

22. We can afford to have major gratitude for all our triggers. When repurposed in the light, they reveal exactly where we have mistakenly placed our values by our wish to be separate. With Holy Spirit's help, repurposing self-attack heals the one cause of every possible pain, illness, relationship conflict or problem.

23. There is always only one problem, and one Holy solution. There is no degree of difficulty in healing anything in this dream. Why? Because all of it stems from one fundamental illusion – the insane wish to be separate. When we drop to our knees in heartfelt gratitude and recognize this without exception, we will have embraced the *Course's* number one miracle principle: *"There is no order of difficulty in miracles."*

a. *"The state of guiltlessness is only the condition in which what is not there has been removed from the disordered mind that thought it was. This state, and only this, must you attain, with God beside you. For until you do, you will still think that you are separate from Him." T-14.IV.2:2-4*

5. ONE TRULY COMMON PURPOSE

1. Since the beginning of time, almost no one has recognized the *single underlying cause* of the collapse of all failed relationships. This is why they suffer from such high risk of continued failure in the world today. Without identifying the single, underlying cause of collapse, the remedy cannot be recognized nor implemented.

2. The bedrock of all our seeming conflict with others is that we each value what we believe is our own "private mind," with a separate body, all with highly personal thoughts and independent agendas. These private minds seem to value differing goals and so they clash.

The ego's self-serving goals are designed to divide and separate, with varying degrees of conflict and loss following.

3. Nearly all relationships in the world, personal and business, are based on this mistaken investment in separate agendas. These include romantic, family, friend, and business relationships. They are predicated on "specialness" – as personal, self-seeking aims. There may even appear to be a holistic, common goal, but if those involved do not agree to unite in one *truly common purpose* then the relationship will eventually fail.

4. In this world we can join with others in what, at first glance, *appears* to be a common purpose. For instance, romance, marriage, sex, having children, making money, saving the planet, etc. To historically ascertain how successful the ego's model of a "common purpose" has been, we need only to look at the multitude of marriages and business partnerships that were initiated in good faith, but which ended up in disaster, loss and separation.

5. How can it be that people can come together with the best of intentions initially, perhaps even to serve an altruistic cause, yet eventually their distinctly personal, i.e. special agendas collide, and they separate?

6. When people attempt to unite under the umbrella of a common purpose, yet each one values their own private, self-seeking agenda, then the common purpose, along with the relationship, business or project is often shattered. Separation as self-seeking agendas is the goal of specialness.

A. Egocentric vs. Inspired Common Purpose

1. The underlying agenda for joining with others in an ego common purpose – romantic relationships, friends, business ventures, saving the planet, etc. – is that they always join for what each person can get *separately*. They unite in temporary allegiance for what *each one* can gain individually from the collaboration. Their priority for personal gain over the unified goodness for all is a divided allegiance. The sum of a relationship's parts must collapse if its members divide themselves through their pursuit of self-seeking agendas. This is the real reason why so many relationships, business ventures and global empires have collapsed.

2. We see the repeated fragmentation and destruction of the ego's relationships in all walks of life. Strength is always weakened when it is not shared with all. Love has become fearful because the individual is possessive of this "love." Their agenda, at least on some level, was to gain something for them self. Had there been a *truly common purpose* as the foundation of the relationship, the power of that *true Love* could not have been shaken.

a. *"Egos do join together in temporary allegiance, but always for what each one can get [separately.] The Holy Spirit communicates only what each one can give to all." A Course in Miracles, T-6.V.A.5:9-10*

3. To bring this teaching into practical perspective, please refer again to the Gap diagrams on pages 46 thru 49. If you have experienced conflict in any relationship, look at each of the ego's idols which dwell in the gap. Can you see that the only *cause* of that relationship conflict was that you or your companion valued an illusory idol in the gap *more* than you valued each other's changeless innocence? This goes for all relationships with children, parents, romantic, etc. For instance, as a parent, if I am triggered and value being "right" while making my child wrong, I reject my child outright. Why? Because I have erroneously valued being "right" about the particular issue in the gap *more* than I cherish this child's innocence.

B. A Universal Law – To Transcend Self-Interests

1. In contrast to the ego's desire to gain independently, the outstanding hallmark of a "truly common purpose" is that it must *transcend self-interest* in order to be genuinely shared. It must be an idea that is mutually beneficial and can be shared with everyone involved; one that is in the best interests of all participants in the relationship. Anything less than this mutual blessing of "transcending self-interest" will eventually succumb to disintegration.

2. Only a truly common purpose can *be* shared. This is a universal law. The ego's version of a common purpose is volatile and temporary. Because those involved still value what each person can get for themselves *separately*, the relationship or business venture is simply not sustainable. No joint ventures can succeed unless we genuinely value other's best interests as *not separate* from our own.

3. A truly common purpose is indestructible. But for this to be so, it must transcend the self-interests of all involved. Only by doing this can it be meaningfully shared.

4. When we step out from our own personal, self-seeking agendas and genuinely desire to see and help others flourish, we will revel joyfully in a massive realization. Beyond the illusion of private minds with separate agendas, all conflicting with each other, is just One Mind. And that Mind is eternally conflict free because it's the true nature of every being on earth.

5. When we choose to see, to reach and to join with that part of everyone's Mind, then not only will *we* be healed together, but the entire world must follow.

C. Our True Purpose

1. Our true purpose involves serving the good of the whole. As our higher purpose, it consistently transcends separate self-interests. And happily, it always involves doing what we love to do. There is no sacrifice involved. This is God's Will which we eventually learn to accept with joy as we undo the false body-self's fear and desire for specialness - along with the crushing unworthiness that comes with it.

2. In addition, as we awaken from separation each one of us is given a special function to fulfill. The essence of this function never changes although the specific "forms" in which it is expressed may be numerous. The content of this function is shared by everyone who willingly embraces this divine mission. The substance of this function is always to convey the underlying message to others of their sinlessness and God given innocence.

3. How this plays out practically in our life will eventually be revealed to us. This assigned function involves implementing our special gifts, skills and abilities, never exclusively for self-gain but to bless the entire Sonship.

4. For example, when I began the *Course* in 1990, I had no idea what my function was. I had been embedded in a long career as a

make-up artist. But over the years, as I truly applied the principles of forgiveness within all my relationships, it became obvious that my passion was to share these life-changing teachings. As my trust in Spirit strengthened, I didn't have to worry about *how* to make a living. I was serving God's Plan. As a result, I eventually followed guidance to write and teach exclusively. This has become my abounding joy.

5. I learned that my number one priority was to serve His Plan's *purpose,* which always involves the undoing of special relating via forgiveness. Then I began to experience Holy Spirit providing the *means* to achieve His purpose and taking care of my earthly needs. Jesus says that once we wholly commit to His purpose then both the function and the means by which we accomplish it are given. This divine providence also includes perfect health and abundance.

   a. *"The means and purpose both belong to Him. You have accepted one; the other (the means) will be provided."* T-18.V.3:6-7

   b. *"You may wonder how you can be at peace when, while you are in time, there is so much that must be done before the way to peace is open. Perhaps this seems impossible to you. But ask yourself if it is possible that God would have a plan for your salvation that does not work. Once you accept His plan as the one function that you would fulfill, there will be nothing else the Holy Spirit will not arrange for you without your effort. He will go before you making straight your path, and leaving in your way no stones to trip on, and no obstacles to bar your way. Nothing you need will be denied you. Not one seeming difficulty but will melt away before you reach it. You need take thought for nothing, careless of everything except the only purpose that you would fulfill."* T-20.IV.8:1-8

6. The ego's version of love and caring, which is really fear in disguise, comes with a stockpile of distorted beliefs. One of these loaded beliefs is that to give or to help another demands that we sacrifice something of our self. It could be time, money or effort, etc.

It could demand that we suffer some form of loss or pain in order to help someone else. This is the insanity of the ego.

7. God's Love is whole. It is the very nature of our one continuous and unified Self, as the one Mind of God. Love cannot suffer. It cannot lose. And it cannot by any means "sacrifice" anything real. God's Love is completely alien to the ego thought system where we seem to lose what we give away, and the one we gave it to appears to gain what we lost.

8. In a radical reversal of the ego's belief, the only way we can *truly keep* something is if we *give it away*. We're talking here about the intent behind the giving. That intent, if pure and unencumbered by self-interests, must be returned to us perfected and amplified. What we give we always give to our self. Giving *is* indeed receiving when it has zero strings attached.

9. The law that giving is receiving is universal; and it is the principle behind both the projection of fear, and the extension of Love. The ego projects fear and the Holy Self extends Love. Whatever we still hoard in our subconscious, especially grievances and unforgiven memories, the ego will project – give away – and superimpose upon people and circumstances. In projecting its judgments externally, it amasses guilt (self-attack) for itself. Hence the ego's endemic legacy is a world full of broken relationships and sick bodies.

10. Whatever the mind shares with others or projects toward others must also be strengthened in our own mind and experience. Because there is just one mind and not many, if we judge someone and condemn them, or if we try to cheat someone or bargain them down, then we our self must experience this projected attack since giving *is* receiving. The question is, "Are we extending what we desire to keep and nurture, such as Love, forgiveness, innocence, abundance, etc.? Or are we projecting fear, blame, guilt and scarcity, etc.?" By extending or projecting, one thing is for sure – we get to *keep everything* that we give.

a. *"The second error is the idea that you can get rid of something you do not want by giving it away. Giving it is how you [keep] it. The belief that by seeing it outside you have excluded it from within is a complete distortion of the power of* extension. That is why those who project are vigilant for their own safety. They are afraid that their projections will return and hurt them. Believing they have blotted their projections from their own minds, they also believe their projections are trying to creep back in. Since the projections have not left their minds, they are forced to engage in constant activity in order not to recognize this." T-7.VIII.3:6-12

11. Giving *is* receiving! Whatever we share or give unconditionally must also be received, although it may come in a different form. The intent to share, to extend without a self-seeking agenda, is the extension of the Mind of God. Our true Self is known only by sharing its joyous wellspring as Love, as innocence.

a. "God's Teacher speaks to any two who join together for learning purposes. The relationship is holy because of that purpose, and God has promised to send His Spirit into any holy relationship. In the teaching-learning situation, each one learns that giving and receiving are the same. The demarcations they have drawn between their roles, their minds, their bodies, their needs, their interests, and all the differences they thought separated them from one another, fade and grow dim and disappear. Those who would learn the same course share one interest and one goal. And thus he who was the learner becomes a teacher of God himself, for he has made the one decision that gave his teacher to him. He has seen in another person the same interests as his own." M-2.5:1-9

6. BUSTING THE MYTH OF GIVING

1. Those of us on the spiritual path are often well aware of the virtues of giving. In fact, the art of giving has become largely spiritualized and is commonly seen as a sign of "selflessness." Yet the need to be seen as a person who gives is one of the heaviest and most loaded idols in the ego's bag of tricks. This need seems difficult to identify

and flush out because it is mistakenly deemed as a highly sought after spiritual attribute.

2. When under the ego's influence we sometimes try to esteem our self by being a gift giver, often "sacrificing" time, money, energy, etc. There can be a hidden agenda of feeling superior or alleviating guilt, or projecting guilt onto the recipient of the gift (now they owe us).

3. The ego cannot be the Holy Child of God, therefore it cannot be confused with "What" we are. The false self is the habitual need to get, to take, to trade and to *possess*. Thankfully, this is not our true Identity.

4. The only gift that is truly helpful and loving, to our self and to any other, is the recognition and acknowledgment of our true Identity as sinless and therefore, guiltless. We have truly given a *real* gift when we are able to look on our Self and another for *What* we are in Truth. If we first know the Truth about our Self it is easy to know the Truth about our brothers. If we are aligned with our false self we will not truly recognize our brothers and will be unable to give the only gift really worth giving.

5. When we are tempted to believe we need to "get" something from another, such as approval, validation, support, gifts, etc., we often forget that it's the ego demanding something. And if its needs are not met in the form it assigns then it believes it is justified to project resentment or anger (separation).

6. As a bottomless pit of deprivation, the ego will never be satisfied because it is *sustained* in our mind *by* its state of lack or victimhood. Attempts to "get" always come from the false self. This is why the ego cannot really "receive." As the illusory thought system of lack and division itself, it has no ability to *give or receive* fully and gratefully. To give and receive truly involves a Holy Instant of presence and gratitude. The ego is incapable of either. And yet we rarely recognize that no real giving can occur unless we have genuinely *received* first. We cannot give what we our self have not *already received* in presence and gratitude. This is a fundamental Law of God. And the outcome of giving consciously in this way is the feeling of having received as well.

7. We long deeply for changeless Love, innocence, abundance and security. Yet these qualities are not things we can get, take, trade, or possess. These qualities cannot be gained externally from others, the body or the world. And the reason is because the false identity seeking them *is* the state of lack itself. The false self is always on the hunt to complete itself, yet this state of deprivation cannot ever be satiated because it's an imposter. It is a self-concept apart from Love, from God. And its fervent but secret mantra is "seek but never find."

8. When we perceive fear, guilt, lack, conflict, pain or illness two things happen: 1) we forget our union with God, and 2) in that forgetting we choose to see with the ego, from fear and lack itself. Once we see through the eyes of lack and we *believe* it, then we will attempt to problem solve from the very sense of deprivation that originally caused the sense of lack. This is why the ego endlessly seeks and yet never finds.

A. The Holy Instant of Abundance

1. "Why can't we give unless we have first *received?*" We must first mindfully receive or remember the Truth of our Identity in God before we can give anything sincerely. All real giving and receiving can only come from this Identity. Everything else is a sham.

2. A true gift is not of "form" but content. It is recognition, with Christ' Vision, of Love and nothing else. It is hanging out with your brother's ego but knowing *that's not him.* It is being able to let the ego behaviors move through, but without belief. It is seeing the Light within and without, and being unafraid to close the seeming gap.

3. All genuine giving must come from having first recognized and *received* the nature of Love as the guiltlessness that we are. Only what we share with God can be given and received. All else arises from fear and is a dream. And this is why the ego has never once given or received in Truth. Now we can more clearly see that the persistent sense of lack that rears its ugly head all too often originates from the ego, and not from our most beloved and complete Holy Self.

4. How do we receive? We receive by showing-up for our Self in any Holy Instant of deep willingness to yield entirely to Love, to forgiveness and to the Holy Spirit within. We set the intention to

receive, to accept what God has already given. Remember there is no lack in God, and therefore none in us. God's perfect Will and His endless Supply are here now. All that is missing is our recognition and acceptance of it. Are we willing to look past the "appearance" of lack and open our heart to receive His Loving Will for us?

5.   The Atonement is the most powerful catalyst for instant healing. We don't need to prepare for it or plan for it. It's available in every instant that we decide to *receive* it. And the only prerequisite is that we truly desire to *accept* it. Jesus tells us that He stands with us in this precious Instant:

a.   *"You can claim the holy instant any time and anywhere you want it." ... "I stand within the holy instant, as clear as you would have me. And the extent to which you learn to accept me is the measure of the time in which the holy instant will be yours." T-15.IV.4:4,5:1-2*

b.   *"The holy instant is a time in which you receive and give perfect communication. This means, however, that it is a time in which your mind is open, both to receive and give. It is the recognition that all minds are in communication. It therefore seeks to change nothing, but merely to accept everything." T-15.IV.6:5-8*

6.   The Holy Instant is restorative because in receiving it we are returned to our Holy Self. And it is from here that all *true* giving and receiving takes place.

B. Giving from the Ego

1. We have erroneously learned to give from the false self. Yet this is giving from a state of fundamental lack. The ego knows only how to give in order to "get" which is really taking or stealing in disguise.

2.   For example, many of us have been tempted to buy and give gifts at Christmas and birthdays even though to do so may cause extreme financial stress. The goal then is out of alignment with the means. When this occurs, we must ask "who" is the one desiring to give gifts and why? What is the underlying intent beneath the gift-giving?

3. If it's from the Holy Self, then the means (or finances) will always be available. But all too often the intent beneath gift-giving comes from the false self. Is it to gain approval, attention? Do we give from a sense of obligation? Do we cringe when we receive a gift because we mistakenly feel obligated to return the favor? Does our identity depend on being seen as generous?

4. To bring the underlying intent more into focus let's ask a revealing question: "In celebrating a special occasion with loved ones (like Christmas), what fears arise if you were not able to give any gifts at all?"

5. These concerns will continue to propel the ego while they remain unrelinquished and unforgiven. Holy Spirit cannot heal that which we hide from Him and refuse to give to Him.

   a. *"The necessary condition for the holy instant does not require that you have no thoughts that are not pure. But it does require that you have none that you would keep. Innocence is not of your making. It is given you the instant you would have it. Atonement would not be if there were no need for it. You will not be able to accept perfect communication as long as you would hide it from yourself. For what you would hide [is] hidden from you." T-15.IV.9:1-7*

6. Recently, I was able to join with a close friend who was experiencing an acute wave of sadness and frustration over financial lack. She was having a hard time just meeting her everyday needs, let alone being able to play her accustomed role of abundant "gift-giver" at Christmas. Hence, she resorted to over-using her credit card to provide for the seeming intensifying shortfall.

7. In a Holy Instant of joining with her, I received a direct message to extend to her (and myself) from Spirit:

   a. *"Do not borrow from the imagined future in order to quell the emptiness of an imagined past. God's endless abundance resides here and now in You. This boundless gift is not truly given unless it is first received."*

8. So, she was asked to be still and enter the Holy Instant to remember and receive the glory of her divine inheritance, her Identity as the

most Holy Child of God. We both then saw that the ego is forever stealing from the imagined future in its desperate attempts to alleviate its sense of lack and loss from the past. Thus, it continues to project its groundless fears into the future while avoiding the present moment where all healing rests.

9. It does this with money and in its special relationships too. That bottomless pit of deprivation seeks to keep us trapped in the past and the future. And these are the only two ghosts of time where we cannot access the Love and innocence that we are.

10. In reflection, when we give to someone *from* the false self we end up giving *to* and colluding *with* the false self. And nothing at all happens except an illusory trade of specialness that only serves to increase guilt, along with broadening the gap between us.

11. The ego is terrified to receive or give. It sees these as its annihilation and appropriately so! In genuine receiving or giving "it" ceases to exist.

12. Ultimately, as we learn to receive the Truth of our Identity instead of the ego's persistent sense of threat and lack, our ability to give and to receive increase considerably. There is a palpable sense of joy and gratitude in giving because we know then that giving *and* receiving are really one and the same. The ego's division between them disappears. We no longer give from a sense of lack or need, but from the certainty of wholeness which increases as we give it away.

13. In genuine receiving we receive first and then we give from our Holy Self as Love. When we give we always give to the Holy Self in others because this is the only aspect of anyone that *can* receive. And it's the only aspect of Self that can give. In the shimmering light of our Holy Self the ego ceases to exist in every Holy Instant where we show-up to receive.

7. LOVE OR SPECIALNESS – WHICH DO YOU WANT?

1. In human relationships we erroneously believe we are in relationship with other bodies. We have no idea that *there are no bodies.* We're really relating to our own "false interpretation" of the

other person as a body. Further, we see the other person one of two ways; either *as they are in truth* (innocent, as we are), or as we *want* them to be. This is non-negotiable.

2. The body was projected as a barrier – a defense – to separate each of us and to block true communication between us. Yet God's Love is all we are. True communication consists of the ever-extending Love that we are. Because of this we dwell in a state of perpetual, uninterrupted innocence - Holiness. This state of incorruptible innocence is eternal and changeless whether we are aware of it or not. Our innocence *is* the Will of God. It cannot change.

3. In this ego dream everything we appear to experience, including the body and its state, arises from just one place – our desire for it. Projection makes perception because we always perceive exactly what we believe, and therefore value, either good or bad. Desire precedes all experience.

4. We cannot possibly experience anything here without a desire for it. And desire is made through our beliefs, including our fears. Recall that what we fear and defend our self from is its attraction. Most of these desires remain unconscious, as the ego's wish to be unfairly treated, until we are willing to have them healed.

5. In order to maintain separation, we must keep the illusion of separate bodies and minds alive. The body's five physical senses were made to see and sense only separation. They were fabricated to block out our shared and changeless innocence.

6. Because Love and innocence are one, they cannot be separate. The moment we judge or blame our self or another, we're temporarily unconscious, unaware of the innocence we share with everyone as the Holy Self. The costs of this amnesia are guilt, fear and self-attack as pain, illness or relationship conflict, etc.

7. Consequently, while we continue to rely on the body's senses to inform us of reality, we will see and value sin, guilt and fear over Love and innocence. If we perceive anything that contradicts innocence in another, our self, the body, the past or the world, *we are hallucinating*. And this is why we have forgiveness and the Atonement; so, we can ask Holy Spirit to correct our warped perception.

8. Special relationships are the favorite breeding ground for this hallucination where love and innocence can suddenly shift to their opposites, hate and guilt. While we value what the body seems to offer us (ours or another's) we will use it to witness to suffering, conflict and separation, as the absence of Love and innocence. Each person in special relationship reenacts his own seeming proof of guilt and unworthiness every time he believes his anger is justified.

   a. *"It is impossible to forgive another, for it is only your sins you see in him. You want to see them there, and not in you. That is why forgiveness of another is an illusion. Yet it is the only happy dream in all the world; the only one that does not lead to death. Only in someone else can you forgive yourself, for you have called him guilty of your sins, and in him must your innocence now be found." S-2.I.4:2-6*

9. We all see, feel and experience exactly what we desire. But have we gone within to discover what it is that we really desire? Why would we have it remain hidden? Why not bring it up to the light of awareness so we can look upon it with the Holy Spirit, and ask Him to repurpose it?

A. Exercise: Take the Test

1. Take the following test to find out whether you want Love *or* specialness.

   a. What do I truly desire?

   b. What do I long for?

   c. Do I want to be Loved?

   d. Do I want to feel Loved?

2. It is impossible to feel Loved and receive Love without responding with a "yes" to the following question:

   a. Do I want, above all else, to see others as innocent, as sinless, regardless of appearances to the contrary?

3. If your answer is "no" to this preceding question, then changeless Love is *not* what you want. Instead you seek special love, which is conflict and separation in disguise.

   a. Do you want to know Love?

   b. Or do you want to be special?

4. These two are diametrically opposed and can never be merged because they seek opposing goals. When innocence is all you want to perceive, then Love is all you will experience.

   a. *"Dreams show you that you have the power to make a world as you would have it be, and that because you want it you see it. And while you see it you do not doubt that it is real. Yet here is a world, clearly within your mind, that seems to be outside. You do not respond to it as though you made it, nor do you realize that the emotions the dream produces must come from you. It is the figures in the dream and what they do that seem to make the dream. You do not realize that you are making them act out for you, for if you did the guilt would not be theirs, and the illusion of satisfaction would be gone."... "In your waking dreams, the special relationship has a special place. It is the means by which you try to make your sleeping dreams come true. From this, you do not waken. The special relationship is your determination to keep your hold on unreality, and to prevent yourself from waking. And while you see more value in sleeping than in waking, you will not let go of it."* T-18.II.5:1-6,16-20

8. DO YOU REALLY NEED A HOLY RELATIONSHIP?

1. A relationship involves constant teaching and learning although we're often not consciously aware of this. We teach all the time, but most of what we teach and thus *learn* is unconscious and arises from the ego's guilt, until we begin to heal through forgiveness,

consistently apply the *Seven Keys*. Consequently, this guilt is largely projected onto others, the body, and the world, reinforcing and therefore, teaching ourselves further separation.

2. Ultimately, we teach our self and others *who we are* through our thoughts, judgments, beliefs and values. We actually learn who *we are* by what we teach or demonstrate. We either teach that we are guilty and fearful through blame (projecting our guilt), or we teach that we are innocence and Love by extending forgiveness. We always get to keep that which we give away, judgments and condemnation included. This is why, when we're triggered, it is crucial to choose to forgive rather than to dump our blame onto anyone else. The more we blame, the greater we suffer because we're accumulating self-attack.

3. To give, to share or to project are all acts of giving. Whatever we give or project, we our self must receive. This is a universal law which the ego fiercely defends from reaching conscious awareness. If we really recognized and believed this law, we would cease all condemnation. Period.

   a. *"The role of teaching and learning is actually reversed in the thinking of the world. The reversal is characteristic. It seems as if the teacher and the learner are separated, the teacher giving something to the learner rather than to himself."* ... *"The course, on the other hand, emphasizes that to teach [is] to learn, so that teacher and learner are the same. It also emphasizes that teaching is a constant process; it goes on every moment of the day, and continues into sleeping thoughts as well."*

   "There are only two thought systems, and you demonstrate that you believe one or the other is true all the time. From your demonstration others learn, and so do you. The question is not whether you will teach, for in that there is no choice. The purpose of the course might be said to provide you with a means of choosing what you want to teach on the basis of what you want to learn. You cannot give to someone else, but only to yourself, and this you learn through teaching. Teaching is but a call to witnesses to attest to what you believe. It is a method of conversion. This is not done by words alone. Any

situation must be to you a chance to teach others what you are, and what they are to you." M-in.1:1-3,5-6,2:2-10

4. In all our relationships, we are constantly teaching who we believe we are – the fragile false self *or* the Holy Self – so that others will reinforce our self-image. Which *self* do we believe is real? Because this is the self we must *want* to be. We are either a teacher of fear or one of Love. The "self" we portray to others is how we want others to think of us. In our special relationships we repeatedly teach our self and others that we are a body, and therefore separate and guilty. By stark contrast, in Holy Relationship we work in unison toward the mutual goal of undoing of our self-deception as separate beings, revealing our shared innocence. Commitment to sacred union and its process is the transformational bridge that we cross to the wondrous Real World dream.

5. In order to awaken entirely from the ego's dream we *do* require the experience of Holy Relationship. This is where we really learn the value of transcending the ego's self-serving interests. It is through Holy Relationship that we come to forgive everybody and everything.

    a. *Salvation is a collaborative venture. It cannot be undertaken successfully by those who disengage themselves from the Sonship, because they are disengaging themselves from me." T-4.VI.8:2-3*

6. All relationships are teaching-learning situations. The long-term learning goal for all relationships is to recognize that we are all one, and all equally sinless. But this vision cannot be genuinely accepted until we join with another in a *mutual commitment* to transcend our own self-serving interests. We must learn that giving and receiving are the same, which is in violent opposition to the ego's core beliefs.

    a. *"In the teaching-learning situation, each one learns that giving and receiving are the same. The demarcations they have drawn between their roles, their minds, their bodies, their needs, their interests, and all the differences they thought separated them from one another, fade and grow dim and disappear." M-2.5:5-6*

7. We have spent perhaps thousands of lifetimes since the separation associating as false identities that seek and depend on special love (fear) which is the driving force behind all unforgiveness in this world. At some point in the long dream of time, every one of us will eventually require at least one mutual Holy Relationship (not necessarily romantic) by which our own fear of Love is undone. Because of its holographic nature, this Relationship has the divine potential to heal all of our relationships since the beginning of time.

8. Holy Spirit sends us a savior, a person with which to embark upon our healing in Holy Relationship. And He knows just when we're sincerely willing to meet and join our savior/s in Holy Relationship. The necessary prerequisite is that we are willing to look upon them and see them as sinless.

   a. *"To each who walks this earth in seeming solitude is a savior given, whose special function here is to release him, and so to free himself." ... "And each one finds his savior when he is ready to look upon the face of Christ, and see Him sinless." T-20.VI.5:3,6*

9. In the meantime, we can accelerate this meeting exponentially by learning to show-up in *all* our relationships. As we learn to communicate authentically using the *Seven Keys,* we initiate the purification process that is required, preparing us for authentic relating in Holy Relationship.

   a. *"Each teaching-learning situation involves a different relationship at the beginning, although the ultimate goal is always the same; to make of the relationship a holy relationship, in which both can look upon the Son of God as sinless. There is no one from whom a teacher of God cannot learn, so there is no one whom he cannot teach. However, from a practical point of view he cannot meet everyone, nor can everyone find him. Therefore, the plan includes very specific contacts to be made for each teacher of God. There are no accidents in salvation. Those who are to meet will meet, because together they have the potential for a holy relationship. They are ready for each other." M-3.1:2-8*

10. In conclusion, the most formidable obstacle we face to fully remembering the Love we are as the Holy Self, is our mistaken belief that we're the body. Misidentification as the body brings with it the guilt responsible for attracting us to death over and over again.

a. *"Perhaps you are willing to accept even death to deny your Father."... "You will think that death comes from God and not from the ego because, by confusing yourself with the ego, you believe that you want death. And from what you want God does not save you." T-12.III.9:2, VII.14:5-6*

11. While the body remains our coveted central identity, we will pursue the ego's special relationships because they continue to supply the guilt necessary to keep the mind imprisoned within the illusory body. Special relationships heavily reinforce and perpetuate guilt, thus extending the illusion of time as suffering.

12. The real question is, "What is our goal?" Do we genuinely want to know that we share God's invulnerable Will with all our brothers? Do we truly want to know God's Love? If so, then we will be willing to learn to forgive everyone and everything. And we will commit to the purification necessary to open to Holy Relationship – applying the *Seven Keys* and *A Course in Miracles* workbook lessons within all our relationships.

13. We have two online programs by donation, which help to foster the beginning of Holy Relationships (not romantic) within our classes. Partners are often referred to as miracle buddies. One, the *TTC (Total Transformation Course)* runs for 12 months. (Visit: *https://nouksanchez. com/online-course-total-transformation-course/*) The other is called *The Holy Relationship Journey - Online Course,* based on *A Manual for Holy Relationship.* (Visit: *https://nouksanchez.com/online-course-holy-relationship-journey/*) Both these courses offer valuable opportunities to meet with like-minded people from around the world and offer the potential to establish life-long Holy Relationships.

14. As we learn to finally show-up for our Self, as we learn to be radically self-honest, defenseless and accountable – as we learn to shatter our emotional paralysis and dare to express our emotions intimately, we must realize that there is no one to protect or defend our self from. In fact, as we show-up for our Self, others will show-up

for us! And then we will witness that everyone and everything we seem to see in the world is wholly and magnificently changed. All because we've learned to show-up for our most beloved Holy Self – the Self that is shared as *One*. The Love we seek is *what* we are. And when we know this … Love will be all we feel and see.

9. DO YOU REALLY WANT A HOLY RELATIONSHIP?

1. Do you really want a Holy Relationship? Before you answer this, perhaps you might like to know what it will cost you. I'll be frank. It will cost you your false self-concept along with all its erroneous beliefs about what Love is.

2. Firstly, the journey from specialness to Holiness is set to reveal to you what Love is *not*. Unless you're willing to learn what Love is not, you will not be willing to open to Love. This is where real willingness comes in. Resistance to learning what Love is not, is the fear of Love (God) that Jesus speaks of in *A Course in Miracles*. While you still choose to believe that others can hurt you, you will not find Love because you have locked yourself away from it.

3. Relationships fail because we don't recognize and value their singular purpose. We unknowingly use them for anything and everything other than their one miraculous purpose.

4. Through the fragile and deceptive false self, we try to get from others that which we believe we're lacking. This is its goal – to *get*. It could be special love, physical closeness, sex, financial security. It could be approval, validation, or emotional support. Whatever it is, we most certainly try to get from others (including our parents and children) that which we have refused to give to our self.

5. The pseudo self attempts to disguise its intent to *take* from others, by secretly "giving to get." But giving to get is no different than taking or stealing. And because in truth there is only one of us here, we rob from our Self. Although we are likely not conscious of this, we still accumulate guilt for it because it has not been offered to Holy Spirit and forgiven. Instead, it is projected outward onto others and they mirror our own Self-betrayal to us.

a. *"The ego never gives out of abundance, because it was made as a substitute for it. That is why the concept of "getting" arose in the ego's thought system. Appetites are "getting" mechanisms, representing the ego's need to confirm itself. This is as true of body appetites as it is of the so-called "higher ego needs." Body appetites are not physical in origin."* T-4. II.7:3-7

6. Giving to get is based on lack and deprivation and always breeds separation. Only the false self can feel lack, unloved, hurt, unseen, betrayed, abandoned, unappreciated and misunderstood. Our Holy Self is entirely impervious to threats like these. It does not need to get anything from anyone. It knows it has everything because it knows it *is* everything. Its great joy is to extend the Love and abundance that it is.

7. The false self does not know Love (capital "L"). It only knows specialness and exclusivity. While believing it is a bottomless pit of unworthiness it cannot know Love. It cannot give Love or receive it. It believes that Love can change, which is impossible. Love can only *seem* to change if I first *abandon myself* in dishonesty.

8. With the ego, it's truly astounding how we can have close relationships that swing wildly from love to hate. One minute we seem to love and in the next we're full of resentment. This is what Jesus says about this insane concept:

a. *"No one considers it bizarre to love and hate together, and even those who believe that hate is sin merely feel guilty, but do not correct it."* T-16.V.3:4

9. I know from previous years of being an addicted "people-pleaser" in all my relationships, there was a specialness dynamic that played out. Eventually I had to look at just "why" I felt so damned resentful in my relationships. I had to look at why I felt cheated, tired and unfairly treated. I was largely *unseen*.

10. I was a perfectionist and the ultimate loyalist. I gave and gave. I sacrificed for others. Aha! That's it right there! Little did I realize

back then that sacrifice is *not* Love but attack. In fact, if I sacrificed for others I was resenting them, in return unwittingly *increasing* the gap between us. On top of that I was hiding the fact that I was being consistently dishonest with myself. In the secret "need to be needed" lay a deadly trap. All sacrifice is a hidden desire to "give to get," which is attack in disguise because it increases guilt.

11. To maintain the ego's desire to be needed, it cost me my Self-honesty, my trust, and my gratitude. I literally had to abandon myself to keep feeding the sick cycle of giving to get, of fueling that need to be needed.

  a. *"In such insane relationships, the attraction of what you do not want seems to be much stronger than the attraction of what you do want. For each one thinks that he has sacrificed something to the other, and hates him for it. Yet this is what he thinks he wants. He is not in love with the other at all. He merely believes he is in love with sacrifice. And for this sacrifice, which he demands of himself, he demands that the other accept the guilt and sacrifice himself as well. Forgiveness becomes impossible, for the ego believes that to forgive another is to lose him. It is only by attack without forgiveness that the ego can ensure the guilt that holds all its relationships together." T-15.VII.7.*

A. The Singular Purpose of Relationships

1. Contrary to popular belief, the singular purpose of all relationships is *not* to meet the imagined needs of the false-self and its body appetites (financial security, special relationship roles, sex, etc.). The purpose is to "close the gap" of separation between us. This will ultimately lead to the final closing of the gap within. As our projections are withdrawn from others, we remove the distorted self-concept to reveal the one shared Holy Self. And the false needs of the body do not intrude on this most cherished relationship. The body falls into alignment now with the Holy Spirit's purpose.

2. All relationships are living classrooms to help us undo our own distorted belief that we are unworthy of Love. They are purely mirroring our own self-condemnation, our own guilt. And it's this profound lie that forms the basis of our false self-concept. This is the self that attempts communication in relationship with other false selves.

3. All the false-self's roles, rules and expectations are based on protecting and defending this false-self (fear and guilt) as it says over and over in a thousand different ways, *"I will love you just as long as you do what I want."* Yet this image of self is the block to our most beloved Holy Self. Why on earth would we want to keep it? Especially once we recognize the conflict and suffering it causes.

4. Most people in the world, including those who have perhaps lived together under the same roof for decades, even sleeping in the same bed together, have never really *seen* each other. They go to the grave without ever having truly closed the gap between them. And this is *why* they die. They maintain a false self-image with its fake relationship roles, rules, beliefs, stories, and values, all revolving around the unreal body. Yet they have never really seen each other. They cannot be seen, really seen, until they have learned to genuinely forgive, to be radically self-honest, defenseless, emotionally vulnerable and transparent.

5. Jesus speaks of this special relationship dynamic here:

   a. *"For an unholy relationship is based on differences, where each one thinks the other has what he has not. They come together, each to complete himself and rob the other. They stay until they think that there is nothing left to steal, and then move on. And so they wander through a world of strangers, unlike themselves, living with their bodies perhaps under a common roof that shelters neither; in the same room and yet a world apart."* T-22.in.3:5-8

6. Jesus gives us this happy alternative to the neediness of the special relationship, the Holy Relationship:

   a. *"A holy relationship starts from a different premise. Each one has looked within and seen no lack. Accepting his completion, he would extend it by joining with another, whole as himself.*

He sees no difference between these selves, for differences are only of the body." T-22.in.3:1-4

B. Showing-Up for Our Self

1. The purpose of all relationships is to undo our fundamental belief that we're separate, a belief that we can *be* victimized. The means to achieve this is via quantum forgiveness (Atonement). As we forgive *our self* for having unknowingly used others to attack us, the veil of condemnation falls away to reveal our most Holy Self. This is the *radical self-accountability* required to initiate and sustain a Holy Relationship. Without this crucial piece (peace) we cannot undo the unconscious self-hatred that masquerades as relationship conflict, disease, pain, depression and financial lack, etc.

C. Did You Know It's Impossible to Forgive Another?

1. Here is the reason why trying to forgive another does not work:

    a. *"It is impossible to forgive another, for it is only your sins you see in him. You want to see them there, and not in you."* ... *"That is why forgiveness of another is an illusion."* ... *"Only in someone else can you forgive yourself, for you have called him guilty of your sins, and in him must your innocence now be found." S.2.I.4:2-4,6*

2. It is only through others that we are gifted the opportunity to forgive *our own* imagined sins and undo the self-saboteur that inflicts self-punishment via projection. We could never undo this tragic self-concept without our brothers and sisters. They show us exactly where our own unconscious self-abandonment lies so as we can forgive it.

3. Most of us are in special relationships and have no idea how to initiate a Holy Relationship, especially if our partner has zero interest in living this path. And that brings up a lot of fear, even terror for many. The deep-seated fear of loss and rejection seems so overwhelming. Yet Jesus reassures us that these relationships can be transformed. However, this involves our own wholehearted participation in applying the *Seven Keys* and Quantum Forgiveness (the Atonement).

a. *"I have said repeatedly that the Holy Spirit would not deprive you of your special relationships, but would transform them."* T-17.IV.2:3

10. AM I READY FOR A HOLY RELATIONSHIP?

1. Holy Relationship begins once two or more people have joined in a truly common purpose with the Holy Spirit. He sets the one goal (innocence and union) of the relationship which is opposite of the goal for special love relationships (guilt and separation).

2. With lifetimes of on-the-job training with the ego thought system, most people have no concept as to what is involved in the transfer from special to Holy Relationship. This section is further dedicated to delving into some necessary and radical, self-inquiry to find out if we (and/or our partner) are ready to engage in a life-changing, Holy Relationship.

3. To be honest, when we begin this pathway, we have no idea what changeless Love *is*. All we have ever known is special love which, as Jesus tells us, is not Love at all. We are thoroughly confused about Love and unknowingly, we are afraid of divine and perfect Love because it threatens our false self-concept along with all its beliefs, values and stories.

4. While we still mistakenly presume that love involves any of the following, we must come to recognize that we value and are invested in *special love,* which is hate in disguise: sacrifice, guilt, blame, shame, defense, jealousy, drama, resistance, arguments, agendas, withholding, concerns, private thoughts, justifying, demands, lusty sex, denial, etc. These are just some examples of the effects of fear and our blocks to Love.

5. As we consent to first recognize and then repurpose these effects of special relating with Holy Spirit, we understand that they are calls *for* Love, for forgiveness. Here are more of the ego's often unrecognized idols which, while cherished over and above aligning with Holy Spirit's Will, are a sign that we value specialness as opposed to real Love: the need to be right, financial security, physical safety, house, family, children, sex, sacrifice, secrets, belief that your partner is responsible for your happiness or your disappointments, holding grievances, stories based on the past, body image, people-pleasing, social circles, job, career, assets, bank account, pleasure-seeking, entertainment, drama, companionship, etc.

6. While *any* of these take priority over God (Holy Spirit) and forgiveness, then we will still value "special love" and therefore resist changeless Love via a Holy Relationship. However, if we have genuinely suffered sufficiently from having mistakenly given our authority to the ego rather than to Holy Spirit, then we are ready to surrender our attraction to pain and separation. There is another, much more joyful way.

7. The means by which our desire for special love is undone, is through learning authentic communication via *consistent* application of the *Seven Keys*. Together with forgiveness, this is a practice necessary for the undoing of our mistaken "self-concept." The false self is *anti*-communication since it is a product of fear and its primary goal is separation. The false self is the embodiment of *self-deception* in this world. Self-deception is the antithesis of changeless Love because it prevents true joining with anyone including our beloved Holy Self.

8. Through diligent practice of the *Seven Keys*, we experience firsthand how we have unknowingly abandoned and betrayed our Self in the past, and how we have inadvertently projected that self-abandonment and betrayal onto others. We quickly come to realize that we behave one way with a certain person, and completely different with another. We see how we abandon our Holy Self by becoming a chameleon depending upon who we are with.

9. This inauthenticity or abandoning of Self, as we will see later, is based on what the false-self wants from other people - what it uses them *for.* Seeing this, we learn just how much we have lied to our true and Holy Self. This also includes recognizing how we have unwittingly used others to attack us ... just to keep our false

self-concept alive. It cannot be sustained without our belief that we have been unfairly treated, and we have projected onto others and manifested adverse experiences to do just that!

10. There is to be no guilt or self-judgment upon seeing this because self-judgment, like any condemnation or grievance, is attack. If we sincerely desire to transfer our trust from the false-self with its special love, over to the Holy Self and changeless Love, then we must also desire to undo our blocks to Love, peace, innocence, joy and heartfelt union with Self and others. Recognizing this helps motivate us to change our mind and embrace the unparalleled value of wholehearted forgiveness. Through practicing the *Seven Keys* we find our authentic Holy Self and then we're able to see and finally join with that same, innocent Holy Self in others.

11. Holy Relationship prioritizes one thing above all else - we must desire to see our partner and our self as innocent. This necessitates the consistent desire – with Holy Spirit's help – to see another and our self as blameless, guiltless and sinless. Without this single desire *above all else*, there is no possibility of Holy Relationship. As we will see, we learn eventually to withdraw all our projections of guilt (blame) from others and our self.

12. With radical honesty we need to ask our self this first question, "Where do I currently believe my salvation lies?" In other words, what do I currently value? While we still value idols we will erroneously believe that we are sustained by the *illusions of love* we experience in any special relationship. While we value these, we will defend them in our relationships, which will inevitably result in grievances and conflict.

13. The second question is "Am I wholly willing to have these idols divinely repurposed by Holy Spirit?" If not, then I am not yet ready for a Holy Relationship. Furthermore, I do not agree to share the one, truly common purpose of forgiveness using the *Seven Keys,* because they will threaten my idols which include my special relationships and my defenses *against* Love.

14. In the event that one person in a relationship is willing and the other is not, then they have opposing goals. When two people have mutually exclusive goals such as this, one desire's a Holy

Relationship while the other still values and therefore defends his false self-concept with its special love, then this resistance prevents the Holy Spirit from entering to make the relationship Holy. He requires two (or more) people to *join* in the one, truly common purpose t*ogether* before He is granted permission to shift the relationship's goal to its total opposite.

a.   *"The holy relationship, a major step toward the perception of the real world, is learned. It is the old, unholy relationship, transformed and seen anew. The holy relationship is a phenomenal teaching accomplishment. In all its aspects, as it begins, develops and becomes accomplished, it represents the reversal of the unholy relationship. Be comforted in this; the only difficult phase is the beginning. For here, the goal of the relationship is abruptly shifted to the exact opposite of what it was. This is the first result of offering the relationship to the Holy Spirit, to use for His purposes."*

"This invitation is accepted immediately, and the Holy Spirit wastes no time in introducing the practical results of asking Him to enter. At once His goal replaces yours." T-17.V.2,3:1-2

A. Exercise: What do I Value Most in Relationship?

1. Let's take a radically honest look at what we currently value *more* than changeless Love, more than our one, shared and Holy Self.

2. This questionnaire is designed to reveal where your hidden idols may dwell. Many of these are valued by the world as symbols of special love. Some of these may be areas or qualities that you deem as positive strengths, yet in truth, they are unrecognized "blocks" to Love and therefore, barriers to real union and Holy Relationship.

3. Take your time and go through each of these possible idols. An idol is anything we value or prioritize above God, and thus readily *defend*. Be radically honest as to how much you value or identify with each of these.

4. On a scale from 0-10, determine which of these has more or less value for you right now. This often changes as we transfer our trust from fear to Love. 0 represents no value for you, while 10 represents a strong value for you:

1) being a provider

2) being a rescuer

3) being a problem-solver

4) being a people-pleaser

5) compromise myself to keep the (ego's) peace

6) being a control freak

7) being a clean freak

8) being a forward planner

9) being private, keeping private thoughts

10) appearing strong, unwilling to be emotionally vulnerable and transparent

11) being competitive

12) being right

13) being needed by others

14) being meticulous

15) being intelligent

16) being creative

17) being a drama queen

18) being sick or in pain

19) being a martyr

20) being a worrier; anxious

21) taking on "false-responsibility" for loved ones

22) compartmentalizing my life

23) belief in innocent victims *and* guilty perpetrators

24) belief in the world, news, politics, etc.

25) belief that I am a victim of the body, another person, the past or the world

26) holding grievances from the past or present

27) find it difficult to forgive completely

28) attached to stories from the past

29) sentimental

30) belief in having been unfairly treated

31) belief that my romantic partner should provide sex

32) being addicted to any one of the ego's many body appetites such as sex, pornography, food, TV, video games, drugs, shopping, judging, gossiping, drama, spending, fitness, body image, alcohol, etc.

33) belief that real love involves sacrifice, putting our own needs on hold, etc.

34) belief that love can change or end

35) belief in certain "rules" and "roles" in relationship that if broken, are grounds to withdraw or end love

B. Exercise: Are you Ready to Commit to Holy Relationship?

1. Again, mark each of these on a scale from 0 – 10. In this exercise, 0 represents no willingness and 10 represents abundant willingness:

1) How **willing** am I to have all my idols divinely repurposed by Holy Spirit? This involves learning not to defend my idols by projecting blame.

2) How **accountable** am I willing to be for everything that seemed to happen to me in the past, the present and in the future?

3) How willing am I to be **emotionally vulnerable** and transparent with myself and others?

4) How willing am I to be radically **self-honest**? Am I willing to align my thoughts, feelings, speech and actions in self-honesty? And am I willing to communicate with everyone through this level of honesty regardless of fear of rejection?

5) When any of my idols are threatened (review my list above), how **defenseless** am I committed to be?

6) Do I **trust** when any of the ego's idols appear to be threatened, that this is an opportunity and never a threat? Do I trust when I am triggered emotionally, that it's *always a gift in disguise*; to reveal yet another block to Love (idol), so I can offer it over to Holy Spirit in exchange for the miracle?

7) Do I have **gratitude** for my forgiveness opportunities? Am I grateful to have my mistaken self-concept challenged so I can finally experience the profound innocence, security, and Love that I am?

8) Am I eager to join in Holy Relationship to welcome the acceleration of undoing the false-self and its addiction to pain, loss and separation?

2. These exercises are not meant to increase guilt, but they are intended to increase self-honesty and mindfulness. There is to be no judgment in this honest self-inquiry. However, most of us do not know who we are, let alone what perfect and changeless Love is. As we undo what we are not – perfect, changeless Love is all that is left.

3. A Holy Relationship does not seek to improve the self we think we are. But it will, by its nature, erase everything we are *not*. Love remains as our one Holy Self. Only in this way can we ever know with conviction that Love can never *be* threatened.

4. Holy Spirit is the one who decides:

   1) Our "readiness" and timing for Holy Relationship, and

   2) The particular person or people we initiate a Holy Relationship with.

5. It cannot be forced. From my own experience, it is not kind to try to make an unwilling companion undo their mistaken self-concept. This accomplishment is a *natural* result of reversing the special relationship with Holy Spirit. In this case the only thing we can change is *our self*. If our partner is not interested, then it's up to us to begin with practicing forgiveness and the *Seven Keys*. We must show-up for our Self despite fears of rejection and conflict. We must learn to communicate authentically.

6. Sometimes, the people we are presently in special relationship with are not ready to:

   1) Agree to the Holy Spirit's purpose and goal for Holy Relationship because it threatens their self-concept together with its beliefs and values.

   2) Engage in forgiveness and practicing the *Seven Keys*, which are the necessary means by which we achieve the Holy Spirit's new purpose for relationship.

7. To conclude, it's important to realize that no matter how willing and ready we think we are for a Holy Relationship, it is entirely up to Holy Spirit to bring that person or people to us when He knows we are ready. It cannot be forced.

II. THE END OF CONFLICT – UNIFIED WILL

1. In Holy Relationships there is a fail-proof formula which, when practiced, ends conflict. It exposes and heals the root of conflict that is prevalent in all special relationships. The mutual purpose and goal in the Holy Relationship is to prioritize God's Will above all else. To achieve this goal involves the consistent application of forgiveness and the *Seven Keys*, which together offer a highly effective formula to end all conflict.

2. When two or more people join and commit to this one goal with Holy Spirit, God's Will is established and embraced above all else. There is no conflict in His Will and therefore none in the Holy Relationship. The partners are divinely synchronized and guided together *in* and *as* God's Will. In other words, they do not favor an independent will, a personal will apart from Holy Spirit.

3. It is the *joining* and the *unified will* of those in Holy Relationship that brings the joyfully, selfless experience of oneness with Love and innocence. The separate, self-governing "identity" with its obsessive white-knuckled grip on life, falls away. Thus, the small self becomes redundant because joyful, glorious and liberated union has come to take its place.

4. When we believe we are autonomous and independent from Spirit we will automatically believe we're also separate from others, including our loved ones. We will believe that it's possible for them to value and to enforce a separate will of their own, complete with agendas opposed to ours. Our personal will, will seem to clash with the personal will of others. And this is what occurs in all special relationships. Belief in the illusion of separate wills and agendas is the singular cause of all conflict.

5. While we are mindlessly convinced by the illusion that we each have separate wills (minds) and bodies, we will see conflict everywhere, in our bodies as sickness, in our families, our communities and our world. We will believe in enemies and that we could be attacked by them in an endless number of forms, i.e. betrayal, abandonment, illness, pain, depression, loss, lack and death.

6. However, a far greater rival for the separate self is hiding beneath the quest for personal will and special relationships with their

endless conflict. The false self keeps busy, compartmentalizing and running its own special relationships and life, by its rules and laws. Its frenetic concern and activity serve to evade the discovery of its supreme adversary, one that we've been running from since time began.

7. Here is the greatest enemy of all time. This is God, as changeless Love and incorruptible innocence. This is our one, shared and Holy Self. This is our one unified Will, our true Will. The one unified Mind we share with every Child of God whether they are aware of it or not. The separate self's greatest fear is not death, but the realization that we all share one unrivaled Will, that we truly are all one, as Love.

8. Our Mind cannot be separate! Our Will cannot be divided! There are no separate people with independent wills and agendas of their own. There are no "private" thoughts. We share the Mind of God as one Self.

9. The one Mind of God, of the changeless Love and innocence we share, is continuous, uninterrupted and unopposed. It cannot *be* threatened. It shares all of God's Power and has dominion over all that the split mind hallucinated, including conflict, sickness and death.

10. This illusion of a split will – or conflict – is a mirror of the investment or the value we place in our own split mind. It must be unified as one in God's Will, which is our one, shared Holy Self. This Self extends continuously without a break, without the imagined opposition that we seem to see coming from the body's five physical senses.

11. Two people with one goal, who take every opportunity to close the gap of conflict via forgiveness, offer and receive the greatest gift ever to grace this dream of duality.

12. When there is conflict between two people, it is due to one or both wanting an "idol" which they believe is more valuable than closing the gap; than joining as one in forgiveness. The idol, if valued and unrelinquished, is an obstacle to peace and will be used to foster specialness as separation.

13. In Holy Relationship, what brings genuine peace and happiness to one must bring the other the same. This is God's Will as the one Holy Self, the one Mind we share. In special relationships this is reversed. Each operates from his own private will, independent of Spirit. Consequently, it seems possible that one person's desire or actions conflict with the other's. This is impossible in the Holy Relationship.

14. Remember that projection always makes perception. It literally makes what we appear to see. We are confronted by what *the ego* desires to see, which is evidence of separation, conflict and death. We only ever see what the ego has projected outward in order to cover and hide from us what is *really there* – God's Will as one, undivided explosion of joy and happy union!

15. If we believe what the ego has hurled forth as its blocks to Love, then we are blinded and concede to it. This is what occurs in every relationship conflict. We never conflict with a person. We actually see and react to what the false-self *projects,* which is what it *wants* from them. It needs to believe in conflict; that we each have separate and personal wills which can collide and battle, win or lose. Recall that in order to sustain the illusion of a false self, it must believe in conflict and unfair treatment. This means when we appear to encounter an obstacle, a problem or conflict, no matter its form, it is always a hallucination arising from our own fearful split mind.

16. This is why the discipline to look past what the five physical senses report is an integral part of the forgiveness process. If not forgiven, we will be hypnotized by fear, which then denies us access to Holy Spirit's help. In fear, we actually believe the illusion. And once we *believe* it, it cannot be forgiven, and Holy Spirit cannot heal it. We must be *willing* to join with Spirit, recognizing that the singular cause of the problem is our *choice to be separate* from our one, shared and Holy Self. This is always the only cause of all adversity – the choice to be separate. This, and only this, requires healing.

17. We need not be concerned with "effects." Once we accept Atonement for our choice to be separate, the seeming consequences or effects are healed by Holy Spirit.

18. We learn to look past the body's senses and appetites in order to make way for direct vision or Christ Vision. This is the outcome of our desire to look past what the body's senses report; we see what is really there which is always unity and healing. But we will not see this while we value a self-serving, personal will.

19. If someone triggers us, no matter the form, they always offer us a healing opportunity. The only purpose of any trigger is to help reveal where we still value a block to Love. Once we see this, we can have it healed by forgiveness.

20. It is impossible to attack or punish anyone or anything without also condemning our self. If we attack our self privately, we attack everyone. There is no "private self." It's impossible to inflict pain anywhere and not suffer from it our self. We are one mind. When we try to take from one person, we rob our self. This is literal. There is no one else out there to take from.

21. Just to drive this crucial point home, if I am triggered by conflict in any form, I must perceive it through the separate, personal will. To the degree I am triggered tells me the extent to which this "self" wants conflict and has projected it. Undoing of my perception – through forgiveness and Atonement – is necessary to affect change at the cause level and heal all conflict.

22. In stark contrast, the one, unified, Holy Self knows *and therefore sees* only God's unified Will. Because it is not separate, it has no opposing "will." It does not believe in projected "appearances;" it expects instead to see God's Will, which is *really* there behind the false appearance, as wholly healed and happy.

23. In the Holy Relationship the idea of separate, personal wills, each with their own independent agendas, disappears. The world of duality can only seem to appear when two or more people agree to witness a gap between them. The entire world of conflict and suffering is made *by* and *in* that gap. And it is upheld by the continued agreement to give witness to this illusory gap.

24. The Holy Relationship is the final Victory Lap, the closing of the dream of time. When two or more join in this unprecedented union and agree to witness *no gap*, the world is healed along with them.

We cannot truly know God until we embrace our brother and close the gap. How can we have closure with God unless we first have closure with our brother?

a. *"This holy relationship, lovely in its innocence, mighty in strength, and blazing with a light far brighter than the sun that lights the sky you see, is chosen of your Father as a means for His Own plan. Be thankful that it serves yours not at all. Nothing entrusted to it can be misused, and nothing given it but will be used. This holy relationship has the power to heal all pain, regardless of its form. Neither you nor your brother alone can serve at all. Only in your joint will does healing lie. For here your healing is, and here will you accept Atonement. And in your healing is the Sonship healed [because] your will and your brother's are joined."*

"Before a holy relationship there is no sin. The form of error is no longer seen, and reason, joined with love, looks quietly on all confusion, observing merely, "This was a mistake." And then the same Atonement you accepted in your relationship corrects the error, and lays a part of Heaven in its place. How blessed are you who let this gift be given! Each part of Heaven that you bring is given you." T-22.VI.4:1,4-8,5:1-5

CHAPTER SIX

C–VI.   BRIDGE TO THE REAL WORLD

I. CONTRASTING SPECIAL LOVE AND CHANGELESS LOVE

1. There is just one practical purpose for incarnating into this world and that is to heal our split mind. This epic schism between Love and fear is responsible for a massive hallucination, a dream in which it appears as if we each have separate bodies with private minds. It seems as if we can indeed be hurt and that we our self can harm others. In addition, there is an insane conviction that the completely neutral body can turn against us in illness, pain, aging and death.

    a. *"Forget not that the healing of God's Son is all the world is for. That is the only purpose the Holy Spirit sees in it, and thus the only one it has. Until you see the healing of the Son as all you wish to be accomplished by the world, by time and all appearances, you will not know the Father nor yourself. For you will use the world for what is not its purpose, and will not escape its laws of violence and death. Yet it is given you to be beyond its laws in all respects, in every way and every circumstance, in all temptation to perceive what is not there, and all belief God's Son can suffer pain because he sees himself as he is not." T-24.VI.4.*

2. Jesus speaks to us about the "bridge to the Real World." This is the rite of passage which we undertake as we unlearn special love and come to remember the boundless joy of our one, innocent, shared and Holy Self as changeless Love. This divine transition seems to be a journey which we undertake while we believe we're in time.

3. The special relationship dynamic which we have valued and upheld throughout time is surely the most formidable antagonist for maintaining the split mind (the separation) including the ideas of bodies and time, via the illusion of reincarnation. This is why the *Course's* central teaching spotlights the pivotal transition from special to Holy Relationships. It is in this miraculous transformation that the split mind, along with its gap of separation, is healed.

4. The *Course* leads us toward the passing of the ego's dream of sin, guilt, fear, death, birth, bodies, time and space. This is the final Victory Lap overcoming the long, arduous dream of separation. But before this occurs we will experience the miraculous reversal of the ego dream and bask in the happy dream or Real World where fear, conflict, pain, disease and death are no longer believed and valued, therefore they are not experienced. And the definitive passageway for this phase of awakening from the body dream is the transfer from special to Holy Relationship.

5. The Holy Relationship is the rite of passage to the Real World and the catalyst for our final awakening *from* the dream altogether.

   a. *"I said before that the first change, before dreams disappear, is that your dreams of fear are changed to happy dreams. That is what the Holy Spirit does in the special relationship. He does not destroy it, nor snatch it away from you. But He does use it differently, as a help to make His purpose real to you. The special relationship will remain, not as a source of pain and guilt, but as a source of joy and freedom. It will not be for you alone, for therein lay its misery. As its unholiness kept it a thing apart, its holiness will become an offering to everyone."*

   "Your special relationship will be a means for undoing guilt in everyone blessed through your holy relationship. It will be a happy dream, and one which you will share with all who come

within your sight. Through it, the blessing the Holy Spirit has laid upon it will be extended."... "And He will waken everyone through you who offered your relationship to Him."

... "In your relationship the Holy Spirit has gently laid the real world; the world of happy dreams, from which awaking is so easy and so natural." T-18.II.6:3-9,7:1-3,7,9:4

A. The Shift from Special Love to Changeless Love

1. How in the world is it possible for love to hurt? How can love change or even end? In this world it seems that we can experience a time of union with someone and then often, these relationships can erode and finally end, sometimes even bitterly. There once "appeared" to be love there, and then it disappeared or turned to hate.

2. The shocking fact here is that if the love between two people *does* diminish or end – it was not real Love but hate in disguise. Let me explain.

3. In the world's distorted version of love, it is commonly accepted that in a relationship, both love/like *and* disdain (expressed as anger, blame, guilt, hurt, resentment, hate, etc.) can be interspersed accordingly. Sometimes these companions appear to be loving or friendly toward each other and then at other times they resent each other.

4. Everyone has experienced this see-sawing between love and resentment in relationships with family, spouse, children, parents, colleagues, friends, etc. But what we haven't recognized is that all the vacillations between love/like *and* resentment are not what they seem. Resentment *and* special love (or like) appear to be two opposing behaviors evoking two very different reactions. The shocking news however, which we discover as we begin to "live" the Holy Relationship, is that *they are the same.*

5. So, when a relationship seems to vacillate from love to resentment, it merely swings from ego's version of *love* which is a *desired* form of fear – to *resentment* as an *undesired* form of fear. Yet it's *all* fear!

6. Special love is *always* fear in disguise. In our special relationships all that occurs is that this pendulum swings incessantly from the ego's hotly *desired forms of fear* such as pleasure, safety and security, to its most viciously rejected forms of fear such as conflict, pain and loss. The whole pendulum *is* fear. As fear itself, it can only swing between these two versions of fear. These two polarities of fear represent the ego's "symbols" of love. Like a pendulum, its entire field of action is completely circumscribed by fear. This is not Love. And this is why so many human relationships fail.

7. Real Love on the other hand, is not an emotion that changes or ends. We cannot trade it or use it to bargain. It's not a feeling that comes and goes. It does not change from person to person. Changeless Love is all that remains once we release everything that Love is *not*. And specialness is anything *but* Love.

   a. *"Love is not an illusion. It is a fact. Where disillusionment is possible, there was not love but hate. For hate [is] an illusion, and what can change was never love." T-16.IV.4:1-4*

8. Only through a body-centered perception could we possibly believe that real Love can change or end. Instead of knowing our Self as changeless Love, we have made up "symbols" of love/like in a convincing effort to block out the innocence of our shared Identity.

9. The ego mind gathers these fractured symbols like pieces of a jigsaw puzzle. It places them together in an attempt to convince us that once set in the right configuration these symbols form the whole picture of love or friendship. But when any of these symbols are threatened by someone's behaviors, beliefs, body appetites, values, conditions, possessions, etc., it withdraws its love or appreciation, and suddenly there appears to be a "falling out of love," or failed friendship or family relationship, etc. Love then seems to be replaced with its opposite as anger, blame, guilt, hate, or hurt, etc.

B. Special Relationship Pendulum Diagram

Please see the Special Relationship Pendulum diagram on the opposite page and the Traits of Specialness vs. the Qualities of Holiness diagram on page 564.

Using the image of a pendulum here, we will call this special relationship pendulum "fear."

Special love is always fear in disguise. In our special relationships all that occurs is similar to a pendulum that swings incessantly from the ego's hotly desired forms of fear such as pleasure, to its most viciously rejected forms of fear such as conflict, pain and loss. The whole pendulum is fear. As fear itself, it can only swing between these two versions of fear. These two polarities of fear represent the ego's "symbols" of love. Like a pendulum, its entire field of action is completely circumscribed by fear. This is not Love. And this is why so many human relationships fail.

Special Relationship Pendulum

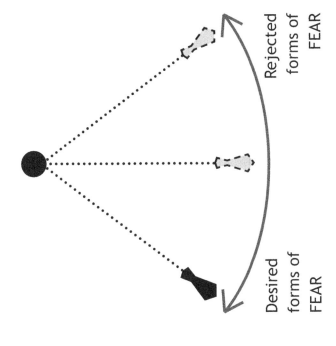

Rejected forms of FEAR

Desired forms of FEAR

TRAITS OF SPECIALNESS	QUALITIES OF HOLINESS
• self-serving interests	• transcending self-interests
• abandoning self for another's interests	• sharing in one truly common purpose - committed to see each other & self as sinless
• falling in love or sexual lust	
• exclusivity, jealousy	• inclusivity
• conditional gift giving	• shared guiltlessness
• people-pleasing, sacrifice	• commitment to unlearn body identification
• body-focused	
• pride, need to be right	• genuine emotional intimacy
• concern, worry or sympathy	• emotional transparency
• colluding, withholding	• authentic bonding
• separate self-seeking agenda	• shared reverence
• self-gratification or neediness	• shared grace, shared gratitude
• impatience	
• false humility	• sacred communion
• co-dependent behavior	• interdependence
• habituated	• empathy
• possession/control, keeping score	• radical self-honesty
	• unequivocal self-accountability
• rivalry or competition, superiority	• willing to be wrong
• fault-finding, accusing or guilt-tripping	• all-forgiving
	• patience, harmony
• victimhood, defending	• shared defenselessness
• dishonesty or distrusting	• unconditional communication
• ungrateful	
• love for status or position	• trusting implicitly
• love for money, security or safety	• joint will & joint motivation
	• joint experience
• love for fame, love for possessions	• spontaneous
	• sincerely selfless
• turning our light down to not threaten another	• genuine humility
• taking things personally	

C. Traits of Specialness vs. Qualities of Holiness Diagram

The diagram on page 564 lists a few of the traits found in the special relationship as compared to the qualities of holiness found in the Holy Relationship.

1. Generally, we take for granted that there *can* be fluctuations between love and resentment in a relationship; that we can like or love someone, and then just as quickly withdraw from them if they don't meet our perceived specialness needs. Yet all these traits of special relating, both seeming positive and negative, are classified together under just one umbrella *–fear*, as the opposite of Love.

2. When we first see this stark contrast between real Love and special love, it can induce an intense and uncomfortable reaction, perhaps even feelings of guilt or hopelessness. For most of us, all we have ever known is special love. Until we truly recognize the pain that special, changing love brings, we naturally won't desire changeless Love. There is no reason for guilt or hopelessness because we do need the experience of special relating to show us what we *do not* want. This is the key motivator as it brings us to the point where we make a conscious choice to join with Holy Spirit, asking Him to repurpose our special relationships.

3. To help us better learn to determine the traits and patterns of special love (without guilt), let's look at its seemingly positive symbols as these are highly valued by the ego. The ego's symbols of love always represent some "form of fear." Even those highly valued symbols of love like sympathy, concern, worry, sexual lust, falling in love, exclusivity, giving to get, sacrifice and playing small (false humility), all arise from fear and not from Love. This is what special relating *is*. It is a form of fear made to exclude the very nature of our Identity as changeless innocence and Love. And that is why the world's version of love is a trap, and a global delusion.

4. The good news though is that once we see and release our limitation on love (fear) to Holy Spirit, He divinely repurposes the relationship so we can learn of real Love. This is true union that can't *be* threatened. And it's in this Love that we joyfully learn of our incorruptible innocence.

5. This massive contrast between the *ego's symbols* of love and *genuine Love* helps explain why we really don't know what Love is. And why our greatest unconscious terror is of God as Love. After all, in the *Course's* introduction it explains its aim. And it tells us just how to make our way back to Love, to God and our cherished Holy Self:

a. *"The course does not aim at teaching the meaning of love, for that is beyond what can be taught. It does aim, however, at removing the blocks to the awareness of love's presence, which is your natural inheritance. The opposite of love is fear, but what is all-encompassing can have no opposite."* T-in.2:6-8

6. The kind of "love" that we have taught our self is really hate in disguise. Special relationships are based on the whims of fear and not on changeless Love. And that is why they appear to be so unpredictable. Any love that *can* be threatened is fear.

7. Here, born in and sustained by our addiction to special love as our fearful substitute for Love, lays an epic oversight. Realizing that it is fear and *not* changeless Love that underpins humanity's relationships since time's first inception, perhaps we can appreciate that the special relationship is the heaviest long-standing defense against Love in the dream. This includes the specialness involved in all our relationships, not just romantic ones. In its attempt to balance hate *and* love it completely obliterates Love in our awareness. The special relationship, as the ego's "chief weapon," represents the very seat of our unconscious aversion to God, to our one, shared and Holy Self with all our brothers.

a. *"You cannot limit hate. The special love relationship will not offset it, but will merely drive it underground and out of sight. It is essential to bring it into sight, and to make no attempt to hide it. For it is the attempt to balance hate with love that makes love meaningless to you. The extent of the split that lies in this you do not realize. And until you do, the split will remain unrecognized, and therefore unhealed."* T-16.IV.1:5-10

b. *"The special love relationship is the ego's chief weapon for keeping you from Heaven."* T-16.V.2:3

8. The false self only knows fear because it was made in fear. It does not know Love. Since the illusion of time began, in no single instant has it ever known changeless Love which is an undivided totality *as* our Holy Self. All it knows and experiences from birth to death is a cleverly disguised and richly seductive smorgasbord of fear. Its symbols of love which are really symbols of fear (hate) constitute the ego's version of special conditional love.

9. The ego's fearful love arises from an endless abyss of deprivation, emptiness and worthlessness. It always seeks to *get*. Even in its giving, it demands something in return. Its love quickly turns to anger if its illusory needs are not met by another.

10. If love can be superseded by anger, then it was not love but disguised hate. In special relating the symbols of love and the symbols of hate fuse together as one and the same. They share the same purpose which makes them synonymous. They are fear and not Love. Love is total. Changeless Love is everything that fear is not.

   a. *"The symbols of hate against the symbols of love play out a conflict that does not exist. For symbols stand for something else, and the symbol of love is without meaning if love is everything." T-16.IV.2:1-2*

11. Love is undivided and eternally innocent. It is changeless and cannot by any means be intermingled with fear. Love and fear are each totally, mutually exclusive thought systems. They cannot coexist in our awareness. The presence of one in our awareness completely obliterates the other. There are no degrees of fear. It is total. There are no degrees of Love. It is total. These two, fear and Love, cannot meet.

12. The same can be said about the "one" who thinks they can both love *and* hate together. The false self that perceives fear in any form is isolated from our beloved Holy Self. This is the split mind.

13. Taking this even further, if we say we do indeed love one person, but we despise or hate another person, then we cannot possibly truly Love the one we think we cherish. Love is not really Love unless it is extended across the board.

a. "Perhaps you think that different kinds of love are possible. Perhaps you think there is a kind of love for this, a kind for that; a way of loving one, another way of loving still another. Love is one. It has no separate parts and no degrees; no kinds nor levels, no divergencies and no distinctions. It is like itself, unchanged throughout. It never alters with a person or a circumstance. It is the Heart of God, and also of His Son."

"Love's meaning is obscure to anyone who thinks that love can change. He does not see that changing love must be impossible. And thus he thinks that he can love at times, and hate at other times. He also thinks that love can be bestowed on one, and yet remain itself although it is withheld from others. To believe these things of love is not to understand it. If it could make such distinctions, it would have to judge between the righteous and the sinner, and perceive the Son of God in separate parts."
W-127.1,2.

14. Taking this another step further, the "one" who believes in and practices special love, as the special self that can appear to love at times, and then be hurt or angered at other times, does not even exist. That false body-identity, the one that tries to *get* love, this same one that does not truly exist, is the darkest, most formidable opponent to our awakening to the breathtaking joy and resounding Love of our shared and Holy Self.

15. In the adoration of special love (as hate) there is a profound confusion. So extreme is this confusion that through the body-self, we do not recognize or value, or even know we're not in touch with changeless Love, the very substance of our eternal being. One permanent and uninterrupted attribute of this Love we are, is our incorruptible innocence. This is our perfect sinlessness; the ever-present safety and joy of our being which gives us literal immunity to all the attacks of the ego. Whenever this innocence is not perceived in our self or others, then it can only be the false self, believing and thus seeing its very own unforgiven projections.

16. Thank God for quantum forgiveness. Those who trigger us consistently offer us opportunities to recognize the single "source"

of the trigger, which is always the false, body-identity, together with its illusory past. Now we can forgive it in our own mind. Only this false self can *be* triggered! Only this self can believe in or experience suffering. Our Holy Self cannot. Thank God.

D. The Bridge from False Self to Holy Self

1. As we make the transfer from special to Holy Relationships, we must simultaneously be willing to release our own self-concept to Holy Spirit. As the body identity, this is the unlearning of special relating.

2. We can utilize the *Seven Keys* contained later in this chapter on page 572 to learn to communicate authentically and consistently access the Holy Instant. Making this divine switch undoes specialness (as Self-betrayal) and trains us to be in alignment with the Holy Self, mindfully present in communication with our Self and others, at all times. Also see *The Divine Switch from Ego to Holy Self* on page 297.

3. Along with the Atonement, these tools are necessary to *unlearn* the false self's *mis*communication which fosters guilt, conflict and sickness. Specialness is Self-dishonesty and Self-betrayal. We release our self from the ego's addiction to Self-disloyalty and unworthiness. And while we abandon our Self to serve the ego's special relationships, we will be unable to recognize our Self and others as the one innocent and Holy Self. Our view and response, unfortunately, will be through our own distorted filter of fear.

4. The transition from special to Holy Relationship is the critical alchemy agent for healing and crossing the bridge from our present dream to the Real World dream. There is, however, an additional seismic transfiguration which takes place.

5. The ones who step onto this transformational bridge together in moving from specialness to loyalty to Holy Relationship, are *not* the ones who step off on the other side. An extraordinary shift takes place. In this epic transition, the split mind – as the gap –is healed. The quantum effects of this are so far reaching that we can scarcely imagine its glorious repercussions for all the sleeping Sonship. Two or more cross the bridge, collapsing the imagined

gap for all! I am guided to include the following quotes together because they speak so masterfully of this transition:

a. *"The special relationship is totally meaningless without a body. If you value it, you must also value the body. And what you value you will keep. The special relationship is a device for limiting your self to a body, and for limiting your perception of others to theirs. The Great Rays would establish the total lack of value of the special relationship, if they were seen. For in seeing them the body would disappear, because its value would be lost. And so your whole investment in seeing it would be withdrawn from it."*

"You see the world you value. On this side of the bridge you see the world of separate bodies, seeking to join each other in separate unions and to become one by losing. When two individuals seek to become one, they are trying to decrease their magnitude. Each would deny his power, for the separate union excludes the universe. Far more is left outside than would be taken in, for God is left without and [nothing] taken in. If one such union were made in perfect faith, the universe would enter into it. Yet the special relationship the ego seeks does not include even one whole individual. The ego wants but part of him, and sees only this part and nothing else."

"Across the bridge it is so different! For a time the body is still seen, but not exclusively, as it is seen here. The little spark that holds the Great Rays within it is also visible, and this spark cannot be limited long to littleness. Once you have crossed the bridge, the value of the body is so diminished in your sight that you will see no need at all to magnify it. For you will realize that the only value the body has is to enable you to bring your brothers to the bridge with you, and to be released together there."

"The bridge itself is nothing more than a transition in the perspective of reality. On this side, everything you see is grossly distorted and completely out of perspective. What is little and

insignificant is magnified, and what is strong and powerful cut down to littleness. In the transition there is a period of confusion, in which a sense of actual disorientation may occur. But fear it not, for it means only that you have been willing to let go your hold on the distorted frame of reference that seemed to hold your world together. This frame of reference is built around the special relationship. Without this illusion there could be no meaning you would still seek here."

"Fear not that you will be abruptly lifted up and hurled into reality. Time is kind, and if you use it on behalf of reality, it will keep gentle pace with you in your transition. The urgency is only in dislodging your mind from its fixed position here. This will not leave you homeless and without a frame of reference. The period of disorientation, which precedes the actual transition, is far shorter than the time it took to fix your mind so firmly on illusions. Delay will hurt you now more than before, only because you realize it [is] delay, and that escape from pain is really possible. Find hope and comfort, rather than despair, in this: You could not long find even the illusion of love in any special relationship here. For you are no longer wholly insane, and you would soon recognize the guilt of self-betrayal for what it is." T-16.VI.4,5,6,7,8.

6. NOTE: This is a good place to cross-reference the sections titled, *"Do You Really Want a Holy Relationship?"* on page 541 and *"Are You Ready to Commit to Holy Relationship? - Self-Inquiry Exercise"* on page 552.

2. THE "HOW" OF HOLY RELATING

A. The Seven Key Principles of Authentic Relating:

*1. Please contemplate the **check points** that follow each Key to identify any resistance in implementing these Key Principles. If there is resistance, stay with that principle till the resistance falls away. We must neutralize the (ego) resistance before we can fully integrate the Seven Key Principles.*

WILLINGNESS

2. The first attribute to acquire is the willingness to have every belief and value undone by Spirit. It is the willingness to be wrong about our beliefs and values, and our interpretation of the past along with all our stories. It's an eagerness to be shown all the unconscious blocks that obscure our awareness of Love's eternal and uninterruptible presence. This calls for the willingness to face up to and confess that, of the ego, we know nothing. Yet by the Spirit in us, the Truth can and will be revealed. It is also the willingness to see others as sinless, as guiltless, despite seeming evidence to the contrary. This is the willingness to forgive.

3. The Willingness check points are:

   1)   Am I feeling any resistance to do this? If there is resistance, there is fear of God's Love. Resistance is a sign that we're not willing to trust God and therefore, to trust our Holy Self.

   2)   Am I grateful for my willingness?

ACCOUNTABILITY

4. This is the recognition and acceptance that all our suffering is caused by just one culprit, no matter how many varied forms it might appear to take. The ego is our own unconscious self-hatred projected outward onto others, our body and the world, to manifest as attack (conflict, betrayal, abandonment, sickness and pain, scarcity and death, etc.).

5. We accept that others, the body, the past and the world are all causeless because their primary underlying cause lay within our own mind. It is here, in our mind, through the ego's distorted filter of perception, that the singular source of all suffering is found and healed. This is true accountability, where we do not judge or blame others, the body, or our self, for our own unconscious self-attack. Therefore, we must learn to forgive our self for unknowingly using others, the body, the past and the world for the purpose of attack and separation.

6. *The Accountability check points are:*

1) Am I feeling resistance to this? If so, which areas do I wish to keep separate from God/Love/healing?

2) Am I grateful to be 100 percent accountable for all my thoughts, feelings and actions, without self-blame?

EMOTIONAL VULNERABILITY / TRANSPARENCY

7. The greatest challenge for many of us is to acknowledge that we have unknowingly learned to relate with our self and others dishonestly. And we cannot heal this until we first see it. Then we will recognize that we have abandoned our Self in the pursuit of specialness. Learning to be authentic involves learning to be emotionally vulnerable and transparent. The ego sees this as weakness, the complete opposite of the Holy Spirit's interpretation, which is that emotional vulnerability is *strength* because it brings us closer to Him, others and our Holy Self. We're so conditioned to "special relating" that we have no idea *who we* really are. Initially, we are afraid to find out because we believe we may lose our special relationships if we do.

8. *The Emotional Vulnerability/Transparency check points are:*

   1) Am I grateful for my emotional vulnerability and transparency?

   2) To what degree am I happy to feel and express my emotions without blame, either alone or with those I know, as well as with those I don't know?

   3) Am I okay to shed a tear in public?

   4) Am I comfortable expressing peace in the midst of seeming turmoil?

   5) Can I express empathy (not sympathy) and extend trust without concern for how others who feel upset might perceive it?

   6) Can I accept my own emotions, seemingly positive or negative, and hold myself Lovingly without embarrassment, shame or self-criticism?

RADICAL SELF HONESTY

9. It is through radical self-honesty and self-inquiry that we peel back all our erroneous beliefs, conditioning, stories and values to reveal our true feelings. And it's by feeling whatever we have repressed, without self-judgment, that we can finally recognize and relinquish our defenses to God's Love as our Holy Self. Honesty is one of the key characteristics of true awakening. Jesus shares its supreme importance with us:

a. *"Honesty does not apply only to what you say. The term actually means consistency. There is nothing you say that contradicts what you think or do; no thought opposes any other thought; no act belies your word; and no word lacks agreement with another. Such are the truly honest. At no level are they in conflict with themselves. Therefore it is impossible for them to be in conflict with anyone or anything."* ... *"Conflict is the inevitable result of self-deception, and self-deception is dishonesty."* M-4.II.1:4-9,2:4

10. So, the ego wants to keep the peace in its relationships. Keeping the peace looks good and safe to the ego but let's really look at this with radical self-honesty. Keeping the (ego's) peace necessitates Self-abandonment and Self-deceit. It has a cost that will be exacted.

11. *The Radical Self Honesty check points are:*

1) Am I feeling any resistance to this?

2) Am I more concerned with how others (egos) will receive my honesty (authenticity), rather than staying 100 percent authentically aligned in my Truth?

3) Am I being 100 percent radically self-honest with myself and everyone that I encounter?

4) Are my thoughts, feelings, speech and actions all in line with my truth? Or do I abandon my own truth to appease the ego of others?

5) Am I grateful for my radical self-honesty?

DEFENSELESSNESS

12. The persistent sense of threat that we experience arises from a deeply buried and nebulous sense of guilt. That guilt is the unconscious fear of God (Love) that arose when we mistakenly believed we separated from God and made duality. It is this guilt that spawns all fear and the many forms of suffering we seem to witness.

13. Our safety lies in our willingness to be defenseless. Defenselessness is not weakness but strength. It is the recognition of our innocent and Holy Self. It calls forth the Christ within and affirms our inherent invulnerability. When we defend we unknowingly reinforce attack. Whatever we fear or defend against, we will attract. In defense, we make an opposite to God's Love and we believe this opposite is a seemingly real opponent.

14. All forms of fear arise from our secret belief that we have sinned (separation), are guilty, and now we require defense. Therefore, we *expect* punishment (from God) for that illusory belief. And because we have free will and use the power of God to materialize our unconscious ego choices, we unknowingly manifest our fears.

a. *"Who would defend himself unless he thought he were attacked, that the attack were real, and that his own defense could save himself? And herein lies the folly of defense; it gives illusions full reality, and then attempts to handle them as real. It adds illusions to illusions, thus making correction doubly difficult."* W-135:1:1-3

b. *"Defenses are the costliest of all the prices which the ego would exact." ... "Defenselessness is strength. It testifies to recognition of the Christ in you. W-153.4:1,6:1-2*

15. Expressing sincere defenselessness within interpersonal communication serves to lift the ego's veil of fear long enough to catch a glimpse of our Self and others as we are now – innocent – in the Holy Instant. Otherwise, especially when we're triggered, we will view them through our own superimposed past, as guilty. But how we judge another is always our own unconscious self-judgment. It will be either a blessing of innocence or a condemnation of guilt.

16. *The Defenselessness check points are:*

1) Am I feeling resistance to practicing defenselessness?

2) If there is no opposite of God/ my Holy Self, then why do I feel the compelling need to be right, or to defend myself from anyone or anything? Who or what am I defending myself from?

3) Am I grateful for my defenselessness?

4) Am I okay to drop all need to defend?

TRUST

17. If I am not perfectly at peace, then fear has entered my mind and therefore I must be trusting in the ego's strength which is weakness. God's Will for me is perfect peace. If I experience anything less than that, I am denying God's Will.

a. *"The presence of fear is a sure sign that you are trusting in your own strength. The awareness that there is nothing to fear shows that somewhere in your mind, though not necessarily in a place you recognize as yet, you have remembered God, and let His strength take the place of your weakness. The instant you are willing to do this there is indeed nothing to fear." W-48.3.*

18. With Holy Spirit we learn to withdraw our trust in fear as guilt, blame and judgment. We allow Him to transfer our trust to Love as innocence, peace and true union. Our trust is strengthened as we apply quantum forgiveness to all our triggers. We learn to trust the eternal light within our one, shared and Holy Self by forgiving the ego's projections of separation.

19. *The Trust check points are:*

1) Am I feeling any resistance to surrender it all over to Holy Spirit?

2) Am I grateful to surrender everything over to Holy Spirit?

3) Do I trust that all my needs are met by God?

4) Do I trust that I can safely surrender every one of my compulsions to control (relationships, family, finances, the body, health, income, job, etc.) over to Holy Spirit?

GRATITUDE

20. As our defenses, our need to control, to struggle and to judge fall away, we find that they were there only to obstruct our natural state of *gratitude*. From here we see that behind every forgiveness opportunity there lay a miraculous healing. In fact, we welcome forgiveness opportunities because we know the quantum healing they bring, and for these we have abundant gratitude.

21. As we unlearn fear and open our self to Love through genuine willingness, accountability, emotional transparency, radical

self-honesty, defenselessness and trust, we find that gratitude accompanies us wherever we go.

22. The Gratitude check points are:

1) Am I grateful to exchange *all* my past experiences, stories, values and beliefs for Holy Spirit's Thought System?

2) Am I grateful for this miraculous Default Thought System?

3) Can I gratefully invite it to completely take over every one of my decisions and reactions from now on?

23. For additional helpful information, please refer to *The Divine Switch from Ego to Holy Self* on page 297.

B. The Intent of the *Seven Keys*

1. Consistent practice with the *Seven Keys* will bring us to the place of really knowing our true Identity, as Love. Through heartfelt, authentic communication the seeming gap between our self and others, and between our self and God, is finally closed. Fear is the only reason we believe we are separate. We cannot master fear. Attempts at mastery over an illusion merely lead us deeper into more illusions. Mastery over fear is impossible. Only fear itself attempts to master fear.

a. *"It has already been said that you believe you cannot control fear because you yourself made it, and your belief in it seems to render it out of your control. Yet any attempt to resolve the error through attempting the mastery of fear is useless. In fact, it asserts the power of fear by the very assumption that it need be mastered. The true resolution rests entirely on mastery through love." T-2.VII.4:1-4*

2. The truth of our Identity is the totality of Love. Only the false self perceives fear, guilt, blame, suffering or loss. Only the false self believes it *is* a body that owns a private mind with personal agendas that can clash with another's.

3. All true communication arises from Love. The false self as fear, cannot communicate. Fear breaks true communication. Fear can only attempt to communicate aspects of darkness which are unknown to and incommunicable with Love.

4. To unlearn the ego's default of fear, we must learn to welcome and embrace our natural state of being – as Love – through applying the *Seven Keys* with all our communication, inner and outer. Through this application our decisions, actions and communication become "inspired" by Holy Spirit and a happy sense of effortlessness comes to take the place of fear and control.

5. Along with the Atonement, the *Seven Keys* provide an ongoing means by which we bring the darkness of the false self to the light of our Holy Self. These keys offer us a bridge by which to cross from the ego – to accept and receive the Love we *are*. As we practice these *Seven Keys* it is the one, shared and unified Holy Self that we begin to experience within and without. Crossing this inner bridge from self-disloyalty to Self-loyalty, we happily discover that others reflect our inner sense of loyalty and worth. The one unified Mind of Love gently awaits our conscious participation.

C. The Origin and Purpose of the *Seven Keys*

1. Recently, it seems I'm learning about a whole new level of Holy Relationship. I recognize that the depth and reverence attained in a relationship (including our Holy Self) depends on our willingness to develop key qualities. These qualities, largely alien to the ego thought system, appear to threaten it along with the special, conditional "love" that it idolizes.

2. A Holy Relationship with our Self and others requires a high level of devotion and vigilance. The focus is on learning to be authentic, honest, trusting, emotionally vulnerable, inclusive and defenseless. This is the complete opposite of the ego's goals of specialness, dishonesty, doubt, defensiveness, secrecy, sacrifice and exclusivity. The Holy Relationship is centered on giving or extending rather than the ego's obsession with "getting;" through it we learn that giving is indeed receiving.

3. Because all relationships start off as special, most people in the world including those who have perhaps lived together under the same roof for decades, even sleeping in the same bed together, have

never *seen* each other. They go to the grave without ever having truly closed the gap between them. And this is why they die. They maintain a false self-image with its fake relationship roles, rules, beliefs, stories and values all revolving around the unreal body. Yet they have never really seen each other. They cannot be seen, *really seen,* until they have learned to genuinely forgive, to be radically self-honest, defenseless, and emotionally transparent.

4. Jesus speaks of this special relationship dynamic here:

   a. *"For an unholy relationship is based on differences, where each one thinks the other has what he has not. They come together, each to complete himself and rob the other. They stay until they think that there is nothing left to steal, and then move on. And so they wander through a world of strangers, unlike themselves, living with their bodies perhaps under a common roof that shelters neither; in the same room and yet a world apart."* T-22.in.3:5-8

5. The happy alternative Jesus gives us to the neediness of the special relationship is the Holy Relationship:

   a. *"A holy relationship starts from a different premise. Each one has looked within and seen no lack. Accepting his completion, he would extend it by joining with another, whole as himself. He sees no difference between these selves, for differences are only of the body."* T-22.in.3:1-4

6. Initially, the journey from specialness to Holiness is set to reveal to you what Love is not. While you still choose to believe that others can hurt you, then Love will not find you because you have locked yourself away from it. Unless you're willing to learn what Love is *not*, you will not be willing to open to Love. This is where *learning and implementing the Seven Keys is required.*

7. Relationships fail because we unknowingly use them for anything and everything other than their one miraculous purpose. The real purpose of all relationships is to remember our own and others' incorruptible innocence. This *innocence* is the changeless Holy Self we share, the one that is in permanent joy, peace and Love. The necessary means by which we accomplish this sacred task of

remembering this innocence is by learning how to communicate authentically and fearlessly.

8. Through the false self we're taught how *not* to communicate. The ego attempts to convince us that we are fundamentally deprived, and thus we adopt various masks and roles in our attempt to recover our worth and completion. Such unrecognized motivation arises from fear and lack. Special love is really fear in disguise; therefore, it is steeped in the erroneous belief in lack. Communication becomes very precarious in these relationships. Unfortunately, when we try to communicate via fear, we unwittingly block Love and healing.

9. Through the deceptive false self, we try to *get from others* that which we believe is lacking in us. *Getting* is the *goal*. It could be special love, physical closeness, sex, or financial security. It could be approval, validation or emotional support. Whatever it is that we have refused to give to our self, we try to get or extract from others – including our parents and children.

10. The pseudo self attempts to disguise its intent to take from others by secretly "giving to get," or giving conditionally. But giving to get is no different than taking or stealing. And because in truth there is only one of us here, when we give with the expectation of something in return, we rob from our Self. Although we may not be aware of this, we still accumulate guilt for it because it has not been offered to Holy Spirit and truly forgiven. Instead, it is projected outward onto others and they reflect our own self-betrayal back to us.

    a. *"The ego never gives out of abundance, because it was made as a substitute for it. That is why the concept of "getting" arose in the ego's thought system. Appetites are "getting" mechanisms, representing the ego's need to confirm itself. This is as true of body appetites as it is of the so-called "higher ego needs." Body appetites are not physical in origin."* T-4. II.7:3-7

11. Giving to get is based on lack and deprivation and always breeds separation. Only the false self can feel lack, unloved, hurt, unseen, betrayed, abandoned, unappreciated and misunderstood. Our Holy Self is entirely impervious to threats like these. It doesn't need to get anything from anyone. It knows it has everything because it knows

it *is* everything. Its great joy is to extend the Love and abundance that it is.

12. The false self does not know Love. It only knows and wants specialness and exclusivity. While this self is a bottomless pit of unworthiness it cannot ever know Love. It cannot give Love or receive it. It believes that Love can change or end, which is impossible. Love can only seem to change if we first abandon our self in self-deception.

13. When coming from the ego, it's truly astounding that we can have close relationships which swing wildly from love to hate. One minute we seem to love, in the next we are full of resentment. This is what Jesus says about this insane concept of special love:

a. *"No one considers it bizarre to love and hate together, and even those who believe that hate is sin merely feel guilty, but do not correct it." T-16.V.3:4*

14. He also reveals that what passes for love in the world's special relationships is really sacrifice in disguise. We have no idea that sacrifice always involves guilt and resentment and is not Love:

a. *"In such insane relationships, the attraction of what you do not want seems to be much stronger than the attraction of what you do want. For each one thinks that he has sacrificed something to the other, and hates him for it. Yet this is what he thinks he wants. He is not in love with the other at all. He merely believes he is in love with sacrifice. And for this sacrifice, which he demands of himself, he demands that the other accept the guilt and sacrifice himself as well. Forgiveness becomes impossible, for the ego believes that to forgive another is to lose him. It is only by attack without forgiveness that the ego can ensure the guilt that holds all its relationships together." T-15.VII.7.*

15. Contrary to popular belief, the foremost purpose of all relationships is not to meet the imagined needs of the false self and its body appetites (financial security, special relationship roles, sex, etc.). It is to "close the gap" of separation between us. This will ultimately lead to the final closing of the gap *within*. As our projections of

blame are withdrawn from others, we remove the distorted self-concept to reveal the one shared Holy Self. And the false needs of the body do not intrude on this most cherished relationship. The body falls into alignment now with the Holy Spirit's purpose.

16. In relating with thousands of *Course* students over the years, I recognize a common challenge that many face. They desire Holy Relationships, however, often their loved ones are not on this spiritual path. The transfer from a special to a healed relationship looks far too daunting for them, consequently they tend to compartmentalize their spiritual practice so they don't rock the boat in their relationships.

17. Here is a common example of most people's resistance to dive into the transfer process from special to Holy Relationships:

   a. *"I want to "keep the peace" so I apply the Course's principles to some of my life (in private) while dissociating it from my significant relationships. The "special roles" I play (spouse, lover, parent, family member, income earner, work colleague, homemaker, etc.) are kept separate from my spiritual practice. I can't afford to come out of the closet in every area of my life with my spiritual path. I'm afraid I'll lose friendships and family."*

18. All relationships are living classrooms to help us undo our own distorted belief that we are unworthy of Love. They are purely mirrors of our own hidden self-condemnation, our own guilt. And it's this profound lie that forms the basis of our false self-concept. This is the self that attempts communication in relationship with other false selves.

19. All roles, rules and expectations are based on protecting and defending this false self (fear and guilt). The starring role here is always played by the ego's replacement for our Holy Self, the body. Everything the false self does is for the *illusory body* and not the Holy Self. To its partner or friends, it says over and over in a thousand different ways, *"I will love you just as long as you do what I want."* Yet this image of self is the block to our most beloved Holy Self. Why on earth would we want to keep the ego? Especially once we recognize the conflict and suffering it generates.

20. Because the major purpose of all relationships is to undo our fundamental belief that we're separate, the means to achieve this

is quantum forgiveness (Atonement). As we forgive our self for having unknowingly used others to attack us, the veil of condemnation falls away to reveal our most Holy Self.

21. Did you know that it's impossible to forgive another? And here is the reason why trying to forgive another does not work:

a. *"It is impossible to forgive another, for it is only your sins you see in him. You want to see them there, and not in you."* ... *"That is why forgiveness of another is an illusion."* ... *"Only in someone else can you forgive yourself, for you have called him guilty of your sins, and in him must your innocence now be found."* S.2.1.4:2-4,6

22. It is only through others that we are gifted the opportunity to forgive our *own imagined* sins and undo the self-saboteur that inflicts self-punishment via projection. We could never undo this tragic self-concept without our brothers and sisters. They show us exactly where our own unconscious self-abandonment lies, so we can forgive it.

23. Most of us are in special relationships and have no idea how to initiate a Holy Relationship, especially if the other person or people have zero interest in living this path. And that brings up a lot of fear, even terror for many. The deep-seated fear of loss and rejection seems so overwhelming. Yet Jesus reassures us that these special relationships can be transformed. However, this involves our own wholehearted participation in applying the *Seven Keys* and *The Seven Essential Principles of Quantum Forgiveness* (the Atonement).

D. The Magnitude of Implementing the Seven Keys

1. The Holy Relationship starts with me. I am one hundred percent responsible (accountable) to relate with others from my Holy Self and not the pseudo self. Even if the ones I'm in relationship with are not on this path it's still up to me to show-up authentically for *myself* with them. As I become more genuine my inner conflict falls away and because we all share the one Christ Mind, others will also come into alignment with my inner shift.

2. As we learn to be thoroughly accountable for all our projections (without self-blame) we will experience more genuine peace. As we finally show-up for our Self in radical self-honesty and defenselessness, as we learn to shatter our emotional paralysis and dare to express our emotions intimately, we must realize that there is no one and nothing to protect or defend our self from.

3. In fact, as we show-up authentically, others will show-up for us! And then we will witness that everyone and everything we seem to see in the world is wholly and magnificently changed. All because we have learned to show-up for our most beloved Holy Self – the Self that is shared as one. The Love we seek is what we *are*. And when we know this ... Love will be all we feel and see.

4. Expressing our emotional vulnerability ensures that we cannot *be* attacked. When we are honest and vulnerable, we call upon truth in our self and in others. Our safety depends on it. Expressing our vulnerability or transparency guarantees our perfect immunity to the ego's illusory threats in whatever form they may take. Emotional intimacy is an important part of true communication with others and our Self. It ties in with radical Self-honesty.

5. Emotional vulnerability and transparency (without blame) is the doorway to the heart. It connects us to each other. It's a powerful expression of defenselessness. And it bypasses the ego's intellectual defenses which are blocks to Love and healing. Contrary to what the ego teaches, emotional vulnerability is strength and not weakness. In our emotional transparency Holy Spirit is given permission to make Himself known to us through others and vice versa. Why would we resist this wonderful opportunity?

6. As we unlearn specialness in our relationships, we will come to value the importance of becoming emotionally available and open. And it is here that we will learn that we are eternally safe to lay down our defenses. It is here that we experience a sanctuary of innocence and healing. In fact, we will know that our safety and strength lie in being emotionally transparent and honest. This is in stark opposition to the ego's idea of safety.

7. When we learn to communicate authentically, we open more to Holy Spirit and trust His guidance. Our past conditioning is literally

undone as we apply forgiveness and practice relating from an authentic place within. The result of this process is that we begin to see others in their true light, which is a joy! Without the past clouding our perception we look for opportunities to sincerely "close the gap" with others. We come to expect miracles in all our relationships and the healing is monumental.

8. The transfer in our relationships from specialness to Holiness is really the path to discovering our most beloved and innocent Holy Self. In this experiential journey of return to Self, the Love we're so fearful to lose… is finally found within. And joy of joys - when we learn to embrace and live out from this divine authenticity then Love increases in our experience with others. We no longer engage in relationships for the ego's mutual use. We *are* the Love we seek, and that Love is felt and witnessed by everyone we encounter.

9. All defenses, regardless of their form, serve the same purpose, which is to protect the ego from the Love and forgiveness that would dissolve it. Defenses are used exclusively to guard the ego's senseless idols, the blocks to our awareness of Love's presence.

10. When we're triggered by someone or something it's always *our own* projected guilt that we react to. This is why forgiveness of our projections is crucial because in it we learn to forgive our own unconscious guilt as self-attack. In contrast, if we become defensive when triggered, no healing of our own self-attack takes place. In fact, in defensiveness we further consolidate our guilt by our belief it is real.

11. We will never truly know our Holy Self's changeless innocence and immunity to all the ego made until we recognize the value of defenselessness. *"If I defend myself I am attacked. But in defenselessness I will be strong, and I will learn what my defenses hide."* W-135.22:4-5

12. In the preceding quote it says that through our defenselessness we will learn what the ego's defenses hide, which is always the changeless innocence, safety and Love of our eternal and shared Holy Self. The ego *is* 100-percent guilt and fear. It uses its projected fears as a shield to protect itself from the light of Love, union and healing which would dispel it. Whenever defense as fear

is valued, then forgiveness as Love is rejected. Our safety lies in our defenselessness.

13. When we align our self with the qualities of willingness, accountability, defenselessness, radical self-honesty and emotional vulnerability then we can afford to trust in the flow of life implicitly. We can trust others because we have learned to trust our Holy Self instead of the ego. We look past the egos of others and focus on the truth within them. It is this trust that our faith calls out within them. What we choose to acknowledge in another is exactly that which we will manifest and experience.

14. During our diligent practice of the *Seven Keys* we learn to become authentic in our communication. And as we learn to show-up authentically we come to trust in changeless Love which is what we are. We learn that Love without trust is impossible, and that doubt and trust cannot coexist. Trust is a crucial component of real Love. And doubt always arises from Love's opposite, fear.

15. Once we prioritize God as our chief goal, we will view every seeming challenge as a forgiveness opportunity. We will look for and accept the miracle beneath every seeming adversity. Seeing it this way ensures that gratitude becomes our natural state. We experience a growing appreciation for those people in our life who mirror to us where we still harbor hidden judgment and unconscious self-sabotage. Because of our shift in intent we will also experience boundless miracles which further confirm that only Love is real and that we *are* Love.

   a. *"Our gratitude will pave the way to Him, and shorten our learning time by more than you could ever dream of. Gratitude goes hand in hand with love, and where one is the other must be found. For gratitude is but an aspect of the Love which is the Source of all creation."* W-195.10:1-3

16. God's Will for us is perfect happiness. And as we come into vertical alignment with our Holy Self, happiness is the natural outcome because we are in alignment with God's Will for us. Eventually, as our unconscious attraction to sin, guilt and fear are undone through forgiveness and applying the *Seven Keys,* we will find that the

unhappy self is joyfully replaced by our incorruptible and majestic Holy Self.

E. A Period of Temporary Disorientation

1. In my own experience and that of many others, when we first begin to utilize the *Seven Keys* within established special relationships, there can be an initial period of disorientation. Our companions are accustomed to us relating through the ego and suddenly we're introducing the brilliant light of honesty, which tends to reveal areas of darkness so they can be healed in Love, and no longer hidden in resentment and conflict. When one person in a special relationship decides to initiate communication through the *Seven Keys* it eventually affects everyone positively. But at first our companion or family may feel this change is a threat. Patience, trust and forgiveness are important during this phase. I suggest printing out the *Seven Keys,* placing them somewhere where everyone can see them, like the refrigerator door. This way we can begin our new communication in honesty, by announcing to significant others that we'd like to practice these Keys for *our self.* And that we would appreciate our loved ones' support. We do not expect that they *practice* the *Seven Keys* unless they express their willingness to do so. These Keys are for *our own* transformation and healing.

2. Another helpful suggestion is to ask our companions to help us stay in alignment with the *Seven Keys*. This way if they're not on this path they can at least begin to participate and eventually recognize the value of learning to communicate more honestly and defenselessly. The *Seven Keys* tend to be happily contagious once the enormous value of consistently applying them is recognized.

3. THE SEVEN BLOCKS TO FEARLESS RELATING

1. Fear, which is expressed in countless and mostly unrecognized forms, is largely concealed from our awareness until we commence our awakening journey. If changeless Love is really all that *can* be communicated in reality, then fear is an immediate block to true communication.

2. Before we can positively value and implement fearless communication, we need to identify the most common blocks to it. Remember that our default is the "fear-driven mind." It is especially wary of any perceived threat to its fiercely defended autonomy. It likes to be in control in order to maintain its shield of fear - protection from the light, Love and union of our Holy Self. From its perspective the Holy Spirit is too abstract and out of control.

3. False pride is one of the ego's favorite defenses, made to oppose feeling and expressing genuine emotional vulnerability. Consequently, it poses a major obstacle to authentic relating and healing. False pride is perhaps the greatest common denominator in all communication breakdowns. This is the *need to be right* no matter what. This pride is self-centered, unapologetic, defensive and often opinionated. It is concerned with itself while ignoring the views or ideas of others.

4. False pride underpins all conflict. It renders us as unreachable and therefore, *unteachable*. This handicap severely limits our ability to communicate, and especially to forgive. Forgiveness is the prerequisite for true communication. Only the split mind perceives and reacts to fear and conflict, and only forgiveness erases the guilt responsible for causing all fear.

5. There can be no real Love without forgiveness. Yet false pride is *unforgiving*. Below is a brief self-inquiry checklist which you can delve into whenever you feel tempted by conflict.

A. Checklist – Seven Habits of Denial

1) Unwilling: resisting, evasive, afraid, controlling, uncooperative, rigid, stubborn, unforgiving, defiant, procrastinating.

2) Unaccountable: blaming others, passing the buck, irresponsible, victim, unfairly treated, defensive, self-compromising/ sacrificing, demanding, unforgiving, resentful.

3) Self-dishonest: self-deception, self-disloyalty, self-betrayal, self-abandonment, private thoughts, people-pleasing, unworthiness, self-attacking, unforgiving of self and others.

4) Emotional paralysis: private feelings, suppressed emotions, protecting feelings, evasive, resentful, unaffectionate, secrecy, unforgiving.

5) Defensive: autocratic, self-justifying, judgmental, accusing, controlling, arrogant, prideful, defiant, unforgiving, resentful.

6) Distrusting: doubtful, fearful, anxious, suspicious, faithless, planning ahead as a defense, unforgiving.

7) Ungrateful: unforgiving, thankless, ungracious, depressive, critical, judgmental, complaining, victim, self-centered.

4. THE SEVEN ESSENTIAL PRINCIPLES OF QUANTUM FORGIVENESS (ATONEMENT)

1. We're about to delve deeply into the principles and process of Atonement. This is the forgiveness process, the means through which we exchange our perception of suffering for miracles instead. The Atonement brings about the gradual reversal of all our ego beliefs, values and laws. In short, it is a monumental unlearning accomplishment, because it thoroughly reverses the ego's cause and effect. This is the undoing of the ego's world of suffering.

2. Only after many years did I discover the critical principles involved in forgiveness, as Jesus teaches it. Like most *Course* students, I thought forgiveness would take place automatically when I set my good intentions to forgive. Yet I was clearly missing something. Countless futile attempts at forgiveness over the years proved there must be some error or omission on my part. With all my heart, I asked Jesus to teach me—to show me what he really means by forgiveness and Atonement.

3. According to Jesus, we spent millions of years teaching our self to separate from God's Love—and now we need to unlearn or reverse, via the miracle, the destructive illusions we have brought into being. For forgiveness and miracles to take place, seven critical principles must first be accepted. These seven principles contain reality-reversal properties in themselves, but when combined together, they act to bring in the mighty power of God's Love and healing.

4. A word of warning: Don't presume you already know these principles, just because they may sound familiar. Believe me, these are principles that must be learned through consistent application. It's only in their consistent application that undeniable miracles will unfold. This is how unswerving trust is developed in the power of God's Love and healing.

5. You've undoubtedly noticed I often repeat certain themes and principles, especially regarding Atonement. It's because I'm aware of the way our minds work: We understand a concept fully, which might lead us to think we've mastered this process. Yet when we are hit with a special challenge, fear or issue that renders us temporarily insane, we tend to completely forget these principles—no matter how thorough our comprehension. In the frequent repetition of this material, my aim is to allow these concepts to sink in deeply, beyond the surface understanding of the intellect.

6. For until these Truths become our natural default, we must be vigilant in our practice. These thought-reversal principles appear so often precisely because we need reminding over and over until they become second nature. Until this happens, please do book mark these pages on the Atonement/forgiveness process. Better still—print them out and keep them handy.

7. The seven basic principles of forgiveness/Atonement are:

   1) **Apply true denial.** Recall there is only one Power, and it is God's Loving Will. Therefore, steadfastly deny anything not of God's Love the power to hurt you or anyone else.

   2) **Place cause and effect in their proper sequence.** No matter the form of problem, all cause is in your mind and nowhere else. If you believe the cause is anywhere but in your mind,

you will be unable to heal the cause or its seeming symptoms. Recall unconscious guilt is self-attack projected outward. There is no one to forgive except yourself, for unconsciously using others, the body, the past or the world to attack you.

3) **Make healing of your mistaken perception your priority over all else.** You must desire to have your perception of the illness or problem healed, more than you want a physical healing, a physical miracle.

4) **Look past appearances.** Look beyond what your physical senses tell you of reality. The ego sends these senses out to report back exactly what it wants us to see; they will always confirm "proof" of separation and suffering.

5) **Remember there is no hierarchy of illusions.** One illusion is never truer or bigger than another. They're all equally illusory. As we accept and practice this principle, we also learn and demonstrate there is no order of difficulty in miracles. One miracle is not harder or more impossible to achieve than any other. By accepting and demonstrating the illusory nature of illusions, and the maximal power of miracles, we undo everything the ego made to attack us.

6) **Accept the Atonement.** In accepting Atonement, we immediately join with and receive God's Will for healing. This unequivocally cancels out the ego's wish to be unfairly treated. This is the miracle! No matter where we see suffering, we must accept the Atonement, the miracle, for our self. If we perceive suffering in another, the past, the body or the world, healing must be accepted in our own mind first. This is the divine undoing of fear and guilt in our perception.

7) **Trust in God's Love and healing**! It is already done. Doubt and trust are mutually exclusive. If we doubt, we cannot accept healing.

8. Here is a helpful prayer:

"Holy Spirit, please help me to forgive myself for having believed in separation by having unknowingly used __ (person, sickness, pain, situation, lack, etc.)__ to attack myself, and thus for abandoning my Holy Self. In this Holy Instant, I genuinely accept the Atonement that you have already given, the complete undoing and healing of the cause of this adversity, along with its effects."

5. PREPARATION FOR HOLY RELATIONSHIP

1. All special relationships – romantic, family, friends, colleagues, etc. – are based on the mistaken belief that we are each special, separate, personal identities. These identities center entirely on the body thereby obscuring the changeless innocence of all those concerned. Further, while we remain predominantly body identified our goals and agendas will arise from and be driven by unconscious guilt (fear). Recall that this self does not recognize Love but only the ego's "symbols" of special love, which are primarily self-destructive.

2. It's from the illusory, conditioned self that we assign our relationship goals and expectations. Its fundamental goal is to satiate the separate, personal identity, namely the body. In its erroneous attachment to this goal set apart from God, it secretly condemns itself with guilt. Next, we unknowingly project our guilt onto others and use them to *prove* that we are indeed separate via blame, conflict, sickness, pain, loss and death.

3. However, at some point the pain of relating through specialness reaches its peak. It becomes intolerable. When we're entirely done with the turmoil and we sincerely desire to open our heart to a better way to relate we will find, paradoxically, that the priceless gifts given us to awaken from this predicament of separation *are* our special relationships. They provide the miraculous vessels for our unprecedented awakening from fear.

a. *"The special relationships of the world are destructive, selfish and childlishly egocentric. Yet, if given to the Holy Spirit, these relationships can become the holiest things on earth-the miracles that point the way to the return to Heaven. The world uses its special relationships as a final weapon of exclusion and a demonstration of separateness. The Holy Spirit transforms them into perfect lessons in forgiveness and in awakening from the dream. Each one is an opportunity to let perceptions be healed and errors corrected. Each one is another chance to forgive oneself by forgiving the other. And each one becomes still another invitation to the Holy Spirit and to the remembrance of God." From the Preface of A Course in Miracles Urtext.*

4. The first phases of undoing specialness involve purification by Holy Spirit. We offer our willingness to Him to gently undo our beliefs and values including our ideas of love and forgiveness. Because this is a phase of undoing it often manifests as what Jesus terms a "period of disorientation."

5. Once we've sufficiently experienced Holy Spirit's purification, through forgiveness, we can appreciate the need for undoing the ego's goals and agendas, especially in relationships. We are then more able to recognize specialness as an outright substitute *for* Love. A natural consequence of this shift is our willingness to drop the attraction to old patterns of fearful, changing, unholy love and really experience changeless Love.

A. Committing to One Wholly Shared Goal

1. In this dream of separate bodies and private minds who believe they are deprived, we are each concerned with first defining our "personal interests," and second, we spend our relationships and our lives trying to fulfill those goals. The incredibly sad truth is that these personal interests are all ego goals, since the identity that believes it *has* personal agendas apart from others and God, *does not exist.*

2. A separate, self-seeking identity cannot share a truly common purpose or goal with anyone else. This mistaken perception is

underpinned by a profound belief in lack. It sees its relationships as merely a means to "get" from the other what it believes is missing in itself. Its secret agenda in all relationships is not true joining but *mutual use*; hence the plethora of relationship breakdowns. Following is an explanation of what really occurs when two people appear to fall in love which is described here not as Love, but as an attractive form of fear. This ego dynamic also occurs in friendships too:

a. *"Most curious of all is the concept of the self which the ego fosters in the special relationship. This "self" seeks the relationship to make itself complete. Yet when it finds the special relationship in which it thinks it can accomplish this it gives itself away, and tries to "trade" itself for the self of another. This is not union, for there is no increase and no extension. Each partner tries to sacrifice the self he does not want for one he thinks he would prefer. And he feels guilty for the "sin" of taking, and of giving nothing of value in return. How much value can he place upon a self that he would give away to get a "better" one?"*

"The "better" self the ego seeks is always one that is more special. And whoever seems to possess a special self is "loved" for what can be taken from him. Where both partners see this special self in each other, the ego sees "a union made in Heaven." For neither one will recognize that he has asked for hell, and so he will not interfere with the ego's illusion of Heaven, which it offered him to interfere with Heaven. Yet if all illusions are of fear, and they can be of nothing else, the illusion of Heaven is nothing more than an "attractive" form of fear, in which the guilt is buried deep and rises in the form of "love."

"The appeal of hell lies only in the terrible attraction of guilt, which the ego holds out to those who place their faith in littleness. The conviction of littleness lies in every special relationship, for only the deprived could value specialness. The demand for specialness, and the perception of the giving of specialness as an act of love, would make love hateful. The real purpose of the special relationship, in strict accordance with the ego's goals, is to destroy reality and substitute illusion.

For the ego is itself an illusion, and only illusions can be the witnesses to its "reality."" T-16.V.7,8,9.

3. The special relationship is an impossible attempt at union. At the outset, each person engages with the other from a wholly deluded standpoint. They believe they *are* the body and not the Holy Self. The body-self, its senses and appetites, and its past, become the central focus. It is an end in itself, the central identity, which excludes the changeless innocence in both people. The body is not seen purely as a "means" through which we extend Love as guiltlessness.

4. From this one mistaken conviction alone, everything those in the special relationship desire, see and judge arises from the unquestioned body-self, its self-seeking interests and its unforgiven projections based on the past. The body *is* the ego's filter through which they view and engage with others, thinking they share perhaps the same goal and purpose, for example, romantic union, raising family, safety, financial security, and similar interests – however, while each one stores and gathers unforgiven grievances, their goal and purpose is most definitely self-seeking and not mutually shared.

    a. *"You who were created by love like itself can hold no grievances and know your Self. To hold a grievance is to forget who you are. To hold a grievance is to see yourself as a body. To hold a grievance is to let the ego rule your mind and to condemn the body to death." W-68.1:1-4*

5. There can be no real joining between two people with independent self-seeking agendas. Unknowingly, they each expect the other to satisfy their mistaken identity's desires. And when they fail, the ego projects its blame and justifies its resentments. Seeming "love" is withdrawn or even broken off. Hence the never-ending cycle of sin, guilt and fear.

6. Personal interests cannot be truly shared with another. Only the separate self has personal interests. On the other hand, the Holy Self increases and extends only by sharing, and transcending separate, personal interests.

a. *"If any two are joined, He must be there. It does not matter what their purpose is, but they must share it wholly to succeed. It is impossible to share a goal not blessed by Christ, for what is unseen through His eyes is too fragmented to be meaningful."* P-2.II.6:5-7

7. In the preceding passage Jesus says, *"It does not matter what their purpose is, but they must share it wholly to succeed."* What does it mean "to share a purpose wholly?" The ego is, by definition, a separate self-seeking concept. It has never and could never share a purpose wholly with another. Being the belief in deprivation itself, the false self is always immersed in self-seeking agendas. It will appear to work with others in its special relationships but only for what it can gain alone. When it gives, it gives only to *get* something in return. And when its personal agenda is threatened by a loved one it can easily turn to hate.

8. To share a purpose wholly means that two or more people set aside their own separate (ego) interests and genuinely join by losing all sense of self-interests and self-gratification. Think of how it makes us feel when we see people unselfishly coming together for good. Suddenly, in that Holy Instant the split-mind is eclipsed by the brilliant blaze of truth. This is the shared Mind as *one*. This is the one Holy Self.

9. Once their own interests are seen as *not separate* from another's, Holy Spirit has been invited to join them. He cannot enter in *special relationships* where people have separate, selfish agendas arising from lack, which bear no relevance to a truly shared purpose or goal.

B. One Goal Wholly Shared with a Brother is Salvation

1. At the highest level, our final obstacle to peace that we must overcome is our fear of God. This, our ultimate communion with God, is impossible *alone*. Yet many attempt this alone, not realizing that we cannot reach God wholly without first closing the gap with our brother. If we exclude even one brother in our forgiveness, we condemn our Self as separate from God. One goal wholly shared with a brother *is* salvation; this is the Holy Relationship. And from it, we learn to forgive every brother.

a. *"This holy relationship has the power to heal all pain, regardless of its form. Neither you nor your brother alone can serve at all. Only in your joint will does healing lie. For here your healing is, and here will you accept Atonement. And in your healing is the Sonship healed [because] your will and your brother's are joined."T-22.VI.4:4-8*

2. Remember the ego cannot give or receive unconditionally. As fear incarnate, it has never known an instant of real and changeless Love. However, our Holy Self *has* and does so eternally, although we will not recognize nor value this until we've undone at least some of the false self's perception. In the following quotes Jesus uses the term *therapist*. He is saying that we're all therapists and patients, or teachers and pupils. The roles shift constantly as we play our part in the healing of our mind through relationships.

3. As we will see, salvation rests on one requirement. This is asked of everyone in order to complete the healing of their perception, from fear to changeless Love and innocence. The Holy Relationship invites us to share *one goal wholly* with another person and in doing so, lose all sense of separate interests. Only here, in the midst of true union with our brother, can we look clear past the body and glimpse the incomprehensible majesty of our brother and our Self. It is in this precious Holy Instant of extraordinary gratitude that we catch our breath as we behold the awe-inspiring innocence of our savior, our brother.

a. *"What must the teacher do to ensure learning? What must the therapist do to bring healing about? Only one thing; the same requirement salvation asks of everyone. Each one must share one goal with someone else, and in so doing, lose all sense of separate interests. Only by doing this is it possible to transcend the narrow boundaries the ego would impose upon the self. Only by doing this can teacher and pupil, therapist and patient, you and I, accept Atonement and learn to give it as it was received."*

"Communion is impossible alone. No one who stands apart can receive Christ's vision. It is held out to him, but he cannot hold out his hand to receive it. Let him be still and recognize his

brother's need is his own. And let him then meet his brother's need as his and see that they are met as one, for such they are." P-2.II.8,9:1-5

C. Where Two or More are Joined

1. The Holy Relationship is undertaken with Holy Spirit by two or more people and not just one alone. While we can certainly keep practicing our own forgiveness opportunities alone in our special relationships, for Holy Spirit to transform a relationship from special to Holy, He requires consent from *both* people in order to radically shift the relationship's goal from special as guilt, to Holy as guiltlessness. When one companion desires only special love, having no interest in applying consistent forgiveness, Holy Spirit cannot go against their will. As we'll see in the following quotes, Jesus teaches that Holy Relationship takes two. I have underlined these references to two people.

  a. *"Yet reason sees a holy relationship as what it is; a common state of mind, where <u>both</u> give errors gladly to correction, that <u>both</u> may happily be healed as one." T-22.III.9:7*

  b. *"God's Teacher speaks to <u>any two who join</u> together for learning purposes. The relationship is holy because of that purpose, and God has promised to send His Spirit into any holy relationship."... "Those who would learn the same course share one interest and one goal." M-2.5:3-4,7*

  c. *"...the ultimate goal is always the same; to make of the relationship a holy relationship, in which <u>both</u> can look upon the Son of God as sinless." M-3.1:2*

2. Chapter V, "Holy Relationship Blueprint," which starts on page 477, tells why it takes two or more to form Holy Relationships.

3. Jesus tells us that the Holy Relationship is a phenomenal teaching accomplishment and a major step toward the Real World. This relationship is "learned" because it is the complete *reversal* of special love.

4. When I experienced my first encounter with Holy Spirit entering a very special relationship to abruptly reverse its goal – with Tomas in 1990 – I remember reading this section in the *Course* many times (Chapter 17, Section 5, The Healed Relationship). Not having met or read about anyone who had yet pioneered this at the time, it was quite a deep dive into trust for Tomas and me. Yet trusting these valuable and specific instructions that Jesus gave us, was the single most powerful catalyst for astounding healing for both of us, and for countless others as the miracle rippled outward to affect many people. I feel that Jesus' instructions are so practical and meaningful that I am including the key stand-out passages in this section.

5. Before we continue, let's address the issue that many people have found it challenging to find like-minded people who share the willingness necessary to pursue the same wholly shared goal of Holy Relationship; people who are genuinely dedicated to do whatever it takes with Holy Spirit to undo the primary cause of conflict and suffering. This is why, through our nonprofit, Take Me to Truth, Inc., we offer a 12-month online "Total Transformation Course," affectionately named the "TTC." This 52-week program is offered by different hosts across the globe by donation. In the TTC we join with others and have the chance to really experience Holy Relationship through forming online relationships with "miracle buddies." These relationships are usually not romantic. For more information please visit https://nouksanchez.com/online-course-total-transformation-course/

D. A Period of Disorientation

1. When two or more invite Holy Spirit in to make their relationship Holy the customary rules for relationship will be tested initially. This is the undoing of our *substitutions* for changeless Love.

   a. *"Be comforted in this; the only difficult phase is the beginning. For here, the goal of the relationship is abruptly shifted to the exact opposite of what it was. This is the first result of offering the relationship to the Holy Spirit, to use for His purposes."* T-17.V.2:5-7

2. This invitation allows Holy Spirit to begin the undoing by replacing His goal for the ego's. He does this quite rapidly and the repercussions may seem somewhat distressing at first, especially if the relationship was largely special and conditional to begin with. The false self only knows its false "symbols" of love. These symbols must be seen for what they represent, which is to bolster the idea of a body-identity and private mind, with its self-seeking agendas. Jesus warns us not to fall into a common trap here. They are not Love. In this beginning phase the relationship often appears to be confusing and the ego craves familiarity. At this early point in the disorientation phase of the Holy Relationship many people want to return to the seeming safety of specialness. Remember that an enormous addiction within specialness is compartmentalizing our thoughts and actions. It is terrified of radical self-honesty, accountability, defenselessness and emotional transparency. To the ego its thoughts are personal and therefore, private. This is the attraction to guilt.

3. Knowing they cannot go back to specialness in this *present relationship*, some people in this initial phase, may look for an *additional, substitute, special relationship* in which they can satiate the ego's cravings and body appetites.

4. As two or more companions sincerely join in commitment to Holy Relationship, Holy Spirit wastes no time in flipping the goal of specialness to its complete opposite. However, the former attraction to specialness can linger on and must be recognized as the block to true union that it is.

   a. *"This invitation is accepted immediately, and the Holy Spirit wastes no time in introducing the practical results of asking Him to enter. At once His goal replaces yours. This is accomplished very rapidly, but it makes the relationship seem disturbed, disjunctive and even quite distressing. The reason is quite clear. For the relationship as it [is] is out of line with its own goal, and clearly unsuited to the purpose that has been accepted for it. In its unholy condition, [your] goal was all that seemed to give it meaning. Now it seems to make no sense. Many relationships have been broken off at this point, and the pursuit of the old goal re-established in another relationship.*

For once the unholy relationship has accepted the goal of holiness, it can never again be what it was." T-17.V.3.

b. *"The temptation of the ego becomes extremely intense with this shift in goals. For the relationship has not as yet been changed sufficiently to make its former goal (of specialness) completely without attraction, and its structure is "threatened" by the recognition of its inappropriateness for meeting its new purpose. The conflict between the goal and the structure of the relationship is so apparent that they cannot coexist. Yet now the goal will not be changed. Set firmly in the unholy relationship, there is no course except to change the relationship to fit the goal. Until this happy solution is seen and accepted as the only way out of the conflict, the relationship may seem to be severely strained." T-17.V.4.*

5. In working with numerous people during this phase of their relationships, I was often asked, "Why can't we shift the new goal more slowly? Why can't we do this gently and organically?" Well, for those who did indeed pull back, trying to be *kind* by slowing down this initial shift, the outcome was either a retrogressive return to the earlier patterns of specialness, or a complete breakdown of the relationship.

6. The ego does not know what true kindness or compassion *is*. Period. When this tectonic shift of goals is deliberately slowed down, it obliterates the most important learning which is *experiencing* the blinding contrast between Holiness/miracles *and* specialness/conflict, between separate-selves and our one, shared Holy Self. Without this life-changing experience of contrast, the gravitational pull back to special relating is far too overwhelming.

a. *"It would not be kinder to shift the goal more slowly, for the contrast would be obscured, and the ego given time to reinterpret each slow step according to its liking. Only a radical shift in purpose could induce a complete change of mind about what the whole relationship is for. As this change develops and is finally accomplished, it grows increasingly beneficent and joyous. But at the beginning, the situation is experienced as very precarious. A relationship, undertaken by two individuals for their unholy purposes, suddenly has holiness for its goal. As these two contemplate their relationship from the point of view of this new purpose, they are inevitably appalled. Their perception of the relationship may even become quite disorganized. And yet, the former organization of their perception no longer serves the purpose they have agreed to meet." T-17.V.5.*

7. This is the time for faith. Once Holy Spirit enters the relationship it is up to us to stay the course. For me, during this period, I kept a journal in which I wrote out all my confusion. I divided my journal into two separate columns. One was for the ego's expressions of fear and blame, and the other was for the Voice or thoughts of Holy Spirit. This journaling was amazingly productive as it gave me a whole new level of witnessing the contrast or "split" in my own mind. As a consequence, this practice helped me to genuinely withdraw my projections onto my partner at the time. Forgiveness was the result.

   a. *"This is the time for [faith.] You let this goal be set for you. That was an act of faith. Do not abandon faith, now that the rewards of faith are being introduced." ... The goal [is] set. And your relationship has sanity as its purpose. For now you find yourself in an insane relationship, recognized as such in the light of its goal." T-17.V.6:1-4,7-9*

8. Because the temptation to return to specialness is often so seductive, particularly in sexual relationships, there may be a strong temptation to abandon our companion and the relationship. This is why Jesus repeats the following warning twice in this section. He even includes an especially loud alert to the ego's tempting voice, saying "Hear not this now!"

   a. *"Now the ego counsels thus; substitute for this another relationship to which your former goal (of specialness) was quite appropriate. You can escape from your distress only by getting rid of your brother. You need not part entirely if you choose not to do so. But you must exclude major areas of fantasy from your brother, to save your sanity. [Hear not this now!] Have faith in Him Who answered you. He heard. Has He not been very explicit in His answer? You are not now wholly insane. Can you deny that He has given you a most explicit statement? Now He asks for faith a little longer, even in bewilderment. For this will go, and you will see the justification for your faith emerge, to bring you shining conviction. Abandon Him not now, nor your brother. This relationship has been reborn as holy." T-17.V.7.*

6. YOGANANDA'S VISITATION AND MESSAGE

1. In the early hours of the morning of August 22, 2016, I was blessed by a mystical visitation from the great guru, Paramahansa Yogananda. This visitation and the profound message he shared with me came on the heels of having watched the documentary about him titled, "Awake; The Life of Yogananda." I felt an uncanny resonance with him that transcended both the body and time. I knew his voice. It was extraordinarily familiar and very natural. It was as though it had never left me. I merely remembered that it had always been there.

2. Of course, my thinking mind immediately scrambled to try to figure out just "how" I could have possibly known him. In this lifetime I was born four years *after* he had already left the body. In addition, I had not read his writings and I had not studied his Kriya Yoga pathway, or his life. This directly known familiarity was a complete mystery to the thinking mind. However, I knew to trust my inner knowing and not to place too much emphasis on attempts to find answers to what is clearly not understandable to the severely limited ego.

3. In the documentary it was disclosed that Yogananda had a close boyhood friend who later became his beloved colleague, Swami Dhirananda. Although these two were very close, Yogananda and

Dhirananda eventually suffered a bitter fall-out. Here is a snippet from Durga Mata's book on Yogananda which gives us a glimpse of the depth of the bond they had:

a. < *Masters, as Yogananda explained, live a dual existence: they have a very human side, which suffers and rejoices, and a divine one, deep inside, where they are completely free in God, in bliss, never forgetting that everything is just a great dream.*

b. *Yogananda, Durga writes, bore deep love for Dhirananda. When Dhirananda, "whom he loved so dearly," left Mount Washington in 1929, after having lived there for 3.5 years as the resident teacher, Yogananda cried in pain: "My best friend has gone!" He was absolutely heartbroken. In a letter he once wrote: "I have given more to Dhirananda than to anyone else." Yogananda was actually so distraught that he took off and went to Mexico, to forget his pain (also written in Durga's book.) The disciples thought he might never return. Kamala writes that Yogananda was away much longer than planned. But "the Lord mended Master's wounded heart. (Durga)" >*

4. Unlike special relationships where love can end or turn to hate, there can be no falling-out of a Holy Relationship. They are eternal because they are devoted to closing the gap of private minds with separate agendas. When I witnessed this story of division in the documentary I was greatly saddened. I asked, "How could such a great sage as Yogananda not know of Holy Relationships?

5. Yogananda and Dhirananda must have had a special relationship; one that presented them both with great lessons of forgiveness. This is what Jesus classifies as the second level of the three levels of relationship teaching:

a. *"Each teaching-learning situation is maximal in the sense that each person involved will learn the most that he can from the other person at that time. In this sense, and in this sense only, we can speak of levels of teaching. Using the term in this way, the second level of teaching is a more sustained relationship, in which, for a time, two people enter into a fairly intense teaching-learning situation and then appear to separate. As with the first level, these meetings are not accidental, nor is what appears to be the end of the relationship a real end. Again, each has learned the most he can at the time. Yet all who meet will someday meet again, for it is the destiny of all relationships to become holy. God is not mistaken in His Son." M-3.4.*

6. I remember thinking that Yogananda and Dhirananda would have a second chance to complete their Holy Relationship, as Jesus shares in the preceding quote. But I was saddened to think it would take yet another incarnation to achieve it.

7. After watching the documentary, I lay awake for quite some time, and then drifted into a lucid state where I felt exceedingly close to Yogananda. I must say that while there was such closeness, I did feel quite bewildered by the sadness I felt. So, I offered it up completely, tears and all. I then drifted off to sleep. However, what followed this complete surrender to Spirit was something I could not even imagine.

8. I was awoken in my sleep by Yogananda's voice just before dawn the next morning. I thought I was wide awake because I saw that he and I were walking in this exquisite garden together. The dappled morning light was dancing on the flowers and leaves as they swayed ever so gently in the breeze. Everything was super conscious, super sensory and super present. He was trying to make a very clear point and he wanted me to pay particular attention to specific principles that he was teaching. He kept checking with me by making direct eye contact and tilting his head in a questioning manner.

9. I seemed to know that I was not dreaming. This was far more credible and real than what my waking life appeared to be. He repeated the first line at least twice, until I got it. And then he went on once I assured him that I would take down his notes.

A. The Message – Relationship as the Path of Return

1. "You are to DISRUPT all relationships!

2. These people do not know of true relationship.

    1)   The entire STRUCTURE of man's understanding of relationship MUST be torn down

    2)   The entire OBJECTIVE of man's understanding of relationship MUST be reversed

    3)   True relationship is at the SEAT of the Son's return to His beloved Father. But first you must DISRUPT all relationships. These are not relationships, but travesties of Love, mockeries of God. God is not fear but LOVE.

3. True Union cannot be attained until DIS-UNITY is deemed unattractive! Relationships of this world are ANTI-RELATIONSHIPS as they involve two false entities seeking to join in order to teach and learn separation.

4. **Please note:** You cannot keep your concept of "self" in this DISRUPTION and REVERSAL process.

B. What is True Compassion?

1. I asked Yogananda about compassion. His answer:

2. This world does not know true compassion.

    1)   To know true compassion, you must undermine the structure of compassion as you presently know it. Your compassion arises from fear and is therefore impure. The structure of compassion is self-defeating because of its basis. Steps you take to express your version of compassion only seek to reinforce the original error.

    2)   To know true compassion, you must reverse the objective of compassion as you presently know it. The purpose of your version of compassion is to remediate a problem which does not exist in reality; therefore, it constitutes a block to receiving the divine remedy.

3. I ask you, "who" is the one expressing compassion? And, "why?" When you answer this last question, you will recognize the truth in my previous two statements.

4. **Please note:** The word "DISRUPT" cannot be misconstrued here. If the objective of all so called "special relationships" is SEPARATION then the special relationship cannot be properly DISRUPTED and REVERSED except by Love. Therefore, the disruption and reversal of relationships in this context IS by means of the LOVE they lack. It is the LOVE that first appears to disrupt these relationships because you still believe the original error... that fear IS Love.

5. When I woke up, I was absolutely awestruck by what had just happened with Yogananda. I grabbed my notebook and scribbled his messages while still sitting in my bed. The content of his message still had not landed in me. But I was able to write his principles down because it was *his* voice in my mind that was still dictating these principles. I did not allow my thinking mind to take in this shocking and most confronting teaching at the time because if I had, I think I would have had enormous resistance and I would have blocked them.

6. Much later, as I researched Yogananda and some of his teaching while he was here in his previous incarnation, I found a direct quote from him: *"To those who think me near, I will be near."* Well, this was a beautiful confirmation of his visitation.

7. Some people may be skeptical about the visitation and message I received from Yogananda. After all, his message appears to be totally blasphemous to human love and relationships. When we genuinely desire guidance from the Angels, Saints or Ascended Masters, they meet us to the degree we "show-up" without a preconceived idea of what it should look like. My heart was yearning to be shown the truth even if it challenged my beliefs tremendously. And it showed up in the form of Yogananda, along with his valuable gift of *content*, the preceding principles involved in "Relationship as the Path of Return."

8. I am heartened by the following passage from Jesus:

    a. *"There are those who have reached God directly, retaining no trace of worldly limits and remembering their own Identity perfectly. These might be called the Teachers of teachers because, although they are no longer visible, their image can yet be called upon. And they will appear when and where it is helpful for them to do so. To those to whom such appearances would be frightening, they give their ideas. No one can call on them in vain. Nor is there anyone of whom they are unaware. All needs are known to them, and all mistakes are recognized and overlooked by them. The time will come when this is understood. And meanwhile, they give all their gifts to the teachers of God who look to them for help, asking all things in their name and in no other."* M-26.2.

9. In conclusion, I am reminded of some very relevant and potent quotes from Jesus which support Yogananda's message:

    a. *"The special love relationship is the ego's chief weapon for keeping you from Heaven."* T-16.V.2:3

    b. *"Love is not learned. Its meaning lies within itself. And learning ends when you have recognized all it is [not.] That is the interference; that is what needs to be undone."* T-18.IX.12:1-4

    c. *"Love is not an illusion. It is a fact. Where disillusionment is possible, there was not love but hate. For hate [is] an illusion, and what can change was never love."* T-16.IV.4:1-4

    d. *"Most curious of all is the concept of the self, which the ego fosters in the special relationship. This "self" SEEKS the relationship, to MAKE ITSELF COMPLETE. Yet, when it FINDS the special relationship in which it thinks it can ACCOMPLISH this, IT GIVES ITSELF AWAY, and tries to TRADE itself for the self of another. This is NOT union, for there is NO increase and NO extension. Each partner tries to sacrifice the self he does NOT want, for one he thinks he would*

PREFER. He feels guilty for the "sin" of TAKING, and of giving nothing of value in return. For how much value CAN he place upon a self that he would GIVE AWAY to get a BETTER one?

The "better" self the ego seeks is ALWAYS one that is MORE special. And whoever SEEMS to possess a special self is "loved," FOR WHAT CAN BE TAKEN FROM HIM. Where both partners see this special self IN EACH OTHER, the EGO sees "a union made in Heaven." For NEITHER will recognize that HE HAS ASKED FOR HELL, and so he will NOT interfere with the ego's ILLUSION of Heaven, which it offered him TO INTERFERE WITH HEAVEN. Yet if ALL illusions are of fear, and they CAN be of nothing else, the illusion of Heaven is nothing more than an ATTRACTIVE form of fear, in which the guilt is buried deep, and rises in the form of "love."" – A Course in Miracles, Urtext, T-16.6.

C. Yogananda's Message – Relationship Disorientation

1. Referring to the initial period of disorientation and purification by Holy Spirit, this feels to be the perfect place to recall the wisdom of Yogananda, as received in my vision. Upon reflection we may see just how these instructions meld seamlessly with Jesus' instructions in the *Course*. I will include a brief summary of Yogananda's message here:

1) **"You are to DISRUPT all relationships!"**
Can we see now just why special relationships require disrupting first?

2) **"The entire OBJECTIVE of man's understanding of relationship MUST be reversed."**
Can we see now that the objective, as the special relationship's goal, must be reversed by Holy Spirit?

3) **"The entire STRUCTURE of man's understanding of relationship MUST be torn down."**
Can we see now how the structure of the special relationship

which is built on sin, guilt and fear, must be torn down in order to allow changeless Love and innocence to take its place? Fear *and* Love cannot coexist.

2. And further, he included this:

   1) **"You cannot keep your concept of "self" in this DISRUPTION and REVERSAL process."**
   Can we see now that in this relationship transition, the false self is gradually laid by to reveal the profound union, Love, innocence and safety of our one, Holy Self?

7. THE RITE OF PASSAGE – BRIDGE TO THE REAL WORLD

1. As we advance in the Holy Relationship, and because we are now joined in one wholly common purpose, we gradually learn to forego the ego's personal and exclusive agendas in favor of true union. We can no longer deny our brother's real needs are also our own. Now, seeing our Holy companion's interests as *not apart from our own* means that if he/she is in fear, i.e. pain, conflict, anger, etc., (a call for Love), then it is impossible for them to experience or to deal with it alone. We are both now *one in purpose* which translates to accepting that our brother's need *is* our own. We must learn to answer all calls for Love, *with Love* and not with defense.

2. This concept of true union, of knowing that our brother's need *is ours* even when they are emotional and acting from ego… is not recognized or valued in the *special* relationship. In specialness, when one perceives threat from the other, we go into false self-preservation mode, which usually includes either colluding in self-pity, or a fight or flight response. Fear is believed and then reacted to.

3. The Holy Relationship teaches that when our brother appears to attack, he/she is immediately "calling *for* Love." We put the ego's self-preservation aside and allow Holy Spirit to answer their call

through us. In doing so, we actually learn to answer our own ancient call for Love; something that is never known in the special, self-seeking relationship. A call for Love is a call for innocence through forgiveness. We don't join them in their pain. But we do join them in truth by mirroring their perfect guiltlessness in the Holy Instant.

a. *"The power of joining its blessing lies in the fact that it is now impossible for you or your brother to experience fear alone, or to attempt to deal with it alone. Never believe that this is necessary, or even possible. Yet just as this is impossible, so is it equally impossible that the holy instant come to either of you without the other. And it will come to both at the request of either."* T-18.V.6:4-7

A. The Saner of the Two

1. In the Holy Relationship each companion takes turns in offering the other forgiveness opportunities as they both learn to value each other's sinlessness *more* than they desire to be right.

2. In 1990 when the *Course* came along to save our relationship, Tomas and I entered a particularly volatile period of disorientation during our initial shift from specialness to Holiness. It seemed that I was burdened with the bulk of forgiveness and it felt unfair at the time. But as I stayed with him in complete defenselessness through his bouts of anger, accusation, conflict and frustration, I couldn't help but notice that I was being healed as well. My old primary coping mechanism when Tomas acted out was to flee in fear and leave him to deal with his own mess. Either that or I would go into defense mode as a last resort. However, I soon learned that all defense is attack. And I did not want it any longer.

3. Together, Tomas and I learned not to abandon each other, especially when one or both of us were in darkness. Six years before we read the *Course*, in 1984, we desired to experience a Love which could never be threatened, a Love beyond human love. We had made a sacred vow together with Holy Spirit that, "No matter what and no matter who might seem to come between us, let us never abandon each other."

4. We learned later in the core teaching set magnificently within this vow, that all expressions of fear as anger, attack, sickness, pain, etc., are always nothing other than a call *for* Love. But when we forget this and lash out in fear or defense, we *abandon* our Self and each other. All attack and defense are the delusional belief that we (ego) are able to gratify our needs at the expense of others. But in this, we unwittingly attack not only the other but our self as well, reinforcing the ego's delusional cycle of sin, guilt and fear.

5. In contrast, when we answer a brother's attack as it really is – as a call for Love – we must heal *with* them, and our whole Mind is restored as one. We overcome our own fear by answering it in others. When we respond *with* Love to the call *for* Love *(attack),* we close the gap of the split-mind.

6. The single purpose of fear is to hide the call for Love beneath it, thus perpetuating the separation. In Holy Relationship we learn to deny all forms of fear the power to conceal Love. In this consistent practice, fear becomes meaningless and the darkened veil, which has shrouded the innocent face of Christ since the beginning of time, is finally lifted. I think the following two passages masterfully explain how the Holy Spirit miraculously heals our perception of the reactions of others especially in the transfer from special to Holy Relationships.

a. *"By applying the Holy Spirit's interpretation of the reactions of others more and more consistently, you will gain an increasing awareness that His criteria are equally applicable to you. For to recognize fear is not enough to escape from it, although the recognition is necessary to demonstrate the need for escape. The Holy Spirit must still translate the fear into truth. If you were left with the fear, once you had recognized it, you would have taken a step away from reality, not towards it. Yet we have repeatedly emphasized the need to recognize fear and face it without disguise as a crucial step in the undoing of the ego. Consider how well the Holy Spirit's interpretation of the motives of others will serve you then. Having taught you to accept only loving thoughts in others and to regard everything else as an appeal for help, He has taught you that fear itself is an appeal for help. This is what recognizing fear really means. If you do not protect it, He will reinterpret it. That is the ultimate value in learning to perceive attack as a call for love. We have already learned that fear and attack are inevitably associated. If only attack produces fear, and if you see attack as the call for help that it is, the unreality of fear must dawn on you. For fear [is] a call for love, in unconscious recognition of what has been denied."*

"Fear is a symptom of your own deep sense of loss. If when you perceive it in others you learn to supply the loss, the basic cause of fear is removed. Thereby you teach yourself that fear does not exist in you. The means for removing it is in yourself, and you have demonstrated this by giving it." T-12.I.8,9:1-4

7. In my early transition period with Tomas, it seemed that I was doing most of the forgiving. It took me quite a while to recognize that the real purpose of all this forgiveness was to heal *my own* split-mind as well as his. I slowly learned when conflict tempted us that it was the perfect opportunity to ask which of us was the saner of the two. In other words, who was more willing to recall the gratitude we have for our brother, even amidst seeming conflict? In the beginning it was me, and later Tomas came in boldly holding the torch of forgiveness for me and reflected my sinlessness when I needed it the most.

8. It takes just one of us to remember to invite Holy Spirit in, to help us both by divinely reinterpreting (heal) a challenging situation or conflict. And just one Holy Instant is all it takes. During that early phase I must have referred to the following prayer a thousand times:

    a. *"Whoever is saner at the time the threat is perceived should remember how deep is his indebtedness to the other and how much gratitude is due him, and be glad that he can pay his debt by bringing happiness to both. Let him remember this, and say:*

        I desire this holy instant for myself, that I may share it with my brother, whom I love.

It is not possible that I can have it without him, or he without me.

Yet it is wholly possible for us to share it now.

And so I choose this instant as the one to offer to the Holy Spirit, that His blessing may descend on us, and keep us both in peace." T-18.V.7.

B. Setting the Goal in Advance

1. In the special relationship we have two separate self-seeking bodies, each with private minds. They may seek to share a common goal but each one has their own separate self-serving agendas and separate self-interests. How can we tell? Well, if the love between these two can be threatened by anyone or anything, then they must not share a wholly common purpose with each other and Holy Spirit. In other words, these companions will value and defend the ego's idols in the "gap" *more* than they cherish one another's innocence (see the Gap Diagrams on pages 46 thru 49). Divided purpose shatters a relationship. Each one has their own personal agenda based on the body-self's seeming needs.

2. When these two decide to seek a goal together, it's the ego that sets it. And it's the ego that pursues the goal. So, it's bound to end in conflict. Each one wants their very own needs met even if this is accomplished at the expense of their partner. In their personal agendas, they see their companion's interests as *apart* from their own.

3. While we each value the ego's separate agendas, we will have no idea of the one overarching goal set by Holy Spirit. In our daily exchanges with others we tend to be attached to our own desired outcomes. And if that outcome is not met then the ego becomes upset and forms a grievance. Oftentimes it will make a second attempt to manipulate the person or situation to get its own way. And if that doesn't work then the result is more conflict (resentment). In these relationships there is often no willingness to recognize that the singular purpose of apparent conflict is to *forgive* our belief in and attraction to it.

4. Do we really know what the only valuable goal *is* for all communication?

   a. *"In any situation in which you are uncertain, the first thing to consider, very simply, is "What do I want to come of this? What is it [for]?" The clarification of the goal belongs at the beginning, for it is this which will determine the outcome. In the ego's procedure this is reversed." T-17.VI.2:1-4*

5. What do I want to come from this? And what is it *for?* In any exchange or situation, do we set the goal in advance by prioritizing peace over all other goals? Or do we latch onto what we think the desired outcome *should* be? Especially within the infancy of our Holy Relationship, we will learn that the ego's previous self-seeking goals must give way now to just one divine goal, one that is set for all interactions and situations. Peace translates to forgiveness and vice versa.

6. Our healing response is always to *forgive first* – and then Holy Spirit's understanding must follow. There can never be any understanding without forgiveness. Nothing can be understood in fear or anger because the presence of these *breaks* true communication. *"And it is recognized that all things must be first forgiven, and [then] understood." T-30.V.1: 6*

7. Recall that no matter what or who appears to threaten us, everything that occurs is either an expression of Love, or it's a call *for* Love (help). If the underlying "call for Love" is not recognized for what it is and is mistakenly classified as attack, then the cause of the problem cannot *be* healed. The prerequisite for healing is our willingness to see everything from this right-minded perception. And the Holy Relationship is the perfect vehicle for this acceleration of healing.

8. The false self believes that its own understanding is a necessary contribution. However, the ego is incapable of understanding anything because its thought system is wrought in fear. Now that Holy Spirit has entered our relationship to shift the goal from specialness to Holiness, He wastes no time in helping us sort out the true from the false. Furthermore, we must learn to decide in advance for the goal of peace in all our interactions.

a. *"The value of deciding in advance what you want to happen is simply that you will perceive the situation as a means to [make] it happen. You will therefore make every effort to overlook what interferes with the accomplishment of your objective, and concentrate on everything that helps you meet it. It is quite noticeable that this approach has brought you closer to the Holy Spirit's sorting out of truth and falsity. The true becomes what can be used to meet the goal. The false becomes the useless from this point of view. The situation now has meaning, but only because the goal has made it meaningful." T-17.VI.4.*

9. When we set the goal of peace in advance, then regardless of what the situation delivers, we stay in peace and trust. From that peace Holy Spirit brings us everything we need. If we do not set the goal of peace in advance, then the ego is free to wreak havoc in our mind and thus in our relationships. When the ego is upset it's because no real predefined goal was set. *"The ego does not know what it wants to come of the situation. It is aware of what it does not want, but only that. It has no positive goal at all." T-17.VI.2:7-8*

10. The value of setting the goal in advance is well explained here:

a. *"No goal was set with which to bring the means in line. And now the only judgment left to make is whether or not the ego likes it; is it acceptable, or does it call for vengeance? The absence of a criterion for outcome, set in advance, makes understanding doubtful and evaluation impossible."... "The value of deciding in advance what you want to happen is simply that you will perceive the situation as a means to [make] it happen. You will therefore make every effort to overlook what interferes with the accomplishment of your objective, and concentrate on everything that helps you meet it." T-17.VI. 3:5-7,4:1-2*

11. In Holy Relationship we prioritize peace and closing the gap with our brother. In setting the goal of peace in advance for all interactions through applying forgiveness, we learn to perceive *all situations* as a means to bring our goal of peace to fruition.

12. As two or more people join with Holy Spirit in the one unified goal

of Holy Relationship it is He who unifies and purifies everything we bring to him. Our miraculous tool is the ever-present Holy Instant; the moment we become lucid in awareness and desire *His* interpretation of the situation instead of the ego's.

13. From this perspective then every forgiveness opportunity becomes a golden window for healing and true union. This is where we learn what real faith *is*. We can afford to have infinite faith in our brother because the real goal of each situation, regardless of how the ego interprets it, has already been set by Holy Spirit. But it takes our faith and presence to remember this and thus to receive it in the Holy Instant.

14. In our brother is the Christ; the same Christ found in us. This is *who* we have faith in. And by keeping that faith we join Holy Spirit in bringing the Christ forward, out from behind the false appearance of a body-self. When we fall prey to temptations to see him/her as a body (good or bad), or when we resent our brother, we betray faith in both him and our Self. We cannot lose faith in our brother without also losing that faith within. When we are tempted to perceive conflict then it's always because *we* lack faith. Jesus says that only what *we have not given* can be lacking in any situation. He refers here to faith.

a. *"Only what [you] have not given can be lacking in any situation. But remember this; the goal of holiness was set for your relationship, and not by you. You did not set it because holiness cannot be seen except through faith, and your relationship was not holy because your faith in your brother was so limited and little. Your faith must grow to meet the goal that has been set. The goal's reality will call this forth, for you will see that peace and faith will not come separately. What situation can you be in without faith, and remain faithful to your brother?" ... "Every situation in which you find yourself is but a means to meet the purpose set for your relationship. See it as something else and you are faithless."* T-17.VII.4,5:1-2

15. We offer and receive the gift of faith in each moment. Remember it's the Christ within each of us who joins in Holy Relationship.

And that is why, when the ego tempts us with conflict, we must have faith to look past the illusory body-self, holding the faith that the Holy Spirit has already solved the perceived problem.

16. It is always our faith in our brother that brings the seeming dilemma's resolution. It's our faith in our brother and thus in our one unified Holy Self that brings about profound healing which the ego could never possibly fathom. It is in this sanctified union that we learn to demonstrate the *Course's* number one miracle principle: *There is no order of difficulty in miracles.* Here, within the blessed union of two or more brothers dedicated wholly to closing the ego's gap, the Laws of God are received and established on earth.

   a. *"If you lack faith in anyone to fulfill, and perfectly, his part in any situation dedicated in advance to truth, your dedication is divided. And so you have been faithless to your brother, and used your faithlessness against him. No relationship is holy unless its holiness goes with it everywhere. As holiness and faith go hand in hand, so must its faith go everywhere with it. The goal's reality will call forth and accomplish every miracle needed for its fulfillment. Nothing too small or too enormous, too weak or too compelling, but will be gently turned to its use and purpose. The universe will serve it gladly, as it serves the universe. But do not interfere."... "The power set in you in whom the Holy Spirit's goal has been established is so far beyond your little conception of the infinite that you have no idea how great the strength that goes with you." T-17.VII.6,7:1*

17. The Holy Instant is a window outside of time, into eternity where God's Laws prevail. The Holy Instant is here in every single moment. Yet choosing to perceive through the filter of fear obliterates its presence in our awareness. Thankfully, in each moment of temptation to perceive anything other than Love, peace and safety, we can choose again. This is what the Atonement is for.

18. We make a comprehensive shift when we sincerely want only peace. From this perspective our priority is to forgive our self for every appearance of conflict, regardless of where it appears to come from.

C. We Do Not Recognize Our Own Best Interests

1. While the false self struggles in life to attain its personal agendas apart from our brothers and God, we will not recognize what *anything* is for. Hence our special relationships are the breeding ground for self-seeking agendas, aka separation. Conflict between people can only occur when two or more companions believe the impossible – that they are each separate identities, with private minds, and mortal bodies opposing each other.

2. In our transition from special to Holy relating we learn that our individual, self-serving agendas are neither good nor bad. They are recognized as what they really are, which is purely *meaningless*. Thus, there is no blame and no guilt.

    a. *"You perceive the world and everything in it as meaningful in terms of ego goals. These goals have nothing to do with your own best interests, because the ego is not you. This false identification makes you incapable of understanding what anything is for. As a result, you are bound to misuse it. When you believe this, you will try to withdraw the goals you have assigned to the world, instead of attempting to reinforce them."*

    "Another way of describing the goals you now perceive is to say that they are all concerned with "personal" (separate, ego) interests. Since you have no personal interests, your goals are really concerned with nothing. In cherishing them (ego goals), therefore, you have no goals at all. And thus you do not know what anything is for."

    "It is crucial to your learning to be willing to give up the goals you have established for everything. The recognition that they are meaningless, rather than "good" or "bad," is the only way to accomplish this." W-25.1:1-2,2,3,5:1-2

3. The body-self values one particular addiction over all others. Judgment as projection.

4. It maintains a white-knuckled grip on this, its single reason for being. Without it, this self could not exist. To maintain its illusory identity, it must project its denied guilt, judging and condemning

others and even its self, hence its attraction to being unfairly treated; whereas genuine forgiveness annihilates this judgment-driven self's very foundation. Forgiveness erases the ego's obsession with separation as separate bodies, private minds and self-seeking agendas. The journey from specialness to Holy Relationship offers us this sacred pathway.

5. The illusory self that is triggered by others is sustained by judgment and blame as unforgiveness. In contrast, the innocent Holy Self, which is what we are in truth, cannot *be* triggered. This guiltless Self is joyfully revealed as we forgive the illusory self its grievances.

6. As uncomfortable as it feels, the false self thrives on being unfairly treated. Quite literally, this self *must* be unfairly treated so it can continue to hurl its unforgiven guilt – as projection – onto others, the body, the past and the world. Thus, in a vicious cycle of believed victimhood, this identity's self-attack flies under the radar of conscious awareness. As a consequence, its identity and intent are fiercely defended and kept hidden from the light of forgiveness which would dispel it.

7. We must remember that the illusory body-identity is the ego's shabby replacement for our eternal and magnificent Holy Self. Therefore, a crucial necessity in this transition is to allow Holy Spirit to *undo* our false self concept, which includes how we view others as well. The body also must be divinely repurposed by Holy Spirit. While our identity, our pleasure seeking and our aversion to pain are centered on the body, we cannot possibly know Love.

8. The body's five senses, its past, along with its appetites, are all aimed at trapping us into maintaining this separate self. Its senses are "rigged" to see, project, and react from guilt and fear. Its entire sensory perception, including its sensual appetites, is focused on this, whether it seems to pursue pleasure, or it attempts to avoid pain. It's all the same.

9. While we continue to believe that we and others are bodies instead of Spirit, we will perpetuate the projection cycle of unconscious self-attack, using others to do so. And this is why we need to offer our body, its senses and appetites to the Holy Spirit for divine repurposing.

D. Giving Up the Things that Made Us Sick

1. The purpose of the Holy Relationship is to undo the false self's fear filter, the split mind. It always sees its own *imagined* sins in others. Every trigger reveals this. When this filter is gone, we see clear past the body, only to what is really there, which is innocence, Love and joy. In this Holy Instant we literally glimpse *our own* incorruptible innocence in our brother, which shifts our awareness from the body-self to the perfect and boundless Holy Self. We cannot know our eternal immunity to fear and its effects until we join with a brother to find it. We unite in this, the highest purpose within the ego dream.

2. And this is why, as we deepen our commitment in Holy Relationship, our gratitude for "forgiveness opportunities" grows. We are lucid, and instead of reacting blindly to triggers, we actually welcome opportunities to close the gap with others.

3. The commitment made is the agreement to give up the things – beliefs, values, stories, judgments and patterns – that made us sick. A personal "will" apart from our brother and God *is* sickness. Every single block (idol) to Love, both seemingly good and bad, must be offered to Holy Spirit to divinely reinterpret. This is how we heal the split-mind and close the gap of separation. *See the Gap diagrams on pages 46 thru 49.*

4. When we embrace the moment and no longer defend the ego, we will see the magnificence of our shared Holy Self reflected in our companion. These glimpses, these Holy Instants where our heart sees with Christ' Vision, are absolutely breathtaking. Gratitude explodes, and we realize that we're seeing our companion for the very first time, perhaps even despite having known them for years.

5. From a practical perspective, let's look at the main reasons why this first phase of Holy Relationship is usually so disorienting for most people. This may be a good time to review, without judgment, our own defenses to Love. *Please take a look at the "Traits of Specialness vs. Qualities of Holiness Diagram" on page 564.*

6. Upon entering a special relationship, we've established that each person mistakenly believes they have their *own personal will*. A body-focused self is kept separate from another by obsession with its own personal agendas. This private and secret "will" of the special relationship is always in opposition to God's Will, whether we are aware of it or not. In its constant pursuit of pleasure and its defense from pain, while seeking its own safety and security, along with its own attempt to problem-solve apart from Spirit, the unconscious target of this *personal will* is to see sin. So, when people form a special relationship, each with their own *secret wills* apart from God, the outcome is bound to be painful. This is what unforgiven guilt ensures in all unhealed relationships.

7. One stark difference between special and Holy Love, which must be seen and undone, is that in special relationships there is an erroneous belief that we can condemn our companion, through blame, and yet still profess to love them. In contrast, the Holy Relationship reveres and prioritizes our companion's *innocence.* Through this ultimate commitment, Love is naturally revealed as the joyous byproduct of cherishing guiltlessness *above* all personal reactions and agendas.

8. The sacred transition from special to Holy Relationship *evaporates* our secret, independent wills so that we come to realize with great joy that we are quite literally one with God, one with Love and one with each other. This is the known experience of being completely supported by Love, by safety, by security, by health, and by endless abundance, all of which we recognize can never be threatened.

9. A significant component of the initial undoing involves the willingness to *recognize and release* our secret will apart from God. This necessitates looking with Holy Spirit and our mighty companion, at old ego patterns, beliefs, grievances, stories, addictions, false idols, etc., so that these can be genuinely forgiven and healed for all time.

   a. *"What could be secret from God's Will? Yet you believe that you have secrets. What could your secrets be except another "will" that is your own, apart from His? Reason would tell you that this is no secret that need be hidden as a sin. But a mistake indeed! Let not your fear of sin protect it from correction, for the attraction of guilt is only fear. Here is the one emotion that you made, whatever it may seem to be. This is the emotion of secrecy, of private thoughts and of the body. This is the one emotion that opposes love, and always leads to sight of differences and loss of sameness. Here is the one emotion that keeps you blind, dependent on the self you think you made to lead you through the world it made for you." T-22.I.4.*

10. When the Holy Spirit enters a relationship, He wastes no time in *reversing the relationship's goal* from specialness to Holiness. He *disrupts the specialness* so that changeless Love can be recognized and valued, thus making way for peace, union, Holy Instants and miracles. Another substantial reason for feelings of disorientation is due to the *structure of specialness* being broken down. The ego's substitute for Love as "ego-stroking" must be undone and this can feel uncomfortable at times. The old symbols of special love are being withdrawn. And when special love is the only kind of love we have known, it sometimes feels like love *itself* is being withdrawn, which is not true.

E. Essential Instructions for Closing the Gap

1. The gap here refers to the false self's obsession with its own private will and self-seeking agendas. It is here in this gap that all the seeds of pestilence are sown. When two or more people attempt to relate to each other or try to resolve issues together, they usually do so through their own will *apart* from Holy Spirit. This occurs in every special relationship with partners, family, friends and colleagues. Relating with others and seeking to problem-solve independent from the one, shared Holy Self, results in a gap of separation – a gap where God's Loving Will and miraculous healing are not welcome.
2. This gap constitutes a major block to Love and healing. Consequently, it represents a loveless space which must attract suffering. Adversity, illness, pain, conflict and scarcity can only ever appear in this gap. They cannot arise nor continue when this gap is healed. That is why we must desire to "close the gap" first, before any seeming problem can be resolved.
   a. *"The gap [is] little. Yet it holds the seeds of pestilence and every form of ill, because it is a wish to keep apart and not to join. And thus it seems to give a cause to sickness which*

is not its cause. The purpose of the gap is all the cause that sickness has. For it was made to keep you separated, in a body which you see as if it were the cause of pain." ... *"The cause of pain is separation, not the body, which is only its effect."* T-28.III.4:2-6,5:1

3. A miraculous thing happens when two or more people decide to "close the gap" together. Let's look at an example of two people whose aim is to resolve a problem they perceive. Let's also say that these two have conflicting views about *how* the issue should be resolved. In addition, they are each attached to their particular viewpoints. In this instance the "gap" constitutes two private minds each valuing conflicting agendas.

4. From the world's perspective, in this situation our priority would be to resolve the seeming problem as we see it. We would attempt to drive and defend our version of how to solve the issue. However, this scenario presents us with the perfect opportunity to introduce the miracle – and the problem's resolution – if we're willing to pause in a Holy Instant and choose again. Here, we consciously elect to shift our primary focus from the *problem and its solution,* to our mindful intention to *trust* that Spirit has *already resolved it* as we offer up attachment to our own personal judgment and agenda. Remember, when we joined in Holy Relationship, Holy Spirit already solved every seeming problem which would appear. But do we trust in the Holy Instant of peace to bring the answer?

5. The miracle, together with the problem's resolution, is always given when two or more unite in *prioritizing peace* above all else. This means they are willing to align in the shared Mind, thereby acknowledging that here, their interests are *not* separate, but one with God.

6. They each forgive themselves for having believed the ego's separate agendas. In other words, their *intent to join* takes precedence over everything else including their preconceived ideas of what the problem *is,* along with their attachment to its resolution. It is through this central focus to close the gap between two people, a sincere pause in which they agree to set aside their independent agendas and truly *join*, which allows the miracle to occur.

7. When two people attempt to resolve a seeming problem *without* pausing in the Holy Instant to release their separate judgments, resentments, agendas or doubts to Spirit, they unwittingly block the inspired and miraculous solution.

8. In everyday life, and especially in attempting to communicate in relationships, we frequently forget that every apparent problem, irrespective of its form, is actually a symptom of its one underlying cause, which is always our belief that we're separate from God and each other. So, when we recall this single cause of adversity, we can immediately access the miracle by pausing, to set our intent to receive Spirit's recalibration.

9. The next step is to trust and open to receive His guidance, which may come in any form, including a thought or perhaps through someone else, because when we pause together, we drop the blocks which prevent access to the one Mind where all answers are already given. The answer is always given where the gap had seemed to be.

10. The private mind is fear-driven and compartmentalized. It uses the body's five senses to hallucinate problems that are not there. Unconsciously, its purpose is to project difficulties onto others, the body and the world, all to convince us that we are separate, guilty and deserving of suffering and death. When we choose to mindfully overlook (forgive) a problem with another we neutralize it. As we set aside the ego's problem and instead, we join another to close the gap, the fearless Mind is accessed and given permission to work miracles.

11. What happens when just one person participates in this miraculous dynamic while the other person refuses? Referring to the Gap diagrams, on pages 46 thru 49, a problem can only appear to exist if *two or more people* agree to its reality. But when one person withdraws their agreement as a witness to the gap and its imagined problems then this weakens the ego's argument along with its symptoms. So even though we may not have a consenting partner in Holy Relationship, we can certainly contribute to healing by withdrawing our agreement to engage in conflict and other erroneous beliefs.

12. I am reminded in the following passage that regardless if we're interacting with a Holy Relationship partner or with a total

stranger, what we acknowledge (either fear or Love) in another, we acknowledge in our self. And what we share, we strengthen. So, let us share a sense of respect and reverence with everyone we meet.

a.   *"The idea of the Holy Spirit shares the property of other ideas because it follows the laws of the universe of which it is a part. It is strengthened by being given away. It increases in you as you give it to your brother. Your brother does not have to be aware of the Holy Spirit in himself or in you for this miracle to occur. He may have dissociated the Call for God, just as you have. This dissociation is healed in both of you as you become aware of the Call for God in him, and thus acknowledge Its being."*

"There are two diametrically opposed ways of seeing your brother. They must both be in your mind, because you are the perceiver. They must also be in his, because you are perceiving him. See him through the Holy Spirit in his mind, and you will recognize Him in yours. What you acknowledge in your brother you are acknowledging in yourself, and what you share you strengthen." T-5.III.2:5-10,3:1-5

8.   ALL SICKNESS IS BLOCKED COMMUNICATION

1.   Our natural state, our Identity, is infinite and changeless innocence as Love which includes Love's expression as peace, gratitude, trust, happiness, joy, health and abundance.

2.   Real communication stems from changeless Love and unopposed innocence as a natural extension of itself. The pure miracle impulse, as Love, starts with God and is always present in each Holy Instant that we show up authentically. When we contract in fear or judgment we block the miracle's extension, and we also obstruct our receiving its benefits by rejecting the Love – as forgiveness – that heals our split mind. Forgiveness erases all our blocks to Love.

3.   If we are not supremely peaceful, happy and healthy then we

must have *unresolved* and *unforgiven* inner conflict. All illness, including physical death as Jesus teaches, is a *defense* against the truth; against our true Identity. But let's go deeper and discern what this truth as our divine Identity is. This is God's truth reflected here in the dream. God and His beloved Children know nothing of separation. As all-encompassing Love with no opposite, God and our Holy Self do not know of any separation nor the ego's illusory idols of illness, pain, conflict, scarcity and death. These represent the ego's *convincing* but imaginary defenses against the memory of our blissful, innocent, undivided union, as nothing less than the Will of God *and* His Kingdom.

4.   Let's take a peek at just *why* the ego insists on projecting illusions of sickness, pain, conflict and death. The ego's greatest terror is of healing our split mind and awakening to our invincible Holy Self as perfect Love. In *our awakening* lies *its* annihilation. Illness, pain, conflict and death are the ego's strongest defenses to keep us from awakening completely from the staggering misperception that we *are* the body and not immortal Spirit. These compelling illusions are among the ego's grandest defenses against our awakening to our constant and unassailable immunity to all phenomena the ego projects in its attempt to prove the separation has in fact occurred.

a.   *"All forms of sickness, even unto death, are physical expressions of the fear of awakening. They are attempts to reinforce sleeping out of fear of waking." T-8.IX.3:2-3*

5.   The ego uses pain, sickness and death for separation, through isolation. By magically imbuing the completely neutral body with the seeming authority to attack through disease etc., the ego instructs the body to retreat from any threat of truth as Love and union by employing its defenses. While consciously we say we want to be healthy, pain free and avoid aging and death, the unconscious and *uninvestigated ego mind* has other plans.

a.   *"Sickness is isolation. For it seems to keep one self apart from all the rest, to suffer what the others do not feel. It gives the body final power to make the separation real, and keep the mind in solitary prison, split apart and held in pieces*

by a solid wall of sickened flesh, which it can not surmount."
W-137.2.

6. The fundamental qualities of truth that can be expressed here in the dream include radical Self-honesty and Self-loyalty, which are inherent in our true Identity as the Holy Self. In contrast, the ego thrives on specialness, self-dishonesty and self-disloyalty as the means it requires to keep the illusion "alive" through guilt. Awakening from the false self and its unrelenting defenses of illness, pain and conflict, necessitates the complete undoing of our fear of union – as the fear of God – which is the ego's attraction to specialness, separation and death. Because the ego has designated the body as its means of attack, we must consciously repurpose the body with Holy Spirit. We then use the body to demonstrate union and health, thereby teaching all-inclusive guiltlessness by demonstration. These defenses of sickness, pain and conflict are initiated and fed by unforgiven guilt. Truth then can be summarized as a *deep acceptance* and understanding of true union as the Holy Self that we are. Awakening is the return to true union, and in the light of this blazing realization comes the acceptance of our complete invulnerability and innocence. This is *What* we are!

7. Pain, sickness, conflict and death all arise from some form of mental conflict caused by unforgiven guilt. Not many of us realize yet that all conflict (as guilt) begins with *self-dishonesty,* and the certain outcome from this is usually played out through some form of attack on the body *and in our relationships.*

   a. *"That forgiveness is healing needs to be understood, if the teacher of God is to make progress. The idea that a body can be sick is a central concept in the ego's thought system. This thought gives the body autonomy, separates it from the mind, and keeps the idea of attack inviolate. If the body could be sick Atonement would be impossible. A body that can order a mind to do as it sees fit could merely take the place of God and prove salvation is impossible."M-22.3:1-5*

8. It must be seen that all pain, illness, conflict and adversity arise from the split mind (ego) but we won't really want to discover

and heal its fundamental source until we have genuinely reached our own pain threshold via the ego. Disillusionment with the ego and its projections always precedes our greatest breakthroughs. Consequently, believing in any self-blame or guilt for experiencing pain or illness is a total waste of time and an ego delaying tactic. Only the ego condemns. Holy Spirit never does. If we ask Him to help us divinely reinterpret the seeming issue, He replaces the ego's judgments with right-mindedness which opens us up to miracles.

9.   Since our Christ Mind is forever one with God and our brothers, it is in eternal and uninterrupted communication with God. It's just that through our *wish for separation* we have temporarily *blocked* this communication of Love from our awareness. All-encompassing Love is *all* there is to communicate. The ego is fully aware that to hear the Father's Voice would be the complete undoing of the fantasy of separation. Our unforgiven beliefs in sin, guilt and fear, including all their consequences such as illness, pain, conflict and death, are our blocks or defenses to true communication, as only Love can be communicated.

10.   Our Christ Mind holds only what we think with God and is shared with God as nothing other than all-encompassing Love. The illusory split mind on the other hand, is the convincing dream of sin, guilt, fear, time, space, bodies and the 3-D world. Here we appear to have thoughts, feelings and experiences apart from God's Love and truth. By our choice to first desire and then to believe in the dream of separation, we effectively chose to experience amnesia of our true Identity and purpose.

11.   Because we have chosen to believe what our conditioning has taught us, we mistakenly think we actually know what will make us happy and what is in our own best interests. We carelessly conclude that we know what the body is to be used *for*. We erroneously assume that the *body* is an *end goal,* rather than understanding it to purely be a *communication device* which can lead us to go *beyond it* to the complete healing of our split mind. We think we know how to Love and communicate – but – what we don't realize is that any communication originating from unforgiven guilt *(blame, judgment, guilt trips, concern, worry, pain or illness)* actually

blocks true Love and communication. As soon as we mistake the body *as* our self, we invite fear into our mind and experience. As a consequence of this confusion, we then invite the illusions of attack and defense. Only an unreal "body self" could dream a fearful dream and then decide that it's in need of any defense.

a. *"The body is in need of no defense. This cannot be too often emphasized. It will be strong and healthy if the mind does not abuse it by assigning it to roles it cannot fill, to purposes beyond its scope, and to exalted aims which it cannot accomplish. Such attempts, ridiculous yet deeply cherished, are the sources for the many mad attacks you make upon it. For it seems to fail your hopes, your needs, your values and your dreams."* W-135.7.

A. How Do We Block Healing?

1. Jesus recently revealed to me that the most persistent threat to the ego is the *threat of union* which is the fear of true communication. The ego's primary defenses to true communication and union, aside from sickness, are the attraction to special relationships and special relating. It uses these defenses to maintain its illusory separate body and private mind concept, as separation.

2. *Healing is always the restoration of true communication.* It is the return to true union in our mind. All conflict, sickness and pain are the result of blocking healing as true communication. The primary incubator for blocking our healing comes in the form of having abandoned our self to Self-disloyalty and Self-dishonesty in our special relationships. If sinlessness and blamelessness are an absolute hallmark of true communication as Love, then through the ego we mistakenly learned how *not* to communicate, and therefore, how *not* to Love. Unfortunately, through special relating we learned how to further abandon and betray ourselves.

3. How many of us actually *believe* and even *react to* the insane critic in our mind? How many of us feel imprisoned by the tyranny of the ego's constant self-judgment; by its relentless barrage of threats and self condemnation? All condemnation is self attack, whether it is toward others or self imposed. It's all the same, as an ego attempt

to sever communication and reject true union with our Holy Self and others.

a. *"The beginning phases of this reversal are often quite painful, for as blame is withdrawn from without, there is a strong tendency to harbor it within. It is difficult at first to realize that this is exactly the same thing, for there is no distinction between within and without." ... "Self-blame is therefore ego identification, and as much an ego defense as blaming others. You cannot enter God's Presence if you attack His Son." T-11.VI.4:5-6,5:5-6*

4. Love *and* unopposed innocence are one and the same; where Love is ... innocence is. It's impossible to Love without valuing and upholding this innocence. Love is automatically denied in judgment. When we blame or judge anyone, including our self, we reject Love. Perhaps we can acknowledge how gladly and swiftly we choose to "judge" our self or others. This, the ego's trigger reaction, is its first defense against the threat of true communication and union as Love. And sincere forgiveness is the divine antidote that gently restores true communication and union. At some point we will recognize the enormous cost of all judgment, and when triggered it will be our great joy to choose forgiveness as unopposed innocence instead.

5. True communication and union begins *within* first. Remember this – every thought that we "believe" either positive or negative, is our wish to have it manifest. Belief in it translates to our *valuing it. Every believed thought is a prayer.* And this is why it's crucial to bring our own self talk and judgments up to the light of Holy Spirit so as they're not denied and projected onto the body as disease and death, or onto our relationships as conflict or betrayal. All of these are hidden self-attack until they are wholly forgiven. Recall that all forgiveness is always *self forgiveness.*

6. All self talk must be screened in mindful presence, and effectively "sorted out" as either truth *or* illusion with Holy Spirit. If we sincerely desire to heal then we need to learn to be mindfully present and accountable (without guilt) for *all* our self talk, as well as our interactions and reactions with others.

7. The predominant reason for attracting conflict, pain and illness is because of our unrecognized Self-betrayal and Self-dishonesty. This unforgiven Self-betrayal and dishonesty must be projected outward and this is why the body seems to betray us with cancer or other forms of disease. The body, as a now moment projected image, is entirely neutral and cannot sicken or heal of itself; it is merely a screen onto which we project our own denied self attack, *or* our Self Love. The body always responds exclusively to what we use it *for*.

B. Special Relating Condemns the Body

1. Special relationships are body-centered and body-bound. They come about as a result of having *abandoned* true communication and union with our Holy Self and others. In special relating we compartmentalize our thoughts and feelings, intensifying the inner and outer split which will eventually show up as *dis-ease* in the body. The body is unfortunately misused in special relationships. The guilt that binds special relationships is always taken out on the body. The ego projects its unforgiven guilt as attack onto the body in its effort to try to prove that sin, guilt, attack and separation are real. And while we believe in these lies then we will perpetuate them because we are secretly, bitterly afraid of true communication and union – as Love.

   a. *"The body will remain guilt's messenger, and will act as it directs as long as you believe that guilt is real."* T-18.X.5:1

2. True communication and union necessitate the consistent and mindful practice of *authentic relating* with our self and others. We cannot possibly be truly authentic and yet still engage in special relating. It is impossible. Special relating is the *absence of Love* because it is fearful communication and ultimately judgmental. As such it is attack, which requires us to vacate our authentic Self. Thus, it *breaks communication* and blocks true union. Therefore, and by reversal, true healing calls for *authentic* relating or Holy relating. By necessity, healing involves the thorough and divine repurposing of what we use the body *for*. While we continue to use the body for self-seeking pleasure (pain) and special relating, we unknowingly use the body for attack. Remember that special relating *severs* communication as Love.

3. Special relating revolves around its central idol, the body, and by its very nature demands Self-dishonesty, disloyalty and guilt to sustain it. What we don't seem to realize is through this, we reject healing by blocking miracle impulses. The pure miracle impulse – as Love, communication and healing – flows constantly. However, while we value judgment and blame and while we continue to value being *body-centered* in our relationships, either positively or negatively, we unknowingly block the miracle. *Unexpressed miracle impulses are the cause of all illness.* We heal by transcending self interests; by extending *beyond the body*. In our desire to see innocence in another, rather than a body, *we* heal.

    a. *"Communication ends separation. Attack promotes it." ..."Healing is the result of using the body solely for communication. Since this is natural it heals by making whole, which is also natural. All mind is whole, and the belief that part of it is physical, or not mind, is a fragmented or sick interpretation. Mind cannot be made physical, but it can be made manifest [through] the physical if it uses the body to go beyond itself. By reaching out, the mind extends itself. It does not stop at the body, for if it does it is blocked in its purpose. A mind that has been blocked has allowed itself to be vulnerable to attack, because it has turned against itself."*

    "The removal of blocks, then, is the only way to guarantee help and healing. Help and healing are the normal expressions of a mind that is working through the body, but not [in] it. If the mind believes the body is its goal it will distort its perception of the body, and by blocking its own extension beyond it, will induce illness by fostering separation. Perceiving the body as a separate entity cannot but foster illness, because it is not true. A medium of communication loses its usefulness if it is used for anything else. To use a medium of communication as a medium of attack is an obvious confusion in purpose."

"Learning must lead beyond the body to the re-establishment of the power of the mind in it. This can be accomplished only if the mind extends to other minds, and does not arrest itself in its extension. This arrest is the cause of all illness, because only extension is the mind's function."

"To see a body as anything except a means of communication is to limit your mind and to hurt yourself. Health is therefore nothing more than united purpose. If the body is brought under the purpose of the mind, it becomes whole because the mind's purpose is one. Attack can only be an assumed purpose of the body, because apart from the mind the body has no purpose at all." T-8.VII.4:1-2,10,11,12:6-8,13:3-6

4. A common motive for why we continue to value special relating is because we still hope to find the "Love," reverence and acceptance *from another* that is missing in our false self. But this is the same sense of reverence and unconditional acceptance that we so readily *deny* in our Holy Self. It's the forgiveness that we deny *extending* to others which must be first given *before* we can receive it. Instead, we look externally to the body, others and the world, for what we mistakenly believe will complete us. This is a hopeless situation indeed!

5. We can only ever recognize and find in another what we secretly believe about our self. And while we choose to *believe* our own destructive self talk, condemnation and resentments, then this must be projected outward onto others and the body. It's the ego's vicious cycle, and at some point, when we have truly had enough, we will muster the courage to break the cycle.

6. To escape the ego's bondage, we must learn to replace the voice of condemnation with the Voice for Love. Jesus speaks of how our grievances actually attack Love. If we *are* Love, then we are attacking our Self with all our judgments and resentments.

    a. *"Grievances are completely alien to love. Grievances attack love and keep its light obscure. If I hold grievances I am attacking love, and therefore attacking my Self. My Self thus* becomes alien to me. I am determined not to attack my Self today, so that I can remember Who I am." W-84.3 (68)

7. The first step in restoring true communication and union is to learn to *stop blocking* our true Identity which is uninterrupted, unopposed innocence as Love. Regardless of the ego's ranting in our mind, it's important that we learn true *Self loyalty* and show-up to mindfully rebuke any negative self talk or blame, reminding our self that this is always the ego's defense against our Holy Self as Love. Applying this discipline is real Self trust and Self Love. In this practice we learn to be radically Self-honest and Self-loyal first. We can never expect anyone else to be loyal, Loving, honest and unconditional with us until we learn how to communicate with our Holy Self.

8. While we passively "accept" resentments and negative self-talk, they remain unforgiven, to be used by the ego for attack on the body and in relationships. Mindful undoing without judgment is necessary and this is what the Atonement and the *Seven Key Principles of Authentic Relating* are for. They are tools to help *undo* the ego's blocks to true communication and miracles. Note: The *Seven Keys* can be found on page 572 and *The Seven Essential Principles of Quantum Forgiveness (Atonement)* are on page 591.

9. God as Love is the only real Cause, but while we still mistakenly *believe we are the body* and we engage in special relating, we will be tempted to give reality to the *ego's* cause (sin, guilt) and its illusory effects as illness, pain, conflict and death. This is precisely why when tempted, we can accept the Atonement as the closing of the gap within. Once that gap is closed within and we wholeheartedly *accept* our incorruptible innocence ... the apparent consequences of separation (as sickness, pain, conflict, etc.) are also healed.

a. *"Now is the body healed, because the source of sickness has been opened to relief. And you will recognize you practiced well by this: The body should not feel at all. If you have been successful, there will be no sense of feeling ill or feeling well, of pain or pleasure. No response at all is in the mind to what the body does. Its usefulness remains and nothing more."*

"Perhaps you do not realize that this removes the limits you had placed upon the body by the purposes you gave to it. As these are laid aside, the strength the body has will always be enough to serve all truly useful purposes. The body's health is fully guaranteed, because it is not limited by time, by weather or fatigue, by food and drink, or any laws you made it serve before. You need do nothing now to make it well, for sickness has become impossible."

"Yet this protection needs to be preserved by careful watching. If you let your mind harbor attack thoughts, yield to judgment or make plans against uncertainties to come, you have again misplaced yourself, and made a bodily identity which will attack the body, for the mind is sick." W-136.17,18,19

10. As we heal and cease compartmentalizing our lives and communication (while returning to innocence and authenticity using the *Seven Keys* and forgiveness) we completely repurpose the body. The body's condition is a direct reflection of our degree of alignment with Holy Spirit. The body automatically falls into perfect alignment with our authentic and vertical purpose, to awaken to the pristine sinlessness and guiltlessness we share with everyone. Only here, in whole forgiveness and authentic alignment, can we be consistently free of unconscious motives to use the body as a witness to attack and guilt.

11. When we agree to abdicate every *ego purpose* for the body, the body naturally aligns with the harmonious governance and authority of the Holy Spirit. It becomes a symbol of sinlessness, free of all signs of attack. This is the natural outcome of using our body *only for communication;* to reach our brothers with Holy Spirit's message of our all-inclusive sinlessness. In this, the body is liberated from separation and divinely dedicated to union, by transcending self-interests.

12. True health and consistent miracle working are the result of relinquishing all attempts to use the body lovelessly. Remember that "pleasure and pain" are *one and the same* because they serve a

solitary function – to make the body real, a convincing opponent to our Holy Self and God's Will. And this is why the body seems to sicken, age and die. As long as we still prefer to extract our pseudo fulfillment from the body with its sensual pleasures and pain, we remain divided. The outcome of this confusion is a divided body used by the ego to seek suffering and death.

a.   *"The Holy Spirit teaches you to use your body only to reach your brothers, so He can teach His message through you. This will heal them and therefore heal you. Everything used in accordance with its function as the Holy Spirit sees it cannot be sick. Everything used otherwise is. Do not allow the body to be a mirror of a split mind. Do not let it be an image of your own perception of littleness. Do not let it reflect your decision to attack. Health is seen as the natural state of everything when interpretation is left to the Holy Spirit, Who perceives no attack on anything. Health is the result of relinquishing all attempts to use the body lovelessly. Health is the beginning of the proper perspective on life under the guidance of the one Teacher Who knows what life is, being the Voice for Life Itself." T-8.VIII.9.*

9.   GIVE PEACE A CHANCE

a.   *"I am upset because I see what is not there. Reality is never frightening. It is impossible that it could upset me. Reality brings only perfect peace. When I am upset, it is always because I have replaced reality with illusions I made up. The illusions are upsetting because I have given them reality, and thus regard reality as an illusion." W-62.1. (6)*

1.   I am upset because I see what is *not* there. What I see is therefore a hallucination and is not real.

2.   I can be affected by this illusion *only* if I mistakenly *believe*

it. To believe is to give the illusion reality and value. In valuing this illusion, I reject the peace of God, the Holy Instant in which all miracles are offered and received. I must make a choice. I either desire the illusion of (fill in the blank) fear, pain, illness, conflict, special relationships, being right, my story, etc. – or – I desire the peace of God which *is* Reality. I cannot have both. My belief in one excludes the other entirely.

3. Deciding that we want *only* the peace of God in all we think, feel, say and do, means that we withdraw our value from the world and the body, which seems to sense the illusory world. Hence the body is no longer used as the lens we previously accepted to inform us of reality.

4. Instead of reacting to illusions seen through the body's senses, the mind is immersed inwardly and exclusively on choosing the *opposite* Reality – the peace of God – over what the body's senses report. This is the choice for Christ Vision. We say and mean, "Above all else I want the peace of God instead of this distorted belief in what the body's eyes see."

5. We rest in this certainty. Not only does God know our deeper desires, but He has already answered them for all time. His gifts are already given. But do we return our awareness to the stillness within to receive them? Every seeming problem is perfectly resolved in this peace. This is the Holy Instant.

6. Our consistent practice of choosing the Holy Instant of peace to divinely correct all obstacles brings quantum resolution to every concern which the illusory body's senses report. The activating agent in all healing is our choice for the *peace of God* in place of what we appear to see.

7. This is healing the singular cause in our mind of all subsequent errors at the level of form. These errors are the *effects* or consequences of our mistaken choice to value the ego's judgment instead of God's. Atonement is the choice for the peace of God over every temptation to perceive otherwise.

   a. *"You will yet learn that peace is part of you, and requires only that you be there to embrace any situation in which you are. And finally you will learn that there is no limit to where you are, so that your peace is everywhere, as you are." W-rl.in.5:1-2*

8. The moment we are triggered or when we desire something other than the peace of God, we abandon our Holy Self. We choose to be immersed in the dream/illusion. Guilt, fear, doubt and self-attack are the byproducts of this Self-betrayal.

9. At some point in our own transfer of trust from fear to Love, we must make a concerted choice to cease compartmentalizing our hierarchy of illusions. All illusions arise from fear and exclude Love. Our erroneous belief that some illusions are valuable because they will give us *more* than what we *are* as God's Love, blocks us from that Love and healing. While we are still invested in valuing (believing) certain illusions (positive or negative) above others, we unknowingly reject the miracle's infinite and overarching authority to heal all.

   a. *"There is no home can shelter love and fear. They cannot coexist. If you are real, then fear must be illusion. And if fear is real, then you do not exist at all." W-160.4:5-8*

10. Following, in this compelling message from Jesus, we see that the presence of fear is a sign that we have abandoned our Holy Self:

   a. *"The presence of fear is a sure sign that you are trusting in your own strength. The awareness that there is nothing to fear shows that somewhere in your mind, though not necessarily in a place you recognize as yet, you have remembered God, and let His strength take the place of your weakness. The instant you are willing to do this there is indeed nothing to fear." W-48.3.*

11. The desire for only the peace of God establishes the condition necessary for consistent miracle working. Once this whole, completely undivided condition is accepted (peace of God), level confusion is erased. Thoughts of the body/world recede in awareness so much so that they are vividly eclipsed by the light of Love which peace restores.

A. Opening to Accept the Atonement

1. The ego's false humility often tempts us to believe that we must qualify for God's Love and healing, that we must earn it. There may be a lurking belief that we are unworthy to receive His divine healing. *"Your difficulty with the holy instant arises from your fixed conviction that you are not worthy of it."* T-18.IV.3:3 When this occurs, we will mistakenly attempt to "prepare" our self to accept healing. But readying our self for purification actually blocks the miracle. The Atonement is the correction. All that is asked of us is to:

1) Desire the peace of God (more than anything else).

2) Receive it.

a. *"In preparing for the holy instant, do not attempt to make yourself holy to be ready to receive it. That is but to confuse your role with God's. Atonement cannot come to those who think that they must first atone, but only to those who offer it nothing more than simple willingness to make way for it. Purification is of God alone, and therefore for you. Rather than seek to prepare yourself for Him, try to think thus:*

I who am host to God am worthy of Him. He Who established His dwelling place in me created it as He would have it be. It is not needful that I make it ready for Him, but only that I do not interfere with His plan to restore to me my own awareness of my readiness, which is eternal. I need add nothing to His plan. But to receive it, I must be willing not to substitute my own in place of it." T-18.IV.5:4-13

2. The Atonement is available to us literally in every moment. This Holy Instant is the instantaneous restoration to awareness of our perfection in God. Real humility would never assume that we are unworthy of having our perception restored to union with God and our brothers. Only the ego's arrogance could possibly suggest that we are not worthy to be God's changeless and eternally innocent Child.

3. We have a choice. Do we elect to believe the ego's judgment of who we are? Or do we trust in God's certain knowledge of What we are? Only one is true. The ego's unworthiness is really arrogance because it surmises that God's certainty of our Identity is wrong. Be willing to look with Holy Spirit and answer the following question:

4. *"What belief, value, concern, story, need, pain, pleasure, anxiety, unworthiness, etc. have I mistakenly desired MORE than the "peace of God," more than my incorruptible innocence?"*

5. Remember that peace always brings understanding. We cannot understand anything at all through fear or lack as they are not understandable. Fear and lack arise from a mistaken belief in a dream apart from our beloved Holy Self. Yet when we prioritize peace above all else, understanding is the outcome.

    a. *"There is nothing to fear. How safe the world will look to me when I can see it! It will not look anything like what I imagine I see now. Everyone and everything I see will lean toward me to bless me. I will recognize in everyone my dearest Friend. What could there be to fear in a world that I have forgiven, and that has forgiven me?"* W-60.3.4

10. MY PROFOUND RELATIONSHIP JOURNEY – FROM FEAR TO LOVE - INTRODUCTION

1. A Holy Relationship need *not* be romantic. It is not exclusive but *inclusive*. It may be between two or more people. In contrast, the special relationship is exclusive.

2. There are at least three fundamental phases of relationship reform within the ego dream. Remember Jesus tells us that relationships are our primary *teaching-learning* experience. They are the most important vehicle required for our final return to Love as our one, shared and Holy Self. If our relationships remain special, then our identity, beliefs and values will be based on fear (special love)

and not on perfect Love. As a result, we will continue to experience suffering and conflict.

3. **Phase One:** This phase of relationship is one which humanity has valued and experienced since the beginning of the dream of separation: *special relationships!* Nearly every relationship in the world is *special* until it has been divinely re-purposed with Holy Spirit. *Special* love is fear in disguise, and this is why it seems that the "love" in our human relationships can change and end. Yet... perfect Love is changeless Love. Love without fear, without attack. This is *what* we are as the one, shared and Holy Self. We won't really know this with conviction until we commit to undoing special love with Holy Spirit. Nearly everyone in the world values special love and special relationships.

4. **Phase Two:** By necessity, the desire for and transfer to a Holy Relationship involves the divine *undoing* by Holy Spirit, of our beliefs and values, especially the false self-concept. The mistaken concept of special love must be healed in order to return our awareness to our Holy Self. The second phase of relationship reform involves one partner desiring to heal the relationship from a special to a Holy Relationship, while no other partner(s) are interested. In this case the partners have separate relationship goals and do not share a truly common purpose with Holy Spirit. This is often the perfect classroom for the partner who desires this change to use every emotional trigger as an opportunity to extend forgiveness and accept the Atonement. It is also an excellent opportunity for this one to begin to authentically "show up" for *themselves,* applying the *Seven Keys.*

5. **Phase Three:** This is where two (or more) partners agree to join with Holy Spirit in Holy Relationship. They agree to commit to a truly common purpose with Spirit. And that is to awaken from the false self and its dream of separation. This is an *agreement* to undo separation as special love by *willingly inviting* the divine undoing by Holy Spirit, of our beliefs and values, especially the false self-concept.

6. As an example, I will share my own experience and lessons in having traveled through the various phases of relationship transition from special to Holy. The first part describes the transition from a

very special, toxic and codependent relationship with Tomas… to a profoundly Holy Relationship. It features the "phase of disorientation" which Jesus speaks of in Chapter 17, Section 5 of the *Course*. The second part explains my own experience of a Phase Two relationship and the lessons I gained from it (many people on the ACIM path may relate to this). The third part features my own and my partner Daniel's experience in an advanced Holy Relationship. What to look forward to!

A. Nouk and Tomas' Miraculous Story

i. The Vow

1. Like most of us, Tomas and I wanted to be loved. We longed to be respected, cherished, accepted, and loved unconditionally. In other words, we desired a changeless and everlasting Love that we had never experienced, yet knew deep down was possible.

2. We met in 1984, after each having experienced a series of broken relationships. We both had fairly "normal" childhoods – with the usual themes of emotional abuse, betrayal, abandonment, and then speckled with the occasional moments of connection. As children, most of us generally remain "unseen" by our parents despite the best of their intentions.

3. Sadly, we grow up to be unseen children masquerading as adults, still playing out the same childhood dynamics in an effort to seek the love and recognition in our relationships which we never received from our parents or caretakers. The result is that we grow up not knowing who we really are or having any sense of innate worth.

4. Unless we are raised by ascended masters in a family who *sees* us as the divine beings we inherently are, and teaches us to believe in what is beyond the ego's illusory world, we will, as adults, continue the external search for love that seemed to be so elusive to us as youngsters -always just out of reach. In other words, as we age, we continue to seek the Love we didn't experience as children. From this place of lack, it is no wonder that we are always trying to *get* love from our worldly relationships – to compensate for

that which was missing in our frustrated or somewhat unsatisfying relationship with our parents.

5.   In the sphere of romance, we seek an idealized partner, hoping, and in some cases even demanding, that this soulmate exalt us just as we wanted our mother and father to adore us. We erroneously assume that he or she will automatically - and spontaneously "see" our Spirit - hence, know who we truly are - and forevermore reflect our state of absolute innocence in all their loving actions towards us.

6.   Tomas and I, indeed, made that very assumption, setting unrealistic expectations for one another from the outset. We were convinced when we first got together that our special, romantic love would be eternal, and that this relationship was going to meet all our "needs" for sure! Oops . . . we certainly didn't have a clue what we were in for. We didn't have the awareness back then to even pose the essential question: "What is this relationship *for*?"

7.   Neither Tomas nor I had discovered our one, shared Holy Self yet. Accordingly, we were following a longstanding psychological pattern: We each were looking to the other as the means to fulfill our selfish desires, namely a romantic partner to give us the love we so desperately wanted.

8.   We came to realize in hindsight, that it's always the false self (the ego) that sets this dynamic up – the saboteur with the unconscious mantra, "*seek and do not find!*" But, at the time, Tomas and I were entirely unaware of its sinister workings. To outwit or overcome the ego's insidious trappings requires spiritual help, tools, and an uncompromising commitment. But that learning came later for us!

9.   Let me bring you back to the beginning. Our relationship was born on a balmy evening in 1984. As we lay on the warm sand of a tropical beach, complete with twinkling stars, we were both inspired to express our deeply cherished intent. Our mutual goal was to experience real, changeless, and indestructible Love – a Love that was eternal and that could never be threatened. The vow we exchanged was this: "*No matter what and no matter who might seem to come between us, let us never abandon each other.*" As we spoke those words in unison, our powerful commitment appeared to reverberate throughout the universe.

10. While we lay on this deserted beach in the quiet of the evening, making our vow, a stunning phenomenon occurred. A shimmering pink light which appeared to beam out from the heavens, flashed upon us…bathing our faces in undeniable grace. For a miraculous moment, Tomas and I beheld the breathtaking face of Christ in each other. Tears began rolling down our cheeks as we caught a glimpse of the sheer magnitude of this commitment to experience a changeless Love that could never be threatened.

ii. Setting the Trap

1. I am reminded of what Jesus tells us in the *Course* about how, when the pupil is ready the teacher appears. Tomas and I were both pupil *and* teacher for each other simultaneously.

   a. *"Certain pupils have been assigned to each of God's teachers, and they will begin to look for him as soon as he has answered the Call. They were chosen for him because the form of the universal curriculum that he will teach is best for them in view of their level of understanding. His pupils have been waiting for him, for his coming is certain. Again, it is only a matter of time. Once he has chosen to fulfill his role, they are ready to fulfill theirs. Time waits on his choice, but not on whom he will serve. When he is ready to learn, the opportunities to teach will be provided for him."* M-2.1.

2. Just before the date of our approaching marriage (three years before commencing our journey in *A Course in Miracles*), I decided to establish a ground rule for our future life together. Feeling strongly that when one makes a romantic commitment to another, one also commits to monogamy, I told Tomas: "If you ever cheat on me, I will need to end our relationship; in fact, I will initiate a divorce immediately."

3. Looking back, I see I was consumed – obsessed, if you will – with my notion of what a romantic partnership should be. I could not fathom how anyone could make a serious loving commitment, but then intentionally – or unintentionally – ignore that promise and even go so far as to engage in extramarital flirtations or sex. For me,

matrimony and infidelity were mutually exclusive. My stance was crystal clear to Tomas and he willingly agreed to comply with my condition. We went on to marry soon after in 1987, and our precious daughter Rikki was born the following year.

4. Unbeknownst to me at the time, the provision that I had set *for* us was about to boomerang and literally act *against* us over time. I had unwittingly set a trap with my conditions on Love. In attempting to protect our partnership from potential harm, I inadvertently brought about the very threat I had so hoped to avoid. I did not know this truth back then: whatever we fear, we ultimately attract. Unintentionally, I was creating and attracting the very damaging and dysfunctional relationship I so desperately wanted to avoid.

5. Despite our honorable intent, our relationship was rapidly falling apart and by 1990, only six years after committing to our sacred vow, our relationship was on the rocks. In an attempt to try to save our relationship through a frenzy of counseling and research, I came across *A Course in Miracles* and felt, without a doubt, that this *Course* presented the perfect vehicle that would teach us the *means* by which we could experience the changeless Love we so yearned for, yet had consistently sabotaged.

6. Most importantly, the *Course* introduced us to the possibility of achieving a Holy Relationship, which represents a Love that can never wane or die. The purpose of a relationship such as this is the *undoing* of the false and separate self, the elimination of fear and guilt – and the experience of True union as the one, shared Holy Self.

7. This is the opposite of the purpose of our worldly relationships, which the *Course* calls "special relationships." The ego uses the special relationship to reinforce fear and guilt, thereby ensuring the perpetuation of separation. Special relationships are nothing more than the ego's destructive substitute for our original relationship with our brothers and God.

8. The *Course* further illustrates just *why* our relationships with partners, friends and family often start out loving, only to frequently disintegrate over time. In its Preface, there is a passage that speaks of the "scarcity principle" that governs our world of illusions. Speaking

about the ego's version of ambivalent love it aptly states, *"we seek in others what we feel is wanting in ourselves. We 'love' another in order to get something ourselves. That, in fact, is what passes for love in the dream world. There can be no greater mistake than that, for love is incapable of asking for anything."* ACIM, Pref. xi

iii. Trial by Fire – From Special to Holy Relationship

1. While I enthusiastically embraced the *Course* from the outset, Tomas initially felt a very real threat – his false self was about to be greatly challenged. His response in those early months of my total immersion in studying the *Course* was to take off to the jungles of Papua New Guinea for three months. This left me alone at home to continue learning this new and radical teaching material.

2. There were no study groups and my family and friends at the time thought I was going nuts. Moreover, I must admit, back then I did misinterpret much of what the *Course* was teaching; so many misunderstandings occurred. Accordingly, I remember this to be a particularly fearful and isolating period for me. At one point, I momentarily gave validity to the doubt of my loved ones and even began to question my own sanity in following this new path. Yet for all the mistakes Tomas and I made, we were kept safe as we learned to recognize and surrender each of them to the Holy Spirit to be divinely corrected.

3. During that time, we were undergoing much change at the level of "form," which included the decision to sell our home. With Tomas away, this left me to deal with initiating the sale process, although just before he went on vacation, he arranged for a realtor to visit me the following week.

4. When that morning came, I was looking out the kitchen window and was struck by a most unbelievable sight. I saw a man slowly walking toward our front door with a briefcase and what appeared to be the same green book that had recently become the meaning of my world. "Was he really carrying *A Course in Miracles?* Am I delusional?" A million thoughts and questions burned through my mind.

5. When I opened the door, there was an unmistakable moment of deep recognition between us. We both entered a Holy Instant together as we met. All pretenses fell away, and we beheld the Christ as one. We knew each other. There was an undeniable feeling that we had agreed to accomplish something remarkable in this lifetime, although consciously, we didn't recall the details. This déjà vu feeling was overwhelming. This moment of synchronistic collision really catapulted my faith and trust, helping me to believe that I was *not* insane, but that life instead was playing out perfectly.

   a. *"Each teaching-learning situation involves a different relationship at the beginning, although the ultimate goal is always the same; to make of the relationship a holy relationship, in which both can look upon the Son of God as sinless."... "Therefore, the plan includes very specific contacts to be made for each teacher of God. There are no accidents in salvation. Those who are to meet will meet, because together they have the potential for a holy relationship. They are ready for each other."* M-3.1:2,5-8

6. Daniel, the realtor, and I thought that he had come to help sell our house, but the Holy Spirit had a far more profound purpose for our meeting. We formed an immediate friendship as we both marveled at the *synchronistic* meeting of two, previously lonely and isolated *Course* students.

7. To my surprise, Daniel shared that his wife at the time, just like Tomas, was reluctant to delve into the *Course*, which left him pretty much on his own with this new and seemingly challenging thought system. I remember feeling the most immense gratitude for this man coming into my life. Now I had a fellow traveler to "live" this teaching with.

8. Daniel and I would meet up every few days to study the lessons and work through the beginning of a great "undoing" of so much of what we had previously believed and valued. We were beginning to see the many false idols we had, and for me it was an intense, emotional roller coaster ride. It was such a relief though to be able to bare my soul in this friendship without fear of attack. So much repressed

baggage came up and I was so grateful that Daniel allowed me to express without any judgment, blame or shame.

9. During those three months of Tomas' absence, Daniel and I became closer. Yet I felt a growing feeling of unease. There was a problem. A shocking thing had surfaced that I was totally at a loss to explain. I realized that I was becoming attracted to this fellow student and that the attraction threatened my entire value system.

10. It was an absolute breach of the condition that I put on Tomas at the outset of our marriage. I was besieged with confusion and guilt even though I had not cheated on Tomas. The mere fact that I felt an attraction to someone other than my husband was enough to spin me out. "Now what do I do?" was my heart-felt question to Spirit. And my answer came almost immediately: "Tell Daniel the truth and allow Spirit to guide you."

11. So, at our next meeting, I summoned the courage to push through my extreme embarrassment and told Daniel that I was feeling an attraction to him despite still loving my wonderful husband. His response was not what I expected or wanted to hear. He divulged that he was feeling a mutual attraction and was in turmoil and confusion, as well.

12. Thankfully, Tomas was due back a few days later from his three month long trekking vacation in the Highlands of Papua New Guinea. In spite of the terror I felt, I decided that I would need to openly tell him of this attraction I had for Daniel, even if in doing so, I would jeopardize our relationship. I'd learned enough by now that my safest path was always to be totally honest and express my emotional vulnerability, rather than to defend it. As long as I was one hundred percent truthful, I would be safe.

13. The day Tomas returned I couldn't help but blurt out that I had something extremely important to tell him that just couldn't wait, despite his urgent desire to unpack his bag and to take a shower. I was so afraid; nevertheless, I sat with Tomas and shared what seemed for me to be something that could possibly end our relationship. Crying, I told him the whole story about developing an attraction for Daniel. But nothing could have prepared me for what came next.

14. Tomas began to laugh and laugh; his laughter escalated until I couldn't help but join him. Then, in the next minute, he blurted, "Have I got something to tell you!"

15. In a surreal moment that seemed to stand completely apart from time, he told me that while we were married, he had had not just one affair, but three! I heard him speak; yet in me, there was a strange sense of peace. Not one judgment arose in my mind and I could not locate a single negative emotion.

16. Then suddenly and unexpectedly, I fell on the floor in raucous laughter only to find Tomas had fallen beside me. We both dissolved into a joined state of hilarious communion; it was a truly Holy Instant where all seeming sins disappeared and what remained was only pure innocence, as infinite and changeless Love.

17. Profound forgiveness took place both for me and Tomas. In that Holy Instant, our authentic and Holy Relationship *began* . . . six years *after* we exchanged our original vow that starry night to discover the nature and purpose of changeless Love.

18. We had asked for this experience of a Love that could never be threatened, but we had no idea at the time that everything we'd learned about love – as special love –had to be completely *un*-learned. Until that moment of total forgiveness between us, Tomas and I had experienced the classic "special relationship," as characterized by the *Course* – complete with unrecognized codependency and compulsory constraints, all of which were the ego's utterly insane defenses against truth and, therefore, against Love.

19. I instantly realized I had set the stage for Tomas's ego to cut loose perfectly by telling him earlier there was a single provision that could not be broken: Stray and it's over! What I was really threatening him with before our marriage was "Cheat and I will withdraw my love for you." That's the ego thought system and special love in operation right there - always trying to limit Love's infinite extension in our minds.

20. In pushing Tomas to specifically agree to my premarital ultimatum, I didn't foresee the adverse effects that it would have eventually on both of us. Somewhere deep down, I felt guilty for placing conditions on our love and knew that it was fear - and not an innocent

or unconditional Love – that motivated me to do so.

21. Tomas, in fact, did breach my terms with not just one affair, but three. His guilt and shame increased with each mistake and I, at the time, was oblivious to it all. For three years, he could not tell me for fear of my leaving him; so, while we were "together" as a couple in "form" (marriage) we were certainly not together in "content" (Love).

    a.   *"For an unholy relationship is based on differences, where each one thinks the other has what he has not. They come together, each to complete himself and rob the other. They stay until they think that there is nothing left to steal, and then move on. And so they wander through a world of strangers, unlike themselves, living with their bodies perhaps under a common roof that shelters neither; in the same room and yet a world apart." T-22.in.2:5-8*

22. Tomas had trapped himself with my condition and doomed himself to a prison of deceit, separation, and isolation. So many times he wanted to confess but could not bear to face me. When he came close to expressing his vulnerability, he heard my threat ringing in his ears and thus he would retreat into separation again.

23. He felt mired in guilt for breaking his promise to me. The consequences of this deceit were that we both felt estranged and separate. We then fixed the blame outward – upon one another for each other's unspoken actions. This, I now realize, was the ego's projection of unconscious guilt, which is the core and fuel of the ego thought system. I now recognize the subtlety of the dance of victim and perpetrator.

24. The dance, however, seemed to come to a halt between us that momentous evening where we forgave each other, for our relationship began to take on a whole new meaning and purpose. That night, we experienced first-hand the *Course's* definition of forgiveness: nothing bad had ever happened. We were blameless and guiltless.

25. Once we extended toward one another this quantum forgiveness, all seeming negative effects literally dropped away. It was as if the past evaporated in our unconditional acceptance of each other. In

this lesson we also realized that we were never a victim of anything, contrary to what the ego tried to convince us of during the first six years of our relationship.

26. We discovered that neither of us had done anything sinfully wrong, as the illusory world would have judged. We had merely erred. Underneath the mistaken thoughts and resulting behavior, all that had really occurred was a consistent cry *for* Love. In that Holy Instant of forgiveness between us, our Holy Relationship truly began, and within this profound recognition of one another, guilt and fear were erased from our hearts and we were bathed in a magnificent state of grace.

   a. *"There is a course for every teacher of God. The form of the course varies greatly. So do the particular teaching aids involved. But the content of the course never changes. Its central theme is always, "God's Son is guiltless, and in his innocence is his salvation." M-1.3:1-5*

27. As to the outcome of my friendship with Daniel, it did not end when Tomas came home from New Guinea. As a matter of fact, we continued to meet regularly and openly, much to Tomas' dismay. Nevertheless, I was guided to continue to deepen my relationship with Daniel and that lasted just as long as it took for each of us to learn the lessons we needed at the time.

28. Daniel and I continued to get together, however we included Tomas in many of our joinings. The process was radical and emotionally challenging but tremendously healing for us all. Specialness was being undone. Genuine honesty, accountability, emotional vulnerability, and defenselessness were abundantly present in all our interactions.

29. I really believed that Daniel would commit to a lifelong goal with me in pursuing the path of the *Course*. But after a year or so, he explained that he was not ready to commit to being undivided in his pursuit of this pathway. Much later, I recognized that a Holy Relationship takes two people or more who commit to the one common and consistent purpose of quantum forgiveness, using the *Seven Keys*. However, for Daniel at the time, it was too much of a leap and too threatening to the life he was invested in. I was so

saddened by his decision then and did not understand it.

30. Daniel moved away some time later, and we lost touch until twenty-five years later (a miraculous outcome featured later!). However, those few months with Daniel presented Tomas with an opportunity to undo many of the fears that fed his ego's desire for the exclusive, toxic special relationship. As for me, it enabled me to learn to stay focused on my particular issue at the time, which was to stay true (without guilt) to my own guidance, despite frustrating my partner's ego's needs.

iv. Holy Spirit's Relationship Goal Reversal

1. For Tomas and me, all this served to cement our Holy Relationship while undoing the special love we once valued. The circumstances provided a great lesson in forgiveness all around and we were blessed with this awareness and with the willingness to take the challenge on.

2. When two people in a special relationship agree to a Holy Relationship, the Holy Spirit enters to transform it to a Holy Relationship as it did with Tomas and me. The original goal of "specialness" is immediately replaced with the goal of Holiness by Him. There is no denying that this period is often uncomfortable and confusing. The temptation to end the relationship and seek the old goal of specialness in another relationship is quite common. This initial phase is such a huge, life-changing experience that I feel compelled to include a riveting section about it here from the *Course*:

    a. *"The holy relationship, a major step toward the perception of the real world, is learned. It is the old, unholy relationship, transformed and seen anew. The holy relationship is a phenomenal teaching accomplishment. In all its aspects, as it begins, develops, and becomes accomplished, it represents the reversal of the unholy relationship. Be comforted in this; the only difficult phase is the beginning. For here, the goal of the relationship is abruptly shifted to the exact opposite of what it was. This is the first result of offering the relationship to the Holy Spirit, to use for His purposes."*

"This invitation is accepted immediately, and the Holy Spirit wastes no time in introducing the practical results of asking Him to enter. At once His goal replaces yours. This is accomplished very rapidly, but it makes the relationship seem disturbed, disjunctive and even quite distressing. The reason is quite clear. For the relationship as it [is] is out of line with its own goal, and clearly unsuited to the purpose that has been accepted for it. In its unholy condition, [your] goal was all that seemed to give it meaning. Now it seems to make no sense. Many relationships have been broken off at this point, and the pursuit of the old goal re-established in another relationship. For once the unholy relationship has accepted the goal of holiness, it can never again be what it was."

"The temptation of the ego becomes extremely intense with this shift in goals. For the relationship has not as yet been changed sufficiently to make its former goal completely without attraction, and its structure is "threatened" by the recognition of its inappropriateness for meeting its new purpose. The conflict between the goal and the structure of the relationship is so apparent that they cannot coexist. Yet now the goal will not be changed. Set firmly in the unholy relationship, there is no course except to change the relationship to fit the goal. Until this happy solution is seen and accepted as the only way out of the conflict, the relationship may seem to be severely strained."

"It would not be kinder to shift the goal more slowly, for the contrast would be obscured, and the ego given time to reinterpret each slow step according to its liking. Only a radical shift in purpose could induce a complete change of mind about what the whole relationship is for. As this change develops and is finally accomplished, it grows increasingly beneficent and joyous. But at the beginning, the situation is experienced as very precarious. A relationship, undertaken by two individuals for their unholy purposes, suddenly has holiness for its goal. As these two contemplate their relationship from the point of view of this new purpose, they are inevitably appalled. Their perception

of the relationship may even become quite disorganized. And yet, the former organization of their perception no longer serves the purpose they have agreed to meet."

"This is the time for [faith.] You let this goal be set for you. That was an act of faith. Do not abandon faith, now that the rewards of faith are being introduced. If you believed the Holy Spirit was there to accept the relationship, why would you now not still believe that He is there to purify what He has taken under His guidance? Have faith in your brother in what but seems to be a trying time. The goal [is] set. And your relationship has sanity as its purpose. For now you find yourself in an insane relationship, recognized as such in the light of its goal."

"Now the ego counsels thus; substitute for this another relationship to which your former goal was quite appropriate. You can escape from your distress only by getting rid of your brother. You need not part entirely if you choose not to do so. But you must exclude major areas of fantasy from your brother, to save your sanity. [Hear not this now!] Have faith in Him Who answered you. He heard. Has He not been very explicit in His answer? You are not now wholly insane. Can you deny that He has given you a most explicit statement? Now He asks for faith a little longer, even in bewilderment. For this will go, and you will see the justification for your faith emerge, to bring you shining conviction. Abandon Him not now, nor your brother. This relationship has been reborn as holy." T-17.V.2,3,4,5,6,7.

3. During that year when Daniel joined us and my relationship with Tomas was in total upheaval, the preceding section of the *Course* literally kept me sane and devoted no matter how dramatic and terrorizing things appeared to be. I reread this section hundreds of times thinking that if we got through this phase, we would one day help others to take the journey from special to Holy Relationships too.

4. As Tomas and I began our new Holy Relationship, there was an unmistakable, unified decision made between us. We agreed with Holy Spirit that we would do whatever was necessary to pursue this lifelong commitment to Holy Relationship. Looking back, I realize that we had agreed to join in the one, common and Holy Purpose necessary for the Holy Relationship, *consistent forgiveness.*

5. I also recognize, on reflection, that we were both committed to Holy communication through applying the *Seven Keys.* Now, there was nowhere for the ego or specialness to hide.

6. Finally, we had made a wholehearted commitment to study and practice the *Course* together and, accordingly, it moved us to seriously question the ego thought system including all our beliefs and values. While this triggered conflict at times, we were still motivated to extinguish the old goal of the special relationship with its well-entrenched patterns and replace it with Spirit's Holy purpose.

7. Despite our commitment, I still found myself falling back into old patterns of denial and projection. As a recovering victim, I would still occasionally bait Tomas to play the old role of perpetrator. I really got to witness just how much the false self is addicted to being unfairly treated; how much it desires to project guilt onto others.

8. We began to part the curtain that previously made Love appear so obscure in our earlier relationship. Together, Tomas and I were learning that real Love requires no defense, because beneath the false self, changeless innocence as Love itself is what we truly are.

9. As our fear of Love dissolved, we become aware that Love *is.* Period. In a Holy Relationship, we learned that innocence *is* Love. There can be no Love while there is blame, guilt, judgment, grievances or resentment. We learned that Love emerged naturally when we prioritized seeing each other as guiltless, as sinless, above all else.

10. Innocence *as* Love arises as the natural outcome of prioritizing forgiveness. Love via forgiveness is ultimately known only through its unconditional extension: by giving it without expecting anything in return, we remember that we *are* innocent. The outcome of this realization is eternal and changeless Love that cannot be threatened by anyone or anything – just like the vow we made to each other

with Holy Spirit seven years earlier: *"No matter what and no matter who might seem to come between us, let us never abandon each other."* If two or more took and kept this vow, a lifelong Holy Relationship would be the glorious outcome. However, every shred of specialness would need to be seen and surrendered to Spirit.

11. The *Course* advises us before doing anything, to always ask, "What is it *for?"* In other words, "what is my intent or purpose?" We asked this question of ourselves in our day-to-day relationship almost every time we were tempted to act from the ego. Using the tools of present moment awareness and radical self-inquiry, we found to our astonishment that most of the loving things we routinely did for each other were really arising from fear and guilt – and not from real Love, which arises from God.

12. For example, my previous, fear-based conditioning had me believe that if I didn't cook most nights, wasn't attentive to Tomas' needs, or didn't look attractive for him, then I might lose my husband. Put differently, most of what I gave in our relationship was driven unconsciously from deprivation and self-doubt – and not from trusting in the abundance of Spirit. I was a people-pleaser. I had mistakenly convinced myself that compromise and sacrifice equaled love. I had no idea that real Love demands nothing.

13. Tomas, too, realized that much of what he did for me in our relationship was motivated by his fear of abandonment. His acts, like mine, were not born out of unconditional Love. These unloving, conditional acts are what we term "ego-stroking" and are usually desired and expected in all special relationships.

14. We rapidly realized that nearly everything we had believed was Loving was actually fear-driven. Consequently, we agreed to practice being more authentic and radically honest with each other without fear of being rejected. In our previously special relationship, this was not possible because we each valued the "special" ego-stroking behavior more than we valued authentic relating.

15. The shift in the relationship's goal meant for us both a withdrawal of ego-stroking. This was very uncomfortable at first, although there was little attraction to regressing to our former way of relating. Once we agreed that the relationship's purpose was no longer to get our ego's needs met, we were free to dedicate ourselves wholeheartedly to its real aim: the undoing of "the blocks to the awareness of Love's presence."

16. The benefits of this goal-reversal strongly made themselves known. We began to learn to trust the Holy Spirit in lieu of the ego and to reinterpret and wipe away all of our judgments. A mighty leap of faith was taken as we applied this most powerful means of transformation and healing. Quantum forgiveness as the Atonement, which was the catalyst for healing, continued to prove to be the miraculous tool that opened our hearts to the possibility of peace between us, rather than the ongoing suffering that simmered under the surface before.

17. Completely repurposing our relationship, it enabled us to continue to transcend the routine, marital bargaining and judgments that we had been accustomed to imposing upon one another. Instead, we joined in an unparalleled and divine Love that was literally out of this world.

v. Releasing the Marriage to Save the Relationship

1. Around 1997, about seven years after our first significant forgiveness experience, we came to a point where we had grown enough (had more trust in Love instead of fear) to see that the ego still claimed a stake in the form of our relationship; in our case, the marriage. This is a contract that is supposed to offer security, but actually bred insecurity. There remained some doubt within us, which surfaced as fear of losing each other. To Tomas, it was the fear of abandonment, and for me it was the fear of freedom.

2. Despite all the adjustments and corrections we had made on our new path, Tomas and I were still experiencing some conflict, insecurity and fear. I found there still remained fears within me, specifically those of feeling like a victim, that I projected onto Tomas to keep the special relationship dance afloat. He would sometimes join the dance as the seeming victimizer.

3. While observing this phenomenon between us, we concluded that the ego was still hiding in the "form" of our marriage. In our case, it ostensibly offered the ego protection from being fully exposed and

then relinquished. We knew that in order to continue our undivided resolve to Love each other no matter what and no matter who might seem to come between us, we would need to accept higher guidance . . . again.

4. It became obvious to both of us that we still cherished some "specialness" between us, and that forgiveness was not complete. For example, I recognized that I still felt obligated to play the role of a good "wife;" however, this was in stark conflict with an inner calling that beckoned me onward into a new phase of life in which I could be free to travel and explore my own spiritual challenges.

5. I needed to surrender the remnants of pseudo-love that presented as my feeling responsible for being a good "wife." Being incredibly loyal, this posed an uncomfortable challenge. Nonetheless, I felt strongly to trust my Self in this decision to follow my inner calling, despite initially disappointing Tomas and other members of my family.

6. While our first lesson was that of forgiveness and working towards dismantling our special relationship, the next lesson for us was to learn that the "form" of a relationship meant nothing in truth. In fact, quite often it is the ego's addiction to the form of the relationship that excludes the "content," which is Love.

7. Once we had discussed our situation and connected with inner Guidance, we both felt strongly directed to go the next step. If Love was indestructible and eternal, then no-thing could threaten it. But did we truly believe this? That's when we took another leap of faith. It was time to surrender the *form* of our relationship.

8. We arrived at a point where the actual marriage, with all its false security, was limiting our opportunity to fall into the trusting arms of Love without opposite. Soon after, we divorced, but not to separate as the ego would like. We relinquished the marriage in order to *save* our relationship! Pretty weird stuff, huh? However, that was *our* guidance and I will say here that I don't recommend this for anyone else unless strongly guided by Holy Spirit. We felt as if we were pioneers at the time and we took our lessons to the extreme.

a. *"Whenever any form of special relationship tempts you to seek for love in ritual, remember love is content, and not form of any kind. The special relationship is a ritual of form, aimed at raising the form to take the place of God at the expense of content. There is no meaning in the form, and there will never be. The special relationship must be recognized for what it is; a senseless ritual in which strength is extracted from the death of God, and invested in His killer as the sign that form has triumphed over content, and love has lost its meaning."* T-16.V.12: 1-4

9. Despite relinquishing the marriage, Tomas and I remained close. In fact, we continued to join often at increasingly deeper levels, unrestrained by previous limitations. We communicated every day and eventually wrote a successful book together, Take Me to Truth; Undoing the Ego. We then went on to travel the world together sharing what we had learned.

10. In conclusion, the Love that Tomas and I experienced could not be threatened. We reached a place together that far transcended the world's idea of Love. Tomas was the first person to have ever truly *seen* me, and I was the first to have truly seen him. We cannot see and therefore Love another unless we see them as sinless and blameless.

11. We were mutual witnesses to each other's innocence. As was mentioned earlier, we come into this world unseen and grow up unrecognized. We manufacture a false self that believes it is unworthy at its core, yet spends its life seeking innocence and Love in impossible places. We crave to be seen, to be accepted, and to be cherished. We desire to know Love as our Self; yet, such Love is unattainable through the false self.

12. The profound nature of the Love that is extended between Tomas and me now is entirely unassailable. It reaches far past our notion of time and space and the limiting idea of bodies. Tomas left the body in December 2010, yet we remain in constant communion.

13. For me, Tomas saw past every ugly, shameful and shocking part of me; he forgave it all. In doing so, he mirrored to me the worthiness and innocence that lay at my core. He showed me that unlike every

relationship I had ever known in the dream of life, in this one, I did not have to earn Love. Through his unconditional acceptance of me, he demonstrated beyond any shadow of a doubt that I was indeed Love.

14. In our early practice of the *Course,* it was me who carried the false identity of victim and he of victimizer. Initially as a victim, it was me who seemed to do all the forgiving. Thus, it was in forgiving Tomas that I learned of my own innocence. The more I overlooked his errors, the more I opened to the Love inside me, in us as the one, shared and Holy Self. In relinquishing the special relationship, we each exchanged the gift of forgiveness, and through our healing we discovered our own true innocence.

15. Most of us seek love from an unrelinquished false self, so the experience we usually have is one where we "seek" love outside, while we simultaneously "deny" our unconscious guilt. This always results in projection and that's when we see conflict in our relationships – especially when it appears to be the other person's fault.

16. Accepting that all conflict originates within our own mind helps us to apply quantum forgiveness. In extending this, our unconscious guilt is undone. Tomas and I learned that it is true, that what we give, we receive. As we extended forgiveness, we received it. The result was the Love that we tried earlier to "get" from each other was clearly evident *within* us. Love was no longer something we sought. By giving it, we realized that we had it all along! Through *giving* it, we grew to appreciate that Love, as innocence, increases as it is shared. This concept is quite the opposite of the ego's interpretation of love.

17. Tomas and I discovered an eternal reflection of the incorruptible innocence that lay perfectly undisturbed by any seeming past. We learned so much from seeing and experiencing each other's needs as not apart from our own. We each learned to drop our defenses, our destructive values, our false images and insane expectations.

18. We grew to see the other without shame, blame or guilt in any way. And ... we kept our original vow: that *"no matter what and no matter who might seem to come between us, let us never abandon*

each other." We had finally learned that the only purpose for any relationship was not to get our ego needs met, but to wake-up from the dream of suffering. In overlooking error in each other, we came home to our Holy Self ... and for that, we remain eternally grateful to one another.

19. As I look back on that earlier transition from special to Holy Relationship, and reflect on all the trials, the times of what seemed like hopeless confusion and suffering, I feel such a tremendous peace. Now I know that Holy Spirit had been guiding us all the way, even though we didn't recognize it at the time. There was not one moment in which He was not present, holding us in His Love. Despite the fact that we did not recognize we were being carried much of the time, He used everything we originally made to separate and hurt ourselves, and He divinely transformed it all into Love.

B. Two Opposing Goals in Relationship

1. All the ego's past, its world and everything its body's senses seem to perceive are assessed through darkness. This false self has become comfortably numb in this severely restricted state. It defends specialness at all costs, terrified that Love will obliterate it. It seeks refuge in the darkness of special relationships and mistakes them for love. The darkness it depends on is really a general anesthesia to protect it from seeking and finding the light of Love.

2. Recall the ego is the state of deprivation by default. It can only see and experience that which it believes. And it is sustained by the belief in separation. It sees itself as bound by a destructible body which seems to have the power to imprison it. It is severely deprived and seeks its illusory completion via relationships and accomplishments. It robs others in relationships by trying to exchange the self it hates for the self it thinks it wants in another, not realizing it's the same illusory image, only in another form.

3. All relationship conflict arises from not knowing our true Identity and therefore not recognizing it in others. Every special relationship within all the dimensions of time is upheld by the identical foundation, an obsession with sin, guilt and fear. And it's this erroneous belief system that completely obscures the Love that we already have and are.

4. If we genuinely want a Holy Relationship, then we have a critical decision to make. The number one prerequisite is an honest desire to learn to see another as sinless, as guiltless. This is the desire to learn to forgive, to want to "close the gap" with another more than we want to judge them. How else will we ever behold the magnificence within unless we are willing to see it in another? For they are one and the same, our Holy Self, the Christ.

5. In relationships, either romantic or platonic, we can only recognize, extend, and receive conscious Love to the degree we are willing to see others and our self as guiltless and innocent. The ego only knows of special love which is really hate in disguise. It cannot give, receive, or even recognize Love. Our capacity to Love sincerely rests upon our willingness to engage in *authentic* communication, which naturally elevates guiltlessness over condemnation.

6. We can only know Love and forgiveness to the extent we have authentically relinquished the separate self-concept, along with its past, beliefs and values. Remember that all relationships are special (destructive) until we choose to have them repurposed to Holy Relationships with the Holy Spirit. And the reason for this is that the "self" in relationship with another "self" is unknowingly consumed and equally blinded by its own darkness.

7. When the relationship's goal starts shifting from special to Holy it can seem that while one partner feels great willingness to make the shift, the other often resists or clings to the old goal and structure of specialness. It appears then that each partner has separate goals.

8. I've learned that the *Seven Keys,* if practiced diligently when communicating, are a wonderful tool to undo the false self, its beliefs and its values. They undo the special relationship naturally and create the sacred space for the healed relationship. When applied, these principles undo our attachment to the past, along with its effects and lead us naturally to a persistent appreciation and focus on forgiveness.

9. It may be helpful at this point to share just what happened for me in the fourth year of a very significant relationship, to clarify an important point: *All forgiveness* is self-forgiveness.

10. In my own experience, as the one initiating the undoing of specialness – my partner at the time seemed threatened by this change. He (Lee) may have felt "protected" by the darkness of the false self and its idols, interpreting this shift toward the light (truth and authentic communication) as the threat of annihilation to the "self" he had worked so tirelessly to construct.

11. We had set up a common trap whereby one partner is on the "spiritual path" and the other is not the slightest bit interested. Not surprisingly, the relationship became increasingly difficult. The spiritual ego intensified and began to claim superiority. I wanted him to change, which is a no-no. I tried to convert him using the excuse that he needed saving, and the gap between us only increased as a result.

12. We reached an unbearable impasse and I was convinced that it was his fault. After all, I was on the "spiritual path" and he was not. I had not yet learned that he was my teacher and I was the student. Spiritual pride had blocked my awareness at the time.

13. Initially, through the ego, Lee triggered me tremendously. I perceived him as being overly critical of me. In those first few years I often felt judged and condemned. And it seemed to be in all the little things. My driving, the way I washed dishes, did laundry, cooked, ate, etc. There was this persistent nagging about how I just didn't do things "right." I felt belittled, unseen and unappreciated. To counter this pattern, I went into overdrive to try to please my partner's critical eye. However, the pressure to fit into another's expectations became too much to bear. I had unfortunately set up another very familiar and ancient ego trap. Thankfully, there was a grand turning point for me.

i. My Epiphany - There is No Lee

1. Let me begin by saying that Lee is an outstanding person, a truly wonderful soul. I now realize that he was sent to help me learn how to forgive myself for perhaps lifetimes of unforgiveness. My Love and gratitude for him have not changed to this day.

2. One day in August of 2004, the relationship conflict became intolerable for me. On top of that, I'd spent fifteen years with the

Course only to reach this point of feeling utterly hopeless and helpless. I was ready to give up entirely.

3. That fateful morning, I was home alone. I felt such crushing confusion that I just dropped to my knees sobbing uncontrollably. I called out to Holy Spirit with every fiber of my being, crying for help to end this conflict. Suddenly, from out of nowhere came a thundering Voice announcing this: *"There is no Lee!"*

4. I was shocked. The Voice was commanding and authoritative. It was unmistakable. *"There is no Lee!"* My God, what if the Voice was right, I thought. No Lee? That meant that all my conflict arose from within *my own* mind. Not just some of it … but *all* of it. So, I continued the dialogue in my mind, "Do you mean to say that I have been unknowingly using Lee to attack myself? You mean all of it?" The answer was a resounding, "Yes."

5. I will never forget that life-changing epiphany. Suddenly, my mind felt like it was swept clean of eons of false victimization. I was given a glimpse of Christ Vision that seemed to permeate many dimensions of time. A comprehensive collapse of time and suffering resounded in that one instant of recognition.

6. It was true. I was 100 percent responsible (without judgment) for every instance in which I had perceived myself as having been victimized. I chose it, and I did this to myself. No self-blame and no guilt. Just a quiet and impersonal glimpse of the ego thought system. But *that was not me*. The *Self* that witnessed the ego's choices was quite unperturbed by it all.

7. And in that precious Holy Instant I decided to return to my previously tumultuous relationship, only this time I returned without my projections – and with a heart full of forgiveness. I gladly recognized he was my Loving teacher and the bearer of illuminating life lessons. I now saw him completely differently. I felt gratitude for all the tests he offered me, for which I had earlier condemned him. And I saw my utter disrespect and irreverence at my prior attempts to try to change him. Ultimately, I reached a stage in my own development of trust where the path was clear for me to go from unlearning specialness into a phase of learning Holiness.

a. *"Understand that you do not respond to anything directly, but to your interpretation of it. Your interpretation thus becomes the justification for the response. That is why analyzing the motives of others is hazardous to you. If you decide that someone is really trying to attack you or desert you or enslave you, you will respond as if he had actually done so, having made his error real to you. To interpret error is to give it power, and having done this you will overlook truth." T-12.I,1*

8. In those first few years of our relationship, Lee had merely mirrored to me all the conflicting goals in the unconscious areas *in my own mind* that I was unaware of and had not forgiven. This was a hugely valuable classroom for me to practice self-forgiveness and I will be forever grateful for this chapter of my life.

9. When one *genuinely* initiates the undoing of specialness in relationship the entire relationship shifts. And this is exactly what occurred for us. We all share the one mind. Even though I never mentioned my breakthrough to Lee at the time, he was changed by it – because I had accepted the Atonement on our joint behalf. My goal was to see him as sinless and guiltless. The result was that we never had an argument again in the ten years which followed that miraculous epiphany.

10. Reflecting on that learning phase I see very clearly that I needed those years of being with a significant other who had no interest in the *Course* or the awakening it was pointing to. After that miraculous epiphany when Spirit bellowed out, "There is no Lee!" I consciously withdrew my projections onto him and asked to see him as he truly was, wholly sinless, guiltless and innocent. And as I mentioned before, a wonderful thing happened. We healed. There was harmony in our relationship. I had finally recognized that the man I had been living with, at the highest level, was none other than the Christ in disguise.

11. I felt that Lee shared in this healing as there is only one mind to heal although this experience did *not* undo his own choice to continue identifying as a false self with its beliefs and values. He really didn't change however *my* perception of him had. There was almost nothing

left in me for him to conflict with. That part of me had largely fallen away. Therefore, the outcome was peace between us.

12. Although there was harmony in our relationship, the teaching-learning balance between us eventually came to an end. When this happens the relationship often ends, which is what occurred for Lee and me. In this case the "form" of the relationship ended, yet the Love continues. That can never cease. Nothing real can be threatened.

13. Because I had experienced quantum forgiveness, we were both able to stay in a harmonious relationship together for ten more years. This was despite him choosing *not* to join with me in a mutual goal of Holy Relationship where he could willingly heal the ego's destructive beliefs and values along with its addiction to specialness.

14. He did not actively practice forgiveness and unknowingly, his love depended on certain conditions being met (as with most people who mistake specialness for Love). We did not share a *mutual* goal of Holy Relationship. I was privileged to apply forgiveness on my own so to speak.

15. In contrast, my relationship with Tomas was one in which we *both* made a commitment together to the Holy Relationship goal until he passed in 2010. Our vow was, "No matter what and no matter who might seem to come between us, let us never abandon each other." In other words, we desired to undo specialness (guilt) and at one point this required letting go of the marriage (form of relationship) in order to save the relationship (content as Love).

16. We were committed to changeless Love. We did not abandon each other. We stayed focused on the goal of Holiness no matter who or what seemed to come to threaten our union. We applied the *Seven Keys* and practiced forgiveness. This was not a union of bodies but of souls. Very simply, we agreed that *nothing* could threaten the Love we shared between us – *because* our Love was changeless. There was nothing either of us could do which could possibly threaten our relationship.

17. Alternatively, a relationship *can* indeed be threatened when one partner is eager to "close the gap" via authentic communication and forgiveness, while the other still values specialness, as was

the case with Lee and me. In this instance, while these two value separate goals, the one still snagged in specialness will unwittingly prioritize the ego's special love – a *changing* love based upon certain "conditions" being met. And if those conditions are threatened then love can be withdrawn.

18. The ego has a hierarchy of perceived threats and conditions that arise from fear and not from Love. In contrast to the Holy Relationship formed with Tomas, and because Lee was not yet willing to make Holiness his only goal, there were some factors that could well threaten the love he had for me. His love for me *could* change... and it did. Yet mine for him has not changed nor could it. My goal was and is Holiness and this is why my Love for him is changeless. His unrecognized goal was specialness and not changeless Love, which is why his "love" for me has changed.

19. The only reason we are not together today is that even after ten years of harmonious relating, it became clear that we were each pursuing separate goals. His beliefs in the false self, together with its values and purpose remained largely unchanged while mine had shifted considerably. I had eagerly embraced the undoing of my false identity and the crippling specialness beliefs and patterns that came with it. While this was my own chosen path and classroom, it was not Lee's.

20. After the specialness was undone between us there was very little left to hold us together in form because of our separate goals. I had thrown myself headlong into undoing the ego's false belief system while he was still heavily invested in preserving and defending it.

21. Unknowingly, he still desired specialness and had confused it with Love. Although we each had different goals in the relationship, this had worked for me up to a point because it had given me an abundance of rich opportunities to unmask and forgive my own denied and projected beliefs.

22. Our relationship had provided me many years in which to undo old specialness patterns and to learn to bridge the gap between the ego and the one shared Holy Self. Through it I learned to be more authentic and largely consistent. I had begun to embrace the wisdom of aligning my thoughts, feelings, speech and actions more

authentically, which greatly dissolved a lifetime of inner conflict.

23. I recognized that sacrifice is a block to Love and only the ego invests in sacrifice at the expense of Love. I learned how to follow and trust my Holy Self in the face of upsetting another ego – undoing an old and crippling pattern of people-pleasing. I also learned to value guiltlessness; to desire to see others as sinless, guiltless and innocent.

24. As my own trust advanced it became even more obvious that Lee and I were pursuing contrasting goals. While he has always been a truly remarkable and loyal partner, he remained quite immersed in the separate self and its beliefs and values. Our fundamental beliefs and values about our purpose, identity, the past, others, the body and the world were opposed, however the Love between us never changed. And I chalk that up to consistently forgiving myself each time it seemed his beliefs triggered me. I eventually reached a stage where the old triggers just fell away.

25. Over time, I learned to integrate applying the *Seven Keys* for myself. I see now that these principles, if practiced diligently, will undo the false self, its beliefs and values. They undo the dysfunctional special relationship dynamic and naturally create the sacred space for the healed and Holy Relationship if both people are willing to do the work together.

26. Practicing these principles goes hand in hand with forgiveness in the Holy Relationship where two (or more) join with Holy Spirit in the *same* goal – to undo their attraction to special love and to reveal the one Christ Mind and Heart.

27. When applied, these principles undo our attachment to the past, along with its effects. Yet they are not valued by those who still wish to keep their false identity, those who wish to protect and defend their false self-concept and the specialness it craves.

28. The issue which made it increasingly difficult to join in the one goal of Holy Relationship and deepen the relationship experience was that Lee was unwilling to practice the *Seven Keys* when communicating. This was his unseen desire to keep specialness going. Specialness was valued and the goal of Holiness was viewed as a threat.

29. In the following quotes from Jesus in the *Course* I have underlined important references which state that Holy Relationship involves two or more who willingly join in the Holy Spirit's goal of Holiness. This, by necessity, is an invitation by both people to undo the specialness dynamic in their relationship. And this was not the case in my relationship with Lee. I make this point because he was unwilling at the time to give his errors gladly to correction that we *both* could be happily healed as one.

a. *"A holy relationship, however newly born, must value holiness above all else."* ... *"Yet reason sees a holy relationship as what it is; a common state of mind, where both give errors gladly to correction, that both may happily be healed as one."* T-22.III.9:1,7

b. *"God's Teacher speaks to any two who join together for learning purposes. The relationship is holy because of that purpose, and God has promised to send His Spirit into any holy relationship."*...*"Those who would learn the same course share one interest and one goal."* M-2.5:3-4,7

c. *"This holy relationship has the power to heal all pain, regardless of its form. Neither you nor your brother alone can serve at all. Only in your joint will does healing lie. For here your healing is, and here will you accept Atonement. And in your healing is the Sonship healed [because] your will and your brother's are joined."* T-22.VI.4:4-8

d. *"Yet when two or more join together in searching for truth, the ego can no longer defend its lack of content. The fact of union tells them it is not true."* T-14.X.9:6-7

30. Here is a powerful question to be answered with radical self-honesty: "Do I want to be special in relationships?" Or, "Do I want to Love (to forgive)?" These are the only two choices we face in all relationships. We cannot have both specialness *and* Love because they are mutually exclusive, just as fear and Love are opposed. The presence of specialness is the exclusion of Love and vice versa.

31. Specialness is a corrupt replacement for Love. It's what we want when we're secretly afraid of true Love. Yet the false self is obsessed with its belief that specialness is love. Our special relating constitutes a significant portion of the unrecognized blocks we hold to the awareness of Love's presence.

32. In those who prefer to defend their ego and the laws of special relating there is a great fear of genuine emotional intimacy, accountability and radical self-honesty. When someone is resistant to giving their errors gladly to the Holy Spirit's correction... they do not value Holiness above all else. I will repeat this quote below because it's apt to be overlooked:

a. *"A holy relationship, however newly born, must value holiness above all else." ... "Yet reason sees a holy relationship as what it is; a common state of mind, where both give errors gladly to correction, that both may happily be healed as one." T-22.III.9:1,7*

33. When someone is fearful to give their errors to the Holy Spirit's correction it's almost impossible for them to drop their defenses, opinions, pride and the past. Their need to be "right" is often far more valuable to them than closing the gap with another; than forgiveness and allowing Love in.

34. They are often fearful of feeling genuine remorse and expressing it, let alone verbally admitting they were wrong. Unfortunately, the ego regards real strength (emotional vulnerability and defenselessness) as weakness, and it sees weakness (pride and the need to be right) as strength.

35. This highly valued distortion makes it quite difficult to deepen an emotional bond with another. And this is the kind of challenge I eventually faced with Lee. While I was willing and ready to take my learning and trust into deeper territory, he was not. Consequently, the form of the relationship came to an end because our teaching-learning balance had reached its limit.

36. Jesus refers to the three levels of relationship; or the three levels of learning where ultimately there is only one goal – to make the relationship Holy. In the following quote He speaks of the second level relationship which is the one Lee and I had engaged in.

a. *"Each teaching-learning situation is maximal in the sense that each person involved will learn the most that he can from the other person at that time. In this sense, and in this sense only, we can speak of levels of teaching. Using the term in this way, the second level of teaching is a more sustained relationship, in which, for a time, two people enter into a fairly intense teaching-learning situation and then appear to separate. As with the first level, these meetings are not accidental, nor is what appears to be the end of the relationship a real end. Again, each has learned the most he can at the time. Yet all who meet will someday meet again, for it is the destiny of all relationships to become holy."* M-3.4:1-6

37. As if healing the relationship weren't enough, I received another unexpected gift in that I recognized that this type of conflict had been a prominent dynamic of my childhood. My mother and I had unknowingly agreed to play out this painful pattern in my earlier years and it had stayed with me in all my adult relationships. Others appeared to judge and criticize me over and over. I would bend over backward to please them, only to resent them fiercely for it.

38. I'm so thankful this ego pattern finally became unbearable in my relationship with Lee. This pattern of feeling judged and criticized, followed by my appeasing and resentment, might have remained unhealed for many more years, or lifetimes. But because of the immense pain I finally *faced* I learned to locate its singular source in my own mind. In those first four years of our relationship, I could see that Lee simply mirrored to me my very own denied self-condemnation. He was showing me my own self-judgments and all the areas I had allowed the ego to micro-manage me. This insight was such a gift!

39. My mind was the only place in which this deep-seated pattern could be healed. I'd unwittingly used Lee to attack myself. Had I continued to blame him – or anything outside my mind – the misery would have remained intact. In that valuable experience I learned that there is only one ego and one Holy Self. If I am triggered by anything, then it is mine to heal. Period.

40. In truth, although he was not conscious of it at the time, Lee was waiting for me to recognize the miracle and to claim it on behalf of us both. My infinite and eternal Love and gratitude for him is deeply felt. I do trust the healing of this relationship was a precious gift to us both.

C. Nouk and Daniel – An Advanced Holy Relationship Teaching

i. From Nouk

1. If you have already read the section titled, "Nouk and Tomas – Transfer from Special to Holy Relationship," then you will know who Daniel is and how he was called into my life as a teacher and powerful catalyst for our miraculous transfer from special to Holy Relationship, with Tomas in 1990.

2. As I write this I'm looking back over a lengthy period of undoing my attraction to special relationships, experiencing the contrast period of transfer between special to Holy Relationship with Tomas, right through to the present, a truly miraculous Holy Relationship with Daniel more than twenty five years after we first met.

a. *"Time really, then, goes backward to an instant so ancient that it is beyond all memory, and past even the possibility of remembering. Yet because it is an instant that is relived again and again and still again, it seems to be now. And thus it is that pupil and teacher seem to come together in the present, finding each other as if they had not met before. The pupil comes at the right time to the right place. This is inevitable, because he made the right choice in that ancient instant which he now relives. So has the teacher, too, made an inevitable choice out of an ancient past. God's Will in everything but seems to take time in the working-out. What could delay the power of eternity?" M-2.4.*

b. *"When pupil and teacher come together, a teaching-learning situation begins. For the teacher is not really the one who does the teaching. God's Teacher speaks to any two who join together for learning purposes. The relationship is holy because of that purpose, and God has promised to send His Spirit into any holy relationship. In the teaching-learning situation, each one learns that giving and receiving are the same. The demarcations they have drawn between their roles, their minds, their bodies, their needs, their interests, and all the differences they thought separated them from one another, fade and grow dim and disappear. Those who would learn the same course share one interest and one goal. And thus he who was the learner becomes a teacher of God himself, for he has made the one decision that gave his teacher to him. He has seen in another person the same interests as his own." M-2.5.*

3. To assist in this life-changing transition from special to Holy Relationship I feel it helpful to give some real-life examples of how this transfer of trust can occur. For that reason, in this section Daniel will share his experience of when he met me (Nouk) and Tomas in 1990, including what he learned in the missing years from 1991 - 2015. Hopefully, at the conclusion of this section we will see a truly remarkable, Spirit-guided Holy Relationship tapestry emerge which spans a twenty-eight-year period in total.

ii. From Daniel

1. "I was the realtor called by Tomas to come sell their home in 1990 while Tomas was away in Papua New Guinea for three months. He arranged for me to visit Nouk and begin the sale process. However, I had no idea that this meeting with Nouk was going to change my life forever. I thought I knew the purpose of this appointment. I couldn't have been more wrong! I had just recently begun my study of *A Course in Miracles* but was not at all ready to be thrown into the deep end of its practical application and process.

2. That fateful day I first met Nouk, the scene and its ramifications burnt themselves into the very cells of my being. Nothing could have prepared me for this initiation. It was the beginning I later realized, of a most sacred "rite of passage."

3. I knocked on the front door; it opened. Yet when I looked into the eyes of the woman standing there greeting me, I was overcome with what could only be described as a cellular memory, an ancient past which felt strangely more "present" than anything my conscious mind had ever known. This "knowing" was more solid and more certain than anything I had ever experienced before. To say I was deeply affected by what transpired when I first met Nouk is an enormous understatement.

4. A divine reunion took place that day. This was a reunion that sprung open the long-buried, cage door which imprisoned my inner knowing and true purpose. It was as if I suddenly became lucid to awakening from a tremendously, laborious dream.

5. I really feel that I received a profound transmission in that one, eternal Holy Instant. But it wasn't until many years later that I found out why.

6. I remember feeling that Nouk's unwavering honesty, at all times, was such a delightful and refreshing attribute, and that has had a major influence on how I have communicated in all my relationships ever since.

7. Over the three months that Tomas was trekking in Papua New Guinea, Nouk and I met regularly. Because we were both so eager to learn to communicate authentically, we agreed to the mutual goal of overcoming a large portion of the ego's beliefs and values together. There was immense freedom and we experienced warp-speed growth in being able to speak and share so honestly.

8. By the time Tomas returned home, Nouk and I had forged a deep friendship which was plagued by an added complication – physical attraction (as Nouk shared in the story of her and Tomas earlier). Needless to say, because we'd agreed to be radically honest and keep no private thoughts, I was worried how Tomas would take the news.

9. My experience with meeting Tomas was profound. Upon his return, Nouk had shared openly with Tomas about our friendship, along with the physical attraction aspect. Even though this threatened the ego and his special relationship with Nouk, Tomas was truly amazing. I had never encountered anybody in my life before who was so utterly transparent, radically honest, and completely defenseless, and yet so damned confronting! He certainly didn't live by the world's rules.

10. As a result of this "quickening" we were all going through, Tomas made a commitment to study and live the *Course* and to mindfully shift from specialness to Holiness. He was dedicated to this roller coaster ride of undoing the false self's addiction to special love and he was adamant about including me in nearly all our frequent, emotionally charged conversations.

11. When I think back to that time, we were all groping in the dark; but because of our joint devotion to a truly common goal, Holy Spirit came through with many miracles and the three of us learned more in that year than we'd learned in a whole lifetime. Love is not special. Love is certainly not exclusive. Love is always 100 percent innocence – the complete absence of blame, guilt and fear. This is the gift I received during this hugely transformative time.

12. Through his authentically raw and uncompromising approach, Tomas showed me in contrast just how I had been hiding from my Holy Self in what I had mistaken as real life, including my accomplishments and relationships. He called me forward to step into my God-given, authentic and Holy Self. He called on me to show-up for myself.

13. During this particularly challenging phase, Tomas would often call on me in the late hours of the night, sometimes in distress, and other times in great sorrow. He trusted me. His "bare bones," emotional vulnerability and defenselessness touched me to my core. I was deeply affected, and I would cry with him during these times.

14. He was teaching me crucial lessons in genuine honesty, accountability, and the infinite power of defenselessness. In his astounding honesty he was a living demonstration of the indestructible nature of the changeless Love he shared with Nouk. I'd never seen that before. It opened my heart and eyes to a whole new level of Love; one that I felt the world had never known before.

15. I wanted that – a changeless, whole and inclusive Love. A Love that was not of this world. But was I ready?

16. Tomas was the impetus of a pivotal, life-changing, Holy Instant in my life. This moment stood alone, apart from time and space. Through Tomas, the Eyes of God peered unflinchingly into mine. The Voice for God spoke to me directly. Late one night in the midst of this tumultuous time with Tomas, God's Voice boomed through Tomas to me, He roared, "Are you the Son of God!?" "Well, are you!?"

17. Daniel did not answer…but the Son of God did. Streaming through tears from the depths of my Soul came the unequivocal answer: "Yes, I AM the Son of God!" This transmission pierced my Soul and was to stay with me, urging me onward for what would be the next twenty-five years.

18. Through Tomas, the Holy Spirit called me forward, to step into my divine purpose and role and demonstrated what it was like to be completely uncompromising. What a great teacher Tomas was! What he taught me during this period went on with me to form the core values which I still practice today.

19. We had some pretty big lessons to learn back then. For example, in a triangle such as what Nouk, Tomas and I had, there may have been a temptation for Nouk to leave Tomas and join me in a separate, "special" romantic union. We already recognized, fortunately, that it would be special love *again* which was exclusive (separating). We discussed this and joined together asking Holy Spirit to guide us through the confusion of special love toward Holy Love. Jesus shared some extremely helpful advice *especially for Nouk and Tomas* which we all took literally:

a. *"This is the time for [faith.] You let this goal be set for you. That was an act of faith. Do not abandon faith, now that the rewards of faith are being introduced. If you believed the Holy Spirit was there to accept the relationship, why would you now not still believe that He is there to purify what He has taken under His guidance? Have faith in your brother in what but seems to be a trying time. The goal [is] set. And your relationship has sanity as its purpose. For now you find yourself in an insane relationship, recognized as such in the light of its goal."*

"Now the ego counsels thus; substitute for this another relationship to which your former goal was quite appropriate. You can escape from your distress only by getting rid of your brother. You need not part entirely if you choose not to do so.

But you must exclude major areas of fantasy from your brother, to save your sanity. [Hear not this now!] Have faith in Him Who answered you. He heard. Has He not been very explicit in His answer? You are not now wholly insane. Can you deny that He has given you a most explicit statement? Now He asks for faith a little longer, even in bewilderment. For this will go, and you will see the justification for your faith emerge, to bring you shining conviction. Abandon Him not now, nor your brother. This relationship has been reborn as holy." T-17.V.6,7.

20. Nouk went to great lengths to share with both Tomas and I Jesus' specific instructions on the temptations during the transfer from special to Holy Relationships. In those days, we each had the green paperback version of the *Course* and Nouk had made special notes on a sheet of paper of all the page numbers for me to study on the pitfalls of special love. It was a huge eye-opener to say the least. I kept that piece of paper for the next twenty-five years. The Healed Relationship in Chapter 17, section five, was one that I read and reread countless times.

21. Nouk and Tomas were all-in with the *Course* and the uncompromising journey it demanded.

22. I remember the day came when Nouk and I met for coffee to talk about what was required to continue our relationship. It was all – or nothing. I remember that part. What did Nouk mean by *all or nothing?*

23. Now, after years of learning and living Jesus' deeper message in the *Course*, I am finally able to articulate the *essence* of that request from almost twenty-eight years ago. Did I, Daniel, have the same mutual goal of Holy Relationship? And was I willing to engage in uncompromising communication *(The Seven Key Principles of Authentic Relating)* and forgiveness in *all* my relationships? Was I willing to be 100 percent honest with my (then) wife, who was not the slightest bit interested in this path? In other words, did I share the same common purpose with Nouk?

24. Was I willing to go all the way with her on this journey? Boy that was a tough one. We shared deeply and honestly; we cried together and still the question was begging for me to answer.

25. Sadly, the answer was "no." It seemed there was too much to lose at the time.

26. This was the hardest and saddest decision I ever had to make. I could see the heart-retching disappointment in her eyes. I said goodbye to my best friend, or to be more specific, the most beloved savior I had ever known in this lifetime. Ah, the fear of Love (God) had raised its ugly head. But even more heartbreaking was that I made a deliberate choice to go back into the dream to pursue the false self's fantasies.

27. I expended myself on special relationships, business ventures, deals, extramarital affairs, financial challenges and conflict. I threw myself into the ego's world which mirrored back to me such a level of extreme contrast that I finally admitted that I had had enough of its inevitable pain and suffering.

28. Even though I lost touch with Nouk for many years to come, I recognize that those two plus decades of re-immersion into the ego's dream idols were crucial in terms of exhausting the ego's addiction to seeking completion externally. This was a necessary period of undoing the false self along with its body identity, through maxing out on meaningless goals, beliefs and values, to the point of hitting the proverbial wall. This is why no mistakes are wasted when we give them all to Holy Spirit, so He can divinely correct and repurpose them into miracles.

29. Just to be clear, the decades we spent apart and completely out of touch had absolutely no impact on the original transmission that we had received together, the beginning of a truly Holy Relationship. This transmission stayed with me, running strongly during all those years apart, and was always in the back of my mind. Where is Nouk, my miracle-buddy?

30. It's almost as if I knew deep down that I just had to exhaust the ego's values and get them out of my system. Underneath it all I was praying with all my heart that the opportunity to reunite with Nouk would come once again.

31. Looking back, I recognize that first year with Nouk was such a profound agent of healing for me. It left me with a cellular imprint which would stay with me for the next twenty-five years. I think

the greatest impact came from her courage and radical honesty, two uncompromisingly divine qualities that completely threaten the false self and its dishonest, special relationships. Even though I was deeply affected, it took me years before I was able to embody and consistently implement these qualities for myself.

32. Although Nouk was far more authentic and uncompromising than I was in those early days, I knew deep in my heart that I would arrive at that same uncompromising way of being when my willingness had matured. I held the faith that we would one day meet up again, and finally *fulfill* what I had felt was an ancient agreement for a Holy Relationship.

33. What a paradox. A quarter of a century in time went by, but in essence it was just a split second. I carried that cellular imprint with me. A spark had been lit deep inside. And nothing could put it out. Sure, the many distractions I chose to experience over those spent years seemed to numb my awareness of it at times. Nevertheless, that spark continued to grow. There was no denying it. Thank God for that spark! It was always reminding me of what had taken place in 1990… it played an important part in how my time apart from Nouk was divinely repurposed.

34. Holy Spirit uses all our forays into ego land, all our seeming mistakes, and divinely repurposes them *if we let Him*. I now realize that *nothing* was wasted. And there is no guilt and there are no regrets. Only when we're ready, do we agree to commit fully to the path of Holy Relationship. Until then we will dabble in *both* worlds, still looking for our completion through the body, special relationships and the illusory world.

iii. The Reunion

1. Through a series of miraculous events in 2014 I finally located Nouk. No longer living in Australia, she had moved to New Mexico, USA. On November 11th I contacted her via email through her website. Five days later she responded and typically, she asked me where I was "at" in life. Specifically, she asked if I were finally willing to do whatever it would take to complete this sacred purpose of awakening from the ego dream. Talk about cutting straight to the chase!

2. I declared that I was wholly willing and explained in detail just *why* I was happily eager and willing. And that... was that! Twenty-five years apart just evaporated in one glorious Holy Instant.

3. With me living and working in Queensland, Australia, and Nouk in the USA, we decided to communicate daily via Skype or phone. After all, we had a lot of catching up to do. Having both asked Jesus to work with and guide us, we made a choice to use the next few months apart as a purification and divine aligning process. We practiced the *Seven Keys* together and took our joint devotion to a very deep level.

4. After three months of this we decided to meet up in person. Nouk flew over to meet me in Australia and we spent three magical, miracle-filled weeks together, strengthening our Holy Relationship. It was clearly obvious by now that we shared with Holy Spirit, the one truly common purpose necessary to make the relationship Holy – forgiveness.

5. Just after we had reunited, I experienced a powerful vision in which Jesus very gently and lovingly offered me Nouk's foot on a silver pillow. Then, while wide awake, the room was suddenly flooded with a brilliant, golden light. Grace permeated every corner of my awareness as I gazed upon her elegant foot. A long silence followed. Tears welled up from deep inside me; I sensed that I was about to be invited to commit to something that may have seemed impossible. Then, He asked me, "Are you content with just this foot of Nouk's? If you never experience making love through the body with Nouk, do you still commit to loving her regardless?"

6. I broke down completely. A resounding answer surged through me and drowned all meaningless fears. "Yes!" This was an exceedingly strong visual and emotional experience, while at the same time a divine transmission. The impact of this had me in uncontrollable tears for over an hour. I knew this was no ordinary message. It was a sign of a deeper agreement, one which was to come to pass soon after.

7. I had no previous experience of what was to come in our relationship. I really thought that I knew what a Loving relationship *was*. At least in this relationship with Nouk, I was

certainly not prepared for the many necessary adjustments required; but I was *willing*. And this is all the Holy Spirit needed.

8. The particular *form* of Holy Relationship is *unique* to those involved. However, regarding the *content*, the Holy Relationship *always* evolves as mutual innocence is increasingly cherished above all else.

iv. **Mighty Companions**

1. The relationship heals to the degree we are willing to advance our trust, and that eventually necessitates the undoing of our belief in the body as our identity. While we still believe we are the body and not Spirit, the ego will use it for pride, pleasure and attack, resulting in a plethora of suffering. The body along with its appetites must ultimately be given over to Holy Spirit to be divinely repurposed once we're ready and willing.

2. However, this is a conscious, organic process which is happily undertaken without a sense of *sacrifice*. It cannot occur until we are naturally eager to graduate from the body's appetites, especially the sexual appetite. Note: See the three phases of healing the sexual appetite in chapter IV, "Sex and TransOrgasmic Union."

3. Because we both consented to healing the sexual appetite, we initially went through the second phase which Nouk terms as "sex to heal." Some conscious couples may spend much of their adult life in this phase of healing, but there is still a further phase which is more uncommon, which Nouk calls "divine androgyny;" an advanced state for those who are eager to heal and transcend the sexual appetite altogether and for all time.

4. Once Nouk and I got together in physical form we were guided to enter a long quarantine period, largely sheltered from the outside world. After all, this was an inner time. This three-year time frame gave us the space to go within deeply and listen to guidance from Jesus.

5. Our relationship's form probably looks quite a bit different from the world's idea of romantic relationship. It's certainly not what the ego had in mind that's for sure! It took me a while to unhook from my deeply entrenched beliefs about what a Holy union would look

like. Having been quite a romantic kind of guy in the past, I was in for a shock with Nouk!

6. While we now live together, we each sleep in our own separate beds and bedrooms, and we each have our own sacred space. This is vitally important in order for us to do our own work at our own pace, as Spirit guides us.

7. Nouk is the most uncompromising person I know. And so am I; more so now than ever before. Together we both underwent a huge period of undoing which was powerfully accelerated due to our joint common purpose with Holy Spirit. This is what happens when two people unite in one truly common goal of Holy Relationship.

8. Both of us have achieved a high degree of undoing many remaining aspects of the false self. For me, surrendering the body appetite for sexual pleasure has been monumental. This particular appetite, as I found out later, represented the very tap root of the false self's obsession with the body as "my-self." This one desire was the deepest, most hypnotic and magnetic of all… pulling me back into the body identity over and over.

9. Thankfully, this appetite no longer misleads me into temptation because something far more divine has come to take its place.

10. Now that I know better than to confuse my identity with a body and its seeming senses and appetites, I fully understand that the body, a wholly neutral thing, cannot betray us. A mind cannot attack because there is only one Mind in truth. But a mind that confuses itself with a body can indeed betray. All special relationships are based on this. And that is why special love seems to shift, change or even end.

   a. *"You cannot perpetuate an illusion about another without perpetuating it about yourself. There is no way out of this, because it is impossible to fragment the mind. To fragment is to break into pieces, and mind cannot attack or be attacked."* T-7.VIII.4:1-3

11. Nouk and I are having daily experiences that reveal that we are one Mind. So, we recognize and celebrate our oneness, knowing the infinite gratitude we have for each other cannot ever be betrayed by the illusion of a body. In a special relationship this is reversed.

We're so hypnotized by seeing each other as separate bodies; we also think we're further divided as distinctly different minds – and "private" minds at that.

12. I have finally found a deep inner peace resting in the knowing that we are not bodies. I know now that I don't need sexual intimacy or sexual release to feel a deep sense of union with Nouk and myself. That seductive lure just doesn't have the upper hand anymore. There is no more neediness. The persistent neediness and selfish agendas of the sexual appetite severely limit our ability to fully open to Love. Once that sexual neediness fell away for me, with Jesus' help, I was able to see and feel the magnificent Love and innocence that was hidden behind it.

13. If I see Nouk as a body, I cannot connect with her via the heart or soul. It may sound completely counter intuitive to the ego, but if I see and desire her *as* a body, then I'm substituting her body (and mine) in place of our infinitely higher union as one Mind and one heart.

14. Today, we have shifted into spontaneous experiences whereby Nouk and I join in complete presence, entirely lucid, via deeply tender, heart transmissions. I simply bring her into my heart in the present moment and feel into our divine purpose of Love without opposite. Often, both Nouk and I erupt into tears of awe-inspiring gratitude, where the body itself vanishes, just as darkness disappears instantly when we switch on the light.

15. I am now finally able to see and feel what and who Nouk really is; she is my divine mirror in life; literally my savior as Jesus tells us in the *Course*. And in seeing her as she *is,* I see my Self. I can't tell you how immensely liberating that is. In this Holy Instant with more Love and respect than I have ever felt present in my life, I am now wholly filled with peace, joy and complete harmony in all things, inside and out. Thank God the body and its agendas are not limiting my divine experience any longer. Each moment I see and feel how divine this gift of joining truly is, it brings me to tears.

16. I know our function together has been repurposed and divinely reinterpreted. I know we have a relationship guided by Holy Spirit, and one that cannot be threatened by anyone or anything. Therefore, our only function is to show up and see each other as completely

blameless and guiltless. How can someone who has agreed to join me in this, the most Holy purpose on earth, possibly be guilty or do any wrong?

a. *"Communication must have been restored to those who join, for this they could not do through bodies. What, then, has joined them? Reason will tell you that they must have seen each other through a vision not of the body, and communicated in a language the body does not speak. Nor could it be a fearful sight or sound that drew them gently into one. Rather, in each the other saw a perfect shelter where his Self could be reborn in safety and in peace."* T-22.I.9:4-8

17. Through turning everything over to Holy Spirit, including the body, I've learned that everything is given to us. In other words, all needs are met by Him. As I look back before our Holy Relationship, most of my life was spent being distracted by seeking outwardly. I loved the chase so to speak; feeling a fleeting sense of accomplishment when I achieved my goal or bought a particular material object of desire. But it never lasted. Now, in place of that persistent sense of (imagined) lack with its equally debilitating addiction of trying to solve that lack apart from Holy Spirit, I'm in total gratitude. What happened?

18. I now realize with immense joy that I already have everything! I literally don't *need* anything any longer. There is no sense of need. Imagine that. And because I don't spend my life needing stuff anymore, *I have everything*. I rest deeply in gratitude for the smallest of things these days, like my first inward breath of the crisp dawn air on a frosty morning. If I'm not in a state of gratitude then nothing real is happening, because I've abandoned my Holy Self. That's why being thankful in each moment *is* my prayer. All of creation shimmers in that experience because *I am there*, because I am totally here and now showing up in a prayer of gratitude for all I have and all I am.

19. The most transformative experiences that Nouk and I are currently having are these extraordinary Holy Instants which totally eclipse the body, its senses, and the belief that we are two separate beings. It is absolutely out of this world – inexplicable. These Soul fusing

moments unequivocally defy the illusion of separation, time and bodies. They are immediate windows into eternity which instantly restore our memory that we're wholly innocent and wholly worthy. In that all-encompassing innocence, all our fears and self-doubts dissolve and there is an infinite knowing of safety and Love.

20. I believe the reason we're dwelling in these grace-filled moments more and more is because of the undivided commitment we've made, i.e. above all else, we want to see each other as we really are – blameless, guiltless and innocent. We want to see each other as God created us, without the ego's distortions; and this can't happen if we see each other as bodies and entertain special agendas between us.

21. Jesus says that when we accept the Atonement for our self we accept it for our brother. Nouk and I know that we can't possibly blame our self or each other – and still perceive each other as innocent. We share the same Mind and this is becoming far more real and dependable than the deluded idea that we're separate bodies with separate minds and private thoughts.

   a. *"Correction cannot be accepted or refused by you without your brother. Sin would maintain it can. Yet reason tells you that you cannot see your brother or yourself as sinful and still perceive the other innocent. Who looks upon himself as guilty and sees a sinless world? ... "If you and your brother are joined, how could it be that you have private thoughts? And how could thoughts that enter into what but seems like yours alone have no effect at all on what [is] yours? If minds are joined, this is impossible." T-21.VI.2:1-4,8-10*

22. In closing, I attribute the quickening of our healing to one very practical tool in particular, which Nouk and I use consistently; *The Seven Key Principles of Authentic Relating*. We are devoted to this system of relating because it completely revolutionizes the way we are conditioned to communicate in this world (through fear). Using this system of communication with each other neutralizes the false self over time.

23. Anything that is inauthentic must be brought to the light of truth when we use this method of communication. Destructive and often hidden beliefs, values and patterns must be unearthed, seen, and

given to Holy Spirit to be returned to us as miracles, when we use the Seven Keys to communicate.

24. Applying these principles to all our communications eventually proves without question that we're not separate bodies with different and private minds. We're all one! We literally share one Mind and that is our Holy Self. There is no longer any need to hide or defend when we realize the Christ is the one shared Self we are. What freedom!

25. In February 2016, Nouk and I were guided by Jesus to initiate a global, online Total Transformation Course, commonly referred to as the "TTC." It started as a one year course but has since grown into a large and loving global spiritual community, devoted to the goal of Holy Relationships.

26. The TTC (with its one-year online course) is still growing with many new facilitators, or hosts. This family has experienced so many miracles together because through the *TTC* we learn that it's not only safe to be real, transparent and defenseless, but that it's literally the invitation to know our Self as the Christ!

27. Practicing the *Seven Keys* allows us to show up for our Self. In finally showing up for our Self, we discover true freedom including peace, joy, abundance and above all, union. *(End of Daniel's writing.)*

II. SPIRITUAL AWAKENING - STEPPING ACROSS THE THRESHOLD

1. I'm going to attempt to put into words my own recent leap. An irrevocable awakening has occurred. This is really quite funny because it happened *without me.* I had no idea what had occurred at the time. Let me explain.

2. I've had many epiphanies and awakenings over the past few decades, but they came and then over time they faded and disappeared. I would then find my mind sliding back into believing the many seductive temptations of fear, doubt and self-loathing.

Disappointment, disillusionment, and at times even depression would come to haunt me. The underlying message the false self deduced was that I just couldn't make it. Why? Because the "me" identity was the one still trying to awaken. Over thirty years the false self had evolved magnificently. It had become an ace spiritual student and seeker. But the one thing I didn't know back then was that this self, no matter how spiritual it appears to become, can never awaken.

3.   Many of us on the spiritual awakening path believe that the self embarks on its journey and at some point, it awakens. The one who begins the spiritual journey, studying the text, meditating, and practicing the lessons, is the ego. It fantasizes about becoming a better self, a more spiritualized self, a happier self, perhaps even teaching while making its body and world a better dream. It would never commence the transfer of trust from fear to Love if it knew that in this transfer "it" would disappear.

4.   This body-self concept *is* fear. Its inception as fear emerged *from* fear. While the mind still values a private mind and body, it will also value fear. Furthermore, as fear, it will interpret Love as a threat.

5.   In the *Course* Jesus speaks about "the bridge to the Real World." This seems to be a journey of awakening that we undertake. In a way, we make a transition across the bridge in every Holy Instant. The bridge symbol is used as a vehicle by which we appear to migrate from fear to Love, from ego to Holy Self, from split mind to unified Mind. It may appear to be a spiritual metamorphosis.

6.   But in the long journey of the transfer of trust from fear to Love, what I have experienced is that the self who gingerly steps onto that spiritual bridge taking its first few feeble steps, is not the one that steps off the bridge on the other side. While some people may call this awakening, I think a more truthful term might be "replacement." The illusory self-concept as a private mind and separate body ceases to exist. The choice to believe in it is divinely *replaced* by what was always there – as unified Mind – although unrecognized because our earlier choice for separation had obscured it from awareness.

7.   The illusory fear-driven self does not survive the bridge's transition. Instead, it is blazed away by the light of Love and innocence.

8. My experience reveals that during this seeming transition there is most definitely a period of purification. Jesus describes the six stages of this awakening transition as the "development of trust" (*Manual for Teachers* in the *Course*). He also describes the overarching three steps of transition required in *"The Lessons of the Holy Spirit,"* in Chapter Six of the *Course*.

9. We are Love and nothing *but* Love! Some of us may be able to identify with the first part of this idea, "I am Love." However, this means absolutely nothing if we're not vigilantly attuned to applying the second part of the sentence, "I am nothing *but* Love." This part is the most important because through forgiving everyone, and every thought or judgment that is not Love, we come to know without a shadow of a doubt that we *are* Love.

Perfect
Love

Shades of Gray

Fear

As Trust advances
even the slightest contrast
becomes intolerable.

We make an unequivocal decision
to stay in the WHITE BOX,
to stay 100% authentic and present.

FEAR

Perfect
Love

100%

100%

SPLIT MIND
Fear AND Love
are each totally
mutually exclusive.

They cannot coexist
in awareness
at the same time.

We see one OR the other.

© 2020 The End of Death - Nouk Sanchez

A. Shades of Gray Diagram

Please see diagram on page 692 , which is discussed in this next section, *B. "The Transition as Shades of Gray"*

B. The Transition as Shades of Gray

1. We will use some images here. We'll use a spectrum that depicts our transfer of trust as awakening from 100 percent imagined fear as the separation, all the way through to 100 percent perfect Love. In the diagram, fear is represented by a solid black box on the far left. And on the far right is perfect Love as a solid white box. In between we have many shades of gray. These represent the varied idols and vacillations we still value as we transition this journey, with the body itself being the top idol.

2. Using it for pleasure, pain, conflict, sickness or death reveals that we still believe the imaginary body is more powerful than our mind that made it, and therefore we must still value the body, whether good or bad. We do not yet *know* that *the body is nothing* in our experience. It is still *"something,"* being used by the split mind to manifest that the separation has indeed occurred.

3. No judgment here, but this self-attack must be *recognized* with Holy Spirit and *given over* to the Atonement if we want to heal. Only when the body is free of all signs of attack, self-directed or otherwise, can it be *known* as the nothingness it really is. In truth, the body is purely a projected image or reflection of the current state of the mind.

4. Referring again to the diagram, when we begin the spiritual journey we seem to be okay playing in the shades of gray for a long time, perhaps still valuing dream idols such as special relationships and the body. We will believe in and react to the ego-body's illusory sensory perception and revel in its sensual appetites, etc. We may even try to spiritualize the body during this transition. While there remains see-sawing between the gray areas and we still hold out hope that through our own "will" we can control our body, relationships and life (independent of God), we will delay the inevitable stage of recognizing the unbearable contrast between illusion and truth, between fear and Love, between guilt and incorruptible innocence.

5. In the gray zones we continue to compartmentalize our relationships, the body, our life, and the seeming world as we see them through the body's sensory perception, keeping certain areas private and apart from Holy Spirit. Thus, we communicate with our self and others inauthentically. Because we value this private compartmentalizing, we unwittingly value *miscommunication* which leads to projection of conflict, scarcity, pain and illness.

6. Playing within the shades of gray, we think we know our own best interests. We don't realize that we cannot safely discern what will bring us happiness, pleasure or pain. The false self's concept of love is often riddled with fear, obligation, pain, conflict, blame, guilt, confusion, doubt and loss. We honestly do not know what undivided Love *is*. Because we still remain heavily body-identified, we often choose pain, mistaking it for happiness.

7. Our experience in these gray zones provides the necessary "contrast learning" generally required so that we eventually reach a point where the contrast between fear and Love becomes so stark as to be literally intolerable (see the lower two boxes in the diagram). The gray zones are no longer an option and we are faced with making an unequivocal choice. Jesus says it well here: *"The third step, then, is a statement of what you want to believe, and entails a willingness to relinquish everything else." T-6.V.C.10:1*

8. For me, I recognized that while the gray zones appeared to be composed of differing *degrees* of fear, any shade of gray might as well be *100 percent fear*. Fear *and* Love are each mutually exclusive, irreconcilable thought systems. Fear does not exist. But we cannot know and therefore demonstrate this while we believe that fear, along with its seeming effects, is real.

9. This experience took me to the two opposed boxes in the lower part of the diagram. With the gray zones gone, and no more wiggle room, glaring back at me was the unmasked, stark raving insanity of fear – *or* – the glorious, breathtaking presence of Love, peace and infinite joy. Then I knew there was *no choice* to be made. This must be the "choiceless choice." At this point there was a divine recognition that only changeless, perfect Love exists. I AM nothing

but this. And so are you. Temptation to fear may still arise but I am no longer hooked by it.

10. At this point too, it was recognized that all fear, irrespective of its form and severity, is solely the *fear of Love.*

   a. *"This lesson is unequivocal in that it teaches there must be no exceptions, although it does not deny that the temptation to make exceptions will occur. Here, then, your consistency is called on despite chaos. Yet chaos and consistency cannot coexist for long, since they are mutually exclusive. As long as you must be vigilant against anything, however, you are not recognizing this mutual exclusiveness, and still believe that you can choose either one. By teaching [what] to choose, the Holy Spirit will ultimately teach you that you need not choose at all. This will finally liberate your mind from choice, and direct it towards creation within the Kingdom." T-6.V.4:5-10*

11. Here, at the final contrast between fear and Love, we can make an unequivocal choice for Love and nothing *but* Love. I guess this could be called step three in the *Course's "The Lessons of the Holy Spirit,"* where we practice being vigilant only for God and His Kingdom. By the way, we *are* His Kingdom, so we're learning to be vigilant *against* anything that is not the changeless innocence and Love that we all are, behind the illusory self and its body. Here we learn and practice "true denial." Jesus speaks of this here:

   a. *"You can do anything I ask. I have asked you to perform miracles, and have made it clear that miracles are natural, corrective, healing and universal. There is nothing they cannot do, but they cannot be performed in the Spirit of doubt or fear. When you are afraid of anything, you are acknowledging its power to hurt you. Remember that where your heart is, there is your treasure also. You believe in what you value. If you are afraid, you are valuing wrongly. Your understanding will then inevitably value wrongly, and by endowing all thoughts with equal power will inevitably destroy peace. That is why the Bible speaks of "the peace of God which passeth understanding." This peace is totally*

*incapable of being shaken by errors of any kind. It denies
the ability of anything not of God to affect you. This is the
proper use of denial. It is not used to hide anything, but to
correct error. It brings all error into the light, and since error
and darkness are the same, it corrects error automatically."*

*"True denial is a powerful protective device. You can and
should deny any belief that error can hurt you. This kind of
denial is not a concealment but a correction. Your right mind
depends on it." T-2.II.1,2:1-4*

12. Any triggers are seen as the valuable gifts they actually are.
When recognized correctly, they always serve the one extraordinary
purpose of exposing any remaining hidden unforgiveness in our
mind so it can be healed instantly. And for these healings we are
eternally grateful. As we accept the Atonement we stay in the light.
We learn to anticipate only the miracle behind all appearances of
fear, pain and suffering. In fact, we come to rejoice in the *certainty*
of the miracle, even in the face of seeming fear. By expecting *only*
the light behind each appearance of darkness, we invoke it. This is
God's Will.

   a. *"There is no strain in doing God's Will as soon as you
   recognize that it is also your own." T-2.VI.6:4*

13. We joyfully recognize that our will and God's Will are one and
the same. Oh what a relief!

   a. *"Miracles are in accord with the Will of God, Whose Will
   you do not know because you are confused about what [you]
   will. This means that you are confused about what you are. If
   you are God's Will and do not accept His Will, you are denying
   joy. The miracle is therefore a lesson in what joy is. Being a
   lesson in sharing it is a lesson in love, which [is] joy. Every
   miracle is thus a lesson in truth, and by offering truth you are
   learning the difference between pain and joy." T-7.X.8.*

   b. *"You are afraid to know God's Will, because you believe it
   is not yours. This belief is your whole sickness and your whole
   fear. Every symptom of sickness and fear arises here, because*

this is the belief that makes you [want] not to know. Believing this you hide in darkness, denying that the light is in you."
T-11.I.10:3-6

14. Everyone's experience of awakening in the dream is highly individualized. My experience of "divine replacement" occurred in Israel in 2019. This really defies explanation. There are literally no words to describe it really because it is a quantum mind healing and cannot possibly be described or understood in a linear way. I can only say that the ramifications of this awakening feel somewhat like a nuclear blast. Nothing at all is as it was before this. I cannot express adequately in words the impact of this shift, but I can share just a little here that may be helpful.

15. But before I do share this experience of the self being divinely replaced by the Self, I am reminded of a particular passage in the *Course*. The false self is terrified of the truth that beams relentlessly from this powerful statement following below. The recovery of our whole Mind and the uninterrupted joy it knows depends on welcoming this statement wholly. The false self and the Holy Self cannot coexist. One must eventually go:

a. *"This is a crucial period in this course, for here the separation of you and the ego must be made complete."* ... *"Now must you choose between yourself and an illusion of yourself. Not both, but one. There is no point in trying to avoid this one decision. It must be made. Faith and belief can fall to either side, but reason tells you misery lies only on one side and joy upon the other."* ... *"There is no part of Heaven you can take and weave into illusions. Nor is there one illusion you can enter Heaven with."* T-22.II.6:1,6-10,8:1-2

16. The location was in Old Jerusalem. The circumstances were of great significance to me; however it doesn't feel right to go into detail about this here. At the perfect point in time, time itself vanished and I found my awareness in the undivided presence of God. It was precipitated by an exceedingly high voltage, blinding light that torched away all remnants of personal will, leaving it in ashes. An experience of incomprehensible light illuminated the Mind. In

this, the body's eyes were rendered blind and I could not lift my eyes upward. They were fixed, cast downward, and incapacitated so that I would open to the Mind's inner Vision instead. The physical blindness lasted a few hours and it was around twenty-four hours before I could open and lift my eyes up again.

17. It took two months after this "replacement" to learn to integrate back into the seeming body and life. This may seem strange, but at the time of this profound awakening I did not know what it was. As I said in my opening paragraph, it happened *without me*. No doubt it will continue to unpack itself as more levels of awakening flood in.

18. I was literally struck dumb and blind. So, there was an adjustment period following it. There are some common symptoms of this integration period occurring still. And one of them is disorientation, particularly performing mundane duties like thinking, cooking, driving and grocery shopping, etc. I need help with these for a while.

19. The mind does not tolerate superficial or meaningless conversations or activities any longer. Alongside of this there is a rapidly growing conviction in the unopposed power of the miracle to heal everything, all phenomena that the illusion of fear made. In addition, there is a heightened knowing now that our one, shared Mind is not at all compartmentalized as it seems. Thus, in this open and unified Mind, there is a natural ability to see and to heal what I could not access before from the personal mind. Some might say this promotes miraculous healing and psychic abilities. But I would say that these are "shared gifts" we all have, although while we negate them via the false self we will not claim or extend them.

20. Looking back, before this awakening, at my time journeying through those gray zones, the following paragraph from Jesus was so precious to me. The undeniable truth in it which I trusted, was largely responsible for helping me to keep aligned with truth, as I felt I was groping in the dark so much of the time along the journey:

a. *"When you unite with me you are uniting without the ego, because I have renounced the ego in myself and therefore cannot unite with yours. Our union is therefore the way to renounce the ego in you. The truth in both of us is beyond the ego. Our success in transcending the ego is guaranteed by*

God, and I share this confidence for both of us and all of us. I bring God's peace back to all His children because I received it of Him for us all. Nothing can prevail against our united wills because nothing can prevail against God's." T-8.V.4.

21. As mentioned earlier, everyone's awakening is highly individualized - although the *content* is always the same, which is the realization that we are all entirely sinless and guiltless. Once this fearless state has bloomed inwardly, the peace of God is its natural result. And inseparable from this peace, is abounding grace and gratitude. Changeless Love, joy, and happiness are the state of being. Unassailable safety and security are also hallmarks of this state, once fear falls away.

22. Some of the joyous consequences of this divine replacement also include the falling away of self-doubt and of feeling unfairly treated (victimized) in any way. Upon reflection here, it becomes starkly apparent that previous bouts of self-doubt and "poor me" pity parties were not at all random. They were all *valued choices* made to uphold the illusion of a separate self. Of course, we don't recognize this until our genuine desire for peace – via unrelenting forgiveness –outweighs our desire to be unfairly treated.

23. For me, the journey seemed an especially long one because, in a way, I was pioneering in this pathway of Holy Relationships, making every conceivable mistake during the transfer. While they were all helpful, now we have a proven roadmap so to speak, one that is fool-proof if we apply the tools consistently (The *Seven Keys*, Forgiveness/Atonement, Holy Instant, Holy Relationships and ACIM lessons).

24. Please don't be discouraged if it appears to you that there is a long and arduous journey ahead, especially if you have recently begun. This is a course in *miracles!* This means the more you want to undo the separate self-concept, the more that miracles will collapse the concept of time. See the following quote:

a. *"One source of perceived discouragement from which you may suffer is your belief that this takes time, and that the results of the Holy Spirit's teaching are far in the future. This is not so. For the Holy Spirit uses time in His Own way, and is not bound by it. Time is His friend in teaching. It does not waste Him, as it does you."*

If you are tempted to be dispirited by thinking how long it would take to change your mind so completely, ask yourself, "How long is an instant?" Could you not give so short a time to the Holy Spirit for your salvation? He asks no more, for He has no need of more. It takes far longer to teach you to be willing to give Him this than for Him to use this tiny instant to offer you the whole of Heaven. In exchange for this instant He stands ready to give you the remembrance of eternity." T-15.I.2:1-5,11

25. If your genuine desire is to heal your mind, your relationships, and to prioritize forgiveness and the peace of God, then Holy Spirit will quicken the healing, bringing miracles you could never have imagined. The Holy Instant is forever present and available to you. He *knows* your intent. He never judges you. He is never disappointed in you. He always holds your impeccable innocence for you when you forget. But do you stop to rest in the sanctity of this blessed moment to feel and to receive His benediction? One Holy Instant is all it takes to wipe away all perception of pain.

26. The Holy Spirit knows you only as the risen Christ. He knows you as whole and totally immune to sickness, loss or pain of any kind. In any Holy Instant that you allow, He calls you deeply into your heart to "receive" this immutable peace and thereby be healed by it. God's Will is your perfect immunity to all the ego's dreams of pain, conflict, loss and even death. God's Will is *done*. That means that once we learn to trust His Will…all that is left for us is to accept and receive it with gratitude. Once we abdicate our choice for guilt and fear, nothing can oppose His Loving Will for us. Nothing.

27. Another encouraging truth is that because we all literally share the one Mind with the awakened ones, including Jesus and the Angels, we can invoke their help in any Holy Instant. To the degree we sincerely desire and welcome their guidance with gratitude – not in fear or doubt – is the extent to which we give them permission to guide us.

a. *"How long can it take to be where God would have you? For you are where you have forever been and will forever be. All that you have, you have forever. The blessed instant reaches out to encompass time, as God extends Himself to encompass you."* T-15.II.3:1-4

C. Holy Relationship – The Quickening

1. Jesus shares that a Holy Relationship with one or more people is the catalyst for our final awakening, not just *in* the dream but *from* it altogether. It leads us to the very last dream, the Real World. Specialness must be undone in order to reveal the unopposed nature of Love and innocence we are.

2. While we erroneously continue to believe that we are separate bodies with private minds, our attraction to conflict, pain and death will persist. We can quicken our understanding and experience of truly being the Holy and unified Self by employing forgiveness and joining in a truly common goal with at least one other person in a Holy Relationship. It need not be romantic.

3. As Jesus tells us in the following quotes, we fulfill the most Holy function that this world contains through Holy Relationship.

    a. *"You have been called, together with your brother, to the most holy function this world contains. It is the only one that has no limits, and reaches out to every broken fragment of the Sonship with healing and uniting comfort. This is offered you, in your holy relationship."* T-18.I.13:1-3

    b. *"When brothers join in purpose in the world of fear, they stand already at the edge of the real world."* T-30.V.7:1

    c. *"In your relationship the Holy Spirit has gently laid the real world; the world of happy dreams, from which awaking is so easy and so natural."* T-8.II.9:4

    d. *"In your relationship is this world's light. And fear must disappear before you now."* T-18.III.4:3-4

D. The Final Awakening

1. In this essay we're about to expose and shatter the ego's most viciously defended central idol and dream – physical death. This speaks of the very final awakening from the body and time itself. Because the ego's belief in death is so heavily defended, I was guided to include more than the usual number of quotes from the *Course*. Reinforcement of the subject at hand is extremely helpful because we sometimes need to hear something a gazillion times before we allow it to sink in.

2. In the long descent into fear and an equally long ascent back up the ladder of separation toward unification, the split-mind operates from a severely limited frame of reference. In our return to Love there are many illusory levels and progressions of awakening.

3. In this world we are probably most familiar with the customary awakening or enlightenment *within* the body dream. But this is just one form of awakening and we're mostly unaware that there is yet a final awakening to take place. This is awakening *from* the body and its central dream altogether. And this cannot be achieved through what we know as physical death.

4. Many masters achieved enlightenment, but they still retained a split-mind by allowing the illusory body to sicken and die. They did not understand the body's nothingness. They did not realize that it was powerless over their mind. The body, which is a "self-made" fantasy, appeared to claim them through death. And while the illusory body seemed to claim them as victims in sickness and death, they could not recognize the body's nothingness.

5. They were still afraid of the power of the undivided Mind as perfect Love. They continued then to be bound to this illusion of the body and death, not recognizing the power of the miracle and their complete dominion over these hallucinations. Herein lays the deep unconscious attraction to the ego's birth, amnesia and death cycle. And yet we can access the miracle in any situation if we are open to this quantum healing of the mind:

a. *"Miracles enable you to heal the sick and raise the dead because you made sickness and death yourself, and can therefore abolish both. [You] are a miracle, capable of creating in the likeness of your Creator. Everything else is your own nightmare, and does not exist. Only the creations of light are real." T.1.I.24.*

6. One thing that Jesus revealed to me about spiritual awakening is that while we still believe we're in a body, and at the seeming mercy of this *central idol* of all illusions, there will be a progression of awakenings and not just one. These awakenings are irrevocable, yet they continue opening into higher states of unified awareness – if we don't stop at the first awakening or enlightenment which He terms as a temptation to rest in "complacency."

7. I'd like to share a section here from Jesus about His resurrection in the earlier *A Course in Miracles* Urtext. It is titled, *"Was there a Physical Resurrection?"*

   a. *"My body disappeared because I had no illusion about it. The last one had gone. It was laid in the tomb, but there was nothing left to bury. It did not disintegrate because the unreal cannot die. It merely became what it always was. And that is what "rolling the stone away" means. The body disappears, and no longer hides what lies beyond. It merely ceases to interfere with vision. To roll the stone away is to see beyond the tomb, beyond death, and to understand the body's nothingness. What is understood as nothing must disappear."*

   "I did assume a human form with human attributes afterwards, to speak to those who were to prove the body's worthlessness to the world. This has been much misunderstood. I came to tell them that death is illusion, and the mind that made the body can make another since form itself is an illusion. They did not understand. But now I talk to you and give you the same message. The death of an illusion means nothing. It disappears when you awaken and decide to dream no more. And you still do have the power to make this decision as I did."

8. When the Mind has returned to this level of dominion and mastery (as Jesus did), it is understood and demonstrated that the

neutral body is indeed unreal. Thus, the body, as an image only and yet still within the Mind, is known purely as an effect of the Mind. It does not ever leave the Mind. The ego mind dreams of physical death and orders the body to follow suit because that mind is still split. The neutral body is not a cause in itself. It cannot betray us or victimize us. It has zero ability to change in appearance – sicken, heal, age or die – independently of the mind. The unreal cannot die. Can a projected "image" sicken or die? No. Once the mind is healed it merely turns off its projection of the body.

9. As Jesus explains, *"(My body) did not disintegrate because the unreal cannot die. It merely became what it always was."* ... *"The body disappears, and no longer hides what lies beyond. It merely ceases to interfere with vision."* He shares that the body disappeared because He understood and knew the body's nothingness. It did not decay or disintegrate. As a projected image, it merely dematerialized. And afterward, He materialized an additional body in order to teach others who were meant to extend His precious teaching. But as we see now, more than two thousand years later, Jesus' teachings on miracles and overcoming the illusory body and death were not embraced, understood, or demonstrated, except by a rare few.

10. Speaking about enlightenment, many who have experienced an irrevocable spiritual awakening have stopped there, fooled into believing that this state of awareness was the crowning glory of all time. The present euphoria, peace, Love and spaciousness seemed to indicate that there was nothing remaining in their mind to unlearn, and therefore nothing left to learn. The spiritual jackpot had been delivered. However, without knowing it, they then became *unteachable.*

11. Within the ego's dream of life in the body, we awaken as the split mind heals and becomes whole. This is achieved as we make the transfer from fear as a separate self-concept, to Love as the one, shared and unified Self.

12. Even with the traditional ideas of awakening within the dream, there still remains the deepest, most unrecognized and fiercely defended obstacle yet to overcome – the ego's central dream of death.

13. This belief, as the ultimate blind-spot, ensures the mind's ongoing split which perpetuates the illusion of time. So much so, that this undisputed certainty in death as a power greater than God stalks the awakened one *beyond* physical death. This overwhelming loyalty to death as reigning supreme over God is responsible for pulling them into further incarnations within the dream, awakened or not. This massive oversight, as the deeply unconscious attraction *to* death, is the darkest and most defended conviction of all, to perpetuate time and space via the illusions of birth and death.

14. This is a whole other realm of the split mind that has been *unacknowledged* by many awakened masters. And because this split was unseen, it remained unhealed and they could not move past it. There is an almost entirely unknown level of mastery which Jesus beckons us to embrace in the *Course*. He demonstrated it through His resurrection. Enlightenment in a body within the ego's dream is just a beginning.

a. *"The world is not left by death but by truth, and truth can be known by all those for whom the Kingdom was created, and for whom it waits."* T-3.VII.6:11

15. The seeming "death realm" is the ego's most cherished dream (See Chapter Six in Volume One of *The End of Death*, and its accompanying diagram – *Collapsing the Dream of Death,* on page 167.) The death dream is its greatest defense against God as Love and is inextricably entwined with the fear of God. Faith in the death dream is the ultimate split yet to be recognized and healed.

a. *"If death is real for anything, there is no life. Death denies life. But if there is reality in life, death is denied. No compromise in this is possible."* M-27.4.2-5

b. *"What could you choose between but life or death, waking or sleeping, peace or war, your dreams or your reality? There is a risk of thinking death is peace, because the world equates the body with the Self which God created. Yet a thing can never be its opposite. And death is opposite to peace, because it is the opposite of life. And life is peace. Awaken and forget all thoughts of death, and you will find you have the peace of God." T-27.VII.10:1-6*

16. The unquestioned belief that the illusory body (purely an "idea" or image dwelling in and projected by the split mind) has dominion over *the mind* that *made* it, reveals that the mind is only partially awakened and is still divided. It has not overcome the ego's most aggressive central dream. Consequently, it sees physical death as safety, as escape from the final Awakening.

a. *"Those who fear death see not how often and how loudly they call to it, and bid it come to save them from communication. For death is seen as safety, the great dark savior from the light of truth, the answer to the Answer, the silencer of the Voice that speaks for God. Yet the retreat to death is not the end of conflict. Only God's Answer is its end." T-19.IV.C.7:1-4*

17. Since the separation, the split mind bases itself on one pivotal and entirely unquestioned central dream. All other illusions stem from this one seemingly infallible belief. Without this one belief – *that death is the certain outcome of all life* – the entire dream would crumble instantaneously.

a. *"Death is the central dream from which all illusions stem. Is it not madness to think of life as being born, aging, losing vitality, and dying in the end?" ... "It is the one fixed, unchangeable belief of the world that all things in it are born only to die. This is regarded as "the way of nature," not to be raised to question, but to be accepted as the "natural" law of life." "...all this is taken as the Will of God. And no one asks if a benign Creator could will this."*

"Death is the symbol of the fear of God. His Love is blotted out in the idea, which holds it from awareness like a shield held up to obscure the sun. The grimness of the symbol is enough to show it cannot coexist with God."

"There is either a god of fear or One of Love. The world attempts a thousand compromises, and will attempt a thousand more.

Not one can be acceptable to God's teachers, because not one could be acceptable to God. He did not make death because He did not make fear. Both are equally meaningless to Him."

"The "reality" of death is firmly rooted in the belief that God's Son is a body. And if God created bodies, death would indeed be real. But God would not be loving. There is no point at which the contrast between the perception of the real world and that of the world of illusions becomes more sharply evident. Death is indeed the death of God, if He is Love."

"And the last to be overcome will be death." Of course! Without the idea of death there is no world. All dreams will end with this one. This is salvation's final goal; the end of all illusions. And in death are all illusions born." M-27.1:1-2,4-7,3:1-3,4:6-10,5:1-5,6:1-6

18. If God is all life without opposite or end, how can death possibly exist? Death, along with its entirely imagined realm, is an ego illusion! If death exists, then God as Love does not. We cannot afford to believe that both these mutually exclusive possibilities exist simultaneously. If we do, then we are looking from a split mind and not the unified Mind. God's Love is *all* there is. Death is an attempt to resolve conflict by not deciding at all!

19. Belief in death is rejection of Love as God. This belief *is* the split mind. It maintains the split. Only God's Love is all there is. Jesus shares with us:

a. *"The body neither lives nor dies, because it cannot contain you who are life. If we share the same mind, you can overcome death because I did. Death is an attempt to resolve conflict by not deciding at all. Like any other impossible solution the ego attempts, [it will not work]." T-6.V.A.1:4-7*

20. The concept of death is a lie that we taught our self by trusting the body's sensory perceptions which were made exclusively to report and sustain separation. Death is not a fact. It is learned and must be now unlearned. The body sickens and withers and dies

only because we *learned this* and then expected it to do so. The body, as purely an "idea" in the mind, is a neutral, changeless, now moment, projected image. It has no past! This is why it can be healed by the miracle instantaneously if the mind is willing to be healed. It, of itself, has zero power to sicken or to heal. It's the mind, either conscious or unconscious, which instructs the body to change anything in form, including physical death.

21. Death is the fear of life. It is none other than the *fear of our Holy Self,* of the Love and innocence we are as one with God. Thus, is death the ego's attempted escape from God. And death is the final obstacle to Love that must be unlearned.

a. *"You see in death escape from what you made. But this you do not see; that you made death, and it is but illusion of an end. Death cannot be escape, because it is not life in which the problem lies. Life has no opposite, for it is God. Life and death seem to be opposites because you have decided death ends life. Forgive the world, and you will understand that everything that God created cannot have an end, and nothing He did not create is real."* M-20.5:2-7

22. As we approach perfect Love as light – which is full awakening from separation – a great many, including enlightened masters, frequently choose sickness and physical death at this point. Why? Because death is an attempt to escape *from* God. The split-mind tries to escape since there remains still some fear of Love, of returning our perception to the realm of Knowledge, as undivided and unopposed union with God.

a. *"All forms of sickness, even unto death, are physical expressions of the fear of awakening. They are attempts to reinforce sleeping out of fear of waking. This is a pathetic way of trying not to see by rendering the faculties for seeing ineffectual. "Rest in peace" is a blessing for the living, not the dead, because rest comes from waking, not from sleeping. Sleep is withdrawing; waking is joining."* T-8.IX.3:2-6

23. In the light of these Victory Lap teachings, some may then mistakenly assume that the *Course* is advocating immortality *in* a body. This is

not the case. As the mind is made whole again, guilt as the single cause for all attack, is erased. As a consequence, all "effects" of guilt such as disease, pain, conflict, aging and death, are also erased. The miracle heals the cause in the mind together with the effects seen in the body. Cause and effect are one, never separate.

24. Jesus tells us that when we reach this most advanced stage, we will decide with Holy Spirit whether we desire to stay in the body or lay it aside. But it is not laid aside through attack such as sickness, aging, pain, accident, etc. To do so would demonstrate that the mind remains split and is not yet healed. In the advanced state when we decide to leave the body, we step away from a perfectly healthy and serviceable body.

25. Jesus makes a strong point in the following passage. He says that in laying it aside the body is *not sick nor old nor hurt*. It shows no signs of attack. It's not used by the ego as proof of sin, guilt and death. Instead, the body is employed by Holy Spirit as a beacon to demonstrate not just our own sinlessness, but the sinlessness of everyone.

   a. *"And yet a neutral thing (the body) does not see death, for thoughts of fear are not invested there, nor is a mockery of love bestowed upon it. Its neutrality protects it while it has a use. And afterwards, without a purpose, it is laid aside. It is not sick nor old nor hurt. It is but functionless, unneeded and cast off."* W-294.1:5-9

26. As we approach this grand awakening from the body and death itself, the definitive experience involves looking lucidly upon our "fear of God," without the many layers of illusions which previously kept it hidden from stark awareness. This is our denied terror of Love as the fear of God and as the attraction to conflict, sickness, pain and death. Here, we will come to see that separation itself is perpetuated by our *fear of our brothers*. Simply put, every unforgiven grievance that we still believe (project) is a painful expression of our own unhealed fear of our brothers. And this is why we need the quantum healing experience of Holy Relationship because its forgiveness reaches out to heal all minds within all the dimensions of time.

*a. "You are afraid of God [because] you fear your brother.
Those you do not forgive you fear." T-19.IV.D.11:5-6*

27. The final awakening proceeds from our undivided agreement to overcome our *fear of union* with our brother and thus with God. This clearly illogical fear of extraordinary communion and all-encompassing forgiveness manifests as the split mind's belief in the body's reality, its sensory perceptions, the laws of the world and finally, death itself. It uses these illusions to attack itself and keep the separation intact.

28. This last eye of the needle necessarily involves the experience of rite of passage through Holy Relationship, a true relationship *beyond* the body. This is the triumphant and joyful relinquishment of the very last obstacle to our willing return to peace, to Love, and to conscious union with our brother and God. The Holy Relationship heals the split mind's terror of union because union with our brother literally *ends* the separation by eradicating the guilt that perpetuates it. Here, in this unprecedented bonding through forgiveness, is the necessary unification of the split mind, brother to brother, that ultimately collapses the ego's gap of separation in its entirety.

29. In the divine union of Holy Relationship lay the proof that we do indeed share one, continuous, Loving Mind with God and all our brothers. This depth of union shatters the bounds of the laws of this world, completely demolishing them, and extending God's Love in a holographic fashion through all minds who are willing. In the advanced Holy Relationship lay our irrefutable demonstration of the *Course's* number one miracle principle, "There is no order of difficulty in miracles."

30. This teaching presented in the *Course,* is the final Victory Lap. The reason is because the Holy Relationship is an experience of union that utterly transcends bodies, and therefore all sense of separation. It is this direct experience of *union with our brother beyond the body* that proves unequivocally that we are *not* body-bound. Nor are we prisoner to its illusory laws of birth, decay and death.

31. These teachings are our lighted pathway *out of* the ego's impossibly long, weary and arduous *dream* of life in the body, which is really a *dream of death,* and not life at all. I am so deeply grateful to Jesus,

as the first Christ amongst us all, to have undone the entire ego dream for all time. Thank God for His having accomplished the Atonement on behalf of all of us. Now, all that remains for us to do is to *accept and receive* this truth deeply into our hearts. After all, the sole responsibility of the miracle worker – as you and me – is to accept the Atonement for our self.

32. In conclusion, I am constantly reminded that Jesus says *and means* He is literally with us in our seeming awakening from fear to Love. He tells us that the ego has no power to interfere in this, the most Holy journey of all time. Jesus is with us and offers us His hand and His strength. I am so grateful I took His hand and that I will never let it go.

   a. *"Whenever fear intrudes anywhere along the road to peace, it is because the ego has attempted to join the journey with us and cannot do so. Sensing defeat and angered by it, the ego regards itself as rejected and becomes retaliative. You are invulnerable to its retaliation because I am with you. On this journey you have chosen me as your companion [instead] of the ego. Do not attempt to hold on to both, or you will try to go in different directions and will lose the way."*

     "Never accord the ego the power to interfere with the journey. It has none, because the journey is the way to what is true. Leave all illusions behind, and reach beyond all attempts of the ego to hold you back. I go before you because I am beyond the ego. Reach, therefore, for my hand because you want to transcend the ego. My strength will never be wanting, and if you choose to share it you will do so. I give it willingly and gladly, because I need you as much as you need me."
     T-8.V.5:5,6:4-10

12. LIFTING THE VEIL – APPROACHING THE REAL WORLD

1. In Chapter 19 of the *Course*, Jesus describes the four obstacles to peace that we use, with the greatest and final obstacle as our fear of God, which is our fear of union as Love. Before we can transcend these obstacles, we must genuinely desire to close the gap with our brother; to see him as sinless. This requires the undoing of the belief in separate selves as well as our obsession with special relationships.

   a. *"Either there is a gap between you and your brother, or you are as one. There is no in between, no other choice, and no allegiance to be split between the two." T-28.VII.3:1-2*

2. Jesus informs us that we must decide to repurpose our special relationships with Holy Spirit which involves learning to show-up for our self authentically using the *Seven Keys* on page 572 and the *Divine Switch* on page 297. When this is undertaken, an initial phase of disorientation occurs because the goal of the relationship has been reversed. During this period, we learn to release the private mind with its self-seeking agendas, along with our concept of the body, and all the ways we use fear and its effects to maintain the belief in separation.

3. We must learn to recognize the stark contrast between guilt-inducing desires and those that bring us peace and healing. Through the false self we think we can discern between what brings us happiness and what brings us pain. Yet we need to understand that the ego's pursuit of pleasure is pain. Remember that its ulterior motive is to hoard unconscious guilt which leads to conflict, sickness and death. The separate, personal body-identity searches for love and pleasure apart from God's Will. In this pursuit it amasses hidden guilt.

4. The things that it searches for to complete itself (through body appetites), are symbols of guilt. The compulsion for them is the ego's compulsion for sin. The cycle is sin, guilt and fear. Guilt follows sin. Fear arises from this unforgiven mistake, and then self-inflicted punishment (sickness, loss, conflict and death) follows inevitably.

5. The world has named and struggled against perhaps thousands of various diseases. Then there's a frenzied search for thousands of different cures for each of these diseases. Yet almost no one has seen and therefore undone their single common denominator and root cause – the special relationship – which is literally, a death magnet.

6. The journey across the bridge to the Real World begins with the undoing of our special relationships and our wholehearted devotion to their opposite, the Holy Relationship.

7. The purpose of the Holy Relationship is to serve as the bridge to the Real World, where all is one. As we undo the false self via the Holy Relationship, we soon come to discern that the one we thought we were, the one who took their first step onto the bridge, is not the one who completes the journey. And neither is our mighty companion.

8. Having largely left the body identity and specialness, all of what had previously seemed to give us meaning disperses into oblivion as we look out from the clear and radiant state of unassailable innocence, peace, Love, security and safety. With the blocks to Love undone, eternal and perfect Love is all there is.

   a. *"Love is not learned. Its meaning lies within itself. And learning ends when you have recognized all it is [not.] That is the interference; that is what needs to be undone." T-18. IX.12:1-4*

9. From Love, we know that we already have everything because we *are* everything. Only the illusory self can possibly believe in lack, conflict and adversity, which is the lack of Love as Self in our awareness. And if we are everything, then any sense of lack or conflict must always be the false self. In fact, the false self is the very idea of deprivation. Its senses and appetites all report a state of lack, and therefore seek the impossible – to "get" in order to gratify its illusory (incomplete/inadequate) self.

10. The ego's need to get is always the hidden desire to hoard guilt. It believes that we must take from someone else in order to get, which requires that someone else has less, and this produces the very guilt that the ego needs in order to establish that it has indeed separated from God.

11. In addressing the final obstacle to peace, Jesus speaks about "lifting the veil" just prior to our facing our fear of God. So, what does lifting the veil actually mean?

12. Let's recall that all of our self-hatred and guilt is projected outward onto the world, our body and our brother. In order to maintain this hatred against our brother, we made a veil from our distorted perception to prevent us from seeing our brother as the Christ, as one with us.

13. So, as we forgive our brother and accept the Atonement, this veil, which previously obscured his brilliant light as one with ours, as the Great Rays – is finally lifted. In our brother's freedom from our projections we are also freed. As we see him in glory, we behold the innocent Christ as our shared Identity.

   a. *"You and your brother are coming home together, after a long and meaningless journey that you undertook apart, and that led nowhere. You have found your brother, and you will light each other's way. And from this light will the Great Rays extend back into darkness and forward unto God, to shine away the past and so make room for His eternal Presence, in which everything is radiant in the light." T-18.III.8:5-7*

14. Because forgiveness of our brother is the way to transcend the fear of God, it is now clear how our brother is our savior from the long drawn out dream of suffering. He saved us from the formidable claws of fear, separation and death. As we recognize that all our triggers and all our demons arose from our very own denied self-hatred, we see that our brother was there all the while to reflect the truth back to us, that we are innocent always, and we're merely dreaming.

15. Our brother did not abandon us in our darkest hour of self-betrayal. Instead, he quietly shone the light of forgiveness until we learned that we are forgiven along with him. This willingness between two or more companions to maintain the innocence of each, establishes the common goal necessary to form the Holy Relationship.

16. In this Holy Relationship the Christ Himself is reborn as our shared Identity. Jesus states that He dwells within our Holy Relationship and that together with Him we will overcome all obstacles. This

includes the ego's fiercest and most heavily defended obstacle to Love and union, physical death. As startling as this may appear to be, He assures us that within the Holy Relationship lies the end of death. He also says that within our Holy Relationship is every miracle we will perform held out to us.

a. *"In your holy relationship is your Father's Son. He has not lost communion with Him, nor with himself. When you agreed to join your brother, you acknowledged this is so."... "There is no obstacle that you can place before our union, for in your holy relationship I am there already. We will surmount all obstacles together, for we stand within the gates and not outside." ... "From your holy relationship truth proclaims the truth, and love looks on itself."... "I am within your holy relationship, yet you would imprison me behind the obstacles you raise to freedom, and bar my way to you."*

To you and your brother, in whose special relationship the Holy Spirit entered, it is given to release and be released from the dedication to death."... "The fear of death will go as its appeal is yielded to love's real attraction. The end of sin, which nestles quietly in the safety of your relationship, protected by your union with your brother, and ready to grow into a mighty force for God is very near." ... "Your newborn purpose is nursed by angels, cherished by the Holy Spirit and protected by God Himself. It needs not your protection; it is [yours.] For it is deathless, and within it lies the end of death."

"In its tiny hands it holds, in perfect safety, every miracle you will perform, held out to you. The miracle of life is ageless, born in time but nourished in eternity. Behold this infant, to whom you gave a resting place by your forgiveness of your brother, and see in it the Will of God. Here is the babe of Bethlehem reborn. And everyone who gives him shelter will follow him, not to the cross, but to the resurrection and the life."

"No one can look upon the fear of God unterrified, unless he has accepted the Atonement and learned illusions are not real. No one can stand before this obstacle alone, for he could not have reached this far unless his brother walked beside him. And no one would dare to look on it without complete forgiveness of his brother in his heart." ... *"Once he has found his brother he [is] ready."* ... *"Behold your Friend, the Christ Who stands beside you. How holy and how beautiful He is!"* T-19.IV.B.4:9-11,5:3-4,7:1,8:3, T-19.IV.C.1:1,9:1-2,4-6,10:5-9, T-19.IV.D.9:1-3,10:3,14:1

17. All the idols we have sought to fill the tiny band of time between birth and death which we call "life," only serve to *obscure* the one most Holy purpose we could ever accomplish – the Holy Relationship. When we commit together to Holy Relationship, we effectively commit to healing our split-mind through freeing it of all belief in fear and separation. This, by necessity, is also the undoing of our special relationships because they always seek to replace God's Will with the ego's will.

    a.   *"But the holy relationship shares God's purpose, rather than aiming to make a substitute for it. Every special relationship you have made is a substitute for God's Will, and glorifies yours instead of His because of the illusion that they are different."* T-17.IV.2:6-7

18. As the Holy Relationship advances, we directly experience union with another, and the separate body and private mind concepts fall away. Through our trust, our belief and experience of a fear-driven body and world are miraculously transferred to their complete opposite. Once these blocks of fear and body identity are evaporated, the pristine beauty of the Real World is revealed in our awareness.

    a.   *"[The face of Christ] has to be seen before the memory of God can return. The reason is obvious. Seeing the face of Christ involves perception. No one can look on knowledge. But the face of Christ is the great symbol of forgiveness. It is salvation. It is the symbol of the real world. Whoever looks on this no longer sees the world. He is as near to Heaven as is possible outside the gate. Yet from this gate it is no more than just a step inside. It is the final step. And this we leave to God." C-3.4.*

19. Not only does Holy Relationship surmount the obstacles to peace, but the miraculous journey through the six stages of the development of trust, of spiritual awakening, (Manual for Teachers, M-4) is hastened exponentially by the Holy Relationship as well. In fact, the ten characteristics of the Teachers of God (Manual for Teachers, M-4) are actually "gifts" which are born within this sacred relationship. The Holy Relationship is truly the answer and the Holy Grail to awakening from the dream entirely.

     a. *"God gives special gifts to His teachers, because they have a special role in His plan for Atonement. Their specialness is, of course, only temporary; set in time as a means of leading out of time. These special gifts, born in the holy relationship toward which the teaching-learning situation is geared, become characteristic of all teachers of God who have advanced in their own learning. In this respect they are all alike." M-4.1:4-7*

20. As a result of the direct experience of union with a brother, the idea that we each have separate, self-seeking "wills" apart from each other and God becomes laughable. We are one with God. Our will and His are now one. There can be no independent will to suffer any longer when this is accepted.

21. Immense and often overwhelming gratitude for our mighty companion fills our heart as we recognize the gifts we receive in Holy Relationship. Within the journey of forgiveness, we recognize the Christ is present, literally. Precious, joint Holy Instants pierce our mundane awareness as we find our self looking directly into the Eyes of Christ, as our brother or sister. In this magnificent reflection we catch our breath as we see our One Self brimming with unimaginable compassion and innocence. This One has never sinned. This One has never known the pain of separation. This One has come to welcome us back into the arms of Love as One. This is the perfect Love that can never be threatened. This is what we are.

22. Jesus goes on to say that the Real World, the world of happy dreams, actually lies within our Holy Relationship.

    a. *"Return with me to Heaven, walking together with your brother out of this world and through another, to the loveliness and joy the other holds within it." ... "In your relationship the Holy Spirit has gently laid the real world; the world of happy dreams, from which awaking is so easy and so natural."* T-18.I.12:4, T-28.II.9:4

23. Jesus really expresses the inestimable value of our Holy Relationships to lead us to Heaven itself.

    a. *"In your relationship you have joined with me in bringing Heaven to the Son of God, who hid in darkness." ... "My need for you, joined with me in the holy light of your relationship, is your need for salvation. Would I not give you what you gave to me? For when you joined your brother, you answered me."* T-18.III.6:1,5-7

A. No Disagreements Any Longer

1. In the advanced Holy Relationship, trust has been largely transferred from fear to Love. Another way to explain this is that each companion sees, expresses, and extends from the Holy Self most, if not all of the time. Because of this all-inclusive devotion to forgiveness, even when tempted, they each choose to forgive appearances of adversity (the gap) holding steadfast to seeing the miracle behind all situations.

2. The personal, false, body identity, which always seeks to satiate its own separate needs, has no place in this sanctified relationship. The body self-concept is the only identity that can possibly fantasize about conflicting interests with another. It's the only one that can believe it has been unfairly treated, and it's the only one that can possibly judge another.

3. In an advanced Holy Relationship, the Christ within both companions is the One who communicates. This is the one continuous and Loving Mind we share, now unobstructed by fear. Christ Vision, which looks upon itself in everyone, replaces

the fraudulent body's five senses. Love makes no demands here. Giving is experienced *as receiving* and our highest joy is to be in service to our brothers on behalf of Love.

4. No arguments are possible here. Each companion sees the other's interests as his own. Their wills are joined. The one Will of God, the one Mind of Christ, lives through these companions. How could they possibly be in conflict when they *are* the unified Will of God? What possible needs could they have that are not already met by God's immediate and infinite supply? And what miracles could they not perform in full service to God? Here, in this most advanced union of brothers, the number one miracle principle is embodied and demonstrated:

"There is no order of difficulty in miracles. One is not "harder" or "bigger" than another. They are all the same. All expressions of love are maximal." T-1.I.1.

5. The only way that two people could have an argument is if one or both value an idol – as guilt – within the ego's gap *more* than they value each other's innocence as the Holy Relationship. Please refer to the Gap diagrams for idols in the gap, pages 46 thru 49.

6. If one companion withdraws their defense and asks instead to enter a Holy Instant in which to accept the Atonement on behalf of both, then the second companion must either join with their partner in forgiveness of the idol, or seek another special relationship that shares the same attraction to guilt.

7. An idol in the gap, whether negative (pain) or positive (pleasure), requires at least two consenting witnesses to give it seeming power. For instance, if I want to defend an idol and you refuse to agree, saying instead that you want peace between us above all else, then I have a choice to make. My decision now is either to let go of the idol and save our relationship or save the idol at the expense of the relationship. I choose either to place my partner's innocence *above* the idol, or to seek out a *substitute relationship*, someone else who worships the same idol as me (a special relationship).

B. The Joint Holy Instant and Grace

1. The Holy Relationship removes the artificial veil or barrier to joyous awareness of the one Mind and will, which we share together with God and our brother. The *Course* offers us a number of practices for healing and one of them is the Holy Instant. In addition to this, is the profound experience of the "joint" Holy Instant, which presents a window into what I would call the incomprehensible merging of souls.

2. In my experience, the joint Holy Instant is timeless and utterly bodiless. The body, its five senses and its appetites cannot intrude upon this Love. When the world speaks of the highest union between two people it mostly refers to lovemaking in a romantic relationship, which is the ego's substitute for the experience of true union. This romantic love is not at all what we're speaking of here in the context of the joint Holy Instant.

3. Because the body is not involved in this timeless union, it has nothing to do with sexual union. This joint, Holy Communion is of the highest order; one that totally transcends bodies and the illusion of separate minds.

    a. *"Nothing can show the contrast better than the experience of both a holy and an unholy relationship. The first is based on love, and rests on it serene and undisturbed. The body does not intrude upon it. Any relationship in which the body enters is based not on love, but on idolatry."* T-20.VI.2:1-4

    b. *"In the holy instant, where the Great Rays replace the body in awareness, the recognition of relationships without limits is given you. But in order to see this, it is necessary to give up every use the ego has for the body, and to accept the fact that the ego has no purpose you would share with it."* T-15.IX.3:1-2

4. Sexual desire is a *distortion* of the pure, uncorrupted miracle impulse which is the desire to join truly through communion of minds. The pure impulse gets distorted because through the body filter the companions seek union *through the body* as a physical substitute for the sacred merging of the one Mind and Spirit.

5. Once this mistake occurs, then unconscious guilt must enter because both companions are seeing one another as a body which *prevents* the miracle impulse from extending. Body appetites are a cleverly disguised means to amass guilt, which blocks Love and true union if left unforgiven. On the other hand, a joint Holy Instant with another occurs *because* there is no physical agenda for sexual desire or orgasm to block it, and the miracle impulse is allowed to extend. For more on the subject of sex, please refer to Chapter IV titled, "Sex and TransOrgasmic Union" beginning on page 379.

6. Where two minds and hearts agree to join to close the gap without bodily interference the result is the joint Holy Instant. The body falls away in our awareness as it is magnificently eclipsed by breathtaking reverence for each other as One, as well as our Loving God whose Will we share.

   a. *"To do nothing is to rest, and make a place within you where the activity of the body ceases to demand attention. Into this place the Holy Spirit comes, and there abides." T-18.VII.7:1-2*

7. Because the body and its appetites are *not* involved in these Holy Instants, the unimpeded miracle impulse is free to ripple forward holographically.

   a. *"A mind and body cannot both exist. Make no attempt to reconcile the two, for one denies the other can be real. If you are physical, your mind is gone from your self-concept, for it has no place in which it could be really part of you. If you are Spirit, then the body must be meaningless to your reality."* W-96.3:4-7

8. I think the following two quotes are particularly powerful as they clearly state that in the Holy Instant there are no bodies at all, but just the attraction of God. A necessary prerequisite for this blessed instant of divine union is detaching from the body completely. The body-self is a "getting" mechanism. And sexual desire is a desire to – get – its illusory needs for self-gratification met. When we place no value on the body as a means to "get" anything, then our own self-seeking fantasies will evaporate as we behold the extraordinary beauty and pristine innocence of our savior, our brother or sister, the

Christ. *"God cannot come into a body, nor can you join Him there."* *T-18.VIII.2:3*

a. *"When the body ceases to attract you, and when you place no value on it as a means of getting anything, then there will be no interference in communication and your thoughts will be as free as God's. As you let the Holy Spirit teach you how to use the body only for purposes of communication, and renounce its use for separation and attack which the ego sees in it, you will learn you have no need of a body at all. In the holy instant there are no bodies, and you experience only the attraction of God."* *T-15.IX.7:1-3*

b. *"You can stretch out your hand and reach to Heaven. You whose hand is joined with your brother's have begun to reach beyond the body, but not outside yourself, to reach your shared Identity together."* *T-18.VI.10:1-2*

C. Holy Relationship Accelerates the Collapse of Guilt and Fear

1. While we value fear, judgment, anger and blame, we also prolong the erroneous belief that we're guilty, and therefore deserving of punishment as self-attack. We can certainly use all our temptations into fear to accept the Atonement instead. But where guilt and fear are most quickly erased is within the Holy Relationship. The reason is because in joining with a Holy Relationship companion, we literally collapse the guilt and subsequent unworthiness that are responsible for the attraction to fear. We do this together by each agreeing to withdraw as consenting witnesses to the ego's idols that make up the illusory gap between us (see The Gap diagrams on pages 46 thru 49).

2. When people agree, together, to unreservedly pull out the ego's plug of special love (hate), when they refuse to believe in and sympathize with the ego's dramas for each other, a very rapid demise of the ego's shield of fear occurs.

3. In conclusion, I include a quote here from my dear friend and colleague, Coreen Walson. She so eloquently explains the quintessence of Holy Relationship in one beautiful paragraph:

a. *"In Holy Relationship, consent and trust is extended to one another that says no matter how crazy I seem to get, no matter how convincing the evidence seems to be, no matter how asleep I seem to be, you have permission to be the presence of the Mind of God and to be the reminder of the perfection that must always be right where the problem boasts itself. When two or more have that commitment and refuse to let go of one another even in the heat of the battle so to speak, the ego has no believer to give it traction or seeming life. It fizzles out and is seen as the nothingness that it is, as the one who is sane calls his or her insane brother back to the light of Truth. This is exactly what Jesus did two thousand plus years ago and is asking us to do for one another now."*

Changeless Love will Overcome Death

When we are no longer afraid of changeless Love, when we have experienced this Love through Holy Relationship, we come to know that we don't lose anything. Instead, we gain our whole joyous Inheritance. We will no longer want proof of our brother's guilt, and therefore our own through death, but come to declare "Behold me brother, at your hand I LIVE."

— Coreen Walson

Made in the USA
Monee, IL
10 August 2023

40817659R10437